MAGIC AND RELIGION
IN THE GRECO-ROMAN WORLD

THE BEGINNINGS OF JUDAISM AND CHRISTIANITY

The Greco-Roman world was one of multi-aspected Paganisms, with their consciousness of myriad gods and goddesses, *daimons* and spirits. In that world the Hebrew-Israelite-Judaean tradition struggled to assert itself—and ultimately split into what became Judaism and Christianity. Verbal distinctions that we take for granted—such as those between magic and religion, myth and theology, superstition, heresy and true belief, astronomy and astrology—had not yet assumed the place to which they eventually arrive within our vocabulary.

The book offers an account of how Judaism and Christianity emerged as distinct, related faiths each claiming to be the proper continuation of the Hebraic tradition. It considers how their theological relationship—their competition with respect to the Truth regarding divinity and its relationship to humanity—is affected by both their mutual interface and their theological relationships with Paganism, and also by the political context of the pagan Roman Imperium in which they develop. The book seeks to understand what comprise the key elements that distinguish and join these traditions, why and how the vocabulary of religion and magic emerges and evolves, and how the shaping of that vocabulary has affected and continues to affect our sense of what Judaism and Christianity *are*.

This book examines ancient texts, some well-known (like the Bible and Homer's *Odyssey*) and others fairly obscure (such as the *Greek Magical Papyrae* and the *Book of Secrets* ascribed to Noah); it also explores a number of modern discussions, either of some of these texts or of some of the concepts that this book addresses. It offers a uniquely broad and integrated perspective on two interwoven issues—magic, superstition and religion, on the one hand, and, on the other, the way early Judaism and Christianity were facing each other while confronting paganism and the evolving concept of heresy.

❖

Ori Z. Soltes teaches at Georgetown University across a range of disciplines, from theology and art history to philosophy and political history. He has also taught at Johns Hopkins University, Cleveland State University, Siegel College, and Case Western Reserve University. Soltes has lectured at dozens of museums, including the Metropolitan Museum of Art, the National Gallery of Art, the Smithsonian Institution, the Art Institute of Chicago, and the Los Angeles County Museum of Art. He is the former director and curator of the B'nai B'rith Klutznick National Jewish Museum, Washington, DC, where he curated over eighty exhibitions. Soltes has authored scores of books, articles, exhibition catalogs, and essays on diverse topics, including *Mysticism in the Jewish, Christian and Muslim Traditions: Searching for Oneness* and *Jews on Trial: Judges, Juries, Prosecutors and Defendants from the Era of Jesus to Our Own Time*.

A scholarly account explores the development of Judaism and Christianity in response to a pagan world as well as the emergent distinction between religion and superstition. The historical arc of Christianity—from a persecuted sect of radicals to the official faith of Rome—raises serious questions about what precisely distinguishes true religions from false ones, myth from reality, and a dominant spiritual metaphysic from the superstitious practice of magic. Soltes (Mysticism in Judaism, Christianity, and Islam, 2008) attempts to answer these questions by looking at the ways in which Christianity and Judaism evolved out of a "Hebrew-Israelite-Judaean tradition" of which they both claimed to be the proper heirs. Their dual development was at least partially borne out of their confrontation with pagan competitors, not only for disciples, but also for political legitimacy from the Roman authorities. The author provides a captivating and philosophically searching analysis that shows that a rigorous theoretical distinction between religion and magic—the feature all regnant religions refer to when trumpeting their superiority—is impossible to draw. In the absence of such demonstrable traits, triumph becomes a function of political power, of who gets to make pronouncements "addressing the divine aspect" of the sacred. Soltes furnishes a wide-ranging history—the display of erudition is breathtaking—that considers not only the nature of religion itself, but also the unfolding of the term "magic" as a mark of illegitimacy and part of a terminology strategy to discredit the spiritual other. The author brilliantly discusses the best of Judeo-Christianity's "serious competition," including traditions like Roman Mithraism, which likely influenced the nature of Christianity just as it was surpassed by it. Soltes also assesses the gradual movement toward monotheism and the central role of demonology in Christianity—part of the religion's particular success stemmed from its articulation of a compelling adversary. Further, the author is careful to avoid overconfidently compartmentalizing historical causes—he candidly discusses the way in which a common theological amalgamation makes neat distinctions nearly impossible. Deep and historically scrupulous, this book is an important contribution to the study of comparative religion.

    — *Kirkus Reviews (starred review)* [1st edition]

At the core of Soltes' book is his conviction that "how the vocabulary pertaining to magic and religion emerges and evolves is of importance to the competing, comparative shaping of Judaism and Christianity—and that this vocabulary has affected and continues to affect our sense of what Judaism and Christianity *are*." . . . Given his interest in the relationship between religious terminology and what we might broadly term "the political," it is not surprising that Soltes draws our attention to a second very important problem: *Who* determines what is "magical" and what is "religious?" *Who* determines what is "mythical" and what is "real?" And *who* determines what forms of engaging the sacred are "superstition" and which ones are religiously legitimate? . . . Much of the Christians' later success in that political struggle resulted from their ability to convince the Roman ruling elites that their religious opponents were practicing forms of engaging the sacred realm in ways that were incompatible with or inferior to the ways that "true religion" was able to engage it.

    — *From the "Foreword" by Jess Hollenback*, *University of Wisconsin-La Crosse,*
author of Mysticism: Experience, Response and Empowerment *(Penn State Press, 1996)*

What is magic, and what is religion? How is alchemy different from sorcery, or true faith from superstition? These are just a few of the issues that Soltes tackles in this astonishingly erudite tome. Throughout the book he weaves together two strands of inquiry: First, how did Judaism and Christianity emerge as separate and often antagonistic religious traditions in the first few centuries of the common era? Second, how did varying definitions of "magic" and "religion" contribute to both the separation and the antagonism?

    In this book Soltes digs deeply into ancient literature, often exposing the etymological roots underpinning particular terms in order to examine their nuances. His explanations are clear and lucid, and the breadth of his research is remarkable. The book sweeps from antiquity to the Middle Ages, from Greco-Roman religions to Judaism and Christianity, from spells and charms to theology, mystical speculation, and religious law. It is truly a dizzying display of both knowledge and insight.

    — *Theresa Sanders*, *Department of Theology, Georgetown University, author of*
Approaching Eden: Adam and Eve in Popular Culture *(Rowman & Littlefield, 2009)*

A hallmark of our age is the blurring of boundaries between categories associated with religion in the broadest sense. Spirituality and mysticism are often seen as somehow apart from the institutional practices of religion. Where does a "miracle" end and "magic" begin? How do these categories relate to "healing"? Soltes' work provides a magnificent historical sweep that significantly advances our ability to view these category boundaries in terms richly informed by both ancient practices and contemporary scholarship. His erudition casts a penetrating light on these issues in general and on the distinctive relationship between Judaism and Christianity in particular.

    — **B. Les Lancaster**, *Professor Emeritus Liverpool John Moores University, author of* The Essence of Kabbalah *(Chartwell Books, 2005)*

What immediately strikes one upon reading *Magic and Religion in the Greco-Roman World: The Beginnings of Judaism and Christianity* are, first, the book's astonishing clarity regarding intractable, abstruse issues and concepts that eluded scholars for millennia—presented here elegantly, authoritatively, and even entertainingly! Second, its author's breathtaking erudition and the resultant expansive range of pertinent observations, documents, and historical facts that went into this work's breadth of concerns. Finally, the level of insight and profundity rarely encountered. This is a magisterial work destined to become a classic.

    — **Alex S. Kohav**, *Department of Philosophy, Metropolitan State University of Denver, author of* The *Sôd* Hypothesis *(MaKoM, 2013) and editor of* Mysticism and Meaning *(Three Pines Press, 2019) and* Mysticism and Experience *(forthcoming, Lexington Books)*

Other Books by Ori Z. Soltes

Fixing the World: American Jewish Painters in the Twentieth Century (University Press of New England, 2002)

Our Sacred Signs: How Jewish, Christian and Muslim Art Draw from the Same Source (Westview Press/Basic Books, 2005)

The Ashen Rainbow: Essays on the Arts and the Holocaust (Bartleby Press/Eshel Books, 2006)

The Problem of Plato's *Cratlyus*: The Relation of Language to Truth in the History of Philosophy (The Edwin Mellen Press, 2007)

Mysticism in Judaism, Christianity and Islam: Searching for Oneness (Rowman & Littlefield, 2008)

Untangling the Web: Why the Middle East is a Mess and Always has Been (Bartleby Press, 2010)

Embracing the World: Fethulah Gulen's Thought and Its Relationship to Jalaluddin Rumi and Others (Tughra Books, 2013)

Jews on Trial: From the Time of Jesus to Our Own Time (Bartleby Press/Eshel Books, 2013)

Tradition and Transformation: Three Millennia of Jewish Art and Architecture (Canal Street Studios, 2016)

God and the Goalposts: A Brief History of Sports, Religion, Politics, War, and Art (Bartleby Press, 2017)

Untangling the Middle East: A Guide to the Past, Present, and Future of the World's Most Chaotic Region (Skyhorse Publishing, 2017)

Ontogeny of Light: Apples, Suns, Mirrors, Electricities — Limitless Light, Oscillating Silences, Immersive Realms: The Art of Alex Shalom Kohav (Canal Street Studios, forthcoming in 2020)

Magic and Religion

in the Greco-Roman World

The Beginnings of Judaism
and Christianity

Foreword by Jess Hollenback

Second Edition

Ori Z. Soltes

ACADEMIA-WEST PRESS

ACADEMIA-WEST PRESS
P.O. BOX 17722
BOULDER, CO 80308-0722

Cover images
(clockwise from upper left):

1 *Mithra Sauroktonos*
Rome, Second-Third c. CE
Musee du Louvre
High-relief marble

2 *Carrying the Temple Menorah into Rome*
Detail from Arch of Titus, Rome, ca 81-82 CE
High-relief marble

3 *Jesus flanked by the Alpha and Omega*
Rome, Via Latina Catacomb, ca 300 CE
Detail from wall painting

4 *The Good Shepherd amidst Grape Harvest*
Detail from Sarcophagus facade
Rome, Praetexta Catacomb, ca 390 CE
Low-relief marble

Soltes, Ori Z., 1951 –
Magic and Religion in the Greco-Roman World: The Beginnings of Judaism and Christianity, 2nd ed.

ISBN: 978-0-9994594-9-2

1. Late Antiquity 2. Ancient Rome
3. Magic 4. Judaism
5. Christianity 6. Title 7. Religion

CONTENTS

List of Figures

FIG 1: *Venus of Willendorf*
Willendorf, Austria, ca 28,000-25,000 BCE
Oolithic Limestone, ca 4.4" tall
Naturhistorisches Museum, Vienna

FIG 2: detail, *Mithra Tauroktonos*
Rome, second-third c. CE
High-relief marble
Musee du Louvre, Paris

FIG 3: detail, *Greek Magical Papyrus* 2 "Leiden," ls 170ff.
fourth c. CE
Ink on papyrus
Staatliche Museen, Berlin

FIG 4: Amulet with Cock-headed, Snake-footed Anthropomorph (Bonner #172)
Rome, first-sixth century CE
Incised jasper

FIG 5: English Caricature of Jews Attended by Devils
Rotulus Judaeorum, (IJHS) 1233
Ink on Parchment

FIG 6: *Scholar in His Study* (aka *Faustus* or *Abramelin the Mage*)
Rembrandt van Rijn, ca 1650-54
etching

FOR BETH PIERCE,
IN MEMORIAM,
AND FOR ADRIANNE PIERCE:

Amor amicitiaque
omnia vincent
et semper vincerunt

Preface to the Second Edition

The advantage of living in an era of easy communication is that ideas can move from one end of the planet to the other with great speed, and groups that, in an earlier era would have known little or nothing of each other have easy access to the means to understand one another. Our era is also one, as a consequence, in which a book such as this, over which the author and his editor pore so carefully before sending it into the world can still leave the residue of small errors that are noticed by one or more readers thousands of miles away from the venues of writing and publishing, and those readers can even do the author the courtesy of pointing those errors out.

A second edition may mean significant changes and updates—but for a book focused primarily on events that took place fifteen or twenty centuries ago and more, that would be most unusual—which is not the case here. Yet a handful of small typographical miscues, captured by the keen eyes of several readers, and the generosity of the publisher, have combined to lead to this new edition. So to those I acknowledged in my first edition, I add the readers who prefer to remain anonymous who uncovered these flaws. My thesis and its details and aspects remain unchanged.

If anything, the events in our world of the past several years—and the upsurge in autocratic leadership and the expression of antisemitism as well as other forms of group-to-group animosity—enhance my conviction that we need to understand how things begin (in this case, Judaism and Christianity). We need to try to shape that understanding within an awareness of a range of concepts for which the everyday references have led to an amnesia regarding true origins and meanings of those concepts. That amnesia is ultimately dangerous for the future of humanity and requires the remedy of re-opening the bank of memory.

Ori Z Soltes
October, 2019
Washington, DC

Foreword

Jess Hollenback

For the last two generations, scholars of the comparative study of religions have shown a growing interest not only in (1) the history of how commonly used terms in their field like "religion," "mysticism," "Hinduism" and "world religions" have originated and developed over the centuries but, at the same time, they have also shown a concern with (2) uncovering the hidden political and metaphysical agendas that are so often embedded in the creation of such terminology and the ambiguities that are so often involved in the ways that they are used. In his book *Magic and Religion in the Greco-Roman World: The Beginnings of Judaism and Christianity,* Ori Soltes makes a very valuable contribution to this significant body of scholarly literature.

At the core of Soltes' book is his conviction that "how the vocabulary pertaining to magic and religion emerges and evolves is of importance to the competing, comparative shaping of Judaism and Christianity—and that this vocabulary has affected and continues to affect our sense of what Judaism and Christianity *are* (p. 1)." He shows how this vocabulary centering around "magic," "superstition," and "heresy" versus "[true] religion" played a vital role in the pivotal 4th century transition of Christianity from a persecuted "superstition" perceived as a grave threat to the stability of the Roman state to a religion co-equal in legality and status with other forms of religion to, eventually under Theodosius I, its triumphant achievement of becoming the only legal religion of the Roman Empire with all its former competitors becoming relegated to the status of dangerous and illegal "superstitions." One of the great strengths of Soltes' book is his fascination with the details of this complex interplay between the terminological and the political.

Given his interest in the relationship between religious terminology and what we might broadly term "the political," it is not surprising that Soltes draws our attention to a second very important problem: *Who* determines what is "magical" and what is "religious?" *Who* determines what is "mythical" and what is "real?" And *who* determines what forms of engaging the sacred are "superstition" and which ones are religiously legitimate? These questions are ultimately political questions that involve considerations of power. On the one hand, the political can be expressed at the divine level, i.e., "my god(s) are more powerful than your god(s)." For instance, how are the Egyptian "magicians" of the Pharaoh distinguished from the ancient Israelite "prophets" Aaron and Moses in the book of Exodus in the Bible? Both the Egyptian magicians and the two Israelite prophets are capable of stunning feats of magic. What ultimately lies behind the Biblical author's judgment of the inferiority of the "magicians" and their magic compared to the magic of the two Israelite "prophets" is simply that author's assumption that the Israelite prophets have the backing of a deity that has more power than the gods of the Egyptians. Similarly, why are the mediumistic feats of the "witch" of Endor calling up the spirit of the dead prophet Samuel in I Samuel 28 and foretelling the future inferior to the entranced visions of Balaam in Numbers 24:4 which also foretold the future?

Ultimately, the judgment for or against is based upon whether or not the action is in conformity to the will of the source of divine power. The "witch" of Endor's mediumistic revelations, though they are accurate, do not have the stamp of divine approval—indeed, they are contrary to God's will whereas Balaam's revelations are congruent with God's will. The political can also be expressed at the level of human power struggles. For instance, when early 4th century Christians were beginning to struggle successfully against their pagan and Jewish opponents for recognition from the Roman authorities as a *religio licita* (legal religion) and, when several generations later, they successfully maneuvered politically so that they had become the *only* legal religion and their opponents were now consigned to the status of illicit "superstitions,' this struggle for legal political recognition in the human realm was not divorced from profound ramifications in the terminological realm. As Soltes noted, "distinctions between religion and magic—and superstition, theurgy, alchemy, medicine, and even philosophy…reach[ed] a particular sort of crescendo as we move into the later third and fourth centuries" (p. 266) when this power struggle reached its climax. Much of the Christians' later success in that political struggle resulted from their ability to convince the Roman ruling elites that their religious opponents were practicing forms of engaging the sacred realm in ways that were incompatible with or inferior to the ways that "true religion" was able to engage it.

Soltes points out with numerous supportive examples that so often when oppositional terms like "magic" and "religion" or "mythical" versus "religious" or "superstition" versus "[true] religion" are set in opposition to one another what is really at the bottom of such distinctions is the ethnocentric assumption that "if it is not mine, it is magic, and therefore is not religion (p. 26)." If one has ever argued with a Christian fundamentalist, one has run into this assumption that while the Genesis creation narrative is assumed without question to be "true" and historically factual, other creation narratives from different religious communities are not true or factual. The latter are simultaneously classified and denigrated as mere "myths." In a similar fashion, Soltes draws attention to the fact that when ancient Christians often ridiculed pagan divinatory techniques as a species of either "magical" or "superstitious" hocus-pocus, they conveniently ignored the possibility that an outside observer ignorant of the Christian tradition and its theological context might have a very hard time differentiating why that same label of hocus-pocus might not also be equally applicable to the way, say, priests in a Catholic seminary are trained in the liturgical techniques that they will use in their rituals of Holy Communion. Where does one draw the line between the "magical" and the "religious" in such rituals that purport to make the divine present in this world? Why are the words uttered in one ritual any less magical than those uttered in the other? Soltes points out that even a scholar as sophisticated as Marcel Mauss who wrote a classic book focusing on the task of distinguishing magic from religion encountered a similar difficulty when he tried to distinguish the essential difference that distinguishes magic from religion. When all was said and done, Mauss was really incapable of convincingly distinguishing how magical practices really differ from religious ones. Almost always a practice that he would label "magical" would often be found among practices that in another context he would label "religious." Again, we were ultimately left with nothing much better than "if it is not mine it is magic and therefore it is not religion." This problem is, as Soltes observes, "endemic to every religion and belief system (p. 198)."

The issues that *Magic and Religion in the Greco-Roman World* raises about the interweaving of the terminological and the political is not just of relevance to students of comparative religion and students of the history of the ancient Mediterranean world. We can see examples of a similar interplay between terminology and politics in contemporary American society. For instance, notice how the word "liberal" with its 18th century

Enlightenment connections with words like "liberty," "free," and "freedom" has, since the time of Ronald Reagan successfully undergone a metamorphosis into a "swear" word in conservative Republican discourse used to vilify one's political opponents. This interplay between terminology and politics has been so successful that it has even forced their liberal Democrat opponents to stop referring to themselves as "liberals" and instead refer to themselves as "progressives." I would bet that the details of how this particular terminological transition came about would show significant parallels with the ways that Christian apologists and later, Christian rulers, succeeded in using vocabulary pertaining to magic and religion as a way of first demonizing their pagan and Jewish opponents and then suppressing or marginalizing them.

Magic and Religion in the Greco-Roman World deserves a place on the bookshelf of students and scholars interested in the history and religions of the ancient Mediterranean world, especially those interested in the history of Jewish and Christian origins. It is also a very valuable work for those students and scholars who are interested in exploring the relationship between religion and politics.

Jess Hollenback, PhD, is Associate Professor of History, University of Wisconsin-La Crosse, and the author of *Mysticism: Experience, Response and Empowerment* (University Park, PA: Penn State Press, 1996)

Preface and Acknowledgments

Some forty years ago, as a graduate student in Classics at Princeton University, I took a course called *Magic and Religion in the Greco-Roman World*, taught by Professor John Gager. Like the department and the school—and like all of us, I suppose—the course and the professor had strengths and weaknesses. It offered a range of interesting readings, of both primary and secondary sources, and certainly an eye-opening exposure to the problematic of distinguishing the two contrastive terms in the course title. A more broad-minded approach to the material and a more fair-minded approach to the students might have made the course stronger. The overall outcome, however—for this student, at least—was an appreciation of how much more complex the matter of dealing with the realm of the Other has been, three and two millennia ago—and how in all the time since (up to our own time), it has remained so.

A decade later, I taught a similar course for the first time at the then-extant Cleveland College of Jewish Studies, where the president, David S. Ariel, encouraged me to think as broadly as I wished. I injected a second element into the course, recognizing as I did by that time that the Greco-Roman era involved the emergence out of the Hebrew-Israelite-Judaean tradition of two twin, competing offspring: Judaism and Christianity. For I realized that the definitional issues of magic and religion—and an array of other terms—interwove that of defining these two religions at their outsets, when both began as Judaean traditions with increasingly different notions of how to understand God, God's revealed Word and the figure of Jesus of Nazareth.

Part of the complexity of competing belief systems that defined (and sometimes continues to define) the relationship between Judaism and Christianity derived from the extraordinarily complicated pagan world within which they were working out their respective senses of self. This complexity requires a careful teasing out in order to appreciate its significance for the two Abrahamic siblings.

A decade or so ago, I resurrected that course, with its double series of definitional issues, at Georgetown University, where I have now taught it several times. I also began to think that it might make sense to capture its elements in written form, in order to raise these questions for a larger audience than that in my classroom. We live in an era as fraught with complications in the matter of religion as ever; the interweave between spirituality and politics is as quietly (and sometimes noisily) rampant as ever. Our ability to communicate across the globe is unprecedented, and the content of communication both positive and negative.

These are things we need to think about, well beyond what we were taught in Sunday school. If we are to move forward, as individuals and as a species, we need sometimes to look backward, to understand where we have come from, in order to more clearly chart where we think we wish to go in the future. It is in the spirit of assisting that process just a little bit that I offer the narrative that follows.

*   *   *   *   *

This volume is dedicated to two wonderful individuals. Beth Pierce, a second mother to me and the only real grandmother from my side of the family that my children ever knew, passed away eighteen months ago, but rare is the day when she does not pass through my consciousness. Her daughter, Adrianne, was my friend and colleague first, as a graduate student in Classics, and has remained a very dear friend ever since. Not only that, she probably knows more Latin than Cicero did—and certainly all the important details from the ever-*sacer*-engaging X-Files!

I also want to acknowledge my Georgetown students who, as I covered this territory in the classroom, so often posed challenging questions that caused me to rethink what I thought I had thought out as far as I could—and in particular to Caitlin Mannering and to my son, Brahm, both of whom made the onerous task of creating the index a survivable experience. So, too, my inestimable editor and friend, Alexander Kohav who, as I hoped he would, proved to be the perfect respondent to the issues raised in this narrative, given his own skills and interests as a philosopher, artist and pedagogue, as well as being an editor and publisher. A serious comrade-in-arms.

A NOTE ON SPELLINGS

I admit to a snobby prejudice regarding the transliteration of Greek woirds and names; we tend to follow Latin versions of these. Thus, for instance, we write "Democritus" or "Neoptolemus" when a more accurate transliteration of the Greek would yield "Demokritos" and "Neoptolemos." (A few key Greek names do end in "-us"—such as "Akhilleus" and "Odysseus," however). So I use what I think are more accurate transliterations, except under three conditions: if a name is so commonly used according to the Latinized transliteration (e.g., "Cleopatra") and/or likely not to be recognized if I change it, I leave it; when I am quoting Roman writers in Latin I abide by the Latinized forms of Greek words and names that they use; if I am quoting someone who uses the Latinized transliteration, I leave it. Therefore, I occasionally spell the same name two different ways on the same page, in the same paragraph or even within the same sentence, if, say, I am quoting a Latin-language writer but then refer to some Greek-named character to which he refers. The same snobbery applies to Hebrew and Aramaic, for which my usual *bete-noire* is this: there are three "h" sounds in Semitic languages, two of which offer different degrees of a guttural sound (as in the German name, Bach). It has been a convention to transliterate the harsher verion with "ch", but I think that that misleads the unaware reader to pronounce it as in "church" or "chair", so I prefer "kh". Ideally, the lighter version should be rendered by an "h" with a "." under it, but in the absence of that ability, I prefer an "h"—again, rather than a "ch" or even a "kh", although that might misguide the reader to pronounce it as a straightforward English-language "h"—as in "hit" or "hah!" Thus "barukh" but "mashiah" (in the second of which, the final "h" should be aspirated and not silent, whereas in "Torah" it is a simple "h" and should be silent). Admit it. You thought this was going to be easier, didn't you? There are no simple solutions, even in this small matter. May the gods of spelling and transliteration forgive me for being so annoying.

14

INTRODUCTION

The Difficulty of Defining Terms

The world of the Greeks and Romans was one of multi-aspected Paganism, with its consciousness of a range of gods and goddesses, as well as *daimones* and spirits moving between the divine realm and ours. It was also one in which the Hebrew-Israelite-Judaean tradition competed with Paganism and continued to struggle to define itself—and ultimately split into what became Judaism and Christianity, which competed both with each other and with the pagan traditions from which they both sought to distance themselves.

This volume focuses on the times, places and literatures that reflect the interface between Paganism as it was evolving within the Greco-Roman world and nascent Judaism and Christianity. It pushes toward an understanding of how Judaism and Christianity emerged out of the Hebrew-Israelite-Judaean tradition as two forms of faith, each claiming to be the proper continuation of that tradition. It considers how their theological relationship—their competition regarding the Truth as it pertains to divinity and its relationship to humanity—is not only affected by their mutual interface and their theological relationships with Paganism but by the political context of the pagan Roman Imperium in which they both developed.

That Imperium and the ideas out of which it grew and which it both continued and transformed was a world of convergence, divergence, synthesis, embrace and rejection of religious principles and ideas. It was a world in which verbal distinctions that we take for granted—such as those between magic and religion, myth and theology, superstition and true belief, astronomy and astrology—had not yet assumed the place to which they have arrived over time toward our vocabulary. The closer we look at these various pairs of terms, the clearer is becomes that they—and other similar pairs—stare at each other across metaphorical borders that were not only blurry in antiquity but have often remained blurred in the modern era, even when used by scholars with impressive backgrounds and impeccable credentials.

Our goal is largely to come to understand how "magic" and "religion" have been or may be distinguished from each other in a coherent manner—or to recognize how in the end they may not be clearly distinguished—while at the same time interweaving that understanding and its perhaps problematic limits with the issue of what it is that comprises the key elements that distinguish and join the two traditions, Judaism and Christianity, particularly at the time of their respective births. Thus the premise of this book is that the matter of why and how the vocabulary pertaining to religion and magic emerges and evolves is of importance to the competing, comparative shaping of Judaism and

15

Christianity—and that this vocabulary has affected and continues to affect our sense of what Judaism and Christianity *are*.

To begin with, one must understand the broad context within which magic and religion operate. For simplicity's sake I will begin by discussing the underlying purposes and principles of religion alone, but sooner than later we will arrive at the realization that the purposes and principles of magic may be similar or even the same—which will be part of the point toward which this inquiry is directing itself.

Religion presupposes a dichotomy to reality. On the one hand, the realm in which humans operate in the everyday sense—the realm, in time, from sunrise to sunset (daytime) and from birth to death; the realm, in space, of the community in which I am comfortable and safe, whether I construe that community to be my small village or planet earth; the realm that encompasses humanity and its preoccupations—all of that is what the Romans called the realm of the *profanus*. It is that aspect of reality that we know—or believe we can or do—and in which time moves in a reliable, linear manner and distance is measurable in agreed-upon, consistent units.[1]

The other side of reality is called the *sacer*. This term refers to the realm of sleep and dreams, of night, of death, and of the unknown vastnesses beyond the community: the ocean, the woods, the mountains, the desert, outer space. The *sacer* is that which is not human: it is the realm of animals, particularly wild animals, and above all, it is the realm of divinity. As such, the *sacer* does not conform to our patterns of pre-expectation; rather than offering safe circumscription it operates unpredictably—sometimes with positive results (so it is a realm fraught with hope) and sometimes with negative outcomes (so that it is a realm fraught with fear).

This understanding of a fundamental dichotomy to reality is endemic to human thought, across the entire panoply of our cultures and civilizations, even as myriad differences of detail distinguish one culture or civilization from another. Moreover, within this dichotomous thinking, the *sacer* offers a two-fold possibility in its relationship to the *profanus*. For it is intrinsically neutral in its disposition toward the *profanus* but potentially positive or negative in its interaction with us, a source of help and harm, of obstruction and promotion. Moreover, while all aspects of the *profanus* and the *sacer* are analogues of each other, the most profound and profoundly disturbing aspect of the *sacer* is divinity—for the obvious reasons: if divinity, as humans believe, has created us, it has the power to destroy us; if it can help us it can also harm us—further or hinder us, bless or curse us; it can exercise the potential of the *sacer* to affect the *profanus* in either positive or negative ways more extremely than is true of other aspects of the *sacer*.[2]

---

[1] Thus 1 o'clock is reliably followed by 2 o'clock and the distance from the Washington Monument to the White House is reliably different from that between the Washington Monument and the Empire State Building in New York City or the Eiffel Tower in Paris.

[2] The term "*sacer*" is of course the ancestor of our word "sacred," as "*profanus*" is the ancestor of our word "profane." I use these Latin antecedents rather than their English descendants for three reasons: because they imply a greater range of analogic aspects; because they underscore the potentially positive or negative but intrinsically neutral nature of the concepts; and so that the reader, not used to these terms, will necessarily pause for a milli-second each time they are used, rather than slipping swiftly and unthinkingly over excessively familiar terms.

If the various aspects of the *sacer* are analogues of each other, there is also an obvious logic to operating vis-à-vis the *sacer* by way of analogues: if that aspect of it that is most important because of its potential to create or destroy us is divinity, and divinity is, by definition, utterly other—the Latin word is *alienum* (from which we derive our word "alien") and it has it analogues in other languages; for example, *xenos* in Greek and *anyad* in Sanskrit—then our ability to understand it and to know what we must be and do in order to survive is limited in the extreme.[3] So we approach it by way of analogues, by way of metaphor, by an array of indirect means.

The *sacer*, to repeat, is the opposite of the *profanus*; it does not operate as the *profanus* does in time and space; there offers an inherently paradoxic manner. In a dream reality, we can find ourselves suddenly in a completely different place from where we were a moment ago, with completely different people—including people who are dead but with whom, typically, we have had a very strong emotional relationship. Time and space lack a linear clarity. Vast distances can be traversed in an instant. Outcomes are absolutely unpredictable.

Particularly in its divine aspect, the *sacer* is a realm of paradox, beyond straightforward understanding. It is ultimately eternal, and fundamentally spaceless in our sense of "space" and timeless in our sense of "time." Every inch of reality is part of the continuum of its awareness; all of time is present tense to its consciousness—in contrast to our limited spatial sightlines and our senses of easily forgotten past and invisible future. Yet we establish precisely—emphatically precise—circumscribed times and spaces in attempting to engage the *sacer*. The times are most often border times (for their very being connotes our intention to cross a border in engaging the *sacer*)—sunrise, sunset, noon, midnight—from which we diverge at the minimal peril of the inefficacy of our rituals and the maximal peril of disaster.

We define precise spaces in which to interact with the *sacer*: locations that are known or believed to offer a point of contact with the *sacer*; border places where that interaction has a maximal chance of success. Each of these places functions as a kind of center—a sacred center—around which our *profanus* reality revolves, and that connects us to the *sacer*. Thus the *omphalos* at Delphi—the Greek word is cognate with the Latin "umbilicus"—suggests a consciousness of that site as propitiously connected to that particular aspect of the *sacer* that offers guidance to human petitioners, divinity articulated, in this case, as the god Apollo.

Similarly, when in Genesis 28, Jacob flees the wrath of his brother Esau, his first night away from home on the way to his uncle's home in Haran is spent in the wilderness—the *sacer*. At night—a *sacer* time—he has a *sacer* experience—a dream—in which he sees some sort of ladder-like entity connecting heaven (*sacer*) and earth (*profanus*) with beings going up and down (moving between *profanus* and *sacer*) on it. When he awakens he is astonished regarding what he has understood to have been a message to him from the *sacer*

---

[3] As we will have occasion to note later on, another word that would be translated into English as "foreign" from Greek is "*barbaros*." While that onomatopoetic locution derived from the fact that non-Greek speakers—most specifically, Persians—sounded to Greeks as if they were saying *bar-bar-bar…* when they spoke, it came to have a distinctly pejorative sense that was later transferred into the Latin (*barbarus*), English (barbarian/barbarous), and other European languages.

and asserts that "I did not know that the God of my fathers, Abraham and Isaac dwelt here." He takes the stone upon which he had slept and other stones and creates a tangible marker of that experience to indicate this site as propitious of divine-human contact: a high place—an *altar* (from the Latin *altus*, meaning "high"—see the English word "altitude")—and to his descendants, that place, called *Beit-El* (Hebrew for "House of God") will be an important spatial point of *sacer-profanus* contact forever thereafter.

Moreover, to repeat, the *sacer* is inherently neutral in its disposition toward the *profanus*, while its response to and interaction with us is *potentially* either positive or negative. We may sleep and have no dreams, or we may dream and the dreams are not particularly memorable, or they can be so sweet that we don't wish to wake up or so nightmarish that we cannot wait to get out of them and remain profoundly disturbed by them long after we are awake. In the woods my fairy god mother may touch me on the shoulder and give me three wishes that transform my life wonderfully—or wild beasts may attack me and tear me apart. When we die nothing may happen—or we may go to a wonderful place called heaven or paradise or a horrific place called hell. When we seek contact with divinity, it may not respond at all, or it may respond in an altogether positive way by giving us precisely what we need or in an enraged manner that is intensely destructive to us.

So: the *sacer* is that which is outside and beyond the *profanus*. The *profanus* may be understood as the community, and the *sacer* is beyond and outside the community. It is not only the realm of gods and animals and foreigners—friend or foe—but even a member of the community who becomes estranged from it is by definition *sacer*. Some individuals are habitually half out of the community: prophets and seers, priests and pharaohs: beings who are both part of the community but stand apart from it and possess a unique connection to the *sacer*. Such beings are termed *sacerdotes* (*sacerdos* in the singular)—a word that attaches the suffix "-dos," from the Latin "*do, dare,*" meaning "to give"—to the noun "*sacer.*" Thus such individuals can give to us what the *sacer* would have us be (its instructions) and give to the *sacer* what we need from it (our petitions).

Religion is that construct that articulates this understanding of reality and seems to have existed as long as humans have. Its purpose is to bind us back to divinity as that aspect of the *sacer* that is the source that has made us. We can see this in the Latin term from which the word itself derives: *religio*, whose three etymological components are *re-*, (meaning "back" or "again"); *l-vowel* (usually "i" or "e" and in this case "i")-*g*, meaning "binding" (as in *li*gaments, or *li*gatures); and the suffix, *-io*, indicating that it is a noun. The purpose *within* the purpose of "binding us back"—to the source that we believe has made us—is survival. Based on the belief that that which has created something can destroy it—can hinder or further it, help or harm it, curse or bless it—religion has, as far back as humans have existed, sought to ensure that the relationship between divinity and ourselves has a positive and not a negative outcome.

We can see this expressed in the earliest of visual human expressions, which are invariably part of the pre-writing articulation of the hope for survival. Thus for instance, among the oldest sculptures—perhaps 26-30,000 years old—is the so-called "Venus of Willendorf." She is a small (4.3" tall) figurine with no lower legs, heavy thighs, a well-defined pubic area, a large belly with a prominent umbilicus, enormous breasts that are further emphasized by stick-like arms that are stretched across them and a head without a face [FIG 1]. That appendage is completely covered by rows of curly hair—like rows of a well-plowed field—that wrap around it. There are seven of these, that number anticipating, perhaps, what written material millennia later will tell us regarding the importance of seven as a *sacer* symbol. For there are seven "planetary" divinities—associated with the seven "wanderers" (in Greek: *planetes*, from the Greek verb, *planeo*) that move across the sphere of fixed stars (stars that appear to remain in a constant spatial relationship to each other across the night and across the centuries) with a reliable periodicity. To this day we refer to these seven wanderers by the Roman versions of their god-names: Mercury, Venus, Mars, Jupiter, Saturn, Luna (the Moon) and Sol (the Sun).

FIG 1: Venus of Willendorf ca 30,000 BCE

The "Venus of Willendorf" is, from her exaggerated body parts to her strange head, a concretization of the abstraction "fertility," made more certain with divine assistance, and without which we cannot survive: if our fields or our cattle are not fertile, and our food runs out, we cannot survive; if we are not fertile and we have no offspring, we die out. This "Venus" and other similar paleolithic (and later, neolithic) statuary—as well as works in other media, such as early cave paintings—suggest a concern for survival that relates to a belief that survival is largely dependent on a proper relationship with divinity. Such ideas will much later be spelled out in words when, with the onset of the Bronze Age, writing systems develop. With those systems, moreover, we arrive at a more detailed and complex expression of the fundamental questions of religion: What *is* divinity? Why *did* it create us? What *would* it have us be and do, so that we are blessed and not cursed, helped and not harmed by it?

Religious rite and ritual regulates the separation between *sacer* and *profanus*, and guides us toward the appropriate times, places and manner of transgressing the boundaries between realms. One might ask how we know what the proper rituals are and where and when to perform them so that divinity is pleased and not offended by our performance. The answer resonates with the larger problematic of religion, and not just its rites and rituals. Every religious tradition offers revelation as its starting point; every tradition believes that there are individuals— *sacerdotes*; prophets and priests—to whom and through whom divinity communicates, reveals itself, instructing them with regard to guiding their constituents in general terms as they relate to the *sacer* and specifically with regard to rites and rituals, whether communal or individual, on a defined periodic basis or occasionally.[4]

This entire matrix of ideas can be understood in a succinct manner by considering the Roman inscription in which the term "*sacer*" first appears (albeit in a pre-classical form); this is the earliest Latin inscription available to us. It is found on an object called the *lapis niger*—the black stone—that, as early as the seventh pre-Christian century, marked the boundary between the amorphous center (the old forum) of the early town (village, really, at that point) of Rome and an area that was separate and dedicated to a goddess, perhaps Diana.

The inscription indicates that whoever upsets this boundary stone—together with his cattle (presumably a symbol of wealth and well-being)—will be *sacer*. The inscription offers us three obvious questions: What exactly does "*sacer*" mean in this context? Why would someone who upset the stone become *sacer*? What might that individual do, assuming that the condition of being *sacer* is not a desideratum, to reverse that condition? The intention is obviously to curse the individual—so "*sacer*" means "cursed"—but in practical terms it means "not be part of the *profanus*." Since the *profanus* is, in effect, the community, the individual so-labeled will no longer be part of the *profanus*: s/he is estranged from the community. As a further practical consequence, s/he is no longer protected by that which binds a community together—its *religio* and its *leges* (laws)—and may be assumed to be at potential risk: if s/he has enemies, this condition will offer them a chance to do him/her in.

So the offender had better leave town quickly, for his own protection. But that departure has a more profound motivation: to protect the community. The offending individual must be separated from those around him because, in the realm of *sacer/profanus* relations as they are governed by religion—a realm of analogues—every boundary connotes the ultimate *sacer-profanus* boundary. Thus to upset any boundary (particularly one that marks the separation between an area set aside for a goddess and the area of human action) is potentially to upset the ultimate boundary between the community and its gods—or in this case, a particular goddess—thereby inviting their (her) wrath upon the entire community. So the offender must disconnect him/herself from the community in order to draw the anger of the goddess onto him/herself and away from the community of which he was formerly part.

This situation is well exemplified in the Greek story of Oidipos. At the outset of Sophokles' play, *Oidipos the King*, the city of Thebes of which Oidipos is the ruler has been decimated by plague. By the end of the play, he, they and we have learned that Oidipos is himself the unwitting source of the plague, because he has—again, unwittingly—killed his own father and married his own mother, producing four children with her. In order for

---

[4] There are other kinds of *sacerdotes*, as well. Poets and artists are in-spirited by the *sacer* to do what they do, particularly, say, poets who write about the divine *sacer*—this is why Hesiod, for instance, spends the first 115 lines of his poem, the *Theogony* ("The Coming to Be of the Gods") invoking divine inspirational assistance, so that he may tell his tale accurately and effectively. Heroes are capable of acts beyond ordinary humans due to their divine connection—sometimes in the form of unique levels of support, as in the relationship between the Greek hero Odysseus and the goddess Athena, and sometimes because the hero is actually part god, as the Greek Akhilleus is, his mother a sea goddess, his father a mortal. Pharaohs and shahs are—or wish their constituents to believe that they are—half-divine, or at least that they operate with divine imprimatur.

the plague to be removed, Oidipos leaves Thebes, going into exile accompanied by the more loyal of his two daughters.

The last of the three loosely-linked plays on this topic that Sophokles wrote (*Oidipos at Colonus*) presents Oidipos years later, having made amends to the gods, having assuaged the gods' anger, permitting him to die in peace, albeit never having returned, and never having desired to return, to Thebes. But what of the offender who has disturbed a goddess by disturbing the *lapis niger*—what if, unlike Oidipos, he wishes to return to the community? How is it possible for him to make amends to the offended goddess and to return? He must first of all consult someone who will be able to answer that question: a *sacerdos*.

The *sacerdos* will inevitably instruct him along three lines all of which converge on the principle of precision. At a precisely prescribed sacerdotal place, at a precisely prescribed—almost inevitably, a border-type—time, he must perform a precisely prescribed ritual. Any number of rituals may fill out this third aspect of the process, but more than likely it will involve making something other than himself *sacer*. "To make *sacer*" in Latin is "*sacer facere.*" Certainly a very common sort of ritual would involve taking some animal—perhaps a lamb, or a goat, or a bull—and slaying it (in a precisely prescribed manner).

This must have happened pretty frequently, under diverse conditions, since ultimately the two words, *sacer facere*, coalesced to produce one word: *sacrificare*—that becomes "to sacrifice" in English. But the Latin term, meaning "to make *sacer*" does not only or necessarily mean to slay—although to go to the gods, while it implies going to immortal life (a positive outcome), at the same time, does mean "to die" in the sense of being separated from human affairs (a presumably negative outcome in most people's view).[5] In any case, the animal that is slain (if that is the process) by the one who disturbed the *lapis niger* is both *sacer* in being a gift to the goddess to atone for the offender's guilt and, if it has indeed been killed, is also *sacer* in that death is an aspect of the *sacer* realm.

It is very likely that part of the process—before slitting the animal's throat—will be to touch it; to lay one's hands upon it, transferring the guilt for the offense from *sacer* individual to the animal by physical contact. We may recognize this sort of process in the account of what happened on the annual Day of Atonement in the courtyard of the Jerusalem Temple of the Israelites and Judaeans. The High Priest, who was understood to have taken upon his shoulders a year's worth of God-offending sins from the entire people, laid his hands on a goat—the *Azaz-El*, as it was called in Hebrew, rendered in English as "scapegoat"—that was then pushed off the precipice of the Temple Mount into the valley below that led out into the Judaean wilderness. Put otherwise, then, the *Azaz-El*, to which those sins had been transferred by the laying on of the High Priest's hands, was made *sacer*—protecting the *profanus* by being made *sacer*—in the sense either of perishing

---

[5] When we first encounter Odysseus weeping on the beach of Kalypso's island and eager to continue home to his wife—after a dalliance of seven years with the nymph—he is rejecting the immortality that she offers him in favor of returning to Ithaka and a certain eventual death. Kalypso's name is cognate with the Greek verb, *kalyptein*: "to bury." Odysseus needs to get back to an existence that places him in the middle of all kinds of action, however complicated or disturbing that action might be, rather than remaining in isolation, cut off from human storm and stress—for to spend eternity in that condition, even if in the company of a voluptuous goddess, is to be functionally dead and buried.

(assuming that it died in the fall into the valley) or of wandering out into the wilderness (if it did not die). Or both. Either way, the sins were conveyed into the *sacer*, away from the *profanus*.

Of course, we must distinguish a ceremony that was an annual event—or periodic according to whatever timetable—and enacted by a *sacerdos* on behalf of the community, from one that involved an individual who has committed a one-time offense that requires expiation, as in the case of the *lapis niger* matter. But in both cases the same fundamental methodological issue is operative—precision with regard to time, space and ritual act, and border/boundary contexts for all three aspects of that precision—and the same fundamental goal: to protect the communal *profanus* from the potentially negative action toward it by the *sacer* in its overwhelming aspect as divinity. The need for precision offers an inherent paradox. For the realm of the *sacer* is by definition spaceless and timeless—it may not be boxed in with *profanus*-style borders—yet our engagement of it with such precision does just that.

Moreover, both the communal/periodic and the individual/occasional types of situation illustrate an even more significant paradox of the *sacer*: that it is inherently neutral but potentially negative or positive in its disposition toward the *profanus*. For the animal that is sacrificed—made *sacer*—particularly if that means that it is killed, may be assumed by us to experience a negative fate, if we understand death as a fate that is negative. But if we think that death is "going to a better place" then that fate is positive. To become one with the gods, since they are also *sacer*—assuming that the gods are at least partly good if not mostly good; and if there is only one God that that God is even understood to be all-good—can only be a positive experience, while at the same time most of us are likely to prefer to live than to die, which means that it is perceived to be a negative experience.

There remains at least one further pressing question evoked by this discussion: how do the *sacerdotes* whom we consult about all of this know what they know so that they may instruct us as to what to do under whatever *sacer*-related circumstances we encounter? How are they privy to the information that they provide for us? It is *revealed* to them. Every religious tradition, as we have observed above, offers as its starting point the conviction that there are certain individuals who are particularly conducive to *sacer-profanus* contact, as there are certain times and places that are.

The beliefs concerning revelation carry within them a layered complication that pertains to the second part of the process of religion: interpretation. We might ask how precisely divinity communicates with the sacerdotal individuals to whom it reveals itself and through these individuals communicates to the *profanus*. Does it have a voice as we do? Does it shape words with a throat, tongue, teeth and lips? When in Exodus 3 Moses "encounters" God at/through the Burning Bush, how exactly does Moses perceive the God that pushes him to return to Egypt and engage the Pharaoh toward allowing the Israelites to go free? And did Moses correctly understand the Lord—standing before the Burning Bush, and later on, when he and the Israelites were standing at the edge of the Sea of Reeds (Ex 14:16), or later still when, following the death of his sister, Miriam, he would importune God on behalf of the people to provide them with water and is told to speak to the rock (Numbers 20:8)?

For Moses—even Moses—is not infallible in his understanding of God's word. In his hurry to return to Egypt from the wilderness of Midian, he completely forgets to circumcise his son—God almost slays Moses for this omission, his error corrected through the remedial action of his wife, Tzipporah (Ex 4:24-7). And instead of speaking to the rock, Moses hits it—twice—with his staff (Num 20:11), provoking the anger of God, for "because you did not trust me enough to demonstrate my holiness to the people of Israel, you will not lead them into the land I am giving them! (Num 20:12)" Thus the greatest of Israelite prophets would be denied entrance into the Promised Land toward which he leads his flock for 40 years in the wilderness for having misconstrued the word of the Lord.

So a prophet, however great, is still human and humans make mistakes, including that of misinterpreting revelations. And what happens when the prophet is gone? The texts that eventuate—for example, the Torah, the Gospels, the Qur'an—are all written down well after the events that they describe and the oral shaping of those texts by the prophets to whom their content has been revealed by God. How incontrovertibly accurate are such texts, written down after the prophet has left us—and thus reliant in part, at least, on the memory of those writing it all down?

As often as not, the text as we receive it in writing may be sufficiently obscure that we need to interpret it carefully in order to understand God's intentions. What exactly does it mean "not [to] seethe a kid in its mother's milk" (Ex 23:19) for the purposes of an everyday traditional Jew in the twenty-first century? Why and how does it come to mean that s/he may not eat a cheeseburger, or either drink a glass of milk with his/her steak or follow it immediately with an ice cream sundae? A series of interpretations pertaining to the underlying intent of the commandment and also connecting it to a different commandment—to "build a fence around the roof of your house that you may not bring guilt of bloodshed on your household if anyone should fall from it" (Deut 22:8)—and its own interpretative chain lead, in combination, to this post-steak, sundae-less conclusion.[6]

It is not surprising that what becomes Judaism builds itself only on the *foundations* of the Hebrew Bible. The edifice itself is built beginning with the varied rabbinic interpretive literatures known as Talmud and *Midrash*. Similarly, what eventuates as Christianity builds itself on the foundations of the New Testament and what Christianity understands as its prelude, the Old Testament, but the edifice itself is constructed beginning with the patristic and scholastic literatures and the interpretive thinking of St Augustine, St

---

[6] The underlying intention has to do with cruelty: what could be crueler than to cook veal, say, in the milk taken from its own mother—something altogether conceivable in a sheep-, goat-, and cattle-herding community. The process of digestion is likened to the process of seething, so to drink a glass of milk—particularly in a *post-*herding reality, where I don't know where it came from—that might conceivably have come from the mother of the animal whose delicate meat I am consuming, would be to abrogate God's commandment. This is connected (the connecting itself an interpretive act) to the rabbinic interpretation (in *Pirkei Avot* 1:1) of the first clause in the verse from Deuteronomy—which is that one must "build a fence *around the Torah*," which is in turn interpreted to mean that one must go beyond fulfilling a divine commandment a mere 100% (which is called a *humra* in rabbinic thought) to make sure not to abrogate it inadvertently—and leads to the decision not to consume milk and meat *products* together (hence, no cheeseburgers) or even one after the other (hence no post-steak milk or ice cream). The discussion will eventuate, over time, to include the question of how *long* after my steak I need to wait before I have digested it, so that I can have that ice cream for which I have been eagerly waiting. (One to six hours, depending upon whom you ask—although the 12th-century French rabbi, Rabeinu Tam, asserted that if one merely recites the grace after meals, clears the used dishes away and removes the tablecloth, one may immediately drink one's milk, having fully abided by the commandment).

Anselm, St Thomas Aquinas and a host of others who lived between the fourth and thirteenth centuries.

Moreover, what distinguishes Judaism from Christianity is not limited to their divergent interpretations of the texts that they share in common and agree are revealed. The very fact that what Jews called the Hebrew Bible (or more accurately, the *TaNaKh*) is called the *Old Testament* by Christians reflects two different interpretations regarding what constitutes the revealed texts known to both groups as the Bible. For Jews, the Torah, Prophetic writings and an array of further writings (the Hagiographa) together constitute the totality of the biblical text whereas for Christians, this material is understood to be an antecedent to the somewhat more important texts of the Gospels, Acts, Epistles and Book of Revelation that follow.[7]

This issue of distinguishing revelation from interpretation and correct interpretation from false may be seen in any number of contexts, and not only that of Judaism and Christianity. Nor is it limited to the Abrahamic traditions that include, for instance, Islam, with its interpretation-based distinction between Sunni and Shi'i Muslims and in turn, the more than half-dozen major schools of interpretive jurisprudence that further define subsets of Islam. This issue carries far and wide.

One might think, for example, of ancient pagan Greece, for which religious reality perhaps the most important site was that at Delphi with its *omphalos* and its Pythian *sacerdos*. She sat on her tripod over a cleft in the earth from which noxious fumes apparently emerged, enveloping her and in-spiriting her—causing her to babble in a manner well-nigh incomprehensible to ordinary people. It fell to the priests to interpret her ravings and transmit the messages of the god, Apollo, to those inquiring of the oracle. In turn, the statements of the priests might be obscure, as the inquirer, departing the site, would have to decide what exactly the words of the god had been and had meant.

Perhaps the most notorious instance of a misinterpretation is that recorded by Herodotos in his *Histories*. In that work the "Father of History" tells the story of Croesus, the enormously wealthy King of Lydia, who is not sure whether or not to wage war against the Medo-Persians and their shah, Cyrus the Great, in 547 BCE. The oracle informs him that if he does so, he "will destroy a great empire." It is only after being defeated by Cyrus that Croesus realizes that he had misinterpreted the oracle: the great empire that he destroyed was his own.

The reference to the belief system of the Greeks—a system that Judaism and Christianity regard as inherently mistaken with regard to its understanding of the divine *sacer*—reminds us that there are other terms besides "religion" that refer to means of transgressing the *sacer-profanus* border into intercourse with divinity. One of these is *magic*. The interesting thing is that the word "magic" itself is derived from Persian—the very Medo-Persians who, during their Achaemenid period were not only involved with the Lydians and the Egyptians and Greeks, but were also involved with the Judaeans. For it was the same Cyrus referenced in Herodotos who is credited, in the Bible, with allowing

---

[7] Still other texts—Maccabees I and II, Susanna and the Elders, Judith, Ben Sirah, and others—that were originally considered part of the Bible by Christians ended up rejected as canonical by the Protestants in the course of the sixteenth century while remaining part of the canon as far as Catholic, Orthodox and Ethiopian Christians are concerned.

the Judaeans to return to Judah from their Babylonian-imposed exile and rebuild their temple in Jerusalem.[8]

Like the forbears of the Judaeans, the Israelites, who included among the twelve tribes that comprised their confederation and eventual kingdom, the tribe of Levi—a priestly tribe, distinguished from the other eleven, in part, by possessing no property of its own—the Persians included among their societal groups a priestly group, each member of which was called a "*maghos*." The word was subsequently borrowed into Greek as "*magos*" (pl: *magoi*), and in turn imported into the Latin that the Romans mainly spoke, as "*magus*" (pl: *magi*)—and eventually into English as "magic, magician," and their adjectival siblings.

Also imported into English is the sense of magic as something somehow not real, not legitimate—a kind of dark or weak underside of religion, where the latter is both very real and possesses legitimate, positive power. It seems that the negative view of *mageia/magia* derived mainly from the fact that it was associated with the Persians.[9] From the Greek perspective, there are at least two reasons to either suspect *mageia* or look down upon it. If it is practiced by the Persians, then it is practiced by a group that was, first of all, regarded as inherently inferior: this was the almost immediate implication of the word "*barbaros*" (pl: *barbaroi*)—which is actually an onomatopoeia.[10] Simply put, Persian (and no doubt other foreign languages) sounded to Greek ears like ...*bar-bar-bar-bar-bar*..., as opposed to their own inherently superior and richer-sounding (to them, at least) language. As much as the Greeks knew about and were in awe of the grand trappings that were part of Persian culture, they (like most peoples) felt themselves inherently superior to others, so anything, including the particulars of others' religious traditions, shared a converse aura of inferiority.[11]

This would have been reinforced by the Hellenic success against the Persians during the wars that marked the late sixth and much of the first half of the fifth century BCE. Thus the Greeks—in particular the Athenians, who achieved a certain distinctive cultural and political-military hegemony within the Aegean during that time period—would have looked at the Persians with jaundiced eyes. For the Hellenic world and its sense of self as a "free" world was under threat by an Achaemenid juggernaut that employed enslaved soldiers (or at least mercenaries, fighting for no more than a paycheck); Hellenes looked at the Persians with supercilious eyes after the eventual Athens-led defeat of the Persians at the land battle of Marathon and the sea battle of Salamis and others.

---

[8] The term "Judah" is an anglicized version of the Hebrew term, *Yehoodah*. By contrast, "Judaea" is the Greco-Latin version of the term in its anglicized form. I tend to use "Judah" in discussing the period before around 300 BCE and "Judaea" for the Hellenistic-Roman period thereafter.

[9] Begging my reader's indulgence: *mageia* transliterates the Greek rendering and *magia* is the Latin rendering of this term.

[10] It is not precisely clear as to when "*barbaros*" is first attested, but certainly by the time of the Persian Wars (ca 500-450 BCE) the term had begun to acquire a negative connotation, suggesting uncouthness, etc., as noted above in fn #4.

[11] The Greeks of course are by no means alone both in considering themselves superior to others, and also in thinking of particular others in paradoxic terms. The Romans, for instance, admired the Greeks culturally, but found them morally inferior. See on the one hand the comedies by Plautus and Terrence that, with their often morally suspect characters, are inevitably set in Athens—never in Rome!—and the familiar quip referring to the Greeks as possessing morals that are as loose as the Greek islands.

The Romans, in turn—who inherited and emulated so much from the Greek world that they gradually swallowed up during the last two centuries BCE—applied the same negativizing sensibility to the terms "*magus*" and "*magia*" that they imported from Greece. What's ours is religion—and in the case of the Romans, that term encompassed a vast array of diverse belief systems—but what we don't embrace, if we called it "*magia*," is suspicious and ambiguously capable of doing damage, yet impotent when compared to true religion.

Similar in being viewed as standing on the opposite side of the fence from *religio* was what Roman law called *superstitio*, with which term the emphasis on a belief system's potential negative impact on the entire community was underscored. Where *religio*—more precisely, *religio licita*—was the term (or rather, phrase) that referred to forms of addressing the *sacer* in its divine aspect that were considered legal and thus acceptable to the state, because these forms posed no threat and might even be beneficial to the state; *superstitio* referred to a form of faith considered somehow politically subversive, potentially damaging to the state and therefore illegal.

By the time the term *magia* (and its sibling, *magus*) has reached English, its practitioners, a far cry from *sacerdotes* intermediating between the community and its divinities, have come to be thought of as people doing little tricks for fun and profit, to entertain and sometimes to heal but more often to harm on behalf of themselves or their clients. *Superstitio* has become superstition, and refers to radical misbelief—to belief in elements of the *sacer* that don't really exist—in contrast to religion and the real *sacer* truths toward which it points.

Other criteria—or rather, questions, with regard to a relationship with the *sacer*—put into play by both ancient and modern writers for distinguishing religion from magic help complicate the issue. Is the result that is desired different, and if so, how? Could it be that magic seeks physical results and religion metaphysical (spiritual) results? What sort of means are employed for contacting the *sacer* in order to yield the desired results—how do incantations, charms and amulets differ from prayers and sacrifices? Are there different layers and/or levels of the *sacer* to which magic and religion differently direct themselves? Is the expected effect on the *sacer* the same, or different: does magic operate through the presumption of compulsion while religion petitions? All of these kinds of distinctions have been proposed in various texts, as we shall see.

This narrative poses three essential questions, then. It asks how in the Greco-Roman world, and more recently, this sense of religion/magic either/or has been understood by significant ancient authors and modern commentators—and what other terms, incidentally, are included in the matrix for which religion, magic and superstition are our beginning point. Where do astrology, medicine, philosophy, science and theurgy, for example, fit into the discussion? A subset of this issue is the question of how rites, rituals, spells, charms, prayers—in short, various forms of engaging the *sacer* with words or actions—serve in that interaction to yield positive outcomes for the *profanus*. How do these processes influence the *sacer*; to what extent *is* the *sacerdos* perceived to be petitioning or compelling the *sacer*—and does this perception change depending upon whether the perceiver understands the context to be magical or religious?

There is an obvious sense in which this multi-valent question may be understood with regard to power on several levels. If the divine *sacer* can help or harm, further or hinder, bless or curse, create and preserve or destroy, then its power is considerable. How do we influence it? How do we invoke the power of that consummate *other* realm successfully on our behalf—to utilize its power in *this* realm? How do we distinguish the efficacy of, say, rituals of invocation from those of re-enactment? When the Babylonian priests of more than three millennia ago retold the story, year by year, of Marduk's defeat of Ti'amat at the beginning of time and his establishment of the order of the world as we know it, they *re-enacted* it as well.

At the beginning of every year—every solar cycle—they did this to assure that the god would repeat his deed of asserting order *now*, at *this* (annual) time, as he did at the *beginning* of time. To what extent ought we (or they, the Babylonians many millennia ago) to understand the act of recounting and re-enacting to function as a means of enabling the god to accomplish his annual ordering process? How is that different from or the same as the occasional sacrifice of predictably periodic offering—to the gods with respect to the principle endemic in the history of religions, *do ut possis dare* ("I give so that you may be enabled to give")?

How legitimate are the diversely articulated retellings in the first place? The early Greeks would refer to an account of the gods as a *mythos*—a gods'-truth account, by definition, since the one telling the tale cannot have been there when what he describes transpired, and would not be so foolish as to make things up about the gods, so s/he must have been inspired (in-spirited) by them with the information that is shared with the community. Put otherwise, the poet is, like the prophet and the priest, a *sacerdos*. Hesiod's *Theogony*, like the anonymously authored Babylonian *Enuma Elish*, is "based" on divinely revealed sources of information regarding the gods and how they engendered our reality. At a certain point in time, the Greeks began to distinguish *mythos* from *historia*, however, whereby the former was understood to lack facticity where the latter was understood to offer reliable facts.

We are more likely, in the world of today, to view the Babylonian and Greek creation stories as myth, not fact, whereas we might view the account in Genesis as more "real." But—and this is essentially our second question—who ultimately determines this, as time moves on? Who is in control of the *profanus* and decides what is and what is not a legitimate means of engaging the *sacer*? Put otherwise: where does the millennia-long interface between religion and politics intersect the ostensive line between religion and magic as between religion and mythology?

All of the elements of these two issues lead to a third issue, a question—a straightforward but not simple one, it seems. How did Judaism and Christianity begin and what was their relationship to each other and to the pagan world around them at the outset of their respective histories: not only what was eschewed but what was absorbed, adopted and adapted across the denominational lines that we might assume existed with clarity and distinguished Judaism from Christianity and from Paganism.

How, ultimately, are these three questions and their constituent sub-question elements variously intertwined in the world of late antiquity? This is a world in which Judaism and Christianity are not only wrestling with each other and with Paganism theologically—i.e., with regard to who has the truth pertaining to the divine aspect of the *sacer*—but politically, as each seeks legitimization and full legal status within the Roman world as that world continually expands through the centuries in diversity and in its conviction that the citizens of the Empire of World Order are the favorites of the gods and the darlings of destiny.

By the end of the fourth century, under the Emperor Theodosius I (r. 379-95), that Roman Empire will have become Christian, and myriad forms of Paganism as well as Judaism will become all but illegal. How and why did that happen—and what does that development have to do with the issue of religion and magic? These are questions to which we shall seek answers in the chapters that follow.

CHAPTER ONE

Theories of Magic and Religion from Frazer to Malinowski

In 1890, Sir James Frazer, a cutting-edge anthropologist and student of religions, published his seminal and lengthy work, *The Golden Bough*. Coming out of an academic discipline that had been gradually developing during the previous few generations, this work offered a rich discussion of cultural traditions and ideas that could be found expressed, with variations, across a broad range of human groups—nearly all of them pre-Christian, non-Western European or both. Frazer's starting point was an ancient rite associated with the priest of the sacred grove of Diana at Aricia, on the shores of Lake Nemi, in Italy. That priest, Frazer informs the reader, was known as the King of the Wood, which, according to Sir James, indicates that he was originally regarded "as an incarnation of the spirit of the woodlands," his function "to control and regulate fertility and vegetation."[12]

He goes on to suggest that "such royal and priestly stewards of nature (or particular departments of nature) are found among primitive peoples everywhere." In the definitional terms laid out in the discussion within the introduction to our own text, an important and perhaps surprising issue within Frazer's synopsis is that he uses the term "primitive" as if to suggest that more advanced cultures and traditions are completely free of such concepts of stewardship.

Moreover, Frazer continues, such stewards "operate by means of *magic*" (his italics). The first part of his narrative is in fact called "The Magic of Kings." The first subset section of that first part is called "The King of the Wood," at the end of which he observes that "among primitive peoples the king is frequently a *magician* as well as a priest..." (Frazer's italics, once again).[13] On the one hand, the discussion at the end of the book (over 650 pages later in the one-volume *abridged* version of his study, where he comes back to the question of how to understand the rite near Lake Nemi that he began to describe in his introduction) emphasizes the sacerdotal position of kings and their ilk, to account both for the image of the golden bough, that "being a bough, ...is poised, as it were, between heaven and earth"—that there are taboos against kings touching the earth because they are not ordinary, earth-touching humans. On the other hand, the observation

---

[12] Both quotes and that in the following paragraph come from Frazer's synopsis, found at the outset of *The New Golden Bough (Abridged): Sir James Frazer's classic work on Ancient and Primitive Myth, Magic, Religion, Ritual, and Taboo. Revised and edited in the light of recent scholarship by Theodore H. Gaster*. (New York: Criterion Books, Inc., 1959), xxi. The original work, incidentally, is many volumes long.
[13] Ibid, 34.

that kings may be magicians leads Frazer to embark on a discussion in the next subset section of that first part, regarding "the basic principles of magic in general."

Much of that subsection, "The Roots of Magic" relates its subject to the initial topic of kings as *sacerdotes*/magicians, forming the foundation of what follows throughout the volume. Thus Frazer writes, regarding the conviction of those who practice or are enthralled by magic, that one of that discipline's underlying principles is that "like produces like." The second key principle is that things once in contact with each other continue to act on each other always. These two principles may be spoken of as two laws: the first is the "Law of Similarity" and the second the "Law of Contagion." The first pertains to what he calls homeopathic magic and the second to contagious magic.

"Both derive, in the final analysis, from a false conception of natural law," Frazer observes. The primitive magician, however, never analyzes the mental assumptions on which his performance is based, never reflects on the abstract principles involved.... He knows magic only as a practical thing, and to him it is always an art, never a science, the very idea of science being foreign to his thinking."[14] One among our expanding list of questions must pertain to these comments by Frazer and whether and how they are of use in addressing not only the categories of religion and magic but, given his last trio of clauses, that of science vis-à-vis both of these.

Frazer offers a cornucopia of illustrations for his schematization of paired magical types—of instances where one may observe these laws/principles in action. Homeopathic magic has been used "by many peoples in many ages to injure or destroy an enemy by injuring or destroying an image of him. For thousands years this practice was known to the sorcerers of ancient India, Babylon, Egypt, Greece and Rome; and it is still employed by cunning and malign savages."[15] He moves from the Ojibway Indians—who, wishing "to work evil on anyone, ...make a little wooden image of [their] enemy and run a needle into its head or heart, or ...shoot an arrow at it, believing that wherever the needle pierces or the arrow strikes the image, [the] foe will at the same instant be seized by sharp pain"[16]—to the Aino of Japan to the "ancient books of the Hindus" and "the Moslems of North Africa."

This will surely sound familiar as a method to everyday fans of popular culture—including movies like "Indiana Jones and the Temple of Doom"—and associated with the phrase "voodoo dolls." A similar "device" is the execration text, in use for millennia in pre-Christian antiquity among the Egyptians, for instance. An image intended to represent one's intended victim is made, the name of one's enemy written upon it—thus adding the "magic" of words, particularly committed to the written form known only to priest/magician practitioners—and it is then destroyed, with the intention and expectation that the would-be victim will experience the same destruction or physical pain as that to which the facsimile is subject.

Whereas a voodoo doll is typically used with regard to an individual, an execration text may apply to an entire community, and, to repeat, includes the writing down of the victim's name, sometimes embedded within a prescribed formula. Thus for instance, the

---

[14] Ibid, 35.
[15] Ibid 35.
[16] Ibid, 35.

city of Jerusalem is mentioned in an Egyptian Execration Text from the eighteenth century BCE: the name of the city (and of others mentioned in the same text) was inscribed on a clay figurine that was then smashed. So Jerusalem and the other cities listed in that inscription were expected to experience an analogous destruction, just as an individual was/is expected to feel whatever pain was/is inflicted upon the facsimile "doll."[17]

In the case of contagious magic, not only might one be able to effect a desired result vis-à-vis an enemy by using some object with which s/he has been intimate, but by means of sometimes obscure sorts of physical contact.[18] Frazer references the pharaohs in describing an example of this that was "familiar to the wizards of Egypt. A drop of a man's blood, some clippings of his hair or parings of his nails, a rag of the garment which he had worn, sufficed to give a sorcerer complete power over him."[19]But he refers also to the notion that a weapon that has inflicted a wound, drawing blood from one's adversary, in still having its tip covered with that blood will be able to inflict further damage if put to use within the framework of a proper ritual.[20] Even someone's footprints—if, say, that individual has injudiciously passed through mud and left his or her footprints embedded within it—can be used to effect a desired outcome against that individual.[21]

Frazer continues, regarding the "priests of Amen-Ra at Thebes in Egypt," to discuss how they "regularly burnt a wax figure of the fiend Apep, who daily endeavored to prevent the sun from rising," as a means of assisting Ra, the sun god, to overcome Apep day after day.[22] The priests accompany their action with the uttering of curses, presumably similar or identical to the spells "uttered by Ra over the real Apep," to paralyze him. What is most important here for our discussion is the fact that within what Frazer labels as magic he includes practices of the ancient Egyptians—who, we might suppose, considered their practices to be part of their religion, not *mere* magic—as well as examples from Hinduism and Islam where the same question regarding religion versus magic might well be addressed; Hindu and Muslim practitioners/believers might offer a different perspective from that of Frazer regarding the terminology that ought to be applied to their actions.

Nor is homeopathic magic, as Frazer discusses it, limited to negative outcomes. He offers a number of examples—from South Africa and West Africa to the Maori of New Zealand—of homeopathic means of helping the child-birthing process along.[23] He also describes how rain might be brought to a community that is in the midst of a drought. In the first and a rare instance where his focus is on a practice within a Judaeo-Christian

---

[17] See archaeologist Yigal Yadin's brief discussion of this in his book, *Hazor: The Rediscovery of a Great Citadel of the Bible*, (New York: Random House, 1975), 14. Yadin notes that there is some disagreement as to whether these Execration Texts date from the nineteenth or eighteenth century BCE; for our purposes, this does not matter.
[18] Think, in more recent narratives (well after Frazer's time) of the book by Ira Levin (and the movie that followed shortly thereafter), *Rosemary's Baby*. When Rosemary's husband was eager to get the acting role that had gone to another, he procured the sweater of his competitor and provided it to the nefarious sacerdotal practitioners who were his nice (not so nice), elderly neighbors and they were able to work their "magic" through that garment: the competitor suddenly fell and broke his leg, leaving the part in the play open for Rosemary's husband. As it would eventually emerge, of course, the elderly couple were *sacerdotes* in the service of the Satanic side of the *sacer*. More about that later.
[19] Ibid, 37.
[20] Ibid, 65-8.
[21] Ibid, 68-70.
[22] Ibid, 37-8.
[23] Ibid, 39-40.

community, he refers to customs "still commonly observed in some parts of Catholic Europe, [that] are interesting because they show how in later times *magic comes to be incorporated with religion* [italics added]. The molding of wax images of ailing members is in its origin purely magical: the prayer to the Virgin or to a saint is purely religious: the combination of the two is a crude, if pathetic, attempt to turn both magic and religion to account for the benefit of the sufferer."[24] Of course the question is what identifies one of these actions as magic and the other as religion, other than Frazer's say-so—and also, are there other instances of identifiable magic "incorporated with [identifiable] religion?"

Among the more compelling examples of what Frazer classifies as homeopathic magic—but which seems to me to combine similarity with contagion—is that practiced in "some districts of Borneo, when the men are away on a warlike expedition, [and] their mats are spread in their houses as if they were at home, and the fires are kept up till late in the evening and lighted again before dawn, in order that the men may not be cold.[25] Further, the roofing of the house is opened before daylight to prevent the distant husbands, brothers, and sons from sleeping too late, and so being surprised by the enemy."[26] Similarly, his discussion of the use of animals, "often conceived to possess qualities or properties which might be useful to man, and [through] homeopathic or imitative magic seeks to communicate these properties to human beings in various ways," often, it seems to me, blurs the line between the two kinds of magic that he discusses without his noting that blur. Thus, for instance, "[t]he Esquimax of Baffin Land fancy that if part of the intestines of a fox is placed under the feet of a baby boy, he will become active and skillful in walking over thin ice like a fox."[27] The baby may become like the fox, which certainly sounds homeopathic, in that the one imitates the other, but if he does so it is because of contact with the fox entrails, which is contagious.

The same may be said for the ancient Greek belief "that to eat the flesh of the wakeful nightingale would prevent a man from sleeping; that to smear the eyes of a blear-sighted person with the gall of an eagle would give him the eagle's vision;"[28] and similar examples that Frazer multiplies. In any case, conduct of both contagious and homeopathic sorts is exemplified from Madagascar to the Babar Archipelago, among the Bantu and the Bohemians, where particularized use of an array of animals as well as plants is perceived as promoting qualities that may be harmful or helpful in the hands of those who know their proper use.

In considering larger-scaled instances of homeopathy, Frazer turns to "the magical control of the weather," offering as his first example a brief description of a village near Dorpat, in Russia—presumably a Christian community—in which three men share the sacerdotal responsibility of causing it to rain when nature has failed to offer the precipitation needed for communal survival. The three men "used to climb up the fir-trees of an old sacred grove. One of them drummed with a hammer on a kettle or small cask to

---

[24] Ibid, 40.

[25] Presumably part of what makes this entire process "work" is the fact that the sleeping mats have been in contact with the men, therefore adding a contagious element to those that are homeopathic.

[26] Ibid, 51.

[27] Ibid, 56.

[28] Ibid, 57.

imitate thunder; the second knocked two fire-brands together and made sparks fly to imitate lightning; and the third, who was called 'the rain-maker,' had a bunch of twigs with which he sprinkled water from a vessel on all sides" to simulate rain—and to cause it to rain. It is noteworthy that Frazer uses the past tense but without specifying how far back in the past this ceased to be a practice, or how old the "old sacred grove" would have been (or why it was sacred—presumably because once upon a time it had been, or was believed to have been, a site where effective *sacer-profanus* contact had taken place).

These various examples—and many more that Frazer offers—provoke a series of questions. What exactly is the power of the word—or of particular words or names—as opposed to particular actions? Frazer distinguishes words that are associated with actions leading to a positive outcome, which he labels "charms," from those with negative intent, which he calls "taboos." This question in turn leads us to ask what it is that distinguishes these actions as magic from actions that would be considered religious? Does it pertain to compulsion as opposed to petition? To what extent is it a matter of negative versus positive intentions? Obviously if magic can be both white and black, then it can be both positive and negative and cannot, per se, be distinguished from religion along such lines. To what extent may we understand the distinction to be one of what is mine/ours versus what is yours/theirs?

In fact, in the subset of that part of his discussion devoted to "Sacred Marriage" that refers to "sex and vegetation," among the instances that he offers is one in Ukraine, where "on St. George's Day (the twenty-third of April) the priest in his robes, attended by his acolytes, goes out to the fields of the village, where the crops are beginning to shew green above the ground, and blesses them. After that the young married people lie down in couples on the sown fields and roll several times over them, in the belief that this will promote the growth of the crops. In some parts of Russia the priest himself is rolled by women over the sprouting crop."[29] So are we to understand that these actions are magical in spite of the fact that they involve a *sacerdos* who is the center of (Christian) religion within the community?

What of the question as to whether "the priest who bore the title of King of the Wood at Nemi and his mate the goddess of the grove have been serious counterparts of the merry mummers who play King and Queen of May, the Whitsuntide Bridegroom and Bride in modern Europe? And may their union have been yearly celebrated in a *theogamy* or divine marriage"? How do we distinguish this as magic from religion? How does the ancient custom "[a]t Thebes in Egypt [where] a woman slept in the temple of Amon as consort of the god and, like the human wife of Bel at Babylon, she was said to have no commerce with a man"[30] differ from the marriage vows to Jesus-as-God taken by an acolyte into the Franciscan Order of the Poor Clares beside the fact that Jesus is a different god-concept from Amon or Bel?

Certainly Frazer recognizes some of these sorts of resonances himself when he concludes at the end of this opening chapter of his work that "the kings of Rome and Alba... [like] all the kings of ancient Latium... each, we may suppose, represented or

---

[29] Ibid, 126-7.
[30] Ibid, 130.

embodied the local Jupiter. For we can hardly doubt that of old every Latin town or settlement had its own Jupiter, as every town and almost every church in modern Italy has its own Madonna... At Rome [Jupiter] occupied one summit of the Capitoline hill, while the other summit was assigned to his wife Juno, whose temple... has for ages been appropriately replaced by the church of St. Mary 'in the altar of the sky' (*in Aracoeli*)." The question is not how to parse the continuity and transformation pertaining to both Juno (Hera, in Greek) and Mary as the Queen of Heaven as much as the difference between the two versions of that consummate female (the one a goddess among other goddesses, the other a human, by paradox the mother of God in God's human incarnation) as representative of the dichotomy between magic and religion—and the further question of how and whether that dichotomy relates to the dichotomy between mythology and religion.

A second important figure in the late nineteenth through mid-twentieth-century discussion of these issues is Marcel Mauss (1872-1950), known as a thinker whose writing straddled the border between sociology and anthropology. In 1902-3 he wrote a monograph that was first published in full-fledged book form in 1950, entitled *Esquisse d'une theorie generale de la magie*.[31] Mauss begins in his prologue by asserting that "[u]p to now, the history of religions has consisted of a blurred bundle of ideas... Words such as religion and magic, prayer and incantation, sacrifice and offering, myth and legend, god and spirit are interchanged indiscriminately." He sets out, as he explains, to offer definitions and explanations that "will provide us with scientific notions—that is, clear ideas about things and their inter-relation."[32]

Mauss explains that, in his earlier study of sacrifice, he came to realize that the "basic idea of all ritual... was the idea of the sacred."[33] Fair enough as a conclusion. But that first study led him to the second, focused on magic, thinking that if he could "succeed in finding the ideas related to a concept of the sacred, as the basis of magic, we [would] be justified in extending the conclusions which [he] proved to be true for sacrifice to all kinds of mystical and traditional techniques. That is because *magical rites are precisely those which, at first glance, seem to be imbued with the least amount of sacred power*" [emphasis added].[34] So at least initially (hence my added italics) he sees magic and its concomitants as possessing or offering less sacred power than religion does. And he immediately recognizes a conundrum. He has emphasized that the idea of the sacred is a social idea—a product, as he puts it, of collective activities, and he has concluded that "magical practices which derive from this idea or a similar one, are social facts in the same sense that religious rites are social facts," except that magic is typically understood to be practiced by individuals outside the social group, acting in their own interests or those of individual clients. So is magic "a collective idea or [is] the notion of the sacred... an individual one?"[35]

[31] I am using the English edition (translated in 1972 by Robert Brain): Marcel Mauss, *A General Theory of Magic*. New York: W.W. Norton & Co, 1975.

[32] Mauss, 7.

[33] I am in this part of the discussion sticking with the term "sacred," recognizing that it represents a narrower band of the broader concept, *sacer*, as I have earlier asserted. For the purposes of our examination of Mauss's discussion thus far, the distinction does not matter.

[34] Ibid, 8.

[35] Ibid, 9.

The important issue, as Mauss goes on to state, is less the rite itself than the milieu in which it occurs. "In other words, we ought not to try and consider independently a series of isolated rites, but consider all those things which constitute magic as a whole; we must, in sum, begin by defining and describing it."[36] He refers to a handful of prior authors, arriving quickly to Frazer and objecting to Frazer's discussion as too dogmatic, too limited and tending "to confuse 'magic' with 'sympathetic magic.'"[37]

He also brings up Winfred P. Lehman who defines magic "as 'the practicing of superstitions'—that is, 'beliefs which are neither religious nor scientific'"—certainly a problematic sort of definition, since it states what one might consider obvious: that magic is not religion or science. But this tells us nothing about what magic actually *is*—albeit Mauss does not seem to notice this problem. He does, however, follow this by noting that none of the writers who precede him offer an attempt "to enumerate fully the different categories of magical facts and, as a result," he concludes, "it is doubtful whether, at this stage, it is possible to propose a scientific scheme which could embrace the whole subject" (which is clearly what Mauss himself intends to do). And he notes, importantly, that other authors' efforts have been hampered by their prejudices, an idea that we have already seen well exemplified.[38]

Where does this lead Mauss in his second chapter, entitled "A Definition of Magic"? He writes as an anthropologist, albeit not in the Malinowskian sense of focusing on a particular culture (or cultures); rather he generalizes while observing that people are subjective about their definitions.[39] He asserts that "a religion designates the remnants of former cults as 'magical'" even when the rites are being performed in a religious manner."[40] He thus implies that religion is a more evolved form of what begins with magic—although he notably does not define what the phrase "in a religious manner" actually means. In the same vein he again emphasizes that the term "magic" should be used to refer to those things that "society as a whole considers magical and not those qualified as such by a single segment of society only." Again this dodges an actual definition and even, in an odd way, absolves him of the responsibility as presumably one who is "qualified"—why else an entire book on the subject?—of actually defining the subject that he is defining.

Nonetheless, he offers directional suggestions. Thus, in magic "we have officers, actions and representations: we call a person who accomplishes magical actions a *magician*, even if he is not a professional; *magical representations* are those ideas and beliefs which correspond to magical actions... [which] we shall call *magical rites* [his italics]."[41] So how is this distinguished from religion and its officers, actions and representations? That we call a practitioner a priest instead of a magician—and must he always be a professional, perhaps meaning "ordained"? Presumably religious representations are those ideas and beliefs that correspond to religious actions, which one

---

[36] Ibid, 10.
[37] Ibid, 12.
[38] Ibid, 13, 14 for both the quotes and this last comment.
[39] On Malinowski, see below, 44ff.
[40] Ibid, 18.
[41] Ibid, 188.

might call religious rites. So where do these three aspects of magic lead and leave us with regard to a real definition?

Let us follow Mauss further to see if this question will be answered. He points out that magical actions need to be repeatable (but so do scientific "actions"!) and they require that the entire community believe in their efficacy—so "strictly private superstitions of gamblers cannot be called magical."[42] So the distinction between religion as public and magic as private and hidden away from the eyes of the community that he otherwiss asserts as a distinction between these two disciplines[43] does not apply in this iteration of Mauss' terms. Magical rites, he says, *do* things. They are creative, but human skill can also be creative and therefore it is often difficult to distinguish "techniques from rites... Moreover, there is probably not a single activity which artists and craftsmen perform which is not also believed to be within the capacity of the magician... [Indeed, m]agic in general, aids and abets techniques such as fishing, hunting and framing"—and again we might ask[44] what precisely it is that identifies certain rites/actions as specifically magical and not religious or scientific?

Mauss in fact acknowledges in the several lines that follow thereafter that other arts—and he refers specifically to medicine and alchemy—are "swamped by magic." "Medicine, almost to our own days, has remained hedged in by religious and magical taboos, prayers, incantations and astrological predictions. Furthermore, a doctor's drugs, potions and a surgeon's incisions are a real tissue of symbolic, sympathetic, homeopathic and anti-pathetic actions which are really thought of as magical."[45] As he continues in this direction and further presents related definitional comments, we seem to get ever more deeply mired in the mud that obscures clear borders either around magic or distinguishing it from any number of other disciplines, most obviously religion and medicine.

Indeed, in objecting to Frazer's discussion of sympathetic magic he outright states how sympathetic rites may be either magical or religious, underscoring how far we are from a definitional distinction between the two disciplines by way of Frazer. He adds that Frazer offers a second criterion for magic—that it constrains—whereas religion worships and conciliates, but asserts that "religious rites may also constrain and, in most ancient religions, the god was unable to prevent a rite from accomplishing its end if it had been faultlessly executed," which may certainly be true, although Mauss offers no examples— nor does he evince awareness of how that can also occur in more recent religious contexts.[46] In any case, he notes, conversely, that magicians often need to supplicate spirits and *daimones*.

---

[42] Ibid, 19.

[43] See below, 37 and especially 38.

[44] Mauss, 19. See also the discussion of Malinowski's discussion of the so-called use of magic by the Trobriand islanders in their cultivation of yams and in their fishing, (below, 46-7).

[45] Ibid, 20.

[46] Ibid, 21. I am thinking of the idea in late Jewish mysticism of the "Master of the Good Name (i.e., God's Name)" (*Ba'al Shem Tov*) who is able to accomplish miraculous outcomes due to his intimate knowledge of God's true Name and Essence: he does not and would not presume to have mastery over God, and yet his mastery of the Name, which conveys God's essence, gives him access to divine power—paradoxically, of course, since God, God's Name and Essence and God's power are beyond anybody's reach. And yet... See below, 240 and fn 405, and also 286.

This all said, Mauss proposes to present his own criteria for distinguishing religion from magic. Rites that are solemn (by whose estimation are some rites solemn and others not? one might ask), public, obligatory, regular are religious, even if Frazer, as Mauss notes, refused to accept some of these as religious. For example—and we have seen this sort of attitude in our brief perusal of Frazer—all Australian aborigine ceremonies and initiation rites are inherently "magical because of the sympathetic ritual involved." But, Mauss correctly observes that "the ritual of the Arunta clan, known as the *intichiuma*—the tribal initiatory rites—have precisely that degree of importance, seriousness and holiness which the idea of religion evokes."[47] Mauss clearly recognizes the prejudicial framework in which Frazer was working. The question will be, is Mauss free of such a framework?

Thus as for Mauss's own definitional superstructure, he continues: "rites do exist that are consistently magical. These are evil spells or malefices… The casting of evil spells is illicit and expressly prohibited and punished. This prohibition marks the formal distinction between magical and religious rites. It is the fact of prohibition itself which gives the spell its magical character."[48] We recognize that this formulation derives from Mauss's earlier statement of emphasis on the social context. In that case, magic can (always?) = evil, whereas religion always = good. Such evil-intended magic is illicit and prohibited—but is all magic (to repeat) thusly characterized? And who determines that a rite should be illicit and on what basis it should be illicit? What is the shape and size of that social context? If, as we shall subsequently see, Christianity is illicit throughout the Roman Empire more often than not, between ca 100 and 313 CE, and if in many parts of Christendom from the fifth through the seventeenth centuries, Judaism is all but illicit—to offer just two significant examples from the narrative that follows—are Christianity and/or Judaism and their respective rites magical rather than religious at those times and in those places, and not magical but religious at other times and places?

Mauss acknowledges that there are religious rites that are maleficent, such as imprecations against a communal enemy (as against Christians who were perceived to be communal enemies of the pagan Roman Imperium so often during the second and third centuries CE, or as the Jews came to be perceived by Christianity over the centuries that followed. But this is not a pair of examples that he offers). Yet he insists on two definitional poles: "the pole of sacrifice and the pole of evil spells."[49] Religion directs itself though hymns, vows and sacrifices toward "an ideal" whereas magic is associated with evil, at their respective extremes, although in between those extremes there are actions that blur the borders between the poles, including religious actions that are private and magical practices that are licit. Acknowledging the strong possibility for confusion, Mauss begins his initial "conclusion" by "accept[ing] Grimm's definition that magic is a 'kind of religion, used in the lower spheres of domestic life.'"[50] So religion addresses a higher aspect of the divine *sacer* toward higher outcomes and magic directs itself to lower aspects and lower outcomes.

---

[47] Ibid, 21.
[48] Ibid, 22.
[49] IbId.
[50] Ibid, 22-3.

He concludes his definitional chapter by asserting that magic and religion have different agents: a priest *qua* priest would not be performing magical exercises. We shall see how that formulation can be inherently prejudicial when, for example, Moses and Aaron contend with the *sacerdotes* of the Egyptian pharaoh: they are referred to as magicians in the biblical—Israelite-focused—text, but to the Egyptians they are priests. There is also site-differentiation: magic being "commonly performed in woods, far away from dwelling places, at night or in shadowy corners, in the secret recesses of a house," etc. Religious rites are performed openly, in full public view. Again using the story in Exodus as an example: both Moses and Aaron on the one hand and the Egyptian *sacerdotes* on the other perform in the same public location (and Moses, by the way, as did so many Israelite prophets, went away from the *profanus* community, out in the *sacer* to commune alone, albeit not to perform a ritual—if not in the woods then on a mountain-top in the middle of the wilderness—with God).

The magician, if required to perform in public "makes an attempt to dissemble: his gestures become furtive and his words indistinct."[51] More so than the Catholic priest reciting the litany in Latin in a time—our own—when virtually nobody in the congregation understands a word of it? Or than the culmination of the Armenian Mass behind a curtain separating the priest and his assistants from the congregation? Isolation and secrecy are essential to magical rites, Mauss asserts, and they are anti-religious. Inherently so? How so? Perhaps because they by definition, in being regarded by the religious and political powers-that-be as illicit, offer an alternative view of the divine *sacer* and how to engage it from that followed by the majority leadership?

But Mauss doesn't say this. He notes simply that magical rites do not belong to those "organized systems which we call cults," although he then points out that "there are examples of cults which are magical" in ancient Greece and in the Middle Ages and in India. "...[R]eligious practices, on the contrary... are always predictable, prescribed and official.... Magical rites... are always considered unauthorized, abnormal and, at the very least, not highly estimable."[52] So the person(s) in power—say, the Roman emperor, for example—states what is religious and what is magical. Is this what in the end distinguishes these two different disciplines? This is part of what we shall inevitably address as we move forward.

Mauss follows this in the remaining chapters of his book by exploring in more detail the issues that he has raised up to this point. In discussing the magician, he asserts that, "as a general rule, magical practices are the prerogative of specialists." True enough, perhaps, but it is odd that he immediately after making this statement illustrates by reference to "the Vedic texts, where the ritual may be performed only by the Brahman."[53] Odd because a Brahman is a priest; the Brahman caste is the priestly caste—analogous to the Levite tribe in ancient Israel—and as such perform rituals that their Hindu constituents would consider religious, not magical. So this sort of identifying feature does not seem to distinguish a magician from a priest or, accordingly, magic from religion—except, perhaps, along the lines of "what is mine is religion and what is yours is magic."

---

[51] Ibid, 23.
[52] Ibid, 24.
[53] Both quotes in this paragraph are from Ibid, 26.

In fact, an aspect of this sort of attitude-based definition is directly acknowledged by Mauss a few pages later, when he notes that [o]nce a church loses its following the members of the new religion consider the former priests to be magicians… [and h]eresy also leads to acts of magic..[and i]n the same way, strangers in a community are grouped as sorcerers."[54] This series of statements offers a range of ways in which the engagement of the *sacer* by the other is viewed—because it is inherently regarded by the majority as wrongly directed and even dangerous, be it those on the other side of a schism, those who offer a minority view of what constitutes the "correct" form of the faith, and those who constitute a different but minority religion. We shall encounter just this sort of range as our narrative moves forward. Indeed, Mauss anticipates a very specific direction that we will eventually take when he notes that "all Jews were magicians in the eyes of the Alexandrians, for example, as well as for the medieval church."[55]

Again, though, his societal classification system obscures certain issues. He notes that children may be in great demand as assistants to the magician "because of their age and because they have not passed though definitive initiatory rites..."[56]—or in our terms, they are not yet full-fledged members of the *profanus*, and are therefore, by definition, still, in part, a part of the *sacer* and likely to be of particular use in accessing and engaging it. I could not agree more, except I am not sure that this truth should be limited to magic: why is the role of the acolytes who assist Catholic or Armenian priests (to name just two examples) in performing religious rituals, played by non-adults—including, in the case of the Armenian Church, going behind the curtain that is then closed, walling off the altar from the congregation, for the most important, secret part of the service?

Similarly, Mauss points out that women—for certain obvious reasons, such as spontaneous bleeding every month, as well as pregnancy and birthing—are "said to be the font of mysterious activities, the sources of magical power. On the other hand, since women are excluded from most religious cults—or if admitted, reduced to a passive role—the only practices left to them on their own initiative are magical ones."[57] Once more one can only agree with the first part of this assertion, for these inherent female attributes place them with some frequency—once that is, having been transformed through puberty and its attendant rites of passage they are old enough to become full-fledged members of the *profanus*—at the border between *sacer* and *profanus* at its most profound: life and death (as signified by both menstrual and birthing blood).

On the other hand, this is certainly not limited to magic. The sort of sacerdotal exclusion that he references may well be found in the patriarchally-shaped Abrahamic traditions (including not only Judaism and Christianity but Islam), but it was hardly the case, for example, in the Roman world with its all-important Vestal Virgins or the Greek world with its oracular females at sites like Delphi, to say nothing of the mystery religions in both worlds. Unless one chooses not to recognize Greek and Roman religion traditions as *religious*, these are certainly examples in which women play a major sacerdotal role—

---

[54] Ibid, 30-1.
[55] Ibid, 31.
[56] Ibid, 29.
[57] Ibid, 28.

even as there are examples in which they do not—and in which, conversely, for that matter, men are excluded from the cult and its rites.

It is only at the end of his third, penultimate chapter that Mauss actually states that "it only remains now to compare magic and religion"—as if the entire prior discussion of magic did not automatically invite implicit comparisons, given how he introduced the subject—and acknowledges that this is a difficult challenge. He asserts, though, that religious "life, like sacrifice, permits no individual initiative, and invention is admitted only under the form of revelation... [but] if we are able to demonstrate that within the field of magic there are similar powers as those existing in religion, we shall have shown that magic has the same collective character as religion."[58] He thus asserts, in opening his last chapter that "we have gradually reduced our study of magic to the pursuit of collective forces which are active in both magic and religion."[59]

Good enough—and "magic, by definition, is believed"—but so is religion, is it not? Ah, but magic "cannot be the object of very clear beliefs"[60] although I do not see how those of religion are inherently clearer. "Magic, like religion, is viewed as a totality; either you believe in it all, or you do not. These can be verified in those cases where the reality of magic has been questioned."[61] He offers several instances from the medieval period and from the seventeenth century—in the latter time frame he refers to a book in Dutch from 1691, by Balthazar Bekker—*De Betoverde Wereld* (*The Enchanted World*)—that "was concerned solely with the existence of demons and the devil"[62]—and our obvious question is whether those two categories of *sacer* being are associated with magic or with religion, given the importance of the devil to Christianity (as we shall discuss in some detail in our penultimate chapter) in general and with regard to its evolving view of Judaism.

He next asks what distinguishes magical beliefs from scientific beliefs. "The latter are *posterior* beliefs, constantly subject to the scrutiny of individuals and dependent solely on rational evidence," although I suppose one might ask how rational the theory of relativity is, built on the principle of space/time curvature, at least to the average individual, not equipped with the mathematical instruments necessary to verify it (and there are, of course, large numbers of people who don't find it verified at all—but in any case, in fairness, Mauss was writing a few years before Einstein published his special theory of relativity in 1905 and more than a decade before his publication of the definitive general theory, in 1916). In other words, scientific beliefs are arrived at through proofs, whereas "magic is *a priori* a belief... [N]obody seeks out a magician unless he believes in him. Even in our own days, spirits do not admit unbelievers into their midst. Their presence [sc that of unbelievers] is believed to render their activities null and void."[63]

While this may be a valid distinction, he does not bring up the notion that the purpose of seeking out a magician is not likely to be the same as that of seeking out a scientist—unless we include in that latter category, physicians, which brings us back to the

---

[58] Ibid, 90.
[59] Ibid, 91.
[60] Ibid.
[61] Ibid, 92.
[62] Ibid.
[63] Ibid.

question of where the line is drawn between magic and medicine: how absolutely rational and scientific are medical procedures as opposed to magical ones, for which kinds of maladies? If, say, one is seeking a cure for someone's madness, what does one believe the cause is and what sort of cure-practitioner will one seek out? On the other hand, are "spirits," part of the *sacer*, associated with magic or religion or both? And how is it that they are affected by our belief in them other than by way of a circular line of reasoning?

As one reads carefully through the remainder of this last chapter in Mauss' book one encounters repeated points about magic that seem perfectly valid—but for religion, as well, and not only for magic. One also finds a broadening of the realm of inherent prejudice—if it's not mine and I don't believe that it is real, I call it magic—to include myth: "magical stories are believed in the same way as myths."[64] The problem with this formulation is that its underlying conviction is that, in running parallel to the formulation distinguishing religion from magic, it offers the view that "if I don't believe in this material as real, then I call it myth, rather than religion."

So the stories of the gods found in Homer and Hesiod are myths to me, today, as a Jew or a Christian or a Muslim, say, because I don't believe that they really explain the divine *sacer* as it truly is, in and of itself and in its relation to the human *profanus*, although as a Christian, say, I fully believe in the Virgin Birth—as a unique, mysterious, miraculous event that accurately expresses the divine *sacer* in general and in its relationship with the human *profanus*. As a pagan Greek, familiar with many stories of Zeus and his relations in different physical forms (as a bull, as a shower of gold, as a woman's husband) with various human women that yield extraordinary progeny (such as Herakles and Dionysios, for instance) I might very well be prepared to embrace Virgin Birth as a legitimate part of religion, but as a Jew or a Muslim I might consider it a myth, might I not?

So in the end Mauss is muddying still further the definitional waters. It is not that his attempts to define magic and magical ritual are necessarily off, it's that they fail to distinguish these from religion and religious ritual, as he does not succeed in clearly separating religion from other ideas, such as myth, or magic from medicine or science in a sufficiently effective manner. Indeed, in summing up by turning to the question of why one might believe in magic, and shifting his focus toward the power that the discipline is understood to bring to bear on the *profanus* realm (my phrase, of course, not his), he refers to the "mysterious milieu" of magic. This is a milieu in which "things no longer happen in the way they do in our world of the senses. Distance does not prevent contact. Desires and images can be immediately realized. It is the spiritual world and the world of the spirits at the same time."[65] This is a perfectly apt description of the *sacer*, as we have discussed it, and therefore of the realm of and addressed by religion as much as of and addressed by magic. So, yet again, he provides a reasonable description of magic but does not indicate what distinguishes it from religion.

The power that the practitioner seeks to draw from, he explains, is referred to in the Melanesian and most Polynesian languages as *mana*. But *mana* is not simply power or "a force, a being, it is also an action, a quality, a state. In other terms, the word is a noun,

[64] Ibid, 93.
[65] Ibid, 107.

41

an adjective and a verb... It reveals to us what has seemed to be a fundamental feature of magic—the confusion between actor, rite and object... The idea of *mana* consists of a series of fluid notions which merge into each other. It can be handled yet [is] also independent. That is why it may only be handled by individuals who possess *mana* during a *mana* action, that is, by qualified individuals during the course of a rite... *Mana* is a force, more especially the force of spirit beings, that is to say, the souls of ancestors and nature spirits. *Mana* is both supernatural and natural, since it is spread throughout the tangible world where it is both heterogeneous and even immanent... *Mana* is separate from the world of mortals. It is the object of a reverence which may amount to a taboo. It is the *mana* of the magician which works through the *mana* of the rite..."[66]

The ellipses that I have used, in the interests of space, to reduce this account should not obscure at least two fundamental issues that I have with Mauss' presentation. The first is that his entire description is directed toward what he labels as magic, and the practitioners of which enterprise he labels as magicians, although for the Melanesians who are the object of the study from which he has drawn his summary, *mana* and its concomitants are the essential center of their *religion*: *mana* and its diverse aspects are not part of some side-belief system different from, much less opposed to the mainstream religious system.[67] So his perspective, like that of Frazer with the discussion of whose work this text began, is subjective and prejudicial. If we are interested in deriving a definition of magic that distinguishes it from religion, we are thus far left with "if it is not mine it is magic and therefore is not religion."

Second, most of the descriptives that he provides for the term can associate it quite comfortably *with* religion as Mauss would no doubt understand it. A panenotheistic view of God that is found in any number of Jewish, Christian or Muslim thinkers would recognize God not only as a transcendent, distant reality, unreachably *apart* from us but as an immanent being embedded throughout the creation—and certainly embedded in humans as a *part of* us, in the form of our souls. The notion that *mana* can only be handled by certain individuals certainly applies both to mainstream Western religious thought and even more so to mysticism within those traditions. Indeed, the blurring of the line among the practitioner, the act and the object (God, with whom s/he wants to become utterly filled) is ever-present in the Abrahamic mystical traditions—albeit each possesses its own vocabulary, just as all of them offer a different vocabulary from that used by the Melanesians. Their vocabulary is distinguished, in turn, from that of other non-Western religious (magical!) traditions that Mauss discusses—for instance, the North American Hurons (Iroquois) who use the term *arenda* in a manner analogous to the Melanesian use of the term *mana*.

The conclusion to which he arrives is that "we feel justified in concluding that a concept, encompassing the idea of magical power, was once found everywhere... it is a category which does not exist in an individual's understanding in the same way as our categories of time and space."[68] No turn of phrase could more appropriately refer to the

---

[66] Ibid, 108-112.
[67] He has drawn it from Robert Henry Codrington's work, *The Melanesians: Studies in their Anthropology and Folk-Lore*, (Oxford: Clarendon Press, 1891), 119ff and 191ff.
[68] Mauss, op citum, 117.

sacer and its various aspects, including but not limited to the divine aspect. The question is: what distinguishes the ubiquity of magic from the ubiquity of religion and its terminology and concepts?

Interestingly, Mauss himself acknowledges this, albeit no doubt without intending to do so, when he further asserts "that *mana* is an idea of the same order as the idea of the sacred." Although he further asserts that "the idea of *mana* [is] more general than that of the sacred, …[still,] the sacred is inherent in the notion of *mana* and derives from it. It would probably be fair to say that the sacred is a species of the genus *mana*"[69]—as it is of the genus *sacer*, albeit there may be certain differences of nuance between *mana* and *sacer*. Only slight differences.

For not only divinity, dreams and the wilderness are encompassed by both terms; so is death. Mauss expresses the *mana* side of this equation by adding that "[m]agical beings and magical things notably include the souls of the dead and everything associated with death."[70] The same may be said of the *sacer*, of course, and even of the more limited "sacred" and thus also of religion: funerals, after all, are the most obvious instrument with which religion negotiates the border between the *profanus* of the living and the *sacer* of the dead. The point, for the purposes of our own discussion, is that that aspect of the *sacer/mana* to which Mauss is confining the term "sacred" is addressed by both magic and religion, at least as far as he has gotten with the definition of either or both, alone or in conjunction with each other.

One might defend Mauss by pointing out that his main task all along has been to define magic and not, per se, to distinguish it from other disciplines. The problem is that one cannot ignore such distinctions if one wishes to define magic clearly and not *confuse* it with other disciplines. And in fact, at the very end of his last chapter he asserts that magic evolved, eventually, to the point of approximating "the sciences and finally came to resemble them in so far as it claimed to result from experimental researches and logical deductions made by individuals. In this as well, magic more and more came to resemble technology, which itself responds to the same positive and individual needs."[71] So he is certainly cognizant of the need to make a distinction although the distinction as he offers it is not overly clear.

More directly significant for our purposes, in the brief conclusion that follows this last chapter he notes that

> [w]hile religion is directed towards more metaphysical ends and is involved in the creation of idealistic images, magic has found a thousand fissures in the mystical world from which it draws its forces, and is continually leaving it in order to take part in everyday life and play a practical role there. It has a taste for the concrete. Religion, on the other hand, tends to be abstract…. Magic is essentially the art of doing things… Magic is the domain of pure production, *ex nihilo*. With words and gestures it does what techniques achieve by labor.

---

[69] Ibid, 119.
[70] Ibid.
[71] Ibid, 140.

...A magician does nothing, or almost nothing, but makes everyone believe that he is doing everything.... We must admit that these actions are the prefigurations of techniques.... Magic is linked to science in the same way as it is linked to technology. It is not only a practical art, but also a storehouse of ideas. It attaches great importance to knowledge...as far as magic is concerned, knowledge is power.... But whereas religion, because of its intellectual character, has a tendency toward metaphysics, magic—which we have shown to be more concerned with the concrete— is concerned with understanding nature.... In the lower strata of civilization, magicians are scholars and scholars are magicians.[72]

And so on. So religion apparently never has concrete goals—like the curing of someone who is ill or bringing the wrath of God onto an enemy who will thereby be defeated. Magic loves knowledge but religion is more intellectual and therefore loves abstract knowledge. Magic does things but the magicians actually do nothing: the focus on the concrete yields only the illusion of concrete results. The knowledge attained by the magical practitioner is only worthy of that name by misguided peoples like the Australian aborigines who are not civilized as "we" are—we, who practice proper religion and have a more correct understanding of the *sacer* and how to engage it. *Our sacerdotes* must be real scholars, unlike the illusionary ones belonging to other, more primitive groups. Or so Mauss would have us understand. I am not sure how objective all of this is, to understate my view.

Bronislaw Malinowski (1884-1942) adds to this discussion in his long 1925 essay, "Magic, Science and Religion" by observing, in his first sentence, that "[t]here are no peoples however primitive without religion and magic[, n]or... savage races lacking either in the scientific attitude or in science.."[73] We might begin by asking whether there are any peoples, however "civilized" lacking these two ideas, before asking how religion and magic are to be distinguished from each other. For he concludes his first paragraph by offering a dichotomy between "the Sacred and the Profane; in other words, the domain of Magic and Religion and that of Science."

Malinowski begins by alluding to the work of Edward B. Tylor, who "maintains that the essence of primitive religion is animism," but then asserting that Tylor's view "was based on too narrow a range of facts, and made early man too contemplative and rational." He continues by referencing Frazer's work, and its assertion that "[e]arly man seeks above all to control the course of nature for practical ends, and he does it directly, by rite and spell, compelling wind and weather, animals and crops to obey his will. Only much later, finding the limitations of his magical might, does he... appeal to higher beings; that is, to demons, ancestor-spirits or gods. It is in this distinction between direct control on the one hand and propitiation of superior powers on the other that Sir James Frazer sees the difference between religion and magic."[74]

Malinowski further notes that whereas magic is "based on man's confidence that he can dominate nature directly... religion... lifts man above the magical level."

---

[72] Ibid, 141-4.

[73] Bronislaw Malinowski, *Magic, Science and Religion and Other Essays*, (Garden City, NY: Doubleday Anchor, 1954; reprint of the 1948 edition by Free Press/Beacon Press, Boston, MA), 17.

[74] Ibid, 19.

Furthermore, "science is born of experience, magic made by tradition... Science is open to all, a common good of the whole community, magic is occult, taught through mysterious initiations.... While science is based on the conception of natural forces, magic springs from the idea of a certain mystic, impersonal power, which is believed in by most primitive peoples." So magic works by compulsion—or the belief that we can compel *sacer* forces— and does religion work, contrastively, by importuning or by somehow dealing with something higher? Magic is devoid of reason and is occult—and based on what Malinowski refers to as a process derived from "mystic power," although he does not define this last adjective—whereas science is based on reason and out in the open. That "certain mystic power" is believed in by most—meaning two-thirds of? 80% of? 99% of?—primitive peoples.

We have now broadened the discussion to a threefold matrix crowned by an apparent distinction between what "most" primitive peoples believe and engage in— magic—whereas, presumably, non-primitive peoples engage in religion and science. That "mystic power" is called by a generic term, *mana*, Malinowski explains, and it is "the essence of 'pre-animistic religion,' and it is also the essence of magic." Presumably civilized people do not believe in *mana*.[75]

Malinowski continues by commenting on totemism along lines defined by Frazer, as "a mode of social grouping and a religious system of beliefs and practices," as a "blend of utilitarian anxiety about the most necessary objects of [early man's] surroundings, with some preoccupation in those which strike his imagination and attract his attention, such as beautiful birds, reptiles and dangerous animals." He asserts that the "savage depends on the group with whom he is in direct contact both for practical co-operation and mental solidarity to a far larger extent than does civilized man."[76] We might note that this is the first time we have encountered the phrase "religious system" (rather than magical system) among these modern thinkers, but that one might debate the last point: unless we apply a very narrow and perhaps circular definition to the word "civilized" we can surely adduce myriad instances—from medieval Christian communities to twenty-first-century urban street gangs—where dependence upon the group "both for practical co-operation and mental solidarity" is as active as for the everyday "savage."

Malinowski completes his review of Frazer's work by commenting on the latter's discussion of the cults of vegetation and fertility. He asserts that "early religion... leads now and again to suicidal acts of self-immolation," because "for primitive man death has meaning mainly as a step to resurrection, decay as a stage of rebirth, the plenty of autumn and the decline of winter as preludes to the revival of spring."[77] Certainly Christianity's emphasis on the rebirth of the immortal soul in Paradise (or Hell, depending upon its earthbound actions), and the growing volume of suicide bombers, particularly within the Muslim world of the past generation, would seem to militate against limiting this sensibility to "primitive man."

Malinowski concludes this first section of his essay by stating "that magic and religion are not merely a doctrine or a philosophy, not merely an intellectual body of

---

[75] See above, 42-3, for a discussion of Mauss' extended engagement of this term.
[76] Ibid, 21.
[77] Ibid, 22.

opinion, but a special mode of behavior, a pragmatic attitude built up of reason, feeling, and will alike. It is a mode of action as well as a system of belief and a sociological phenomenon as well as a personal experience."[78] This conclusion, placing the two disciplines on the same side of the definitional fence, returns us to the question of what actually distinguishes magic from religion.

After briefly comparing the analyses of a series of theorists—Levy-Bruhl, J.L. Myres and A.A. Goldenweiser, each of whom offers different observations regarding the "savage," "primitive man"—Malinowski offers his own subject for analysis: the Trobriand islanders of Melanesia. He notes their success at cultivating yam plants, which he recognizes is a result, in part, of their "clear knowledge of weather and seasons, plants and pests, soil and tubers…" but also of "magic, a series of rites performed every year over the gardens in rigorous sequence and order." Moreover, "[m]agic is undoubtedly regarded by the natives as absolutely indispensable to the welfare of the gardens…. [N]o native garden has ever been without its ritual, in spite of some thirty years of European rule and missionary influence and well over a century's contact with white traders."[79]

Malinowski comments on the fact that "there is a clearcut division…[between] the well-known set of conditions, the natural course of growth, as well as the ordinary pests and dangers to be warded off by fencing and weeding…[and] the domain of the unaccountable and adverse influences… The first conditions are coped with by knowledge and work, the second by magic." He wonders, then, to what extent the Trobrianders distinguish the two aspects of their method, the physical processes of planting and harvesting under such-and-such circumstances and the metaphysical process of ritual, with respect to the success of their enterprise. He notes what he terms the social setting that offers the line of division, observing that, with regard to magical ceremonies, "all are public in that it is known when they are going to happen and anyone can attend them."[80]

This last comment reinforces what would have been our own question even without it: what distinguishes the ceremonies as magical from those that we might label religious? Since, as we have seen, one of the key distinctions between magic and religion offered by Marcel Mauss is that the former takes place in secret and the latter in public, then Malinowski's statement, read through a Maussian lens would automatically put the actions of the Trobriand islanders into the religious category.[81]

The same may be said for Malinowski's discussion of the success of the Trobriand islanders as fishermen. It may be true that "in the lagoon fishing, where man can rely completely upon his knowledge and skill, magic does not exist, while in the open-sea fishing, full of danger and uncertainty, there is extensive magical ritual to secure safety and good results."[82] But of course the same could be said of the Christian fishing communities of Brittany, except that the terminology would be different: when they fish in the bay they don't spend much time praying to God for success and certainly not to be protected from the potentially mortal dangers of the open sea, but before venturing out into the ocean and

---

[78] Ibid, 24.
[79] Ibid, 28.
[80] Ibid, 29, for both quotes in this paragraph.
[81] See above, 35-38.
[82] Ibid, 31.

when they return from it, their religious rituals are far more extensive. What, then, defines the one as magical and the other as religious, beyond the principle that the one is "mine/ours" (i.e., Christian) and other not?

Perhaps Malinowski's second question reflects the same sort of oppositional (ours vs yours) implications. He asks: "Can we regard primitive knowledge, which, as we found, is both empirical and rational, as a rudimentary stage of science, or is it not at all related to it?"—to which his response is that "there is no doubt that even the lowest savage communities have the beginnings of science, however rudimentary... [H]e has his profane world of practical activities and rational outlook besides the sacred region of cult and belief."[83]

This leads him, in the next section of his essay, to an observation regarding religion, to separate it from animism, animatism, totemism, and fetishism: "The *ism* definition of religion in its origins must be given up, for religion does not cling to any one object or class of objects, though incidentally it can touch and hallow all. Nor, as we have seen, is religion identical with Society or the Social, nor can we remain satisfied by a vague hint that it clings to life only, for death opens perhaps the vastest view on to the other world. As an 'appeal to higher powers,' religion can only be distinguished from magic and not defined in general, but even this view will have to be slightly modified and supplemented."[84]

So on the one hand we are still left without a precise definition of religion but a proposed distinction between religion and magic, whereby the first pertains to appealing to higher powers and the second presumably does not. Religious ritual as Malinowski proceeds to explore it circles around life cycle events: conception, pregnancy, birth, puberty, marriage, and death—border crossings between different aspects of (what in our terms we would refer to as) *sacer* and *profanus*. He writes of rituals associated with food, which "has also a conspicuous role in ceremonies of a distinctly religious character. First-fruit offerings of a ritual nature, harvest ceremonies, big seasonal feasts in which crops are accumulated, displayed and, in one way or another, sacralized, play an important part among agricultural people."[85] Sacrifice and communion are, as he puts it, the two main forms in which food is ritually ministered; "in primitive societies the roots of sacrificial offerings are to be found in the psychology of gift," of sharing with his spirits and divinities "in the beneficial powers of his Providence."[86]

Frazer and Mauss, in the end—and in spite of Mauss's paired-definitional conclusion—are really more preoccupied with the question of how to understand what magic is than to distinguish it, per se, from religion. Malinowski on the other hand places more emphasis on trying to distinguish the two disciplines from each other. One might say of Claude Levi-Strauss (1908-2009) that, in his nominal discussion in the third part of his renowned *Structural Anthropology*, he follows the Frazer-Mauss path, although we might anticipate a more Malinowskian path given the title of that part of the book, "Magic and Religion." The first chapter of this part (Chapter IX in the book, overall) is called "The

---

[83] Ibid, 34, 35-6.
[84] Ibid, 36.
[85] Ibid, 42.
[86] Ibid, 43.

Sorcerer and his Magic," which he begins with an assertion that "[a]n individual who is aware that he is the object of sorcery is thoroughly convinced that he is doomed according to the most solemn traditions of his group. His friends and relatives share this certainty. From then on the community withdraws. Standing aloof from the accursed, it treats him not only as though he were already dead but as though he were a source of danger to the entire group."[87]

We immediately recognize two familiar issues in this formulation. One, that the individual who is "the object of sorcery" resembles the individual who has inadvertently dislodged the *lapis niger*—the discussion of whom was the starting point of our discussion of religion. Put otherwise, might we substitute one "who has upset (the) god(s)," like Oidipos—or Miriam, the sister of Moses when, in Numbers 12 she speaks disdainfully of Moses and his Cushite wife, is struck with leprosy and ultimately must spend a week apart from the community—for one "who is the object of sorcery" and come up with a very similar if not identical formulation?

Two, given the formulation that Levi-Strauss offers, are we to conclude that magic and sorcery are not only one and the same but negative, and thus to be distinguished from religion as a term that refers to a positive consequence for its adherents? Certainly the hypothetical case that he offers is negative, and leads him to his analysis of what it is that yield effectiveness in magical practice: a belief in it. That belief has "three complementary aspects: first, the sorcerer's belief in the effectiveness of his techniques; second, the patient's or victim's belief in the sorcerer's power; and, finally, the faith and expectations of the group, which constantly act as a sort of gravitational field within which the relationship between sorcerer and bewitched is located and defined."[88]

We might note that in the second of the three aspects, Levi-Strauss mentions both patients and victims, implying that the sorcerer may serve as a healer and not only as a purveyor of damage—so if the matter of negative/positive is not necessarily a criterion for distinguishing magic from religion, we are once again faced with the question of where the line gets drawn between the sorcerer and the physician. Is it, indeed, "mine" versus "yours"? It would certainly seem to be highly dependent on psychosomatic factors— everyone involved has to *believe*—as opposed to being real. Is *that*, then, the defining criterion for sorcery and magic: that they are not really real, but are effective when they are effective due to this threefold interweave of belief in their efficacy?

But Levi-Strauss also asserts that "[c]ertainly the sorcerer maintains an intimate relationship with the forces of the supernatural." How then is he to be distinguished from the religion-based *sacerdos*—the priest (or prophet)—who does the same? The difficulty of ascertaining what is psychosomatic and what is really real—or, otherwise put, between belief and hope for results that may or may not obtain and belief that yields definitive results—is exemplified in the story that Levi-Strauss relates about a "Kwakiutl Indian from the Vancouver region of Canada, obtained by Franz Boas."[89]

---

[87] Claude Levi-Strauss, *Structural Anthropology*, (Garden City, NY: Doubleday Anchor Books, 1967), 161.
[88] Ibid, 162.
[89] Ibid, 169ff. Boas (1858-1942) was a pioneering German-American anthropologist often called the "Father of American Anthropology" and also the "Father of Modern Anthropology."

"Quesalid (for that is the name he received when he became a sorcerer) did not believe in the power of sorcerers—or, more accurately, shamans, since this is a better term for their specific type of activity in certain regions of the world."[90] Even before continuing with Levi-Strauss' borrowed narrative, it seems to me that we might pause and ask why "shaman" is a more appropriate term than "sorcerer"—what are the criteria that distinguish the two terms? He does not tell us, apparently assuming that everyone knows the difference.

As the narrative moves forward, and the activity in which Quesalid ultimately becomes primarily engaged seems to be curing the sick, we might suppose that that is what a shaman does, but a sorcerer does not, but we might also wonder how a shaman is in that case distinguished from a physician. Is it that the one uses science that is *real* with regard to the relationship between cause and effect in someone becoming ill and being cured where the other does not? Then a shaman must not actually be able to heal. But if a shaman can heal, even if we construe the success to derive from the psychosomatic processes that Levi-Strauss has already outlined, so that the patient experiences real physical improvement, how is this less real than the improvement experienced by a patient upon whom a "science-based" physician focuses his/her attention?

In any case, "Quesalid was [d]riven by curiosity about [the shamans'] tricks and by the desire to expose them" so he began spending time with the shamans and was ultimately asked to join their fraternity. He accepted, and "his narrative recounts details of his first lessons, a curious mixture of pantomime, prestidigitation, and empirical knowledge, including the art of simulating fainting and nervous fits, the learning of sacred songs, the technique for inducing vomiting, rather precise notions of auscultation and obstetrics, and the use of 'dreamers,' that is, spies who listen to private conversations and secretly convey to the shaman bits of information concerning the origins and symptoms of the ills suffered by different people."[91]

There are three particularly interesting outcomes of the Quesalid narrative where our own is concerned. The first is that he not only learns—with the intention of exposing as false—the shamans' techniques. Most important of these is that "the shaman hides a little tuft of down in the corner of his mouth, and he throws it ups, covered with blood, at the proper moment—after having bitten his tongue or made his gums bleed—and solemnly presents it to his patient and the onlookers as the pathological foreign body extracted as a result of his sucking and manipulations."[92]

The second is that he becomes extraordinarily successful as healer. He is already a success as an apprentice, which he ascribes to the belief—based on a dream—on the part of his patient, asserting that Quesalid would succeed. He is even able to cure a member of the neighboring Koskimo Indian community, when its own shaman (using a different method, limited to saliva, rather than down and blood) has failed. The despairing, failed shaman ends up leaving the village "with his entire family, heartsick and feared by the community, who think that he may be tempted to take revenge. Needless fears: He returned

---

[90] Ibid, 169.
[91] Ibid.
[92] Ibid.

49

a year later, but both he and his daughter [whom he had at one point dispatched to Quesalid begging for his secrets] had gone mad. Three years later, he died."[93]

The third outcome is that Quesalid the doubter has become, at least in part, a believer: that there are real shamans and false ones, as opposed to all of them being false.

The narrative ends up with an absence of certainty with regard to the issue of whether or not Quesalid believes that he himself is one of the former. At the very least he has continued to practice, successfully and with pride in his success. "He seems to have completely lost sight of the fallaciousness of the technique which he had so disparaged at the beginning."[94]

The comparative categories seemingly defined by Quesalid's exemplary story are, to begin with, legitimacy versus illegitimacy and more powerful versus less powerful. Interwoven with these categories is the question of method and motive (curing someone for money or simply to cure him). To what extent, we might ask, would these categorical distinctions apply to the distinction between magic and religion? Would that not complicate the matter of classifying what Quesalid does, as compared to what a Catholic priest or a Western medical doctor does?

Without further elaboration on the specific case of Quesalid, Levi-Strauss returns to, and elaborates the three-aspect theory with which he began his discussion. What he refers to as a "fabulation of reality"—thus it is clear for Levi-Strauss that what happens in the story of Quesalid, both to him and to the older Shaman who ultimately went mad and died, has no solid reality to it—is "founded on a threefold experience: first, that of the shaman himself who…undergoes specific states of a psychosomatic nature; second, that of the sick person, who may or may not experience an improvement of his condition; and, finally, that of the public, who also participate in the cure…"[95] Put simply: it's all psychosomatic. Does this mean that it isn't *real*? If so, is this what would distinguish what Levi-Strauss has been discussing, as magic and/or sorcery, from religion (and medicine/science)?

Levi-Strauss continues, noting that "[t]hese three elements of what we might call the 'shamanistic complex'… are clustered around two poles, one formed by the intimate experience of the shaman and the other by group consensus." We are enjoined by him to accept the sincerity of belief on the part of the shaman ("or at least the more sincere among them," he writes—and how, by the way, might we distinguish the sincere ones from the insincere?) and to appreciate how "the hardship and privations which they undergo" would really provoke the states that they assume, "even if we refuse to admit them as proof of a serious and fervent calling."[96]

He adduces an interesting instance of linguistic evidence to support the notion that a given culture believes in the efficacy of a given shaman. Thus in the Wintu language it turns out that there are five verbal classes that pertain to modes of knowing—as opposed to conjecturing—by sight, by bodily experience, by inference, by reasoning, and by

---

[93] Ibid, 172.
[94] Ibid, 173.
[95] Ibid.
[96] Ibid.

hearsay.[97] "Thus the native who becomes a shaman after a spiritual crisis conceives of his state grammatically, as a consequence to be inferred from the fact—formulated as real experience—that he has received divine guidance. From the latter he concludes deductively that he must have been on a journey to the beyond, at the end of which he found himself— again, an immediate experience—once more among his people."[98]

This description incidentally—or not—accords very well with the *sacer-profanus* matrix with which our own narrative began. It accords in particular with that subset, mysticism, in which the practitioner seeks access to the hiddenmost recess of the *sacer*, known as the *mysterion*. What is essential for the mystic is his/her ambition and intention not merely to gain that access in order to be personally enlightened but to return from intimacy with the *mysterion* with the ability to benefit the community, based on his/her experience. But mysticism is an intense subset of religion, not a construct that exists in opposition to religion, like magic or superstition.[99]

While Levi-Strauss evinces no recognition of this, he does see—perhaps not surprisingly, given what appears to be his understanding of the sort of successful action by *sacerdotes* such as Quesalid as psychosomatic—a connection to the principles of psychoanalysis. First, in that a cured patient is well-positioned, according to him, to become a shaman in his own right. Second, because "disorders of the type currently termed psychosomatic, which constitute a large part of the illnesses prevalent in societies with a low degree of security, probably often yield to psychotherapy. At any rate, it seems probable that medicine men, like their civilized colleagues, cure at least some of the cases they treat and that without this relative success magical practices could not have been so widely diffused in time and space."

But "Quesalid did not become a great shaman because he cured his patients; he cured his patients because he had become a great shaman." Moreover, "[t]he true reason for the defeat of Quesalid's rivals must then be sought in the attitude of the group rather than in the pattern of the rivals' successes and failures."[100] So it appears that, for Levi-Strauss, the only "real" element in all of this is what he had referred to as "the states that [the shamans] assume." But what are these "states" to which he refers? They are integral to what Levi-Strauss calls the shaman's performance of reproducing in himself the appearance of the conditions he is curing. "He actually relives them in all their vividness, originality, and violence. And since he returns to his normal state at the end of the séance, we may say, borrowing a key from psychoanalysis, that he *abreacts*."[101]

So the shaman has more in common with an actor than with a physician or a priest—but he truly believes (or perhaps, as in Quesalid's case, he didn't at first, but comes to believe) that he is effecting a cure by this process. Furthermore, the patient believes that

---

[97] Interestingly—as a kind of side note—Levi-Strauss refers to the Wintu language as a dialect, reflecting either his meager knowledge or his prejudicial perspective, since that reference functions to "reduce" the status of the Wintu verbal instrument. This is in spite of the nuanced and sophisticated feature of the language that he adumbrates.

[98] Ibid, 174.

[99] For more on the issue of mysticism and its relationship to these other terms, see below, 239-40, 288-9, 373.

[100] Ibid, 174 for all the quotes in this paragraph.

[101] Ibid, 175. Whereas in psychoanalysis this term usually refers to the patient's experience of living through the trauma that induced the disturbed condition that is being cured by this process, in this case it is the shaman who, as Levi-Strauss says, "is a professional abreactor."

the shaman is really living through his diseased experience, and so does the community: "The public must participate in the abreaction, to a certain extent at least, along with the patient and the sorcerer."[102] Exactly how much "to a certain extent at least" might be, Levi-Strauss does not try to suggest.

This is the most coherent connection to Western modes of addressing illness that Levi-Strauss finds for the sorcerer and his magic: a parallel to psychoanalysis, with its abreactive process multiplied by three. Although even at that there is a crucial difference: "Magic readapts the group to predefined problems through the patient, while psychoanalysis readapts the patient to the group by mean of the solutions reached."[103] It is not clear (to me at least) precisely how the group is readapted, or how the problems are predefined any more than problems of illness are predefined in psychoanalysis or purely physical medical conditions—or in religion when, say, a Catholic priest heals an individual possessed (or believed to be possessed) by the devil.

Levi-Strauss concludes, in any case, that "if this analysis is correct, we must see magical behavior as the response to a situation which is revealed to the mind through emotional manifestations, but whose essence is intellectual." It is thus a mindset that is encompassed by the magical process that Levi-Strauss analyzes. Where "normal" thinking offers a deficit of meaning, "so-called pathological thought... overflows with emotional interpretations and overtones in order to supplement an otherwise deficient reality." It is in this latter thought that the shaman/sorcerer operates, apparently. But it is still not clear as to whether there is any objective reality to such thought, particularly given that it is termed pathological and that its reference point is restricted to the psychosomatic realm.

This question of the role played by belief in the effectiveness of magical—or religious—practice (is the practitioner acting and hoping that the performance is convincing enough to yield the curative response for his patient, or does he genuinely believe that he is doing what is necessary to effect the cure) will reappear for us in chapter thirteen, as we follow Christianity and Judaism toward and into the medieval period.

I have in any case spent considerable time in reviewing a handful of discussions from the past 120 years or so regarding the subject of magic and religion with the intention of suggesting both that the distinctions that are offered are neither consistent nor clear and that a good deal of what is discussed as magic bears a remarkable resemblance to customs, traditions, ceremonies and rituals that are associated with what these same authors are likely to call religion. If the forms are so similar, then what is it that distinguishes the content? As often as not the distinction is based on preconceptions regarding what are and are not viewed as legitimate modes of addressing the divine aspect of the *sacer*. If it's mine, I call it "religion." If it is not, I am more inclined, in viewing it as inherently illegitimate, to call it "magic"—or label it with some other term, such as "superstition" or "myth," that connotes either inferiority to religion or full-fledge illegitimacy.

In considering this issue within the context of emerging and developing Judaism and Christianity within the Greco-Roman world—and the question of how they differ from each other and both differ from Paganism—we might consider some of the plethora of texts

---

[102] Ibid, 176.
[103] Ibid, 177.

from antiquity that would offer us a sense both of how ancient groups distinguished magic from religion and how that distinction reflects onto and resonates within this threefold matrix (Paganism, Judaism, Christianity) of identity differentiation. We therefore need to jump back some three thousand years in order to re-begin our exploration from within that ancient context.

CHAPTER TWO

Magic and Religion in Greek Paganism and Israelite "Monotheism"

One very reasonable place where one might begin the quest in antiquity for answers regarding perceived distinctions between magic and religion and their concomitants—or at least of awareness of the difficulty at obtaining them—is the *Odyssey*, one of the earliest of Greek literary works. We shall not consider the question of who authored that great epic poem, recognizing that, in referring to Homer as the poet we are ignoring (because it is outside our purview of interest) a host of questions regarding who or if "Homer" actually was and when "Homer" actually lived. Embracing the tradition of Homeric authorship and a time frame of ca 750-650 BCE, we shall arrive almost directly at the material most relevant to our discussion.

Almost—for we do require one brief excursion before arriving there. That excursion is the following observation: that the story told in the *Odyssey*, that involves an Akhaian hero, Odysseus, spending years returning home from the Trojan War—and engaged, while in that adventure, with a number of gods and goddesses—is, together with works like the *Iliad* and Hesiod's *Theogony*, part of Greek religion at one extended point in its development. The proper Greek term for such narratives is *mythos*—which term we might best translate as "gods'-truth account," on the grounds that any narrative that describes and discusses the gods, their birth and struggles to organize the world we know as a *kosmos* (order), and their interactions with heroic figures of the past cannot have been directly observed or known by the poet telling the tale. Neither Homer nor Hesiod can have witnessed the events they describe, and the only way they can know about them is if the gods themselves inspire—*in-spirit*—them with the knowledge that they then share with their audiences. It is not just an incidental poetic form that causes the poet to begin by invoking the assistance of the muses, handmaidens of the Olympians.

By the mid-fifth century BCE, however, some Greek writers are beginning to distinguish *mythos* and its verbal sibling, *mythein*, from another pair: *historia* and *historiein*. Thukydides, for instance, the Greek historian of the Peloponnesian Wars, understands *mythos* to offer information of questionable facticity, where *historia* is fact-bound. So focused is he on this distinction that he neither considers the possibility that *mythos* might contain important truth even if lacking reliable facts, nor notices that, when he informs the reader of his precise (*akribos*) method for ascertaining and providing us with facts, that method is inherently flawed and its facticity fabric inevitably ridden with holes.[104]

We have in turn inherited this prejudicial view of the term *mythos*. Thus whereas when we speak of our own beliefs regarding the divine aspect of the *sacer*, we use the term *religion*, when we discuss the Greeks and their gods we call their narratives *mythology*—by which we mean an array of fantastic stories in which nobody (at least nobody modern or intelligent) believes. While that perspective may be fine for us, in our own time, place and circumstances, it behooves us to recognize that the audiences of Homer and Hesiod believed as surely in their gods as we do in ours. This will have implications for our further discussion regarding the definitional borders between religion and magic.

All of which brings us back to the *Odyssey*—specifically, books 10 and 11 of that epic poem. This is the point in Odysseus' tale to the Phaiakians regarding his adventures when he and his crew arrive at what proves to be the island of Kirke, a non-Olympian goddess. (Travelling as they have been through the *sacer*, they arrive at a still more *sacer* location—a space outside of ordinary space—inhabited by a *sacer* being). Odysseus sends part of his crew ahead to reconnoiter. Moving through the dense woods (the deeper *sacer* within this *sacer* realm) they arrive within earshot of Kirke's house, where they "heard Kirke inside singing in a sweet voice as she went up and down along a great design on a loom, immortal such as goddesses have..." (10:221-3)

They call to her and she invites them into her house—all but suspicious Eurylokhos enter—and she promptly turns them all into swine, by mixing them

> a potion, with barley and cheese and pale honey
> added to Pramneian wine, but put into the mixture
> malignant drugs, to make them
> > forgetful of their own country.
> When she had given them this and they had
> > drunk it down, next thing
> she struck them with her wand and drove them
> > into her pig pens... (234-8)

Eurylokhos, who has observed this terrifying turn of events, hustles back to the ship and tells Odysseus what has happened. Odysseus—the hero for whom every potential danger is a potential adventure to add to his portfolio—takes up his great bronze sword and his

---

[104] See Thukydides, *Peloponnesian Wars* I.21, in which the author informs us that, unlike his predecessors, he will offer a methodology of ascertaining and conveying facts that is a model of precision. He explains that every action he describes he either saw with his own eyes or heard about from "reliable witnesses." We might wonder how reliable "reliable witnesses" are, particularly with regard to events transpiring in the midst of the chaos of battle—and how reliable he himself is as an objective witness, since, unlike a god who might hover above the scene, he would be immersed within it. Our doubts can only increase when he further notes that every speech that he quotes he either heard himself, or heard repeated from reliable sources—or, in cases where neither was available, "I placed in the speaker's mouth words that I know he would have spoken under the circumstances." It is in fact remarkable how important speeches, such as the so-called "Funeral Oration" of Perikles or the speech of Nikias to the Athenian troops about to be devastated in the Bay of Syracuse, offer all the familiar features of Thucydides' own rhetorical style!

great bow and, leaving Eurylokhos to recover from his fright by the relative safety of the ship, heads into the woods. But

> As I went up through the lonely glens, and was coming
> near to the great house of Kirke, skilled in medicine,
> there as I came up to the house, Hermes, of the golden
> staff, met me on my way, in the likeness of a young man... (275-8)

> He took me by the hand and spoke to me and named me,
>   saying:
> 'Where are you going, unhappy man, all alone,
>   through the hilltop.
> ignorant of the land-lay, and your friends are here
> in Kirke's place, in the shape of pigs and holed up in the
>   close pigpens...? (280-3)

> But see, I will find you a way out of your troubles,
>   and save you.
> Here, this is good medicine, take it, and go into Kirke's
>   house; it will give you power
>   against the day of trouble.
> And I will tell you all the malevolent guiles of Kirke.
> She will make you a potion and put drugs in the food,
>   but she will not
> even so be able to enchant you, for this good medicine
> which I give you now will prevent her.
> I will tell you the details of what to do.... (286-93)

Hermes gives Odysseus full instructions, including how to extract an oath from the goddess, once he has proven (presumably temporarily) invulnerable to her powers of negative enchantment, that she will make no further effort to harm him. And having spoken,

>   ...he gave me the medicine, which
> he picked out of the ground, and he explained the nature
> of it to me. It was black at the root, but with a milky
> flower. The gods call it *moly*. It is hard for mortal
> men to dig up, but the gods have power to do
>   all things. (302-6)

The result of this encounter with Hermes is straightforward. Odysseus enters Kirke's lair and she strikes him with her wand, but without the result she intended or expected. She is astonished at first but then realizes that this must be resourceful

Odysseus—concerning whom Hermes "was forever telling me you would come to me, on your way back from Troy with your fast black ship" (331-2).[105]

These fascinating passages raise a number of interesting issues for us. We note that a mere human—albeit a heroic human, by definition a subset of the category *sacerdos*, because he is either half-divine or, in this case, has the unfailing support of a goddess, Athena who, as his patron, sends another god, Hermes to assist him in this situation—can overpower a goddess if the conditions are right. The conditions in this narrative are simple: that Odysseus has ingested a drug brought to him by an Olympian god, whereas the goddess seeking to harm him is a lesser, non-Olympian goddess. So there is a hierarchy within the *sacer* and a hierarchy of power that is available to certain sacerdotal individuals in the *profanus*.

But the distinction between the drugs possessed by Kirke and those possessed, through Hermes, by Odysseus is also one of positive versus negative. Kirke's drugs are intended to harm; those gained by Odysseus through Hermes are intended to help. However, the terminology of this passage offers this positive-negative distinction purely through context. The translation from which I quote above, by Richmond Lattimore, renders the Greek word *pharmakon* (sing.) *pharmaka* (plur.) as "malignant drugs" (in line 236) and as "good medicine" (in line 287 and again in line 291).

So a *pharmakon* is a substance used by an individual with a *sacer* connection and the context determines whether or not the intention is benevolent or malevolent. Is the line between medicine and magic that between positive and negative intention and outcome? Where does religion fit into this equation? For a Greek who believes in diverse gods and goddesses of both Olympian and non-Olympian stature, both Hermes and Kirke are real aspects of the *sacer*, part of their religion—and certainly Odysseus does not doubt the reality of Hermes, without whose assistance he would have been truly lost (nor the reality of Kirke, *because* of whom he would have been truly lost).

Then what sort of term(s) should be used to refer not only to the action in which the practitioner is engaged—magic, religion, medicine?—but to the practitioner him/herself? If one might suppose that the proper Latin-language term for the practitioner is *sacerdos*, then that could certainly apply to Odysseus-as-hero, but not to Kirke, who, as a goddess, is, simply *sacer*—although she represents a lower order of *sacer* being than do Hermes and Athena. A number of definitional lines appear blurred.

We might note one other detail of potential importance for our discussion. Once Odysseus has succeeded in withstanding Kirke's attempted enchantment and she wants to go to bed with him, he will not do so until he has extracted a non-hostile-aggression oath from her—and once she has sworn that oath she cannot, under any circumstances, goddess though she be, contravene it. So his power to compel her moving forward beyond the moment involves a condition in which she willingly agrees to be bound by him. This is somewhat paradoxical, given that she is a goddess and he a mere man—except for the fact that he is not a *mere* man, but a hero, which is why he has access to Athena/Hermes-based *pharmaka* that give him an unnatural (or better put: a *super*natural) advantage over Kirke.

---

[105] I am using the translation by Richmond Lattimore (New York: Harper & Row, 1967), 158-61ff.

Odysseus spends a year in the company of Kirke—bound to her and by her who is bound to him and by him—until his shipmates/warriors (their human form restored by the goddess after Odysseus' initial "victory" over her) beg him to move on and resume the journey homeward. The goddess presents the hero with gifts and most important, instructions. These instructions, carrying the narrative into book 11, pertain to Odysseus' desire to know something of his own future and fate. This is information not available to ordinary men but a hero-*sacerdos* has access to such things through his/her contact with the timeless *sacer*. In this case the specific source of the information sought by Odysseus is, as it were, a double *sacer/sacerdos* source. Teiresias, the blind seer (prophet; i.e., *sacerdos*) who has figured in other strands in the tapestry of the Greek tradition, and who is, at the time of this narrative, dead and buried—and therefore within the *sacer*—is the source.

To access that source, Odysseus must follow the precise instructions of the *sacer sacerdos*, Kirke: sailing beyond the outermost edge of the *sacer* ocean to a community into which the very sun never peers, "but always a glum night is spread over wretched mortals" (11.19)—at this *sacer*most edge of the *sacer profanus*, (for it is the edge of the known world, as it were, but the part of that world through which Odysseus has been travelling is the unknown), they beached their ship and walked along "until we came to the place of which Kirke had spoken" (22). There Odysseus follows the goddess's instructions, digging

> ...a pit, of about a cubit in each direction,
> and poured it full of a drink offering for all the dead, first
> honey mixed with milk, and the second pouring was
> > sweet wine,
> and the third, water, and over it all I sprinkled white barley.
> I promised many times to the strengthless heads
> > of the perished
> dead that, returning to Ithaka, I would slaughter a barren
> cow, my best, in my palace, and pile the pyre with treasures,
> and to Teiresias apart would dedicate an all-black
> ram, the one conspicuous in all our sheep flocks.
> Now when, with sacrifices and prayers, I had so entreated
> the hordes of the dead, I took the sheep and cut their throats
> over the pit, and the dark-clouding blood ran in, and the souls
> of the perished dead gathered to the place, up out of
> > Erebos... (23-37)

A diverse array of the dead swarms up through the "window" that Odysseus has created through the ritual of a precisely dug pit filled with precisely measured out offerings and carefully chosen words—and facilitated most directly by the blood from properly slaughtered sheep: for blood is life and thus gives the dead a temporary "living" condition by means of which they can speak to the living. The gathered dead include the helmsman of Odysseus, Elpinor, who, it transpires, had fallen asleep on Kirke's roof after the crew's long party held on the last night in her home. He had awakened, not knowing where he was, fallen from the roof and died of a broken neck—and, unnoticed, had not been accorded a proper burial accompanied by proper funeral ceremonies.[106] This is what enables him to be at the *sacer-profanus* border so quickly, before the others: without the proper border-crossing procedures, he never made it fully into the *sacer*.

But aside from their brief conversation—Odysseus had had no inkling that Elpinor was dead—the hero will allow nobody among the dead, even his beloved mother, (who died of heartbreak, we learn shortly afterwards, when Odysseus never came home from Troy) to drink from the blood until Teiresias has come forward to speak with him. When the Theban *sacerdos* comes forth, holding a staff of gold—and (oddly, all things considered; one might expect him, particularly in his *sacer* condition, to already know this) he asks Odysseus what the hero is doing "here, to look on dead men, and this place without pleasure" (94)—Teiresias is permitted to "drink of the blood and speak the truth to [him]" (96).

Odysseus will walk away from the conversation that ensues with an ambiguous conclusion to the prediction regarding his future. He will converse with his mother, trying at the end of their conversation to embrace her and coming up—three times—empty-handed, since it turns out that the dead retain only the forms they possessed when alive, without the substance. He encounters a very unhappy Akhilleus who, in this condition of substanceless deprivation, rues the sacrifice of his flesh-and-blood life for the immortal glory of his name recalled down the ages through poetry—as in this very poem. He encounters an Ajax still angry at him for reasons we know about through extant works of Greek literature beyond the surviving corpus of epic poetry.[107]

For our purposes, among the more interesting questions raised in this series of encounters, particularly that with Teiresias, is that of how to classify and define what is happening in the narrative. Odysseus' actions and words, through which he successfully accesses the *sacer* for the purpose of finding out his future, constitute what for a Homeric audience would surely be regarded as parts of a religious ritual. But for an audience that does not look to the Olympian gods as real, this adventure and its ceremonial components are likely to be labeled as myth, as a parallel to magic and superstition at the very least in being excluded from what we might embrace as religion.

*   *   *   *   *

We might ask what sort of parallels, if any, to either of these accounts—that of Odysseus, Hermes and Kirke and a hierarchy of *sacer*-based power; and that of Odysseus and Teiresias meeting on the border between the *profanus* of the living and the *sacer* of the dead—may be found in the ancient literature upon which Judaism and Christianity are founded. These two are, after all, a pair of religions that share in common a belief in the *sacer* in its divine aspect not as multiple but as singular.

It turns out that there are several. To begin with, one reads in Exodus 7-8, for example, about the initial encounter between Moses and Aaron on the one hand and the *sacerdotes* of the Egyptian pharaoh on the other—and one might ask first how the

---

[106] Had Kirke been in a position to read Deut 22:8, this might not have happened! (See above, Introduction, 23.)
[107] Most importantly, the tragedy, *Ajax*, by Sophokles.

terminology that refers to Moses and Aaron as prophets differs from that used to refer to the Egyptians. Since, as it turns out, they are referred to as magicians, what is the intended difference between what they are and do as compared to what Moses and Aaron are and do? What exactly do they *do* that distinguishes them from Moses and Aaron?

Moses is fresh from a wilderness encounter with the Lord, in which his reluctance to confront the Pharaoh due to his discomfort with his own speaking ability has led to God telling him that Aaron will be his *navi*—his *mouthpiece* (which is the meaning of this term that will later be translated into Greek as *prophetes*, and eventuates into English as "prophet")—and the two brothers are about to appear before the pharaoh.

> Then the Lord said to Moses and Aaron: "When Pharaoh says to you, 'Prove yourselves by working a miracle,' then you shall say to Aaron, 'Take your staff and cast it down before Pharaoh, that it may become a serpent.'" So Moses and Aaron went to Pharaoh and did just as the Lord commanded. Aaron cast down his staff before Pharaoh and his servants, and it became a serpent. Then Pharaoh summoned the wise men and the sorcerers, and they, the magicians of Egypt, also did the same by their secret arts. For each man cast down his staff, and they became serpents. But Aaron's staff swallowed up their staffs. (7:8-11)

So at first glance what distinguishes Moses and Aaron from the pharaoh's *sacerdotes* is the scale of their power, and that is presumably attributable to the relative scale of the power of the God of Israel and the gods served by the Egyptians.[108] In other words, we are apparently confronted with a hierarchy of *sacer* power analogous to that found in Book 10 of the *Odyssey*, except that in the Greek case the greater and lesser powers were part of the same religious tradition, whereas in the Israelite case they are attached to two different religious traditions and the text we are reading is foundational to one of the two. Not surprisingly, the tradition to which it is attached presents its one God as more powerful than the gods of the other tradition.

Moreover, as one continues through the narrative, this perspective is reinforced a number of times. Thus in turning to the first plague we read that when the pharaoh's heart is hardened and he refuses to let the Israelites go, God instructs Moses and Aaron to

> Go to Pharaoh in the morning, as he is going out to the water. Stand on the bank of the Nile to meet him, and take in your hand the staff that turned into a serpent. And you shall say to him, "The Lord, the God of the Hebrews, sent me to you, saying, 'Let my people go, that they may serve me in the wilderness.' But so far, you have not obeyed. Thus says the Lord, 'By this you shall know that I am the Lord: behold, with the staff that is in my hand I will strike the water that is in the Nile, and it shall turn into blood...'"

---

[108] As a separate, small but important matter, "pharaoh" is treated in both the Hebrew of the biblical original and in the English translation (and other translations), as if it were a proper noun: a name. The term, however, is like the terms "king" or "shah" or "kaiser;" it is a common noun referring to the Egyptian ruler, *the* pharaoh. Hence the disparity between my use and that in the passages quoted from the Bible.

Moses and Aaron did as the Lord commanded. In the sight of Pharaoh and in the sight of his servants he lifted up the staff and struck the water in the Nile, and all the water in the Nile turned into blood. And the fish in the Nile died, and the Nile stank, so that the Egyptians could not drink water from the Nile. There was blood throughout all the land of Egypt. But the magicians of Egypt did the same by their secret arts… (7: 15-22)

It is, of course, the last line, (verse 22), that is most intriguing. Apparently, the pharaoh's *sacerdotes* are able to do what Moses and Aaron do—so far, at least; and what they do they do "by their secret arts," which is presumably not the method used by Moses and Aaron. Does this mean that the former are practitioners of magic and the latter of religion? As the narrative continues, "Seven full days passed after the Lord had struck the Nile" (verse 25), and (continuing in chapter 8):

…the Lord said to Moses, "Say to Aaron, 'Stretch out your hand with your staff over the rivers, over the canals and over the pools, and make frogs come up on the land of Egypt!'" So Aaron stretched out his hand over the waters of Egypt, and the frogs came up and covered the land of Egypt. But the magicians did the same by their secret arts and made frogs come up on the land of Egypt. (8: 5-7)

Once again, the *sacerdotes* of Egypt, "by their magic arts" are able to do what Moses and Aaron, prophets of the God of Israel and the religion that focuses on Him, are able to do. One might further note, by the way, that Aaron's role as the mouthpiece of the mouthpiece of God is clear from the phraseology of verse 5: God works through Moses who works through Aaron. The subtle beginning of a turning point with respect to the comparative power of Moses and Aaron over against the Egyptian *sacerdotes*—the limits of the capacity of the latter as compared to the former—may be discerned by implication in what follows: that the pharaoh turns to Moses and Aaron and not to his own *sacerdotes* to rid the land of the plague of frogs:

Then Pharaoh called Moses and Aaron and said, "Plead with the Lord to take away the frogs from me and from my people, and I will let the people go to sacrifice to the Lord." Moses said to Pharaoh, "Be pleased to command me when [it is that] I am to plead for you and for your servants and for your people, that the frogs be cut off from you and your houses and be left only in the Nile." And he said, "Tomorrow." Moses said, "Be it as you say, so that you may know that there is no one like the Lord our God. The frogs shall go away from you and your houses and your servants and your people. They shall be left only in the Nile." So Moses and Aaron went out from Pharaoh, and Moses cried to the Lord about the frogs, as he had agreed with Pharaoh. And the Lord did according to the word of Moses. (8: 8-13)

But it is with the third plague that we arrive at a definitive condition of disparate power that will then follow the narrative all the way through the 10 plagues and on toward the parting of the Sea of Reeds:

> Then the Lord said to Moses, "Say to Aaron, 'Stretch out your staff and strike the dust of the earth, so that it may become gnats in all the land of Egypt.'" And they did so. Aaron stretched out his hand with his staff and struck the dust of the earth, and there were gnats on man and beast. All the dust of the earth became gnats in all the land of Egypt. The magicians tried by their secret arts to produce gnats, but they could not. So there were gnats on man and beast. Then the magicians said to Pharaoh, "This is the finger of God." (8: 15-19)

Moreover, interestingly, the *sacerdotes* of the pharaoh are presented as recognizing that events have gotten beyond their capacity for dealing with them because a *sacer* power greater than that upon which they ordinarily call is operative. The definitional question remains imprecisely answered for us, however: are we to understand the Egyptian *sacerdotes* as magicians or priests/prophets, as dealing with false powers or merely weaker powers than that with which Moses and Aaron—or rather, Aaron through Moses—deal. There is certainly nothing that suggests that where Moses and Aaron are dealing with a positive sense of the *sacer* and its positive effect on the *profanus*, the Egyptian *sacerdotes* are, *per se*, dealing with a negative sense of the *sacer* and/or its negative effect on the *profanus*, unless we assume that to oppose the will of the God of Israel is by definition to be engaged is something negative, even evil.

The reason that the word "monotheism" is placed in quotation marks in the title to this chapter becomes clearer after reviewing these passages in the book of Exodus: while Judaism and Christianity will evolve toward an understanding of the divine aspect of the *sacer* as singular and all-encompassing, this sensibility required centuries of evolution. The starting point of what ought to be called the Israelite religion—there is no mention of Jews (or Christians) in Exodus, or anywhere else in the Torah, for that matter, as we shall shortly discuss in more detail—is considerably more equivocal. With this in mind, in fact, we might recall that when the Ten Commandments are described as having been presented to the Israelites at Sinai in Exodus 20 (and repeated for their benefit again later on, in Deuteronomy 5), they are warned to "have no other Gods *before Me*," not simply to have no other gods.

We might infer from this that God Itself recognizes the developmental limitations of that people with which a Covenant is being articulated: at that time and in that context (whether we view it as historical or mythological) the divine demand is limited to an exclusive *profanus–sacer* relationship between the Israelites and the God who performed the miracles of the plagues and the crossing of the Sea of Reeds and who communed with Moses on Sinai, without necessarily denying the existence of other gods or the validity of their relationships with other peoples.[109] But we further understand that those gods are deemed at best far more limited in power than the God of Israel.

These complications may be further explored by pushing deeper into the biblical narrative—specifically toward I Samuel 28. The events in this chapter fall, in a sense, on the heels of those in I Samuel 15, in which Saul abrogates God's direct command, delivered through the *sacerdos*, Samuel, that he go out and battle against and slaughter the Amalekites. He is assured of victory and commanded to destroy every last one of them as well as all their animals. He commits what might be considered a standard act of king-to-king courtesy, in sparing the life of the Amalekite leader, Agag—as well as the best among the animals, which are offered up by the people to God. To get to the point of primary interest for our own narrative: Samuel is furious, in God's Name, that Saul has disobeyed a direct order. He bellows out the rhetorical question:

> Has the Lord as great delight in burnt offerings and sacrifices,
> As in obeying the voice of the Lord?

—and the reminder that:

> Behold, to obey is better than sacrifice,
> and to heed than the fat of rams.
> For rebellion is as the sin of witchcraft,
> and stubbornness is as iniquity and idolatry.
> Because you have rejected the word of the Lord,
> He also has rejected you from being king. (15:22-23)

So for our purposes, the two important points in this explosion are that what Saul has done in disobeying God is as bad as witchcraft and that, as a consequence, he has lost his kingship—for himself, as it turns out, and for his son.[110] At the end of this stretch of narrative Samuel hacks Agag to death and we learn shortly, that furthermore, Samuel left the royal presence and that Saul never saw him again before his (Samuel's) death.

---

[109] In using the phrase "historical or mythological" I am recognizing the range of current understandings of the narrative found within the Torah. The most traditional of Jews and Christians understand the entirety of the Torah to have been transmitted at Sinai; the most non-traditional see the entire narrative as a myth; there are various views regarding both factuality versus non-factuality and divinely revealed versus humanly contrived between these two perspectival poles.

[110] What is translated as "witchcraft" here is *kesem* in Hebrew, which comes from a root meaning "divide, distribute" (as in drawing lots at a sanctuary in order to seek answers from the *sacer*, and perhaps as in dividing the *sacer* into diverse powers) and comes to mean "divination" or some means of addressing the divine *sacer* that is inherently illegal and presumably morally wrong because it does not rely simply and entirely on the God of Israel. There is—not surprisingly—a kind of circularity to the idea: if it is not officially approved by God's *sacerdotes* and thereby by God it is not merely off the sacerdotal mark (and presumably ineffective, or at least limited in its efficacy) but morally wrong because the definition of "morally wrong" is "disobedience to God." Thus, the phrase "*hata'at kesem*—"the sin of witchcraft/divination" is not only based on circular reasoning but is redundant, since anything to do with "*kesem*" is by definition a "*hayt'*."

One might also keep in mind that the textual beginning of Saul's demise is back in I Samuel 16:14: "Now the Spirit of the Lord had departed from Saul, and an evil spirit from the Lord tormented him." So on the one hand, there are other elements of the *sacer*, evil as well as good, but on the other hand they are all under the control of God. It is, of course, this very ambiguity that will continue into Judaism and Christianity, in spite of their pure monotheistic convictions.

All of this shapes the painful context of I Samuel 28. There, a distraught King Saul, both abandoned by God and bereft of the *sacerdos* and father-figure who had guided him from the time of his anointment as king to this day, is desperate for some sort of contact with the *sacer* on the eve before a crucial—and what will prove to be fatal—battle against the Philistines that will take place on Mount Gilboa the following morning. Having supposedly driven all sorcerers, magicians, witches and the like—either false practitioners of the *sacer* or practitioners of a false sense of the *sacer* (or at least competitors with those *sacerdotes* approved by the God of Israel as legitimate)—out of Israel, Saul instructs his men to seek one out. Irony aside, the search and its successful outcome—they find a woman who is just such a practitioner—yield the definitional question again, as to what exactly it is that distinguishes the "witch" at Endor from, say, Samuel as a *sacerdos*/prophet/priest.

Here is what the passage says:

> Now Samuel was dead, and all Israel had mourned for him and buried him in his own town of Ramah. Saul had expelled the mediums and spiritists from the land. (28:3)

And further:

> The Philistines assembled and came and set up camp at Shunem, while Saul gathered all Israel and set up camp at Gilboa. When Saul saw the Philistine army, he was afraid; terror filled his heart. He inquired of the Lord, but the Lord did not answer him by dreams or Urim or prophets.
> Saul then said to his attendants, "Find me a woman who is a medium, so I may go and inquire of her."
> "There is one in Endor," they said.
> So Saul disguised himself, putting on other clothes, and at night he and two men went to the woman. "Consult a spirit for me," he said, "and bring up for me the one I name."
> But the woman said to him, "Surely you know what Saul has done. He has cut off the mediums and spiritists from the land. Why have you set a trap for my life to bring about my death?"
> Saul swore to her by the Lord, "As surely as the Lord lives, you will not be punished for this."
> Then the woman asked, "Whom shall I bring up for you?"
> "Bring up Samuel," he said.
> When the woman saw Samuel, she cried out at the top of her voice and said to Saul, "Why have you deceived me? You are Saul!"
> The king said to her, "Don't be afraid. What do you see?"
> The woman said, "I see a ghostly figure coming up out of the earth."
> "What does he look like?" he asked.
> "An old man wearing a robe is coming up," she said.
> Then Saul knew it was Samuel, and he bowed down and prostrated himself with his face to the ground.
> Samuel said to Saul, "Why have you disturbed me by bringing me up?"

"I am in great distress," Saul said. "The Philistines are fighting against me, and God has departed from me. He no longer answers me, either by prophets or by dreams. So I have called on you to tell me what to do." Samuel said, "Why do you consult me, now that the Lord has departed from you and become your enemy? The Lord has done what he predicted through me. The Lord has torn the kingdom out of your hands and given it to one of your neighbors—to David. Because you did not obey the Lord or carry out his fierce wrath against the Amalekites, the Lord has done this to you today. The Lord will deliver both Israel and you into the hands of the Philistines, and tomorrow you and your sons will be with me. The Lord will also give the army of Israel into the hands of the Philistines." (28:4-19)

If we compare this passage to that in *Odyssey* 11, we may recognize the following similarities and differences, (among others). Odysseus had received instruction regarding how to conjure up Teiresias from a goddess, an aspect of the *sacer*, albeit a less-than-Olympian goddess—part of the mainstream Greek religion at the time of "Homer"— whereas Samuel is conjured for Saul through a *sacerdos* who functions illegally, outside the mainstream, in order to accomplish the king's bidding. Teireisas is active among the dead, all of whom are "active" albeit substanceless, and he offers a positive statement to Odysseus of his future; Samuel has been inactive, as if he has been asleep, and is disturbed by Saul and offers a concise statement of the latter's doom couched in the terms of his failure to do God's bidding.

Moreover, the medium—the woman at Endor—is functionally not altogether different from the medium played by Whoopi Goldberg in the 1990 film, *Ghost*, who is able to communicate with the deceased Patrick Swazy character and communicate his words to the Demi Moore character, who cannot see, hear or communicate with him. But *Ghost* is just a Hollywood movie; I am not expected to believe in the reality of its narrative, whereas I Samuel 28 is part of a revealed text—the word of God—at least as far as traditional Jews and Christians are concerned! What, apart from what I do or do not believe and the texts in which I do or do not believe, *really* distinguishes these two from each other?

The words that are translated here as "mediums and spiritists" or "a medium" are *ba'alot 'ov* (plural) and *ba'alat 'ov* (singular) in the original Hebrew. "*Ba'al(at)*" means "master/mistress of" and "*'ov*" seems originally to have meant "skin-bottle" or "wine-skin"—and therefore something hollow, or something with a hollow sound. Presumably someone who deals with the dead—ghosts—is dealing with substanceless—hollow— beings. These phrases come to be understood to refer to practices that a) deal with the *sacer*, particularly with the dead; b) in so dealing, invoke powers other than the God of Israel; and c) are illegal, in part at least because of the Commandment articulated by Moses at Sinai regarding other gods.[111] One must keep in mind the wording of this commandment, since it enjoins the Israelites not simply not to have other gods—or necessarily to believe

---

[111] Most versions of the text include the commandment to "have no other gods before me" as the second part of the First Commandment. The Babylonian Talmud treats it as the first part of the Second Commandment.

that they exist—but none "before me." At the very least this implies belief in the reality of other gods, at the most it acknowledges a place for them within Israelite spirituality, albeit a subsidiary place to that of the God of Israel.

At first glance this appears to be a radical understanding of that spirituality—particularly if one's perspective is that of contemporary Judaism or Christianity (or Islam). But one must be careful not to retrofit a contemporary understanding of God and God's demands upon a time and place, 30 or 35 centuries ago, in which conditions were radically different.

For one must also keep in mind that there is a range of biblical terms to refer to the process of engaging the *sacer*, both with regard to divinity and with regard to the dead, both legally and illegally. Thus what the woman at Endor was engaged in—necromancy; contact with the dead—was condemned by Israelite law, for instance in Lev. 19:31 and Isa. 8:19, 20.[112] On the other hand, a *kosem* would go into a trance before predicting future events—obviously in that trance state, the practitioner experienced *ek-stasis*, being outside him/herself and enveloped by the *sacer* with its non-linear sense of time. Balaam (Num 24:4) exemplifies this. There were other types of *sacerdotes*, as well, specializing in different aspects of the *sacer* and what it can offer to the *profanus* questioner.

For our purposes, the most important of these refers not to an individual but to an object, the *Urim vi-Tummim*, some sort of divining instrument associated with a dozen semi-precious stones worn on the High Priest's breastplate (Ex 28:15-25). These were used to predict the future, to decide cases of innocence or guilt that were otherwise not soluble, and also to offer definitive advice in matters of property ownership and questions of waging war versus keeping the peace. The point is that the High Priest (*kohayn ha-gadol*), wearing his robes and that breastplate was understood to be consulting God Itself for advice in these matters. What most obviously distinguishes that figure from others is that he is legitimate in the eyes of the authorities and the people but is understood to derive his legitimacy from the Israelite God, whereas others, like the practitioner at Endor, did not—and were, moreover, understood to be abrogating God's commandments by offering counter-measures and counter-elements of the *sacer* as sources for their practice.

---

[112] Both passages forbid one from "turning to ghosts (*'ovot*) and "inquiring of familiar spirits" (*yod'oneem*, from the Hebrew root, *y-d-'*, which refers to knowing something—or sexually knowing someone).

CHAPTER THREE

Evolving Greek Engagements of the Divine *Sacer*:
From Homer to Theophrastos

The *Iliad* and the *Odyssey* mark much of the beginning of Greek literature and the written form of the language that we call "Greek." They may be dated, as written narratives (as opposed to the oral traditions upon which the texts as we have them are almost certainly based) to around 775-700 BCE. Together with Hesiod's slightly later (ca 700-675 BCE) poetry, particularly the *Theogony*, these epic masterpieces offer a distinct picture of the Greek sense of the *sacer* as it assumes its classical form. Important differences exist between that form and the earlier form associated with the Bronze Age as well as the later form associated with the Hellenistic period, but all three phases share a number of traits in common.

These include the following features that are particularly relevant to our discussion. One, there is a multiplicity of Gods. Two, these gods are immortal, but they are all born at some time; they apparently grow to a certain ideal age and then remain that way forever. Thus Zeus appears older than Hermes or Apollo, for example. On the other hand, although Aphrodite is a young goddess—the personification of youthful female beauty— her birth, as featured in Hesiod's *Theogony* (ls 188-206) seems to pre-date that of any of the other gods. There is, of course, a perfect logic to this: to speak of "pre-date"—or of "before" and "after"—is to speak in a linear manner endemic to the *profanus*, but Aphrodite and all the gods and goddesses, in being parts of the *sacer*, are not subject to such linear thinking: directions in both time and space don't exist in that realm as they do in ours.

Three, there is a hierarchy within that multiplicity as it is understood in the classical period, encapsulated by the Epic, Lyric and Tragic poets (as opposed to the pre-classical or post-classical periods): the Olympians are inherently more powerful than gods and goddesses like Kirke or Kalypso, to say naught of those associated with rivers and streams or trees and other natural elements. Four, even the most powerful of the gods— Zeus, king of the Olympians—is limited in both knowledge and power. Thus Zeus can be deceived (as can the other gods and goddesses); like his father, Kronos, he can see the future but apparently cannot see everything even in the present. Indeed, when Zeus was born, he was spirited away to the island of Crete to be raised by the Nymphs while his father, eater of his new-born children, one of whom (Zeus) was fated to overthrow him, was tricked into swallowing a large stone wrapped in swaddling clothes.

For Kronos could not, in the end, alter history: he and his order of Titans would be overturned by Zeus and Zeus's fellow gods and goddesses, who would install the order—the Greek word for which is *kosmos*—with which we are familiar. Neither can Zeus alter the course of history beyond a certain point: that point is where *Fate* operates above and beyond his control. Thus, for instance, when he wishes to save the life of his son, Sarpedon—a Lycian warrior born to Zeus by a mortal woman, who has come to assist the Trojans in the defense of their city—he cannot. When Sarpedon is about to be struck down by the Akhaian warrior, Patroklos, Hera reminds Zeus that, as powerful as he is, to save a man fated to die would upset the very order of things of which he is, as it were, the consummate champion. All that Zeus can do is see to it that Sarpedon's corpse is wafted gently back to Lycia, sweet-smelling rather than rotting, to enjoy a splendid funeral.[113]

If the poetry of the Classical Greeks embroiders an ever-more complex tapestry of gods and their relations with humans in the course of the next few centuries, by the time the Lyric poets have transformed and expanded the variety of means of such expression, another group of thinkers has entered the arena of posing questions regarding the world and the place of humans within it. That group, known commonly as the pre-Socratic philosophers, differs most obviously from the poets in that their approach to reality is rooted not in supernatural forces but in nature.

The pre-Socratics began by asking which of the elements underlay all the others: which element was the substratum—the *hypokeimenon*—from which all the other elements, and thus our physical universe, derive. Thales (ca 624-526 BCE) proposed that it was water; Anaximenes (ca 585-28 BCE) proposed, rather, that it was air. Thales' pupil and Anaximenes' older friend and possibly also his teacher—Anaximander (ca 610-546 BCE)—looked in a more abstract direction for the answer. He spoke of the *apeiron*—the "boundless" as the *hypokeimenon*, introducing a kind of metaphysical concept to the discussion of physical nature. Other pre-Socratics followed in diverse directions. What they share in common is their turn away from what might be termed a religious—or mythological, if we follow a standard mode of thought and reject any sort of reality to the accounts of the *sacer* that we derive from Homer[114] and Hesiod—perspective in favor of a "scientific" one.

When Sokrates (469-399 BCE) steps onto the historical stage he ostensibly completes the first round of rationalizing the world, but without eschewing either the principles or the personalities associated with the classical articulations of Greek religion. For our purposes, however, there are two key elements that he adds to the discussion. One is the matter of values: ethics and morality beyond the standard Greek conviction that is evident in much of pre-Socratic Greek thought, that if someone is successful it must be

---

[113] See *Iliad* XVI: 426-507, 580-83.

[114] The astute reader might have noted that I have completely ignored the three most obvious parts of the "Homeric question" that are so important to some aspects of classical thought. Thus we need not concern ourselves with: a) what precisely the relationship is between the written forms of the *Iliad* and the *Odyssey* and either their prior putative oral history or other epics that existed orally or in writing but have not survived; b) who exactly Homer was—if an individual poet at all; and c) whether both these poems were written, or written down, by the same poet, assuming that either or both were composed by a single poet. It is what these poems and the *Theogony* tell us about the classical Greek sense of the *sacer* (and for our purposes we need only consider this issue in broad terms) that matters here.

because the gods approve his/her actions and therefore those actions must be "good." Indeed, Sokrates points out that divine approval in the context of a polytheistic *sacer*—in which the gods and goddesses are repeatedly shown in Homer and Hesiod to disagree about all sorts of thing (going back to their beginnings as delineated in the *Theogony* and to the beginnings of the Trojan War's Olympian context)—offers very thin ice for a simpler, divinity-based definition of holiness or piety (*hosiotes*) and by extension, the "(morally) good."[115]

The second contribution of Sokrates of particular relevance to our discussion is that, in recognizing the difficulty of defining a moral code by reference to the gods *because* they are so many and so often disagree with each other he offers a new articulation of a consummate *sacer*. This articulation he refers to as the "Forms/Ideas" (*eideia*). To be more precise, we don't always know exactly what Sokrates said, because he himself wrote nothing down and we therefore rely on others who have represented him to us. The most prominent of Sokrates' followers and the one to whom we turn almost entirely as our source for Sokrates' thinking, is Plato (428-348 BCE).[116] One of the complications of this relationship—between Sokrates and Plato and between the two of them and ourselves—is that there are concepts represented in the Platonic dialogues as articulated by Sokrates for which Plato may in fact have been the originator. The "Forms/Ideas"—*eideia*—is one of the most important of these, but for our purposes, it is the concept, not its originator, that matters.

With these last three clauses in mind, there are two further issues that must push us forward. One is *what* the concept of the *eideia is*. Briefly put, every abstract and concrete element within our *profanus* reality, from tables and chairs to acts of piety/holiness and justice are understood by Plato's Sokrates to derive from, and operate in emulation and imitation of, consummate, perfect, eternal, immutable versions of these elements in some *sacer* reality beyond our own. Thus all tables and acts of piety are temporary and imperfect expressions of the Forms "tableness" and "piety." Part of what we see Plato's Sokrates engaged in again and again is trying to systematically isolate what, precisely constitute the features causing us to call a table a table and a pious act a pious act, so that he can define "tableness" and "piety."

While "tableness" is ultimately not of profound interest to Sokrates, piety and other concepts that pertain to moral behavior are; ultimately he is seeking an unequivocal definition of what the Good is—the Form under which all other moral behavior Forms are subsumed. Two sub-issues of this first issue present themselves as particularly important to our discussion. The first is that, in the hierarchy of Socratic-Platonic thinking, the gods are understood to be part of the universe and perhaps makers of our *profanus* world as well as progenitors of many of its other-than-physical issues (such as love and strife). But they are not only not supreme, they are almost beside the point when seeking answers to moral questions. The Forms are a construct beyond both humans and gods; they are simply *there,*

---

[115] This point is most obviously articulated in *Euthyphro*—named for the sophist (a self-proclaimed wise—*sophos*—man of that name), one of the early dialogues penned by Plato, which would record one of the presumably last discussions in which Sokrates engaged before his death.
[116] There are a few other sources, both far more limited than Plato and for the purposes of our discussion, irrelevant, such as Xenophon.

distant and disengaged in an active sense, yet every moral (or immoral) act is measured against them—every moral act is understood to direct itself to them, to participate in them (every act of piety, for example, participates in the Form "piety.").

But (and this is the second sub-issue of our first issue) we can never seem to arrive at an absolute definition of any of these *absolutes*—Plato's Sokrates nearly always ends his conversations in a state of *aporia* ("no way out;" literally "without a passage"). Indeed, Plato and Sokrates, supreme rationalists though they are—they offer their arguments, at least initially, by way of a careful and systematic *logos* (a reasoned "account")—often fall back on *mythos* to try to complete their inquiry. Thus in the *Phaedo*, for instance, after offering half a dozen rational arguments for believing in the immortality of the soul, Sokrates offers a *mythos*, an account of a particular soul's journey after death, for which he has no means of definitively stating that it is fact-based. The Forms and the gods and *mythoi* regarding the immortality of the soul all share a common property: they all require a trans-rational embrace of one sort or another.

The second issue that is important for us in negotiating the terrain of Sokrates and Plato is the fact that the latter felt the need to write things down, presumably at the outset recalling discussions—either that he heard or that were reported to him—between Sokrates and various protagonists. At some point in the course of his career he had gone beyond those remembered conversations, but continued to use the dialogue form and continued to place Sokrates at the center of each work, leaving us the task, if it is important to us, of determining where Socratic thought ends and Platonic thought begins.

Among the many areas of that terrain where we can be certain that the ideas of both men intersected, albeit from differing angles, was the application of the Good to city-states. It is clear that Sokrates, for example, spent his career asking sometimes annoying questions and leading his conversants down paths of inquiry toward aporetic and for them frustrating ends because he wanted Athens to be as morally perfect a *polis* as possible. Having seen how that desire and the method of its fulfillment led ultimately to Sokrates' death, Plato refocused: he created an ivory tower, the Academy, as a place where one could ask questions without the threat of offending someone who possessed sufficient power to destroy the questioner.

Having further seen that the ideal ruler of the ideal state that he briefly thought he could shepherd into existence (in Syracuse) was not possible, he determined that, in the absence of such a ruler—a philosopher-king, one who rules reluctantly, because he must, not because he wants power, and who addresses every situation with a reasoned and wise approach—the next best thing would be to have an exhaustive series of laws that anticipates every eventuality as a guide for a nearly-ideal state. Thus late in his career he wrote an extensive work—a dialogue in form, a treatise in content—in which he hoped to consider every possible issue that might come up in the day-to-day life of a state.

The *Laws*, as this late work is called, includes within its discussion a small section (933A-E) of particular relevance to our own discussion. In that section he first discusses "fatal injuries inflicted by the use of *pharmaka*"—this is the same term with which we are familiar from the *Odyssey*, the positive/negative nuance of which is determined by context—and then subsequently, "less harmful cases of voluntary and premeditated injury

71

inflicted by giving food or drink or by applying ointments." Plato is true to his systematic rationalist form in then noting that

> poisoning is of two kinds. First there is the sort we have just explicitly mentioned: the injury a body suffers from some physical substance by natural processes. The other kind is a matter of spells and charms and 'enchantments': not only are the victims persuaded that they are being seriously injured by people with magical influence, but even the perpetrators themselves are convinced that it really is in their power to inflict injury by these methods.

There are four terms of marked interest to us here. What is rendered as "spells" is, in Plato's Greek, *magganeisis*. The root of the word, *mag-*, is a direct Greek derivative from Old Persian, where that root is the basis of the word *maghos*. In Persian that term means "priest"; it refers to a member of the priestly tribe, as we have previously noted—a legitimate engager of the *sacer*. But, in part, no doubt, due to the tendency of the Greeks to think negatively about the Persians (who, after all, nearly swallowed Greece up at the end of the 6th and beginning of the 5th centuries BCE—even coming so close as to sack the Athenian acropolis—before being beaten back in the course of half a century of conflict) has led to the appropriation of that term, as we have observed, and its relegation to the category of nefarious practice with regard to *sacer* influence on the *profanus*.

The term rendered here as "charms" is *epoidais* (in the dative plural form), an oral recitation of neither inherently negative nor inherently positive nuance—reminiscent, in this positive-negative ambiguous sense, of *pharmakon*, as we have seen in the *Odyssey*—except by context. "Enchantments" is a translation of *katadesesi legomenais* (again, in the dative plural form)—literally "bindings by things said," i.e., "bindings by words." To be slightly anachronistic: if we think back to Kirke and Odysseus' men in *Odyssey* 10, had she turned them into swine with mere verbal formulae, rather than through a combination of *pharmaka* and touching them with her *sacer*-empowered wand, then we would speak of their transformation as having been effected by *katadesesi legomenois*.

Lastly, Plato's comment that people are persuaded that they have been injured by those with "magic influence" offers a rendering of the phrase *dynameuon goeteuein*. The first term refers to the *capacity* or *power* to do something. The second term—*goeteia* in its nominal form—refers to the practice of invoking the *sacer* to accomplish some end in the *profanus* that is understood to be nefarious; it is to be invoking the power of the *sacer* in a manner that is not legal because it is harmful (and harmful because it is not legal).

There is a double issue to be noted in all of this. The first is that of nuance; how neutral terminology acquires a negative (or positive) connotation by context or prejudice (which, in turn, provides a challenge to the translator to convey that nuance). The second issue is: what does Plato recognize and acknowledge with regard to positive/negative ambiguity apropos accessing the *sacer* (or seeking to access it) in order to effect some result in the *profanus*. For in the next line, he continues by noting that

> it is not easy to know the truth about these and similar practices, and even if one were to find out, it would be difficult to convince others; and it is

just not worth the effort of trying to persuade people whose heads are full of mutual suspicion, that even if they do sometimes catch sight of a molded waxen figure in a doorway or at a junction of three roads or on their parents' graves, they should ignore it every time, because they cannot be sure these things work.

There are two issues that Plato is noting here, within the framework of a third issue familiar to us from our introductory discussion. One is the fact that people easily jump to conclusions regarding objects and their placement and are wont to assume that they have a negative role in the *sacer-profanus* relationship when they may not—if I cannot explain what a particular object is doing in a particular place, I am inclined to assume the worst—and the second is that what is at issue is not necessarily the *intention* but the *efficacy* of an action or an object. The framework that we can recognize is that of analogues and borders: a threefold crossroad and a grave and even a doorway, as border places—where opposing realms meet, be they inside/outside, life/death or a/b/c directions—are all analogues of each other and, potentially, of the ultimate boundary between *sacer* and *profanus*, with a potential for unpredictably propitious or dangerous consequences.

Having spent considerable side effort on analyzing and discussing this issue, Plato goes on to assert that the law code regarding *pharmaka* needs to be a "double law, reflecting the two methods by which poisoning may be attempted," and then to distinguish between a case when "the person who tries to use poison happens to be a diviner or soothsayer" and an amateur who "acts in ignorance of how his spells will turn out" and between a case in which the practitioner "happens to be an expert in medicine," and one in which the amateur "acts in ignorance of the effect he will have on the body."

So Law # 83, Plato tells us, will require that a doctor who poisons someone, (or a member of that individual's family or his cattle or bees!), even if the victim does not die, must be put to death; whereas a layman who does the same may or may not be executed or otherwise punished, at the discretion of the court. And Law #84 will state that a "diviner or soothsayer" who injures someone by spell, incantations, charms, etc., must also die; whereas the punishment to a presumably ignorant layman practitioner is left to the discretion of the court. He goes on to explain what the purpose of the prescribed punishments is.

For our own purposes what is most important is that, within the matrix sketched out by Plato the explicit categories being distinguished are those of accomplishing one's ends through physical means and through non-physical means and of being a professional aware of the consequences of certain actions and of not being professional. But implicit is another set of categories—between medicine as a practice designed to heal physical illnesses and wounds and its use with the intention of inflicting harm; and between oral means whereby a priest seems to access the *sacer* on behalf of an individual or the community and those by which a nefarious practitioner uses those same sorts of means to inflict damage.

Given both the terminology and the descriptive context provided by Plato near the outset of his discussion, an obvious question that we might ask pertains to how one distinguishes the physician or the priest who is a functionary of (legitimate) medicine or *religio*/religion from the poisoner or the soothsayer who is a functionary of (illegitimate) *goeteia*/*mageia*/magic. Or is it simply the outcome (or intended outcome) that distinguishes them from each other?

This question offers three different angles of discussion that we might pursue. One is with reference to Plato's own writings and the role of irony in Sokrates' discourse as Plato represents it. For at the other end of his corpus, in one of the earliest works he wrote, the *Euthyphro*, composed perhaps as early as the 390s BCE, Plato shows Sokrates challenging the self-proclaimed wise man (sophist) of that name to define *hosiotes*. For the purposes of our discussion, it does not matter whether we translate that term as "piety" (as some do) or as "holiness" (as others do). What matters is that Euthyphro's most concerted effort at a response is to define it as "what is pleasing to the gods." As with other definitional attempts by his protagonist, Sokrates easily finds holes in the offering. In this case, there are at least two.

One is rhetorical: is an act *hosios* because it pleases the gods or does it please the gods because it is *hosios*? The other is, as it were, practical: since the Greek literary tradition often shows the gods to be at odds with each other (consider, for example, the ultimate Greek narrative, that of the Trojan War, in which some gods and goddesses not only support but actually fight on the side of the Trojans and others on the side of the Akhaians), then could one do something that pleases one god but displeases another? Soon after this, Euthyphro suddenly "remembers" another appointment for which he needs to hurry away, leaving Sokrates—as he so often is, at the end of the Platonic dialogues—with his definitional question unanswered; he is—and we are—rather, in a state of *aporia*.

The irony is not of the sort that is typical of and internal to the dialogues (where Sokrates speaks in a tongue-in-cheek manner completely missed by his interlocutor(s) but which we are intended to recognize). It is that Plato, not only at the outset of his career as a writer but throughout most of his career leaves Sokrates in a state of *aporia* at the end of his dialogues. He never defines *hosiotes* in the *Euthyphro* or elsewhere, but more than four decades later, in the *Laws*, he carefully defines types of crimes that seem to involve the *sacer* and if he distinguishes their categories, he nonetheless does not offer a ready series of definitions by which to distinguish the legitimate practitioner from the illegitimate.

The significance of this becomes clearer when—this is the second angle of discussion offered by the *Laws*—we encounter a writer a generation or so after Plato who, among other things, wrote a series of short works offering descriptions of different human "types" or "characters." One of these pertains to what is commonly translated as "The Superstitious Man." This may not answer the question of how to distinguish religion from magic or medicine from sorcery, but it offers an account of the sort of individual whose concerns vis-à-vis the negative potential of the *sacer* is at least in part embedded in that question and its putative answers. The third angle is to examine at a more practical level the discussion of the question by way of the sort of court cases that might be seen either directly (in Athens) or indirectly (in the Roman Empire, many generations later) to reflect the sort of sensibility offered by Plato. We shall pursue this third angle of discussion in the next chapter.

As for the second angle: Theophrastos (371-287 BCE) was born in Eresos, on the island of Lesbos, and arrived into Athens at a young age, studying initially with Plato.

Eventually, after Plato's death and Aristotle's decision to found his own school, Theophrastos moved over and in the end succeeded Aristotle as the head of the Lyceum and its Peripatetic school of philosophy. Among his *Typoi*, "The Superstitious Man" is of particular interest: the Greek term from which this title derives is *deisidaimonia*, which literally means "fear/awe of *daimones*" and the term *daimon*, as we have already noted, is used to refer to lesser forces of the divine *sacer* than is the term *theos*. The latter would be used to refer to an Olympian god or goddess, the former would not. Odysseus encounters figures who might be referred to by either term when he meets Kirke and Kalypso, since they are not Olympians, but are more powerful than any number of still lesser *sacer* beings.

So, Theophrastos defines *deisidaimonia* as "an abject fear of the supernatural"— or, to be more precise (albeit awkwardly translated), as "fear *pros to daimonion*," which would mean "toward [that which pertains to the realm of] *daimones*."[117] He then describes the individual who is subject to such fear, who seeks to protect himself against "pollution" by

> constantly washing his hands and sprinkling himself from a sacred spring, and by chewing leaves of the sacred laurel; these precautions keep him busy the whole day. And should a cat chance to cross his path, he goes not a step further until he has tossed three stones across the road or until somebody else passes by. In the same way, seeing a harmless snake in the house makes him call on Sabazios Dionysios; and at the sight of the poisonous "sacred snake" he hurries to have a shrine put up marking the spot; nor can he pass the ritual stone at a crossroads without pouring an offering from his oil-flask and kneeling to reverence them first.

There is a handful of issues raised by this first part of Theophrastos' description. As a general rule, the entire discussion suggests that, for the *deisidaimon*, not only are we surrounded by the ever-present *sacer* but the ubiquity of the *sacer* includes, front and center, its negative potentiality, which one must counter by accessing its positive potentiality.

While *constantly* washing one's hands may certainly be considered obsessive, to what extent ought we to associate that sort of physical precaution with *deisidaimonia* and to what extent with medicine? In other words, is the pollution against which the so-called *deisidaimon* protects himself a series of illnesses associated by him with nefarious *sacer* powers—nefarious *daimones*—but that actually derive from *germs* (unknown to either the *deisidaimon* or perhaps to most of his contemporaries), and so they are fended off by good hygiene? We are thus considering the last question posed by Plato's *Laws* from a different perspective: not medical/priestly versus magical action or cure from illness versus imposition of illness through nefarious means, but illness from germs versus illness from *daimones*.

---

[117] From the Greek verb, *deido*, meaning "to fear" and, of course, *daimonia*. One could translate "*to daimonion*" as "the demonic," but the nuance of that term in English is misleading in being fully negative; the Greek is (like the *sacer* overall) more neutral, its most noteworthy characteristic being the ubiquity of *sacer* forces—of which ubiquity the *deisidaimon* is so acutely aware.

When, in order to further protect himself, the *deisidaimon* chews sacred laurel leaves, he is by definition invoking the protection of Apollo, to whom the laurel is sacred. So is it a matter (as in the story of Odysseus, Hermes and Kirke) of a more powerful aspect of the *sacer* being put to use against a less powerful aspect, wherein the first also happens to be a positive force and the second a negative force? How does this understanding fit into the larger question of categories within the *sacer* and their relationship to the terms "religion" and "magic"?

We recognize that elements of Theophrastos' description could certainly apply to religion and not only to superstition—such as the importance of *threeness* ("three stones") or the erection of a sacerdotal shrine at a spot deemed propitious because of what has been interpreted as a communication from *sacer* to *profanus* (in the "person" of the poisonous "sacred snake"—sacred because as it ages, it continually sheds its old skin and emerges fresh and new and larger than before; and because, as a poisonous snake, it has the power over life and death as the gods and Fate do).

In a fundamental way, then, we might ask whether at least some of the procedures identified by Theophrastos might not be drawn from the vocabulary of standard, mainstream *religio*—or put otherwise, reflect the *hosiotes* that Plato's Sokrates could not define, rather than the *deisidaimonia* that Theophrastos is defining by listing its "attributes." Certainly the two concepts overlap: the "ritual stones"—and at a crossroads, a meeting of realms, at that!—reflect standard aspects of traditional *religio*, and making an offering or genuflecting to reverence them could certainly just as easily qualify as *piety* as it could as *superstition*, particularly if one believes in the reality of the *sacer* power(s) that such a site and such gestures are intended to propitiate.

The world of standard *religio* in which Theophrastos is living and writing is one also noteworthily marked by a good deal of syncretism where addressing the *sacer* is concerned—as syncretism is evident in other ways in that world. Thus the Sabazios Dionysios to which he refers represents a synthesis of Sabazios—an originally Phrygian and/or Thracian sky god typically represented on horseback, who comes to be associated with vegetation in general and then with barley in particular—with Dionysios, himself originally a foreign (i.e., Non-Hellenic) god who comes to be associated in particular with wine (thus Sabazios, by way of barley, is associated with beer and perhaps, therefore, particularly synthesizable to Dionysios and wine).[118]

These issues are carried onward as the description of the *deisidaimon* moves forward. He responds to the gnawing of holes in his barley sack by mice by consulting "some interpreter of omens" and by offering sacrifices. "He is also likely to keep purifying his house all the time, on the excuse that Hekate has come to haunt it." Again: obsessiveness seems to define the *deisidaimon*, but that obsessiveness is illegitimate simply because Theophrastos doesn't share it; and the positive/negative ambiguity of the *sacer* could not be more obvious than in the reference to Hekate. As she is presented in this sentence, she appears to be a negative force from which one requires purifying protection.

---

[118] There will be further implications for the Sabazios Dionysios association into the Roman period and for Roman pagan views of the Judaean religion. See below, 147-8.

Hekate can be associated with the negative—with what might be termed magic and witchcraft, necromancy and sorcery. But wasn't Kirke a sorceress, but also a goddess, who turned Odysseus' men into swine and imprisoned them, but then helped Odysseus to get what he wanted—and wasn't Odysseus, with Kirke's help, a necromancer, like the woman at Endor, who conjured up the dead to find out his fate? And Hekate is in any case at least as frequently associated with crossroads and entry-ways—border sites, where she is invoked to *protect* one from the negative possibilities that every such site offers—as well as with fire and light (protective elements), as well as with knowledge of herbs and poisonous plants (that is to say, for both benevolent medicinal and malevolent purposes: *pharmaka*).[119]

She is, in some parts of the Greek tradition, a goddess with a kind of rulership over earth, sea and sky (she stands, as it were, at the crossroads of all three and she is depicted with three faces looking simultaneously in three directions); and is also thought of as a kind of salvationist deity, in her capacity as *Soteira*. A key figure with altars in every Athenian household, she protects homes and brings prosperity to families. So Theophrastos' depiction of the *deisidaimon* as needing to purify his home to allay *haunting* by Hekate would seem to turn a positive *sacer* force into a negative. Is it that turn that identifies this Theophrastian *typos as* a *deisidaimon*, rather than as a person who is *hosios*?

"Owls hooting while he is out for a walk upset him; he won't go on without first saying 'Athena save us!'"—which makes sense, since the owl is Athena's emblematic bird, and also does *not* make sense, since why would one need protection from Athena's owl? "Also, tombs and dead bodies and women in childbirth are bad omens that make him keep his distance…to guard against being polluted." Again this makes sense, in that all three are sacerdotal—border places or beings—and any sacerdotal border is potentially dangerous, since the negative aspect of the *sacer* can cross it into the *profanus* and one doesn't want to be near the point at which negative aspects enter. But this may also be seen as nonsensical, since such borders are also potentially propitious, so it isn't distance that one needs (if the *sacer* wants to find you it will, wherever you hide within the *profanus*) but proper rituals enacted at/to them.

The same ambiguity with regard to what is really religion and what is not may be recognized in the lines that follow:

On the unlucky days of the month—the fourth and the twenty-fourth—
he has his servants prepare hot wine. Then he shops for myrtle wreaths,
frankincense, altar-cakes; and once he is back home he spends all the rest
of the day arranging garlands on the statues of Hermaphroditos."

Unlucky days are part of mainstream religious thinking not only for Romans but for any number of ancient societies with awareness of the everyday presence of the *sacer* and concern for its negative potential. The Babylonians, for instance, considered the seventh,

---

[119] This is consistent with the general view of the *sacer* as inherently neutral and potentially positive or negative, as we have discussed. Every God and goddess can act benevolently or malevolently, depending upon circumstances. Artemis/Diana, for example, associated (see above, Introduction, 20ff) with the *lapis niger*, is a patroness of hunters when it is appropriate, but she also protects wild beasts from being hunted when it is appropriate to do so.

fourteenth, nineteenth and twenty-first days of each month to be bad luck days, when as a consequence of its potential dangers the king was forbidden to eat certain foods, ride in his chariot and offer sacrifices, and some sources suggest that the populace at large did not work on those days. Such an unlucky day was called *Shappatu*.[120]

So the *deisidaimon*'s behavior is consistent with a form of mainstream religious behavior. It is interesting, moreover, that the deity whose images he garlands is a border-divinity: by definition, being both male and female, s/he stands with a foot in each of two normally distinct and separate realms that are analogues of the consummate distinct and separate realms, *sacer* and *profanus*.

The last part of Theophrastos' description comments on the issue of dreams, bird-omens and other signs from the *sacer* that require interpretation—in which the *deisidaimon* asks "which god he should pray to. And before his initiation into the Orphic mysteries he visits the priests of the god every month, taking the whole family along." What is doubly interesting in this is firstly, that both dreams and bird-omens on the one hand and Orphism on the other are part of mainstream Greek (and Roman) religion, so that it is less the particular beliefs that this *typos* possesses that qualify him for the author's caricaturizing tone, than the intensity with which he practices, both in adhering to every sort of system and in his obsessive engagement intensity in each and every case.

Secondly, the Orphism that was legitimate in an earlier era—that earlier form had even inspired Plato—had apparently become debased by Plato's own time and thus the more so by Theophrastos' day. In Plato's *Republic* itinerant priests who trade on Orpheus' name are condemned as charlatans. With this development in mind, the mysteries to which Theophrastos refers can be understood to be illegitimate parodies of true *religiones*.

He begins the end of his brief portrait by reference, again, to Hekate—"Hecate's garlic at the crossroads," which both recalls the importance of a crossroads, in *sacer-profanus* relations, both legitimate and illegitimate, positive and negative; and alludes to a far-flung practice, across many cultures, of using garlic to protect one's self from the negative side of the *sacer*. If garlic can, by means of its objectionable raw odor, keep friends away, it can keep evil spirits (and vampires, that are a particular subset of "evil spirits") away.

Theophrastos ends by asserting that "[a]t the sight of anyone suffering from madness or epilepsy he shudders and spits into his bosom." We recognize in this last observation the idea that *mania* has a causal association with the *sacer*—the madman was assumed to be in contact with powers beyond the human, which would account for his unintelligible words or behavior—which, not surprisingly, can be positive or negative. As for epilepsy, it is referred to as the "divine madness" (even in Plato, *theia mania* is represented as accounting for unusual behavior; see, for example, *Phaedrus* 244-55 and 256b) and assumed to be the result of divine possession. But since that possession could be viewed as positive or negative—the "possessors" could be malevolent or benevolent *daimones*—it would be wise to protect one's self from infectious contact with an epileptic.

---

[120]This would evolve in the Israelite-Judaean tradition, as *Shabbat* (the Sabbath): the seventh weekly day when one does no work, but because of divine prescription rather than because it's a bad luck day.

And spitting—the expelling of body liquid—has a long history of being regarded as apotropaic.

In analyzing the period that carries us, in Greece, from Homer to Theophrastos, the classicist E.R. Dodds (1893-1979) in his work, *The Greeks and the Irrational*, refers to it as an era of change from being a Shame Culture to being a Guilt culture.[121] A Homeric warrior like Odysseus is characterized, he suggests, by a desire to perform well in battle in order to "show off" for his best friend—who may (or may not) be his lover—rather than to suffer the embarrassment of performing poorly. Odysseus himself may not be the best example of this. Rather, someone like Akhilleus, who has a best friend whom he loves, Patroklos—whose death in fact brings Akhilleus back into battle in the *Iliad* after he had sat out for some time due to the insult and public humiliation meted out to him by Agamemnon. Moreover, Akhilleus, who, according to another thread in the tapestry of the Trojan War tradition, had not wished to join the war in the first place, was shamed into joining by Odysseus.[122]

The point is that what the Homeric heroes do they do not out of fear of the gods in the sense of moral guilt but from fear of being shamed by poor conduct. When Akhilleus agrees to come fight at Troy, it is because Odysseus shames him into that agreement; when Agamemnon insults Akhilleus in the first book of the *Iliad*, it is because he has been shamed before his troops, and, in turn, Akhilleus' decision to turn away from further participation in the fighting as a consequence of Agamemnon's action reflects the fact that he has been shamed before those same troops by Agamemnon, and his (Akhilleus') honor—*kleos*—has been besmirched. That would eventually change—but much later, beginning with Sokrates—and a greater concern for what the gods (and men) would think of one's actions from a moral standpoint, led to the substitution of guilt for shame. This would culminate when Greco-Roman culture met and interwove Israelite-Judaeanism and its offspring, Judaism and Christianity, and their obsession with moral goodness—which is the direction in which our discussion leads next.

---

[121] E.R. Dodds, *The Greeks and the Irrational*. (Berkeley and Los Angeles: University of California Press, 1951), chapter two. (See also chapter six).

[122] Akhilleus fails to show up at Agamemnon's door along with the other Akhaians who, like him, had agreed to do so, years before, when Helen had chosen Menelaos to be her husband. At that time all of the suitors had agreed that, should anyone ever try to take her from him they would gather together to prevent her being carried off or to bring her back, but Akhilleus doesn't show up, knowing well the prophecy that if he fights at Troy he will die there, albeit achieving "undying glory" (*kleos aphthiton*). Odysseus is dispatched by Agamemnon to find Akhilleus, who is hiding in disguise among the women folk of his (Akhilleus') friend, Lykomedes, King of Skyros. Odysseus sees through the disguise and asks him whether he does not feel ashamed to be on the verge of sitting out the great war and missing out on his chance for glory. In the fullest version, the *Akhilleid*, by the Roman poet, Statius (ca 45-ca 96 CE), his mother, the sea goddess Thetis, sent him to live at the court of Lykomedes in order to dodge the prophecy that he would die at Troy. He was disguised at Skyros under the name Pyrrha—"the fiery-haired," (or in other versions, Issa, or Kerkysera). There he fell in love with and had an affair with (and/or married) Deidamia, one of the daughters of Lykomedes, and they had a son, Neoptolemos (or two sons, Neoptolemos and Oneiros). In one version, Deidamia disguised herself as a man so that she could follow Akhilleus to Troy and fight by his side.

CHAPTER FOUR

Israelite-Judaean History and the Engagement of the *Sacer* from King David to King Antigonos

During the course of the centuries that carry us from Homer to Theophrastos within the Greek world, the world of the Israelites is also in the process of undergoing a series of significant changes. To begin with, the tribal confederation led by Moses and subsequently by Joshua and a progression of figures known as Judges, has evolved into the unified kingdom led first by Saul—part of the unhappy end of whose story we have briefly explored. The end of King Saul's reign and his destruction on Mount Gilboa at the hands of the Philistines is followed by a more expanded and perhaps still more unified kingship under David and Solomon (ca 1005-930 BCE). Saul and David in turn were physically anointed—the Hebrew for which verb is "*mashah*" and the participial form of which is "*mashiah*"—by the *sacerdos* Samuel (whom we have also already encountered) with oil, guided to do so, according to the text of I Samuel 9:15-17, 10:1 (Saul) and 16:3, 6, 12-13 (David), by God Itself. The participial form of that verb, as we shall later repeat, will evolve as a noun—and will be translated into Greek as "*khristos*"—to refer to someone who is anointed by, or at the direction of, God.

The death of Solomon, however, leads to a civil war and a dissolution of the kingdom into two separate states. This happens for a number of reasons beyond our focus, although it should be noted that the first book of Kings (11:1-13) suggests that the underlying reason is that Solomon displeased the God of Israel, primarily because, although he built a magnificent Temple, a cult center, for God, literally and figuratively attached to his own palace complex, he also built temples for the non-Israelite gods worshipped by non-Israelite wives taken by him in dynastic marriage arrangements, notably, the daughter of the Egyptian pharaoh.

The northern kingdom, more or less associated with the territorial areas of 10 of the 12 tribes, continued to be called "Israel" and appears to have contained most of the more valuable territory for both grazing of flocks and farming, as well as being surrounded by friendly neighbors. The south, largely comprised of the areas associated with the tribes of Benjamin (from which Saul came) and Judah (from which David and Solomon came) came to be referred to as "Judah"—named, in other words, for the larger of those two tribes, which was also, after all, the tribe from which the God-chosen successor to the God-abandoned-and-rejected Saul had come. If the areas commanded by Judah were less agronomico-economically useful and flanked by far more threatening neighbors than was true for Israel, it possessed Jerusalem, the capital established by David and enhanced by Solomon, with, among other things, its exquisite Temple. If Israel were better situated in the conventional physical sense, Judah was better situated in the unconventional metaphysical sense, and its royal line continued the House of David and Solomon whereas the royal lines of Israel derived from other families.

Roughly three-quarters of a century after Solomon's death the northern kingdom had established itself under the line of Omri and Ahab with a capital in Samaria—archaeological remains of that palace complex, including magnificently carved ivory furnishings, abound from that site—and Ahab led a confederation of northern Israelites and their neighbors in a successful encounter with the rising Assyrian Empire at the battle of Karkar, in 853 BCE. But from a spiritual perspective, Ahab is seen in negative terms by the Bible. He is constantly criticized and opposed by the Samuel of his day, the Prophet (*sacerdos*) Elijah.

Most stirringly, Elijah destroys scores of *sacerdotes* loyal to Ahab's dynastic-marriage spouse, Jezebel, the Tyrian princess and priestess whom he brought back to Israel from the Lebanon and wed, and who was loyal to the gods she served, most notably, Ba'al. Elijah, moreover, predicts the demise of both king and queen in intense terms (I Kings 21:22-24). The deaths of Ahab and Jezebel are in fact particularly gruesome—the only such deaths described in the entire Hebrew Bible—as he is defeated in battle and the dogs lap up his blood, and as she is pushed from an upper window of her palace and her broken body is devoured by dogs (I Kings 22:38 and II Kings 9:30-37).

There is a peculiar series of parallels between the stories of the glorious King Solomon and the villainous King Ahab in which the first may be said to have offered a "model" exceeded by the latter. Solomon turned to the Tyrians to build his God's Temple and expand his father's palace; Ahab apparently turned to them to build his palace (this is evident from the style and quality of the aforementioned ivory furniture decorations). Solomon married foreign princesses, including the daughter of the Egyptian pharaoh; Ahab married a Tyrian princess, who was also a priestess. Solomon built Temples to the gods of his wives; Ahab permitted the priesthood of the Tyrians to function within his country, among his people, and he was influenced by his wife to displease God by "straying after fetishes" (I Kings 21:25-6). Solomon lost 10 of 12 shares, as it were, of his father's kingdom for his descendants; Ahab's repentance (after Elijah so severely excoriated him for his behavior) saved his kingdom temporarily but his descendants would eventually lose Israel altogether to the empire that he had managed to hold at bay at Karkar.

At issue are both human-human issues and human-divine issues. Solomon's son, Rehoboam, is represented as having treated the Israelite people poorly, with excessive taxes. He had become disconnected from the people, both figuratively and literally—the walled royal precinct that encompassed the Temple and palace complex helped facilitate that—which was the icing on the cake of his acts that displeased God (I Kings 12:1-16). Ahab and Jezebel are represented as treating their people poorly, which acts offered a complement to their spiritually offensive acts. But the matter of spiritual offence reminds us of how consistently fragile the relationship between the Israelites and their God must have been. They were surrounded and constantly tempted by peoples with other gods; the non-existence of such gods is not a given, but it is a given that a good Israelite (and especially an Israelite king!) should have nothing to do with them.

Somewhat more than a century after Ahab's death—in 722-21 BCE—a mightier Assyrian monarch with a more powerful army destroyed the city of Samaria and its royal palace and, in brief, the outcome was that the Israelites were lost to history. That is, the members of the ten "northern" tribes—largely cut off for two centuries from Jerusalem and its Temple as a concrete expression of a special relationship with the God of Israel, due to the ongoing conflicts between Judah and Israel, and now, as a practical matter, with families and communities broken up by the Assyrians—lost all sense of being part of the covenantal tradition that carried back through David to Moses and, ultimately, to Abraham. After that date, then, the remaining, fragmentary covenantal community would be referred to as Judah and its inhabitants as Judaeans.

Judah was nearly swallowed up, as well—its second largest city, Lachish, was destroyed in 701 (a relief-carved account illustrating this has survived from the Assyrian capital of Nineveh)—but Jerusalem held. Assyria's mighty empire subsequently collapsed in 614-612 before the onrushing might of its cousins, the Chaldaean Babylonians. The Babylonians succeeded where the Assyrians had failed back in the late eighth century: they captured Jerusalem, destroyed the Temple and carried off anyone likely to be of use or of threat to Babylonia. *Anyone of use or threat*—meaning that members of the lower classes were no doubt left behind in Judah, or, in some cases, apparently fled, temporarily, southwest into Egypt. What this also means is that, should the community in exile survive with its Judaean identity intact, its sense of self might grow increasingly different from that of Judaeans who never went into exile.

Had the Judaeans—both those who remained in Judah and those in exile— followed standard psycho-spiritual procedure, they would surely have abandoned the God of Israel after this debacle, or at least hyphenated their God to one of the key Babylonian gods, such as Marduk. After all, a deity incapable of protecting Its people and Its Temple from enemies worshipping other gods must be weaker than those other gods, by definition. But this is not what transpired. On the contrary, the Judaeans—at least those in exile, members of the upper, more educated and perhaps more thoughtful classes— committed two shifts away from conventional ancient thought with enormous consequences for the rest of history.

Most importantly, they seem to have finally arrived at a universal sense of God. What had begun for Abraham, Isaac and Jacob as a series of personal relationships, covenants, and beliefs, and that had evolved though Moses and the pre-exilic prophets into a sense of a national god—the God of Israel, before whom there must be no other gods, but arguably a god *among* other gods and, at least in the context of both the Moses/Aaron/pharaoh and the Ahab/Jezebel/Elijah narratives, a God more powerful than any other—was now definitively understood to be the only God, the God of all of creation and the Author of all of history.

Aspects of that God's wider focus and interest will be explicitly expressed in at least two biblical texts. The Book of Jonah centers on a reluctant prophet who is pushed by God to warn the Ninevans—i.e., inhabitants of the capital city of the hated enemy empire that swallowed up the northern kingdom of Israel!—that they must clean up their spiritual and moral act or face destruction at the hand of God. He tries to outrun God and cannot, and when he finally delivers his warning, the Ninevans, led by their king, change their pattern of behavior, and are saved (to Jonah's narrow-minded consternation) from divine destruction. The Book of Ruth centered on a Moabite woman—from yet another people traditionally inimical to the Israelites—who embraces the God and people of Israel. The narrative ends with a genealogy that identifies Ruth as the great-grandmother of none other than King David, the consummate *mashiah*.

Within the context of this burgeoning universalism, a second shift took place in Babylonia for Judaean spirituality. The destruction and exile came to be understood not as acts *against* God, but as acts *precipitated* by God. The Babylonian king, Nebuchadnezzar, was understood to have been a mere instrument in God's hand, a rod used to chastise the Judaeans for having failed to live up to their covenantal obligations, as prophet after prophet, particularly Jeremiah, had warned would happen. For prophet after prophet had asserted, each in his own voice with his own particular emphases, that God would punish them if their God-displeasing behavior continued. The Babylonians had been God's method; they were not impelled by gods who do not even *exist*—although the Babylonians themselves surely did not realize this.

The Judaeans in exile, rather than abandoning worship of the God of Israel, or hyphenating His Name to that of one or more of the Babylonian gods, not only continued the worship of their God. They came to understand that God could be effectively addressed anywhere and everywhere, through prayers and readings and discussions of God's words, and not only at a site like that of the Temple in Jerusalem, through sacrifices and priestly offerings.

Jeremiah and other prophets had also reminded the Judaeans that if they turned their hearts back toward the Lord, God would turn back to them. This they presumably did in exile, for that dark period lasted less than 50 years—which confirmed the new view of God developed in exile. The Babylonian Empire collapsed, overrun by the Achaemenid Medo-Persian Empire of Cyrus the Great, in 539 BCE. The understanding of these events, conveyed at the end of the Hebrew Bible, was that—once again—an all-powerful, all-knowing God of mercy and justice had facilitated a restorative sequence of events just as God had facilitated the destruction and exile of five decades earlier.

For not only was Cyrus' conquest of Babylon part of a divine plan, but "the spirit of Cyrus was raised" by God, according to the Bible, to proclaim that "the Lord God of Heaven… has charged me with building Him a House in Jerusalem, which is in Judah" so that in 538 BCE he invited the Judaeans to return home to participate in that grand project: "any one of you of all His people, the Lord God be with him and let him go up." (II Chronicles 36: 22-23).

Not every Judaean would take Cyrus up on that invitation, however, for many of them had established themselves comfortably in Babylon—or had moved still further to the east, to trade and even to live—and were loath to return and rebuild what had evolved in 48 years to become a kind of frontier wasteland. There would, moreover, be a layered and very important problematic that would begin to emerge as a part of the return that played out over the next few generations. Three elements in particular present themselves in the context of our discussion.

The first element, an issue of definition, has three components to it. To begin with, not *everyone* in the reshaped Judaean community had necessarily come to embrace a universal sense of God. Perhaps members of the lower classes in particular, who were not taken into exile—they offered neither threat nor usefulness to the Babylonian conquerors— continued to believe in a more narrowly focused, ethnocentric God of Israel: a "God of Israel" not just as a turn of phrase that highlights a covenantal relationship between God and Israel, but as a literal statement of that God as exclusively involved with Israel, while other gods, perhaps, were involved with other peoples. They no doubt continued to bring offerings to the Temple mount during the 48 years of the exile—for once a sacerdotal spot of connection between divinity and humanity, always a sacerdotal spot.

Cognate with this ongoing question regarding the nature of God there emerged a question of leadership: should it be Davidic—a descendant of the Israelite king, looked back at increasingly as an ideal monarch whose idealized status was underscored by the fact that he had been *mashiah*—anointed—at the instigation of God Itself? Or should the reconstituted community of Judah be led by a less political kind of figure? After all, politically speaking, Judah was no more than a subset of a province (a satrapy) of the great Achaemenid Persian Empire, and answered to its governors and ultimately to its Shah. Should Judah therefore be led not by a royal scion but by a descendant of the High Priest in Solomon's Temple, himself understood to have been a descendant of Aaron, brother of Moses?

There were two groups of leaders who espoused these respective positions. The Sadducees asserted that the head of the community should be the High Priest and the Pharisees argued for a secular, Davidic head of state. At some time the Pharisees began to argue for the need to incorporate contemporarily relevant interpretations of the Torah into Judaean life, whereas the Sadducees tended toward being guided by a more literal approach to the text of God's word, asserting that the Pharisaic approach allowed for the possibility of excessive distortion of God's covenantal intentions. The term Pharisees—*Perushim*— may be understood either (or both) as an insult applied to them by the Sadducees, because it can be seen to derive from the Hebrew root, *p-r-sh*, meaning "to separate" (and therefore they are being labeled as separatists from the community) or as a self-declared statement of their interest in interpretation, since the same Hebrew root may be taken to mean "to interpret."

The double issue of defining God and defining proper Judaean leadership may have begun to play out, together with other socio-economic divisions within the renewed community, from the very beginning of the return from exile. Perhaps that explains why it took the Judaeans twenty-three years to rebuild the Temple—more than three times the time it took Solomon's Tyrian artisans to build the First Temple—in spite of considerable support from the most powerful empire the world had yet seen. There was, moreover, the question of the so-called Samaritans (also known as Samarians) who were apparently a product of intermarriages between northern Israelites and various pagan groups that had occurred due to the Assyrian policies of breaking up the communities and even families of those they conquered.[123] Still loyal, it seems, to the God of Israel, they were interested, according to the Book of Ezra (4:2), in helping out with the Temple project but were unequivocally rejected by the Judaean leadership as presumably spiritually impure.

So the treble issue—of defining the nature of God, the nature of proper Judaean leadership and the nature of Judaeans themselves (who is and who is not a real Judaean, and what does that mean: is it a spiritual or an ethnic entity?)—enveloped the community and clearly grew, rather than shrank, as time moved on. Not quite a century after the return from exile it seemed that the Judaean community was on the verge of imploding. This is when Ezra the Scribe entered onto the Judaean stage. Having been an important figure in the Perso-Babylonian world in which he was born and bred—a "scribe expert in the teachings (*Torah*) of Moses" (7:1-6), who "dedicated himself to study the teachings (*Torah*) of the Lord" (7:10), he apparently asked permission of the Shah to "return" to Judah.[124]

Ezra is said by the biblical tradition to have accomplished a final redaction—the definitive edited text—of the Torah. In the book that bears his name in the Hebrew Bible he is said to have read the entire text, out loud, from beginning to end, before the Gate of Water, at the conclusion of the fall harvest festival of *Sukkot*—one of the three major festivals decreed in the Torah by God, that evolved as festivals of pilgrimage to Jerusalem and its Temple, and which commemorate aspects of the Israelite migration from Egypt to the Promised Land.

According to that biblical text, the people wept when they heard the divine words as they recognized how far from the prescriptions of the Covenant they had fallen (10:1). Ezra would articulate rigorous demands of the Judaeans—that they extract from within their own families those who were not firm in their commitment to be part of the community of Covenant.[125] More importantly—and this is the second element of the post-exilic (aka Second Temple) period problematic—he put in place a revolution: the scribal

---

[123] In Ezra 4:1-2 what I am terming "Samaritans" are referred to simply as *Tzarey Yehudah ooBinyamin…* ("The adversaries/foes of Judah and Benjamin…"). It was thus a long process of, 85 superimposed on this period based on an increasingly hostile relationship between Samarians and Judaeans that came to a head in the last pre-Christian century that ends up specifically identifying the *tzareem* as Samaritans. This will prove essential as we enter into the texts of the New Testament with its narrative passages referring to the Good Samaritan and to the Samaritan woman (see below, 199-200).

[124] If we follow the traditional dating of this, then Ezra would have arrived during the reign of Ataxerxes I (r. 465-424 BCE).

[125] See Ezra 10:2 and 10:10-11 and Nehemiah 13:27. I think it unlikely that what he had in mind was ethnic cleansing; his demand that they "send away [their] foreign wives and children" more likely refers, in calling them "foreign", to their spiritual convictions and their unwillingness to abandon other gods—the same sort of issue we have observed dogging the Israelite-Judaean community down through prior centuries—and commit themselves exclusively to the God of Israel. The word typically translated as "foreign" is *"nokhriyah,"* one of three different terms in biblical Hebrew that are translated as "foreign." Each, however, has a different connotation. *"El nokhree"* refers to a foreign god (Deut 31:16); so, too, the term is used to refer to idolatries (Jer 8:19) and foreign altars (II Chron 14:2). So *"nokhree"* may refer to someone who follows foreign gods. By contrast, a *ger/gerah* would refer to someone who dwells as a sojourner in one's land without ever becoming part of the community; and a *zar* would refer to a stranger or even an enemy. I could be wrong, of course, about Ezra's intentions; maybe they were more extremist than makes me comfortable. If so, then the spiritual universalism to which I refer that is expressed in Jonah and Ruth—and certainly in the latter case, is interwoven with ethnic non-particularism—is contending with a very ethnic ethnocentricity within the biblical text itself.

revolution. That is, Ezra made available, presumably for the first time, the entire text of the Torah/Pentateuch/Five Books of Moses to anyone and everyone who was literate.[126]

More to the point, the scribal revolution introduced another important change into the thinking of most of the Judaean leadership with respect to the relationship between Judaeans and God as that relationship is articulated and mediated by the text of the Torah. Thus whereas the central figures in the Hebrew-Israelite-Judaean narrative from Abraham to Ezra are all *sacerdotes* of one sort or another—prophets and priests with a direct line of communication to God, even more important, in the long run, than the most stellar of kings—the post-Ezra era (the traditional date of his redaction is 444 BCE) will become dominated by scribes and scholars. In other words, direct revelation as a guide to how to live a covenantal life will be supplanted by interpretation of the revelation.[127]

Sometime after Ezra, two processes began to move forward. One was to determine what texts, exactly, could be viewed as divinely revealed or inspired besides the Torah. Prophetic books, of course, associated with individuals like Isaiah and Jeremiah, but also books of history and wisdom, from Joshua to Ecclesiastes, would eventually make their way into the canon of what became the Hebrew Bible—by 140 CE. The most fundamental criterion for inclusion that emerged was that any such work had to have been written—or could safely be construed to have been written—before the time of Ezra (i.e., before 444 BCE).

So, too, a double tradition began to take shape with respect to how to answer the question of how to live a covenantal life most effectively. That double tradition—conducted orally for centuries and not committed, as far as we know, to written form until well after the time of Jesus (as we shall later see)—included both the *Midrash* and the beginnings of what would become the Talmud. The first of these works offers discussions that try to understand the underlying and often obscure meanings of God's words—as they are found in the Torah, and eventually other works as well—through direct exegesis of those words. The latter begins by posing an everyday problem, sometimes banal and sometimes more elevated, and offers a preliminary solution or series of solutions (posed by different discussants) to it. This preliminary discussion, called *mishnah*, would in most cases eventually beget a secondary discussion, called *gemara*, which might take place many generations removed from the first, but would be carried on virtually as if all discussants, from whatever time periods, were in the same place at the same time together. The *mishnah* and *gemara* together comprise the first layers of what, over many centuries, would become the Talmud.

---

[126] For our purposes the question raised in particular during the past few centuries among theologians—of how much of the Torah originated with Moses (i.e., with Moses as the conduit through which God Itself provided the content) and how, when and where the parts that he did not write were written or transformed from an oral to a written text, if he did not write all of it down—need not be addressed here. The point is that the writings associated with Moses and with subsequent Israelite and Judaean prophets are understood to be part of an extended divine revelation that needs to be separated from human interpretation.

[127] This may also therefore be called the "nomocratic revolution." Prophets and priests derived their authority from assumptions regarding their direct relationship with God (*theos*); scribes and scholars derived their authority based on assumptions regarding their intimate knowledge of and ability to interpret the Torah (for which the Greek word is *nomos*, meaning "law").

A preponderant amount of midrashic material offers interesting and sometimes odd stories to make its points; such story-telling is called *aggadah*.[128] The preponderant quality of the Talmud is that it is tightly focused on legal issues, based on a combination of interpreting God's word and applying it to a given situation through the exercise of human reason and ingenuity. The legal issues are referred to as *halakhah* (literally: "the way to go."). But there are many halakhic elements embedded within the *Midrash* and aggadic elements punctuate the Talmud.

So the questions of definition and the scribal revolution with its shift away from an era of prophets and priests to an era of scribes and scholars leads—and this is the third post-exilic, Second Temple period element of interest to our discussion—to an array of schisms throughout the entire era. Even after Ezra's shoring up of the Judaean community on the verge of implosion, that community remains divided by an array of issues and not easily resolved questions.

How does one understand God? How does one understand God's word? What does it mean to be a Judaean? When will a *mashiah* arise to restore Judaean sovereignty— or better still, a *mashiah* who will be so charismatic that all of the world's leaders will turn to him and will acknowledge the singular legitimacy of the God of Israel? Did God in fact cease to speak to us directly, through prophetic beings, after Ezra, or are there still prophets among us and might there be texts of God's word that are being written down today?—for not everyone within the community embraced the idea that God no longer communicates with us through *sacerdotes*. One must, to repeat, add to these rather intellectual issues the more mundane ones that divide any given community, the socio-economic issues: rich and poor, rural and urban, educated and uneducated.

For us, as for the outsiders who were contemporaries of Second Temple Judaeans, the third question within this list would prove particularly problematic, at times, for both theoretical and often practical reasons. Does "Judaean" refer to someone who worships the God of Israel, whose main shrine is in Jerusalem, the Judaean capital: a religious definition? Does it refer to someone who claims descent from the tribe of Judah—or perhaps the tribes of Judah and Benjamin: an ethnic, blood-line definition? Does it refer to someone residing within Judah, whether under Persian governorship or, later, under the governorship of the Hellenistic Seleucids who held sway soon after Alexander the Great dismantled the Persian Empire, or, still later, under the governorship of the Romans—or briefly, under the governorship of the Hasmonaeans (ca 140-37 BCE) and Herod (37-4 BCE)—as an independent polity: a political definition?[129]

---

[128] This is an Aramaic term, for which the Hebrew-language equivalent is *Haggadah*. The literal meaning for both is "telling [a story]".

[129] To clarify the confusion somewhat, let us take King Herod "the Great" and his era (who ruled Judaea—as Judah comes to be referred to in English as we enter the Hellenistic-Roman period—as its king in 37-4 BCE) as an example. Herod's grandfather, Antipater, king of the Idumaeans (whom the Bible earlier refers to as Edomites) had been defeated by the Hasmonaeans a few years before the turn to the last pre-Christian century. According to the Judaean historian, Josephus (37-ca 100 CE) (*Antiquities of the Judaeans*, 13: 9, 1), John Hyrkanos I, instead of killing, exiling or selling into slavery the Idumaeans, demanded that they be circumcised and convert to the faith of Judaea, which they did—thereby becoming Judaeans by religion (but not ethnically). So Herod, on his father's side, was a third-generation believer in the God of Israel—but ethnically, he was an Idumaean. He ended up extirpating the Hasmonaean line in becoming king of Judaea. On his mother's side, he was ethnically a Nabataean (she was in fact a Nabataean noblewoman)—and, as such, religiously, a pagan. He was thus both a religious and ethnic mix and, as king of the Judaeans, he expanded—or, if we believe Josephus, altogether

All of these issues would and did have implications for the eventual, culminating schism within the Judaean community that would yield two sibling faiths, Judaism and Christianity. There is, however, one further important issue that would surely have implications for Second Temple Judaeans and that culminating schism—that would begin about a century before the time of Jesus and continue until about the beginning of the second century CE. That further issue pertains to the group of Judaeans associated with the site of what is much later called Qumran, near the Dead Sea, and the scrolls that were discovered in caves near that site, beginning in 1947. But this issue is itself importantly affected by a yet prior one, that of the Persian religion of Zoroastrianism.

Zoroastrianism (also known as Mazdaism)[130] developed in Persia perhaps as early as around 1500 BCE or as late as the sixth century BCE; it had in any case emerged as the state religion by the time the Judaeans were in the midst of the Babylonian exile; it would remain the official religion of the Persian state through the Achaemenid, Parthian and Sassanian eras—i.e., through about 651 CE.[131] Its basic principles center on visions regarding/focused on Ahura Mazda, (*Ahura* means "Being" and *Mazda* means "Mind" in the Avestan language), an all-powerful, all-good God—the "uncreated Creator." These visions are accorded to the young prophet, Zoroaster (as we have his name through the Greeks; in Persian, it is Zarathustra).[132] The tradition maintains that, when Zoroaster was 30 years old, he went into the Daiti River to draw water for a Haoma ceremony; when he emerged, he received a vision of *Vohu Manah*. After this, *Vohu Manah* took him to the other six *Amesha Spentas*, where he experienced the continuation to completeness of his visions.

In these visions, the shape of our reality is explained. The transcendental Ahura Mazda is immanent in the world—the *pure* world that he created was created through him—as *Spenta Mainyu* ("creative energy" or "bounteous principle/spirit") that derives from *Asha* ("Truth/Order"). *Spenta Mainyu* is thus the manifestation of Ahura Mazda interactive with the world. *Spenta Mainyu* in turn emanates from itself into, and is undergirded, as it were, by a series of seven *Amesha Spentas* ("Bounteous Immortals")— angel-like creatures, "divine spirits," each of which represents a different aspect of creation; these are in turn undergirded by lesser (but still "worthy of worship") spirits called *Yazata*s (which *means* "worthy of worship").[133] Thus we may recognize a relationship with

---

rebuilt—the Temple in Jerusalem to the Judaean God—just as he built, among other structures, the stupendous port at the site of the small Judaean coastal town of Straton's Tower. The expanded town was renamed Caesarea, to honor the Roman emperor, and most of its inhabitants were pagan, albeit, as inhabitants of Judaea, they were, politically, Judaeans—i.e., Judaeannationals.

[130] The Avestan name for the religion is *Mazdayasna*, meaning "worship/devotion (*yasna*) [of/to] Mazda."

[131] The Achaemenids would be defeated by Alexander the Great, ca 331-330 BCE, and their empire dismantled by him. Parts of it would fall to his various Macedonian successors at the time of his death in 323 BCE. A second Persian empire, the Parthian or Arsacid, would emerge around 250 BCE and last for five centuries—often giving the expanding Roman Empire fits—supplanted by the Sassanian Empire. The Sassanians (also known as Sasanids or Sassanids) would fall to the Muslim Arabs gradually, from 643—or even 636 CE, with the emphatic defeat of the Sassanians by the Arab Muslims at the Battle of al-Qadisiyyah—but the death of the last Sassanian Emperor, Yazdegerd III, in 651 CE, marks the unequivocal and definitive end of the empire, at which time Islam would supplant Zoroastrianism as the state religion in that region of the Middle East.

[132] He is also known as *Zartosht* and *Zardosht* in Persian, and as *Zaratosht* in Gujarati.

[133] The *Amesha Spentas* are: *Spenta Mainyu* (the manifestation of Ahura Mazda within the world; one might compare this to how the sun can, in Mesopotamian-Persian-Greek-Roman thought, be considered as both the "Eye of Heaven" and thus separate from the *planetes* and also one of the seven *planetes*), *Asha Vahishta* ("highest

but an important difference from polytheism: the idea of many gods has been subsumed into many lesser *sacer* beings that are of an altogether different "order" from the singular Supreme Being.

The same may be said of the one *sacer* entity that opposes Ahura Mazda: *Ahriman*. Ahriman is not an equal antithesis of Ahura Mazda. Ahriman embodies evil—*druj* ("falsehood/chaos")—which comes into the world through the machinations of the rebellious underling of Ahura Mazda, also known as Ahriman, and manifest as *Angra Mainyu*. So *Angra Mainya* is the destructive energy that opposes God's creative energy. *Angra Mainyu* continually attacks that creative energy, making it *impure*, thus bringing about illness, aging, famine, natural disasters and death.

There is more. *Asha* encompasses everything in the phenomenal universe: the motion of the planets and astral bodies; the progression of the seasons; and the pattern of the daily nomadic life of a herdsman, governed by regular metronomic events such as sunrise and sunset. All of physical creation (*geti*) is intended to operate according to a master plan, shaped by Ahura Mazda, and violations of the order (which are all aspects of *druj*) are violations against creation, and thus violations against Ahura Mazda. This concept of *asha* versus *druj* should not be confused with the good-versus-evil battle articulated in Western thought, for although both forms of opposition express moral conflict, the *asha* versus *druj* concept is more systemic and less personal, representing, for instance, chaos (that opposes order); or "uncreation," evident as natural decay (that opposes creation); or simply "the lie" (that opposes truth and righteousness). Moreover, in his role as the one Uncreated Creator of all, Ahura Mazda is not the creator of *druj*, which is ultimately "nothing," anti-creation, and thus, likewise, uncreated. It might be construed as emptiness, in opposition to the fullness of Ahura Mazda's creation.

Ahriman is particularly successful at accomplishing his negative end when he can induce humans to be drawn to his cause. Indeed, the series of visions vouchsafed to Zoroaster present Ahura Mazda as commanding the prophet to articulate this situation to humans and to invite them to choose between Ahura Mazda (good) and Ahriman (evil). Zoroaster taught that humans must all be part of the cosmic struggle between good and evil because of our capacity for free choice. Predestination is in fact rejected in Zoroastrianism. Humans bear full responsibility for all situations in which we find ourselves. Every time we choose—between right and wrong, truth and falsehood, and light and dark—we affect not only our own eternal destiny but, potentially, the cosmic balance.[134]

---

truth"), *Vohu Manah* ("righteous mind"), *Khshatva Vairya* ("Desirable Dominion"), *Spenta Armaiti* ("Holy Devotion"), *Haurvatat* ("health," "perfection"), and *Ameretat* ("Immortality"). They are, in our terms, *concepts* as much as *beings*.

[134]To be more full-fledged with regard to how this all came about: according to the Zoroastrian cosmogonic *mythos*, Ahura Mazda existed in light in goodness above, while Angra Mainyu existed in darkness and ignorance below. They have existed, independent of each other (but by no means co-equal) for all time. Ahura Mazda first created (emanated) the seven *Amesha Spentas*, and the *yazatas*. He then created the universe itself in order to ensnare evil. He engendered the floating, egg-shaped universe in two parts: first the spiritual (*menog*) part and 3,000 years later, the physical (*getig*) part. He then, finally, created Gayomard, the archetypical perfect man, and the first bull.

While Ahura Mazda created the universe and humankind, Angra Mainyu, whose instinct is to destroy, miscreated demons, evil *yazads*, and noxious creatures (*khrafstar*) such as snakes, ants, and flies. Angra Mainyu created an opposite, evil being for every good being created by Ahura Mazda—except for humans, for which he could contrive no equal entity. So Angra Mainyu invaded the universe through the base of the sky, inflicting

Thus on the one hand, one's personal afterlife is determined by the balance between good and evil thoughts, words and deeds, in the course of one's life. Achaemenid-era Zoroastrianism developed the abstract concepts of heaven and hell, as well as personal and final judgment, all of which, however, are only alluded to in the *Gathas*. *Yasna 19*, (which has only survived in a Sassanian-era *Zend* commentary on the *Ahuna Vairyain* vocation), prescribes a path to Final Judgment known as the *Chinvat Peretum* (*Chinvat Bridge*), which all souls have to cross, and judgment (regarding thoughts, words, and deeds performed during a lifetime) is passed as they are doing so. In fact, two judgments are necessary, one for each of the two aspects of human beings, spiritual (*menog*) and physical (*getig*).

For those whose good thoughts, words and deeds outweigh the bad, heaven awaits; those who did more evil than good go to hell (which has several levels corresponding to degrees of wickedness).[135] There is an intermediate purgatorial-like "space" for those whose deeds are weighed out equally. The system is not absolute—hell is not an eternal condition—and allows for human weakness; not all faults are registered or weighed forever on the scales. Sins can be effaced through confession and through the transfer of supererogatory merits accomplished through prayers and ceremonies offered by the living on behalf of the departed.[136]

On the other hand, at the end of our era, a great—3,000-year-long—battle will take place between the forces of Ahura Mazda and those of Ahriman in which the all-powerful Ahura Mazda will prevail. It is an uneven battlefield, because Ahura Mazda *is* supreme—it is almost as if Ahura Mazda permits the existence and machinations of Ahriman in order to provide a moral exercise for humans: the opportunity and obligation to utilize our free will in choosing between good and evil. Rejecting *druj* is part of the responsibility imposed by Ahura Mazda on the human soul—*urvan*—that is articulated by Zoroaster.[137] This is summed up in a simple phrase: "good thoughts, good words, good

---

Gayomard and the bull with suffering and death. However, the evil forces were now trapped in the universe and could not disappear from it. Moreover, the dying primordial man and bull emitted seeds. From the bull's seed grew all of the beneficial plants and animals in the world, and from the man's seed grew a plant whose leaves became the first human couple. Humans thus struggle in a two-fold (spiritual and physical) universe in which evil is also entrapped. The evils of this physical world are not products of an inherent human weakness, but are ascribed to Angra Mainyu's assault on creation. This assault turned the perfectly flat, peaceful, and eternally daylight-illumined world into a mountainous, violent place that is always half covered in night.

[135] A young maiden leads the righteous dead safely across the bridge to the *Amesha Spenta* who carries the dead to paradise. An old woman leads the sinful dead down a bridge that narrows until the deceased falls off into the abyss of hell. Zoroaster reminds humanity in the Avesta that "[b]rilliant things instead of weeping will be [the reward] for the person who comes to the Truthful One [i.e., to Ahura Mazda]. But a long period of darkness, foul food, and the word 'woe'—to such an existence your religious view will lead you, O deceitful ones, of your own actions." (*Gathas: Yasna 31.20*)

[136] The Zoroastrian system of penance involves reciting the *patet*—a formulaic statement articulating the firm resolve not to sin again—and confessing one's sins to a particular, high-level priest called a *dastur*, or to an ordinary priest should a *dastur* not be available.

[137] Prior to being born, the *urvan* of an individual is still united with its *fravashi* (guardian spirit)—such spirits have existed since Ahura Mazda created the universe. During life, the *fravashi* acts as a guardian and protector. On the fourth day after death, the soul is reunited with its *fravashi*, in which the experiences of life in the material world are collected for what is a continuing battle in the spiritual world. It is not clear whether the (re-)emergence of the soul in the new post-apocalyptic battle reality constitutes a reincarnation, but there is nothing inherently against this understanding, since Zoroastrianism does not equate material substance with *druj* and spiritual substance with *asha*.

deeds" (*Humata, Hukhta, Hvarshta* in Avestan)—for it is through these that *asha* is maintained and *druj* is kept in check.

In any case, the culmination of the cosmic battle will arrive and time as we know it will end. Near the end, a final assault by Angra Mainyu will lead the sun and moon to darken, and humankind will lose its reverence for religion, elders, and family. The world will fall into a tormented winter in which Angra Mainyu's most fearsome miscreant, *Azi Dahaka*, will be free to terrorize the world. But at last, a *saoshyant*—a kind of savior figure associated with Ahura Mazda's activating presence, born to a virgin impregnated by the seed of Zoroaster while she was bathing in a lake—will bring about a final renovation of the world (*frashokereti*), in which the dead will be revived. Ahriman and all of his followers will not be destroyed, but will be drawn away from *druj* and, purified by a kind of spiritual fire, will return to Ahura Mazda, returning to life in the undead form, and taking (or re-taking) their places in the perfect, all-good reality that follows the current one: a paradise on (a new) earth bathed in ever-present light. Since everyone eventually ends up there, Zoroastrianism can be said to be universalist with respect to salvation.

Fundamentally, too, Zoroastrianism presents a positive view of reality: humankind is ultimately good, will choose *asha* over *druj* in the end and this ultimate goodness will triumph over evil. As a cognate matter, it also rejects asceticism and monasticism as ways of life, since it requires us to be involved in and engaged with the world of the here and now: the *profanus*. The avoidance of any aspect of life, including the avoidance of the pleasures of life, is a shirking of the responsibility and duty to oneself, one's *urvan*, and one's family and social obligations. These obligations are all punctuated in the course of the year by six major festivals (*Gahanbars*) that emphasize not only worshipping Ahura Mazda but the requirement that his human acolytes be happy.

Our access to this narrative comes primarily through parts of the surviving fragments of the revealed text—the *Avesta*—that is to Zoroastrianism what the Bible is to Judaism and Christianity, and from texts written down much later, between the ninth and eleventh centuries of the Common Era.[138] The *Avesta*, its canon probably not completed until the era of the Sassanians—226-651 CE—consists of liturgical works, including hymns of praise and sermons ascribed to Zoroaster (the *Gathas*),[139] together with

---

[138]According to tradition, Ahura Mazda created the twenty-one *nask*s which Zoroaster brought to King Vishtaspa (the shah credited with pushing Zoroastrianism into the position of becoming the official religion of the Achaemenid Medo-Persian Empire). Two copies were created, one of which was put into the royal archives, and the other put into the Imperial treasury. During the conquest of Persia by Alexander the Great (ca 330 BCE), the text of the Avesta was burned, and, according to subsequent Zoroastrian tradition, the scientific sections that the Greeks could use were dispersed within the Greek world. Under the reign of King Valax of the Parthian (Arsacid) Dynasty, an attempt is said to have been made to restore the Avesta. During the era of the Sassanian Empire, Shah Ardeshir ordered Tansar, his high priest, to finish the work that King Valax had started. The Shah Shapur I sent priests to locate the scientific text portions of the Avesta that were in the hands of the Greeks. Under Shapur II, Arderbad Mahrespandand revised the canon to ensure its orthodox character, while under Khosrau I, the Avesta was translated into Pahlavi.

[139]Aspects of Zoroastrian theology are scattered throughout the *Gathas*, rather than presented in a systematic doctrinal arrangement. (We must keep in mind that Judaism and Christianity as we understand them are not simply and systematically presented in the Hebrew Bible or New Testament (nor, for that matter, is Islam simply and systematically presented in the Qur'an). Some of the verses are directly addressed to Ahura Mazda. These expound on the divine essence of Truth (*Asha*), the Good Mind (*Vohu Manah*), and the spirit of righteousness. In other verses, apparently addressed to the public that may have come to hear him speak, the prophet exhorts his auditors to live a life as Ahura Mazda has directed, while pleading to Ahura Mazda to intervene favorably on their behalf.

invocations and descriptions of ceremonies to be performed at festivals, prescriptions for purification, and spells against demons.[140] The Avesta lays the foundations of Zoroastrian *Daena* (*Din* in modern Farsi): the eternal Law, whose order was revealed to humanity through the *Mathra Spenta* ("Holy Words"). *Daena* is variously translated as "religion," "faith," "law," and even "instruction."

Temples center on a sacred fire, established through an elaborate ceremony, which must be kept burning continually and is formally fed at least five times a day; prayers are also recited five times daily. There are rites for purification and for regeneration of a fire. There are three primary types of the former, (in decreasing order of importance): *Padyab* (ablution), *Nahn* (bath) and *Bareshum* (a complex ceremony performed over several days at prescribed—sacerdotal—places), which includes the participation of a dog (whose left ear is touched by the devotee; dogs are sacred in Zoroastrianism, like cows in Hinduism) whose gaze is understood to put evil spirits to flight.

These rituals typically involve both fire (*atar*) and water (*apo*), the quintessential agent elements of ritual purity, and are intended to lead the participant toward greater wisdom: fire is a medium through which spiritual insight and wisdom are gained, and water is the source of that wisdom. For according to the Zoroastrian cosmogony, water and fire were the second and last primordial elements to have been created, and fire has its origin in the waters. Both elements are considered life-sustaining, and both are represented within a Fire Temple. Zoroastrians usually pray in the presence of some form of fire—which is

---

Other verses, from which some aspects of the prophet's life have been inferred, are autobiographical in tone—such as passages describing Zoroaster's first attempts to promote the teachings of Ahura Mazda, and an initial rejection by his kinsmen (with the exception of a cousin, who became his first disciple)—but all center on Zoroaster's mission to promote the visions of the Truth (*Asha*) that he has received. The initial rejections lead him to doubt, and he asks for assurance from Ahura Mazda, and for repudiation of his opponents. The seventeen hymns appear to have been composed at different periods in his life; a tone of contentment and belief in his vindication arrives only in the last few hymns, and he remains the persevering preacher to the end—where he officiates at the wedding of his youngest daughter.

[140] Only a fraction of the presumed original texts survives today. Those that remain are the *Gathas/Yasna*, the *Visperad* and the *Vendidad*. The *Gathas*—the seventeen hymns believed to have been composed by Zoroaster—are in terse, metrical verse. They total 238 stanzas, comprising about 1300 lines or 6000 words. They were later incorporated into the 72-chapter *Yasna*, which offers the primary liturgical material within the greater compendium of the Avesta. The sequential order of the *Gathas* is structurally interrupted by the *Yasna Haptanghaiti* ("Seven-Chapter *Yasna*," chapters 35-41, that is linguistically as old as the *Gathas* but written in prose) and by two other minor hymns at *Yasna* 42 and 52. Overall, the 17 hymns are identified by their chapter numbers in the *Yasna*, and are divided into five major sections. Along with this material, primary Zoroastrian literature also includes the communal household prayer book called the *Khordeh Avesta*, which contains the *Yashts* and the *Siroza*. Religious texts in Middle Persian and Pahlavi were created well into the Islamic period—mainly in the 9th through 11th centuries. The latest extant manuscript is dated, in fact, to 1288.

The most significant and important books of this era include the *Denkard, Bundahishn, Menog-i Khrad*, selections of *Zadspram, Jamasp Namag, Epistles of Manucher, Rivayats, Dadestan-i-Denig*, and *Arda Viraf Namag*. All Middle Persian texts written on Zoroastrianism during this time period are essentially commentaries—secondary works—and not scripture. Nonetheless, they have had a strong influence on the religion as it has continued to evolve toward our own era (as do the rabbinic, patristic-scholastic and shari'a literatures in the Abrahamic traditions). Many works are responses to the difficulties experienced in a particular place during a particular era—and all of them include exhortations to stand fast in one's religious beliefs. Some, such as the *Denkard*, are doctrinal defenses of the religion, while others are explanations of its theological aspects (such as the *Bundahishn*) or practical aspects (e.g., explanation of rituals). About sixty such works all told are known to have been written, of which some are known only from references to them in other texts. What is relevant to our own discussion, of course, is the earlier material.

considered immanent in any light source—and the culminating ritual of the principle act of worship, the *Ab-Zohr*, represents a "strengthening of / offering to the waters."

The main Zoroastrian ceremony that is not, per se, a purificatory ritual is the *Yasna,* in which *haoma* (sacred liquor) is offered to—shared, as it were, with—Ahura Mazda before the sacred fire, together with recitations of substantial passages from the Avesta. The ceremony includes offerings of milk and bread and originally also included meat and animal fat.[141]

The sacrament that marks the transition from life to death includes a sacred dog (preferably one with a spot above each eye, making it a "four-eyed" dog, with a gaze thereby doubled in efficacy) that is brought before the corpse five times daily. After this, the corpse is exposed to the elements, naked on a tower—a Tower of Silence—or consumed by cremation and purification through fire. On the morning of the fourth day the *urvan* of the deceased has reached the Bridge where it is judged, and whence it will be sent into paradise or the abyss to await the cosmic battle between Ahura Mazda and Ahriman and the inevitable outcome of that battle.

The broader priesthood responsible for the transmission of the Avestan narrative and also for both leading and instructing Zoroastrian traditions and rituals is a hereditary, tribal group, analogous to the Levites in the Israelite-Judaean tradition (who are all understood to be descendants of the tribe into which Moses and Aaron were born). The term in Avestan (one of two main ancient Persian languages) for such an individual—a *sacerdos*, or, in English, a priest—is *maghos*. Such individuals play the role that priests in every culture play, of forging and maintaining a connection between the *profanus*—the people of which they are part—and the *sacer* in its divine aspect.[142]

The Greek "father of historiography," Herodotos, in his *Histories* (ca 440 BCE), in including a description of Persian society, also includes what are recognizably Zoroastrian features, including exposure of the dead. He is the one who informs us (*Histories* Bk 1, section 101) that the Magi were the sixth tribe of the Medes, apparently the priestly caste, as we have just noted, of the Mesopotamian-influenced branch of Zoroastrianism today known as Zurvanism, and who wielded considerable influence at the courts of the Achaemenid Medo-Persian emperors.[143] According to later Zoroastrian legends (in the *Denkard* and the *Book of Arda Viraf*), many sacred texts were lost when Alexander the Great's troops invaded Persepolis (ca 330 BCE) and destroyed the royal library there. The Roman historian Diodorus Siculus (who wrote in Greek), in his *Bibliotheca historica*, (ca. 60 BCE), appears to substantiate this Zoroastrian legend (Diod. 17.72.2–17.72.6).

---

[141] *Yasna* (Avestan for "oblation" or "worship") is both the name of the primary liturgical collection of texts in the Avesta (see the previous note) and the name of the principal ceremony (also called *Izeshne*) during which those verses are recited and appropriate liturgical actions performed. In its normal form, *Yasna/Izeshne* is only performed in the morning. A well-trained priest can usually recite the entire *Yasna* in about two hours. With additional material, (typically the recitation of the *Visperad* and *Vendidad*), the ceremony requires an additional hour or so.

[142] The earliest use and form of the term that survives is in *Yasna* 33:7 of the Avesta, where "*magâunô*" appears, referring to the religious caste/tribe of the Medes into which Zoroaster was born: *ýâ sruyê parê magâunô* ("so I can be heard beyond [the] Magi").

[143] Until the unification of the Persian Empire under Cyrus the Great, all Iranians were referred to as "Mede" or "Mada" by the peoples of the Ancient World.

It was the contact with the Greeks that resulted in the transformation of the sense of the Old Persian word "*maghos*": imported into Greek as *magos*, (from which the Latin term "*magus*" appears), it acquired the negative connotation that is also evidenced in Roman literature.

Thus Zoroastrianism, which became the state religion of the Parthians—the fiercest rivals of the Romans for domination of the Middle East—once they supplanted the Achaemenids, left perhaps a treble legacy in the world of the Romans. Zoroastrianism, as we shall see, may have provided the Mithraic offshoot (or at least inspired the development of a form of Mithraism) that became very popular in particular within the Roman army during the mid-imperial period; it may have directly—or indirectly, through the Qumran material—had an influence on developing Christianity; and some of its vocabulary— specifically the word that we render in English as magic—entered Roman thought by way of Greek.

*   *   *   *   *

I have expended considerable space on Zoroastrianism because it leads in two very important directions for our own narrative. One pertains to beliefs that develop among the Judaeans in the schismatic Second Temple period and the other to the evolution of the Medo-Persian term, *maghos*, in Greek, and then Roman, vocabulary. That the Judaeans had considerable contact with Zoroastrianism we can hardly doubt. Not only were they living cheek by jowl with the increasingly dominant faith in what is now Iraq/Iran for at least part of their exile, but in the aftermath of exile, since many Judaeans remained in Perso-Baylonia, that contact would have continued, and since there was a good deal of cultural and commercial back-and-forth between Perso-Babylonia and Judaea—we have archaeological evidence of this, and how else would Ezra have been so conversant with the complications that pushed him to immigrate to Judaea a century after the Return?—we might infer that a range of issues and ideas passed from East to West and from West to East during the post-exilic centuries.

As we have seen, those centuries were not easy ones. Even after Ezra's nomocratic reforms, if there was socio-economic, cultural, political and spiritual calm in Judaea, it lasted for only a century. By around 330 BCE, the Achaemenid Empire had fallen, under its last Shah, Dareios III, to the military genius of young Alexander (the Great) the Macedonian. Nonetheless, Alexander, like the Persians, seems to have believed that skills that could contribute to the running of an empire were not dependent upon religion or ethnicity; aside from the inevitable difficulties associated with regime-change accomplished through war, the conditions for being a religion apart seem not to have altered for the Judaeans. Nor did they in the aftermath of the sudden and unexpected death of Alexander in 323 BCE, at the age of 33.

During the period that followed Alexander's death—called "Hellenistic" from a Eurocentric (which is to say, Hellenocentric) perspective, due to the transmission of Hellenic (Greek) ideas, like gymnasia and theater complexes, as far east as northern India—Judaea remained, spiritually speaking, in a largely unique position, as far as the world from Mesopotamia to Italy (*Magna Graecia*, as Roman historiography later called it) was concerned.[144] That world was marked, among other things, by a particularly intense tendency toward syncretism: terms and ideas from one culture would permeate those of another, in art, language, philosophy and also religion. The temple in northwestern Egypt (now Libya) of Amon-Ra that Alexander visited after conquering Egypt, and from which he exited proclaiming that its priests had informed him that Amon-Ra had adopted him as his son—who already claimed to be a direct descendant of Zeus by way of Herakles—became, in the Hellenistic period, a temple of Zeus-Amon-Ra. Functionally, this meant that Macedonian Greeks and Egyptians alike could bring offerings and that they could worship together, at least in theory.

The Judaeans clearly stood apart in this matter. There could be no hyphenation of the God of Israel—who was, after all, fully arrived at a condition of being understood both to be universal and to be singular: the earlier injunction to "have no other gods before me" had been supplanted by the idea that one might have no other gods, *period*—because there are none in reality. The effect of this was to further divide the Judaeans, between those who were in favor of being culturally affected by the Greek world—and thus, in effect, part of the culturally syncretistic Hellenistic world at large—and those who favored a clear and socio-culturally complete separation for Judaeans from that world, out of fear that any sort of serious contact, be it social, cultural or commercial, might threaten the *spiritual* separation of Judaea from other peoples.

Politically, as a practical matter, Judaea found itself constantly caught in the tug-of-war of ambition between the two large neighbors whose first Hellenistic rulers were two of Alexander's oldest and best friends and most important generals, Ptolemy (who ruled Egypt) and Seleukos (who ruled Syria). For the most part, however, religiously speaking, both of Alexander's successors and their successors—even they as engaged in trying to swallow each other in order to effect a reunification of the heartland of Alexander's trans-Hellenic conquests—left the Judaeans to themselves, not interfering with their odd penchant for believing in only one God: an invisible, intangible one, altogether inaccessible to the senses and even the intellect, at that.

Nonetheless, the internal religious complications of the Judaeans were affected both by their own issues and by their geographical location and its political implications. Shortly after Antiokhos IV came to the Seleucid throne in 176 BCE, Joshua-Jason became the High Priest of the Temple in Jerusalem, a position essentially usurped from the previous High Priest, Onias III. Oniashad had journeyed to Syria to address Antiokhos' predecessor, Seleukos IV, (for reasons beyond our narrative, but pertaining to internal politics in *both* Syria and Judaea), but had fled into Egypt soon after Seleukos was assassinated, when he recognized that Antiokhos did not favor him.[145] In Egypt he apparently received permission

---

[144] The underlying idea of calling the post-Alexander, pre-Roman age "Hellenistic" ignores the flow of ideas from east to west—such as the concept of grammar, of how language functions, pioneered by the Indian thinker, Panini, which was carried westward during and after Alexander's brief visit there, and its terminology translated into Greek by the Stoics in the next few generations. (All of our own grammatical terminology, in which word-types, cases, tenses, and moods tell what the function of a given word is in a sentence, are anglicized versions of Latin translations of the Greek translations of Sanskrit terms.)

[145] For a discussion of some of the details, see Solomon Zeitlin, *The Rise and Fall of the Judaean State*, Vol 1, (Philadelphia: Jewish Publication Society, 1962), 74-6.

from Ptolemy V and his Queen, Cleopatra, to build a temple—a counter-Temple to that in Jerusalem that, he and his followers asserted, had now been profaned in being occupied by an illegitimate High Priest.[146] For the High Priesthood that Onias III had abandoned was quickly usurped by Joshua-Jason—whose position was, in turn, usurped by Onias-Menelaos, through the support of Antiokhos.

Onias III built his Temple in Heliopolis—although the largest Egyptian Judaean community, by far, resided in Alexandria—because the Judaean tradition recalled Heliopolis as the residence of the patriarch, Jacob, and his sons, when they first arrived from Canaan into Egypt; and it also associated Heliopolis with Moses. So this choice of location would give the Temple a patina of legitimacy. But one can only suppose that the dueling Temples presented the average Judaean with a good deal of confusion as to which of these was ultimately the legitimate one. The implications of all of this would surely have been serious with regard to the notion of living a life governed by the Divine Covenant.[147] Moreover, the situation in Jerusalem with its dueling would-be High Priests (Joshua-Jason and Onias-Menelaos)—even with Onias III out of the way—soon became still more problem-ridden. For Antiokhos IV's back-room support of first one pretender and then the other was only the tip of the iceberg of his interest in Judaea and its capitol.

When Antiokhos had come to the Seleucid throne, he had diverged from his Macedonian Greek predecessors in at least one particularly significant way. They had viewed their direct connection to the divine *sacer* with a grain of salt—Egyptian pharaohs and diverse Mesopotamian and Medo-Persian monarchs had been viewed for millennia as directly connected to divinity if not virtual divinities in and of themselves, and so the Macedonian rulers had typically paid effective lip service to that sensibility to reinforce their power as rulers. But Antiokhos believed (or at least demanded of his constituents that they believe) that he truly *was* an incarnate god. He called himself *Theos Epiphanes* ("God manifest").[148] Unlike his predecessors, about six years into his reign he demanded that the Judaeans place his—divine—image in their Temple in Jerusalem. (It no doubt would not have occurred to him that they had no images of their imageless god: first of all, an imageless god would have been, to him, no god at all—the imageless Judaeans would have

---

[146] I admit to a transliteration inconsistency here—and elsewhere—where a name—in this case, "Cleopatra"—is so familiar that I have not altered it as I might have, to "Kleopatra."

[147] To get a bit of a sense of the spiritual absurdity (or at least complexity) of this situation, one might think well forward in history to the period known as the "Babylonian Captivity" of the papacy and its schismatic aftermath. It began with the decision on the part of Pope Clement V to remove himself from Rome to Avignon in 1309 (in part due to conflicts between French and Italian cardinals regarding who *should* be the Pope) and ended with the decision of Pope Gregory XI, under the influence of Saint Catherine of Siena, to move the papacy back to Rome in 1376. In the Great Western Schism that ensued only a few years later, after the deaths of Gregory (1378) and Saint Catherine (1380), there were Popes and Anti-Popes in Rome and Avignon (and also, briefly, toward the end, Pisa). Each had his own retinue and supporters throughout Western Christendom, (entire countries favoring this one or that one), until the Councils of Constance more or less solved the issue in 1414-18—although one anti-Pope, Clement VIII, continued to have some support until as late as 1429, when he resigned his claim to the papal tiara and a unified papacy resided in Rome. The politics of religion has been truly remarkable at times in human history.

[148] The epithet comes from the Greek verb, *phainomai*, meaning "to appear." His detractors, according to the Greek historiographer, Polybius (ca 200-118 BCE; *Histories* 26:1), referred to him as *epimanes*—the crazy one. The Roman historiographer, Livy (59 BCE-17 CE; *Ab Urbe Condita* 41:20) also mentions that there were those who thought that Antiokhos was "unquestionably insane."

appeared to him as atheists—and second of all, the Temple *had* images, after all, although not images of God).[149]

More than that, he entered the Temple in the company of the High Priest, Onias-Menelaos, and—needing to replenish his coffers after an extensive and expensive war against Ptolemaic Egypt—stripped the sanctuary of its gold and silver vessels, the golden altar, the display table, the sacred curtains hanging before the Holy of Holies, and the golden seven-branched menorah.[150] Over the next two years or so he forbade the practice of Judaeanism, making it a crime to observe the Sabbath or to practice circumcision, and eventually commanded that the daily sacrifice in the Temple courtyard be abolished; about half a year later a pagan altar was put in its place.

There were certainly those in the Judaean community who were willing to accede to the demand that the image of Antiokhos be installed within the Temple—why rock a relatively stable boat when one could simply place his image there and ignore it?—particularly, no doubt, members of the business community. For they would already have figured out ways to compromise with the kind of puritanism promoted by the likes of Ezra so many generations earlier. How can I do good business with my pagan counterparts if I cannot dine with them (they eat foods proscribed by my religion)—when so much more business is done in the dining room than the board room—and if I am expected, by Judaean law, to leave town and to get at least 2400 cubits away from the city limit anytime there is a polluting pagan ceremony or ritual being performed or celebrated?[151]

So there were Judaeans who would not have been overly upset by one more little compromise—and even, perhaps, the growing list of anti-Judaean religious prescriptions. Even these other demands were perhaps part of a slippery slope of acceptability to those wanting to be part of the Hellenistic world. There was also a substantial group of zealots who called themselves *Hassidim*—"pious ones"—who willingly submitted to torture and death rather than transgress any of the Torah's laws. They would not physically oppose the Seleucids if opposition meant any sort of abrogation of those laws—a thousand of them, trapped in a cave by Syrian soldiers where they had gone to celebrate the Sabbath, refused to fight the enemy on the Sabbath, leaving it to God to deal with the situation; they were all burned alive.[152] But there were others, also purists but willing or even eager to fight about it, for whom these Seleucid demands were all part of a red line over which they would not step and—to make a long story short—after the installation of the pagan altar and the offering of a pig to Zeus on it, they rebelled against Antiokhos.

There was a concatenation of consequences. To be brief: the revolt, led by a priestly clan called the Hasmonaeans, which began in 168 BCE, took three years to come to a conclusion. During that time, by important coincidence, Roman power, that had by

---

[149] I am fairly consistently breaking with the standard tradition of transliterating Greek names by way of their Latin equivalents. Thus I am writing Seleukos, rather than Seleucus; Antiokhos, rather than Antiochus; and later, Hyrkanos, rather than Hyrcanus; Aristoboulos rather than Aristobolus, etc. My reasons: "-us" is a Latin suffix; its Greek equivalent is "-os" (there are, however, some Greek names with "-us" suffixes, such as Odysseus and Akhilleus)—and "k" is a more logical transliteration of Greek "kappa" (k) than "c"—and these are Greek names.

[150] One may read two different accounts of this. One is II Maccabees 5:11-17 and the other is Josephus, *Antiquities of the Judaeans*, 12.5.4).

[151] A cubit is between 18" and 24", so one would need to remain roughly two-thirds to nearly a mile away.

[152] The account of this is found in I Maccabees 2:29-38. These would constitute the first religious martyrs on record; the Antiokhan persecution of Judaeans for religious reasons is unprecedented.

then swallowed the entire Italian peninsula and the entire western Mediterranean in turn, and had begun pushing itself deeper and deeper into the eastern Mediterranean, had arrived at the doorstep of the Seleucids. Thus two things helped cement the eventual Judaean victory by 165 BCE. Certainly the brilliant guerilla warfare waged by the Hasmonaeans, led by the middle of five brothers, Judah (popularly known as "the Maccabee") was one. But the other was the arrival of the Romans and their agreement to take on the Judaeans as minority-partner "allies," which meant that Antiokhos not only had bigger issues to deal with than Judaea and the (so-called) Maccabean revolt, with the Romans in general at his doorstep, but that the Romans were specifically positioned to assist the Maccabees, at least as far as Antiokhos knew and feared.

Two further consequences might be noted. One, as part of the "ally" agreement, the Judaean leadership sent representatives—in effect, friendly hostages—to Rome, establishing the beginnings of a Judaean community there that would eventuate as Jewish and Christian communities that are, one way or the other, still there today. Two, that the Hasmonaeans became the leaders of a Judaea that was fully independent for the first time in over 400 years—since 586 BCE. More to the point: the last of the surviving five "Maccabee" brothers, Simon, made himself High Priest (*Kohayn Ha-Gadol*) of the Jerusalem Temple.[153] At the time of Simon's death in ca 136 BCE, his son John Hyrkanos—who, importantly, added a Greek "surname" to his Hebrew "forename"—succeeded him both as High Priest and as ruler of what was still nominally a commonwealth, functionally turning the Hasmonaean political administration into a hereditary kingship.

One can discern one small and two large complications in this, all three fraught with both irony and consequences for our narrative. The small one is that "surname," particularly when we observe that the successors of John Hyrkanos altogether dispensed with their Hebrew names, preferring simple Greek forms, like Antigonos, Hyrkanos and Aristoboulos. So the revolution fought by the original Hasmonaean "Maccabees" to protect Judaea from excessive Hellenization led to independent Judaean rulers, heirs and descendants of those Hasmonaeans who themselves exemplify Hellenization in the most emphatic personal way: if one's name contains one's essence, as all ancient (and most post-ancient) peoples believed, then what can one surmise regarding these Judaean leaders and their sense of Judaean identity, given their name preferences?

The first of the two bigger complications is this: that a community that had, at the time of the return from exile, wrestled within itself regarding whether its leadership should be Davidic or Tzadokite—a leadership that in any case would have been by definition secondary to the Achaemenid satraps (governors) to whom it would have to answer, and through these to the Shah—now, hundreds of years later, fully independent, had a leadership that was *neither* Davidic nor Tzadokite. The Hasmonaeans were from a priestly family, but not that of Tzadok, the High Priest in Solomon's Temple; they were certainly not from the Davidic line—the line going back to those who had been the "anointed of the Lord":

---

[153] There are many sources to which one might turn for a more detailed discussion of the issue of what the terms "Hasmonaean" and "Maccabee" mean, and of this entire period. None is more useful than the first volume of Solomon Zeitlin's *The Rise and Fall of the Judaean State*. (Philadelphia: Jewish Publication Society, 1962). It goes without saying that volumes two and three are equally valuable for following this story in greater detail through to the end of the Second Temple Period.

mashiah elohim. So sooner than later there would be pushback regarding the (il)legitimacy of Hasmonaean leadership.

That pushback—and this is the second larger complication—would take its most coherent form (at least as far as we can understand it at a distance of more than two millennia) as two political parties that evolved from two groups offering two spiritual perspectives. The Sadducees—*Tzadokim*—who emphasized what they asserted was the connection between their ideology and that which could be traced back to Tzadok, emerged as a concerted force by the late second century, as did their opposing counterpart, the Pharisees—*Perushim*. The idea that the latter derive their name from their inclination to follow a mentality of guiding Judaean life by careful study, analysis and interpretation—*perush*—of the Torah would be reinforced in the late nomocratic era.

The Sadducees tended to be not only more literal but also more conservative in their views, and their understanding of the text of God's word usually worked in favor of the socio-economically better off. The Pharisees tended to be more liberal in their views and their understanding served the needs of the more socio-economically downtrodden—and eventually became the basis for rabbinic Judaism, as we shall see.[154] It has further been argued that the Sadducees and the High Priestly class that the Sadducees championed had become excessively Hellenized under the influence of the Seleucids and Ptolemies, so that the revolt against Antiokhos IV was also in part a revolt against the Sadducees, in which the people were led not only by the Hasmonaeans but, more broadly, by the Pharisees. This would help account for how Simon and his son John Hyrkanos, who were not of the High Priestly family, were able to assume that position: with widespread Pharisaic support.[155]

As these two groups became increasingly politicized they became increasingly interwoven with Hasmonaean affairs, which had become ugly. Concisely put: "[t]the dynasty had begun as the popular leadership of a people's rebellion; it now evolved into a ruling house which was autocratic, self-seeking and widely despised."[156]By the late second century, the son of John Hyrkanos, Aristoboulos, soon after his father's death, seized the rulership from his mother, threw her into prison where she was left to die of starvation, and also threw two of his four brothers into prison (although he never killed them). He preserved the freedom of Antigonos, with whom he had always been very close, and ignored his much younger brother, Jonathan Jannaeos (better known as Alexander Jannaeos), whom their father had sent north to the Galilee some years earlier to be raised away from home.[157] Aristoboulos fought a successful war against the Ituraeans, and in his victory echoed his father's actions vis-à-vis the Idumaeans: he gave them the choice of expulsion or circumcision and conversion to the faith of the Judaeans—most of whom chose the second option.

---

[154] For an accessibly detailed discussion and good examples of this socio-economic distinction reflected in Sadducean versus Pharisaic interpretations of issues within the legal strictures of Judaean life, see Zeitlin, *Rise and Fall*, vol I, 177-201.

[155] Zeitlin asserts this. See *Rise and Fall*, vol I, 176-77.

[156] Ibid, 317.

[157] John Hyrkanos apparently detested him, according to Josephus in *Antiquities of the Judaeans*. 13.12.1: "It had been his fate to be hated by his father from the time he was born, and never to come in his sight so long as he [John Hyrkanos] lived."

With the expansion of Judaea's borders, one must keep in mind—this will be important later on—that the term "Judaea" itself begins to acquire two historical meanings: "lesser Judaea" (I sometimes prefer "Judaea proper" as a designation) refers more or less to the original area held by the Judaeans and Benjaminites, which was returned to semi-autonomous control under the Persians and Alexander the Great and which gained its independence in the defeat of the Seleucids. "Greater Judaea" would include areas added by John Hyrkanos and Aristoboulos (and later, areas further added by Jannaios Alexander and subsequently, Herod). After his victory over the Ituraeans, Aristoboulos formally changed the structure of the Judaean administration from that of a commonwealth to that of a monarchy: what had *de facto* been the case since at least the death of Simon now became *de jure* the situation.

Meanwhile, a rift had been growing between the Pharisees and the Hasmonaeans. Late in John Hyrkanos' reign he disassociated himself from the Pharisees (for reasons that are not clear) and abolished the interpretative innovations and laws that they had guided into place over the previous few decades. The disassociation became deeper under Aristoboulos, since the Pharisees believed strongly (or now came to believe strongly) that the only sort of *legitimate* king for Judaea must be Davidic. Aristoboulos in any event ruled for only a year (105-4 BCE), dying of an illness that caused him to hemorrhage continually from the mouth. His wife, Salome Alexandra, feared for her life should Antigonos assume the kingship, so she organized a conspiracy to murder him. She managed to convince the ailing Aristoboulos that Antigonos was seeking to murder *him* and altered a message from Aristoboulos to Antigonos that led Aristoboulos to have his brother assassinated.[158] When Aristoboulos died, he was therefore succeeded by his 22-year-old younger brother, Jannaios Alexander (104-78 BCE), who married his 37-year-old sister-in-law. (We might suppose that Salome Alexandra exerted a good deal of power over her young husband and therefore over Judaea during the following few decades).

Jannaios Alexander could hardly have been more hostile to the Pharisees, most of whom now distinctly opposed the non-Davidic Hasmonaean rule that had recently declared itself a monarchy and some of whom altogether felt that the administrative leadership of the state should be straightforwardly theocratic (i.e., led by the priesthood, its broader political administration provided by the Seleucids or the Ptolemies or later, the Romans). That opposition increased as the young king, maintaining a careful neutrality in the ongoing dynastic wars in Seleucid Syria as well as in the larger Middle Eastern arena, pursued an increasingly aggressive policy toward his neighbors, pushing the envelope of forcing conversions as he sought to expand the borders of greater Judaea. His wars required larger armed forces than were indigenously available, so he employed increasingly large numbers of mercenaries, which meant increasingly onerous taxes on Judaean citizens, who became increasingly disenchanted with him.

---

[158] The king had asked his brother to come see him and had instructed the royal guards to kill Antigonos if he was armed as he passed by Straton's Tower, a coastal village about 65 miles from Jerusalem. Salome Alexandra was able to intercept and change the message so that it specifically *instructed* Antigonos to come armed, who was therefore murdered. When the news of this reached Aristoboulos, he got so upset that he hemorrhaged severely. Josephus asserts that he died in grief, somehow having come to realize that Antigonos had not intended him wrong and feeling guilty for his brother's death.

That opposition, led apparently by the Pharisees, broke out into violence during the Festival of *Sukkot* (Tabernacles), in 90 BCE, in which, according to the late first century CE Judaean historian, Josephus (37-100 CE), some 6,000 Judaeans perished at the hands of Jannaeos' mercenaries. Pharisaic opposition to the king was balanced by Sadducaean support for him. Whereas, in the previous few generations, the Sadducees had stood with the Pharisees on important political matters—from the war against Antiokhos IV to the appointment of Simon the Hasmonaean as High Priest and governor of the commonwealth—regardless of their differences on religious interpretation and related issues, now the two groups were in open and potentially blood-spilling opposition to each other. The Sadducees advocated expansion of the kingdom and a coercive policy of converting conquered neighbors to Judaeanism.[159] The Pharisees opposed this, believing in conversion through the word alone and not the sword.

Briefly put: a civil war ensued that lasted nearly six years (90-85 BCE), in which perhaps 50,000 Judaeans died. It was largely a civil war between the Sadducees and the Pharisees at the end of which 8,000 Pharisees fled the country.[160] With the end of concerted opposition to his power, Jannaios returned to a policy of external war for the next five years. But in the last few years of his life, he was struck down by quartan fever exacerbated by a growing taste for large amounts of alcohol. It is interesting that during these last years he struck bi-lingual coins, with the words "Jannaios the King" in Greek on one side and Hebrew on the other, as if, with the use of the latter language he was making a slow, slight spiritual/cultural pilgrimage back to the roots that he and his father and uncle, at least as evidenced by their names and their policies, seem to have abandoned so thoroughly. As he lay dying—while in the midst of besieging Ragaba—he recommended to his soon-to-be widow, Salome Alexandra, that she bring back the Pharisees, give them power again, and thereby gain their support for the Hasmonaean house of which she would soon be the ruler.

That she did. During Salome Alexandra's rule (78-69 BCE), she appointed her son by Jannaios Alexander, John Hyrkanos II, as High Priest. She restored all the laws that had been introduced by the Pharisees[161] and elevated them to a position as a power elite. Although Pharisaic thinking emphasized humility and forgiving wrongdoers, a substantial body of them, through the politicization process, had become quite taken with vengeance-against-one's-enemies as an ideology. They thus convinced the queen to destroy all of those who could be construed to have had a part in killing those who had rebelled against Jannaios Alexander; the former, of course, included many Sadducees. A bloodbath of Sadducees followed.

---

[159] Earlier, the Sadducees had not even believed in proselytism, on the grounds that the Judaean religion is ethnic, later embracing the Pharisaic view of Judaeanism as universal and with that embrace even advocating forced conversions of non-Judaeans. At the same time, they considered new members of the faith, like the Idumaeans and Ituraeans, as inherently inferior to ethnic Judaeans; the Pharisees opposed such a discriminatory viewpoint—rather an ironic feature of their ideology, given how they are portrayed in the Gospels.

[160] There is much more to this, but one important note is that Jannaios Alexander was known for his extraordinary cruelty: according to Josephus (*Antiquities* 13.14.2) he entertained himself after one victory by crucifying scores of captured opposition soldiers, slaughtering their wives and children before them—crucifixion, a preferred Roman mode of execution, as we shall later discuss, offers a slow process of dying—while enjoying a picnic in the company of his concubines.

[161] Josephus, *The Judaean Wars*, 1.5.1-2.

This was in turn followed by a plea to the Queen from her second son, Aristoboulos II, on the Sadducees' behalf, that they had loyally served her late husband, were loyal to her and should be protected from Pharisaic depradations; she was convinced to permit the Sadducees to leave Jerusalem and to take control of various fortresses outside the city. There would be consequences of this later on. When Salome lay ill and apparently dying, Aristoboulos decided that the time had come to seize power and used those fortresses as his staging platform: he took control of 22 of them in two weeks, and gathered an increasingly large army. A group of elders under the leadership of Hyrkanos II came to the Queen to ask her what to do—but she died shortly thereafter. Hyrkanos II was declared king, as the older son. War once more set in, between the followers of her two sons, as Aristoboulos II immediately declared war on his older brother. Within a few months Hyrkanos, having been defeated in a battle near Jericho, in order to avoid a protracted and destructive civil war, abdicated in favor of Aristoboulos, while retaining the high priesthood.

It seems that Hyrkanos was content with this arrangement, as he apparently lacked his younger brother's political ambition, but not all of his followers were content. They pushed to convince Hyrkanos that his brother was planning to assassinate him, encouraging him to take aggressive measures against Aristoboulos in order to protect himself. In the end this would lead first to the loss of full Judaean independence through the involvement of the Romans and second to the demise of the Hasmonaean dynasty in favor of Herod the Idumaean, as we shall shortly discuss in further detail.

For our present purposes what is most important is that, by the end of the Hasmonaean era, all of these issues—many of which offer their own complex interior details—were interwoven in a tight web of confusion where the hopes and aspirations of everyday Judaeans were concerned. John Hyrkanos II ruled for all of three months in 69 BCE before his throne was successfully usurped by Aristoboulos II. Six years later, Pompey the Great arrived in the Syro-Judaean neighborhood to reinforce the Roman presence and the Seleucid Empire formally came to an end, becoming a Roman province. Three separate deputations of Judaeans paid Pompey a visit: the supporters of Hyrkanos wanted Roman help to restore his position as king, the supporters of Aristoboulos wanted Roman help to assure that he retained his throne—and a third group wanted Roman help to remove both of them as non-Davidic.

Pompey initially supported Aristoboulos' claim, but when he asked the latter to accompany him south on an expedition against the Nabataeans and Aristoboulos for unknown reasons instead fled to the fortress of Alexandrion, Pompey followed him, piqued and obviously thinking that something was amiss. Negotiations between the two—Aristoboulos hoping to retain his throne and Pompey now determined to put Judaea firmly under Roman authority—led Aristoboulos to take refuge in Jerusalem. Pompey captured the Temple in July, 63 CE, slaughtering many of its priestly inhabitants. But as he saw them not only not defending themselves but actually continuing to perform their offices, he was surprised and impressed. He called for his soldiers to cease and desist, and ordered the Temple to be cleansed and repurified.

He also—very importantly for subsequent history—declared the Judaean religion to be a *religio licita*, recognized by the Roman authorities as legal, its precincts sacrosanct and, as a practical matter, the funds annually sent from throughout the Judaean diaspora for its upkeep (a half-shekel per annum) as sacred. Those funds were to be protected by Roman authority and anyone pilfering them would be regarded as treasonous and worthy of the death penalty by Roman law.

Meanwhile, Aristoboulos was removed from power and Hyrkanos resumed his royal role, also assuming the High Priesthood from that point until his death in 40 BCE. Functionally Hyrkanos was answering to the Roman authorities in his capacity as political leader—so Judaea had unequivocally lost her independence—and the Romans divided Judaea into five administrative units administered by Gabinius, the protégé of Pompey who by the early 50s had been put in charge of the area. This further undermined the economic and cultural stability of Judaea. Hyrkanos was succeeded in 40 BCE by Antigonos, who would rule for only three years. To be brief: Herod the Idumaean, who had been very active in these fraternal Judaean leadership conflicts for several years, as his father had been before him, was declared king of Judaea by the Romans in November, 40—although it took him three years to cement his position. He married the last Hasmonaean princess, Mariamne in 38 BCE, in order no doubt to assert a more legitimate status to his kingship over the Judaeans. Antigonos sought to go to Rome to argue the case for his legitimacy as king, but he never made it—he was beheaded in 37 BCE as a political subversive. Herod the Idumaean was now king of Judaea.

The ongoing spiritual and related complications that had defined the Hasmonaean century only worsened in the Herodian period that followed, even as Judaea regained a large measure of political independence due to the successful relationship between Herod and a progression of Roman rulers. When he achieved his kingship of the Judaean state in 37 BCE, what had seemed to some Judaeans a situation that could not get worse, did. Now not only was the king not Davidic, he was not even ethnically Judaean—or fully Judaean by religion.[162] Moreover, Herod soon took charge of the High Priesthood, appointing whomever he chose, based on who would be most amenable and useful to his needs. Simply put, he controlled the priestly vestments and whoever wore them was regarded as *Kohayn Ha-Gadol*: the uniform indeed made the man. The High Priesthood could hardly have become more debased.

Josephus, writing in his *History of the Judaeans* toward the end of the first century CE, notes that by the time of the Hasmonaeans—certainly by the time of Aristoboulos, son of John Hyrkanos, but maybe as early as the time of Hyrkanos' father Simon, the first Hasmonaean, non-Tzadok-descended, High Priest—a religious faction (or possibly more than one), besides the Sadducees and Pharisees, had emerged within the problem-ridden Judaean state. This faction (these factions?) withdrew altogether from mainstream Judaean society, frustrated by the degree to which mainstream Judaea had become disconnected from its sense of covenantal obligation.[163] Specifically, if the High Priesthood was by this group's definition illegitimate and therefore inherently corrupt, then everything associated with the Temple, from the Judaeans' offerings and the daily priestly sacrifice to the annual Yom

---

[162]For the increased complexity of defining "Judaean" in ethnic versus religious versus political terms, in the Hasmonaean-Herodian era, and of Herod himself, see above, 88, and fn #129).

[163] For an explanation of why I render his work as *History of the Judaeans*, rather than its more common rendering as *History of the Jews*, see below, 132 and fnn #204, 205.

Kippur ritual of the scapegoat (*azazel*), was corrupt. Josephus (writing in Greek) referred to this group as the *Essaioi*.

The Judaean philosopher and historian, Philo of Alexandria (ca 20 BCE-50 CE; also known as Philo Judaeus), writing in the first part of the century, also references such a group by the same name, explaining that the word is derived from the Greek *hosiotes*, meaning "piety" or "holiness."[164] Both Maccabees I and II, written, presumably, still earlier, also seem to mention this group. These books, originally in Hebrew and surviving in Greek, refer to a group—the same group as that referenced in Philo and Josephus, or a different group?—as *assidaioi*. A much later writer than any of these, the tenth-century south Italian Jewish historian, Josippon, who seems to have based much of his work on Josephus, refers to such a group as the *Hassidim*.[165] This suggests both that the term *assidaioi* used in Maccabees is a Greekified version of the Hebrew word and that this group grew out of the original *Hassidim* who were around at the time of the Hasmonaean revolt against Antiokhos IV, but, as purists—"pious ones"—became increasingly disenchanted with the Hasmonaeans, to the point that they ultimately withdrew from the community altogether.

Apart from theories of their origin, the range of the terminology raises an unanswerable question: whether these "names" all refer to the same group or whether there were different groups that shared in common the need to withdraw from the mainstream and establish themselves in isolated locations within the wilderness, the *sacer*. A second, related, question is whether any of these groups is what scholars in English have come to refer to as the Essenes. At least the term *essaioi* would seem to fit that bill pretty readily. A third question is whether the Essenes—or which of these groups, if they were separate groups and not one group called by different names by different writers in different times and places—might be associated with the site of Qumran, by the northwest corner of the Dead Sea. There, beginning in 1947, a series of scrolls was located in a difficult-to-access cave complex and, further, an apparent monastic complex presumably associated with those scrolls was archaeologically excavated.

For our purposes these questions are less important than the content of the scrolls. Regardless of the specific name of the group with which they are to be associated, they are clearly tied to that group or one of those groups that withdrew into the wilderness in pious frustration at the corruption that had been swallowing up Judaea since the beginning of the Hasmonaean period. Most of these parchments were stored in sealed jars. If, as seems likely, they came from the nearby "monastery" of Qumran, then they may have been placed by the monastic community in the caves in order to preserve them when the community was attacked, destroyed or dispersed—most likely during the time when, later on, the Romans were suppressing the Judaean Revolt (65-70 CE).

For the most part, they are simply carefully inscribed biblical texts: nearly every book that would eventually make its way into the canon of the Hebrew Bible is represented—notably, Esther, last and most problematic book to enter the canon, as we shall later observe, is missing—as well as books that would not enter it, but would enter

---

[164] He writes this in his work *Every Good Man is Free*, 75.
[165] Josippon was believed until a generation ago to have been much earlier—early third or even late second century. (So, for example, Zeitlin contends, in *Rise and Fall*, vol I, 477, n #50).

either the Catholic/Orthodox canon, such as the Wisdom of Ben Sira'; and books considered non-canonical by nearly all Jewish and Christian denominations, such as Enoch.[166] Among further documents of interest are those that indicate that the Qumran community began to use a calendar different from that in use in Jerusalem: they asserted that the pilgrimage and other festivals decreed in the Torah were being celebrated in accordance with a Hellenized calendar and therefore wrong—and, as with other elements of Temple-governed Judaean life, had become corrupt.

Most interesting, perhaps, and most relevant to our own narrative, are the so-called "Manual of Discipline" and—even more relevant—the so-called "Battle Scroll." The first of these offers instructions as to how one becomes a member of the community of the self-selected elect (if I may put it that way; the group referred to itself as the "New Covenant"—*brit hadashah*, in Hebrew) in which all members cede private ownership of anything and everything they possess to the group. One actually entered the community in three stages: first as a kind of interested acolyte, for an unspecified amount of time; second, provided one has demonstrated the correct inclinations and behavior patterns, one became "Party of the Community" and if, at the end of a year one were deemed suitable, one became part of the "Purity of the Many"—for another year. After these three stages one entered the Covenant fully and gained access to participation in the "Messianic Banquet."

Interestingly, the "Manual" corroborates most of the details reported by Josephus in his discussion of the *Essaioi*. The group presents itself as distinctly monastic—not only in that it lives apart from the world out in the *sacer*, but in its emphasis on gaining salvation through a complete separation of one's self from the material concerns of the corrupted world of the *profanus* (Judaean or otherwise). The more ascetic one's appearance the better the state of one's soul. Concomitant with this was the custom of ritual immersion: cleansing the body to signify cleansing the soul.[167] It seems certain from the "Manual" that, at the very least, the transition from being part of the Party of the Community to being part of the Purity of the Many and from that condition to that of being a full member of the New Covenant was marked by some ceremony of immersion.

One of the ways in which the community itself seems to have been divided was in its view of marriage (based on its divided view of women). Part of the group is said by Josephus to have permitted marriage and a family—after a three-year trial period in which the woman proves her moral trustworthiness—and the other not at all (these apparently despised women, in which case the continuation of the sect had to be through adopting children into it—sons, obviously). There is also a discussion of events that will take place at the end of time as we know it, such as the "Messianic Banquet" of which the ceremonial meals engaged in by the members of the Covenant were a (perhaps annual) foretaste—and in the discussion of which, reference is made to two anointed ones, a High Priest and a Davidic figure. The messianic "type" is referred to as the Prince of Light. All of these details will have implications for the discussion that follows in the next chapter of our narrative.

---

[166] In the Ethiopic Church, Enoch is included in the canon (as well as several other works not included in the Hebrew Bible or New Testament by other Christian denominations).
[167] The Greek verb "to immerse" is *baptizein*—which datum will prove significant as we move forward with our discussion.

It is the "Battle Scroll," however, that is most important for our discussion. It reflects a sensibility of human reality as guided by two opposed principles—good and evil, expressed as light and darkness—albeit both are under the supreme rule of God who eventually assists good to triumph over evil. What underlies the two forces in the human context is a pair of inclinations, or guiding "spirits": the *Yetzer HaRa'* ("Spirit/Inclination of/toward Evil/Perversion") and the *Yetzer HaTov* ("Spirit/Inclination of/toward Good/Truth") that pull humans toward good or evil acts. Ultimately, at the end of time as we know it, these two forces will engage in a cosmic battle—indeed a full-scale war between the "Sons of Light" and the "Sons of Darkness," in which the latter are led by the "Wicked Priest" and the former by the "Good Teacher."

The scroll begins:

> The first engagement of the Sons of Light against the Sons of Darkness—
> that is, against the army of Belial—shall be an attack on the troop of
> Edom, Moab, the Ammonites and the Philistine area and upon the
> Kittians of Assyria, and of those violators of the Covenant who give them
> aid. When the Sons of Light who are now in exile return from the 'desert
> of the nations' to pitch camp in the desert of Judah, the children of Levi,
> Judah and Benjamin, who are now among those exiles, shall wage war
> against these peoples—that is, against each and every one of their troops.

A large question—where might the basic ideas and images shaping the text of the scroll overall come from, beginning with the notion of Sons of Light and Darkness?—immediately presents itself, together with related issues that are noteworthy. The reference to "Belial"—an entity that personifies evil/darkness and opposes good/light—not only offers a cognate question to the first. The likely etymology of the name is itself telling: "*belee 'El*" means "without God" in Hebrew. All three ideas—of followers of good and evil, of a leader of the forces of darkness, and of the etymology of his name—suggest the strong possibility of Zoroastrian influence.

So it is possible that the extended contact with Zoroastrianism had this very interesting consequence within Judaea. There is a key difference, however. The ultimately universalist view of Zoroastrianism, in which, in the end, even the followers of *druj*, defeated, are "saved," has been replaced by a hyper-religiocentricity. Not, incidentally, ethnocentricity, since the basis for separating the Sons of Darkness from the Sons of Lightness is religious ideology as much as or more than ethnicity or nationality. The dark "enemies list," moreover, while it includes traditional national foes of the Israelite-Judaeans, typically uses biblical pseudonyms to refer to them rather than proper names, and seems to intend a range of contemporary, rather than biblical foes.

The *Kittim* (the "Kittians") are most prominently referred to. Biblically, the term originally probably meant inhabitants of Cyprus (derived from the city-state, Kition, that once dominated the southeastern side of the island), or somewhere else in the islands of the Aegean Sea West of Israel-Judaea (see Daniel 11:30). Used in the "Battle Scroll" that term may have evolved from an association with the Babylonians (aka the Chaldeans; see Habakkuk 1:4-6)—who had ended the First Temple period with destruction and exile—to the Hellenistic Greeks to the Romans (who would be the most obvious large power contemporary with this text, and who were presumably expected to engage the God-led Qumranian forces in the final battle in which the latter would ultimately win). But the term also includes "violators of the Covenant who give them aid" which would mean any Judaeans who are perceived to fall into the negative category.[168]

But that would pretty much be all Judaeans who are not part of the community of the Sons of Light who are now in self-imposed exile in the wilderness. And conversely, it would seem that only the Qumran community—the Essene community, if these are one and the same—is included in the group that will fight on the right side of this confrontation and that will achieve salvation. If one considers the history of warfare as far as we know it, the battle envisioned at Qumran offers the first time that a war will be based on religious ideology. If the inspiration for that vision is Zoroastrianism, then on the one hand, Zoroastrianism is actually first in this department (of envisioning a war based on religious ideology), but on the other hand—to repeat—its own vision ends up including all those who believe wrongly together with those who believe rightly living in a final world filled with light. By contrast, the instructions to would-be members of the Qumran community in the first section of the "Manual" is not only to "love all the children of light" but to "*hate all the children of darkness*, each according to the measure of his guilt..." (italics added). This is hardly an inclusive vision.

Moreover—in continuing the "Battle Scroll" narrative—this will only be the first battle in a longer war, for after it, "[t]hey [the Sons of Light] shall advance upon the [king of] the Kittians of Egypt." So the Kittians are located on both sides of Judaea, where the Seleucids and Ptolemies are respectively ensconced, and we have at least a tentative confirmation that the term "Kittian" is non-specific, nationally and ethnically speaking, referring to the successors of Alexander the Great and their kingdoms and peoples here even as elsewhere they will more obviously be the Romans. The time of this expanding warfare will in any case be "the time of salvation for the people of God...[who] will come to dominion, whereas those who have cast [their lot] with Belial shall be doomed to eternal extinction... [N]o survivor shall remain of the Sons of Darkness."

The text goes on to describe the participation, as it were, of the forces of nature—which, after all, were also created by God: "[lightning] will flash from one end of the world to the other, growing ever brighter until the era of darkness is brought utterly to an end. Then, in the era of God, His exalted grandeur will give light for [evermore], shedding on all the Sons of Light peace and blessing, gladness and length of days." The post-martial end of days is not envisioned as a light-filled era shared by *everyone*, however.

Nor will this be a simple battle; for "the Sons of Light will have luck three times in discomfiting the forces of wickedness; but three times the host of Belial shall brace themselves to turn back the tide." In fact, "the squadrons of infantry shall become faint-hearted, but the power of God will strengthen their hearts, and *on the seventh occasion* the great hand of God shall finally subdue [the army of Belial]" (italics added). One notes a strong emphasis on numbers—in particular 3 and 7—and an interest in combining their

---

[168] The Dead Sea scroll that makes most of the *Kittim* is the Habakkuk Scroll, not the Battle Scroll. The analysis of who they are is more complicated than I am presenting in an attempt to be concise, and since for our purposes this oversimplified account is sufficient.

power with the power of God's name and God's word, and in connecting them to nature itself.

This becomes even more obvious once one moves beyond this opening, "introductory" chapter and onto the next, in which religious offices during the war are laid out and recruitment for the Army of Light is described. Thus there are fifty-two "Fathers of the community"—the number of the weeks in the year. Forces will be organized under twelve major priests (the number of months, as well as the number of Israelite tribes once united and led by the divinely anointed king of Israel, David. There will be 26 major officials (half of 52) and "twelve major Levites [i.e., priests], one for each tribe, to serve constantly."

The war will last for thirty-three years (which happens to be the length of David's kingship over a united Israel with its capitol in Jerusalem).[169] The scroll lists the specific campaigns, elaborating beyond the introductory comments—it would seem that every group of which the writer is aware will be fought by the Sons of Light. This is in turn followed by an elaborate description of the disposition of the battle groups and the "trumpets of assembly." There is a dozen of these, each inscribed with different words that identify the cohort and its role: "on the trumpets of assembly for the entire community, they shall write: *The Enlisted of God*; on the trumpets of assembly for officers, they shall write: *The Princes of God*; on the trumpets of enrollment they shall write: *The Rank of God*; on the trumpets of the dignitaries they shall write: *The Heads of the Families of the Community*"—and so on, down to the twelfth group, with its trumpets that "signal the route of return from the war against the enemy and the way back to the community in Jerusalem, [on which] they shall write: *Joy of God at the return of peace/at a safe return.*"

Similarly, the entire community, enrolled as troops in the divinely-inspired army, will be led forth by twelve standards held high, on which there will be inscriptions. On the first, "the great standard that precedes the entire army [lit. people] they are to write *People of God* together with the names of Aaron and Israel and those of the twelve tribes of Israel according to their pedigrees. On the standard of the camp commander of the three tribes of Levi, Judah and Benjamin, they are to write [ ].[170] On the standard of each separate tribe they are to write: *Banner of God*, together with the name of the [ ], the name of the chieftain of the ten thousand and those of the [ ]....On the standard of the thousand they are to write: *God's anger is vented in fury against Belial and against all that cast their lot with him, that they have no remnant*; together with the name of the commander of the thousand and of its hundreds... On the standard of the hundred they shall write: *From God comes the power of battle against all sinful flesh...*"—and so on.

The numbers continue, down to "the standard of fifty" and the "standard of ten." Each inscription offers a word-play with regard to that number. Thus "thousand" in Hebrew

---

[169] He had ruled first from Hebron—for seven years—over only part of the kingdom before consolidating his power in newly conquered Jebus (Jerusalem) which then became his capitol. One must keep in mind that such a relatively obscure source for a number of significance would not have been obscure to the members of an inherently esoteric community.

[170] The text is missing here. These are the three tribes singled out for leadership within the "Manual of Discipline." Levi is, of course, the priestly tribe from which the family of Moses and Aaron came. Judah was the tribe of David and Benjamin that of Saul—and after the Assyrian debacle, the only two left functioning (the other ten having been "lost").

is *'eleph*, and "God's anger" is *'aph 'El* (requiring a metathesis of two consonantal components—but hardly in terms of the numerological value of the consonants—to be the equivalent of the number).[171] "One hundred" is *me'ah* in Hebrew; "from" is *me'et*. The word "fifty" is spelled out strewn through parts of the inscription. The inscription on the standard of ten makes reference to "the ten-stringed harp."

Additional inscriptions will be included on standards when they actually begin the battle process—one series when they set out, a second when they draw near to the battle and a third when they return from battle. Details are offered with regard to the deployment of troops and the manner in which they fight. These details continue to play on the power of numbers and the power of the word that shall bring victory. For example, there will be seven battle lines, and "[t]he first squadron shall fling seven war-darts into the enemy line. On the blade of each dart they shall write: *The flash of the spear evinces the Power of God*." Furthermore, "when the priests go out between the lines, seven Levites shall go out with them, and in their hands shall be seven trumpets made out of rams' horns… The trumpets shall keep sounding for the slingers until they have hurled a full seven times." One is reminded (as is surely intended) of the narrative of Joshua's victory over Jericho, where priestly horn blasts in sevenfold sequences brought the walls of the city down—and of the broader importance of the number seven, to say nothing of the importance of ram-horn trumpets.

Ram-horn trumpets offer an association that carries back to Genesis 22 and the story of the Binding of Isaac, and forward to the rituals of the Temple in Jerusalem, from the parapets of which a ram's horn would be sounded at the time of every new month and to announce the beginnings of key Israelite-Judaean festivals, and in particular, the beginning and the ending of the solemn "Days of Awe" that had come to mark the beginning of the year during the Second Temple Period.

The priests will continue to blow these horns in directing the battle from a safe distance, lest their sacrosanctity be compromised by contact with blood and its double implications: that in being spilt it marks the slippage from the *profanus* of life to the *sacer* of death; and that the blood of the Sons of Darkness in particular is, by definition, corrupt:

> …and while the enemy are fallen slain, the priests shall go sounding the signals from a distance; they shall not go into the midst of the slain lest they be defiled by their impure blood; for the priests are holy and they are not to defile the oil of their priestly anointment with the blood of vain heathen.

There are other details that reflect a synthesis between ideas recognizable from Zoroastrianism and those derived from Roman military thinking. Four of the five battle formations described largely recall those of the Roman military, specifically, the "straight line [corresponding to the *agmen quadratum*] flanked by so-called '(human) towers' [corresponding to the *testudo*]" and the "curved line resembling the lower half of a circle"

---

[171] In Hebrew, as in most Semitic languages, it is the consonants that are important—most traditional texts (including the Dead Sea Scrolls and, for that matter, modern newspapers) are written altogether without vowels. So, too, every consonant has a numerical value, which opens up various interpretive doors based on those values.

that corresponds to the Roman *forfex* and that "in a curved line resembling the upper half of a circle" [the *cuneus*], as well as the formation "in a slight curve with ends foremost, protected by wings (of cavalry) advancing on both flanks"—wherein those wings are precisely what the Romans would refer to as *alae equitum* ("wings of horses").

"[A]ll of the 'towers' are to bear inscriptions. Those of the first 'tower' are to carry the legend, *Michael*; [those of the second, *Gabriel*; those of the third], *Sariel*; and those of the fourth, *Raphael*." One might again ask whence these names derive—or rather, from where the very idea derives of a quartet of what are apparently *sacer* powers obedient to the one God who leads the Sons of Light into the battle. And again one might turn to Zoroastrianism as a putative source and its concept of the *Amesha Spentas*. Later, in fact, as we shall see, the book of Enoch (40:9-10) will refer to these archangels as well as to three others, giving a total of seven, which *is* the number of *Amesha Spentas*.[172]

What follows this description is both a prescription for and the text of the speech that will be uttered to the troops to inspire them—what the Romans would refer to as an *allocutio*—in which passages from the Torah and elsewhere in the not-yet-fully-formed Hebrew Bible are quoted and references made to Moses' leadership of the Israelites wandering through the wilderness and encountering, combating and defeating those who attacked them along the way. Most of the speech is actually directed heavenward, reminding God of past times when Israel has triumphed over its enemies through divine interventionist support, including the all-important moment when "Goliath the Gittite, a man of mighty strength, didst thou deliver into the hand of thy servant David, because David trusted in Thy great name and not in sword or spear," and including the victory over—in escaping through the Sea of Reeds from—Egypt.

In the context of this speech *to* God, the speaker observes that

[with thee] in heaven are a multitude of holy beings and armies of angels
are in Thy Holy abode, to [serve as] Thy [legions]; and down on earth
Thou hast [likewise] placed at Thy service the elect of a holy people.

We may recognize as sources for this statement both words, albeit without elaboration, within the Bible itself—for example, the reference, in Isaiah 6:1 to God as *El tzva'ot*: "Lord of hosts/armies"—and ideas that are more fully elaborated in the Zoroastrian tradition of the *Amesha Spentas* and the *Yazatas*. We also recognize both the direct sense of parallel between what is happening in the *sacer* and its mirrored activity in the *profanus*, and the narrow religio-centricity that this facilitates: the warriors of the Lord on earth are the Qumranian subset of the Judaean remnant of the tribes of Israel who echo and are supported by what is happening in heaven. Indeed, "...the King of Glory is with us, along with the holy beings. Warrior angels are in our muster, and He that is Mighty in War is in our throng."

The culmination of the *allocutio* is a poem addressed simultaneously to God and to the troops of the Sons of Light, beginning with the words

---

[172] We must keep in mind that these names that we take to be those of archangels are not found in the Torah or elsewhere in the Hebrew Bible, so that is not the source for the idea; and also that they are all constructed of two elements bespeaking their *sacer* roles: "Lord" (El) + some attribute, such as "strength" (*g-b-r*) or "heal" (*r-f- '*).

> Arise, O warrior!
> Take thy captives...
> Set thy hand upon the neck of thy foeman,
> and thy foot upon mounds of the slain...

and ending the words of post-victory with a call to

> ...put on your finery,
> step forth [ ]
> [   ] Israel, to rule for evermore!
> [   ] the warriors, O Jerusalem!
> Be exalted, O Lord, above the heavens!

There follows an instruction to the priests to offer their own benedictory *allocutio*—both a statement to the Sons of Light regarding God and an invocation to the

> God of our fathers, [that] we will bless Thy name forever... Thou hast made us unto Thee an eternal people, and hast cast our lot in the portion of light, that we may evince Thy truth; and from of old hast Thou charged the Angel of Light to help us. In his hand are all works of righteousness, and all spirits of truth are under his sway. But for corruption thou hast made Belial, an angel of hostility. All his dominion is in darkness, and his purpose is to bring about wickedness and guilt. All the spirits that are associated with him are but angels of destruction.

Once again one cannot but imagine that the ultimate source of inspiration for this series of ideas—light and darkness as opposed within the world, but ultimately all of it under the unified authority, and deriving from the creative effort of a single, good God—as Zoroastrian, even as the ideas have been filtered through the religio-centric proclivities of the Qumran sect: "[Let destruction befall] the Sons of Darkness, but let Thy great light shine [for the Sons of Light]."

If a review of this material suggests an important point of origin in Achaemenid Medo-Persia and its state religion, the next question is: does it go beyond Qumran? Or put otherwise: when the destruction of the monastic complex occurred, presumably during the Judaean struggle for political independence against Rome in 65-70 CE, did the inhabitants simply perish, or were they able to migrate elsewhere? Did they expect to return to reclaim the scrolls that they so carefully hid away in those caves? If we take the "Battle Scroll" as a guide to part of their thinking, then we might suppose that they imagined that a day of reckoning would indeed come, when they, led by no less then God Itself and God's angelic hosts, would rise up in battle against all of their enemies, including the Romans, and destroy them, putting in place a final era of light that the chosen and loyal few would enjoy.

But the monastery was never re-inhabited. Its chambers, their roofs collapsed and their walls burnt or crumbling, would be covered by the sands of the Judaean desert over the course of nearly two millennia, while the scrolls in their jars remained hidden in the nearby caves until the accidental discovery of the first of them by a Bedouin shepherd boy.

Might there be other ways or places where the ideas contained in those scrolls—particularly in the "Battle Scroll"—survived and moved forward? The answer to that question forms part of the discussion of the next chapter in this narrative.[173]

---

[173] There is by now a vast library of books and articles, both scholarly and popular, regarding the Dead Sea Scrolls. For accessible introductions I recommend John Allegro's *The Dead Sea Scrolls: A Reappraisal* and Edmund Wilson's *The Scrolls from the Dead Sea*—both paperbacks. Theodor H. Gaster's paperback, *The Dead Sea Scriptures* offers effective translations of many of the key texts.

CHAPTER FIVE

From Herod to the *Khristos* to *Revelation*:
The Ultimate Judaean Schism

What drove the Essenes, or whatever the group associated with Qumran might be called—and whatever other groups might or might not have taken refuge in whatever other wilderness sites that have not yet been uncovered archaeologically—to separate themselves from the mainstream Judaean community and its life was, as we have noted, the sense of how unbearably corrupt that life had become. A leadership that, in moving from its troubled Hasmonaean period to its even more troubling Herodian period could hardly be expected to be shepherding a people living the sort of covenantal life that past prophets like Isaiah and Jeremiah had insistently called for, or that the finalized text of the Torah, thanks to Ezra the Priest-Scribe, had made available to those who studied its precepts carefully and enacted them.

As for Herod the Idumaean king over Judaea, he offered an ambiguous leadership on various fronts for the Judaeans. On the one hand, he regained their independence for them in that the Romans trusted his skills sufficiently to accord him a junior ally sort of status. His military and organizational capabilities made him a valuable bulwark for the Empire against desert peoples, like the Nabataeans, to the south and east of Judaea, who might threaten the borders of the *Res Romana*.[174] On the other hand, to repeat, from a purist's perspective, the price for re-gained independence was that the king was himself not a Judaean, ethnically, at least, so for many Judaeans—and not only Essene types—loyalty to him would have been difficult if not virtually impossible.

One of the ways in which he sought to gain that loyalty was by putting into play another significant skill that he possessed: devising and sponsoring major engineering/architectural projects. On the one hand, he substantially augmented the Temple mount in Jerusalem, hauling huge blocks of stone into place in order to do so. He

---

[174] I am using this Latin turn of phrase—which means "Roman thing (*res*)"—to underscore the way in which Roman historiography would look at this period—from before the death of Pompey, in 58 BCE, and of Julius Caesar, in 44 BCE, to the conferral of the honorific "Augustus" on Caesar's nephew, Octavian, thereafter known as Augustus Caesar, in 27 BCE. It would be officially viewed as one in which the republic (*res publica*: "people's thing") was restored, rather than as what it was: the culmination of the destruction of the republic and its replacement by a monarchy—an empire—in which Augustus would in turn be succeeded by a series of autocrats like himself, from Tiberias to Romulus Augustus (deposed in 476 CE). We must keep in mind that the history of Judaea-Palestina and the early developments of Judaism and Christianity are played out against this Roman reality.

substantially refurbished the Temple facade—or, if we take Josephus at his word, actually rebuilt it from scratch, gathering all of the materials in advance and preparing everything in order to minimize the time between when his workmen began to dismantle the old structure and the completion of the new one. Nonetheless, that effort, however partial or total the make-over was, seems only to have enhanced resentment of Herod, since the notion of his laying a hand on the central Judaean sacerdotal edifice, even to aggrandize it visually, was unacceptable to most.[175]

Moreover, his predilection for Greco-Roman style would surely have re-enforced the anger of those who were in any case frustrated by or concerned about the matter of Hellenization. We can see that predilection expressed in one unquestionable and one hypothetical way. The serious expansion of the Temple mount, and with it, the outermost Temple courtyard (the so-called "Courtyard of the Gentiles") included the creation of a double-colonnaded porch—a *stoa*—all along the periphery of its inward face.[176] More egregious is the likelihood that Herod added an additional base to the seven-branched menorah—the most important artifact in the Temple besides the Holy of Holies itself.[177]

On the other hand, he took the small fishing village of Straton's Tower and transformed it into a major center of shipping commerce by developing its coastal front into the largest and most effective harbor in the Eastern Mediterranean. Since the majority of the population was pagan, one can see this as an effort that was intended to appeal to the pagan Judaean population as the Temple and Temple Mount project was presumably intended to appeal to Judaeans who worshipped the God of Israel.

On the third hand, Herod built a series of important fortresses and palaces in different parts of the desert. Arguably the most important of these was the palace-fortress complex of Massada in the wilderness, not far from the southwestern part of the Dead Sea. Like other such structures, this one reflected two things: Herod's paranoia—his fear both of insurrections against him by Judaeans and of invasion from the ruler who ended up being the last of the Ptolemies, Cleopatra VII, who was soon engaged in a torrid relationship with the Roman leader, Marc Antony (and would perish with him after the Battle of Actium that

---

[175] One might be reminded—although the circumstances and their significance are radically different—of the moment when Uzzah put out his hand to steady the Ark of the Covenant in David's day, when it appeared in danger of tipping over as it was drawn in a wagon pulled by oxen and they stumbled (II Samuel 6:1-7). God struck him down: however well-intentioned his gesture would appear from a *profanus* viewpoint it was unacceptable from a *sacer* viewpoint. The parallel is that, simply put, there are limitations on what a non-Kohayn may do vis-a-vis such an entity, be it Ark or Temple, even if it is ostensibly to accomplish a positive end, such as preventing the one from falling over or aggrandizing the other. Herod's act would no doubt be viewable as more egregious, since Uzzah was at least not only an Israelite but a Levite, where Herod was a hybrid Idumaean/Judaean (by religion only)-Nabataean/pagan.

[176] There were three courtyards in the Temple: the outermost one could be entered by anyone (the Courtyard of the Gentiles); the middle one could be entered by Judaean men and women (the Courtyard of the Women); and the innermost one could be entered only by Judaean men (the Courtyard of the Israelites). Only priests could actually enter the Temple itself, and the Holy of Holies could be entered only by the High Priest—and only once a year, on the Day of Atonement.

[177] The evidence for this idea is the depiction of the Menorah on the carved-relief image on the inner wall of the Arch of Titus (ca 80 CE), which shows Romans carrying the captured Temple spoils into Rome after the suppression of the Judaean Revolt and the destruction of the Temple. The bottom double base, below the upper base with its Achaemenid-style frond motif, offers the zodiac, a popular Hellenistic-Roman motif that would have attracted Herod and been consistent with his taste for Greco-Roman decor, (and could be seen to symbolize the twelve tribes of Israel)—and there is no reference to such a base previously, so it seems likely that Herod added it.

brought Octavian into singular power, in 31 BCE)—and his love of luxurious accommodations. The storehouses and cisterns of Massada overflowed with food and water; the bathrooms with their beautiful mosaic floors provided a Roman-style trilogy of water types—hot, warm and cold; and a virtual hanging palace on the northern face, where it could be kissed by breezes even in the hottest summer months, was decorated in the latest *trompe-l'oeil* Roman wall-painting and fluted pilaster style.

One of the more surprising features of Herod's reign is that, in the course of it, religious leaders who were highly respected by the community continued to survive, providing guidance for how to live a properly covenantal life—in spite of what the Qumran sect thought of anyone and everyone living in Jerusalem and mainstream Judaea. The Sadducees had all but disappeared, but the Pharisaic leadership was itself increasingly divided between more conservative and more liberal perspectives regarding what constituted genuine religious Judaeanism. Shammai is the name that has survived as the voice of the former—who saw trees where Hillel, the voice for the latter, saw the forest, as both scholars interpreted the Torah.[178]

One might expect that Hillel the Elder, arguably the most important Judaean intellectual and spiritual figure between about 30 BCE and 10 CE—who may be said to have been the leader of the Judaean *community* while Herod was the King of the Judaean *state*—would have been somehow put to death by Herod. After all, the king murdered his own wife, Mariamne, last of the Hasmonaeans, disposed of others among his ten wives and also presided over the demises of various sons, nephews and even grandsons—particularly as, in his later years, what appears to have been stomach cancer helped intensify his paranoia of conspiracies against him. But Hillel prevailed as a teacher. In his last years one might even theorize that among the youngest pupils sitting at his feet was one from the Galilee (not part of Judaea proper, but part of Greater Judaea), named *Y'hoshua*: Joshua, in English—or as that name is rendered in an anglicized Greco-Latin form, Jesus.[179]

If one steps back at this point and considers all of the religious, ethnic, political and, simply, definitional complications that shape the last pre-Christian century in Judaea—and with Herod's death in 4 BCE, the Romans would step back more fully into the situation and reclaim full administrative authority over Judaea, installing a procuratorship—we might well sympathize with the sense of confusion on different levels that not only framed Judaeans' lives but provoked the question: when and how will this all end? More specifically: will we ever really be led again by an anointed of God—a *mashiah elohim* (or in Greek, *khristos kuriou*)—of the Davidic line? More and more Judaeans wondered. (And David and his era would have come to appear more and more golden in retrospect, as time and complications moved forward.) What kind of leader would a *mashiah/khristos* be: a political leader who would restore Judaean fortunes and, specifically, its independence—perhaps one to whom all nations, including the Romans, would look with respect and awe—or, as some contended, an ideal spiritual leader, who

---

[178] It is often difficult to identify ideas that were actually offered by Shammai and Hillel, since the rabbinic literature frequently uses the phrases "School of Shammai" and "School of Hillel" (*Bet Shammai* and *Bet Hillel*; lit: "House of Shammai" and "House of Hillel") to refer to viewpoints presumably associated with their directions of thought.

[179] The name in Hebrew, incidentally, means "savior."

would lead Judaeans back to clarity with respect to the Covenant, but with no political aspirations for the community?

Add to this yet another issue: that the implications of the nomocratic revolution had in any case not been embraced by every Judaean. Specifically, whereas the Judaean leadership and presumably a majority of the Judaean people accepted the idea that the age of prophecy had ended—that direct revelations from God to and through prophets and priests had ceased, yielding primacy of place to scribes and scholars who could interpret God's word—there were surely some who continued to believe that God was continuing to communicate in the old, prophetic manner to certain spiritually privileged individuals in certain times and places. Thus for some but not for most, a charismatic individual publicly proclaiming answers to these sorts of questions might well strike a resonant note.

There was a certain John—known as "the Baptist"—who might be said to fit that bill. "His wild, unkempt appearance, his uncompromising call to repentance, and his fanatical assurance of the nearness of the Day of Judgment, made a particular appeal to the people when he finally began his public ministry."[180] Interestingly, we are offered no information in our sources, the Gospels, as to where John had been or what he had been doing before his public ministry began.[181] Even Luke, with its unique account (in 1:5-24 and 1:57-80) of John's nativity, offers no information—although Luke notes (in 1:80) that "he was in the wilderness until the day of his public appearance to Israel" and one might also infer from the statement in Matthew 3:1—that he "came, preaching in the wilderness of Judaea"—and in Mark 1:4, similarly, that he "came baptizing in the wilderness," that he had spent his pre-preaching adulthood away from the community, out in the *sacer*.

Where in the *sacer* and with whom—or was he all alone? An obvious possibility that presents itself is that he was at Qumran (or elsewhere where members of the Community of the New Covenant may have been). That could account for his having apparently been in the wilderness, possibly (if we infer from Luke 1:80 that he was out there from a rather early age) because he was one of those young boys adopted by the sect—and if (again, taking Luke at face-value), his father Zechariah was a priest, one might suppose that he would have been perceived to show particular promise as a future adult member of that community.

Certainly, he is represented in Matthew and in John 1:23, at the outset of his preaching, as quoting the same passage from Isaiah 40:3 that was referenced by the Qumran literature, warning his auditors to "make a clear way for the Lord in the wilderness," to share one's material wealth, to live honestly and in quiet expectation of the end time soon to arrive. The most noteworthy feature of John's ministry—hence his epithet "the Baptist"—was his notion of total immersion as part of the ritual of marking the change in one's life and the beginning of the purification of one's soul. We have observed how important this rite was to the Qumran community. On the other hand, John had left the community, if that's where he had been. He had come out of the wilderness, into Judaea and begun to preach to everyday people: the objects of his salvational efforts were well

---

[180] John Allegro, *The Dead Sea Scrolls* (Baltimore, MD: Penguin Books, 1965), 157.
[181] Josephus also mentions John in *Antiquities* 18.5.2.

outside the scope of what interested the Qumran community, according to the texts that we have available to us from Qumran.

So it may be true that the Qumran community, at least part of the ideology of which may have been inspired by Zoroastrianism, in turn inspired a founding father of what would eventuate as Christianity—but that possibility should not be confused either with certainty or with excessive parallelism. In any case, John is depicted in the Gospels as presenting himself as a mere forerunner of the figure who will lead Judaeans out of their problem-ridden reality. The consummate moment of his career as one who baptizes is when he baptizes Jesus, whose appearance on the stage of history must be explored from two angles as this narrative moves forward. For we must understand the sort of theological and historical role that someone like Jesus—anyone like him, and not necessarily Jesus himself (for reasons that will be clear in a moment)—might be understood by a non-Christian to play, as well as following his life (and earth-bound death) from a Christian perspective.

Thus as we have observed, against the backdrop of the complications that continued to multiply themselves during the Second Temple period, we must keep in mind the likelihood that an ever-increasing number of Judaeans would have wondered whether and when an anointed—a *mashiah/khristos*, with God at his back—would appear on the scene to restore moral order and covenantal propriety. We must also remember that some number of Judaeans never embraced the notion that the era of divine revelation through prophetic intermediaries had ended with Ezra's nomocratic revolution. These two strands of thought would interweave themselves at the time of and with regard to the person of Jesus for that part of the Judaean schism that became Christianity.

From an eventual Christian perspective that is simply how things *had* to happen because of the relationship between God and humans and how that relationship has played out from the time of Eden until the time of Jesus.[182] For the part of the Judaean schism that became Judaism, Jesus came to be understood to fill a spiritual and psychological human need regardless of what or who he truly was.[183] As that schism widened—not offering much definitive clarity to its own members until the late first century, a good two to three generations after the Crucifixion (during most of which period, parties on both sides of the schismatic fence understood themselves to be Judaeans; i.e., not "Jews" and "Christians")—its parameters crystallized along certain distinct lines.

Those whom we might call "Judaeans for Jesus" believed that Jesus was the messiah and that the age of revelation had continued at least through the time when he walked the earth. Those whom we might call "Judaeans not for Jesus" believed that Jesus

---

[182] This issue will receive its most precise representation many centuries later, when St Anselm of Canterbury (1033-1109) wrote his *Cur Deus Homo* in which he eloquently connects the Christian doctrine of Original Sin, and the eternal damnation that it makes necessary for the human bloodline that begins with Adam and Eve, to the arrival of Jesus as both God and Man onto the stage of history, whose arrival makes salvation from the hellish inevitability possible.

[183] Since Judaism lacks both a doctrine of Original Sin and a substantial concept of hell, the "necessity" of a God Man to effect salvation doesn't exist. The Hebrew language does not even possess a real word for "hell," having to make do with the words for "Grave" (*she'ol*) and Jerusalem's red light district, *gei Ben-Hinnom* ("the valley of Ben-Hinnom"—no doubt the "valley of the shadow of Death [through which when I walk] I fear no evil, for thou art with me" referenced in Psalm 23)—which phrase becomes corrupted, eventually, as the word *gehenna*, to serve as an approximation of "Hell," but there is nothing in it to compare with how Christianity develops the idea.

was *not* the messiah and that the age of revelation ended at or soon after the time of Ezra. These two issues functioned both independent of and in conjunction with each other. Each of the two groups interpreted texts that they shared in common—like Isaiah 7, for instance—differently with regard both to the question of whether Jesus is the fulfillment of messianic promises articulated in those texts and with respect to some of the aspects of Jesus, such as his Virgin Birth (or the eventual claim of it by his followers): is it anticipated in such texts? Eventually, issues such as this last one would be affected by whether one's source was Hebrew (as it was for Jews) or Greek (as it became for Christians).[184]

Thus the eventual Jewish or Christian view of Jesus would in part be determined by their respective interpretations of these sorts of Hebrew biblical passages. Further, as we have earlier noted, what for Jews eventuate as the Hebrew Bible would come to be known as the "Old Testament" or the "Old Covenant" by Christianity, in contrast to the "New Covenant" or "New Testament." The emerging Jewish and Christian perspectives regarding Jesus therefore reflected different notions of what constitutes the divinely revealed or inspired canon, beyond the issue of differently interpreting the texts they *share*. The question of what belongs in the canon had already been evolving during the post-Ezra Judaean period, as we have noted, when after his redaction of the Torah the obvious question soon presented itself regarding what else besides those five books might be considered important, divinely-inspired writ: yes, of course, Isaiah and Jeremiah and the like—particularly given how their prophecies had been fulfilled, both with regard to destruction and exile and with regard to return, restoration and rebuilding—but what other books qualified?

Aside from the issues of how to understand and define God; what the term "*mashiah*" really connotes and whether Jesus of Nazareth *is* the *mashiah*; and the ongoing question of what constitutes biblical canon; what were becoming Judaism and Christianity would also eventually be separated by issues of community observance and celebration. Thus whereas early on, both Judaean groups celebrated the Sabbath, and subsequently, those becoming Christians added a "Lord's Day," eventually the Christian community would abandon observance of the seventh day as the Sabbath altogether, and transform the following day, as the Lord's day, into its equivalent. Similarly, the calendar bifurcated, as traditional Israelite-Judaean festivals—both those mandated in the Torah and those that

---

[184] I am referring most specifically to the interpretation of the Hebrew word *almah* found in Is 7:14, which in its Greek rendering is *parthenos*. The first means "young woman", whereas the second connotes not only youth but virginity. Although a young woman might have been assumed to be unmarried and therefore a virgin, Hebrew does possess a distinct word for "virgin": *betulah*. The Jewish view would be that Christians are using a "mere" translation of the original; the Christian view would be that the translation is itself divinely inspired, since Christian tradition maintains that seventy scholars working separately came up with precisely the same translation for the entire text (called, accordingly, the Septuagint, meaning "seventy" in Greek), which can only have happened if they were all guided by the same *sacer* force, the Holy Spirit. The latter viewpoint would further argue that Isaiah deliberately chose *almah* to emphasize the youthful aspect of Jesus' mother-to-be and that the seventy translators were equally inspired to emphasize her virginity and therefore chose to render *almah* as *parthenos*. Some contemporary Christian exegetes have gone in a completely different direction, in suggesting that the root of *almah* is '-*l*-*m*, meaning "concealed." The implication would be that the *almah* is the female half of an engaged pair and that during their year of engagement the two betrothed individuals remain in their parents' homes, concealed from each other. The discussion of this issue is a poster child for the intriguing issue of the interpretation of revealed texts, particularly since all arguments can be seen as flawed by the outsider but are convincing to the believer.

had come into shape during and shortly after the Second Temple period (like Hanukkah)—were abandoned by the emerging Christian community in favor of their own celebrations, as others, like Purim and Lag Ba'Omer were added to the evolving Jewish calendar.

Needless to say, the same would be true of life cycle events, from circumcision to funerary rituals. Given that the act of circumcision was considered the "mark of the Covenant" by Jews, based on the mandate in Genesis 17:10-14, 23-27and Genesis 21:4 for Abraham and his sons, Ishmael and Isaac, to circumcise themselves in order to signify their relationship with God; and given that Christianity would define itself as, by definition, marked by a new Covenant; there is a logic to the abandonment of that custom by the Church.[185] The decision to do so offers only one, rather distinct manifestation of the Jewish-Christian bifurcation with regard to interpreting the biblical text that the two groups share in common. So, too, whereas what became Judaism would continue the development of the post-nomocratic revolution discussions of the meaning of the Torah and other biblical texts—those discussions, oral for generations, would eventually be organized by Judah the Prince and written down in the third century CE and constitute the beginnings of what we refer to as rabbinic literature—what became Christianity abandoned those discussions in favor of an altogether different set of discussions.[186] The patristic literature would address biblical and other matters from the perspective of the New Covenant.[187]

The Jewish canon would be completed by about 140 CE—more than a century after the Crucifixion. The Christian canon would not be completed until the Council of Hippo, in 393-7 CE, more than three-and-a-half centuries after the Crucifixion. So the primary textual bases for Judaism and Christianity were slow in assuming the form which we would recognize today.[188] A number of issues played out during the time between the two canonization processes. Two particularly important events took place in close chronological proximity to each other. In the Edict of Milan, in 313, the Roman Emperor Constantine eliminated faith-based persecution throughout the Empire and in effect legalized Christianity for the first time (more about this issue below). Hardly more than a decade later, in 325, a council of several hundred of the leading Christian Bishops across the Roman world met at Nicaea, on the northwestern coast of Turkey, to discuss and debate key principles that define Christian belief.

For the purposes of our discussion, the most important issue pertained to the nature of Jesus as the Christ (*mashiah*; anointed one), concerning whom there were two perspectives vying for supremacy. The North African Bishop Arius and his followers asserted that the eternal and unchanging Father was, by definition, separate from and superior to the Son (and Holy Spirit), since the Son was born, grew up and died—in other words, was not eternal and was mutable. Athanasius of Byzantium and his Bishop,

---

[185]As a practical matter, when the two offspring of Judaeanism began to compete for new adherents from the pagan world, it would also make Christianity more attractive to some (no need to suffer the discomfort of cutting off one's foreskin) and Judaism more attractive to others (the "cool" factor of this identifying mark, somewhat analogous to but perhaps more unique than body-piercings and tattoos in our own era).

[186]Judah the Prince is said to have organized the Mishnah in 212 CE, into 6 orders, subdivided into 63 tractates.

[187]There will be more to discuss regarding this last issue in the following chapters.

[188] Aside from differences of understanding between the two communities regarding what ultimately constitute the biblical books; and differences in interpreting the books they share in common, there also emerged two different senses of how to order the books they share in common, so the canons differ not only in terms of inclusion-exclusion, but in terms of organization.

Alexander, challenged that perspective, asserting on the contrary that Father, Son and Holy Spirit were paradoxically indistinguishable from each other, even as they could be distinguished. They were, he explained, of the same substance—*homoio-ousia*, as he observed in Greek—and therefore the proper Christian understanding of God is that It is *triune*: three and one simultaneously. In our terms, what is an illogical paradox for *profanus* thinking is perfectly reasonable in *sacer* thinking.

Constantine threw his considerable political weight behind the Athanasian view, which prevailed—and thus by ca 325 ca, about three hundred years after the Crucifixion, Jesus as *mashiah/khristos* was embraced in Christian thought as fully human and fully divine—not half and half, (which view would constitute a heresy) but fully both.[189] About 55 years later, under the Emperor Theodosius, Christianity—triune Christianity—became the official religion of the Empire. Interestingly, however, the problem of heretics—of those who misbelieve from within the faith, (as opposed to infidels, who are altogether outside the faith)—did not disappear so quickly. Within Italy itself, the very heartland of the Church, the Ostrogothic king Theodoric, who ruled from his capital in Ravenna, was an Arian Christian. During his reign (ca 495-526) Orthodox (Trinitarian) and Arian Christians flourished side-by side; after his death, with the advent of conquest by the Eastern Roman (Byzantine) Emperor Justinian over the following decades, Arianism was wiped out, officially at least. It still prevailed, however, in Visigothic Spain until 587, when King Reccared I embraced a triune understanding of God.

The implications of the Arian and other heretical beliefs and the complications that they engendered for the early Church over the centuries would have implications for the relations between Christianity and Judaism, as we shall see. But meanwhile, fifteen years or so after Christianity became the official religion of the empire, to repeat, its Bible achieved canonization. Even that process, as it turns out, would not be absolute, as history would later play out. On the one hand, the Protestant Reformation of the sixteenth century would lead to a rejection of certain books retained in both the Catholic and the Orthodox traditions. On the other, some books rejected by all three of these denominations are part of the Ethiopic canon.

Thus works like the book of Judith, which recounted the saving of Jerusalem back in 701 BCE, and that of the Wisdom of Ben Sira', and others—including the story of the successful Maccabean Revolt against the Seleucids that ended up recorded primarily in the Books of Maccabees—were among the books deemed apocryphal by both Jews and Protestants, but deuterocanonical or intertestamental by Catholics and Orthodox Christians. As a practical matter, the First Book of Maccabees places most of its emphasis on how the skills of the Maccabees, in particular Judah, accounted for the victory against

---

[189] We need to distinguish three terms the boundaries among which we shall often see blurred in the last part of the period that we are discussing. "Heresy" refers to improper beliefs on the part of someone who professes to be within the circle of believers who use the authority of their numbers to declare the beliefs of such an individual (or group) improper and thus heretical. (Thus the Trinitarian mainstream will declare Arian Christians heretical). If the group of heretics is large enough that they cannot be simply crushed by the mainstream—so that, in effect there emerge *two* mainstreams of more or less equal flow, then the proper term is "schism." (This will, for example, separate the so-called Western and Eastern Churches, in 1054.) Both of these terms need to be distinguished from "infidel"—referring to a non-believer (literally: "faithless") who is outside the circle of belief altogether. Thus pagans and later Muslims will be labeled as infidels by the Church—and Judaism will occupy a strange, spiritual no-man's land, neither infidels nor heretics but clearly not Christians.

the Seleucids; the Second Book of Maccabees places more emphasis on the miraculous divine role.[190]

Ultimately the issue of the canon is still more complicated. For there are actually four Books of Maccabees. The third and fourth end up outside the canon of all three primary Jewish and Christian Bibles. There are other books, such as three different versions of Enoch, that, together with the last two versions of Maccabees, ended up outside of nearly every canon and are commonly called pseudepigrapha—"false after-writings." But some of these, such as the first version of Enoch, *is* part of the Ethiopic/Eritrean Christian Bible. Thus the very idea of "Bible" proves to be more complicated than one might suppose, and the process of shaping different versions of the Bible took centuries, as Judaism and Christianity were in the process of taking the forms that we would recognize and that would separate them from each other with some clarity—at least theoretically.

Within what takes shape as the Christian Bible, the last book, following the Gospels, Acts and Epistles, offers us some particularly interesting interpretive possibilities with regard to the ideological shaping of the post-Qumran world of Judaea. For the Book of Revelation, on the one hand, follows a general pattern visible both in some places in the Hebrew Bible/Old Testament and in a number of deuterocanonical and pseudepigraphal works: it offers a vision of the end of time as we know it—the "End of Days." It also offers an interpretive gloss on at least two very important passages in the Hebrew Bible—that in Genesis 2 and 3 where the serpent engages Adam and Eve; and that in Job 1, where the Satan ("adversary," "opposer") engages God and therefore Job. But in its description of a final cosmic battle, it offers a distinct reminiscence of the Qumran "Battle Scroll"—and in turn, of the Zoroastrian account of that same sort of battle between the forces loyal to Ahura Mazda and those serving Ahriman.

The full title of the book is "The Revelation of John," for it is presented as a report by the Evangelist of the vision he experienced on Patmos.[191] The report is intended to go out to the "seven gatherings/congregations" (i.e., nascent Christian—or more properly put, given the time period, nascent "Judaeans for Jesus"—gatherings/congregations).[192] The bringer of the message from the *sacer*—an angelic being—was flanked by seven lamps and held in his hand seven stars. "The seven stars are the angels of the seven churches, and the seven lamps are the seven churches (1:20)"—to each of whom the writer is instructed to send a particular message (chapters 2 and 3). In chapter 4, a vision of a heavenly throne

---

[190] There were various reasons why books like First and Second Maccabees could not and did not go into the Jewish canon—even if Maccabees told a story that one might very well wish to have included. The most obvious reason is that the time frame for Maccabees (ca 175-140 BCE for the two texts) was too late: by definition, books that recounted events that took place centuries after Ezra could not be considered canonical.

[191] In fact, the title in Greek (which may be the original language of the text, although it is possible that the original language was Aramaic, and that the Greek represents the first translation of the original version) is "The Apocalypse of John." The term "apocalypse"—"out of [that which is] hidden/buried"—comes to refer to texts that assert that their content—a vision of the end of time as we know it—derives from the hiddenmost recesses of the *sacer*, not commonly available even to *sacerdotes*. In the Hebrew Bible, this would apply most obviously to lengthy parts of Ezekiel and Daniel (and much more limited parts of Isaiah).

[192] These are listed in 1:11 as Ephesus, Smyrna, Pergamon, Thyatira, Sardis, Philadelphia, and Laodikea. The term *ekklesia*, which I have rendered as "gathering/congregation" is often rendered as "church"—but the connotations of that term as it is typically used in association with the more fully formed phase of Christian history would make it anachronistic in this context.

is revealed, presumably the Divine Throne, surrounded by 24 other thrones upon which 24 elders in white robes sit and, most extraordinarily,

> In the center, around the throne itself, were four living creatures, covered with eyes, in front and behind. The first creature was like a lion, the second like an ox, the third had a human face, the fourth was like an eagle in flight. The four living creatures, each of them with six wings, had eyes all over, inside and out; and by day and night, without a pause they sang "Holy, holy, holy is God the sovereign Lord of all, who was, and is, and is to come!"

What we may recognize in this vision is an adapted synthesis of elements from Ezekiel 1—the four creatures and wheels made of eyes—and those in Isaiah 6: seraphim with six wings intoning, "Holy, holy, holy, the Lord of Hosts, the whole earth is filled with His glory!" Not surprisingly, then, the framework of the vision is consistent with ideas, particularly those in apocalyptic contexts, found in the mainstream Israelite-Judaean tradition. The text quickly moves along a path parallel to but different from that tradition. For the throne offers a lamb with the marks of slaughter on it, and "[h]e had seven horns and seven eyes (5:6)" and it took from the one seated on the throne a scroll with seven seals."

"Then I watched as the Lamb broke the first of the seven seals; and I heard one of the four living creatures say in a voice like thunder, 'Come!' And there before my eyes was a white horse, and its rider held a bow" (6:1-2). Each of the first four seals, as it was broken, yielded a horse of a different color (the white followed by red, black and pale). Each has a different rider and a different imprimatur: to conquer, to cause men to slaughter each other, to weigh with scales, and—for the rider of the last horse was "named death, and Hades came close behind"[193]—to that last "was given power over a quarter of the earth, with the right to kill by sword and by famine, pestilence and wild beasts" (6:8). We might recognize the play between numbers like seven and four. The Qumran "Battle Scroll," as we have seen, refers to four archangels, whereas the idea of seven archangels appear in Enoch 20:1.[194]

The fifth and sixth seals—but not the seventh—are opened with similarly negative outcomes and then the author sees "four angels stationed at the four corners of the earth, holding back the four winds..." (7:1) and a fifth angel, rising out of the east, warns the others not to do any damage to sea or land or tree until we have set the seal of our God on the foreheads of his servants" (7:3). He/we are then told the number of individuals, in their thousands, from each of the twelve tribes of Israel who have received the seal. Given the culmination of this passage with reference to a vast throng shouting together "Victory to our God who sits on the throne, and to the Lamb!" it is reasonable to suppose that this crowd is being prepared for battle.

---

[193] "Hades" is the Greek word, so its connotation as the realm of death and in a specifically negative sense—the realm of the dead who are deprived of all good things—has been apparently carried over from the pagan Greco-Roman tradition.

[194] The seven are, in order of mention, Uriel, Raphael, Raguel, Michael, Saraqael, Gabriel and Remiel.

Chapter 8 begins with the opening of the seventh seal and in fact a battle ensues in which the powers of darkness are defeated by the powers of light. The latter are led by "seven angels that held the seven trumpets and prepared to blow them. The first blew his trumpet; and there came hail and fire mingled with blood, and this was hurled upon the earth. A third of the earth was burnt, a third of the trees were burnt, all the green grass was burnt" (8:7). If it is arguable that there is a relationship between the Qumran "Battle Scroll" and the Book of Revelation, then one of the obvious differences is that, whereas in the former, each of the trumpets mentioned, like each of the banners, is distinguished by an inscription, in the latter the distinction is articulated in terms of physical outcome.

Thus the second trumpet is blown and what appears to be a great blazing mountain is hurled into the sea; a third of the sea turned to blood, a third of the living creatures in it died and a third of the ships on it foundered. With the blowing of the third trumpet, a great star, called "The Wormwood" fell from heaven, on a third of the rivers and upon the springs of water, making the water bitter (i.e., poisonous) (8:10-11); and with the blowing of the fourth, a third of the sun, moon and stars were stricken so that a third of both day and night was made dark (8:12).[195] And—once again marking a distinction and connection between four and seven elements—a tiny pause occurs in the description of the trumpet blasts, during which John tells us that

> I looked, and I heard a solitary eagle flying in mid-heaven, shrieking loudly, "woe, woe, woe unto those who dwell upon the earth because of the rest of the blasts of the trumpets of the three angels who are about to blow" (8:13).

With the blowing of the fifth trumpet, an extensive description of the first woe ensues, marked by an abyss from which dark smoke belches forth and those men lacking God's seal on their foreheads are tortured for five months (9:1-12). This is followed by the sixth trumpet blast, that brings with it the second woe—the unleashing of four angels bound by the Euphrates River who slaughter a third of humankind (9:13-21). Again a brief "interlude," as "I saw another mighty angel descending from heaven, enveloped in a cloud with the rainbow around his head, and his countenance was like the sun and his feet were like pillars of fire," (10:1) and he held a small scroll in his hand which he instructed the author to swallow—which presumably gave him the wherewithal to "prophesy again to the peoples and nations and tongues and many kings" (10:11).

> And I was told, "Rise and measure the sanctuary of God and the altar and its worshippers. But do not measure the outer court, exclude that, for it is given over to the Gentiles, and they will trample the holy city for 42 months. And I will allow my two witnesses, dressed in sackcloth, to prophesy for one thousand two hundred and sixty days" (11:1-3)

---

[195] The Greek for "Wormwood" is *apsinthos*. (See the unhealthy, addictive drink, absinth, which was known to be popular among artists in Paris in the early twentieth century.) Interestingly, the Hebrew equivalent word, *la'anah*, when it appears in Amos 6:12, connotes perversion of justice; when it appears in Deut 29:17-18 it implies bitterness as in the bitter fruits of idolatry. So the implication here would seem to be that this star is the star of the "New Babylon" which has poisoned the waters of its own life through its idolatrous behavior.

The extensive destructive imagery that follows culminates with a great earthquake which marks the end of the second woe (when 7,000 people perished) and the sounding of the seventh trumpet announcing the imminent arrival of the third woe. The loud praising of the Lord is heard from within the heavens, God's power, wrath and judgment proclaimed by the 24 enthroned elders (11:19).

Chapters 12 through 15 describe a series of spiritual figures. The faithful are symbolized by "a woman [appearing in heaven] clothed with the sun, and the moon under her feet, and on her head a crown of twelve stars" (12:1)—the number of stars recalling the number of Jacob's sons and of the Israelite tribes as well as of the Greco-Roman zodiacal constellations. They flee into the desert, "for there she has a place prepared by God, that she might be nourished for one thousand two hundred and sixty days" (12:6), while a great war is being fought in heaven, with

> Michael and the angels fighting with the dragon. And the dragon and his angels fought, and he did not prevail, neither was there found a place anymore for him in heaven. And the great dragon, the ancient serpent, who is called "Devil" and "The Satan," who deceives the whole world, was cast out onto the earth, and his angels were cast out with him. And I heard a loud voice in heaven, saying "Now is the salvation and the power and the kingship of our God and the authority of His Anointed... (12:7-11).

Here we find an explicit connection being made between the image of the serpent that is found in Genesis and represented there as enticing Eve and Adam to disobey God's command regarding that particular fruit—thereby introducing evil into the world, by both Christian and Jewish interpretation—and the figure who appears in the beginning of Job as an opposer, adversary, questioner of God's logic when God rhetorically praises Job's goodness, i.e., his proper behavior toward God.[196] We must also keep in mind that the Greek *angelos*, translated as "angel" simply means a messenger, without either inherent heavenly or positive/negative nuances. Only by way of St Jerome's later translation into Latin (the Vulgate) who creates the Latin term *angelus* to refer to a divinely-sent sacerdotal messenger—and through Jerome the use of that word in other languages, including English—do we get the positive, heaven-connected connotation with which we are familiar. Thus the Satan's *angeloi* are his messengers, his acolytes, his army.

---

[196] The Greek words *drakon* (dragon) and *sphis* (serpent) are functionally interchangeable as symbols of the *sacer* in its chaotic potential. Apollo established order and his own shrine at Delphi by defeating a gigantic serpent/dragon referred to as *Pytho* (hence, "python" in English, referring to a gigantic snake) that had been ravaging the area. What perhaps distinguishes the *drakon* from the *sphis* is that the former has four appendages and the latter has none—and in Genesis, the punishment of the serpent in Gen 3:14, that "on your belly you shall crawl" has been interpreted particularly in the Christian tradition to suggest that prior to the Fall that creature possessed appendages as we humans do. So if that creature is the Satan, he may also be both a dragon and a serpent—particularly when we recognize that we are dealing with *sacer* time and *sacer* space in this apocalyptic passage, in which the sort of *profanus* linear progression that might give as a "before" and "after" for the serpent's condition need not apply.

Nor is the battle over with the casting of the Satan out of heaven. On the contrary, earth provides him with a perfect setting in which to find many more supporters. Thus, in chapter 13, his allies—personified first and foremost by a monster ascending out of the sea with ten horns and seven heads, and next by a monster ascending from the land—seek to delude the faithful and turn them in the direction of evil (we would call it *druj* in Avestan). The earth-born monster "deceives the earth-dwellers through the signs that he is allowed [by the sea monster] to perform..." and "he tells the earth-dwellers to make an image for the monster..." (13:14). One might wonder to what extent the notion of fashioning an image of/for a false leader is intended to recall the fashioning of the golden calf—an image of/for a false god—by the Israelites as they waited in increasing fear for the absent Moses to return from the peak of Sinai.

The opposite sort of vision occupies the next chapter, which offers Mount Zion and on it "the lamb and with him... a hundred and forty-four thousand who had his name and the name of his Father written on their foreheads" (14:1). John sees an angel, "flying in mid-heaven, with an eternal gospel to proclaim to those on earth..." and a second angel, announcing the fall of Babylon, and then a third, warning that those who worship the beast and its image "shall drink the wine of God's wrath, poured undiluted into the cup of his vengeance.[197] He shall be tortured in sulfurous fumes before the holy angels and before the Lamb" (14:9-10). John hears a voice from heaven instructing him to write the words "happy are the dead who die in the death of the Christ..." (14:13) and he sees the image of "one like the Son of Man" sitting on a white cloud. A fourth angel comes forth from the heavenly temple, proclaiming "to him who sat on the cloud" to stretch out his sickle and reap (which he did) and a fifth angel followed by a sixth, the latter instructing the former to reap the grapes with *his* sickle.

John then saw seven angels with seven plagues. They poured out seven golden bowls "full of the wrath of God" (15:7): foul malignant sores (16:2), the sea turned to blood, killing everything within it (16:3), the rivers and springs turned to blood (16:4), the sun transformed so that it burned men fearfully (16:8-9), the world turned to darkness (16:10), the great Euphrates River dried up (16:12), and "then I saw coming from the mouth of the dragon, the mouth of the beast, and the mouth of the false prophets, three foul spirits like frogs. These spirits were devils, with power to work miracles" (16:13-14). The location of the final battle is famously indicated—Armageddon—and then the seventh angel pours out his bowl on the air, and, with flashes of lightning and peals of thunder and a violent earthquake, its power unprecedented, "the great city was split in three; the cities of the world fell in ruin...[as] huge hailstones...fell on men from the sky" (16:16-21).

What is most important for our purposes is the passage in 17:9-14 that follows, beginning with a gloss explaining that the seven heads of the beast are seven hills on which "the great whore" sits, and the ten horns ten kings who "will wage war upon the Lamb, but the Lamb will defeat them, for he is Lord of lords and King of kings."[198] More angels and their proclaiming voices follow, and "the roar of a vast throng in heaven, and they were shouting: 'Alleluia! Victory and glory and power belong to our God'...and the 24 elders

---

[197] The Greek word translated here as "gospel" is *euangelion* (*evangelion*), meaning literally "good message."
[198] This description of the beast, with seven heads and ten horns is referred to above, quoting from 13:1.

and 4 living creatures fell down and worshipped God as He sat on the throne..." as a cosmic "marriage" is planned for the Lamb and his bride.[199]

But the battle *after* the battle ensues before this event may take place. For out of heaven, "before me was a white horse, and its rider's name was Faithful and True—for he is just in judgment and just in war" (19:11). And, so, too, "[t]hen I saw the beast and the kings of the earth and their armies mustered to do battle with the rider and His army. The beast was taken prisoner and so was the false prophet... The two of them were thrown alive into the lake of fire... the rest were killed by the sword that went out of the Rider's mouth" (19:19-21).

The text is like the last parts of a Beethoven symphony (forgive the simile): one thinks one has reached the end of the story and yet there is more. For

> [t]hen I saw an angel coming down from heaven with the key of the abyss on a great chain in his hands. He seized the dragon, that serpent of old, the Devil or Satan, and chained him up for a thousand years; he threw him into the abyss, shutting and sealing it over him... (20:1-3).

But the battle is *still* not over, for he is only bound for a thousand years. There were thrones and a judgment before which streamed martyrs ("who had been beheaded for God's word and their testimony to Jesus"; 20:4) who came to life again—reminiscent of the vision of the dead being reclothed in flesh in Ezekiel 37—and "reigned with Christ for a thousand years... This is the first resurrection" (20:4-6). But the Satan is let loose again after the thousand-year respite from his moral depradations, "and he will come out to seduce the nations in the four quarters of the earth and to muster them for battle" (20:8).

Again, though—and this time, definitively, "fire came down from heaven and consumed them; and the Devil, their seducer, was flung into the lake of fire and sulfur, where the beast and the false prophet had been flung, there to be tormented day and night forever" (20:10). And then at last "I saw a new heaven and a new earth...[and] new Jerusalem" (21:1) that is described in the passages that follow, and marks a reality in which "there shall be an end to death, and to mourning and crying and pain" (21:4). The angel of instruction and description "said to me, 'These words are trustworthy and true'" (22:6)— a threefold affirmation that what John has seen is not some illusion or dream. For "[i]t is I, John, who heard and saw these things" (22:8) that culminate with the message, delivered three times: "behold, I am coming quickly" (22:7, 12, 20).

One might see The Book of Revelation as not only offering elements that synthesize the Qumran "Battle Scroll" material with elements from Hebrew Biblical apocalyptic—as well as pseudepigraphic apocalyptic literature—but also synthesizing and expanding the details of these elements with more detailed expressions of sensibilities found in the Zoroastrian texts and traditions. Thus the vision of who survives the apocalypse is much broader than that found in the Qumran material—reflecting the growing Christian interest in enticing everybody onto the correct path, where the Qumran community is a small, essentially elitist, subset of the Judaean community—but narrower

---

[199] *Alleluia* is simply a Greekified form of the Hebrew word, *Halleluiah*, (actually two words: *Hallelu Yah*), meaning "Let us/them praise God."

than what Zoroastrianism offers: in both the "Battle Scroll" and Revelation the evil one and his minions ultimately perish, where in Zoroastrianism they are defeated but ultimately drawn into the light of Ahura Mazda.

The text has added its own elements that are found in none of these prior bodies of cataclysmic apocalyptic expression, of course, reflecting both the specific association of the Satan with the serpent of Genesis and the general tenor of emerging Christian thought. The paradox of a powerful evil force that, with more than a small amount of success, opposes a God that is both all-good and all-powerful—but is ultimately defeated—is both Christological and, ultimately, as we have seen, Zoroastrian. The notion that evil's very existence is a function of human choice and specifically, the choice to follow the lead of the Satan, is also both Christological and Zoroastrian in conception. Sandwiched between these two religious perspectives and arguably creating the bridge between them is the Qumran material, (and not only its "Battle Scroll"). The harsh conclusion of the latter, in contrast to the far more benign outcome found in the Zoroastrian final battle ideology, would seem to have been transmitted to Christianity and its vision of the final battle's ultimate outcome.

Along the way, there are resonances of the importance of certain numbers—particularly the number seven—within all three. While the number seven has a long history of *sacer* significance within the Middle East and Eastern Mediterranean—and even within the non-apocalyptic portions of the Hebrew Bible itself, beginning with the creation cycle in Genesis and continuing with the Fourth Commandment to keep the seventh day holy—the repeated and almost obsessive emphasis upon it within both the Qumran text and the Book of Revelation places them together in their own territory with respect to both numbers and *that* number.

Where certain numbers are connected in their power to God's word in the Battle Scroll they are associated with the Lamb as a symbol of God—and, one might presume, associated with Jesus as the incarnation of God, although this last issue is not clear, since the divinity of Jesus is not definitive for Christianity until 325 CE, as we have seen, so it would depend, in part, upon how we date Revelation. We might also recall to mind issues in other Qumran texts that seem to connect directly to Christianity, most obviously the notion of baptism and the transformation of a communal meal (such as would have been taking place one way or another in the general Judaean—i.e., Judaean by religion—community every spring at the Passover season) into a "Banquet" associated with the messiah. If these were ideas developed at Qumran (and its sibling communities, if they existed) and carried forward into Christianity, they were also *transformed* as they were carried forward: *adapted* and not simply *adopted*.

If on the one hand, the Qumran material offers a question as to where and when and why, precisely, the sect (and its possible siblings elsewhere in the *sacer* wildernesses of Greater Judaea) originated—which we can answer up to a point through Maccabees, Philo and Josephus—on the other hand, we might ask whether the community was simply destroyed with its monastery during the first Judaean Revolt against the Romans or continued elsewhere and/or otherwise. Part of the answer to this second question might be that members—some or all?—of the surviving Qumran/Essene community emerged as or among the Judaeans for Jesus, broadening their vision of who might be included in the

New Covenant and the Community of the Elect and bringing with them their vision of the immanent apocalypse of the world as we know it.

There is also a second possibility that involves a non-mainstream part of the Jewish world that emerges out of obscurity to historiographic observation many centuries later. The Karaite movement, characterized by its recognition of the Bible alone as its legal and spiritual authority and by a rejection of the rabbinic interpretive discussions contained in the Talmud (see below, 302-3), limits itself to the most straightforward interpretations as the ancient Israelites, they assert, would have understood them. Two issues are of particular interest to us in their story. One is that, depending upon time and place, the Karaites have either been viewed as "Karaite Jews" or simply as Karaites—as if they are a religion separate from Judaism, as the Samaritans are and as, of course, the Christians came to be, eventually. This will offer a definitional problematic cognate with that which we shall encounter regarding infidels, heretics and Jews, as we shall see (below, chapters 12 and 13).

Two: where and when did they emerge and why? According to the Spanish Rabbi Avraham Ben David (1110-80) in his *Sepher HaKabbalah* (*Book of Tradition*) the Karaites first crystallized as a group in Baghdad in the eighth-ninth centuries, during the early Abbasid period. Mainstream Western Jewish scholars accept this view. Some Jewish Arab scholars, however, assert that the Karaites were already living in Egypt in the first half of the seventh century. This is where the majority were found in the modern era up until the founding of the State of Israel, and the early claim is based on a legal document that was in the possession of the Cairo Karaite Jewish community until the end of the nineteenth century, according to which the first Muslim governor, 'Amr Ibn al-'As, ordered the leaders of the Rabbinite (i.e., rabbinically-led, mainstream Jewish) community to desist from interfering with Karaite practices and holiday celebration rituals. The document was said to have been stamped by the governor's palm and dated to 20 AH (641 CE), which would be less than a decade after Muhammad's death.

In any case the further question is where the Karaites came from, either geographically or spiritually/conceptually. It has not been uncommon to see them as originated, like most early medieval Jews and Jewish communities, in Judaea, and it has not been uncommon to suggest that they and their ideology evolved from the defunct Sadducean community made functionally extinct by the hegemonic Pharisaic leadership well before the time of Jesus. If so, they must have remained sufficiently in touch with that mainstream to be aware of the canon of the entire Hebrew Bible long after the Torah was finalized. I would suggest the possibility, rather, that they might have derived from the Qumran community; that instead of simply melting into the desert at the time of the failed First Revolt, they migrated as a small, purist community—and Egypt would make at least as much sense, in that case, as Mesopotamia would, where they would, in fact, have been able to continue their Jewish lives in functional separation from the rabbinic world evolving in Judaea/Palestine and Mesopotamia—somewhat as the still more distant Ethiopian Jewish community would. (Egypt is where, at the time of the destruction of the First Temple, Judaeans fled for refuge, Jeremiah among them, according to one tradition, as we may recall). But I am merely speculating.

Not that these two possibilities for Qumranian continuation—as early Christians and as Karaites—are necessarily mutually exclusive. After all, Judaeanism yielded both Judaism and Christianity, so in theory, at least, Qumran Judaeanism could have contributed both to emerging Christianity and to a later sect or branch of Judaism. Meanwhile, in the course of the time period during which mainstream Judaism and Christianity are taking shape as twin progeny out of the common parent that is the Hebrew-Israelite-Judaean tradition—defined in part by their respective senses of biblical canon and of God—they were not only contending with each other in the theological sense, each believing of itself that it was following the only proper path of relationship with God. They were also jockeying for acceptance by the pagan Roman authorities.

The Romans made a distinction between the *religio licita* status—that, as we have observed above, was accorded by Pompey the Great to Judaeanism in 63 BCE—and that of being considered a *superstitio*. The latter term had the connotation of political subversion. In fact, whereas the term becomes the English-language term, "superstition" with its implications of addressing (usually fearfully) the wrong and/or negative and/or non-existent aspect of the *sacer*, it is best translated into English as "subversion" in the ancient pagan Roman context.[200]

Generally speaking, the Romans, who attributed their success to serving and therefore being the favorites of *all* the gods, were extremely open-minded regarding religious perspectives: they were in fact omnivores of modes of addressing the divine *sacer*. The reason for this was simple in a twofold, practical way. If one embraces dozens of gods and goddesses, then a few more or less are not likely to upset the powers of the *sacer*. And on the other hand, having studied their Greek literature well, and seen the consequences of ignoring any god or goddess, they recognized it as far better to embrace all possible deities—even those that are weak or even potentially non-existent—than to eschew one that exists and possesses some power.[201]

Thus the only circumstance in which a religion would be pronounced a *superstitio* was if it were to be considered politically subversive. The *religio licita* status of Judaeanism continued under the Roman authorities after Pompey's death, from Julius Caesar and subsequently Marc Antony to Octavian both before and after he became Augustus Caesar and to his successors on the imperial throne. Somewhere between the time of Nero (r. 54-68 CE) and Hadrian (r. 118-138), as we have seen, the bifurcation of Judaeanism into Judaism and Christianity became clear both to Judaeans becoming Jews and Christians and to the pagan Roman authorities.

As such, the question apparently arose: which of the two groups was inherently entitled to the *religio licita* status that had been accorded to their common spiritual ancestor, particularly when both parties in question claimed to be the true, legitimate heir to that spiritual heritage—or in Latin terms, *verus Israel* ("true Israel")? We might recall

---

[200] Thus Theophrastos' "Superstitious Man" would not be labeled using the term *superstitio*, were that little work to have been translated into Latin, since he is characterized not by politically subversive features but by those pertaining to obsession with the negative potential of the *sacer*, as we have seen.

[201] They were certainly familiar, for example, with Euripides' *Hippolytos*, in which the individual of that name adores Artemis, bringing to her prayers and offerings galore, but ignores Aphrodite. The outcome (to be brief) is that Aphrodite in her anger sets in motion deeds that lead to the death of Hippolytos and his young step -mother, Phaedra, and deep grief for his father, the hero Theseos, left to mourn both of them.

that the definition of "Judaean" had become increasingly problematic during the Second Temple period. As we have noted, it could refer to one's ethnicity—as a descendant of the tribe of Judah, or perhaps of Benjamin or even of another of the former Israelite tribes, but in any case, the bloodline connecting one to one's "Judaeanism"—wherever one happened to reside. It could refer to one's spirituality: as a worshipper of the God of Israel, whose primary sacerdotal site was the Temple in Jerusalem—but one's ethnicity might be otherwise: thus one might be an Idumean or an Ituraean or a Nabataean (and we have noted how the Idumaeans and Ituraeans were all but force-converted to Judaeanism at the end of the second pre-Christian century). It could refer to one's nationality: as a pagan altogether, but dwelling in, say, Straton's Tower—later known as Caesarea—a coastal Judaean town, or elsewhere within Greater Judaea, so that one's national identity would be Judaean but neither one's religion nor one's ethnicity would be.

This issue of correctly defining the term "Judaean" would have implications for the emerging pair of post-Judaean contenders for *religio licita* status. Initially the implications carry from complication to simplicity, and later, as we shall see, back to further complication. Thus the pagan Roman authorities certainly had little or no idea of the theological and ideological matters that were gradually separating what became Christians and Jews from each other. As late as in writings of the historians Tacitus (ca 115-117 CE) and Suetonius (ca 120-1 CE), it is clear that these two pagan authorities are not aware of an operable theological distinction between what were, during their time only beginning to be called "Jews" and "Christians."

When Suetonius mentions the expulsion of *iudaei* from Rome in the late 40s CE, during the reign of Claudius (r. 41-54) in chapter 25 of his biography of the emperor, "because the *iudaei* at Rome caused continuous disturbances at the instigation of Chrestus," those expelled were almost certainly "Judaeans for Jesus." For Judaeans, per se, could not be expelled—by Roman law, since they had been resident in Trastevere since the 160s BCE (the Hasmonaean/"Maccabaean" period)—but a recently arrived group could be. One might imagine that such a group of Judaeans did arrive into Trastevere, and perhaps its leader, according to normative custom, was invited to preach during the Sabbath service, and began to speak about Jesus, which is why and when a ruckus broke out that spread into larger-scaled rioting, and thus to the expulsion of those among the rioters who could be legally expelled (and whose leaders had been preaching about Jesus as the *mashiah/khristos*).

Tacitus (in *Annales* XV. 44) notes that, under Nero, in 64 CE, to "stifle the report [that he himself had set fire to Rome], Nero put in his place as culprits… the persons whom the common people hated for their *flagitia* [outrageous/disgraceful acts]. They called them *Christiani*. Christus, from whom the name was given, had been put to death in the reign of Tiberius [14-37 CE] by the Procurator Pontius Pilate [26-36 CE] and the pestilent *superstitio* was quelled for a while." Suetonius, in his own biography of Nero, 16, refers to "the *Christiani*, a kind of men given to a new and criminal *superstitio*, [who] were put to death with grievous torments."

Note that the term *superstitio* is used by both writers to refer to criminal—vaguely criminal—and/or secret acts. Note that Suetonius, in writing about the Claudian expulsion, refers to the group that was expelled as *iudaei*—but he does not or cannot identify the more specific ethnic or religious nature of that group as "Judaean for Jesus," aka "proto-Christian" or "Judaean not for Jesus," aka "proto-Jewish"—although translators typically—and mistakenly—render *iudaei* simply as "Jews."[202]

Moreover, Suetonius refers to the instigator of the riots as a rebel leader whose name is treated as if it is a proper Latin noun: *Chrestus.* He misunderstands that word to be a name, which he has heard in a Latin version of its proper Greek form—and understands this so-called Chrestus to have been a contemporary of events that took place 15 years or so after the crucifixion. On the other hand, in his biography of Nero he uses the word "*Christiani*", but apparently makes no connection between that group and the figure he mentions in his biography of Claudius. Meanwhile, Tacitus has "better" information on Christ—although he, too, refers to him as if "Christus" is his proper name—to wit that he had been executed 30 years before the Nero fire incident. So clearly not only the term *iudaeus* (and its plural form) but also the terms *Christus/Chrestus* (and *Christiani*) are still not clear to pagans by the time these two writers are hard at work narrating the previous century's events.[203]

But the pagan Roman authorities could look at the linguistic situation and a level of potential confusion beyond that pertaining to the definition of "Judaean" would have simplified their decision as to which group should continue to be treated as a *religio*. For in all the languages in use in that part of their world—most relevantly, Aramaic, Hebrew, Latin and Greek—there was/is no distinction between "Judaean" and "Jew/ish."[204] So it would be obvious to them that (what we call) Judaism was a straightforward, direct continuation of Judaeanism, and Christianity, by its very utterly other name, was something altogether new. Accordingly, at the outset of the bifurcation into clarity, Judaism continued to enjoy the *religio licita* status that Judaeanism had possessed. The question is why Christianity, one among myriad belief systems—from the worship of the traditional Olympians to various versions of mother goddess worship, from Hellenized Egyptian forms of religion to Zoroastrianism and one of its own putative offshoots, Mithraism—was not simply accepted alongside the others (including Judaism), as a *religio licita*.

Unlike virtually every other form of *religio* across the empire, Judaism and Christianity posited not only that the divine *sacer* is singular, but that there is only one correct covenantal way of addressing and accessing It: "ours." Other forms of faith are at least mistaken and at most dangerous in being mistaken, since they can lead a community away from God's favor and toward God's disfavor. We can see in the Gospels how the charge of *superstitio*—which would mean that Jesus and those who follow him are

---

[202] See fnn #205, 206 to clarify this point.

[203] Interestingly, had Suetonius referred, in his Claudius biography, to Jesus, rather than to Chrestus, we might possibly speculate that there was a leader of the proto-Christians by that name who was not the same as the one crucified nearly 15 years earlier, since "Jesus" is merely a rendering of the not uncommon Hebrew name, *Yehoshua* (Joshua). But as we have seen, *khristos* is a common noun (once it has eventuated as a noun) and when it comes to be treated as a name, it is applied to only one individual.

[204] Thus *Yehoodae* in Aramaic, *Yehoodi* in Hebrew, , in Latin and *Ioudaios* in Greek are all translatable as both "Judaean" and "Jew/ish"—there is no way to distinguish which of these English-language terms is meant when it appears in one of these languages. For instance, when Josephus recounts his *History of the Ioudaioi*, I have consistently rendered it as *History of the Judaeans*, rather than *History of the Jews* (which is its more common and, I believe, anachronistic rendering), given the "pre-Jewish" time period that is his focus. Similarly, I believe that the typical rendering of *iudaei* in Tacitus as "Jews" is wrong—and importantly misleading in the context of our narrative.

politically subversive—is implicitly rebutted by words ascribed to Jesus such as "render unto Caesar that which is Caesar's and unto God that which is God's" (Matt 22:21). In the last Gospel, that associated with John, and in subsequent passages in some of the Epistles, an accusatory tone regarding the death of Jesus is directed toward the Jews—which is to say, fellow *Ioudaioi/Iudaei*/Judaeans "not for Jesus" (and not the Romans).[205]

So we might in the first place suppose that the sort of rioting referred to in Tacitus was—and/or became more frequent, as time went on—between the two increasingly divergent versions of Judaeanism. In that case, one could speculate that only one, rather than both sides of the conflict would come to be viewed through Roman pagan lenses as subversive and trouble-making. And perhaps the push to have nascent Christianity treated as a *superstitio* because it was viewed as leading its followers away from a proper understanding of God might have come from their main competitor (with regard to Judaean *religio licita* status) before the Roman authorities: the Judaeans-not-for-Jesus. From their perspective the danger was not political but spiritual: Judaeans-for-Jesus might be viewed by them as potentially angering God (just as the Judaeans-for-Jesus might believe that the Judaeans-not-for-Jesus were angering God).

If the Romans accepted Judaeanism-not-for-Jesus as a *religio*, as it was becoming Judaism, and hearkened to its leaders, and if its leaders argued that Judaeanism-for-Jesus, as it was becoming Christianity, was not only not proper "post-Judaeanism" but politically subversive, then the Roman authorities could well have pronounced Christianity a *superstitio*. We have absolutely no textual evidence of this, however it is difficult to find a logical reason otherwise for Christianity's early status.[206]

On the other hand, this hypothesis may be anachronistic, precisely because the conceptual distinctions between Judaism and Christianity are awhile in coming, so if the Jews are the cause of Christianity's *superstitio* status, perhaps that was not the case early on. And as we shall observe shortly, that early status seems in fact to have been largely inconsequential, anyway. Christianity seems for the most part to have been simply ignored. There was little active persecution of Christians, so it may even not have been considered a *superstitio* until later—by the third century, under the emperors Septimius Severus

---

[205] Again the problem of language should not be ignored: at the time of the Crucifixion, the term *Ioudaioi/Iudaei* would have meant "Judaeans" and not "Jews" but already by the time John's Gospel is being written down (ca 90-105 CE) the group against which the text's anger may be understood to be directed is at least the "Judaeans not for Jesus" and perhaps, by then, those we might recognize as the Jews. The Romans may not yet be able to distinguish between the two groups, but Judaeans are probably starting to be able to do so among themselves, at least for the most part.

[206] Moreover, at least once Judaism is both fully formulated and an at-risk, scattered minority (by the late fourth century, as we shall note later), it possesses neither a solid concept of hell nor of eternal damnation, as we have observed. Its visions of the end of time lead far more in the direction of Zoroastrian-style thinking—with its concept of Ahura Mazda as supreme, with a vision according to which those who don't worship Ahura Mazda will eventually come to do so, and in which even the ultimate demon, Ahriman, is not so virulently demonized that he needs to be destroyed—than what is recorded for Christianity in the Book of Revelation and develops all the way to Dante's *Inferno* in the early fourteenth century. So Judaism—at least by a certain point—would not be haunted, as Christianity becomes, by a sense that those who don't accord with its sense of the *sacer* and its understanding of how to address the *sacer* are doomed. But that still doesn't necessarily mean that Jewish leaders would not try to present their Christian competitors to the Roman pagan authorities in as negative a light as possible.

(briefly, in 305), Maximinus Thrax (r. 235-8), Decius (r. 249-51) and Diocletian (r. 284-305), which is when (as we shall see) its adherents experience serious attacks.[207]

As for Judaism, it will encounter a serious bump along the *religio licita* road during the last part of the reign of Hadrian. For in the aftermath of the failed second revolt against Roman authority, in 132-35—led by a literal and metaphorical giant of a warrior named Simon Ben Kotziba, whose followers called him Bar Kokhba (an Aramaic nickname meaning "Son of the Star") and saw him as a *mashiah/khristos*—Hadrian recognized a clear relationship between Judaean-Jewish (as opposed to Judaean-Christian) religious beliefs and their nationalist hopes and aspirations. He therefore proscribed the practice of Judaism.[208]

This meant, in practical terms, that Jews were forbidden to celebrate the Sabbath and the Jewish festivals, circumcise their eight-day-old sons or follow their own gastronomic paths, both generally and during particular festivals, such as Passover. They were also forbidden to enter Jerusalem—whereas Christians were not, which makes it clear that by this time the Roman authorities could distinguish Judaism from Christianity, at least up to a point. Jerusalem was in fact renamed Aelia Capitolina, and on the site of the long-destroyed Temple, a temple to Jupiter Capitolinus was built. Moreover, Hadrian renamed Judaea "Syria Palestina," adapting and Latinizing the name "Philistina" that was derived from "Philistia," (referring to a relatively small area on the western fringe of Judaea—today the area is called Gaza) and applying it to an area that ceased to exist officially, as far as its name-based identity was concerned.

I think it unlikely that Hadrian was, per se, anti-Jewish—anymore than Titus had been. But just as Titus was completing the task begun under Nero by his (Titus') father, Vespasian, of suppressing the political insurrection in Judaea (which led to the destruction of the Temple as a function of unintended consequences/collateral damage, however significant those consequences are for our narrative), Hadrian was interested in ending political insurrections from Judaea once and for all. He very astutely recognized the interplay between religious and political sensibilities in that province and tried to suppress the second by eliminating the first, as a purely administrative matter, not as an ideological issue.

---

[207] Marcus Aurelius came to be popularly thought to have persecuted the Christians, but on the contrary, his writings show his admiration for them.

[208] There had in fact been a serious series of disturbances involving *Iudaei/Ioudaioi*—rioting back and forth between them and the pagan Greek communities in Cyprus and in Cyrene in North Africa, toward the end of Trajan's reign, in 115-117. Some therefore speak of the Bar Kokhba revolt as the third and not the second insurrection by Judaeans against Roman authority. On the one hand, however, the Cyrene/Cyprus disturbances were not, per se, rebellions against Roman authority. On the other hand, it may well be that key figures in those disturbances migrated back to Judaea and helped stir things up until they exploded in 132. As for Bar Kokhba, no less a religious leader than Rabbi Akiba—arguably the most highly regarded spiritual figure among the Judaeans at that time (who was martyred by the Romans during the Bar Kokhba Revolt)—considered Ben Kotziba as messianic, which means that at least some Judaean Jews understood that term in political-military terms at that time, rather than in the purely spiritual terms that it would eventually acquire for/in Christianity. (The Gospels are at pains, on the contrary, to present Jesus' ambitions as entirely spiritual and not at all political, as is clear in other places besides Matt 22:21—most obviously in the words ascribed to Jesus in the Garden of Gethsemane at the time of his apprehension by the authorities: "Put away your sword, Peter; those who live by the sword die by the sword," quoted in Matt 26:52).

Moreover, after his death a few years later, his adopted son and successor, Antoninus Pius (r. 138-161) rescinded the anti-Jewish legislation, and the *religio licita* status of Judaism was restored. For the next few centuries, Judaism and Christianity, as they developed their respective biblical canons and specific concepts of God, together with their customs and traditions in the matter of weekly and annual celebrations and life-cycle issues—would contend with each other within and against the still prevailing pagan polytheism that defined the Empire. And that Empire continued to worry about *superstitiones* of diverse sorts that it found problematic to the socio-cultural, religious and political functioning of the *profanus* in its ongoing relationship with the powerful *sacer*—with its potentially positive or negative inclinations toward the *profanus*.

It is against the backdrop of that larger political and, above all, spiritual picture that Judaism and Christianity are taking the shapes that will become familiar to us, as we shall observe in more detail in the chapters that follow.

CHAPTER SIX

Words, Concepts, Conflicts and Sacerdotal
Competition in the Roman World

As Judaism and Christianity were developing on parallel tracks, and contending with each other regarding which version of the post-Judaean tradition has developed the proper relationship with the divine *sacer*, they were also both contending with the far-flung pagan traditions throughout the Roman world—and as a practical matter, to repeat, competing with each other for acceptance by the authorities administering that world. On the one hand, then, we must remind ourselves of the configuration of that administration and its implications for that competition, and on the other hand consider particular issues that had emerged for that world vis-à-vis the *sacer*.

There are three matters of particular relevance to our discussion that pertain to the position of Judaeans and their successors, Christians and Jews, in the Roman world, and there are several interesting Roman documents that offer an insight into how the pagan Roman world continued or diverged from the Greek understanding of the *sacer* in its legitimate and illegitimate, more powerful and less powerful, and positive and negative senses.

Thus to begin with, after the death of Herod the Great in 4 BCE the Romans eliminated the autonomy that Judaea had enjoyed under their Idumaean/Judaean king. Herod had in part facilitated this—from the grave, one might say. Since, in his increasing paranoia during his last years, he engaged in a spree of assassinations directed at family members who might have potentially risen up against and supplanted him as supreme leader, he also all but eliminated those who might have been most viable as his successor(s). From the Roman perspective, two problems had emerged. Whereas during most of his reign Herod had been a very effective ruler, military strategist and sponsor of major architectural and engineering projects, as we have briefly noted—and therefore presented Judaea to the Romans as a well-managed state, solid, stable, and strong enough to serve as a substantial buffer against would-be transgressors into Roman territory from the non-descript lands to the south and east of that corner of the empire—during the last years of his reign it seemed clear that he was losing control of his country to the point that internal unrest was rampant and external pressures mounting.

And in part thanks to his assassinationist policies, upon his death—he orchestrated his own grand state funeral, supplied with paid official mourners along a parade route that

135

led from Jerusalem to Herodium, his burial site—there was nobody whom the Romans felt that they could trust to be the sort of effective ruler that Herod had been for most of his reign. So they stepped in and established a procuratorial form of government for Judaea, whereby a Roman governor—procurator—would effectively administer the state that was now configured as a sub-province of the larger Roman province of Syria. The procurator would answer to the Syrian governor and to the senate (and emperor) at Rome.[209] His term of office was three years.

When Augustus died in 14 CE and was succeeded by his unhappy step-son, Tiberius, the new Emperor changed the procuratorial structure. Now the one assigned to Judaea could serve for life, unless he was spectacularly corrupt and the case against him was brought to and successfully argued before the Roman senate. What this change meant in practical terms was this: a procurator under Augustus who was particularly nasty and/or disliked by the Judaeans would be gone in a few years; whereas under Tiberius one might expect to be burdened with him for a very long time. On the other hand, all things being equal, a procurator serving for a long time might be expected to be more reasonable in his demands from the people, whereas one who would have three years to serve and squeeze a province might be far harsher and crueler as he sought to extract everything of value or use from the people in that brief period of time.

Pontius Pilate, probably the best known Roman procurator (prefect) in history, thanks to the Gospels, served under Tiberius beginning around 26 CE and seems to have left off serving a decade later, a few months before Tiberius' death, having been recalled for suppressing a Samaritan revolt with excessive harshness. He is said to have arrived back to Rome between Tiberius' death in March, 37 and the accession of the Emperor's nephew, Caligula.[210] What little information we have from primarily Judaeo-Roman and secondarily Roman sources suggests that he was among the nastier and crueler of the prefects and procurators who governed Judaea over time.[211]

---

[209] Technically speaking, in fact, it appears that the original status of Judaea's governor was as a prefect, a lower rank than that of a procurator, and that the province's administration was not elevated to that of a procuratorship until 44, during the reign of the Emperor Claudius. So although I will follow the convention of referring to Pontius Pilate, below, as a procurator, he would have been merely a prefect.

[210] Josephus writes of this in *Antiquities* 18.4.2. Aside from the Gospels, Josephus and Philo are our main sources for knowledge of Pilate. Tacitus mentions him briefly (see the following note) and there is an inscription, known as the Pilate Stone, which is only important in that it offers an apparent archaeological confirmation of his existence. A piece of limestone (currently in the Israel Museum, Jerusalem), it offers part of an inscription presenting Pilate as the dedicator of a public building constructed to honor the Emperor Tiberius and his wife, in Caesarea (Caesarea Maritima) which was in effect the political capital of Judaea while Pilate was its prefect. Pilate seems mainly to have divided his time between Caesarea and Jerusalem, the spiritual capital of the province.

[211] Strictly speaking, the only purely Roman historiographic source that even mentions Pontius Pilate is Tacitus, in his *Annales* (ca 115 CE). To repeat: in 15.44, in the context of discussing the famous fire that burned substantial parts of Rome during Nero's emperorship (54-68 CE; the fire broke out in 64 CE) for which the Emperor accused "a class hated for their outrageous/disgraceful acts, called Christians by the common people." Tacitus notes, as we have seen, that "Christus, from whom the name had its origin, suffered the extreme penalty [i.e., death by crucifixion] during the reign of Tiberius, at the hands of one of our procurators, Pontius Pilate..." So he neither offers the Gospel version of that event in which Pilate is exonerated of guilt nor criticizes Pilate's behavior, personality or style of administration. Interestingly for our discussion, Tacitus continues by referring to the Christians as subject to a "most mischievous *superstitio* [that was] thus checked for the moment [by Jesus' death]." So, too, it is noteworthy that he uses "Christ" as a proper name—as if this is the name of some politically subversive Judaean leader—and in fact, seems to have referred to him as *Chrestus* and his followers as *Chrestiani*; it was likely a later Christian monk at the Benedictine Abbey of Monte Cassino, where the oldest manuscript of Tacitus' work, dating from the 11th century, is found, who altered the spelling (as x-rays have shown). This

Indeed, whereas in all four Gospel accounts, Pilate is represented as trying to avoid responsibility for the death of Jesus, one way or another, Philo and Josephus both report that he repeatedly caused near-insurrections among the Judaeans because of his disregard for their customs—and in effect his ignorance of what their *religio licita* status permitted them—as well as his means of responding to their objections to that disregard.[212] Philo in particular claims that Pilate possessed "vindictiveness and a furious temper," and that he was "naturally inflexible, a blend of self-will and relentlessness." He writes that Pilate feared a delegation that the Judaeans might try to send to Tiberius because "if they actually sent an embassy they would also expose the rest of his conduct as prefect by stating in full the briberies, insults, robberies, outrages and wanton injuries, as well as the executions without trial constantly repeated, and the [acts of] ceaseless and supremely grievous cruelty."[213]

Pilate's term as prefect of Judaea ended, according to Josephus, after an incident involving not the Judaeans, but the Samaritans. A large group of them was persuaded to go

---

suggests that Tacitus had no clear understanding of who the Christians were relative to other Judaeans, much less who Jesus was—i.e., that he had heard the word "Christ," and took it, in a Latinized form, to be a proper name. [212] In Matthew 27:24, Pilate washes his hands to show that he is not responsible for the execution of Jesus and only reluctantly sends him to his death. The Gospel of Mark (15:2 -14), in representing Jesus as innocent of political sedition against the Roman state, also depicts Pilate as reluctant to execute Jesus. In Luke 23:2-22, Pilate not only asserts that Jesus has not conspired against Rome, but he receives concurrence from Herod Antipas— Herod the Great's great-Grandson and the Tetrarch of Galilee (one of the subdivisions of Greater Judaea into which the province had eventually been carved up by the Roman administration) —who also finds nothing treasonable in Jesus' actions, although Herod does mock Jesus. In the Gospel According to John, Pilate states "I find no guilt in him [Jesus]" (18:38) and he asks the Judaeans if Jesus should be released from custody. Their response in the negative shifts the blame clearly onto their shoulders from the perspective of the text.

Josephus asserts that while Pilate's predecessors had respected Judaean convictions by removing all images and effigies on their standards when entering Jerusalem, he permitted his military retinue, when it first arrived, to bring them into the city at night. When the citizens of Jerusalem discovered these the following morning, they appealed to Pilate to remove the ensigns—"graven images"—of the Emperor from the city. After five days of deliberation, Pilate had his soldiers surround the demonstrators, threatening them with death; they kneeled and exposed their necks, willing to accept death rather than submit to desecration of what they construed as part of the Second Commandment. Pilate did finally remove the images on this occasion (*Wars* 2.9.2-3).

In the following passage, however, Josephus recounts another occasion in which Pilate "raised another disturbance" by spending money from the sacred Temple funds to build an aqueduct (presumably the well-known one near Caesarea). This time, when Judaeans again protested his actions, Pilate had soldiers hidden in the crowd of Judaeans while addressing them. He followed his words of response with a signal in responding to which his soldiers randomly attacked, beat, and killed scores of Judaeans in order to silence their petition (*Wars* 2.9.4).

Philo recounts an incident similar to and somewhat later than the first described by Josephus, in which Pilate was chastened by Emperor Tiberius himself after the prefect antagonized the Judaeans by setting up gold-coated shields in his newly constructed palace in Jerusalem. The shields were ostensibly to honor Tiberius, and this time apparently did not contain engraved images but were nonetheless deemed offensive by at least some— a critical mass of—Judaeans. Philo writes that the shields were set up "not so much to honor Tiberius as to annoy the multitude." The Judaeans protested the installation of the shields at first to Pilate, and then, when he declined to remove them, by writing to Tiberius. Philo reports that upon reading the letters, Tiberius "wrote to Pilate with a host of reproaches and rebukes for his audacious violation of precedent and bade him at once take down the shields and have them transferred from the capital to Caesarea" (*On The Embassy of Gaius* Book XXXVIII, 299– 305). One might wonder how real the possibility is that the Emperor, all but ignoring affairs in Rome as he cavorted in Capri, would have paid such close attention to such a moment in Judaea. On the other hand, it is possible that Tiberius, disengaged as he was in other respects, retained a sense of propriety for what he could have construed as *mos maiorum*—the always-to-be-respected "customs of our ancestors." And in any case, Philo was an adult contemporary of these events, so he is not merely reporting something from an earlier era that he heard about from others.

[213] Philo, *On the Embassy of Gaius* Book XXXVIII, 299–305. The context of this concern was that of the Judaean protest regarding the gold-coated shields. (See previous note).

to Mount Gerizim (which they regard as the sacred center chosen by God through Joshua, rather than Jerusalem as favored by the Judaeans) in order to see sacred artifacts alleged—by a man Josephus does not name, but labels a liar—to have been once buried there by Moses himself. But at a village named Tirathana, before the crowd could ascend the mountain, Pilate sent in "a detachment of cavalry and heavy-armed infantry, who in an encounter with those who first arrived into the village, killed some of them in a pitched battle and put the others to flight. Many prisoners were taken, of whom Pilate put to death the principal leaders and those who were most influential" (*Antiquities* 18.4.1). The Samaritans then complained to Vitellius, Roman governor of Syria, who sent Pilate to Rome to explain his actions regarding this incident to Tiberius. However, by the time Pilate got to Rome, Tiberius had died, and Caligula did not send Pilate back to Judaea (*Antiquities* 18.4.2). At this point he all but disappears from history.[214]

So the development of the procuratorship in general and the procuratorship (prefectorship) of Pontius Pilate in particular is the first issue of significance in our attempt to articulate the Roman relationship with Judaeanism as the latter is on the edge of bifurcating into Judaism and Christianity. The Christian view will take shape as one in which he is innocent of Christ's death as are the Romans in general, the blame for his demise being pinned on the Judaeans (the "Judaeans not for Jesus")—who will later be mistakenly understood to be, simply, Jews. The Roman and particularly the Judaeo-Roman view is different, and there is no reference to him at all in the primary Jewish—i.e., rabbinic—sources.[215]

The different perspectives may be understood in terms of the increasingly acrimonious relationship between the two groups as they were becoming increasingly distinct from each other—and on the Christian side, at least, may also be understood in terms of the need to shift the Roman view of Christianity away from being thought of as a *superstitio* to being thought of as a *religio licita*. Thus if, as most scholars agree, the canonical Gospels were written down between the 70s and as late as 110, or so[216]—and if these achieve a canonical place in Christian textuality by the 180s (whereas other so-called Gospels, such as those associated with Thomas and James as well, perhaps, as texts associated with Mary Magdalene and even Judas, were excluded from the canon) along the road to the complete biblical canon of 395—then they were being written down precisely

---

[214] There is a series of later traditions and legends regarding his death and burial, but these all carry beyond the needs of our discussion.

[215] Josephus, in *Antiquities* 18.3.3, in referring to Jesus as "a wise man... a doer of wonderful works, a teacher of such men as receive the truth with pleasure" asserts that "Pilate, at the suggestion of the principal men among us, had [him] condemned to the cross... and the tribe of Christians, so named from him, are not extinct at this day." So his view specifically of Pilate vis-à-vis the death of Jesus is neither exculpatory nor accusatory—and he sees the Christians (in a line just a bit before these) as a group made up of "many of the Judaeans and many of the Gentiles" who continued to follow Jesus' teachings after his death. Compare this perspective with that of Tacitus a generation or so later. (see fn #211)

[216] Mark is understood to have been the first, followed by Matthew and Luke, who share a common vision with each other and with Mark, hence these three are commonly termed synoptic, from Greek *syn* (meaning "with") and *ops* (meaning "eye" and, by extension, "vision"). The last of the four Gospels to have been written down is understood to be John, and it carries the narrative in a series of new and different directions from the other three—from its very beginning ("In the beginning was the word and the word became flesh...") to its strongly excoriatory tone vis-à-vis the Judaeans-not-for-Jesus. Regarding the issue of when the Gospels were written down, see fn #326.

at the time when Judaism and Christianity were becoming distinct from each other and ultimately hostile to each other. Under such conditions, one would not be surprised to see both a presentation of Jesus in the Gospels that emphasizes his non-political intentions and, more to the current point, a presentation of the Romans and even of the procurator who ordered the Crucifixion as benign. Judeao-Roman and Roman sources would not be confronted with a need to depict events and Pilate's personality so positively.

This leads to the second issue that pertains to the position of Judaeans and their successors, Christians and Jews, in the Roman world: the wide range of forms of spirituality rampant across the Roman world to which I alluded toward the end of the previous chapter—some of which may or may not have had an influence on the shaping of one or the other tradition and/or affecting their relationship with each other. This range would only expand as the nominal Roman Republic moved ever more emphatically toward being an Empire between the time of Pompey (d.58 BCE) and the senatorial decree honoring Octavian by referring to him as Augustus Caesar (27 BCE).

Tacitus, as we have noted, would later write briefly about the persecution of *Christiani* at the time of Nero; and Josephus, a generation before Tacitus, would write about Pontius Pilate's unhappy relationship with both the Judaeans and the Samaritans. But Josephus would also write briefly about the Egyptian cult of Isis that arrived into Rome during the reign of Augustus Caesar. Immediately after mentioning Jesus, Pilate and the Christians, he pauses in his discussion of things Judaean to tell of an outrage that occurred in the Temple of Isis, the consequence of which was that its priests were crucified at the order of the outraged successor of Augustus, the Emperor Tiberius (r. 14-37 CE). Moreover, the Temple of Isis in Rome was demolished and the statue of the goddess was thrown into the Tiber River.[217]

What is important for our purposes is that a cult born in Egypt had found its way to Rome, as had—or would, over the long history of the Republic/Empire—many others. Moreover, the following might be noted regarding the cult of Isis: that, by the Hellenistic period, at least, she was not simply known as the wife of Osiris. Her role is essential in the narrative of the cosmic battle between Osiris and his evil half-brother, Seth, in which Osiris is either (depending on the particular thread in this tapestry of *mythos*) torn apart by Seth or drowned by him in the Nile River. An essential aspect of the Osiris-Isis *mythos* came to focus on the story of her endless, timeless time spent seeking the pieces of her spouse (or bringing up his body from the bottom of the river) and restoring him to life (he is, after all, a god). He is "reborn" as Horus. So Horus is both the son of Osiris and Osiris himself. As the god is both father and son, the woman who births him—but not through the usual method—is both his mother and his spouse. This ought to have a familiar Christological ring.

Other religious traditions also found their way to Rome from elsewhere. Prominent among these was that of Dionysios/Bakkhos, whose cult—previously thought to have originated in Anatolia (Turkey) or elsewhere east of Greece—can now be traced back at least as far as the Mykenaean period within the mid-late Bronze Age Aegean (ca

---

[217] The account pertains, in brief, to the bribed cooperation of the priests in facilitating the rape of a virtuous married woman; the rape occurred in the inner precinct of the temple, by a man (he who bribed the priests) masquerading as the incarnation of the god Anubis. See *Antiquities* 18.3.4.

2000-1200 BCE).[218] The first large-scale worship of Dionysios in what would become Greece seems to have begun in Thebes about 1500 BC. Dionysios was associated with Osiris by the Roman period, according to Plutarch (ca 46-120/127 CE); his Mysteries and those of Osiris/Isis/Horus were parallel. The rites associated with Dionysios were based on a seasonal death-rebirth theme common among agricultural cults (also endemic to the Osiris/Horus *mythos*), and also on spirit possession. So, too, he was identified with the god Aion and referred to as "Zeus Sabazios" in other related traditions.[219]

The Dionysian focus on wine was part of a broader interest in both the grapevine and its wild, barren alter-ego, the toxic ivy plant (thought to counteract drunkenness—thus the opposite of the grapevine—and seen as blooming in winter instead of summer). The fig was also a symbol of the god. Further, the pine cone that tipped his thyrsus linked him to Kybele, a mother goddess whose cult *did* originate in Anatolia. The bull (from whose horn wine was drunk) and goat (whose flesh provided wineskins, and whose gastronomic browsing pruned the vines) were also part of the cult, eventually seen as manifestations of Dionysios.

The early Theban rituals were probably similar to rites still held on Greek islands such as Keos and Tenedos in the Classical period. In Bronze-Age Thebes the first wine was offered to Dionysios and the now-growing vine; a bull was sacrificed with a double axe, (its very visual form, with upturned edges, suggesting the horns of a bull), and its blood mixed with the wine. There are indications that at one time the sacrificer of the sacred bull was himself then stoned to death, although this became a merely symbolic act quite early (and may always have been). The more economical practice of goat (rather than bull) sacrifice was later added to the rites. The goat (like the bull) was, to repeat, regarded as a manifestation of Dionysios. However, it was also seen as the "killer of the vine" by eating it—welcome in times of pruning, less so in times of growth. The death of the goat could thus be interpreted as a combined sacrifice of Dionysios (the goat) and of the officiant (killer of the goat). The animal was usually torn apart, as the vine had been at harvest, and its flesh, like the wine derived from the grapes, consumed by the celebrants. They thus took the god into their bodies; the god fed his constituents with his own flesh—a custom and an idea with another familiar Christological ring.

The sacred loci of the Dionysian Mysteries varied over time and place, as the rituals themselves did. The earliest rites took place in the wilderness—in the *sacer*: forests, marshes and high mountains (where perhaps, too, the low oxygen content was suitable for trance induction). In classical times temples were built for Dionysios, the earliest being circular buildings open to the sky, and later no different from any other Greek temple, as

---

[218] The name of the god is found on Mykenaean-era so-called Linear B tablets—"Linear B" refers to a proto-Greek syllabic (as opposed to alphabetic) writing system that disappeared at the end of the Bronze Age—as "DI-WO-NI-SO-JO."

[219] Plutarch (35, 364E) asserts that "Osiris is identical with Dionysios." When the Roman leader, Marc Antony, became involved with the last Ptolemy—Egyptian queen, Cleopatra VII—she saw to it that he was revered by Greek Egyptians as Dionysios and by native Egyptians as Osiris, the 'king of kings' (*nswt nswjw*). The discussion of his association with Aion, who represents the ongoing circle of time—and who was born of a virgin at the time of the winter solstice (offering yet another resonance toward Christianity)—is taken up in fact by early Christian writers. (See W.K.C. Guthrie, *A History of Greek Philosophy* (Cambridge: University of Cambridge Press, 1979), 478). His association with Zeus Sabazios (who is also his father) is referenced in Robert Graves in his *The Greek Myths*, (Baltimore, MD: Penguin Books, 1955), Vol 1, 27.7,9.

Dionysios/Bakkhos became assimilated into mainstream Greek religion. The *lenos* (the building that housed the wine press) also became a temple to the god. Underground chambers were often used for initiations, which may have originally taken place in natural caves (particularly those by the shoreline: boundary zones, such as a shoreline inherently is, were particularly sacred to Dionysios).

As the rite of Dionysios manifested itself in Greece, it intensified its concern with the totality of the grapevine's cultivation and life cycle (understood to embody the living god) and the fermentation of wine from its dismembered body (associated with the god's essence in the underworld). Wine was also poured out at the spot from which the growing vines emerge from beneath the earth—from the underworld—completing the cycle. Most importantly, however, the intoxicating and disinhibiting effects of wine on the acolyte were regarded as due to possession by the god's spirit (and, later, as *facilitating* this possession).

Spirit possession involved liberation from civilization's rules and constraints. It celebrated that which was outside everyday society and a return to the source of being— and would later assume mystical overtones. Although the Dionysian rites were associated with women, the cult officers' titles were of both genders—belying the oft-made claim that the cult was solely for women.

Spiritual possession was also channeled into dramatic masked rituals within the Bakkhic *thiasos*—the parading of the god's retinue—sowing the seeds of acting and what eventuated as classical tragic and comic theater.[220] Public Dionysian festivals were timed to coincide with the "clearing of the wine" (a final stage in the fermentation process), which occurred during the first cold snap after the winter solstice, when Dionysios was said to be reborn. This was later formalized to January 6, a day on which Dionysios changed water into wine. The celebration echoed those associated with the grape harvest and its ritual processions from the vineyards to the wine press that had occurred earlier, in the autumn. It was at these times that initiations into the Mysteries were probably held.

The Dionysian Mysteries of mainland Greece (and, later, the Roman Empire) not only made use of intoxicants but of trance-inducing techniques (such as music and wild, unstructured dance) to remove inhibitions and social constraints, liberating the individual to return to a natural state. In a condition of *ekstasis* (meaning "outside [*ek*] one's usual state of being") or *enthusiasmos* (meaning "having within [*en*] one's spirit [*thumos*] the spirit of the god") they abandoned themselves to wild movements and shouts of "*Euoi!*" (one of the god's names) and at that moment of intense rapture became identified with the god. The trances are described in familiar (to us) anthropological terms, with characteristic movements (such as the backward head flick typically found in trance-inducing cults). Rhythms are also found preserved in Greek prose and poetry referring to the Dionysian rites (such as in Euripides' *The Bacchae*).

Particularly in their early form, these rituals offered liberation for those marginalized by Greek society: women, slaves and foreigners—in each of which groups individuals were normally oppressed and repressed in everyday life. Festivals were orgies with every kind of drunkenness and every aberration of sex, the one leading up to the

---

[220] The first is derived from the Greek "goat (*tragos*)-ode/song (*oide*)" and the second from the Greek "revel/carousal (*komos*)-ode/song (*oide*)." We may recognize in the first the implied spirit and presence of the god himself and in the second the wild carryings on associated with the god.

other—or at least this was assumed to be the case by outsiders. For over all there apparently reigned the Phallus, which—in its symbolism in a flaccid state—represented *post ejaculationem* the death-state of Bakkhos, the god of pleasure, and his resurrection when it was in *forma arrecta*. Thus fundamental themes of sorrow and joy undergird these Mysteries.

Many Greek rulers considered the cult a threat to civilized society and wished to control it (if not suppress it altogether).[221] Suppression failed; control succeeded with the development of a domesticated Dionysianism as a state religion in Athens. This was but one form of Dionysianism—a cult which assumed different forms in different localities (often absorbing indigenous divinities and their rites, as did the god himself). The Greek followers of Dionysios claimed that, like wine, he had a different flavor in different regions; so, too, he appeared under different names and manifestations in different regions.[222] As Dionysios came to be revered at Delphi, for instance, he presided over the oracle for three winter months beginning in November (marked by the rising of the Pleiades) while Apollo was away "visiting the Hyperboreans." At this time a rite known as the Dance of the Fiery Stars was performed—about which we retain knowledge of very few details.[223]

The phallus appears to have been not only prominent later on, in the Bacchic carnival in Rome (carried by the *Phallophoroi*—"phallus-bearers"—at the head of the procession), but it also appears to have been the secret object in the *liknon* (the sacred, winnowing-fan-shaped basket, revealed only after final initiation). Other possible contents would have been sacred fruit, leaves or loaves—all representing the flesh of the god. Some

---

[221] See fn #227 regarding Euripides' *Bacchae*; Pentheus exemplifies this emphatically—and catastrophically.

[222] In the syncretistic Greco-Roman world, where, as we have noted, gods or goddesses from diverse national or ethnic origins could and often did end up with their cults and their adherents synthesized to each other, Dionysios was not only eventually equated in Rome with Bakkhos but with Liber ("the free one"; he was also known as *Liber Pater*—"free father"). Liber was a god of fertility, wine, and growth. His festival was the Liberalia, usually celebrated on March 17, although in some circles, March 5. Across Greece, *Eleutherios* ("the liberator") was an epithet used for both Dionysios and Eros, from which we might infer that their cults were sometimes synthesized. There is a certain logic to this, for in Samos and Lesbos he was referred to by the epithet *Enorches* ("with balls" or perhaps "in the testicles"), in his role as the god of fertility. (Some have theorized that this refers to Zeus having sewn the newborn babe Dionysios into his thigh, i.e., his testicles, when the king of gods snatched him from the ashes of his mortal mother, who was incinerated by the full glory of Zeus that she had asked to see). The epithet *Liknites* ("he of the winnowing fan") also refers to him as a fertility god, connected with the mystery religions. Even Augustine, in *City of God* 6.9, credits Dionysios with being responsible for sexual relief, saying that he "liberates" men from semen during intercourse.

Along with syncretistic relations with other divine figures, he was, like many gods and goddesses, typically referred to by different names reflecting different aspects of his power and action and/or in accordance with traditions of particular locales. Thus he was widely referred to by his epithet, Bromios—"thunderer" or "he of the loud shout"—and somewhat less far-flung, as Dendrites—"he of the trees"—in which guise he was also understood to be a powerful fertility god. Dithyrambos (from the ceremonial songs called "dithyrambs") was the name that referred to him or to solemn songs sung to him at festivals; the name technically refers to his premature birth. As Lyaeus ("he who unties") he was seen as a god of relaxation and freedom from worry, and as Oeneus he is the god of the wine press. Similarly, he was sometimes called Akratophoros, identifying him as the giver of unmixed wine. He was worshipped in Arcadia as Phigaleia; and in Sicyon he was worshipped as Akroreites. In Rome, as Bakkhos, he carried the Latin epithet Adoneus: "Ruler"—interestingly, the word comes from the Hebrew *Adon*, meaning "Lord," rendered as a Greek epithet, *Adoneos*, and then Latinized. At Potniae, in Boeotia, he was worshipped as Aegobolus ("goat killer"), and at Aroe and Patrae in Achaea, as Aesymnetes ("ruler" or "lord").

[223] It may, however, have been devoted to the dead and may have continued, much later on, in Christian countries, as All Souls Day, on November 2.

sources suggest that the phallus was made from fig wood, while even older sources indicate it may have once been the phallus of the sacrificed goat.[224] The contents probably changed over the centuries. We must keep in mind, incidentally, that the focus on the phallus is ultimately part of a broader, millennia-long focus of religion on fertility: it is a function of the importance of religion with respect to human survival and of fertility to the same end, since if we and/or our animals and fields are not fertile, we die out.

It is not clear whether a hierarchy of priests was in charge of the Dionysian Mysteries. The Orphic texts of the late period record a *boukolos* (or "cowherd") as an offerer of sacrifice, reciter of prayers, and hymn singer, who seems to have been the equivalent of a priest. Other inscriptions record an *archiboukolos* ("chief cowherd") presiding over the *boukoloi*; in some records there is also mention of *boukoloi hieroi* ("holy cowherders") as well as *hymnodidaskaloi* ("hymn teachers"). According to Athenian sources, when the cult of Dionysios was state-controlled, a high priest (*hierophant*) and a high priestess (later referred to in Rome as the *matrona*, with two assistant priestesses) were appointed as overseers. One late text describes a complex hierarchy of three *archiboukoloi*, seven *boukoloi hieroi* and eleven *boukoloi*. The names of many senior priests and priestesses reveal them to have been aristocrats, although the high priest in at least one text has the name of a slave (suggesting equality within the cult, or just as likely, an exchange of roles between masters and slaves).

The basic rituals for men involved identifying with the god Dionysios in acting out his life, death and rebirth (including some form of ordeal). This involved a ritualized descent into the underworld—a *katabasis*—often performed in caverns or catacombs, as we have noted above (sometimes, or later, more symbolically, in temples).[225] This process was an original part of the ritual.[226] In contrast, the female initiate was prepared as Ariadne (bride of Dionysios), and united with him in the underworld. After this rite, involving the secret object in the *liknon*, she participated in a similar communion or wedding feast.

---

[224]The carved wooden phallus would be called *prosymnos*, named for a shepherd of that name who lived near the reputedly bottomless Alcyonian Lake, hazardous to swimmers, which lay in the Argolid. One thread in the tapestry of Dionysios *mythoi* asserts that, when the god went down into Hades to rescue his mother, (the mortal Semele, who had been killed by the sight of her lover, Zeus, in all of his glory), Prosymnos guided him to the entrance by rowing him out to the middle of the lake. The reward demanded by Pr osymnos for this service was the right to make love to Dionysios, which the latter promised to allow upon his return from the underworld. However, when Dionysios returned to earth by a different route, he found that Prosymnos had meanwhile died. Dionysios kept his promise by carving a piece of fig wood into the shape of a phallus and using it ritually while seated on the shepherd's tomb.

This story is not told in full by any of the usual sources of Greek narratives, though several of them hint at it. It is reconstructed on the basis of statements by Christian authors; these have to be treated with less than full embrace, since their purpose was to discredit pagan mythology. (See Hyginus, *Astronomy* 2.5; Clement of Alexandria, *Protreptikos* 2.34.2-5; and Arnobius, *Against the Gentiles* 5.28). Annual nocturnal rites took place at the Alcyonian Lake in classical times—interestingly, Pausanias claims that he refuses to describe them. (See Pausanias, *Guide to Greece* 2.37; and also Plutarch, *Isis and Osiris* 35.

[225] A form of this may be reflected in Aristophanes' comedy, *The Frogs* (405 BC). The action of *The Frogs* is driven by the descent of Dionysios into Hades (to bring a first-rate tragic poet back up to Athens, after the deaths of Sophocles and Euripides). He is in part guided by a surreal chorus of amphibious guardians and assisted slightly (but not accompanied) by his half-brother Herakles (another son of Zeus by a mortal woman, who also appears in the iconography of the Dionysian Mysteries).

[226] The initiate in the ritual was then known as a "bakkhos" (which is an alternative name for Dionysios), shown the secret contents of the *liknon* (winnowing-fan-shaped basket) and presented with the *thyrsos* (the sacred, pine cone-tipped wand).

Flagellation also seems to have been a basic ordeal (at least for women, according to depictions of Dionysian initiations, such as that which may be depicted on the walls of the "Villa of the Mysteries" in Pompeii).

By the classical period there were in any case both daytime festivities, as in the Athenian Dionysia, and biennial nocturnal rites that reflected on the death and absence of Dionysios in his aspect of Dionysios *Chthonios*, Lord of the Underworld. The god was "mourned" for a year. During the second year, his resurrection (as Dionysios *Bakkhos*) was celebrated at the *Tristeria* and other festivals (including one marked by the rising of the dog star, Sirius). The *Tristeria* were held on Mount Parnassus in winter. The first day was presided over by the Maenads in their *mainomenos* (madness) condition, during which animals—and, some believe, humans—were hunted, torn apart with bare hands and eaten raw. This was the *Sparagmos*, once associated with the earlier goat sacrifice and marking the harvest (and trampling) of the vine. The second day saw the Bacchic nymphs in their Thyiadic (or raving) state. Although still orgiastic, this was a more sensual and benign bacchanal (assisted by satyrs). Mythographers claim that the Maenads (or wild women) resisted the Bacchic urge and were driven mad, while the Thyiades ("ravers") accepted the Dionysian ecstasy and kept their sanity.[227]

The cults of Gods like Dionysios and Herakles, both of whom had divine parentage on their fathers' side (in both cases, Zeus) and human parentage on their mothers' side, achieved ever-increasing popularity in the Hellenistic period, with its marked growth in sources of alienation: large multi-ethnic, poly-lingual kingdoms with large cities in which people were increasingly cut off from nature and increasingly out of same-language-based sympathy with their own rulers. The need increased for gods that are not so entirely removed from our sufferings and concerns, as the Olympians are.[228] Gods who had a distinct and defined human aspect offered an engaged connection—*pathos*—to humans, rather than the calm, cool, distancing *ethos* exhibited for the most part by the Olympians.

Such gods, furthermore, share a form of our defining attribute: *mortality*—for they die, as we humans all do—while being *immortal* because they *are* gods. In absorbing them into ourselves—most readily by consuming foods that may be construed as their very bodies, and drinking liquids that may be associated with their blood—we become one with them, and are offered an opportunity to achieve a particular kind of immortality. We can, to repeat and to anticipate, recognize a distinct resonance with Christianity in this notion— and realize that, during the period we are discussing, this mode of negotiating the mortal/immortal border is hardly unique to Christianity.

The obsession with the question of how one might achieve immortality was certainly present in earlier cultures such as those in Mesopotamia and Egypt, but it was particularly marked in Greek thought—from epic to tragic poetry and from Socratic thought to that of Zeno the Stoic and Epikouros. That obsession would have found in gods

---

[227] We no doubt see reference to this in Euripides' play, *The Bacchae* (415 BCE), in which, in the end, the mother of Pentheus—the human, royal half-brother of Dionysios, who tries to contain the wildness of the god within legal, civilizational constraints—driven mad by the god, leads her fellow maenads in hunting down and tearing apart her own son.

[228] With regard to Olympian lack of *empathos* ("suffering as one") with humans, consider how, for example, in the *Iliad*, while men are suffering and dying on the battlefield below, the gods, regardless of their affections and antipathies for various Akhaian or Trojan heroes, are frequently shown feasting above, on Mount Olympos.

like Dionysios and Osiris/Horus and their concomitants a kind of solution to the problem of the ironic co-existence within humans of mortality and a thirst for as well as questions regarding immortality. So such cults expanded in the Hellenistic period and their popularity carried into the Roman period.

Introduced into Rome (ca 200 BCE) from the Greek culture of southern Italy or perhaps by way of Greek-influenced Etruria, the Bacchanalia—celebrations of Dionysios/Bakkhos—were held in secret and attended initially by women only, in the grove of Simila, near the Aventine Hill, on March 16 and 17. Subsequently, admission to the rites was extended to men and celebrations took place five times a month. Within the Bacchic Mysteries Dionysios merged with Liber, the local fertility god.[229] Like its Greek counterpart, the Roman Bacchic cult emphasized sexuality, also inventing terrifying ordeals for its Mystery initiation. The notoriety of these festivals, where many kinds of crimes and political conspiracies were supposed by outsiders to be planned, led fairly quickly—in 186 BCE—to a decree by the Senate through which the Bacchanalia were prohibited throughout all of Italy except in certain special cases that required approval by the Senate. This was the *Senatus consultum de Bacchanalibus*, inscribed on a publicly displayed bronze tablet.[230]

Members of the cult were apparently accused of acts of sexual abuse and other criminal activities (including murder). We cannot be certain at all as to whether these charges were true; there may have been individual cases of corruption but there is no evidence of widespread abuse. Scholarly opinion is that these were trumped-up charges leveled against a cult perceived as a danger to the state—a *superstitio*. In spite of the severe punishments inflicted on those found in violation of the senatorial decree, the Bacchanalia were not stamped out, at any rate in the south of Italy, for a long time. The decree only succeeded in pushing the cult underground. There is no evidence of a complex hierarchy in the Bacchic Mysteries of Rome, which seem to have been presided over by a *Domina* and *Dominus* (mistress/priestess and master/priest), so it is possible that only the Athenian form of the Mysteries and the Orphic religion had such a structure.

Much later, the rites gained further notoriety due to claims that the wife of Spartacus (leader of the Slave Revolt of 73 BCE) was an initiate of the Thracian Mysteries of Dionysios and considered her husband an incarnation of Dionysios Liber. The Mysteries were revived in a tamer form under Julius Caesar around 50 BCE, with his ally, Marc Antony, becoming an enthusiastic devotee and gaining popular support for them. They remained in existence (along with their carnival-like Bacchanalian street processions) until at least the time of Saint Augustine (354–428 CE), who mentions them as an issue, and were an institution in most Romanized provinces. In their final phase the Mysteries shifted their emphasis from a chthonic, underworld orientation to a transcendental, mystical one. So, too, some of the aspects of the Bacchanalia seem to have been transferred to the celebration of the Roman Saturnalia.

I have expended so much time and offered so much detail on Dionysios for two reasons. The first is in order for my reader to appreciate how complicated the cult of just

---

[229]See the more extensive discussion of this above, fn. #222.
[230]A tablet with the inscribed decree was discovered in Calabria in 1640.

one god—albeit a very important one—is, both geographically and as it moves through time from the very early Greek (or even pre-Greek) to the late Roman periods. One cannot overstate the spiritual complexity of the world into which Christianity and Judaism will be born out of Israelite-Judaeanism. The second, as we shall soon see in somewhat more detail, pertains to particulars that may be argued to have spilled from this cult into the process of shaping the nascent bifurcating Judaeo-Christian religion—particularly the Christian side of this equation.

There is more. We have earlier encountered the synthesis of Dionysios and Sabazios thanks to Theophrastos.[231] Thus he referred to Sabazios Dionysios as a combination of an originally Phrygian and/or Thracian sky god—who comes to be associated with vegetation in general and then with barley in particular—with Dionysios. As Sabazios, as we previously noted, is associated, by way of barley, with beer and perhaps, therefore, with Dionysios and wine, conversely mead and beer (with its cereal base) were incorporated into the domain of Dionysios.

Now whereas in the Hellenistic Greek pantheon, Dionysios and Sabazios—together with Zeus, as we have also noted—become indistinguishable in terms of their roles and activities but retain separate, albeit linked names; in the Roman pantheon, Sabazius eventually simply becomes one among many names for Bakkhos. The arrival of Sabazius into the Roman world appears to have been mediated in large part through Pergamon, the Anatolian Hellenistic kingdom renowned for both its wealth and its fabulous library, whose last ruler, Attalos II willed the kingdom to the Romans at his death in 133 BCE.[232] The Greek-writing Roman historiographer Diodorus Siculus (90-30 BCE) conflated Sabazios with the secret 'second' Dionysios, born of Zeus and Persephone, a connection that is not borne out by surviving inscriptions, which are entirely devoted to Zeus Sabazios. Still later Roman-period, Greek-language writers, like Strabo in the first century CE, linked Sabazios with Zagreos, among the Phrygian ministers of the sacred rites of Rhea and Dionysios.

The medieval (10th-century) Byzantine Greek encyclopedia known as the *Suda*[233] asserts that "Sabazios... is the same as Dionysios. He acquired this form of address from the rite pertaining to him; for the barbarians call the bacchic cry *sabazein*. Hence some of the Greeks too follow suit and call the cry *sabasmos*; thereby Dionysios [becomes] Sabazios. They also used to call *saboi* those places that had been dedicated to him and to his Bacchantes... Demosthenes [in his speech] 'On Behalf of Ktesiphon' [mentions them]. Some say that 'Saboi' is the term for those who are dedicated to Sabazios, that is to Dionysios, just as those [dedicated] to Bakkhos [are] 'Bakkhoi'. They say that Sabazios and Dionysios are the same. Thus some also say that the Greeks call the 'Bakkhoi'

---

[231] See above, 75-6.

[232] For reasons beyond our discussion, this helped lead Rome toward a century of civil wars that only ended when Octavian finalized his all-powerful rule over the empire and was declared "Augustus" by the Roman senate, in 27 BCE.

[233] The *Suda* is somewhere between a grammatical dictionary and an encyclopedia in the modern sense. It explains the source, derivation, and meaning of names and words in general, according to the philological understanding of the period, using such earlier—and, usually, now-obscure—authorities as Harpocration and Helladios. It is the articles on literary history that are most valuable, since they offer details and quotations from authors whose works are otherwise lost to us today.

'*Saboi*'."[234] From this brief passage we can infer that in a world that has been dominated by Christianity for centuries at the time of this account, there is a good deal of confusion as to what is what and who is who with regard to one of the important pagan cults of late Greco-Roman antiquity. As in so many ways, what would have been perfectly clear to the insider may be entirely obscure to the outsider.

Sabazios was represented, in any case, by the fifth century BCE, on Greek vases, sometimes with the goddess Demeter ("earth-mother") and later depicted on a relief with Demeter and Persephone, as well as with Kybele (another mother goddess). A cult scene pictured on the volute krater made by the Polygnotan Group (Ferrara 2897) represents Sabazios together with Meter, both seated on their thrones, holding scepters (perhaps made of barley) and plates (perhaps filled with barley) and surrounded by their worshippers. In non-Attic regions Sabazios is described as appearing on a horseback.

The cult of Sabazios (similar to that of Kybele or Dionysios) was accompanied by music, particularly by players of double flutes and castanets, and by ecstatic dancers holding small snakes. Thus one of the most important symbols of the cult of Sabazios was a snake, which, in shedding its skin periodically is not only a chthonic symbol but one of rebirth. Another symbol of Sabazios was a crown (with two small snakes raising their heads) worn by the god himself and by some of the members initiated into his cult. Small snakes also encircled the lower arms and/or hands of his worshipers.

In any case, it seems that with the name Sabazios the Greek language acquired words like *saboi, sabasmos, sabazein* that were used in or associated with a ritual context for bacchic crying out. The cult of Sabazius continued to flourish back in Athens during the Roman period, well after it had been introduced into Rome itself and into various, far-flung places throughout the Roman world. Thus for instance there is a representation of Sabazius, with his hands raised and encircled by a snake, in a Gallo-Roman relief on a first-century BCE stele from the cemetery of Arolaunus Vicus—present-day Arlon, Belgium—a significant center between Reims and Trier in the Roman era.

At least some of the important early Christian writers were quite aware of the cult. Clement of Alexandria (150-215 CE)—a convert from Paganism and very well-acquainted with classical sources—wrote about what he had been told regarding the secret mysteries of Sabazius as practiced among the Romans. In referring to how their rites involve a serpent, he comments that, as a chthonic being such a creature is associated with the virtual opposite of the elements central to the original mounted skygod of Phrygia. He asserts that "'God in the bosom' is a countersign of the mysteries of Sabazius to the adepts." Clement further analyzes a detail of the cultic ritual, noting that "this is a snake, passed through the bosom of the initiates."[235]

Perhaps even more interesting with regard to the subject of our own narrative is this: that the first Judaeans who settled in Rome (around 165 BCE, as we have noted above) were said by some Roman sources to have been expelled in 139 BCE, along with Chaldaean (Babylonian) astrologers. For the expulsion was meted out by Cornelius Hispalus, under a

---

[234] *Suda*, under 'Sabazios,' 'saboi'; see also David Sider, "Notes on Two Epigrams of Philodemus," in *The American Journal of Philology*, 103.2 (Summer, 1982:208-213), 209f.
[235] Clement of Alexandria, *Protrepticus (Clement)*, 1. 2. 16.

law that proscribed the propagation of the "corrupting" cult of "Jupiter Sabazius." We find mention of this in the epitome of a lost book of Valerius Maximus, according to which

> Gnaeus Cornelius Hispalus, *praetor peregrinus* in the year of the co-consulate of Marcus Popilius Laenas and Lucius Calpurnius, ordered the astrologers by an edict to leave Rome and Italy within ten days, since by a fallacious interpretation of the stars they perturbed fickle and silly minds, thereby making profit out of their lies. The same praetor compelled *the Judaeans, who attempted to infect the Roman custom with the cult of Jupiter Sabazius, to return to their homes* [italics added].[236]

What is interesting in this passage is, of course, the last sentence, from which it might be and has been conjectured that the Romans identified the Judaean *YHVH/Adonai Tzva'ot* ("Lord of Hosts [i.e., Armies]") with Jove Sabazius.

This mistaken connection between Sabazius and *Sabaot* (which is, in turn, a corruption of *Tzva'ot*) has often been repeated. In a similar vein, Plutarch—who would have been writing at virtually the time when the Judaean bifurcation was beginning to take a pronounced shape toward the separate cults of Judaism and Christianity—maintained that the Judaeans/Jews worshipped Dionysios, and that the Judaean Sabbath day was actually a festival of Sabazius—i.e., the term "Sabbath" was understood by him to be a derivative of Sabazius.[237]

Plutarch also discusses the identification of the Judaean/Jewish God with the "Egyptian" Typhon, an identification which he later rejects, however. More interestingly, for our discussion, is the fact that the monotheistic Hypsistarians worshipped the Judaean God under this name. This group—referenced in Acts 16:17, as "servants of the most high God"—were pagan monotheists living in the area of the Bosporus and Cappadocia in the Hellenistic and Roman periods (ca 400 BCE-200 CE) who asserted that they worshipped God most high—*hypsistos* means "most high" in Greek (and this is the Septuagint translation of the Hebrew "[*El* (Lord)] *Elyon*"). They were apparently sympathetic to Judaean spirituality but remained pagan and did not, for example, practice circumcision. It may be that a native Cappadocian cult of Zeus Sabazios merged with the cult of *YHVH Tzva'ot*, forming associations (*thiasoi*) of strict monotheists who fraternized with the Judaeans but did not follow the Torah.

The significance for us of these *thiasoi* is connected to the fact that when someone asked the oracle of Apollo of Klaros on the western coast of Anatolia whether the *Hypsistos* alone was without beginning and end, the oracle responded: "He is the Lord of all, self-originated, self-produced, ruling all things in some ineffable way, encompassing the heavens, spreading out the earth, riding on the waves of the sea; mixing fire with water, soil with air and earth with fire; of winter, summer, autumn and spring, causing the changes in their season, leading all things toward the light and settling their fate in harmonious order." Such a comment, which could as easily have been made regarding the Judaean God and the God of both of Judaeanism's offspring, Judaism and Christianity, reminds us yet

---

[236] Valerius Maximus, Epitome of *Nine Books of Memorable Deeds and Sayings*, I.3.2 (see Exemplum 3).
[237] See Plutarch, *Symposiacs*, iv, 6.

again that the religious matrix of the world we are exploring is not simply a pagan-Jewish-Christian one.

With this greater complexity in mind, we might note another cult that emerges to some prominence during the later Roman republican or early imperial period that is particularly relevant. Mithraism arguably spread, as an offspring of Zoroastrianism, from Persia. To be sure, the name *Mithras*—the Latin equivalent of Greek *Mithras*—is a form of *Mithra* (in Avestan, and in Old Persian: *Miça*), the name of an Old Persian divinity—specifically, the very important (second in importance only to Ahura Mazda) Zoroastrian *yazata* of covenant and oath, and associated with the sun.[238] We find an early example of the Greek form of this name in a fourth-century BCE work by Xenophon called the *Cyropaedia*, which is a biography of the Achaemenid Medo-Persian king Cyrus the Great (who permitted the Judaeans to return to Judaea and rebuild the Temple in Jerusalem, in 538 BCE).[239]

In addition to being associated with contracts, the Zoroastrian *yazata* Mithra is also a judicial figure, an all-seeing protector of Truth, and the guardian of cattle, the harvest and of the waters.[240] This Mithra is referenced in the Zoroastrian scriptures, specifically, as "Mithra of the wide pastures, of the thousand ears, and of the myriad eyes," (*Yasna* 1:3), and as "the lofty, and the everlasting... the province ruler," (*Yasna* 1:11), as "the *yazata* of the spoken name" (*Yasna* 3:5), as well as "the holy" (*Yasna* 3:13). The Avestan hymn to Mithra (*Yasht* 10) is the longest, and one of the best preserved, of the *Yashts*. The *Khorda Avesta* (*Book of Common Prayer*) also refers to Mithra in the "Litany to the Sun," in which reference is made to an "Homage to Mithra of wide cattle pastures," (*Khwarshed Niyayesh* 5), "Whose word is true, Who is of the assembly, Who has a thousand ears, the well-shaped one, Who has ten thousand eyes, the exalted one, Who has wide knowledge, the helpful one, Who sleeps not, the ever wakeful. We sacrifice to Mithra, Lord of all countries, Whom Ahura Mazda created the most glorious of the supernatural *yazatas*. So may there come to us for aid, both Mithra and Ahura, the two exalted ones," (*Khwarshed Niyayesh* 6-7). Further, "I shall sacrifice to his mace, well aimed against the skulls of the Daevas," (*Khwarshed Niyayesh* 15). Some recent theories

---

[238] Related deity-names in other languages include Sanskrit *Mitra*—the name of a god praised in the Rig Veda, earliest of the Vedic texts (See Rig Veda 3.59). In Sanskrit, "mitra" in fact means "friend" or "friendship." So, too, in the form *mi-it-ra-*, the term is found in an inscribed peace treaty between the Hittites, dominant late Bronze Age power in Anatolia, and the kingdom of the Mitanni, from the early fourteenth century BCE. While the Iranian *Mithra* and Sanskrit *Mitra* are believed to come from an Indo-Iranian word, *mitra*, meaning "contract, agreement, covenant," for our purposes what is important is less the etymology than to recognize that variant forms of both the name and cults associated with those variant forms are part of the complex religious reality that evolved toward its Roman aspect and that impinges upon the focus of our narrative. See Robert Turcan, *The Cults of the Roman Empire*. (Oxford: Wiley-Blackwell, 1996), 196ff, who explains: "The name Mithras comes from a root *mei-* (which implies the idea of exchange), accompanied by an instrumental suffix. It was therefore a means of exchange, the 'contract' which rules human relations and is the basis of social life... We find [Mithras] invoked with Varuna in an agreement concluded ca. 1380 BC between the king of the Hittites, Suppiluliumas, and the king of the Mitanni, Mativaza....It is the earliest evidence of Mithras in Asia Minor." Also see Paul Thieme, "The Aryan Gods of the Mitanni Treaties," in the *Journal of the American Oriental Society*, 80.4 (1960), 301-17.

[239] See *Cyropaedia* 7.5.53.

[240] The term *Mithra* is Avestan. In Middle Iranian languages, such as Middle Persian and Parthian, *Mithra* became *Mihr*, from which Modern Persian *Mihr* derives. The Avestan term and the Vedic common noun *mitra* both, in turn, derive from proto-Indo-Iranian **mitra*, a combination of the root *mi-* ("to bind"), and the "instrument suffix" *-tra-* ("causing to"); thus, *mitra/miθra* ultimately means "that which causes binding," preserved in the Avestan word for "covenant, contract, oath."

have also claimed that Mithra represents the sun itself, but the Khorda Avesta refers to the sun as a separate entity, as it does regarding the moon, with which the sun has "the best of friendships," (*Khwarshed Niyayesh* 15).[241]

Like most other divine beings, Mithra is not mentioned by name in the *Gathas*, the oldest texts of Zoroastrianism, which are generally attributed to Zoroaster himself, as we have noted. Mithra also does not appear by name in the *Yasna Haptanghaiti*, a seven-verse section of the *Yasna* liturgy that is linguistically as old as the *Gathas*. The lack of Mithra's presence in these texts has been taken by some to suggest that Zoroaster had rejected Mithra, although more recently, this *ex silentio* speculation has been rejected by most scholars.[242]

Together with *Rashnu* ("Justice) and *Sraosha* ("Obedience"), Mithra is one of the three judges at the *Chinvat* bridge, the "bridge of separation" that, as we have noted previously, all souls must cross after death. Unlike Sraosha, Mithra is not a psychopomp—one who escorts souls. Should good thoughts, words and deeds outweigh the bad for a given individual, it is Sraosha alone who conveys his/her soul across the bridge. In the intensely syncretistic Hellenistic era, during the Seleucid and Parthian periods, Mithra also seems to have been conflated with the Greek Apollo, who, like Mithra, is an all-seeing divinity of the Truth.[243]

The origins of the Mithraic cult in the form that became so popular in Rome was first understood to be a straightforward outgrowth of Zoroastrianism by Franz Cumont, the first Western scholar to study and write about it—around the same time as Sir James Frazer (whom we encountered toward the outset of our discussion) was writing.[244] Cumont asserted that the Roman mithraic religion was "the Roman form of Mazdaism," and was disseminated from the East. He identified the ancient Aryan deity who appears in Persian literature as Mithra with the Hindu god Mitra of the Vedic hymns. According to Cumont, the god Mithra arrived in Rome "accompanied by a large representation of the Mazdean Pantheon,"[245] and that, while the tradition "underwent some modification in the Occident... the alterations that it suffered were largely superficial."[246]

---

[241] For a brief review of these various texts, see above, fnn #135, 141, 142.

[242] Building on that speculation was another series of speculations, which postulated that the reason why Zoroaster did not mention Mithra was because the latter was the supreme god of a bloodthirsty group of *daeva*-worshipers that Zoroaster condemned. However, as Roger Beck has noted, "no satisfactory evidence has yet been adduced to show that, before Zoroaster, the concept of a supreme god existed among the Iranians, or that among them Mithra—or any other divinity—ever enjoyed a separate cult of his or her own outside either their ancient or their Zoroastrian pantheons." See Beck's article "Mithraism" in the *Encyclopedia Iranica*, 2002.

[243] Further, in the Zoroastrian calendar, the sixteenth day of the month and the seventh month of the year are dedicated to, and under the protection of, Mithra. The position of the sixteenth day and seventh month reflects Mithra's rank in the hierarchy of the divinities; these are respectively the first day of the second half of the month and the first month of the second half of the year. While Mithra is not the divinity of the Sun in Zoroastrian scripture, this being the role of Hvare-khshaeta ("radiant Sun"), in the Zoroastrian tradition, Mithra eventually came to be associated with the Sun. How, when or why this occurred is uncertain, but it is commonly attributed to a conflation with the Babylonian Shamash, who, in addition to being a sun god, was a judicial figure like Mithra. This would suggest a relatively early, Achaemenid-period development.

[244] Cumont published a two-volume work, in French, *Textes et monuments figures relatifs aux mysteres de Mithra*, in 1894-1900; an English-language reduction, *The Mysteries of Mithra*, was published in 1903 and republished as a Dover Edition (New York City), in 1956.

[245] Franz Cumont, *The Mysteries of Mithra* (1903), 107.

[246] Ibid, 104.

A few generations later, Cumont's theories came in for severe criticism from John R. Hinnells and Richard L. Gordon at the First International Congress of Mithraic Studies held in 1971.[247] Hinnells asserted that "the portrayal of Mithras [the proper Roman name, as opposed to "Mithra"] given by Cumont is not merely unsupported by Iranian texts but is actually in serious conflict with known Iranian theology."[248] Others argued otherwise at that same time. A second scholar, Lewis Hopfe, asserted that "all theories of the origin of Mithraism acknowledge a connection, however vague, to the Mithra/Mitra figure of ancient Aryan religion."[249] A few years later, a third scholar, Ugo Bianchi, pointed out that it "was clear to the Romans themselves that Mithras was a 'Persian' (in wider perspective: an Indo-Iranian) god."[250] This last point has also been made by Mary Boyce, who noted that "the Persian affiliation of the Mysteries is acknowledged in the earliest literary references to them."[251]

The argument has been carried on in the decades since.[252] For our purposes, a definitive conclusion regarding origins is less essential than an understanding of what the Mithras cult was in Rome and the influence it may have had on—or the nature of the competition that it offered to—Christianity (or Judaism, or other pagan religions, for that matter).[253] That which came to be known as the Mithraic Mysteries was practiced in the Roman Empire from about the first to the fourth centuries CE. The underground temples or Mithraea appear suddenly in the archaeological record in the last quarter of the 1st century CE, suggesting that the cult only came into existence—or achieved a distinct shape—by that period.[254] What seems minimally to have transpired is that the name of the Zoroastrian god Mithra, a kind of assistant to Ahura Mazda, adapted into Greek as Mithras, became attached to a new and distinctive imagery.

---

[247] See the description of these "devastating critiques of Cumont's Iranian hypothesis" in David Ulansey's *Origins of the Mithraic Mysteries* (New York: Oxford University Press, 1991), 10.

[248] John R. Hinnells, "Reflections on the Bull-Slaying Scene," in *Mithraic Studies*, vol 2, 292.

[249] Lewis M. Hopfe, "Archaeological Indications on the Origins of Roman Mithraism," in Lewis M. Hopfe, ed., *Uncovering Ancient Stones: Essays in Memory of H. Neil Richardson* (Eisenbrauns, 1994), 150ff.

[250] He is quoted in Roger Beck, "On Becoming a Mithraist: New Evidence for the Propagation of the Mysteries," in Leif E. Vaage, et al, *Religious Rivalries in the Early Roman Empire and the Rise of Christianity*, 182.

[251] Mary Boyce & Frantz Grenet, *Zoroastrianism under Macedonian and Roman Rule*, Part 1 (Brill, 1975), 468-9.

[252] Thus Beck theorizes that the cult was created in Rome, by a single founder who had some knowledge of both Greek and Oriental religion, but suggests that some of the ideas used may have passed through the Hellenistic kingdoms. He observes, in the *Encyclopaedia Iranica*, that "Mithras—moreover, a Mithras who was identified with the Greek sun god, Helios" was among the gods of the syncretistic Greco-Armenian-Iranian royal cult at Nemrut founded by Antiokhos I of Commagene in the mid-1st century BCE."

Reinhold Merkelbach, in his book, *Mithras* (Hain, 1984, *chs 5-7*), similarly suggests that its mysteries were essentially created by a particular person or persons and created in a specific place, the city of Rome, by someone from an eastern province or border state who knew the Persian religious narratives in detail, which he wove into his new grades of initiation—but that he must have been Greek and Greek-speaking because he incorporated elements of Greek Platonism into it. The narratives, he suggests, were probably created in the milieu of the imperial bureaucracy, and for its members. Clauss tends to agree. Beck calls this "the most likely scenario" and states: "Till now, Mithraism has generally been treated as if it somehow evolved Topsy-like from its Iranian precursor—a most implausible scenario once it is stated explicitly." He states this in his article, "Merkelbach's Mithras," in *Phoenix* 41.3, (1987), 304, 306.

[253] In fact, lack of absolute clarity on the origins of Roman Mithraism merely reinforces the idea that we are dealing with a far more complex religious world than one might suppose—or than what we heard about in Sunday School...

[254] See Roger Beck, "The Mysteries of Mithras: A New Account of their Genesis," in *Journal of Roman Studies*, 1998, 115-28.

A handful of Roman writers who were contemporary with them discuss Mithras and the mysteries. The earliest literary reference is by the poet Statius, writing in Latin (some Roman-era writers wrote in Greek, as we have seen) about 80 CE. In his epic poem, the *Thebaid* 1.719-20, he describes Mithras in a cave, wrestling with something that has horns. The context of the description is a prayer to the god Apollo. The cave is described as *persei*, which in this context is usually translated "Persian."[255]

The biographer Plutarch, writing in Greek around 110 CE, asserts that "secret mysteries... of Mithras" were practiced (in what would be about 67 BCE, during the era of Pompey the Great) by the pirates of Cilicia (a province on the southeastern coast of Asia Minor), who "likewise offered strange sacrifices—those of Olympos, I mean—and they celebrated certain secret mysteries, among which those of Mithras continue to this day, being originally instituted by them."[256]

The historian Dio Cassius (63.5.2; ca 180-235 CE) records how the name of Mithras was spoken during the state visit to Rome of Tiridates I of Armenia, during the reign of Nero (54-68 CE). He writes that Tiridates, as he was about to receive his crown, told the Roman emperor that he revered him "as Mithras."

Still later, the neo-platonic philosopher Porphyry (third-fourth century CE) offers an account of the actual origins of the Mysteries in his work *De Antro Nympharum* ("On the Cave of the Nymphs"). Citing Eubulus as his source, Porphyry writes that the original temple of Mithras was a natural cave, containing fountains, *which Zoroaster found* in the mountains of Persia (emphasis added). To Zoroaster, this cave was a symbolic image of the whole world, so he consecrated it to Mithras, the creator of the world.[257] (Porphyry thus not only sees a distinct relationship between Mithraism and Zoroastrianism but sees Mithra as the pre-eminent Zoroastrian deity). Later in the same work, Porphyry links Mithras and

---

[255] More literally, "Persei" means "Persean"—referring to Perses, son of Perseus and Andromeda, and known, according to the Greek tradition, as the ancestor of the Persians. See David Ulansey, *Origins of the Mithraic Mysteries* (New York: Oxford University Press, 1991), 29ff.

Lewis M. Hopfe observes, in his article, "Archaeological Indications on the Origins of Roman Mithraism," that there are only three Mithraea in Roman Syria—in other words, the eastern part of the Empire, near Persia—whereas there are many sites further west, and thus suggests that the archaeological record leads to the conclusion "that Roman Mithraism had its epicenter in Rome... the fully developed religion known as Mithraism seems to have begun in Rome and been carried [eastward] to Syria [and in other directions] by soldiers and merchants." The article appears in Lewis M. Hopfe, ed., *op citum*, 147-58.

David Ulansey argues interestingly, in his *Origins of the Mithraic Mysteries*, 771, that the Mithraic mysteries began in the Greco-Roman world as a religious response to the discovery by the Greek astronomer Hipparkhos of Nicaea (190-120 BCE) of the astronomical phenomenon of the precession of the equinoxes—a discovery that amounted to discovering that the entire cosmos was moving in a hitherto unknown way. This new cosmic motion, he suggests, was seen by the founders of Mithraism as indicating the existence of a powerful new god capable of shifting the cosmic spheres and thereby controlling the universe.

However, as Beck summarizes (in his article, "Mithraism," in the *Encyclopaedia Iranica*), A.D.H. Biver, L.A. Campbell and G. Widengren have variously argued that Roman Mithraism represents a continuation of some form of Iranian Mithra worship. Finally, according to Antonia Tripolitis, Roman Mithraism originated in Vedic India and picked up many features of the cultures that it encountered in its westward journey through Babylon and Persia to the Hellenized East and ultimately across the breadth of the Roman Empire. See Antonia Tripolitis, *Religions of the Hellenistic-Roman Age*, (Wm B. Eerdmans Publishing, 2002), 3ff.

[256] Plutarch, *Parallel Lives (Live of Famous Greeks and Romans)*, "Pompey" 24.

[257] "For, as Eubulus says, Zoroaster was the first who consecrated in the neighboring mountains of Persia, a series of spontaneously produced caves, florid, with fountains, in honor of Mithra, the maker and father of all things; a cave, according to Zoroaster, bearing a resemblance to the world, which was [in its entirety] fabricated by Mithra. But the things contained in the caver, arranged according to commensurate intervals, were symbols of the mundane elements and climates" (*De Antro Nympharum* II).

the bull (see below) with planets and star-signs: Mithras himself is then associated with the zodiacal sign of Aries and the planet Mars, while the bull is associated with Venus (see *De Antro Nympharum* II).[258]

The Romans themselves clearly regarded the mysteries as having Persian and essentially Zoroastrian sources, but the dissimilarities between Mithra as a *yazata* within the Zoroastrian religion and how he functions in Rome has led most scholars since the early 1970s to view the latter as a distinct product of the Roman Imperial religious world—and, as we shall shortly note, as a rival of early Christianity.

In Rome, Mithras was a sun god, and, in Persia, Mithra was a *yazata* of the morning sun. The Roman Mithras killed the Primeval Bull, mirroring—or straightforwardly adapting the idea of—the death of a Primeval Bull in Zoroastrianism. The earliest monument showing Mithras slaying the bull is thought to be (so-called) CIMRM 593, found in Rome itself. There is no date, but the inscription tells us that it was dedicated by a certain Alcimus, steward of T. Claudius Livianus. Maarten J. Vermaseren and Richard L. Gordon believe that this Livianus was the same Livianus who was elsewhere identified as the commander of the Praetorian Guard in 101 CE; if they are correct, this would give an earliest date of 98-99 CE.[259]

Overall, about 420 sites have yielded materials. Among the artifacts found are about 1000 inscriptions, 700 examples of the bull-killing scene (usually referred to as the tauroktony), and about 400 other monuments.[260] It has been estimated by one scholar that there would have been at least 680-690 Mithraea in Rome.[261] These meeting places were underground and without windows. In cities, the basement of an apartment block might be converted; elsewhere they might be excavated and vaulted over, or converted from a natural cave.

---

[258]Porphyry was writing close to the time of the demise of the cult, as we shall shortly observe, and in analyzing his work, Robert Turcan has suggested, in his *Mithras Platonicus* (Leiden, 1975) that Porphyry's understanding derives from what suited his Neoplatonism to read into Mithraism. However, other scholars, such as Merkelbach and Beck, believe that Porphyry's work "is in fact thoroughly coloured with the doctrines of the Mysteries"—as asserted by Beck in his "Merkelbach's Mithras," 308, n.7. Beck holds that classical scholars have neglected Porphyry's evidence and have taken an unnecessarily skeptical view of him. He further asserts that Porphyry's *De Antro* is the only clear text from antiquity that tells us about the intent of the Mithraic Mysteries and how that intent was realized. (He asserts this in his 2006 work, *The Religion of the Mithras Cult in the Roman Empire*.) Finally, David Ulansey finds it important that Porphyry "confirms... that astral conceptions played an important role in Mithraism" in his *Origins of the Mithraic Mysteries*.

[259]Richard L. Gordon, "The Date and Significance of CIMRM 593 (British Museum, Townley Collection," in *Journal of Mithraic Studies* II, (1978), 148-74. Other early archaeology includes the Greek inscription from Venosia by *Sagaris actor* probably from 100–150 CE; the Sidonian *cippus* dedicated by Theodotus, priest of Mithras, to Asclepius, 140-141 CE; and the earliest military inscription, on an altar set up by C. Sacidius Barbarus, a centurion of XV Apollinaris, found on the bank of the Danube at Carnuntum (a Roman army camp on the Danube in the Noricum province and, after the first century CE, the capital of the province of Upper Pannonia), probably well before 114 CE.

According to C.M. Daniels, (in his article, "The Roman Army and the Spread of Mithraism," in John R. Hinnells, *Mithraic Studies: Proceedings of the First International Congress of Mithraic Studies*, vol 2, 1975), the Carnuntum inscription is the earliest Mithraic dedication from the Danube region, which, along with Italy, is one of the two areas where Mithraism first took root. The earliest dateable Mithraeum outside Rome dates from 148 CE. The Mithraeum at Caesarea Maritima is the only one in Judaea-Palestine and the date is inferred rather than certainly written down.

[260] See Manfred Clauss, *The Roman Cult of Mithras: The God and His Mysteries*, xxi.

[261] This is based primarily on the 1979 topographic survey by F. Coarelli.

The Mithraea all symbolized the cave in which Mithras carried and then killed the bull (see below). Indeed, "Mithraeum" is a modern coinage and mithraists referred to their sacred structures as "*speleum*" or "*antrum*" (cave), "*crypta*" (underground hallway or corridor), "*fanum*" (sacred or holy place), or even "*templum*" (a temple or a sacred space).[262] These were, in any case, commonly located close to springs or streams; fresh water appears to have been required for some Mithraic rituals, and a basin is often incorporated into the structure.[263]

Not surprisingly, the most common image found in these sites, usually carved in relief on the altars, is that depicting the god slaying a bull—the tauroktony—which seems

FIG 2: Mithra the Bull-slayer. 2nd Century CE

to be specific to Roman Mithraism. The image may be a relief, or free-standing, and various subsidiary details may be present or omitted. The centerpiece presents Mithras clothed in Anatolian costume and wearing a Phrygian cap (with a drooping, forward-leaning, curling "point"), kneeling on the exhausted bull, holding it by the nostrils with his left hand, and stabbing it with his right. As he does this, he looks over his shoulder towards the figure of Sol.[264] In the fullest representation, details include a dog and a snake extending upwards toward the bloody wound, a scorpion seizing the bull's genitals, a raven flying around or sitting on the bull, and three sprigs of wheat coming out from the bull's tail, or sometimes from the knife wound. Two torch-bearers are often depicted on either side, dressed like Mithras: Cautes with his torch pointing up and Cautopates with his torch pointing down. Sometimes Cautes and Cautopates carry shepherds' crooks instead of torches [FIG 2].[265]

The event takes place in a cavern, into which Mithras has carried the bull (as previously noted), after having hunted it, ridden it and overwhelmed its strength. Sometimes the cavern is surrounded by a circle, on which the twelve signs of the zodiac appear. Outside the cavern, top left, is Sol the sun, with his flaming crown, often driving a quadriga. A ray of light frequently reaches down to touch Mithras. To the upper right is Luna, most often, with her crescent moon; she is sometimes depicted driving a *biga*.

---

[262] See the 2007 PhD dissertation by Jonas Bjornebye: *Hic Locus est Felix, Sanctus, Piusque Benignus: The Cult of Mithras in Fourth-Century Rome*—particularly the chapter entitled "The Mithraea as Buildings."
[263] Ibid.
[264] Note the comment by Brit-Marie Nasstrom in her "The Sacrifices of Mithras" that "...the sacrifice [of the bull] is a guarantee of salvation for the participants [in the ceremony carried out in the presence of the altar with its tauroktony image]." This will have significance for the discussion of the relationship between Roman Mithraism and Christianity, as we shall see.
[265] In the latter version, the first has his crook pointed up and the second his crook pointed down. Given the idea that Mithras is either the personification of the sun or is at least on intimate terms with Sol Invictus, Cautes and Cautopates are believed to represent the light of sunrise and sunset respectively, or alternatively, as David Ulansey has proposed, the spring and autumn solar equinoxes.

Some of the reliefs were constructed so that they could be turned on an axis. On the back side was another scene: an elaborate depiction of a feast. This suggests that the bull-killing scene was the focus of the first part of the celebration, and then the second, festal scene was the focus of the second part of the celebration.[266] So, too, besides the main altar and its imagery, several Mithraea offered several secondary tauroktony depictions; some smaller, portable versions—perhaps intended for private devotions—have also been found.

Whatever the original relationship between Roman Mithraism and its possible origins in Zoroastrian Persia, the bull-slaying centerpiece of the Roman cult probably marks a significant difference from the Persian Mithra tradition—although Cumont asserts that the imagery of the tauroktony was a Graeco-Roman representation of an event in Zoroastrian cosmogony described in a late, 9th-century CE Zoroastrian text, the *Bundahishn* ("Primal Creation"). In this text Ahriman (and *not* Mithra) slays the primordial creature Gavaevodata, which is represented as a bovine. Cumont claimed that a version of the myth must have existed in which Mithra, not Ahriman, killed the bovine. According to John R. Hinnells, however, no such variant of the myth is known, and this is therefore mere speculation on Cumont's part: "In no known Iranian text [either Zoroastrian or otherwise] does Mithra slay a bull."[267] So, too, Ulansey observes that "... there is no evidence that the Persian deity, Mithra, ever had anything to do with killing a bull," but in every Mithraeum across the Roman world, the central icon was a representation of Mithras killing a sacred bull.[268] One could even speculate, given how late the text referenced by Cumont is, that a Mithraic element, carried into the western Zoroastrian world that abutted and interpenetrated the eastern Roman world, made its way *back* from the Roman world into late Zoroastrianism.

To repeat and elaborate further: images of a sacred banquet are the second most important scene after the tauroktony in Mithraic art, also usually carved in relief. The banquet scene features Mithras and the Sun god banqueting on the hide of the slaughtered bull. On the banquet scene on the *Fiano Romano* relief, one of the torchbearers points a caduceus toward the base of an altar, where flames appear to spring up. It has been suggested by Robert Turcan that since the caduceus is an attribute of Mercury, and in mythology Mercury is depicted as a psychopomp ("leader of souls"), the eliciting of flames in this scene is referring to the dispatch of human souls and expressing the Mithraic doctrine on this matter. Turcan also connects this event back to the tauroktony, in that the blood of the slain bull has soaked the ground at the base of the altar, and from that blood the souls are elicited in flames by the caduceus—so that one might say that the bull has been sacrificed for the sake of the salvation of these human souls.[269]

Other scenes are also sometimes shown—sometimes as predella-like images around the central depiction of the tauroktony—including Mithras being born from a rock.

---

[266] This was first asserted by Hans-Josef Klauck and Brian McNeil in their 2003 work, *The Religious Context of Early Christianity: A Guide to Greco-Roman Religions.*

[267] John R. Hinnells, "Reflections on the Bull-slaying Scene," in *Mithraic Studies: Proceedings of the First International Conference on Mithraic Studies* (Manchester: Manchester University Press), 290-312. This comment is made on page 291.

[268] Ulansey, *Origins of the Mithraic Mysteries*, 8.

[269] See Roger Beck, *The Religion of the Mithras Cult in the Roman Empire*, 27-8.

He is depicted emerging from it, already in his youth, with a dagger in one hand and a torch in the other, typically nude, but wearing a Phrygian cap. There are variations that depict him coming out of the rock as a child, sometimes with a thunderbolt and in one instance with a globe in one hand. Sometimes he also has other weapons like bows and arrows and he is accompanied by various animals, such as a dog, a serpent, a dolphin, an eagle, other birds, a lion, a crocodile, and even a lobster or a snail. On some reliefs, there is a bearded figure identifiable as Oceanus, the water god identified since Homeric times with the great river believed to encircle the world, and on some there are the four wind gods. Sometimes Victoria (victory personified allegorically), Luna, Sol and Saturn also seem to play a role. Saturn appears to hand over the dagger to Mithras so that he can perform his mighty deeds.[270]

There is also sometimes a naked lion-headed (*leontocephaline*) figure, entwined by a serpent, (or two serpents, like a caduceus) with the snake's head often resting on the lion's head, with the lion's mouth often open in a fierce roar. He is usually also represented with four wings, and with two keys (sometimes a single key) and a scepter in his hand. Sometimes he stands on a globe inscribed with a diagonal cross. The four wings may carry the symbols of the four seasons and a thunderbolt is engraved on the lion-headed figure's breast. At the base of the statue are the hammer and tongs of the Roman smith-god, Vulcan, and the rooster and the wand of Mercury. A rarer variant of the figure offers a human head. Animal-headed figures are, of course, prevalent in depictions of Egyptian gods and also of Gnostic figures from the period (and, in the case of Egypt, for several millennia earlier), but a precise parallel to the Mithraic *leontocephaline* figure is not found outside the Roman Mithraic context.[271]

The name of this last figure has been deciphered from dedicatory inscriptions to be "Arimanius" (although the archaeological evidence is scant), which would seem to be the Latinized equivalent of "Ahriman," the key negative figure in the Zoroastrian pantheon, as we have seen. Arimanius is known from inscriptions to have been a god in the Mithraic cult (CIMRM 222 from Ostia, 369 from Rome, 1773 and 1775 from Pannonia).[272] Thus while some scholars identify the lion-man as Aion (Zurvan, or Kronos), others assert that it is Ahriman.[273] Although the exact identity of the lion-headed figure is debated by scholars, it is largely agreed that the god is associated with time and seasonal change.[274]

---

[270] See Maarten .J. Vermaseren, "The Miraculous Birth of Mithras," in Laszlo Gerevich, *Studia Archaeologica*.
[271] See Hubertus Von Gall, "The Lion-headed and the Human-headed God in the Mithraic Mysteries," in Jacques Duchesne-Guillemin, ed., *Etudes Mithriaques*, 1978, 511. Gnosticism is a term used to refer to a number of different sects that share in common the following fundamental features: The creator of our universe (*YHVH*) is a false god, who rebelled against the true God (and created our world as part of that rebellion). Thus a) Jews and Christians alike worship a false, fundamentally evil God; and b) our world is false; it is an emptiness (Greek: *kenoma*) in contrast to the true world, the fullness (Greek: *pleroma*) created by the true God. Access to— knowledge of—the *pleroma* is possible to those initiated into the *cultus*. (The Greek word, *gnosis*, which means knowledge, in this context refers to hidden, deeply esoteric knowledge.)
[272] See Howard M. Jackson, "The Meaning and Function of the Leoncephaline in Roman Mithraism," in *Numen*, Vol 32, Fasc 1 (July, 1985), 17-45.
[273] There is also some speculation that the figure is intended to represent the Gnostic demiurge, Ialdabaoth. The demiurge, in Gnostic terms, is the artificer of our false, material world—the *kenoma* ("emptiness")—as opposed to the true, spiritual world, the *pleroma* ("fullness") that is accessible only through the informed Gnostic devotee's hidden *gnosis* ("knowledge"). See David M. Gwynn, *Religious Diversity in Late Antiquity* (Brill, 2010), 448.
[274] Beck has, furthermore, suggested that the details of the tauroktony, each component corresponding to a different heavenly element and thus offering a connection between the macrocosm of the universe and the microcosm of

Mithraic temples are common across the Roman Empire, albeit unevenly distributed. Considerable numbers are found in Rome, Ostia, Numidia, Dalmatia, Britain and along the Rhine/Danube frontier; they are somewhat less common in Greece, Egypt, and Syria.[275] From the number and distribution of these sanctuaries we can infer both that the cult was popular and far-flung and that its center was probably the city of Rome itself. Each Mithraeum had several altars at the end opposite the entrance, underneath a—usually relief-carved—representation of the tauroktony, together with a number of secondary altars, as we have observed. Burned residues of animal entrails are commonly found on the main altars, suggesting regular sacrificial use. However, Mithraea do not commonly appear to have been provided with facilities for ritual slaughter of sacrificial animals (a highly specialized function in Roman religion), and one might suppose that a Mithraeum would have made arrangements for this service to be provided by a professional *victimarius* of the civic cult. So, too, prayers were addressed to the sun three times a day and Sunday was especially sacred.[276]

Some aspects of the cult are evident through examining the archaeological remains of numerous Mithraea—such as that most rituals were associated with feasting, (consistent with the imagery of a feast that we have noted), since eating utensils and food residues are almost invariably found. These tend to include both animal bones and also very large quantities of fruit residues.[277] The presence of large numbers of cherry pits in particular would tend to confirm mid-summer (late June, early July) as a season especially associated with Mithraic festivities. The Virunum *album*—i.e., a membership list (*album*)

---

the sacred site, are as follows: bull = (constellation) Taurus; Sol = sun; Luna = moon; Dog = (constellations) Canis major/Canis Minor; snake = (constellations) Hydra, Serpens, Draco; raven + (constellation) Corvus; scorpion = (constellation) Scorpius; wheat's ear = (constellation) Spica; Cautes and Cautopates = (Constellation) Gemini; lion = (constellation Leo; crater = (constellation) Crater; cave = universe. See Beck's essay, "Astral Symbolism in the Tauroktony: A statistical Demonstration of the Extreme Improbability of Unintended Coincidence in the Selection of Elements in the Composition," in his volume, *Beck on Mithraism: Collected Works with New Essays* (2004), 257.

Ulansey, in his *The Origins of the Mithraic Mysteries*, 25-39, has proposed that Mithras was derived, as a figure, from the constellation (and presumably, then, the mythological, sea monster-slaying figure) of Perseus, which is positioned just above Taurus in the night sky. He sees iconographic and mythological parallels between Perseus and Mithras: both are young heroes, carry a dagger and wear a Phrygian cap. Ulansey points, further, to the similarity between the image of Perseus killing the Gorgon and the Mithraic tauroktony, both figures being associated with underground caverns and both having connections to Persia as further evidence. Michael Speidel, on the other hand, in his 1997 *Mithras-Orion: Greek Hero and Roman Army God*, associates Mithras with the constellation (and figure) of Orion because of the proximity of that constellation to Taurus, and the consistent nature of the depiction of the figure as having wide shoulders, a garment flared at the hem, and narrowed at the waist with a belt, in the form he takes as a constellation.

Beck has criticized Speidel and Ulansey for their adherence to a literal cartographic logic, describing their theories as a "will-o'-the-wisp" which "lured them down a false trail." (See Beck's essay, "In the Place of the Lion: Mithras in the Tauroktony," in *Beck on Mithraism: Collected Works with New Essays* (2004),270-76. He argues that a literal reading of the tauroktony as a star chart raises two major problems: it is difficult to find a constellation counterpart for Mithras himself (despite efforts by Speidel and Ulansey to do so) and that unlike in a star chart, each feature of the tauroktony might have more than a single counterpart. Rather than seeing Mithras as a constellation, Beck argues that Mithras is the prime traveler on the celestial stage (represented by the other symbols of the scene), the Unconquered Sun moving through the constellations. Conversely, though, Marvin Meyer, writing on "The Mithras Liturgy" in the volume edited by Amy Jill Levine, et al, *The Historical Jesus in Context*, holds that the Mithras Liturgy reflects the world of Mithraism and may be a confirmation for Ulansey's theory of Mithras being held responsible for the precession of equinoxes.

[275] See Manfred Clauss, *The Roman Cult of Mithras*, 26-7.

[276] Antonia Tripolitis, *Religions of the Hellenistic-Roman Age*, 55ff.

[277] Clauss, *op citum*, 115.

found at the site of Virunum, in the Roman province of Noricum—in the form of an inscribed bronze plaque, records a Mithraic festival of commemoration as taking place on the equivalent, in our calendar, of 26 June 184. Beck argues that religious celebrations on this date are indicative of special significance being given to the Summer solstice. For their feasts, Mithraic initiates reclined on stone benches arranged along the longer sides of the Mithraeum; typically there would be space for between fifteen and thirty participants, and occasionally more, but very rarely more than 40 individuals.[278]

Significantly, no written narratives or theological descriptions survive, with only limited information to be derived from the inscriptions, and only brief or passing references in Greek and Latin literature.[279] This lack of a substantial body of written material limits the basis for certainty with regard to our interpretation and understanding of the physical evidence. It would seem doubtful, in any case, that Mithraism had a monolithic and internally consistent doctrine. It may have varied from location to location (as we have observed for the cult of Dionysios). However, the iconography is relatively coherent, and basic elements can be deduced.

Admission into the community was apparently completed with a handshake with the *pater*, just as Mithras and Sol shook hands. Initiates therefore called themselves *syndexioi*, (using a Greek rather than a Latin term) meaning "those joined by the right [hand; i.e., by a handshake]."[280] The term is used in an inscription by Proficentius and mocked by the early fourth-century pagan-born Christian writer and possibly astrologer, Firmicus Maternus, in his *De Errore Profanarum Religionum*, a work attacking Paganism.[281] The process of initiation was gradual, however, and required the overcoming of a series of prescribed ordeals. The Cappodocian father, Gregory Nazianzos (ca 329-390 CE) refers, in *Oratio* 4.70, to the "tests in the mysteries of Mithras."[282] The Suda also asserts that "nobody was permitted to be initiated into the [mysteries of Mithras] until he should show himself holy and steadfast by undergoing several graduated tests."[283]

According to St. Jerome (347-420 CE), there were seven grades of initiation into the cult—as in other ancient traditions from Egypt to Mesopotamia to Persia to Greece and Rome, the number of grades must have corresponded to the number of *planetes*. The initiate into each grade appears to have been required to undertake a trial ordeal, involving exposure to heat, cold or threatened peril. An 'ordeal pit,' dating to the early third century,

---

[278] Ibid, 43.

[279] Inscriptions and monuments related to the Mithraic Mysteries were catalogued in a two-volume work by Maarten J. Vermaseren, the *Corpus Inscriptionum et Monumentorum Religionis Mithriacae* (or CIMRM).

[280] In ancient Persia, taking the right hand was the traditional way of concluding a treaty or signifying some solemn understanding between two parties, as noted by Walter Burkert in his *Ancient Mystery Cults* (Cambridge: Harvard University Press, 1987), 16f.

[281] Firmicus is known only by this one fragmentary work. Dedicated to the Emperors Constantius II and Constans—and thus presumably written during their co-reign (337-50 CE)—its declared intention is to show the inferiority of the diverse pagan cults to Christianity and to encourage the rulers to outlaw them. The rich, insider-seeming details that he offers regarding Mithraism in particular suggests that he had earlier been a Mithraist himself. He is commonly assumed to be one and the same as the Julius Firmicus Maternus Siculus who wrote a work on astrology around 337 CE. If so, then Firmicus obviously wrote this work while still a pagan, and the other after his conversion to Christianity.

[282] Clauss, *op citum*, 102.

[283] Ibid, 102, referring to *Suda* 3.394.

has been identified in the Mithraeum at Carrawburgh.[284] A floor mosaic in the Mithraeum of Felicissimus in Ostia depicts these grades, with heraldic emblems that are connected either to the grades and/or that serve as symbols of the planets. The grades also have inscriptions beside them commending each grade to the protection of the different planetary gods.[285]

The highest grade, *pater*, is the most common that has been found on dedications and inscriptions. It seems that a Mithraeum might have several persons with this grade, for the form *pater patrum* ("father of fathers") is often found, suggesting the *pater* with primary status—a kind of *primus inter pares* idea, translated from the Roman political structure to this religious context. One can identify several instances in which persons, usually those of higher social status, joined a Mithraeum with the status *pater,* especially in Rome during the so-called "pagan revival" of the fourth century (referenced in context below).[286] It has been suggested by Alison Griffith that some Mithraea may have awarded honorary *pater* status to sympathetic dignitaries.[287]

Military men were strongly represented among Mithraists—his sword-wielding, victorious form would have found a particularly strong resonance among soldiers (and the mobility of the Roman troops would have helped spread the religion to the far reaches of the Empire)—but so, too, were merchants, customs officials and minor bureaucrats. Few, if any, initiates seem to have come from leading aristocratic or senatorial families in the cult's earlier and middle phases, however such individuals were definitely a part of it during the aforementioned "pagan revival" of the mid-4th century—shortly before its demise in the face of a newly aggressive Christianity—but there were always large numbers of freedmen and slaves.[288]

Since only male names appear in surviving inscribed membership lists, historians such as Cumont and Richard Gordon have concluded that the cult was for men only.[289] Interestingly, however, Porphyry refers to female initiates in Mithraic rites. This might be due to a misunderstanding by the ancient scholar; as A.S. Geden noted in the early twentieth century, while the participation of women in the ritual may not have been unknown in the *eastern* versions of the cult, the predominant military influence in Mithraism as it swept through most of the Empire and in particular its western parts, makes

---

[284]Accounts of the cruelty of the emperor Commodus (r. 180-192 CE) describe him as amusing himself by enacting Mithraic initiation ordeals in homicidal form. By the later third century, the trials appear to have been reduced in intensity, as 'ordeal pits' were apparently floored over. Carrawburgh is a settlement in Northumberland. In Roman times, it was apparently an auxiliary fort built along Hadrian's Wall, called Brocolitia, Procolita, or Brocolita, at the Wall's northernmost point, and just over a mile west of the nearest mile castle. Three sanctuaries have been found there; the Mithraeum dates from the early third century.

[285]According to Clauss, in ascending order of importance, these grades were *Corax* (crow; the tutelary deity Mercury); *Nymphus* (bridesman; the tutelary deity is Venus); *Miles* (soldier; the tutelary deity is Mars); *Leo* (lion; the tutelary deity is Jupiter); *Perses* (Perseus; the tutelary deity is Luna, i.e., the moon); *Heliodromos* (sun-runner/sun-path; the tutelary deity is Sol, i.e., the sun); *Pater* (father; the tutelary deity is Saturn). Each of these is in turn associated, in theory, with an attribute illustrated on the Ostia mosaic (eg, a torch for *Heliodromos*, or a Phrygian cap for *Perses*).

[286] See below, 61, 63.

[287] See Griffith's "Mithraism in the Private and Public Lives of Fourth-Century Senators in Rome," in the *Electronic Journal of Mithraic Studies*. http://www.uhu.es/ems/Papers/Volume1Papers/ABGMS.DOC

[288] Clauss, op citum, 39.

[289] Cumont, *The Mysteries of Mithra*, 173; Richard L. Gordon, "Mithraism," in Lindsay Jones, *Encyclopedia of Religions* 9 (Second Edition), 6090.

this unlikely.[290] Given my earlier comment that the cult was not monolithic, with variations in varied locations, David Jonathan's notion that "women were involved with Mithraic groups in at least some locations of the empire" makes a certain amount of sense.[291]

Mithraic initiates were apparently required to swear an oath of secrecy and dedication, and some grade rituals involved the recital of a catechism, wherein the initiate was asked a series of questions pertaining to the initiation symbolism; the initiate had to reply with specific answers.[292] However, almost no Mithraic scripture or first-hand account of its secret rituals survives, with the exception of the aforementioned oath and catechism, and the document known as the Mithras Liturgy, from fourth-century Egypt, the identity of which as a Mithraic text has been questioned by many scholars (beginning with Cumont).[293] The walls of Mithraea were commonly whitewashed, and where this has survived there tend to be preserved extensive repositories of graffiti that, together with inscriptions on Mithraic monuments, form our main source for Mithraic texts.[294]

If the cult may have begun as early as the late Republic, its first substantial expansion across the Empire seems to have happened later, quite quickly, late in the reign of Antoninus Pius (138-161 CE) and under Marcus Aurelius (161-180 CE). By this time all the key elements that we have been discussing would have been firmly in place. The popularity of Mithraism continued to spread, (facilitated, in part, as I have previously suggested, but its popularity among Roman soldiers) reaching its apogee toward the end of the second century and into the third. The culmination of that popularity came with the position, during this period, of *Sol Invictus* ("the undefeatable/invincible sun") as part of the official state religion.

Around this time an otherwise unknown individual named Pallas wrote a monograph to Mithras, and a little later Eubulus wrote a *History of Mithras*. Although these

---

[290] A.S. Geden, *Selected Passages Illustrating Mithraism*, 51f

[291] Jonathan David, "The Exclusion of Women in the Mithraic Mysteries: Ancient or Modern?" *Numen* 47 (2): 121-41.

[292] An example of such a catechism, apparently pertaining to the Leo grade, was discovered in a fragmentary Egyptian papyrus (P. Berolinensis 21196). (See William M. Brashear, *A Mithraic Catechism from Egypt*). Its level of intelligibility is fairly limited, to say the least:
... He will say: 'Where ... ?
... he is/(you are?) there (then/thereupon?) at a loss?' Say: ... Say: 'Night.' He will say: 'Where ... ?' ... Say: 'All things ...' (He will say): '... you are called ... ?' Say: 'Because of the summery ...' ... having become ... he/it has the fiery ... (He will say): '... did you receive/inherit?' Say: 'In a pit.' He will say: 'Where I your ...?... (Say): '...(in the...) Leonteion.' He will say: 'Will you gird?' The (heavenly?) ...(Say): '... death.' He will say: 'Why, having girded yourself, ...?' '... this (has?) four tassels. Very sharp and ...' '... much.' He will say: ...? (Say: '... because of/through?) hot and cold.' He will say: ...? (Say): '... red ... linen.' He will say: 'Why?' Say: '... red border; the linen, however, ...' (He will say): '... has been wrapped?' Say: 'The savior's ...' He will say: 'Who is the father?' Say: 'The one who (begets?) everything ...' (He will say): '('How ?)... did you become a Leo?' Say: 'By the ... of the father.' ... Say: 'Drink and food.' He will say '...?'

[293] The so-called "Mithras Liturgy" is one of the syncretistic *Greek Magical Papyri* (which we shall examine several chapters hence); specifically, in the so-called Great Magical Papyrus of Paris, numbered *PGM* IV.475-834. The name "Mithras Liturgy" originated in 1903 with Albrecht Dietrich, its first translator, based on the invocation of Helios Mithras (Ἥλιος Μίθρας) as the god who will provide the initiate with a revelation of immortality. Whereas Dietrich asserted that the text contains an authentic Mithraic ritual, Cumont rejected that notion, asserting that it was a syncretistic text that therefore included references to Mithras. Recent scholarship is divided on this issue, but most scholars seem to side with Cumont.

[294] See E.D. Francis, "Mithraic Graffiti from Dura Europos," in John R. Hinnells, ed., *Mithraic Studies*, vol 2, 424-445.

two works are now lost, they are both referenced by Porphyry.[295] According to the fourth-century *Historia Augusta*—a late Roman collection of biographies, in Latin, of the Roman Emperors, their junior colleagues and usurpers of the period 117 to 284—the emperor Commodus (r. 180-192 CE) participated in its mysteries—or more accurately, as we have previously noted, desecrated them by translating the initiation ordeals into vehicles for torturing his victims—but it in any case never became one of the state cults under him.[296]

If the time and place of origin of the Roman cult of Mithras is difficult to identify with certainty, it is equally difficult to pinpoint when and how, exactly, it came to an end. Beck states that "Quite early in the [fourth] century the religion was as good as dead throughout the empire."[297] This may be a bit premature as a date on Beck's part, although in general, inscriptions from the fourth century overall seem to be few. It seems more likely (to me, at least), that the process would have been slower that carried the cult from widespread popularity to extermination. This era coincides with the significant rise of Christianity (as we shall discuss in more detail later), between Constantine's Edict of Milan in 313 and Theodosius I's adoption of Christianity as the state religion in ca 381, and Christianity would no doubt have ultimately been responsibility for administering the *coup de grace* to Mithraism.

Clauss asserts that inscriptions show Mithras as one of the cults listed on inscriptions by Roman senators who had not converted to Christianity, as part of the earlier referenced "pagan revival" among the elite.[298] Ulansey maintains that "Mithraism declined with the rise to power of Christianity, until the beginning of the fifth century, when Christianity became strong enough to exterminate by force rival religions such as Mithraism."[299] According to Speidel, Christians fought fiercely with this feared enemy and suppressed it during the fourth century—although, like Beck, Speidel may be slightly premature: active suppression cannot have come until the end of that century and the beginning of the next, under Theodosius. Increasingly, Mithraic sanctuaries were destroyed and religion was no longer a matter of personal choice by then: an age of religious intolerance had set in. According to Luther H. Martin, Roman Mithraism came to an end with the anti-pagan decrees of Theodosius during the last decade of the fourth century.[300] Indeed, virtually any and every form of non-Christian faith came under assault at this time.

---

[295] Porphyry mentions Pallas in *De Abstinentia* 2.56 and 4.16.3 and discusses Eubulus, as we have seen, in *De Antro Nympharum* 6.

[296] See above, fn #284, regarding Commodus. This is what the *Historia Augusta* says: *Mithriaca homicidio vero polluit, cum illic aliquid ad speciem timoris vel dici vel fingi soleat* ("He desecrated the rites of Mithras with actual murder, although it was customary in them merely to say or pretend something that would produce an impression of terror"). As for its official place within the state religion, although Sol Invictus apparently became part of the official cult, as previously noted, Clauss notes (in *The Roman Cult of Mithras*, 24) that "[t]he cult of Mithras never became one of those supported by the state with public funds, and was never admitted to the official list of festivals celebrated by the state and army—at any rate as far as the latter is known to us from the *Feriale Duranum*, the religious calendar of the units at Dura Europos in Coele Syria," [where, as we have noted, there was a Mithraeum]. He further notes that "the same is true of all the other mystery cults too. "On the other hand, Clauss comments that at the individual level, various individuals did hold roles both in the state cults and the priesthood of Mithras—reminding us once more of the complexities of the politics of religion in the Roman world.

[297] "Merkelbach's Mithras," 299.

[298] *The Roman Cult of Mithras*, 29-30.

[299] "Solving the Mysteries of Mithras," *Biblical Archaeology Review*, Vol 20, #5 (September/October, 1994), 40-53. The article is, in effect, a summary of Ulansey's book, *The Origin of the Mithraic Mysteries*.

[300] Martin made the observation in his foreword to *Beck on Mithraism*.

At some of the Mithraea that have been found below churches, for example the Santa Prisca Mithraeum and the San Clemente Mithraeum—both in Rome—the ground plan of the church above was made in a way to emphasize in concrete terms Christianity's domination of Mithraism.[301] According to Mark Humphries, the deliberate concealment of Mithraic cult objects in some places around the empire suggests that precautions were being taken by the Mithraists against Christian attacks. However, in areas like the Rhine frontier, purely religious considerations cannot explain the end of Mithraism and barbarian invasions may also have played a role.[302]

Although Cumont claimed in his book (on page 206 of the English-language paperback edition) that Mithraism may have survived in some remote areas of the Alps and Vosges into the fifth century, there is virtually no evidence that would suggest a continuation of the cult that late. Of particular significance, large numbers of votive coins deposited by worshippers have been recovered at the Mithraeum at Pons Sarravi (Sarrebourg) in Gallia Belgica (modern Belgium, more or less), in a series that runs from the reign of Gallienus (253-68) to that of Theodosius I (379-95). These were scattered over the floor when the Mithraeum was destroyed, as Christians apparently regarded the coins as polluted; and they therefore provide reliable dates for the functioning of the site as a Mithraeum.[303] The coin series in all Mithraea end at the end of the 4th century at the latest. The cult disappeared earlier than that of Isis. She was still remembered in the middle ages as a pagan deity, but Mithras was already forgotten by late antiquity.[304]

In the end—and for our purposes this is most important—the cult of Mithras was, like the cults of Dionysios/Bakkhos and Osiris/Isis/Horus, part of the syncretistic religious world of pagan Rome. Almost all Mithraea contain statues dedicated to gods of other cults, and it is common to find inscriptions dedicated to Mithras in other sanctuaries, especially those of Jupiter Dolichenus, as Clauss points out.[305] Mithraism was not necessarily an alternative to Rome's other traditional religions, but rather one of multiple forms of religious practice in which a given Roman might participate. Thus Mithraic initiates can also be found participating in the Olympos-based civic religion, and as initiates in other mystery cults.[306]

The purpose of devoting so much space to the discussion of these particular religious traditions is twofold. First, it is intended to further underscore how diverse and

---

[301] This sort of action is not unusual: under the crypt of the cathedral of Notre Dame de Paris the remains of a Roman *templum* are found—and under those remains, the remains of a pre-Roman, Gallic sanctuary. There are two principles that underlie such acts of architectural supercession. One is to demonstrate the conquest or eradication by the victors of the specific sense of the divine *sacer* held by the defeated, and to assert that the victory was through the agency of the victors' own sense of the divine *sacer*. The other is to assure that one does not make the error of ignoring a site with a history of significance as a sacerdotal location: once a sacerdotal site, always a sacerdotal site. The pre-Christian history of Santa Prisca is interesting. The building was first built around 95 CE or perhaps as late as 98 CE, serving as a town house for the Emperor Trajan until his death in 117. About a century later a member of the imperial family—Commodus? (less likely, his successor, Septimius Severus?)—built a Mithraeum and a Christian sanctuary side-by-side in the basement. The Mithraeum was covered with wall paintings and reliefs that were redone around 220.

[302] He was writing in Susan Ashbrook Harvey & David G. Hunter, eds., *The Oxford Handbook of Early Christian Studies*, 95f.

[303] See Clauss, *op citum*, 31-2.

[304] Ibid, 171.

[305] *The Roman Cult of Mithras*, 158.

[306] See above, the last part of fn #296.

complex the array of traditions against which Judaeanism and its twin progeny were competing even as those offspring contended with each *other* during the first several centuries CE. That complex diversity is particularly profound when viewed at a distance of so many centuries with so few absolutely reliable resources at our disposal. Paganism was far from a monolith, and one of the distinct elements within it was any number of cults that, while their members no doubt acknowledged the existence of other gods and goddesses, were marked by the singular devotion of those members to the particular god, goddess or group of gods and goddesses associated with that cult.

Second, as should be obvious, it is intended to suggest how the issue of syncretism, so widespread across the Hellenistic and Roman worlds, in general and with regard to religion—a specific aspect of which we have discussed with regard to the putative influence of Zoroastrianism on the Qumran Judaeans and in turn on early Christianity; which we have noted for the worship of Dionysios/Bakkhos; and which we have in turn just noted for Roman Mithraism—was most likely far more interestingly active within early Christianity and Judaism (but particularly Christianity, for reasons we shall discuss shortly) than merely with regard to its putative relationship to Zoroastrianism and the Qumran texts. Moreover, Mithraism in particular stood out in the late second and early third centuries CE as one of a handful of forms of faith during the Roman imperial era that seems to have offered serious competition to emerging Christianity, and like Zoroastrianism—but perhaps more directly—it may have left an imprint on the emerging Christian faith.

The double helix of our narrative leads us therefore in two ultimately interwoven directions. We can and must pursue the issue raised in the previous paragraph. We must also, however, return to the discussion of the concepts of religion and magic that will in the long run prove so important to our understanding of how Christianity and Judaism are being shaped in their early history within the Roman world. To this second issue we turn first, before returning to pick up the issue of *sacer*-directed competition.

CHAPTER SEVEN

"Magic" and "Religion"—and "Medicine" and "Philosophy"— in Early Imperial Roman Pagan Conception: From Pliny to Apuleius and Lucian

Before considering how competition between early Christianity and Mithraism or other forms of Paganism might have developed, it makes sense to ask when and why competition of the sort that at least excoriated another form of faith, or at most sought to exterminate it, would have emerged in a world so rich both in spiritual diversity and in religious syncretism. We have already offered an important verbal instrument for denigration: "magic." What did it come to mean to the Romans and how and when did it come to be related to the concept, "*superstitio*"? Where, to pick up a thread of the discussion that began with the *Odyssey* and continued with Plato's *Laws*, does medicine fit into this matrix of terminology—as opposed to drugs or poisons?

We have preliminarily considered this question by way of our exploration of several Greek writers—Homer and, differently, Plato and Theophrastos—and the ambiguities that their discussions raised for us regarding legitimate and illegitimate engagements of the *sacer* in order to effect either positive or negative results within the *profanus* (Homer and Plato) as well as regarding *beliefs* with respect to the power of the *sacer* to affect the *profanus* (Theophrastos). In the Roman world, references to the Magi begin to accumulate by the last pre-Christian century and expand into the first century CE, and the understanding of what/who they are begins to get muddy.

Thus Cicero speaks of them as "wise and learned men among the Persians," (*De Divinatione.* I. 23, 46 and I. 41, 90; ca 44 BCE). So, too, (as we shall see), the Magi could be vaguely "wise men from the East" in Matthew II:1,2. (ca 80 CE) and be included in a list of professional "trainers" that Greeks have brought or might bring to Rome to teach people—"the teacher of languages, orator, painter, geometer, trainer/ augur, rope-dancer, physician, *magus*, they know it all—in Juvenal's *Satires* (III. 76-7; ca 90 CE), whereas in Ovid's earlier *Metamorphoses* (VII. 195; 8 CE) the mention made of *cantusque artesque magarum*—"the incantations and arts of the magi"—seems to imply spells and skills that are at least not part of religion.

Arguably the pre-eminent student of such matters in the early Roman imperial world was Pliny the Elder (32-79 CE), a scientist renowned for his study of the world around him—and so eager to learn about natural phenomena that he perished at Pompeii, having gone there on August 24, 79 CE, to observe the volcanic process of Mount

Vesuvius' eruption and dying when he remained there too long, asphyxiating before he could escape.[307] By Pliny's time, as we shall see, the term "magus" had lost a good deal of its specific original association with the East—and also, for that matter, the proper-noun association that it originally possessed when "Magi" were understood to refer to members of the Persian priestly tribe. This is well illustrated, among other places, by his note in Book 6, at the outset of chapter XCV, where he is discussing the Gauls. He comments that *nihil habent Druidae—ita suos appellant magos—visco et arbore in qua gignatur, si modo sit robur, sacratius*. ("The Druids—that is what they call their magi—hold nothing more sacred than mistletoe and a tree on which it is growing, provided that it is a hard-oak").

Pliny's work, *Natural History*, is an encyclopedic exploration of astronomy, botany, geology, mineralogy and zoology, as well as their uses, in 37 volumes. It offers a number of interesting points for our narrative. We are particularly focused on Books 28 and 30. In the first of these he arrives at a digression in his discussion "of all thngs growing between heaven and earth, leaving only whatever is dug out of the ground itself, [which I would have completed] if dealing with remedies derived from plants and shrubs did not make me digress to the wider sphere of medicines obtained from the very living creatures that themselves are healed." "Medicines" is a translation of the Latin phrase "*maiore medicina*" here, which might also be rendered "more potent cures/remedies"—in other words the context identifies "*medicina*" as substances that induce a positive outcome for the user/patient. He distinguishes between beneficial elements derived from plants and flowers—he refers to these as *remedia*—and "benefits [again: *remedia*] to humans that are to be found in humans themselves."

It is this latter subject that he pursues at this point, and his first example, in section 2, is the "blood of gladiators [that] is drunk by epileptics as though it were a draught of life, though we shudder when in the same arena we look at even the wild animals doing the same thing. But, by Hercules, they [epileptics] think it most effectual to suck from a man himself warm, living blood, and putting their lips to the wound they drain the very life, although it is not the custom of men to apply their mouths at all to the wounds even of wild beasts."

We might recognize at least three issues in this interesting—dare I say odd?—assertion by Pliny. One is that blood has an association with life that makes it particularly useful in rituals pertaining to living/dead contacts—think back to *Odyssey* 11 and Odysseus' "ritual" of facilitating contact with the dead who have drunk from the pool of blood that the hero has provided. Moreover, it might be supposed that gladiatorial blood was perhaps assumed to have particular potency, since gladiators are the consummate athletes of their era and therefore a kind of echo of earlier-era semi-divine heroes.

On the other hand, Pliny does not specify as to whether the gladiators whose blood is being consumed by epileptics hoping to be cured of their illness are alive and wounded, dying, or dead. We might suppose that the middle of these three categories applied: a healthy, living gladiator, even wounded, might not sit there calmly while an individual with

---

[307] Pliny was quite overweight, and when he succumbed to the noxious fumes his personal slave could not drag, much less carry him to the boat waiting to take them back to safety. At least we can infer this from a letter by his nephew and heir, Pliny the Younger. An alternative view that has been proposed is that he went to rescue others, not to study the phenomenon—but if so, whether or not they got away, he in the end did not.

an acknowledged serious illness sucked blood from his wounds. A dying gladiator might not be able to put up resistance to this invasive act, and stands (or rather, lies, no doubt) on the border between life and death—*profanus* and *sacer*—and might be presumed to have the potential to be as sacerdotally useful in his way as, say, Teiresias had been in his way to Odysseus. A dead gladiator has arguably already passed beyond that border (although, in a pre-funerary, pre-burial condition, still hovers near to it).

The third issue is that, although Pliny reports rather than judges, what he describes might be classified as something other than medical, since no physician is involved in the process, even though the discussion of the process began with the word *medicina*. If a method for curing an illness succeeds, is it medical or magical (one might think back to Levi-Strauss and his discussion of Quesalid!)?

In any case, Pliny goes on to refer to "[o]thers [who] seek to secure the leg-marrow and the brain of infants. Not a few among the Greeks have even spoken of the flavor of each organ and limb"—going into all the details, not excluding nail parings. Infants, too— recently arrived into our world from the other side, presumably—may also be efficacious because of their proximity to the border of the *sacer* and the power of the *sacer* over life and death and by extension, health and disease. Presumably to secure the leg-marrow and brain of an infant means that the infant is dead—so s/he is doubly at the border, having just arrived from *sacer* to *profanus* and just gone from *profanus* to *sacer*.

Further, what is ultimately operative within these accounts is the sort of sympathetic magic that Frazer described: the power associated with gladiatorial blood and infant bone-marrow and the like, and the power that these commodities are understood to possess may be transferred to the one who comes into serious contact with them. Not that Pliny necessarily believes this: "Well deserved is the disappointment if these remedies fail"—but not necessarily because they are false remedies, but because they are, as it were, morally wrong: "[if] to look at human entrails is considered unspeakable ("*nefas*" is the Latin term), what [must it be] to eat them?"

He then asks a rhetorical question (in II.6) which reminds us of the role of "mine/yours" prejudices in these matters. "Who was the one who discovered such things, Osthanes? For it is you who must bear the blame…" Osthanes was a Persian of the early fifth century BCE—apparently a Persian *maghos*—regarded by the Romans as associated with many works of, well, *magic*. That is, he is connected to works associated with exotic and unintelligible modes of yielding results in the *profanus* by engaging certain powers in the *sacer*. There is an inherent circularity to the understanding of Osthanes as such a figure: whatever he is credited with having done, it was done from within a foreign culture, using a language and engaging in actions unknown and fundamentally unintelligible to the Romans, so he and his words/actions are, by definition, magical—if that's the correct word. But it must be: he was, after all, a *magus*.

Pliny lists odd features of tentatively Osthanes-initiated practice, like "chewing human limbs, one by one." He asks, again rhetorically, "What origin could your medicine have had? Who made *veneficia* ("magic potions" or, more usually, simply "poisons") more innocent than *remedia* ("remedies")?" And he continues: "Granted that foreigners and *barbari* had discovered the rites (*ritas*), did the Greeks also make these arts their own?"[308] The terminology is slippery here, except whatever is presented as having a negative association is in turn associated with foreigners and *barbari*—and the Greeks are understood to have acquired them from these types of individuals and transferred them to the Roman world. Pliny specifically refers to Demokritos, a certain Apollonius, a certain Meletus, a certain Artemon and a certain Antaeus—all of whom shared in common, in his discussion, the enactment of odd remedies for odd maladies. Thus, for example, "Artemon treated epilepsy with draughts of water drawn from a spring by night and drunk out of the skull of a man killed but not cremated [i.e., still stuck at that *profanus/sacer* border]. From the skull of a man who has been hanged Antaeus made pills to cure the bites of a mad dog"—and so on.

He is only discussing processes with a positive outcome, apparently: "we shall speak of aids, not of sins" (*nos auxilia dicemus, non piacula*)—such as the milk of pregnant women or human saliva or contact with a human body—in other words, various sources for what Frazer would have called positive contagious magic. He asks, next, in section III, the sort of question that Malinowski asked—or at least commented on—regarding the success of the Trobriand Islanders at growing yams: "have words (*verba*) and formulated incantations (*incantamenta carminum*) any effect? ...all our wisest men reject belief in them, although as a body the public at all times believes in them unconsciously. In fact, the sacrifice of victims without a prayer (*sine precatione*) is supposed to be of no effect; without it too the gods are not thought to be properly consulted."

Several issues are brought to mind by this question and the observation that follows it. One is the question of whether the distinction between physical and verbal actions means that the discussion involves magic, religion or medicine—which question is reinforced by a second question: what is the difference, if any, between *incantamenta carminum* and *precationes*? If we might be inclined to associate the first with magic and the second with religion, why does Pliny use them within a stone's throw of each other as if they are synonymous? Or does he intend them to be understood as two different, separate modes of adding a verbal component to the physical act; but then both magic with its incantations and religion with its prayers, in which gods are involved, are at least two sides of a common coin.

It is certainly not a matter of positive versus negative, since in the very next sentence he observes that "there is one form of words for getting favorable omens, another for averting the evil eye, and yet another for a commendation." He shifts from the question of whether verbal instruments are efficacious to the implied observation that, for them to be so, they must conform to a precise pattern—one might say that they must be, in effect, a ritual, analogous to the physical acts that are part of a ritual, say, of properly offering a sacrifice. For he notes that

---

[308]*Barbaros* (pl: *barbaroi*), is a Greek word, to repeat, that was an onomatopoeia. It referred to those speaking a language that the Greeks could not understand, most particularly the Persians, whose language sounded to Greek ears like "bar-bar-bar." The Romans picked up the term, Latinized it as *barbarus* (pl: *barbari*) and further amplified its pejorative connotation. Where for the Greeks the term implied a people and culture inferior to the Hellenic peoples and cultures, for the Romans it soon began to carry the connotation of savage and unsettled. So Pliny's use of the term both points most specifically to the Persians and, somewhat ironically, associates the Greeks with the negative discussion he is putting forth.

[w]e see also that our chief magistrates have adopted fixed formulas for their prayers; that to prevent a word's being omitted or out of place a reader dictates beforehand the prayer from a script; that another attendant is appointed as a guard to keep watch, and yet another is put in charge of maintaining a strict silence; that a piper plays so that nothing but the prayer is heard… [there are] cases when the noise of actual ill omens has ruined the prayer, or when a mistake has been made in the prayer itself; then suddenly the head of the liver, or the heart, has disappeared, or these have been doubled, while the victim was standing.

What is most interesting here for our purposes is that Pliny doesn't offer an intelligible distinction between whether or when he is discussing religion or magic. The discussion of carefully-followed rituals and the failure of same when the details are not carefully enough followed applies to both domains. The same may be said of the examples with which he proceeds. If the Vestal Virgins are part of Roman religion, then when they are able to root a runaway slave to the spot *precatione*—"by [means of] a spell"—then that word should be translated not as "spell" but as "prayer" (which is how *precatio* is often otherwise rendered; see the rendering four paragraphs above). Certainly the same is true of King Tullus Hostilius, who is said (in Section IV.14) to have "used the same sacrificial ritual as Numa, which he found in Numa's books, and was struck by lightning because he made certain mistakes in the ceremony."

The importance, in particular, of words within religious ritual, is underscored by Pliny in his following assertion that "many assure us that by words the destinies and omens of mighty events are changed." Aside from the fact that he is so clearly continuing along the path of religion, having transitioned without noticing, it seems, from where he began the discussion with an eye toward magic, he has here introduced the extraordinary notion that fate itself can be altered through the judicious application of a proper verbal ritual!

Shortly thereafter, (in IV.18), he explains that "in the laws themselves of the Twelve Tables [the earliest set of Roman laws] there are the words 'whoever shall have enchanted the crops' and elsewhere 'whoever shall have cast an evil spell (*malum carmen*)'… [and a reliable source tells us how] it was the custom, at the beginning of a siege, for the Roman priests (*sacerdotibus*) to call forth the divinity under whose protection the besieged town was and to promise him the same or even more splendid worship among the Roman people." Thus the first legal/religious text of the Romans is said to have made provision for dealing with those whose intentions are negative—and whose method of *incantare* is unstated. Is it by invoking the negative side of the *sacer*? For the *sacerdotes* invoke the *sacer* to assist them and, interestingly, fight the enemies of the Romans by offering a kind of bribe to the gods of those enemies to induce them to switch sides.

Moreover, "down to the present day this ritual has remained part of the doctrine of pontiffs (*pontificum*)"—this last word another term for *sacerdotes*, meaning "those who build a bridge (*pons*) [between *profanus* and *sacer*]." He comments, a sentence later, that "[t]here is indeed nobody who does not fear to be spell-bound by imprecations. A similar feeling makes everybody break the shells of eggs or snail immediately after eating them, or else pierce them with a spoon that they have used." The obvious question for our narrative, in reading these two closely juxtaposed statements, is where the line is understood by Pliny to be drawn between religion and magic. Presumably the conduct of a pontiff/*sacerdos* is inherently part of religion, but the sorts of customs he mentions thereafter recall those spoken of by Theophrastos as practiced by a superstitious man. He then references both Greek and Roman poets—Theokritos, Catullus and Virgil—with regard to representing "love charms in their poems. Many believe that by charms pottery can be crushed, and not a few serpents, even; that these themselves can break the spell," (IV.19).

One might suppose that such beliefs are to be associated with magic and/or superstition, not with religion, but the boundary between the two disciplines certainly remains far from clear. "On walls too prayers are written to avert fires." If they are prayers, this must be religion, but everything about the context suggests magic/superstition. More interesting, "[i]t is not easy to say whether our faith is more violently shaken by the foreign, unpronounceable words, or by the unexpected Latin ones..." (IV.20)—in other words, power to influence the gods, or to convince us that we are influencing them, may be tied in to us/them: the more not-us/unintelligible/exotic, the more effective. Is gibberish understood only by the *sacerdos* and is it all the same whether it is prayer or incantation, part of religion or part of magic? One might be reminded of Plato's discussion in the *Laws*, in which he sought to distinguish different types of verbal and physical actions as illegal or legal, punishable or not.

A few lines later Pliny notes how Homer said that "by a magic formula [*carmine*—which is ambiguous; it is an utterance other than one spoken in everyday prose, but could be a song or a chant and not necessarily an incantation or magic formula] Ulysses stayed the hemorrhage from his wounded thigh; [and how] Theophrastos [said] that there is a formula to cure sciatica; [and that] Cato handed down one to set dislocated limbs [as did] Marcus Varro one for gout." Pliny's information may be slightly amiss, but what is important is that he believes that he is reporting on a series of workable cures which he seems to include in a non-religious, but also non-medical category.[309] Or rather, his categories are more than a bit vague.

So, too, in IV.21, Julius "Caesar, after one serious accident to his chariot, is said always to have been in the habit of repeating three times a prayer formula for a safe journey, *a thing we know that most people do today*" (italics added). So both Caesar, about whom he reports a century after the latter was dead, and also people contemporary with Pliny, take precautions before they travel—and again, the word that is rendered here as "prayer formula" is *carmen*. The question then becomes: how are we to understand how to parse the ambiguity—words uttered in a religious or a magical context—in reviewing Pliny's account of these customs? And where is the line drawn between individuals whom an analyst such as Theophrastos would label "superstitious" and somebody he (or we) would label pious, religious or devout?

We can follow these issues into the next section of Book 28, as Pliny asks:

---

[309] His reference, apparently to *Odyssey* 19.457, is to a passage where Autolykos and his sons, not Odysseus, in fact, effect such a cure. The Theophrastos, Cato and Varro references are more accurate. (See Theophrastos, *Athenaios* XIV. 18; Cato CLX; and Varro *Rerum Rusticarum* I.ii.27).

why on the first day of the year do we wish one another cheerfully a happy and prosperous new year? Why also, on days of general purification, do we choose persons with lucky names (*nomina prospera*) to lead the victims? Why do we meet the evil eye by a special attitude of prayer, some invoking the Greek [goddess] Nemesis, of which there is an image at Rome, on the Capitoline, although she has no Latin name? Why on mentioning the dead do we protest that their memory is not being disturbed by us? Why do we believe that in all matters the odd numbers are more powerful, as is implied by the attention paid to critical days in fevers?... Why do we say "Good Health" to those who sneeze?... [The physician?] Attalos assures us that if, upon seeing a scorpion, one says "two!" it is stopped and does not strike.... (V. 22-23)[310]

—and so on. Pliny offers a small cornucopia of customs and traditions that are designed to protect the individual from the negative potential of the *sacer*—often, but not necessarily, by invoking its positive side. The range of what he describes is fertile, but there is no clearcut qualitative difference between those customs that would be considered part of mainstream Roman religion and those that are not—except, perhaps, a distinction between communal and individual acts and customs. Even that is not absolute, however.

In chapter VI (still in Book 28), Pliny moves on to discuss those "[p]ersons possessed of monstrous natures and poisonous appearances (*monstrificas naturas et veneficos aspectus*)" of a peculiar sort—"for example the members of those families that frighten serpents. These by a mere touch or by wet suction relieve bitten victims." He mentions specific clans, such as the Psylli, the Marsi and the Ophiogenes, from Cyprus. These would seem to be similar to the Levites among the Israelites and the Magi among the Persians: they are marked by their bloodline with an ability that the rest of us lack to connect with the *sacer*—albeit those discussed by Pliny have a relationship with the wild animal *sacer*, not the divine *sacer* with which the Magi and Levites are able to connect. And they also possess peculiar features, according to Pliny, such as possessing a foul smell in the springtime, and having sweat and saliva with broader curative powers.

So, too, there are other odd and interesting things that Pliny shares, such as the discovery by Pythagoras "that an uneven number of vowels in given [personal] names portends lameness, blindness, or similar disability, on the right side, and an even number of vowels the same disabilities on the left."[311] Or, perhaps more astonishing: that "it is said that difficult labor ends in delivery if at once, if over the house where the pregnant woman lies, one were to through a stone or missile that has with one stroke killed a human, a boar and a bear." This last magical(?) solution to a not uncommon medical complication is

---

[310] The idea that sneezing drives out *daimones*—or whatever negative aspect of the *sacer*—is reflected, on might note, in 2 Kings 4:34-5, in the account of Elisha's revival of the dead son of the Shunammite woman. Elisha lay upon him, placing "his mouth on his mouth, his eyes on his eyes and his hands on his hands," walked about within the house, and lay upon him a second time. Then the child sneezed—seven times—and opened his eyes. As a "Man of God," Elisha is a conduit through which the greater power of the Israelite God prevails over whatever weaker *sacer* forces had apparently taken the living soul of the child. (We will see this echoed—but without the sneeze-effect—in Mark 5:36-42, Matthew 9:24-5 and Luke 8:49-55, when Jesus revives the dead daughter of the *archesynagogos*. See below, 193-6).

[311] It would appear from that assertion that one should name one's children altogether without vowels if they are to be both ambidextrous and healthy!

170

further refined by him, to wit, that "[a] successful result is more likely if a light-cavalry spear is used, that has been pulled out of a human body [and]... has not touched the ground" (VI.34).

"So, too," Pliny continues, "as Orpheus and Archelaus write, arrows drawn out of a body and not allowed to touch the ground act as a love-charm upon those under whose beds these are placed" while those individuals are in those beds. Given the popular association in later antiquity between Orpheus and various medical texts, are we to assume that Pliny means that this is a medical matter or a magical matter—or is there no clear difference in his mind between the two?[312] One might be reminded by Pliny's discussion of Frazer's description of certain types of contagious magic, although this is a very different variant of both method and purpose. Where Frazer wrote of the ability of a bloodied arrow to continue to inflict damage on the one whose blood is upon it, this is about the positive power of blood from a wound, still on the arrow that inflicted the wound, that has the power to inflict the wound of love—the love-object will be smitten with love; the love-object will be dead as s/he had been, and a new individual, in love, will be born—when applied properly. It must not be corrupted by touching the *profanus* ground, and it must be placed in the bed where the love-object is asleep—in other words must come into intimate *contact* with him/her; and if we assume, moreover, that this individual is asleep (how else will the practitioner sneak the arrow into the bed under him/her?) then s/he is also in a *sacer* condition.

We might also recall that, as far as proper Greek and Roman religion and medicine are concerned, the ultimate divine patron of healing—but who can also inflict illness by means of his weaponry—is Apollo, "the far-darter": his instrument is a quiver of arrows that never miss their mark.[313] Is the choice of arrows in particular connected in any way to Apollo, (as, say, the chewing of laurel leaves associated by Theophrastos with the *deisidaimon* would be) and if so, where, again, is the line between magic and religion or medicine being drawn?[314] Further, aside from the nature of the *sacer* condition of the love-object that we might infer, we are provided with no explanations from Pliny as to how or why these methods for child-production and love-evocation work and no suggestion that the actions are to be accompanied by incantations or prayers. The proposed methods themselves, at least, would seem to suggest a practitioner of extraordinary skill—or strong connections to the *sacer*: how likely is it that any practitioner will have access to a spear or stone that has killed a human, a boar and a bear all at once?

The examples of means of accomplishing what almost always seem to be positive ends continue throughout Book 28 of Pliny's narrative. Again and again we may discern elements of these means that are consistent with the general principles of *sacer-profanus*

---

[312] The Orpheus better known as a poet who played his way in and out of Hades to reclaim—and ultimately lose— his dead bride, Eurydike, was also believed, in antiquity, to have been the author of various medical texts. Arkhelaos was possibly the lyric poet of that name who lived for a long time in Egypt.

[313] In the beginning of the *Iliad*, Apollo punishes the Akhaians—for allowing Agamemnon not to return Khryseis, the daughter of Apollo's priest, Khryses, to the priest—by raining arrows of plague down upon them; conversely those arrows are associated with healing under other circumstances—the inherent neutrality and potentially positive/negative use of such weaponry is, of course, consistent with how the *sacer* essentially operates vis-à-vis the *profanus*.

[314] See above, 75.

categories—rather than religion vs magic/sorcery/superstition or religion vs medicine vs magic/sorcery/superstition categories. Three further examples from among the many: first, that

> [t]he hair cut off first from a child's head, if tied around the affected part, is said to relieve attacks of gout, as does the application of the hair of all, generally speaking, who are pre-pubescent (IX.41).

We may recognize easily enough why such hair would be considered efficacious (although not so easily why it is efficacious specifically for attacks of gout). Children and "all, generally, who are pre-pubescent" are inherently part of the *sacer*, since they are not yet enfranchised (i.e., adult) members of the community—that is, of the *profanus*. So the implication would be that parts of them—particularly a part, like hair, that is constantly proliferating—should be able to invoke the power of the *sacer* to effect a result in the *profanus* that, in this case, is a cure. (Is this, then, medical, magical, or religious?) Again, though: Pliny refers to no accompanying prayer or incantation. Nor is it clear as to why, in the very next sentence, he notes that "the hair of *adult men*, applied with vinegar, is good for dog bites, or with oil or wine for head wounds" (emphasis added), since there is nothing inherently *sacer*-connected about adult men who, on the contrary, are the absolute center of the *profanus*.

Secondly, at the beginning of chapter XI, "[w]e are assured that the hand of a dead person carried off by premature death cures scrofulous sores, diseased parotoid glands and throat affections by a touch." In this we again recognize general *sacer-profanus* principles: someone who is dead has crossed the border from *profanus* to *sacer*; someone who has died prematurely might be supposed, in his/her reluctance to complete the journey into the *sacer* of death, to be hanging around that border—but on the other side of it—and therefore to be able to assist the curative process through the contact (contagious magic?) of applying the hand from the body from which the soul has only recently and reluctantly departed.

Thirdly, at the very end of chapter IX, where he again takes up the goal of aiding a smoother, quicker birthing process, he conversely notes the importance of the incantational part of the process, observing that

> [i]f the man by whom a woman has conceived unties his girdle and puts it around her waist, and then unties it with the ritual formula: "I bound, and I, too, will unloose," then taking his departure, child-birth is made more rapid.

Not only is there a verbal component to this process, moreover, but—be it medical or magical—it clearly avails itself of what Frazer refers to as sympathetic magic, but the sympathetic act would presumably not be sufficient without the verbal formula that merely states what the sympathetic act *is*. So then, is it medical or magical—or another instance of a magical process that is believed to solve a medical problem in a world where the capability of purely medical practitioners is more limited than it would be, say, in our own time?

Let us note four further directions in which Pliny moves, as he continues through his marvelous compendium, that are particularly relevant to our narrative. (There are many more that one could note, but time and space, unlike in the *sacer*, are limited in the *profanus* of our discussion). I shall not consider them in the order in which they appear. One is when he arrives—after many more reports on diverse remedies for diverse maladies—at the beginning of chapter XVII, where the word *veneficium* is again used, but with a clearer negative implication than before: we can render it as "act of sorcery" or the like. Thus

> To sit in the presence of pregnant women and when medicine is being given to patients, with the fingers interlaced comb-wise, it to be guilty of sorcery (*veneficium*), a discovery made, it is said, when Alcmena was giving birth to Hercules. [The sorcery is] worse if the hands are clasped around one knee or both, and also to cross the knees first in one way and then in the other.

There are at least three interesting issues that this passage raises for us. One, that the term *veneficium* is unequivocally used negatively here, which, as we have seen is not always and necessarily the case. This speaks both to the ambiguities of Pliny's narrative and to the challenge to us of understanding what he really means, as we read his narrative. Two, the source of the *veneficium* is drawn, once more, from a general principle of *sacer-profanus* relational thinking. Criss-crossing the fingers and/or crossing the legs symbolizes the shaping and transgressing of borders, just as crossroads and thresholds/doorways do—and all such border areas and configurations offer the chance to the negative powers of the *sacer* to enter the *profanus* by means of their symbolic place in the highly and necessarily metaphorical vocabulary of *sacer-profanus* relationships.

Three, Pliny traces the source of this truth to an account of Herakles' birth that he apparently takes as simply factual and offers without comment. That is, he neither considers the story—the *mythos*—as a myth rather than as a gods'-truth account, nor does he consider why the context of the *mythos* would seem to make sense. For after all, Herakles is himself a consummate sacerdotal border creature: he is born of a divine father and a human mother, and eventually, when he achieves mortality (he dies) will achieve immortality (he is elevated to Olympos, to dwell among the gods).

The second Plinian direction of particular interest to us is when one arrives (backtracking several pages) to chapter XII and comes upon his first use of the term "Magi." He writes:

> Here are some contrivances/lies (*commenta*)[315] of the Magi, who say that a whetstone on which iron tools have been often sharpened, if placed without his knowledge under the pillows of a man sinking from the effects of poisoning/sorcery (*veneficio*), actually makes him give evidence about what has been given to him, where and when, but not the name of the criminal. It is certainly a fact that the victim of lightning, if turned upon the wounded side, at once begins to speak... To prevent a

---

[315]*Commentum* comes from the verb, *cominiscor*. Its two principle elements are *men-*, pertaining to thought; and *com-*, which is an intensifier. Therefore, the verb means "to devise something with careful thought," and by implication and context, not only "contrive or invent" but also "feign." Thus one can translate *commenta* either in a more neutral or in a more negative manner.

wound from being painful they prescribe wearing as an amulet... the nail or other object that he has trodden on. Warts are removed by those who, after the twentieth day of the month, lie face upwards on a path, gaze at the moon with the hands stretched over their head and rub the wart with whatever they have grasped.

So first of all, his bringing up the Magi has a certain ambiguity to it. If we assume that *commenta* does mean "lies" then he is equating the Magi at least with quacks and at worse with sorcerers. If, on the other hand, we read through the entire section, where it is not clear that Pliny regards any of these "treatments" that he describes as more or less real than all the others that he has described throughout the first eleven sections of this book—and where, as far as being injured by lightning is concerned, he accepts as fact the treatment to which he refers (XII.47)—then perhaps he simply uses the term "Magi" to refer to those kinds of individuals to whom the Persians would have been referring in their use of "*maghos*": their priests.

Further, given that the next section talks about "great remedies [that] have been made by the profit-seeking Greeks," we might suppose that he intends the word "Magi" as a broader term, a virtual synonym for "Persians." Since it would seem that he had no affection, as a Roman, for the "profit-seeking" Greeks, but respects the efficacy of their remedies—the very exotic otherness of which may, in fact help to elevate the presumed level of their efficacy—then this could very well be his view of the Magi, as well: foreign, not to be liked and, perhaps, not to be trusted, but with methods for curing certain maladies that are effective.

There is an inherent logic in this attitude: by definition *they* who are not *us*—the "other," be it Greek, Persian or anyone non-Roman, (in this case, for as we shall later see, this principle is by no means limited to pagan Romans)—are necessarily part of the *sacer*, rather than of the *profanus*, (analogous, therefore, to animals and gods who are not part of the human *profanus*). As such, they who may be the object of our contempt and with whom we may at times be at war, are viewed in their very *otherness* to have a connection to the *sacer* with its capacity for effecting positive outcomes—in this case, cures—for members of our *profanus*.

The third direction to which I would call our attention is where, in chapter XVII.64 he speaks of tying up wounds "with the Hercules knot [that] makes the healing wonderfully more rapid... for Demetrius [a physician, as far as we know, active around 200 BCE] wrote a treatise in which he states that the number four is one of the prerogatives of Hercules, in giving reasons why four cyathi or sextarii at a time should not be drunk." What is interesting is not only the reference to Herakles, a fixture by the Hellenistic period (and continuing into the Roman period) among the gods (whose mother, we cannot forget, was human and his father, the ultimate god, Zeus/Jupiter), so that Pliny has invoked a religious element in his discussion and with it, a number (in this case, four) that has a range of symbolic significances in Greco-Roman pagan religion and much farther afield—and which will come to have great importance in both Christianity and Judaism, as we shall see. So is the use of this knot medical, magical or religious?

Further, at the beginning of the next chapter, XVIII.65, in beginning a discussion of the positive uses of urine—as, for example, an element that can counteract the sorcery (*veneficia*) that prevents fertility—he notes that it (urine) possesses great power that is "not only *ratio* but indeed *religio*." So what do these two Latin terms mean in this context? We began this text by noting the broad meaning of *religio* as that which binds us back to the divine *sacer*, and have seen how it evolves toward a secondary, narrower meaning: a form of addressing the divine *sacer* that is considered legitimate by the state. Here Pliny uses it in contrast to *ratio*, and *ratio* usually means "reason/account/calculation." One might say, in other words, that *ratio* pertains to the ordered functioning of the human mind, as it understands (or tries to make sense of) the workings of the *profanus*. So in that case, *religio* in this Plinian context would refer to that which goes beyond or defies our ability to reasonably understand, make sense of, account for how it works—in other words, the irrational, unintelligible *sacer*.

Then what Pliny would seem to mean is that the power of urine that he is about to discuss falls both into the category of the *profanus* with its intelligible capacities and beyond them; its powers carry even (*etiam*) into—or are connectible to—the incomprehensible functioning of the *sacer*. This distinction, per se, should not be particularly surprising to us; but it offers another way of eroding the line between medicine and religion, to say nothing of medicine and magic—and certainly eliminates altogether the line between religion and magic or superstition. Interestingly, of course, the *ratio/religio* power of urine is contrasted, by implication, with the first example of the sort of element that it can overcome: *veneficia*.[316] One might say that it can do what the Hermes-given *pharmakon, moly*, was able to do for Odysseus against Kirke's *pharmaka* (but there the distinction was clearly between the power of Olympian-sourced *pharmaka* and those with less-than-Olympian power, and the terminology was identical for both—*pharmakon/pharmaka*—as we have seen.

The fourth direction to which I would call attention carries us to the beginning of Book 30, where Pliny begins by asserting that he has, in the previous part of his work "often indeed refuted the fraudulent lies of the Magi, whenever the subject and the occasion required it..." What is odd is that, in the passages mentioning the Magi in Book 28 he hardly seems to have done this, as we have seen. In fact, if we search through the entire extent work we find that Pliny mentions the Magi several dozen times, in many instances either reporting what they recommend as a cure for one malady or another or implying that the cure recommended by them is efficacious and in fewer instances referring to their recommendations either as fraudulent or as lies. But nowhere does he actually offer any refutation of their claims.

Thus, for instance, he briefly mentions the Magi in Book 20 half a dozen times in the context of the use of various plants particular uses of which they recommend for certain cures. For instance, in his discussion of parthenium in section CIV he observes that the Magi "recommend that we gather it with the left hand without looking back, while saying

---

[316] Incidentally, it is also not surprising that the first property that he mentions pertains to the power of "the urine of children not yet arrived at puberty"—which is particularly effective in counteracting the poisonous spit of that type of asp known as a ptyas (a spitting cobra of sorts, obviously). The urine of positive *sacer* beings—children not yet part of the *profanus*—counteracts the effects of a negative *sacer* being, a wild, poisonous serpent.

for whose sake it is being gathered; then a leaf of it should be placed under the tongue of the patient to be swallowed presently in a cyathus of water," as a cure for tertian ague. Note that the instrument is the left—*sinister*, i.e., abnormal, other—hand and that one must not look back while gathering it as well as reciting, almost as a formula/incantation/prayer the name of the one to be cured. A similar method for curing the same sort of ailment is mentioned as Magi-recommended with regard to the ilkanet plant in Book 22.XXIV.

So, too, in Book 24, at the beginning of chapter CII he records—in the same breath with which he mentions Demokritos and Pythagoras—how the Magi use the aglaophotis plant (that they call marmaritis) "to call up the gods." In the same chapter he notes that the Magi drink liquids in which the angelis plant [whatever that may be] has been dissolved "to gain power to divine." When he refers, in Book 25.V to the fact that both Demokritos and Pythagoras "visited the Magi of Persia, Arabia, Ethiopia and Egypt, and so amazed were the ancients at these books that they positively asserted even unbelievable statements," we realize that the term "Magi"—at this point in his discourse, at least—refers in a broad sense to priests of exotic other lands and offers nothing negative in its connotation.

Conversely, in referring later on in the same book (at the beginning of chapter LIX) to the plant "renowned among the Romans as *hiera botane* ('sacred plant'), [which] [s]ome call... *asistereon*, and Latin writers *verbenaca*," he notes that "the Magi especially make the maddest statements about the plant: that people who have been rubbed with it obtain their wishes, banish fevers, win friends and cure all diseases without exception"—implying that he finds these claims to be absurd. But this is the first time he has weighed in with anything suggesting a negative view of Magian thoughts, claims or methods. This view is more overt at the beginning of Book 26.IX, when he asserts that "[a]bove all Asclepiades was helped by Magian deceits"—so deceitful or not, the Magi and their methods were helpful to Asklepios, the consummate physician.

The point is that, even when he refers to them, as he does, for instance, in Book 29, chapter XX, as fraudulent, or when he speaks of their lies, he says nothing that explicitly refutes any of their claims except to pronounce them as false. Perhaps the most emphatic he gets with regard to "proving" them fraudulent is when in chapter XXVI, in writing about the horned owl, he comments: "Speaking of this bird I will not omit a specimen of Magian fraud, for besides their other monstrous lies they declare that a horned owl's heart, placed on the left breast of a sleeping woman, makes her tell all her secrets, and that men carrying it into battle are made braver by it. From the horned owl's egg they prescribe recipes for the hair." For he concludes this part of his report by asking rhetorically: "[n]ow who, I ask, could have ever looked at a horned owl's egg, when it is a portent to have seen the bird itself?" This is hardly a hard-core proof, however.

And he certainly offers nothing to suggest that the Magi are particularly fraudulent or nefarious when, a few chapters later (XXXVIII) he offers no qualitative distinction between their proposed cures and those of others, such as those of Apollonius of Pitane:

> Opaqueness of the eye-lens is cured, say the Magi, by the brain of a
> seven-day-old puppy, the probe being inserted into the right side of the
> eye to treat the right eye and into the left side to treat the left eye; or by

the fresh gall of the *axio,* a kind of owl whose feathers twitch like ears. Apollonius of Pitane preferred to treat cataract with honey and dog's gall rather than using hyena's, as he did also to treat white eye ulcers. The heads and tails of mice, reduced to ash and made into an ointment with honey, restore, they say, clearness of vision; much better the ash of a dormouse or wild mouse, or the brain of an eagle or the gall with Attic honey.

So there would not seem to be anything inherently negative about what and who the Magi are and *magia* is—and thus the beginning of Book 30 is really for the most part an explanation of just that: who the Magi are and where the term comes from. It is not a definitive condemnation of them but it does come quickly around to viewing them negatively and to associating them with the "wrong" kind of methods for tryng to engage the *sacer,* (even if so many of their cures have been reported as if they are efficacious). Pliny begins by asserting that

> [i]n a few respects, however, the theme deserves to be enlarged upon, were it only because the most fraudulent of arts has held complete sway throughout the world for many ages. Nobody should be surprised at the greatness of its influence, since alone of the arts it has embraced three others that hold supreme dominion over the human mind, and made them subject to itself alone. Nobody will doubt that it first arose from medicine, and that professing to promote health it insidiously advanced under the disguise of a higher and holier system; that to the most seductive and welcome promises it added the powers of religion, about which even todaythe human race is quite in the dark; that again meeting with success it made a further addition of astrology, because there is nobody who is not eager to learn his destiny, or who does not believe that the truest account of it is that gained by watching the skies.

So *medicina* is viewed here as the beginning point from which first, *religio* arose, and when this was combined with a careful study, understanding and calculation of the patterns of the stars and planets—the *artes mathematicae*—the result of this synthesis was *magia*.

Pliny then goes on to devote the first eighteen sections of book 30 to a consideration of the Magi. On the one hand, he asserts that "[w]ithout doubt *magia* arose in Persia with Zoroaster. On this our authorities are agreed, but whether he was the only one of that name, or whether there was also another afterwards, is not clear. Eudoxus, who wished *magia* to be acknowledged as the noblest and most useful of the *schools of philosophy*, declared that this Zoroaster lived six thousand years before Plato's death, and Aristotle agrees with him" (emphasis added). Thus, according to Pliny, Eudoxos simply saw the teachings of the Magi as part of—the noblest part of—philosophy: the love (*philia*) of wisdom (*sophia*) with which we (and they) associate figures like Sokrates, Plato and Aristotle.

If *magia* originated in Persia and its beginning point was Zoroaster, yet it has ceased, by Pliny's time, to have a specific association with the Persians any more, as we have previously noted. On the contrary, in section III he notes that

> [a]mong Italian tribes also there still certainly exist traces of magic in the Twelve Tables, as is proved by my own and the other evidence set forth in an earlier Book. It was not until the 657th year of the City [96BC] that in the consulship of Gnaeus Cornelius Lentulus and Publius Licinius Crassus there was passed a resolution of the Senate forbidding human sacrifice; so that down to that date it is manifest that such abominable rites were practised.

—and he continues, in section IV, to assert that

> [m]agic certainly found a home in the two Gallic provinces, and that down to living memory. For the principate of Tiberius Caesar did away with the Druids and this tribe of seers and medicine men. But why should I speak of these things when the craft has even crossed the Ocean and reached the empty voids of Nature? Even today Britain practises magic in awe, with such grand ritual that it might seem that she gave it to the Persians. So universal is the cult of magic throughout the world, although its nations disagree or are unknown to each other. It is beyond calculation how great is the debt owed to the Romans, who swept away the monstrous rites, in which to kill a man was the highest religious duty and for him to be eaten a passport to health.

Thus not only is *magia* everywhere—or was, until the Romans made it their business to extirpate it—but one of its most defining features was human sacrifice. This attribute imputes a distinctly negative quality to *magia*, but, in the international context that Pliny sketches, we must also understand that it is *theirs*—Persians, Gauls, Britons, et al—as opposed to *ours*. However, given that the Romans are clearly comfortable with assimilating other national religions and religious practices into their own diverse religiosity, the distinguishing issue here for Pliny is the "negativity" factor (of human sacrifice) rather than, per se, the "otherness" factor.

Equally interesting is the fact that, toward the end of Chapter II (section 11), Pliny notes further, in his presentation of *magia* as an international enterprise, that [t]here is yet another branch of magic [*magices factio*], derived from Moses, Jannes [an Egyptian magician], Iotapes [Iotape (i.e., *iota pe*, in Greek) = Yahweh], and the *Iudaei* (Judaeans), but living many thousand years after Zoroaster.[317] This is the first time we encounter an explicit reference to the Israelite-Judaean tradition in Greek or Roman writings of this sort, and we shall consider, shortly, what the circumstances would have been that would cause Pliny (and others) to look at Moses as a founder of a branch of *magia*, as opposed to *religio*—although as we have previously noted, Roman law had much earlier already acknowledged Judaeanism as a *religio licita*, which means that Pliny's distinction is not a standard legal-vs-illegal one, but a substantive one of either method or goal.

With that in mind, it is also interesting that, a few lines before this (in II:9) he had noted that, in an earlier era—specifically that of Demokritos and Hippokrates—"both of these arts, I mean medicine and magic, flourished together." What is of importance to us

---

[317] Note that translators typically misrepresent *Iudaei* as "Jews."

is that he sees these as distinctly separate disciplines, the one associated with Hippokrates and the other with Demokritos (who is otherwise known as an atomist philosopher in general discussions of Greek thinkers).[318]

Magian methods that Pliny had briefly adumbrated in Book 28, chapter CIV (such as *luceruis, peivi, aqaa, pila*) he expounds upon more fully, in chapter V of Book 30. There he agrees with Osthanes, that "there are several forms of *magia*; he professes to divine from water, globes, air, stars, lamps, basins and axes, (*aqua, sphaeris, aere, sinus, lucernis, pelvihus, et securibus*) and by many other methods, and besides to converse with ghosts and those in the underworld." This last reference, of course, should recall both *Odyssey* 10-11 and the role of Kirke in facilitating Odysseus' ability to do just that, and I Samuel 28, where the sacerdotal woman at Endor is able to do the same for the Israelite King Saul.

The Magi, moreover,

> have certain means of evasion: for example, that the gods neither obey those with freckles nor are seen by them… [and] Tiridates the Magus… had initiated Nero into their banquets; yet the man giving him a kingdeom was unable to acquire from him this art. Therefore, let us be convinced that it [*magia*] is detestable, vain and idle; and it nonetheless has shadows of truth, but their power comes from the arts of poison not magical [arts]. One might ask what were the lies of the old Magi… [VI.16-18] It should be [for example] a particular evidence of fraud [*vanitas*] that they look with awe upon the mole, of all living creatures, although it is cursed by nature with so many defects, being permanently blind, sunk indeed in other darknesses, and resembling the buried dead. In no entrails is such faith placed; to no creature do they attribute more supernatural properties… [VII.19]

Thus we finally arrive, well into Book 30, to some explicit statement as to what affords a negative evaluation to *magia*: that it is misdirected. We might infer that there are further, related misdirections, such as that "a tooth extracted from a living mole and attached as an amulet cures toothaches" [VII.20], and that "toothaches are also cured, the Magi tell us, by the ash of the burnt heads without any flesh of dogs that have died of madness, which must be dropped in Cyprus oil through the ear on the side where the pain is…" [VIII.21]. But in fact both this last method and the many others that follow in Pliny's discussion are offered in a straightforward manner; if they are intended to be read as a litany of false cures, that falseness is to be inferred from the fact that they follow the mole discussion—or perhaps more subtly, from the fact that they are so, well, unusual in their

---

[318] The Atomists—Leukippos, Demokritos and Epikouros are the main ones—are, for our purposes, noted for two aspects of their thought. They reduce reality to two physical components: atoms (irreducibly tiny elements of material; from the Greek *a-* [not] + *temno* [to cut], thus "uncuttable") and the endless void through which they fall. Some inexplicable force causes the atoms occasionally to swerve (the swerve is called *to klinamen*; think of the English word, "incline"), and they glom on to each other, thus forming our physical, substantive reality. Given this limited sense of the world, they also assert that, when at death the physical *elementa* of the body once again fall apart, so does the soul—which, in other words, is not immortal, disintegrating when the body that contains it does. Concomitant with this is a conviction that there are no gods and those who believe in gods are being deceived.

methodology. One notes, once more, in any case, that these acts of *magia* are indistinguishable from legitimate medical treatments (assuming that these *are* to be read as illegitimate) and that, moreover, even assuming that these are false they are not presented as nefarious—after all they are all offered as means of curing an ailment, not harming a victim.

The same two observations may be made of the array of observations that follow as, for example, that [the Magi assert] "that the taste in the mouth is made agreeable if the teeth are rubbed with the ash of burnt mice mixed with honey" [IX.27] or that "spots on the face are removed by *oesypum* with Corsican honey, that is considered the most bitter" [X.28].[319] In the following chapters there are scores of cures for dozens of maladies—and even for gaining love—that Pliny relates as taught by or derived from the Magi, without necessarily suggesting that there is anything either negative, false or weak about them.

If still later—in book 37, chapter XIV—he notes that he will now "discuss those kinds of gemstones that are acknowledged as such, beginning with the finest. And this shall not be my only aim, but to the greater profit of mankind I shall incidentally confute the abominable falsehoods of the Magi, since in very many of their statements about gems they have gone far beyond providing an alluring substitute for medical science into the realms of the supernatural," his refutation is limited to asserting that their claims are false, as for example, in (chapter XL): "The Magi falsely claim that the amethyst prevents drunkenness, and that it is this property that has given it its name."[320] So he has not explained why or how the magian claims are false; he has merely asserted that they are.

* * * * * *

Pliny's clinical discussion is the analysis by a professional student of all things natural—and supernatural. It does not necessarily convey what the person on the street thinks. His mind, on the other hand, comes off as that of an ordinary, garden-variety thinker, albeit with an encyclopaedic range of interests—and he seems to show much of the uncertainty the ordinary man used to feel with regard to the arts of the Magi. He speaks of their *vanitas* and *fraudes*, but nevertheless, as we have seen, gives details of several score of their prescriptions and amulets, in contexts dealing with everyday remedies and medicines. In several passages, he certainly expresses a strong disapproval of *magia*, which he would appear to dislike and distrust, but he also fears it because of its apparent efficacy. A few generations after him, Apuleius (125-ca 180 CE), in being brought up on charges of engaging in *magia*—in order to win the love of a financially well-off widow—and in defending himself eloquently against those charges, offers a splendid opportunity to begin to assess that very issue.

Apparently, Apuleius was an initiate in several mystery cults, including those associated with Dionysios, and was also a priest of Aisklepios.[321] He travelled a good deal

---

[319] *Oesypum* is some sort of cosmetic, apparently made from washed wool; perhaps something like lanolin.
[320] In Greek, the "*a-*" prefix, called "*alpha* privative," means "not" or "un-" and *methuein* means "to intoxicate."
[321] St. Augustine, writing in the late fourth or early fifth century, also refers to Apuleius as a *sacerdos provinciae Africae* ("priest of the province of Carthage"), so he seems to have been quintessentially Roman in his taste for diverse spiritual traditions.

to further his learning, and on one of his trips, to Alexandria, he was taken ill at the town of Oea (modern-day Tripoli) and was hospitably received into the house of Sicinius Pontianus, with whom he had been friends when he had been a student in Athens. The mother of Pontianus, Pudentilla, was a very wealthy widow. With her son's consent—even encouragement—Apuleius agreed to marry her. Meanwhile Pontianus himself married the daughter of one Herennius Rufinus. Rufinus, indignant that Pudentilla's wealth should pass out of the family, convinced his new son-in-law, together with a younger brother, Sicinius Pudens, a mere boy, and their paternal uncle (in other words, Pudentilla's brother-in-law), Sicinius Aemilianus, to join him in charging Apuleius with sorcery: to wit, that he had gained the affections of Pudentilla by charms and magic spells.

The charge was preferred in ca 158 CE, and the court to judge Apuleius was convened at Sabratha, near Oea/Tripoli. The charges were formally brought up by Aemilianus—or at least he is the one to whom Apuleius seems mainly to address himself. For our purposes we arrive into the middle of Apuleius' long speech as, in the middle of section 25, he begins to "deal with the actual charge of *magia*," based, as he puts it, on a series of old wives' tales. He begins by challenging Aemilianus and "his most learned advocates" as to exactly "how, precisely, they would define *"magus."* This is merely a rhetorical question, of course, as Apuleius immediately demonstrates his linguistic and historical scholarship by noting that "if what I read in a large number of authors be true, namely that *"magus"* is the Persian word for priest, [then] what is there criminal in being a priest and having due knowledge, science, and skill in all ceremonial law, sacrificial duties, and the binding rules of religion, at least if *magia* consists in that which Plato sets forth in his description of the methods employed by the Persians in the education of their young princes?"[322]

He quotes Plato's alleged account of how these Magi, four in number—"one the wisest, a second the most just, a third the most temperate, a fourth the bravest"—are called upon to teach princes, when they reach age 14 "the *magia* of Zoroaster," which "is nothing other than the worship of the gods." So, (he continues in section 26), established by Zoroaster and his mother, Oromazes, *magia* is "an art acceptable to the immortal gods, full of worship and prayer, full of piety and glory"—in other words, *religion*. Elsewhere, he notes, Plato refers to "'magical charms [as] merely beautiful words.' Then why should I be forbidden to learn the fair words of Zalmoxis [a Thracian Magus allegedly quoted by Plato] or the priestly lore of Zoroaster?" Furthermore,

> If these accusers of mine, after the fashion of the common herd, define a
> *magus* as one who by communion of speech with the immortal gods has
> power to do all marvels that he will, through a strange power of
> incantation, I really wonder that they are not afraid to attack one whom
> they acknowledge to be so powerful!

So Apuleius is simultaneously explaining that there is a distinction between harmful and helpful power, but not in this case, between weaker and stronger power, nor between false and true *sacerdotal* practice. There is also an inherent contradiction in his accusers' stance vis-à-vis him: if they believe that his power is both real and nefarious, they should not be

---

[322] Apuleius not surprisingly uses the Latin word, *magus*, rather than the original Persian word, *maghos*.

getting on his bad side! If they do not believe this, then they are falsely accusing him. The defense might have ended here and a reasonable judge would have no doubt exonerated Apuleius, but he continues, both to be sure and because he seems to be having too much fun slicing his opponents into logic-devoid ribbons.

His logic, he would say, derives from the fact that he is a philosopher—one of that kind of person who is often, he notes (in section 27), attacked by the ignorant (thereby conjuring up the image of Sokrates in the Athenian courtroom five and a half centuries earlier). We may understand his equation of what he does with *philosophia*—to be distinguished from *magia*, but also from *medicina* or *religio*?—as generically intended: the love of wisdom (in other words, love of any and all forms of knowledge-acquisition). Thus in this section of his argument, he implicitly merges the meaning of philosopher and magician when he observes, after referring to accusations against philosophers, that "[s]ome of them [the uninitiated] think that those who explore the origins and elements of material things are irreligious, and assert that they deny the existence of the gods. Take, for instance, the cases of Anaxagoras, Leukippos, Demokritos, and Epikouros, and other natural philosophers," and immediately adding: "Others call those '*magi*' those who bestow unusual care on the investigation of the workings of providence and unusual devotion on the worship of the gods..." In this second group he includes "Epimenides, Orpheus, Pythagoras and Osthanes," [who] were regarded as magicians, while a similar suspicion attached to the 'purifications' of Empedocles, the 'daimon' of Socrates and the 'good' of Plato."

There is, on the other hand, a certain ambiguity here: maybe his intention is to *distinguish* magi from philosophers—we might argue that Orpheus is not a philosopher, whereas Plato and Pythagoras are, but we cannot be sure that Apuleius would distinguish their categories of practice from each other as we might. And it is clear on the other hand that, if separate, the two categories share common ground in being perceived by the common people as suspect and opposed to categories of individuals who are legitimate *sacerdotes,* engaging the *sacer* properly.

In any case, Apuleius proceeds at this point to delineate the details of the accusation against him and its absurdity. Thus, he has "bought particular kinds of fish" and he "keeps a mysterious object in his house which he venerates," and also, "a boy fell to the ground in Apuleius' presence"—to which odd charges he responds that he "will prove that they have nothing to do with *magia*," and more to the point, he "will show that even on the assumption of my being the most consummate *magus*, I have never given cause or occasion for conviction of any evil practice... [and moreover I will prove that] "I married [Pudentilla] for love, and not for money [section 28)]." So we can infer both that certain actions are seen by everyday people as part of *magia* in their very oddness—those three "actions" are also presumed by his accusers to appear out of the ordinary to their audience—and also that, to be thought of as pertaining to *magia*, such actions are further believed to have a nefarious, as opposed to neutral, much less benign, intent.

Simply summarized: he admits to buying fish, but asks rhetorically whether buying fish is an unusual action, limited to sorcerers. Even if we "assume with Aemilianus that fish are useful for making magical charms as well as for their usual purposes, ...does that prove that whoever acquires fish is *ipso facto* a magician [section 32]?" He brings up particular words and various poets and philosophers before deciding that he has spent enough time on this angle of defense and asks rhetorically (in section 40): "[w]hat if I take such interest and possess such skill in medicine as to search for certain remedies in fish? For... remedies are to be found in fish. Now, do you think it more *the business of a magician than of a doctor, or indeed of a philosopher*, to know and seek out remedies" [italics added]?

This last rhetorical question places front and center the notion of a distinction among these three types of practitioners and practices, implying that what distinguishes *magia* from *medicina* and *philosophia* is the negative outcome sought by the first practice and the positive outcomes sought by the latter two practices—and again he offers examples from Homer and Aritstotle to reinforce his point. Moreover, he adds: "[I] have made no secret of my research, but conduct it openly before all the world"—further implying that the method of *magia* is secret, rather than open, just as he further reinforces the matter of distinguishing *magia* by its purpose when, at the beginning of the next section (41), he asks whether dissecting a fish is "a crime in a philosopher that would be no crime in a butcher or cook."

He moves on to the accusation that

> I had taken a boy apart to a secret place with a small altar and a lantern and only a few accomplices as witnesses, and there so bewitched him with a magical incantation that he fell in the very spot where I pronounced the charm, and on being awakened was found to be out of his wits... [My accusers should have further lied that he] uttered many prophecies. For this we know is the prize of magical incantations, namely divination and prophecy.

Again, the method is assumed to be secret, the use of incantations is presumed and, interestingly, not only is another supposed outcome presented—that would confuse the line between *magia* and *religio*, since proper prophecy is the province of *sacerdotes* who are part of *religio*—but such things are believed, he adds, not only by ignorant people but by learned men. For

> the philosopher Varro, a writer of the highest learning and erudition, ...[wrote about inquiry] by means of magic into the probable outcome of the Mithridatic war, and a boy who was gazing at an image of Mercury reflected in a bowl of water foretold the future in a hundred and sixty lines of verse. ...[He also wrote of how Nigidius] by means of incantations inspired certain boys so that they were able to indicate to him where a pot containing a certain portion of [lost] money had been hidden in the ground.

Apuleius expresses doubts regarding the veracity of any of this, although he acknowledges the likely legitimacy of *sacerdotes* (my word, not his) of various sorts, particularly when a venerable source such as Plato "asserts that there are certain divine powers holding a position and possessing a character midway between gods and men, and that all divination and the miracles of magi are controlled by them" (section 43). One cannot help but think—

and wonder whether or not Apuleius is thinking—of Sokrates, again, in particular the description of him offered by Alkibiades in Plato's *Symposium* that presents him as a kind of *hemi-theos* (half-god).

He asserts, however, that such an individual should be a young person, (which Sokrates was not, at least when Alkibiades was delivering his encomium of him), since "the human soul, especially when it is young and unsophisticated, may... [be] reduced to its primal nature, which is in truth immortal and divine; and thus, as it were, in a kind of slumber it may predict the future." The notion that such an intermediary be a young boy is consistent with the larger logic of the *sacer-profanus* matrix as we have been considering it: a child is not an enfranchised member of the community—the *profanus*—and is thus by definition part of the *sacer* and may be expected to be far more adept at accessing the divine aspect of the *sacer* and its information than an ordinary adult would be.

Apuleius further asserts that such a "prophetic boy must [additionally]... be fair and unblemished in body, shrewd of wit and ready of speech, so that a worthy and fair shrine may be provided for the divine indwelling power—if indeed such a power does enter into the boy's body," for it is not a given even under ideal conditions that the unpredictable *sacer* will transmit its messages through the conduit prepared for that event. Regarding the accusation to which he is responding, Apuleius says that "Thallus [the boy in question] whom you mentioned, needs a doctor rather than a magician. For the poor wretch is such a victim of epilepsy that he frequently has fits twice or thrice in one day without the need for any incantations, and exhausts all his limbs with convulsions. His face is ulcerous, his head bruised in front and behnd [from constant falls in epileptic fits]..." So much for spells and *magia*: he had such a fit in Apuleius' presence, that's all, and fell down due to an epileptic seizure, and "why then attribute his fall to magic rather than to disease" [section 45]?

Besides, Apuleius continues, "why should I use charms when, as I am told by writers on natural history, the burning of the stone named *gagates* is an equally sure and easy proof of the disease? ...Again, the spinning of a potter's wheel will easily infect a man suffering from this disease with its own giddiness"—and so on. Either these methods of inducing an epileptic to have a fit work or they do not, but his point is, of course, that they all pertain to a medical matter that has nothing to do with *magia*. He further mocks his accusers' attempt to have him indicted by confusing these categories, including their calling upon fifteen slaves as witnesses. "The inference is that fifteen slaves know something, and that something is still a mystery. Or is it nothing mysterious and yet something connected to *magia*? ... [But] either the procedure to which I admitted so many witnesses had nothing improper about it, or, if it had, it should not have been witnessed by so many" [section 47]—so that, again, a defining attribute of *magia* is that it is not only nefarious in intention but that, as a consequence, it is done in secret.

More to the point, with regard to the fact of a legal procedure, is the notion that the "*magia* of which you accuse me is, I am told, a crime in the eyes of the law, and was forbidden in remote antiquity by the Twelve Tables, because in some incredible manner crops had been charmed away from one field to another. It is then as mysterious an art as it is loathsome and horrible" [(section 47]. So, aside from apparently being mysterious in method (as if religion never is!) and nefarious in intention, *magia* is, simply, illegal—because it is mysterious and *deemed* nefarious in intention.

Aemilianus apparently further accused Apuleius of causing a second individual, a woman, into falling down, but again, our defendant argues that a physician named Themison brought her to Apuleius for a *consultation* and that she had a fit while in his presence. Again Apuleius points out that she was an epileptic (and perhaps, from the description, she also had tinnitus), and now offers an excursus on the malady rooted in a discussion of Plato's *Timaeus* and referring to epilepsy as the "divine sickness," or "holy sickness," based on the common idea that it is imposed by (a) *sacer* being(s)—but Apuleius interprets the turn of phrase as referring, rather, to how "this sickness does outrage to the rational part of the soul, which is by far the most holy" [section 50]. In our terms, the most *sacer* aspect of the one suffering from the disease emerges, as it were, when s/he is afflicted.

He comments on Aristotle's comments on it, and on Theophrastos' writing on it, including a claim for curing fits with the skins of newts—writings and claims, he notes, that come from philosophers, rather than from physicians or poets, "that my adversaries may cease to wonder that philosophers [such as I am] have learnt the causes of remedies and diseases in the natural course of their researches" [section 51]. Either, he asserts, based on the evidence that he has provided, "my opponents must assert that it is the part of a *magus* and evildoer to heal disease, or... they must confess that their accusations with regard to this epileptic boy and woman are false, absurd, and indeed epileptic." Again, then, *magia* is assumed to have a nefarious intention (so that Apuleius is either a magician who contradicts what he is by doing something that is not nefarious in intent, or he is not a magician).

There is, finally, in section 53, the matter of that "something mysterious wrapped up in a handkerchief among the household gods in the house of Pontanius," Apuleius' friend and, technically, his step-son-in-law, which "you assert ...was some instrument of magic." He frames Aemilianus' accusation, mockingly, as " 'Apuleius kept certain things wrapped in a cloth among the household gods of Pontanius. Since I do not know what they were, I therefore argue that they were magical'." Thus the essence of something having to do with *magia* is, once again, that it is mysterious in being unfamiliar and in being unfamiliar is mysterious—and therefore assumed to be nefarious. But why, Apuleius asks, would I leave these things lying around where anyone might examine them, if they were something of secret importance?

Toward the end of his *Apologia*, (in section 102), he asks what it was that he was to gain from using love-philtres and whatever other magical procedures to induce Pudentilla to marry him? The marriage contract provided him with none of her wealth; her will continued to name her son—and not her new husband—as her heir. For the purposes of our own discussion this last section of his defense is less important than the earlier parts (which he sums up in the last section of his argument). We can be as convinced as was the judge, Maximus, regarding Apuleius' innocence of the accusations, but we are most intrigued by the themes that repeat with regard to what *magia* is understood to be and how its alleged bases and methods, and/or its alleged goals, could be so easily confused with those of religion, philosophy and medicine. The reference to the Twelve Tables and to illegality reminds us that the issue of *religio* versus *superstitio* or *magia* combined theological with political concerns: not just inherent questions regarding the divine *sacer* but regarding power within the *profanus* based on the answers to those questions.

The common assumptions regarding *magia* could lead to satirical works that mock that perspective, one way or another. Apuleius' own interest in the subject of *magia*, and his pleasure in focusing satirically upon how the term is commonly understood, is reflected in one of the first novels in the Western canon, his *Metamorphoses*—also known (in English translation) as *The Golden Ass*—in which the hero, by ignoring the proper verbal accompaniments to a physical process (smearing his body with a particular unguent) is transformed into an ass rather than a bird and has myriad adventures until he is able to find the precisely correct circumstance in which, through the favor and assistance of a goddess, (who helps him not because she is compelled but because she takes pity on him) he is able to return to a human form. It is a very entertaining adjunct to this discussion, raising by-now-familiar questions regarding how and where to draw a line between magic and religion with regard to method and intention and what forces of the *sacer* are engaged in the process in what way.

So, too, the dialogue authored around 150 CE by Lucian of Samosata (ca 125-ca 190 CE; Samosata was in the Syrian province of the Empire; now part of Turkey), called "The Liar" ("*Philopseudes*"), offers a satirical handling of this subject. The dialogue (in Greek) is shaped in the Platonic style, like a Chinese box, with a narrative within a narrative. Thus it is ostensibly between the main narrator, Tykhiades (whose name means "child of fate"), and Philokles ("lover of glory"). The former asks, rhetorically, why so many people like lies—why they "prefer a lie to truth, simply on its own merits." He begins with a reference to all the tales of gods and other creatures found in Hesiod, Homer and other earlier poets—material that he treats as clearly false and therefore as mythological, rather than as part of the religion that presumably defined Greece during the time of Homer and Hesiod.

This leads to Tykhiades' tale of having recently visited the house of an elderly friend, Eukrates, who suffers from gout. There he gets into an argument regarding the supernatural. The setting seems altogether like a satire of Plato's *Phaedo*, in which Sokrates, awaiting the draft of hemlock that will bring on his death, holds forth in his jail cell to a gathering of his disciples regarding the immortality of the soul. For at the home of the ailing Eukrates (whose very name evokes that of Sokrates) there is a crowd of visitors, representing different schools of thought. Kleodemos is a Peripatetic philosopher, Dinomakhos is a Stoic, Ion is a Platonist and Antigonos, a physician, is also there. Each of these individuals has medical advice for Eukrates. Kleodemos, for instance, tells him to "take up the tooth of a field mouse that has been killed in a prescribed manner in the left hand, attach it to the skin of a freshly flayed lion and bind the skin about one's legs"—a kind of cure that echoes some of the treatments reported by Pliny—while the others suggest variations on this mode of treatment.

The proposed treatment is both homoiopathhic and contagious: the speed of a lion is understood to be transferable by contact to the legs immobilized by gout. Tykhiades asks how useful incantations might be and is laughed at, except by Antigonos, who proposes a change in Eukrates' gastronomic habits: he ought to "cut down on your consumption of wine and go on a vegetable diet." The argument that follows between Kleodemos and Antigonos pits magic against medicine—or asks where the line would be drawn between those disciplines—and also between magic and religion, since when Dinomakhos asks Tykhiades whether he is, in fact, an atheist, since apparently "you do not believe in the existence of the gods, since you maintain that cures cannot be wrought by the use of holy names," Tykhiades responds, "no, say not so... The gods may exist, and these things may yet be lies. I respect the gods," Tykhiades continues. "I see the cures performed by them...—[but] without the lion's–skin-and–field-mouse process."

Tall tales follow, seeking to convince Tykhiades that supernatural phenomena are true (an echo of the series of arguments from analogy that Sokrates makes regarding why the soul should be understood to be immortal)—and each tale Tykhiades either mocks or rebuts—or both (again satirically echoing the rebuttals offered by Sokrates' disciples to each of his arguments). Ion recalls how, in his childhood a worker bitten by a poisonous snake was saved by a Babylonian (Chaldaean) who was able to expel the poison from the wound by an incantation—and the use of a "splinter of stone chipped from the monument to a virgin; this he applied to [the worker's] foot." Moreover, the next morning, early, "the Chaldaean went into the field, pronounced seven names of sacred import, taken from an old book, purified the ground by going thrice around it with sulfur and burning torches, and thereby drove every single reptile off the estate."

To this Saint Patrick-like narrative Ion adds others, regarding a flying Hyperborean, "travelling thought the air in broad daylight, walking on water, or strolling on fire" who could also make a woman fall in love with the one who loves her—provided that the lover can pay a fee to the wizard/magician. Interestingly, the procedure for this involves ordering the goddess Hekate "to appear, with Kerberos [the three-headed dog that guards the way into Hades] in her train, and the moon was brought down, and went through a variety of transformations." Thus it would seem that this mode of Hyperborean magic includes at least one element of religion: the involvement of a goddess.

Ion speaks of "those who cure demoniacal possession," such as "that Syrian adept from Palestina," who "stands over [lunatics] as they li.e., and asks the spirit whence it has come. The patient says not a word, but the spirit in him makes him answer, *in Greek or some foreign tongue* as the case may be..." (italics added). He tells of a statue in his house that, by night, "descends from his pedestal, and walks all around the house," to which Antigonos adds that "I myself have a Hippokrates [the father of Greek medicine] in bronze, some eighteen inches high. Now the moment my candle is out, he goes clattering about all over the house... mixing up all my *pharmaka*; especially when his annual sacrifice is due."

Tykhiades' tale of tales that he was told at Eukrates' house includes Kleodemos' story of having had fever for seven days when "I awoke to find a handsome young man standing at my side, in a white cloak." This was presumably some version/vision of Hermes, the guide of souls (*psykhopompos*), who "raised me from the bed, and conducted me through a sort of chasm into Hades," where he was told that it was not yet his time to die—reminiscent of the *mythos* told by Sokrates in the *Phaedo*, of the journey of the soul through the underworld related to him by a reliable source. In fact, Eukrates himself speaks shortly after this of how he was reading Plato's *Phaedo* shortly after the death of his beloved wife, when she appeared and sat down next to him, to inform him that he had "neglected to burn one of her golden sandals, which she said had fallen under a chest," presumably preventing her from completing her journey to the other side.

Arignotos the Pythagorean shows up and is shocked that Tykhiades does not believe in the supernatural. He tells the tale of how he unearthed a *daimon*, expelling it from a house that, having been haunted by the *daimon*, now became habitable. He went into the house at night and as the spirit made its appearance, "armed with my most appalling adjuration, uttered in the Egyptian tongue [not surprisingly!], I drove him spell-bound into the corner of the dark room, marked the spot at which he disappeared," and at dawn, had his associates dig at that spot, where they found a moldering corpse, and transferred the skeleton to a proper grave. We have seen how this principle of proper burial and proper funerary procedure is necessary in order to facilitate passage into the *sacer* of death; it marked the first encounter of Odysseus with a dead person, Elpinor, in Book 11 of the *Odyssey*.

The culmination of the dialogue arrives with the tale told by Eukrates himself (formally recalling how in the *Phaedo* and elsewhere the culmination of Sokrates' rational arguments—*logoi*—is the *mythos* he tells, followed by his cheerful action (*ergon*) of quaffing the hemlock as if it were the finest of wines)—it is a story that he claims truly took place to himself as a young man who, as a sorcerer's companion (not, as in later versions of this tale, a sorcerer's apprentice!) who misuses elements of the master's magical toolbox after eavesdropping on him but, without fully knowing how to do what he seeks to do, gets into trouble (as Lucius did in *The Golden Ass*).[323]

Not surprisingly, the sorcerer/magician in Lucian's tale is an Egyptian—a priest of Isis and a mystic, called Pankrates. In other words, we once again encounter the Roman penchant for ascribing out-of-the-ordinary engagements and engagers of the *sacer* to exotic other locales with long histories, such as Babylonia or Persia on the one hand and Egypt on the other. And once again the line between religion and magic and their respective practitioners is blurred: what would be a priest engaged in religion to the Egyptians is treated as a magician/sorcerer engaged in magic/sorcery by our Roman narrator.

Eukrates claims to have visited the statue of Memnon, in Egypt, which delivered an oracle to him in seven hexameters. It was on that trip that he encountered Pankrates, who

> was said to have passed 23 years of his life under the instruction of Isis herself... Whenever we came to an inn, he used to take up the bar of the door, or a broom, or perhaps a pestle, dress it up in clothes, and utter a certain incantation; whereupon the thing would begin to walk about... It would go off and draw water, buy and cook provisions, and make itself generally useful... There was another incantation after which the broom was a broom once more, or the pestle a pestle. At last one day I hid in a

---

[323] This is the earliest version of such a tale that would more famously emerge as a poem (1797) by the German writer, Johann Wolfgang von Goethe (1747-1832)—the *Zauberlehrling* ("Magician's Apprentice")—and which would still later be presented as an 1897 symphonic poem, "The Sorcerer's Apprentice," by the French composer, Paul Dukas (1865-1935), whose music would still later be used to accompany a 1940 cartoon version of the story (with Mickey Mouse as the apprentice), created by Walt Disney studios as part of the film, *Fantasia*, and still later, a 1955 ballet version of the narrative, filmed by German filmmaker Michael Powell.

dark corner, and overheard the magic syllables; they were three in number.

Eukrates took the pestle, dressed it up, pronounced the three syllables and ordered it to fetch water—but of course he did not know the correct words to get it to stop, and when he took an ax and cut the pestle in two he merely doubled his problem, until Pankrates appeared and returned the pestle to its/their original form—and then in apparent anger disappeared, never to be seen again by Eukrates.

Tykhiades remains unconvinced of the truth of all of this. Eukrates asks, "talking of superstition... what do you make of oracles, for instance, and omens? Of inspired utterances, of voices from the shrine, of the priestess's prophetic lines?"—thus in a sense completing the discussion by implying that the line between religion and magic or superstition is a thin one indeed, and that if one does not believe in the latter then one will not believe in the former. If we think back to Theophrastos and our question as to whether what he described and ascribed to the *deisidaimon* could not just as easily be associated with a pious as with a superstitious man, then Lucian's satire places us on a differently angled side of the same question: if one does not believe in the *sacer* as it is treated by the superstitious, can one believe in the *sacer*—the divine *sacer*—as it is treated by religion? For Eukrates tells of a certain magic ring in his possession, "the seal of which is a portrait of the Pythian Apollo, and actually *speaks* to me..."—among other further accounts of experiences at religious sites.

All of these stories, in the end, Tykhiades tells Philokles, make him ill, for they are all lies. "Truth and good sense: these are the *pharmaka* for our ailment," he concludes. Apuleius' novel about the adventures of Lucius and Lucian's dialogue that culminates with Tykhiades' story of Eukrates' story in which, like Apuleius' Lucian, he emulates a *sacerdos* without proper or full knowledge of what to utter to yield the desired outcome— share in common an unresolved negotiation along the boundary between the realms of the *profanus* and the *sacer* and, particularly in Lucian's dialogue, along the blurred border between religion and magic. If this negotiation transpires within the pagan panoply of perspectives, what of the Judaean perspective as it is emerging in its double transformation toward Christianity and Judaism, in contending with each other and with the varied pagan traditions some of which we have discussed? This is the layered question to which we turn in the following chapters.

CHAPTER EIGHT

The Shaping of Proto-Christianity and Its Magical Competition

When we turn to the New Testament we encounter some of the same sort of problematic definitional issues that we encountered in Exodus and I Samuel 28. Thus, for instance, there is a very interesting moment in the narrative of Jesus' life and times that we encounter in Mark 5:24ff.

> 24 So Jesus went with [a man begging him to heal the man's moribund daughter], and a great multitude followed Him and thronged him.
> 25 Now a certain woman had a flow of blood for twelve years,
> 26 and had suffered many things from many physicians. She had spent all that she had and was no better, but rather grew worse.
> 27 When she heard about Jesus, she came behind him in the crowd and touched his garment.
> 28 For she said, "If only I may touch his clothes, I shall be made well."
> 29 Immediately the fountain of her blood was dried up, and she felt in her body that she was healed of the affliction.
> 30 And Jesus, immediately knowing in himself that power had gone out of him, turned around in the crowd and said, "Who touched my clothes?"
> 31 But his disciples said to him, "You see the multitude thronging you and you say, 'Who touched me?'"
> 32 And he looked around to see her who had done this thing.
> 33 But the woman, fearing and trembling, knowing what had happened to her, came and fell down before him and told him the whole truth.
> 34 And he said to her, "Daughter, your faith has made you well. Go in peace and be healed of your affliction.
> 35-40 [And thereafter, regarding the presumed-to-be-dead daughter of the *archisynagogos*,[324] he said] "Do not be afraid; only believe... The child is not dead, but sleeping."
> 41 Then he took the child by the hand and said to her, "*Talitha, kumi,*" which is translated "Little girl, I say to you, arise."[325]

---

[324] We can infer from the contexts in which this term appears in a number of Judaean catacomb inscriptions that such an individual was something akin to the President of his synagogue and a socio-economic leader in his community—and not to be confused with a "rabbi," or teacher, who leads spirituo-intellectually by virtue of the respect accorded his scholarship and understanding of God's words.

[325] The interior transliteration is, oddly, slightly off in nearly half of the 25 or so English-language versions that I have examined: they use "*kum,*" the masculine form of the imperative in the Aramaic Jesus is represented as

Variations on this episode occur in Matthew and Luke, as we shall momentarily consider.[326] Regarding the passage itself, however, there is much to think about with regard to the question of how to distinguish magic from religion and a sorcerer or *magus* (as the Romans have begun to use that word) from a priest or prophet—or someone who is more than merely a priest or prophet.

Thus in the first case, the woman who is healed is healed by touching the garment of Jesus—which is what Frazer would call sympathetic magic. At that moment, Jesus perceives that some of his supernatural power—to heal and to do what else?—has shifted out of him and into the individual who has made that contact with him. It is not clear as to whether the emphasis that is intended is on the diminishment of his power in this moment or in the transmitting of power to the woman without any diminishment of Jesus' overall power, although we are likely to read it as the latter. Nor is it clear as to how, in spite of a certain omniscience that, if not now, then at least later on will be ascribed to him—when he is unequivocally understood to be God—he has no idea who the power-thief is. On the third hand, when the woman confesses that it is she who touched his garment, he insists that it is her faith that has healed her—which would suggest that no power was transferred from Jesus to her through his garment, since her belief can be said not to derive from her touching him. Or is it that the contact galvanizes her faith (and/or vice versa) in order to turn it into a healing process?

On the one hand, we may recognize a resonance with Levi-Strauss' description of the three elements necessary for a sorcerer's healing or harming magic to work: that he believe in his power, that his patient/victim believe in it, and that the community believe in it. All three requirements are met, given that she believes, Jesus believes and the crowd around them believes. Does that mean that Jesus is a magician, like Quesalid is—or, if I am Christian, is there some inexplicable-to-an-outsider-reason why this cannot be so? Simply, Jesus is divine—although this will not be official Christian doctrine until 325 and will not be more or less universally believed by Christians until the end of the sixth century—and what he effects are faith healings made possible *because* he is divine, which are at the center of my religion as a Christian, not part of magic.

Jesus assures the woman that it is her faith entirely that has accounted for her being healed, in spite of the narrative itself that offered a distinct emphasis on the physical contact between the two of them. The "ante" of that faith principal is significantly upped in the second part of the narrative, which begins with Jesus' comforting words to the *archisynagogos* that belief will effect what he hopes for, the restoration to life of his little daughter—nonetheless, once more, physical contact between Jesus and the object of his

---

speaking, as does the original Greek version of the text; the feminine form in Aramaic is (correctly) "kumi". Clearly in the cases transliterated as "kumi", the translators were aware of the error in the Greek text in rendering the Aramaic phrase. (Some Greek versions offer it correctly, however!) "Talia" means "young woman" in Palestinian Aramaic (it is the female equivalent of "Tlei," meaning "young man.")

[326] I have begun with Mark because the consensus among biblical scholars is that Mark was the earliest of the Gospels to be composed (in the early 70s, just after the destruction of the Temple), and that Matthew followed ten or fifteen or so years later, based on Mark, and that Luke, in turn, followed shortly after Matthew, based either on Matthew or on a combination of Mark and Matthew. These three synoptic Gospels would be followed by John, perhaps as late as 100-110, with its rather different tone and vision.

healing skill is made: he may tell the little girl to rise—or, more correctly, to come to him—but he has taken her by the hand, presumably transmitting his healing power from his physical being to hers.

Both parts of the narrative present Jesus as not, per se, asserting the possession of power to compel the *sacer* in some manner to do his bidding and therefore heal the bleeding woman or restore the little girl to life.[327] In that sense he certainly conforms to the sort of distinction that, say, Malinowski makes between practitioners of magic who make that assertion—or even go so far as to claim that they can compel the forces of the *sacer* to act to accomplish something (be it positive, healing, or negative, harming) in the *profanus*—and religious practitioners who assert that they are merely conduits through which the divine *sacer*, petitioned, may or may not choose to act.

Both parts of this episode are also presented, more laconically, in Matthew 9:20-26, where the woman comes from behind and touches the hem of his garment, for "she said to herself, 'If only I may touch his garment, I shall be made well,' But Jesus turned around, and when he saw her, he said, 'Be of good cheer, daughter; your faith has made you well.' And the woman was made well from that hour (20-22)." Thus Jesus immediately recognizes who touched his garment, there is no reference to power being transferred or transmitted, and the emphasis is more distinctly on the power of faith to effect the healing.

So, too, the *archisynagogos* is referred to as a "ruler" in Matthew 9:23, and when Jesus suggests that the girl "'is not dead, but sleeping'… they ridiculed him (24)." The crowd is moved outside, and Jesus "went in and took her by the hand, and the girl arose (25)." So in this version of the story it is apparently simply the touch of Jesus that cures her of death, without any words at all.

Luke 8:43-54 falls between Mark and Matthew, as far as the length and detail of the episode are concerned. Thus when the woman touched the border of Jesus' garment from behind (44),

> 45 And Jesus said, 'Who touched me?' When all denied it, Peter and those with him said, 'Master, the multitudes throng and press you, and you say, 'Who touched me?'
> 46 But Jesus said, 'Somebody touched me, for I perceived power going out from me.'
> 47 Now when the woman saw that she was not hidden, she came trembling; and falling down before him, she declared to him in the presence of all the people the reason she had touched him and how she was healed immediately.
> 48 And he said to her, 'Daughter, be of good cheer, your faith has made you well. Go in peace.'
> 49-53 [someone came from the *archisynagogos*' house and he again insisted] 'do not be afraid; only believe, and she will be made well,' [and

---

[327] Jesus asserts that she is merely sleeping. Could she be in the midst of an epileptic or cataleptic seizure unrecognized by her family? That would present an interesting parallel to the second accusation leveled at Apuleius—in the opposite direction, so to speak: he was accused of using magic to knock a boy down and Jesus causes a girl to stand up (and, as we shall see, in the next passage under discussion, is accused of using nefarious means to heal a blind and mute man).

he enters accompanied only by Peter, James and John and asserts that
she the girl is merely sleeping and he is ridiculed.]
54 But he put them all outside, took her by the hand and called, saying
"Little girl, arise!"

While there are slight differences of emphasis, the essentials are constant: Jesus heals by
touching but also through the faith of the individual who is healed (or whose daughter is
healed); it's not clear at all whether the healing could have happened had there been no
physical contact but perhaps clearer that the physical contact would not have been
sufficient without faith.

A somewhat later passage in Matthew—12:22-30—shows Jesus casting out the
daimon that has caused a man to be blind and mute, "and he healed him, so that the blind
and mute man both spoke and saw." (22) This extraordinary act causes the crowds of
Judaeans who witness it to wonder, "Could this be the Son of David?" (23) The response
of the so-called Pharisees who did not apparently witness the act but "heard it... [was to
say]: 'This fellow does not cast out demons except by Beelzebub, the ruler of the
daimones.'"

These two verses yield a number of interesting questions. First, what exactly do
the crowds mean by "Son of David"? We may readily enough understand that they mean
the long-hoped-for descendant of King David—the anointed/*mashiah*/*khristos*—who is
expected to effect changes in the chaotic, schismatic, politically rather oppressed Judaean
world. What kind of changes? Installing a new, God-approved political regime that even
the Romans will step back from, recognizing its legitimacy? Cut such an impressive swath
that even the Romans and other pagans will come to recognize that the God of Israel is the
only true God and turn in worship toward Jerusalem? Be so filled with the spirit of the Lord
that he will be able to accomplish extraordinary acts of healing—miracles? In the latter
case, will he be functioning like some of the Israelite-Judaean prophets were able to, from
Moses, who parted the Sea of Reeds to Elijah and Elisha, each of whom restored a dead
child to life?

Second, who are the Pharisees and who is Beelzebub? The Pharisees, of course,
are the religious faction that evolved during the Hasmonaean period into a political party—
in both aspects of which, they operated and interpreted in opposition to the Sadducees. The
Pharisees ultimately reemerged as a religious perspective when the Hasmoneans were
extirpated by Herod the Idumaean and the Sadducees, their leaders slaughtered, effectively
disappeared, although their angle of religious interpretation persisted, carried on by a kind
of successor group called Boethusaeans.[328] The point is that the Pharisees essentially
became the people's party; their interpretative perspective tended to favor the poor, where
the Saducean/Boethusaean perspective tended to favor the wealthier classes.

For the most part, Pharisaic interpretation would move forward from the Judaean
period into the Jewish-Christian period as mainstream rabbinic Judaism. So there is both
an irony to the manner in which the Pharisees are depicted here—and elsewhere in the
Gospels—as a hard-crusted conservative group that accuses and ultimately persecutes the

---

[328] They were named after the high priest Simon, son of Boethus, father-in-law of Herod. See Zeitlin, *Rise and Fall*, Vol 2, 101.

Jesus who is depicted, in opposition, as the champion of the people: in particular, the poor and the disenfranchised. That image of them seems more likely to reflect a retrofitted view of them in the context of the growing division between the Judaeans for and not for Jesus than the actuality of who they were, ideologically, at the time of Jesus.

They who accuse him of being in league with Beelzebub will ultimately be accused of that association themselves by Jesus' adherents (as we shall see) some centuries later, when those adherents are in a position of political and not just religious power. And as for Beelzebub, the name may originally have referred to a Philistine deity worshipped in the city of Ekron or as another name for a particular manifestation of the Semitic god, Ba'al. The name may mean "Lord of Zebub" (*Ba'al Zebub*; with *Zebub* a site of which we have, to date, no knowledge), or, as is more commonly thought, it means "Lord of the Flies" (*zevuv/zebub* is a collective biblical Hebrew noun for "fly"). Or it might be a (presumably derogatory) corrupted form of "Lord of the High Place [i.e., Heaven]" (for which the proper form would be *Ba'al Zebul*). In an alternative "Beelzebul" form, it is simply a derogatory name meaning "Lord of the Dung Heap" (*zevel/zebel* means dung).

The actual scriptural references are ambiguous and few; the name (in any of these forms) hardly appears in the Hebrew Bible. The northern Israelite king, Ahaziah, severely injured in a fall, sends messengers to inquire of Ba'al Zebub (referred to as god of the Philistine city of Ekron) regarding his survival from his injuries. He is condemned by Elijah to die for not turning instead to the God of Israel (2 Kings 1:2-16). Its more frequent appearance is in the New Testament, in the Gospels (not only here, but also in Mark 3:22; and Luke 11:15-19), in each of which passages the same account is offered: Jesus is accused of being possessed by, or in league with Beelzebub, through whom he drives out negative *daimones*. In all of these parallel references, "Beelzebub" or "Beelzebul" appears to be a name for the Satan.[329]

Which leads to the third question, which I have already partially answered: what, in this context, does *daimon* mean—which is typically translated as "demon"? The latter translation—for we recall that, like *pharmakon*, *daimon* is, in classical Greek an ambiguous term: it refers to powers in the *sacer* that are inferior to *theoi*, but can, like the Olympians themselves, operate in a positive or a negative manner vis-à-vis humans—is justified by the assumption that the context here is intended to be nefarious. For in fact, Jesus himself thusly interprets the Pharisaic comment when he

> ...knew their thoughts, and said to them: "Every kingdom divided against itself is brought to desolation, and every city or house divided against itself will not stand.
> If Satan casts out Satan, he is divided against himself. How then will his kingdom stand?
> And if I cast out *daimones* by Beelzebub, by whom do your sons cast them out? (25-27)

This, then, is one of those moments that both casts Jesus in a light that clarifies that his power is used for good—and wants to suggest, further, that he is a conduit through

---

[329] The name also appears in apocryphal literature with this satanic connotation.

which divine power operates—and casts the Pharisees in a negative light as oppositional to him. At the end of this passage, after all, Jesus rails at them: "Brood of vipers! How can you, being evil, speak good things?" (34)—and he concludes his comments to and about them with the assertion that "...by your words you will be condemned." (37) Moreover, because of their subsequently understood rabbinic association, this nefarious opposition will later also be part of a framework in which Jews and Judaism will be cast in a negative light by the expanding Church, as we shall subsequently see.

The passage also raises an interesting question regarding how to identify what exactly Jesus does. As we again recall (See Chapter One, above), Levi-Strauss identified three aspects of magic/sorcery: the belief of the practitioner that it works; the belief of the victim/patient that it works; the belief of the community that it works. Jesus' emphasis on the faith of the ones he cures, together with his clear conviction that he is an effective instrument—through which, however, God chooses to work, rather than God being compelled by Jesus—and the conviction not only of the crowd that Jesus is being successful, but even of his Pharasaic enemies (albeit their view is that Beelzebub, rather than God is the *sacer* force working through Jesus) conforms nicely to Levi-Strauss's formula. If I am not a believer in the reality of Jesus as *mashiah/khristos* and indeed as the Son of God, how would I understand this passage within the religion/magic matrix?

Meanwhile, if we look further into the text of the New Testament—to the generation following that of Jesus for which the *Acts of the Apostles* offers the canonical account—we arrive, in the beginning of chapter eight, to "the beginning of a time of violent persecution for the church in Jerusalem; and all except the apostles were scattered over the country districts of Judaea and Samaria." (v. 1) There are three issues that this verse raises for us. One, if Christianity is viewed at that time as a *superstitio*, then this would explain why it was being persecuted. Two, this first supposition further assumes that the persecution came from the Romans, who were the political power in Judaea and Samaria, and therefore would have pronounced Christianity a *superstitio*.

However, the end of chapter 7 had described the stoning of the apostle Stephen—regarded as the first Christian martyr—at the end of which we read that "Saul was among those who approved of this murder." (v. 60) The murder came after Stephen delivered a sermon criticizing his fellow Judaeans for a long history of not recognizing, or acting in opposition to, true prophets among them, for "[h]ow stubborn you are, heathen still at heart and deaf to the truth! You always fight against the Holy Spirit. Like fathers, like sons. Was there ever a prophet whom your fathers did not persecute?" (v. 51-52). When Stephen then had a vision of "Jesus standing at God's right hand," (v. 55) and said "I can see the Son of Man standing at God's right hand!" (v. 57) the people rushed him, flung him out of the city and he was stoned by them—and in fact the Romans are never mentioned in the account of his death.

The third issue, therefore, is layered with sub-issues. The Church as a distinct entity and separate from the Synagogue does not yet exist; there are Judaeans who believe that Jesus is the *mashiah/khristos* and those who do not—all of whom would indeed be called Judaeans, rather than Christians and Jews, which, as we have earlier noted, is a concept that takes shape considerably later than in this period. Stoning, in Judaean law and custom, was not the Hollywood image of everyone in a crowd picking up rocks and throwing them at a victim until he or she succumbs, but a formal means of execution for a capital crime in which the guilty victim is placed in a pit and the two witnesses who provided the evidence that yielded the guilty verdict are tasked with pushing over onto him or her the boulder that will crush and kill the victim.[330]

When was the narrative written down, given that it would not be a definitive part of the Christian canon until 395 CE? What had happened between the time of the event and the canonical account? A long struggle between the two sects of Judaeans emerging as Judaism and Christianity to assume the position of *religio licita* in Roman administrative eyes. From a Christian perspective, the account as it stands furthers the exoneration of Roman pagan authorities begun in the Gospels with regard to making things difficult for the early Church, and shoulders the Judaeans—or rather, as the later translation of that term will offer—the *Jews* with that negative responsibility.[331]

My point is that in the double helix of our own narrative—the relation between magic and religion and the emergence of early Judaism and Christianity and their relationship with each other—both issues resonate in the seventh and eighth chapters of Acts. For as Saul is again referenced in 8:3 as one who "was harrying the church, entering house after house, seizing men and women, and sending them to prison"—and again we must ask by what authority he could do that; it could only have been by Roman authority, although Saul is a Judaean—and "as for those who had been scattered [due to the persecution], they went through the country preaching the Word," (v. 4) one apostle, Philip, came preaching and proclaiming the advent of the *mashiah/khristos*, and performing miracles, in a city in Samaria.

Like Jesus in the Gospels, Philip cleansed those possessed by "unclean spirits" and cured "many paralyzed and crippled folk." (8:7-8) But there was also a man named Simon who "had been in the city for some time, and had swept the Samaritans off their feet with his *magical arts*, claiming to be someone great" (italics added). So perhaps the first distinction between Simon and Jesus, even before we get to the distinctions that the text itself will explicitly offer, is that last phrase: that whereas Simon claims to be someone great, Jesus does not. The more fundamental question is: what exactly does the Greek text mean by *tekhnai magikai* (magical arts) and how do the verses that follow help us answer that question?

Simon's large (presumably Samaritan) audience listened to him eagerly and asserted that

---

[330] This is discussed in the Talmudic Tractate *Sanhedrin*, Chapter Six, in the fourth *Mishnah*. Specifically, the first witness pushes him backwards into a pit deep enough to kill him from the fall; if the fall does not kill him, the second witness drops the stone that, the *mishnah* says, must land directly on his heart. The accompanying *gemara* states that the stone must be big and heavy enough that it requires two men to bring it to the edge of the pit, and the one "throwing" it down also, therefore, requires assistance from "his comrade" (the first witness) in order to accomplish that end.

[331] It thus reinforces that perspective as it was expressed in Mark 14-15 regarding the capture and "trial" of Jesus at the hands of the Pharisees and the High Priest in the Temple, together with the choice by the "Jews" to have Bar-Abbas released by Pontius Pilate at Passover time and Jesus executed. Like so many other details of the story of the demise of Jesus and the difficulties of the Apostles, the idea of the Roman Procurator following a custom of releasing one Judaean prisoner chosen by the people at Passover time is not evidenced in any source but the Gospels—which, we must recall, are not contemporary with the events they describe. See Soltes, *Jews on Trial*, 41-66.

> this man is that power of God that is called
> "The Great Power."
> They listened because they had for so long been
> carried away by his *mageia*.
> But when they came to believe Philip with his good news about
> the kingdom of God and the name of Jesus Christ, they were baptized,
> men and women alike.
> *Even Simon himself believed, and was baptized*, and thereupon
> was constantly in Philip's company. (italics added).
> He was carried away when he saw the powerful signs and
> miracles that were taking place. (8:10-13)

We still don't know what Simon's *mageia* was, nor whether it offered an alternative, per se, to what the followers of Jesus had to offer, although a symptom of the good news that they preached was that they could perform powerful signs and miracles that presumably he could not. He is baptized into their community, and when the apostles in Jerusalem heard that the Samaritans had accepted the word of God, they sent Peter and John to pray that the converts "might receive the Holy Spirit. For until then the Spirit had not come upon any of them. They had been baptized into the name of the Lord Jesus, that and nothing more." (v. 14-16) Since the Samaritan community still exists today, we may infer that not all of them converted. It is also interesting to note that there are apparently two components to becoming a true Judaean for Jesus: baptism as a concomitant to one's new spiritual conviction is the first, but actually being filled with the Holy Spirit is the second and it is not automatic.

How does one become filled with it? By a process that, under other conditions such as those described by Frazer, might be labeled as contagious magic. For "Peter and John laid hands on them and they received the Holy Spirit." (v. 17) In this case, then, their faith was not sufficient, even accompanied by the physically purifying act of being baptized, to accomplish a complete transformation. There is more that makes this passage so interesting. "When Simon saw that the Spirit was bestowed through the laying on of the apostles' hands, he offered them money and said, 'Give me the same power too, so that when I lay my hands on anyone, he will receive the Holy Spirit.'" (v. 18-19) So Simon, at least, views what they do, as opposed to whatever it is that he does, as something powerful and desirable—and he mistakes that power for something that can be purchased.

Peter responds in anger about "you and your money; may you come to a bad end, for thinking that God's gift is for sale!... Repent of this wickedness and pray the Lord to forgive you for imagining such a thing. I can see that you are doomed to taste the bitter fruit and wear the fetters of sin!" (v. 20, 22-3) So we still don't have clarity as to what it is that Simon does that constitutes *mageia*; we know only that his sense of what the apostles possess with regard to the *sacer* is mistakenly venal—but after Peter's scolding, he immediately repents, asking them to "pray for me yourselves and [to] ask that none of the things that you have spoken of may befall me." (v. 24)

We cannot definitively say that Simon's arts are negative although we can perhaps infer that they are weaker than those of the apostles; a Christian readership of this part of the narrative of *Acts* could thus conclude that religion—specifically that connected to and through Jesus—is more powerful than whatever magic Simon could perform, and that a defining attribute is that what they possess cannot be purchased, whereas, perhaps, Simon's lesser skills could be taught to a person willing to pay for the lessons.[332] There remain, however, certain ambiguities if we are not subjective Christian readers.

The narrative continues as, in *Acts* 9, Saul, continuing to be a persecutor of the disciples of the Lord, heads off to Damascus to arrest whomever he finds, when

> suddenly a light flashed from the sky all around him.
> He fell to the ground and heard a voice saying, "Saul, Saul, why do you persecute me?
> "Tell me, Lord," he said, "who you are."
> The Voice answered, "I am Jesus, whom you are persecuting..." (v. 3-6)

> ...Saul got up from the ground, but when he opened his eyes he could not see...
> He was blind for three days, and took no food or drink. (v. 8-9)

This is the extraordinary moment that transforms Saul, from a Judaean not for Jesus—and a rigorous persecutor of Judaeans for Jesus, at that—to a member of the Judaean group that he had been previously oppressing. The moment, the fall from his horse and the hearing of a voice, might be compared to the account in Apuleius' *Apologia* of the boy who fell at Apuleius' feet, due, according to Apuleius, to an epileptic fit. Such fits are also sometimes accompanied by the hearing of voices and blindness. What distinguishes Paul's experience, however, is the specific nature of the voice and the amount of time thereafter in which he continued to experience blindness.

While my point here, in passing, is that our reading of the narrative offered in these first nine verses of *Acts* 9 will differ depending upon our religious perspective, already implanted within us when we get to the passage, it is secondary in importance to what follows in *Acts* as a consequence of the passage. Saul's transformation is signified by his taking on of a new name—Paul—that, in Latin (*paulus*) means "little—i.e., humble—one." He is not only now a Judaean for Jesus, but a humble man who was previously arrogant.

We see him in action in his new guise in the beginning of Chapter 13, where, in Antioch, Syria there were "in the congregation there, certain prophets and teachers" (13: 1), including Saul. While they were fasting and worshipping God, "the Holy Spirit said, 'Set Barnabas and Saul apart for me, to do the work to which I have called them.' Then after further fasting and prayer, they laid their hands on them and let them go." So once again, the power to do what the apostles do is conveyed through touch—what Frazer would call contagious magic were the context, say, Native American or Polynesian.

---

[332] One might be reminded of Sokrates and the so-called Sophists, such as Euthyphro, Gorgias, Protagoras and Hippias, whom he is represented in Plato as confronting in diverse dialogues. They all charge hefty fees to teach their skills that operate in a moral void, whereas Sokrates is all about moral thinking and is willing to discuss with anybody, what he claims not to be able to actually teach (he draws ideas and their truths out of his would -be pupils as a midwife draws babies out of the wombs of expectant mothers). He does this simply for the love of dialogue and truth, and not for a fee.

Barnabas and Paul, in any case, proceed to Salamis, where "they declared the word of God in the Jewish synagogues" (v. 3)—or so the usual translation into English renders the passage, but again we must keep in mind that Jews and Christians, per se, do not yet exist as distinctly separate groups with ideologies and customs all of which we would recognize. The Greek term *Ioudaioi* would be more accurately rendered as "Judaeans." To be sure, the term "synagogue" is appropriate, but most members of the community who are Judaean by religion would be worshipping in synagogues if they were not within easy reach of the Temple in Jerusalem; churches, as we would understand that word, don't yet really exist. It may very well be the case that Judaeans for Jesus have begun to meet separately from their fellow Judaeans, and perhaps less openly, in homes and other sorts of places, but the phrase "Jewish synagogues" suggests a distinction between Paul and Barnabas and those in Salamis to whom they are preaching that would not have been nearly as clear at that time as the translation of the text would suggest. There will, of course, be implications for this as Judaism and Christianity do develop as increasingly separate entities in the course of the next several centuries.

In any case, Barnabas and Saul traversed the entire island of Cyprus,

> as far as Paphos, and there they came upon a sorcerer, a *Ioudaios* who posed as a prophet, Bar-Jesus by name....
> This Elymas the sorcerer—so his name may be translated—opposed them, trying to turn the Governor away from the Faith.
> But Saul, also known as Paul, filled with the Holy Spirit, looked him in the face and said,
> "You utter imposter and charlatan! You son of the devil and enemy of all goodness, will you never stop falsifying the straight ways of the Lord?
> Look now, the hand of the Lord strikes you; you shall be blind, and for a time you shall not see the sunlight." Instantly mist and darkness came over him and he groped about for someone to lead him by the hand.
> When the Governor saw what had happened, he became a believer, deeply impressed by what he learned about the Lord. (v. 6, 8-12)

In this case we recognize that what is labeled as sorcery, which is the practice with which Elymas is associated, is both considerably weaker than what the apostles are able to do and associated with dark, negative *sacer* forces—specifically the personification of those forces as the Devil. Thus he is criticized by Paul as a "son of the devil" for "falsifying the straight ways of the Lord." He is said to make the false claim of being a prophet—that is, his claim is to act on behalf of the Lord, but on the contrary, he falsifies the understanding of what God would instruct and expect of people. This is different from what the Egyptian *sacerdotes* do and how they are presented back in Exodus 7-8, who are merely weaker but not necessarily nefarious (except to the extent that are part of the pharaonic system denying the Israelites their freedom).

Saul, "filled with the Holy Spirit," has the power to blind Elymas—he who was himself blinded in the process of becoming a Judaean for Jesus blinds a practitioner from among the Judaeans not for Jesus. The Governor, astonished by this last gesture, embraces the God of Paul and Barnabas. On the one hand, we might be reminded of how Jethro, the father-in-law of Moses and a Midianite priest, came to associate himself with the God of Israel after being astonished at the extraordinary divine acts of salvation enacted on behalf of the Israelites (Exodus18:9-12).

On the other hand, it is interesting that the text parses the name of Elymas to *Bar-Jesus* in Aramaic—which means "Son of the Savior"—suggesting an easy confusion between him and what the apostles themselves are, in the spiritual sense: for they are all "sons of the Savior," as it were. More important, with regard not to the issue of magic versus religion, but that of early Jewish-Christian relations, it is not only that the last verse in this passage offers the Governor, in whose retinue Elymas was serving (and in that capacity "opposed them, trying to turn the Governor away from the Faith") now turned—presumably away from Elymas and his faith and toward the True Faith, in which "he became a believer, deeply impressed by what he learned about the Lord." Of considerable significance is the question as to what faith that would have been to which he turned at that point in time. That of Judaeans for Jesus, as opposed, presumably, to Judaeans not for Jesus, which group included Bar-Jesus/Elymas—rather than to "Christianity" as opposed to "Judaism."

The implication is that a distinction between the two groups exists that is clear enough so that one could believe in either of the two forms of faith. However, in spite of the fact that Elymas/Bar-Jesus is specifically identified as a Judaean (albeit the usual translation turns him, instead, into a "Jew"), one could also suppose that the Governor—a Roman governor, operating on behalf of and presumably himself part of an extensive pagan administration—abandoned his pagan faith in becoming a believer in the God of Israel and presumably in the significance of Jesus as understood by part of the community that worships the God of Israel. That understanding would not yet recognize the sort of Jewish versus Christian distinction that we recognize, and perhaps we are wont to retrofit onto this passage that distinction when it was not yet such a clear one at the time of the event being described.

Arthur Darby Nock, in his essay, "Paul and the Magus," examines this account. He seems unaware of this last issue, but offers an informative consideration of the question of how *magos* is to be understood, parsing it as meaning "one of two things: (1) a Persian fire-priest; (2) a magician or quack."[333] He discusses what we have seen discussed in Apuleius, (although his sources are Strabo and Herodotos), noting that the word is borrowed from Persian, "to describe the priestly Median tribe." He adds the specific detail that "[m]embers of this tribe performed the daily worship of fire, and one of them had to be present at every sacrifice and sing a chant narrating the birth of the gods."[334]

"The Magi are therefore a dignified priestly tribe like that of Levi in [ancient] Israel... It is therefore with some surprise that we find *magos* used in the fifth century B.C.

---

[333] Arthur Darby Nock, "Paul and the Magus," in Frederick J. Foakes-Jackson and Kirsopp Lake, eds., *The Beginnings of Christianity*, (London: Macmillan Press, 1920-33), vol 5, 164.

[334] Ibid, 164. The reference to fire worship is Strabo xv, 3, 15, p 733 and that to reciting the divine narrative is Herodotos I, 132.

to mean 'quack'."[335] The passage Nock quotes from Gorgias is of particular interest because of "the matter-of-fact way in which Gorgias uses *mageia* as an amplificatory synonym for *goeteia*," with the former as "a more colorful word" than the latter in general usage. The question recognized by Nock is whether the skills ascribed to *magoi/magi* by the Greeks and then by the Romans in turn—for example, the kindling of wood—derive from having observed the Persian priests in action at all. We have no way of knowing—in fact, nearly all we know of the Persian *Maghoi* during the Achaemenid period comes from what the Greeks say about them, so we cannot even be sure of what precisely their rituals were at that point.

If we keep in mind the Zoroastrian tradition as we have considered it earlier, then *maghoi* would in fact—by definition—act as part of the Mazdean sacerdotal spiritual army whose job it was to aid the forces of *asha* against the forces of *druj* led by Ahriman and his array of negative *daevas* (*daimones*) and *sacerdotes*. So there is, to be sure, an irony, that such a term would offer the negative connection that it comes to offer in the Greek and Roman traditions. In trying to assess precisely what the *maghoi did*, Nock observes "the Persian use of spells for medicinal and other apotropaic purposes"[336]—thus falling, it seems to me, into the same trap into which the Greeks, Romans and Frazer, Levi-Strauss and Malinowski all fall: while on the one hand we may struggle to articulate precise separations between medicine and magic and between medicine and religion as categories, on the other, if we label the verbal aspect of whatever the maghean procedure was as a spell—rather than, say, as a prayer—then we have relegated that procedure to the realm of magic/sorcery/wizardry and precluded considering it as part of religion.

This definitional issue—but Nock has slowly switched, without noting so, more fully into the realm of medicine versus magic (but also, really, medicine versus religion) rather than magic versus religion (or religion versus quackery)—assumes further interesting shape. "In [any] apotropaic rites the Magi were no doubt paramount... Such proceedings were in ancient civilizations and are in many areas today the equivalent of our antiseptics and inoculations. Man thinks himself to be surrounded by a whole world of evil powers against whom he must arm. *Mageia* as later understood includes such methods of self-protection, but it includes...influencing the affections of others, and ...inflicting physical harm on them."[337] One might suggest that demons in this context are the equivalent of what we refer to as germs—we do indeed live in a world that surrounds us with them—so that the blurred line between magic/religion and medicine is a matter, more than anything else, of whether we do or don't ascribe a personified quality and with it a conscious, negative intention to these potentially dangerous forces.

But Nock then disconnects these proceedings "from the normal standards of Persian priesthood... and it is quite clear that if the Magi had contact with magic they were not professional magicians in the later sense of *magoi*."[338] So we are back where we began,

---

[335] Ibid, 165. Nock then quotes from Sophocles' *Oedipus Rex* 387, Euripides' *Orestes* 1497, Hippocrates' *On the Sacred Disease*, ch 2, and finally Gorgias' *Helena* to illustrate this usage.

[336] Ibid, 168. Nock refers (in his fn #7) to the Zoroastrian text, *Vendidad*, VII, 44, and IX, and notes that these passages are "for cleansing from defilement by a demon: incidentally the process is thought of as driving away diseases."

[337] Ibid, 169.

[338] Ibid.

with the search for how a legitimate religious category came to be spoken of in pejorative terms, or put simply in Nock's terms, "in the ordinary colloquial language of educated men, 'magic' and 'magical'… customarily afford terms of abuse for religious ceremonies which are regarded as superstitious"[339]—which seems to be tautological as Nock expresses it, since this turn of phrase doesn't explain what it is that would cause a religious ceremony to be regarded as "superstitious" nor does it really tell us what "superstitious" means, other than that it causes the Greeks and Romans, whatever it means, to insult it as "magical."

Nock does offer a kind of definition shortly thereafter, suggesting that "'magic'… means the attempt to divert the course of nature by methods which to our science appear to be of a non-rational kind, or which to the user appear to rest on some hidden and peculiar wisdom"—and we might ask how this is different from, say, religious miracles: for example, curing a woman who has been bleeding non-stop for years by causing the bleeding to cease through contact with one's garment. More problematic is Nock's next sentence: "We distinguish it [magic] from science which proceeds by rational methods, and from religion which if it seems to influence the course of events does so by asking some superior being or beings to do what is needed instead of either operating directly by some kind of sympathetic action or again compelling the superior being or beings."[340]

Importantly, Nock recognizes that the distinction he has posed between religion and magic or between religion and medicine would not have been recognized in antiquity. He notes, for instance, various communal efforts to bring rain that are in essence prayers for rain or processions to bless crops. We have earlier noted that examples offered by Frazer and labeled as magic conform to this religion-based pattern. Nock adds that *epoidai*—this term is usually rendered as "spells"—are used, as in Sophocles' *Ajax* 584, by physicians. He acknowledges the blurriness of this line with respect to other terms, as well, as for example *pharmakon*, with which we became familiar in *Odyssey* 11.[341] This includes practices, instruments and practitioners. Thus *goes* (the sibling of *goeteia*) can be used non-pejoratively to mean "wizard," or to refer to a quack or imposter.

All of this brings Nock and us back to the original question: what exactly did *mageia/magia* mean as the Greeks and Romans came to use it: "broadly speaking, three things: the profession by private individuals of the possession of technical ability enabling them to supply recipes or perform rites to help their clients and damage their clients' enemies; the use by such clients or by others of such proceedings to damage enemies; and—corresponding to the vague modern use already mentioned—the religions belonging to aliens or on any general ground disapproved."[342] We have noted in particular this third use, which amounts largely to a "it's not ours and we don't understand it and are therefore threatened by it" sort of definition.

But Nock goes on to consider, at a more technical level, the legal handling of *magia* in Rome, some of whch we have noted, as for example the *Senatus consultum de Bachanalibus* that originally dealt with the foreign cult of Dionysios, but could be and was broadly used by magistrates to punish *sacer*-related activity considered nefarious in

---

[339] Ibid.
[340] Ibid, 169-70.
[341] Ibid, 170.
[342] Ibid, 171.

intention or outcome. (We may also recall how Plato, in his *Laws*, sought to do this). Nock also takes up legislation in the fourth century by Constantine and beyond Constantine—but we shall leave this part of the discussion aside for the moment, since we shall consider this later on in that chronological context, in which Christianity is assuming a very different position from what it held earlier.

What is significant is Nock's conclusion that "there is no sphere of magic at once distinguishable from the sphere of religion and from that of science, though magic and religion together can be opposed to science… [*mageia* was so-called, with its pejorative connotation] due to the impression made on unfriendly Ionian spectators by Persian priests, with their queer garments and tiaras and mouth masks… performing uncomprehended rites, uttering unintelligible prayers, and indispensable at sacrifice… It was the external aspect of Persian *cultus* which counted, not the meaning of the rite."[343]

In short: *us versus them* and *we neither understand nor like them*—who after all speak a language that sounds to us like *bar-bar-bar*, from which we have shaped our word "*barbaros*," with its negative connotations. Interestingly, even as the Greeks who despised the Persians were also somewhat in awe of the grand and glorious court of their Shah and its concomitants, so the terms *mageia* and *magos* had a certain venerability to their connotation, as Nock also points out—as opposed to *goes* and *goeteia*, which were used as unalloyed insulting terms.

Of equal interest is the double change in this picture effected through the Hellenistic period, as Nock points out. One change is that the stature of the *maghoi* apparently diminished between the collapse of the Achaemenid Empire through the conquests of Alexander the Great and, in the aftermath of Alexander's death, the eventual re-emergence of another, different sort of Persian dynasty—the Arsacid or Parthian dynasty (which would extend well into the Roman period, lasting, in fact, from 247 BCE to 224 CE). The second is the arrival into and circulation within the Hellenistic Greek world of "various collections of magical recipes under the names [i.e., alleged authorship] of Osthanes, Zoroaster, and the Magi. We know them from quotations in the elder Pliny… and elsewhere," as we have seen.[344] We have seen both a distinct ambiguity of attitude on the part of Pliny when he refers to the Magi and "it is quite clear that when he quotes Magi he means not 'magicians' in a vague way, but some definite body of doctrine."[345]

As Nock's discussion moves forward, he not surprisingly comes to Apuleius, who "in his *Apologia* 26 sets the two senses [of *magus* as Persian fire-priest and as magician or quack] side by side"[346]—as we have seen. This in turn brings him to the discussion of Elymas in Acts, referred to as a *magos pseudoprophetes*: a "false-prophet mage." Nock nots that it "is not surprising to find a Jew in this context… their spells, or spells which purported to be theirs, enjoyed widespread authority, largely due no doubt to the mysterious

---

[343] Ibid, 174-5. "Ionians" refers to inhabitants of the Greek city-states ranged along the western coast of Anatolia, who had direct contact with the Achaemenid Persians well before and leading into the era of the Persian Wars of ca 500-450 BCE.

[344] Ibid, 178.

[345] Ibid. Nock also refers, (on 179), among others, to the Roman writer, Hermippus, who refers to the "setting forth of two million lines of Zoroaster"—which statement, true or false, at least suggests that there was a good deal of such material out there.

[346] Ibid, 181.

nature of the Jewish race and its firm claim of intimate relationship to a powerful deity whose name was surrounded with a secrecy which accentuated its value, a deity moreover who was believed to have interfered and to be prepared to interfere cataclysmically with the course of history."[347]

If up to this point Nock has proven invaluable as a discussant of the complicated boundary between magic and religion (and either of these terms/disciplines and science/medicine), at this point he seems to have fallen prey to a now-familiar problem. In the first place, is "Jew" the proper and appropriate translation of the term *Ioudaios*? Certainly it would not be for the time period of the story being told, although depending upon when exactly Acts was written down, it could be, if the post-Judaean schism into Judaism and Christianity had shifted into place by then. More importantly, Nock's reference to Judaism as a "race," and one with a "mysterious nature" would seem to reflect his own perspective and prejudices—perhaps surprisingly still to be found among individuals as educated as he within English society in the mid-twentieth century—than would have been the case at the time either of the events depicted in Acts or the writing down of those events.

If we *were* to assume that the writing down is late enough for the schism to be clearly in place, then that would also mean that the competition regarding both the correct view of the *sacer* and the entitlement to *religio licita* status was also fully in place. In that case, "Jew" would be "not surprising"—but not for the reasons that are stated by Nock, but because of the competition between Christianity and Judaism, both of which groups would lay "firm claim [to an] intimate relationship to a powerful deity... believed to have interfered and to be prepared to interfere cataclysmically with the course of history."

For certainly the assumption of a human form and the willingness to self-sacrifice on Golgotha constitute as cataclysmic a double intervention as anything that Judaism would suppose. What Christian belief would not share with its Jewish sibling is the expanding emphasis on God's "name [as] surrounded with a secrecy which accentuated its value"—a perspective that may be seen, in part, as a response to the Christian view of God as assuming physical form. The developing Jewish view posits a God the very name of which is not easily accessible, in part because names were understood to encapsulate the essence of their bearer, and God is non-encapsulatable.[348]

Nock notes—correctly—that Elymas is "not an ordinary professional vending curses and philtres... [but] a man of religious potentiality who has some sort of vague position in the household of a great Roman." He also notes how such a position was apparently not entirely uncommon for *iudaei*, referring to the description in Juvenal, *Satire* VI of "a Jewess who has secured a Roman lady's confidences."[349] Again, however, Nock renders the feminine singular of the Latin word *iudaeus* as "Jewess," where "Judaean" would be more accurate, since Juvenal (ca 55-130 CE?) may well not have distinguished

---

[347] Ibid, 182.

[348] We think, once more, for example, of Odysseus—whose name is etymologized in *Odyssey* 19.403f as derived from the Greek verb "*oduein*", meaning "to give or receive pain"—whose essence is one who suffers and causes suffering to others almost beyond endurance. But God's essence cannot be as simply encapsulated as can the essence of Odysseus. This important issue will be further discussed below, 286-8.

[349] Ibid, 183.

Jews from Christians, but thought of both groups as Judaeans, as we have seen his contemporaries, Tacitus and Suetonius, do. On the other hand, as a pagan Roman he would very likely have thought of *iudaei* as an ethnic group (but "race" is a nineteenth-century Western concept out of place in the Roman world of Juvenal), rather than, per se, as a religion, and would have—clearly did, based on the reference in *Satire* VI—grouped them as exotics, together with Chaldaeans, Egyptians, Persians and the like.

If perhaps Juvenal—a pagan, to repeat—*was* aware of the emerging Jewish-Christian dichotomy, he would have not been aware of details that shaped the religious distinctions between the two groups—and still would have thought of the Jews as an ethnic group with its own *religio* (like the Chaldaeans, Persians, Egyptians, Britons and others had) and of the Christians mainly as a group of adherents to a *superstitio*. In any case, we need to be aware of how Nock, for all of his perspective understanding of the magic/religion boundary complication, slips into an anachronistic explanation of the Elymas story, driven by his own views of Judaism and Christianity that are superimposed by him on the narrative that he is reading and discussing.

Consistent, in fact, with the observation of a few paragraphs back that nascent Judaism and Christianity were in competition with each other regarding both the correct understanding of the *sacer* and a privileged position within the Roman polity is Nock's comment that the "story as a whole is of the type so common later of a demonstration by results of the superior merits of Christianity. The appeal to works as a proof of Messiahship and the gift and promise of supernatural powers to the disciples are made emphatically in the Gospels."[350] But of course that promise and those superior merits would stand against all competitors, be they Judaeans-not-for-Jesus or their later offspring, Jews, or any of the myriad pagan *religiones* that prevailed throughout the Roman period.

I have offered such a detailed review of Nock's article first because he offers a convenient summing up of magic/religion issues that we have been engaged in discussing throughout this text and because while he is an antidote to discussions of magic/religion that fail to recognize how blurred the line between them (and other disciplines) is. Second, he is also useful in the discussion of the beginnings of Judaism and Christianity in which we have also begun to be engaged, because of the important historiographic misconceptions that he offers.

His concluding paragraph is important in his presentation of three purposes served by the tale in Acts. "First it represented the Roman authorities as very sympathetic at the outset of Paul's active ministry in the Gentile world; secondly, it gave to Paul a *Gottesurteil* comparable with that declared by Peter on Ananias and Sapphira; thirdly, and this was perhaps most important, it represented Christianity in very sharp contrast with *magia*. The claim of Christians to work miracles, coupled with the novelty of the movement, caused them to be classed with *magi*. Now Acts very definitively associated *magia* with a Jewish religious adventurer here…"[351]

This treble conclusion is certainly of importance to our own narrative. We may well disagree in part with its first aspect. For we can recognize, to repeat, that emergent

---

[350] Ibid, 184.
[351] Ibid, 188.

Christianity is either for the most part ignored by the pagan Roman authorities—we have very few references to the Church; even those of Suetonius and Tacitus, coming not until ca 115-120 CE, as we have noted, are confused—or oppressed by them. The latter situation continues until 313 CE, as we have seen. So the sympathetic perspective depicted in Acts may well be prescriptive—hoped for—rather than descriptive. Certainly the elevation of Paul is important, and certainly the desire, balancing that expressed in Nock's first purpose, for the emerging *religio* to be distinguished from *magia*, particularly given how that term was being commonly understood, makes sense.

So, too, it would have made increasing sense as the post-Judaean, Jewish-Christian schism solidified—in the era between the Judaean revolt that led to the destruction of the Temple in 70 and the Bar Kokhba Revolt of 132-5 (and beyond the latter)—to redirect the notion of *magia*, *superstitio* and general nefarious *sacer*-engagement toward Judaism to help turn that notion away from Christianity. That really only applies, however, to the period after ca 135, if we think of *Ioudaioi* as Jews rather than as Judaeans-not-for-Jesus. As we shall subsequently see, moreover, there will also be times in the following few centuries when Christian writers will ally themselves with Judaism against diversely hostile pagan forces.[352]

*   *   *   *   *

As so often, a close look at our material yields a more ambiguous conclusion regarding both issues—that of magic/superstition versus religion and that of Judaism versus Christianity—than one might have supposed at the outset of this narrative. And the range of competition with these fledgling faiths is more complicated, too, than to be simply labeled "pagan." One such competitor was Apollonius of Tyana (ca 15-100 CE), a philosopher who followed the ascetic, vegetarian life-style prescribed by Pythagoras. We have an account—*The Life of Apollonius of Tyana*—authored in Greek by Philostratos (ca 170-247 CE) at the behest of the Roman empress, Julia Domnia (wife of Emperor Septimius Severus).

The biography was authored by Philostratos around the years 210-20. It was in part based on earlier works, such as the book on Apollonius' youth ascribed to Maximus of Aegae; the memoir ascribed to Danis, a key disciple and companion of Apollonius; and the work by Moeragenes called *Memorabilia of Apollonius of Tyana, Magician and Philosopher*. Little if any of the works by or associated with these authors has survived, however, so that our reliance on Philostratos himself is rather substantial.[353] Although he related various miraculous feats of Apollonius, he emphasized at the same time that his hero was not a magician, but a serious philosopher and a champion of traditional Greek values.

In Philostratos' description of Apollonius' life and deeds there is a number of similarities with the life and especially the claimed miracles of Jesus. It is not clear as to whether these parallels were intentional, but the original aim was hardly to present

---

[352] See the discussion of Origen's *Contra Celsum*, below, in chapter twelve.
[353] In fact, it is Philostratos himself who mentions these sources in chapter 3 of Book One; he also mentions there that the Empress had asked him to write this work.

Apollonius as a rival of Jesus. However, in the late third century Porphyry, an anti-Christian Neoplatonic philosopher (whom we will briefly refer to in the next chapter), claimed in his treatise *Against the Christians* that the miracles of Jesus were not unique, and mentioned Apollonius as a non-Christian who had accomplished similar extraordinary deeds. Still later, around the year 300, Roman pagan authorities under the Emperor Diocletian used the renown of Apollonius in their struggle to wipe out Christianity.

Hierokles, one of the main instigators of the persecution of Christians as members of a *superstitio*, in 303, wrote a pamphlet in which he argued that Apollonius exceeded Christ as a wonder-worker and yet wasn't worshipped as a god, and that the cultured biographers of Apollonius were more trustworthy than the uneducated apostles. This attempt to make Apollonius a hero of the anti-Christian movement provoked sharp replies from bishop Eusebius of Caesarea (best known as the biographer of the Emperor Constantine) and from Lactantius. Eusebius wrote an extant reply to the pamphlet of Hierokles, in which he claimed that Philostratos was a fabulist and that Apollonius was a sorcerer allied with nefarious *daimones*. This started a debate on the relative merits of Jesus and Apollonius that has continued in various forms across the centuries.

In Late Antiquity talismans allegedly made by Apollonius appeared in several cities of the Eastern Roman Empire, as if they were sent from heaven: magical figures and columns were erected in public places, meant to protect cities from afflictions. The great popularity of these talismans was a challenge to the Christians. Some Byzantine authors condemned them as sorcery and the work of demons, others admitted that such magic was beneficial; none of them claimed that it didn't work. In the Western Empire, Sidonius Apollinari, a fifth-century Christian admirer of Apollonius, produced a Latin translation of Philostratos' *Life*, which is unfortunately lost.

Philostratos' work offers us a heroic Pythagorean from Roman Cappodocia who asserts that God cannot be accessed by means of sacrifices, and indeed has no desire to be worshipped that way. Rather, God wishes to be accessed through the power of *nous*—mind—as God is pure *nous* and as *nous* is the greatest of human faculties. More precisely, Apollonius' model, Pythagoras, "would not stain the altars with blood; rather the honey-cake and frankincense and the hymn of praise were the offerings made to the gods by this man, who realized that they welcome such tribute more than they do hecatombs and the knife laid upon the sacrificial basket. For they say that he certainly had social intercourse with the gods and learned from them the conditions under which they take pleasure in men or are disgusted..." (Bk I; ch 1).

Apollonius follows closely this Pythagorean *modus vivendi*. One might note that this description places Apollonius' thinking simultaneously at odds with and consonant with Jewish and Christian thought, as the latter are emerging in the course of the second through fourth centuries. At odds, of course, since, when the Temple still stood, the predecessors of the Jews and Christians—Israelites (and then Judaeans), as we have seen—placed important emphasis on animal sacrifice. Indeed, where Christianity is concerned, the very centerpiece of its developmental narrative offers a particularized successor to this in the self-sacrifice enacted by Jesus on behalf of humankind on Golgotha.

On the other hand, the emphasis placed by Apollonius on *nous* as the primary connector between the human *profanus* and the divine *sacer*—and the specific notion that *nous* is the essential human faculty that connects us to divinity because God is pure *nous*—seems extremely close to the shared Jewish and Christian idea that what transforms Adam from a clod of earth (*adamah*) into a sentient, thinking, be-souled being is the idea, expressed in Genesis 2:7 that God breathes Its spirit (Hebrew: *n'shamah*) into Adam. So what connects us to God is our *n'shamah*—*psykhe* in Greek and *anima* in Latin; thus Adam is *animated*—that is our essential faculty; and God is pure *n'shamah/psykhe/anima*, as it were. Moreover, the interpretive literatures of both Judaism and Christianity will come to associate our souls with our free will—which free will enables Adam and Eve, for example, to choose to disobey God's commandment regarding fruit gastronomy in the Garden of Eden—which is in turn associated with intellect, which is, essentially, *nous*.

Pythagoras derived his information from the *sacer* itself, according to the tradition embraced by Philostratos, for "he said that Apollo had come to him acknowledging that he was the god in person," and furthermore, his devotees "honored him as an emissary from Zeus" (ibid). Apollonius himself is said in Philostratos' account to have an even stronger divine connection than Pythagoras. He "had interviews with the magi of Babylon and with the Brahmans of India and also the naked [ascetics] in Egypt" (Bk I; ch 2)—so he is understood to have traveled far and to have spent time with diverse types of groups known for either their ascetic qualities or their esoteric wisdom, or both. Interestingly, typical translations of Philostratos into English render "magi"—correctly, since this would properly reflect what the term has come to mean in Greek-speaking Rome—as "wizards" (rather than as "priests"). Indeed, the term is generalized, as when reference is made to how the early Greek philosophers Empedokles, Demokritos as well as Pythagoras "consorted with magi (i.e., sorcerers/wizards)."

Philostratos points out, further, that, while "uttering many *daimonia*"—which term presumably refers to incantations addressing lesser, but not necessary nefarious, demonic powers of the *sacer*—these thinkers never engaged in *he tekhne*: the presumably supernatural art which, in this context is used with a dark nuance, and thus might be translated as "the dark arts." Among his skills was the ability to foresee things before they happened, which capacity he is said by Philostratos to have shared in common with Sokrates and Anaxagoras, the pre-socratic philosopher (and yet Apollonius is not simply referred to as a philosopher)—predicting rainfalls and the collapse of houses. This skill, the author emphasizes, in comparing his subject to these two figures, is not derived from his skill in the "magi art" (*magoi tekhnei* in the dative/ablative)—i.e., sorcery/magic/wizardry.

The beginning of the actual biography, coming in chapter 4, notes his unusual birth, as the son of a man of the same name in a family that was very wealthy. To his mother there came an apparition of "Proteus, who changes his shape so much in Homer, in the form of an Egyptian *daimon*." When, not at all frightened, she asked him what sort of child she would bear, Proteus responded "myself"—and to her question as to who he was, he responded "Proteus, the god of Egypt." So Apollonius' biography begins with a divine annunciation to his mother, informing her that her son will be a god—a god associated with the exotic Egyptian world and who is renowned within Greek lore from its literary beginnings.

If this annunciational moment parallels that in the narrative of Jesus' life as it would later come to be understood—that the son is presented as co-identical with the divine father—within Philostratos' account this patrimony is presented as a less than absolute idea. For the author also notes that the people of the area around Tyana claim that Apollonius is the son of Zeus, but that he referred to himself as, simply, the son of Apollonius (Bk I; ch 6). The notion of a figure who has both a human functional father and a divine biological father can be found in the Greek tradition as far back as the narrative of Herakles' life and, differently, that of Dionysios (as we have noted) and comes forward to the period just prior to Apollonius' lifetime, of course, with the account of the birth of Jesus.

The birth itself took place in a meadow, according to the story that Philostratos relates. Thus

> just as the hour of his birth was approaching, his mother was warned in a dream to walk out into the meadow and pluck the flowers... she fell asleep lying on the grass. Thereupon the swans who fed in the meadow set up a dance around her as she slept, and lifting their wings, as they are wont to do, cried out aloud all at once... She then leapt up at the sound of their song and bore her child.... The people of the country say that just at the moment of the birth, a thunderbolt seemed about to fall to earth and then rose up into the air and disappeared aloft; and the gods therefore indicated, I think, the great distinction to which the sage was to attain... how he would transcend all things on earth and approach the gods... (Bk I; ch 5)

Less out of the ordinary, if nonetheless outstanding, was his acuity in learning as he was growing up—including the fact that he naturally took to a standard Attic dialect of Greek with a hint of the country-bumpkin accent that might have been expected for someone who was born and grew up where he did (Bk I, ch 7). But it is as an adult that we see him accomplishing the extraordinary things that would gain him such a following and offer comparison to the acts of Jesus of Nazareth.

Thus a poor woman came to him with a 16-year-old son who for two years had been "possessed by a *daimon*"—which inherently neutral term we may understand, given the context, to be used here with its negative connotation: a demon, the nature of which was that of *eiron* (one who mocks) and *pseuste* (one who lies).The reason for the possession, according to his mother, was that her son was so good-looking that the *daimon* was in love with him, "and won't permit him to retain his reason (*nous*), nor allow him to attend school or learn archery or even to be at home, but drives him out into wild places" (Bk III, ch 38)—or, to put it in our terms: out into the *sacer*, which is to say that this aspect of the *sacer* that has possessed the boy keeps him a mental prisoner within his (the *daimon*'s) own realm.

Not surprisingly for one possessed, the boy speaks not in his own voice but in a "deep hollow tone, as men do, and looks at one with eyes other than his own (ibid.)." As it turns out, the *daimon* is not evil, per se. On the contrary, not only is he motivated by affection—but being from a different realm (the *sacer*) and not our own (the *profanus*), one might say that he does not have the capacity to recognize that his possessional action yields such an unhappy outcome for both the boy whom he possesses and the boy's loved ones—and more to the point, the *daimon*'s existence, as such, is a function of a failed passage from the *profanus* of life to the *sacer* of death (reminiscent of Elpinor in *Odyssey*, Bk 11).

For when the mother had intended the previous year to bring her son to Apollonoius to be cured, the *daimon* found out through the son, and explained to her "that he was the *eidolon* [ghost, substanceless image—think again of the figures encountered by Odysseus at the edge of the *sacer*] of a man who was killed some time ago in battle, but at the time of his death was in love with his wife; yet when he had been dead only three days his wife offended their union by marrying someone else, the result of which was that he [his ghost!] came to detest the love of women and had translated himself into this very boy" (ibid). The *daimon* had promised to endow the boy with many blessings if the mother left things alone, but the promises were not kept and the *daimon* asserted control of her household, so that she ended up finally seeking the wise man's help.

When Apollonius asked her if her son was with her she said that she had not been able to get him to come with her, and was concerned because the *daimon* was leading him into dangerous locales where he could easily perish. Apollonius gave her a letter to take and read to the *daimon*—the contents are not indicated, but Philostratos assumes that it contained serious threats, and the reader is to suppose that the creature departed. So it appears that Apollonius can drive out *daimones*. He could also heal the lame, for he received a visit from a man of thirty, a lion-hunter, who had been attacked by a lion and so severely dislocated his hip that he limped seriously. "However, when he stroked the hip with his hands the youth immediately began to walk straight" (Bk III, ch 39). The cure bears an obvious resemblance to the laying on of the hands—although one might also associate the cure with more medically-associated techniques, such as rolfing or chiropractics.

Not so the man who arrived at Apollonius' doorstep whose eyes had been put out, and who "went away having recovered the sight (literally, the light) in both of them. Yet another man had his hand paralyzed; but left [the sage's] presence in full possession of the limb. And a certain woman had suffered in labor already seven times, but was healed in the following way through the intercession of her husband. He bade the man, whenever his wife should be about to bring forth her next child, to enter her chamber carrying in his bosom a live hare; then he was to walk once round her and at the same moment to release the hare; for that the womb would be extruded together with the fetus, unless the hare was at once driven out" (ibid).

There are more instances of healing related by Philostratos. On the one hand, we may recognize a number of such acts that resonate with those effected by Jesus in the Gospels. On the other hand, particularly where the last-offered example is concerned, we may recognize a rather Frazerian sort of cure: rabbits are universally associated with successful reproduction, so the use of one in the cure ritual against failed pregnancy offers an implied homeopathic aspect to it. One would have expected, perhaps, the more overt act of contagious magic—the touching of the womb with the rabbit—but perhaps the whole point was to distinguish Apollonius' method from what might be thought of as a more garden-variety act of magic.

In any case, embedded within the narrative by Philostratos are more than a few events that not only suggest comparison with acts associated with Jesus, but that more broadly suggest a blurry line between acts that might be called religious and those termed magical. Not just the acts but the terminology that forms their contexts offers that sort of blurriness. This issue expands, rather than shrinks, as we follow the *profanus* of the Roman Empire in its diversely articulated relationship with the *sacer* through the centuries during which Christianity (and Judaism) are taking identifiable shape.

CHAPTER NINE

Pagan Imperial Rome in the Second through Fourth Centuries: Magic, Sorcery and Theurgy from Julian's *Chaldaean Oracles* to Iamblichus

The question of how the various disciplines function that are parallel to but presumed to be different from religion—and possibly from each other—continues to be addressed as the Roman Empire muddles forward from dynasty to dynasty. That these disciplines have a distinct association with foreign, often ancient and thereby esoteric cultures in the Roman mind is clear from works like the so-called *Chaldaean Oracles*, as well as from the work by Iamblichus variously called *Theurgy* or *On the Mysteries of Egypt*. In both cases, moreover, our trove of vocabulary expands—beyond magician, sorcerer, wizard and the like (as opposed to priest)—to include theurgist.

The *Chaldaean Oracles* are in fact ascribed to one Julian (Julianus), who is known as Julian(us) the Theurgist—a writer active during the reign of Emperor Marcus Aurelius (161-180 CE)[354]—with whom as many as three different works may be associated and found in some 200 fragments of hexameter verse and commentary, upon which the later Neoplatonic philosopher, Proclus (412-85 CE) apparently wrote a further commentary.[355] Julian is said to have completed *The Chaldaean Oracles* begun by his father, Julian(us) the Chaldaean, after the latter's death. The *Oracles* offer an odd combination of Neoplatonic and Perso-Babylonian elements.[356]

The likely Perso-Babylonian source for much of Julian's text is reflected in the prescriptions that it offers of a fire and sun cult, which would seem to have distinctly Zoroastrian roots—and later tradition refers to both Juliani, father and son, as *magi*, which, as we have seen, either means that their source of esoteric knowledge was Persia, or that they were viewed as having skills with respect to the *sacer-profanus* relationship beyond the ordinary but also outside proper *religio*—or both.

The *Chaldaean Oracles* speak, essentially, of an absolute, transcendent deity referred to as the Father, with which being there resides Power, a productive principle from

---

[354] Julian apparently served in the army during the Emperor's campaign against the Quadi and claimed to have saved the Roman camp of which he was part from death through drought by causing a thunderstorm—a claim made by no less than four other *religiones*.

[355] According to the *Suda*, he wrote three works, of which *On Theurgy* was one, and his father authored a four-volume work on *daimones*.

[356] The term "Chaldaea" is the Greco-Latin rendering of the Assyro-Babylonian word, *Kaldu*, which referred to an area southeast of Babylonia in the direction of the Persian Gulf.

which Intellect (*nous*) emanates. The double function of Intellect is to contemplate the Forms located in the purely intellectual/spiritual/metaphysical realm (in our terms, the *sacer*) of the Father—this notion coming right out of Plato's vocabulary—and to shape and administer the material/physical realm (in our terms: the *profanus*). Intellect is thus the Demiurge (*demiourgos*) in Its capacity as shaper and administrator of the *profanus*.

There is a kind of boundary between the spiritual/intellectual/metaphysical and material/phenomenal/physical realms—a kind of membrane or veil—*personified* as Hekate.[357] Hekate separates the two "fires": the purely spiritual aetherial fire of the Father and the fire in which and from which the material universe is created.[358] Moreover, she functions sacerdotally, as a sieve or conduit through which all emanation into the *profanus* realm passes.

There is more. From Hekate the "world-soul" is derived, from which "nature" in turn emanates, that administers and governs the sublunar—i.e., *profanus* and lower *sacer* (earth, water, *aer*/lower heavens)—realm. From Nature, Fate derives, with the capacity to enslave the lower part of the human soul. But the human soul is akin to the divine essence, and thus the goal articulated by the *Oracles* is for the soul—*psykhe*—to return to a condition of "nakedness," freed of its dross, material—*hyle*—carapace. It does this by way of *nous*. The *Oracles* have as their purpose to teach one how to purify the lower part of the soul from the pollution effected through contact with Nature and Fate. They offer instruction in living a life of contemplation and austerity (what Sokrates would no doubt refer to as a true philosopher's life). Salvation—release from a condition of enslavement to Nature and Fate—is possible if one's well-trained, well-tutored, well-disciplined soul ascends through the seven levels of the planetary spheres, casting off various polluted aspects of its lower aspects as it ascends toward a pure intellectual/spiritual condition.

If the opposition between the phenomenal and intelligible worlds, and certainly the vocabulary that articulates that opposition, has such a strong Platonic ring to it, the understanding of that intelligible world into which the soul is freed, saved from the *hyle* that holds it captive in the phenomenal world, offers a Middle Eastern source that extends

---

[357] With regard to the word "phenomenal," one must think again in Socratic/Platonic terms: "Phenomenon" comes from the Greek verb, *phainomai*, "to appear"—thus the phenomenal world is the world of appearances, which is also the world of becoming, which is in constant flux and subject to change, as opposed to the realm of the Forms, which is the world of true being occupied by unchanging absolutes—the Forms/Ideas are those absolutes.

[358] This is an important instance of borrowing, transformation, ambiguity and syncretism. For Hekate was a goddess in earlier Greek religion, most often depicted holding two torches or a key, and in later periods portrayed in a triple form, sometimes sporting three different kinds of animal heads. As a consummate border creature, she came to be associated with crossroads and entryways, but also with fire and light as well as with the Moon and its phases. She came to be thought of as presiding over the three *profanus* realms—earth, sea and sky—and also to play a broader positive role as Savior (*Soteira*), Mother of Angels and, in the *Chaldaean Oracles*, Mother of the Cosmic World Soul. Hekate may have originated among the Carians in Southwestern Anatolia, where variants of her name are found as names given to children. William Berg, in his article, "Hecate: Greek or "Anatolian"?", *Numen* 21.2 (August 1974:128-40) observes, (on p 129), that "[s]ince children are not called after spooks, it is safe to assume that Carian theophoric names involving *hekat-* refer to a major deity free from the dark and unsavoury ties to the underworld and to witchcraft associated with the Hecate of classical Athens." On the other hand, she was one of the main deities worshipped in Athenian households as a protective goddess and one who bestowed prosperity and daily blessings on the family. The Romans gradually associated her with the more nefarious or at least questionable areas of enterprise found as part of the Greek view of her, such as *magia*, sorcery and necromancy, but also with knowledge of herbs and poisonous plants. Rather obviously, she also closely paralleled and was identified with the Roman goddess, Trivia (a border goddess whose name means "three paths").

back beyond Zoroastrianism. The "paradise" concept has its earliest expression nearly three millennia before the Christian era in the vocabulary of the Sumerians, where a place of perfection to which very few gain access is called *dilmun*.[359] That idea is carried forward from one culture to the next in the Mesopotamian-Persian world. The *Oracles* promote the notion of such a locale as an attainable goal for the properly tutored soul.

The awareness of all of this and the consummate guide for how to benefit from such an understanding is associated with the two Juliani. Julian the younger is the first individual, as far as we know, to be referred to as a *theourgos*—a term which he himself may have invented, in order to distinguish himself from *theologoi*, who merely "talked about the gods, [whereas] he 'acted upon' them, or even, perhaps, 'created' them."[360] In any case, he claimed to have received these oracles—he called them *theoparadota*—directly from the gods.[361] Their style is incoherent and bizzare enough to suggest the sort of utterances that someone in a trance might transmit from the not-overly-intelligible *sacer*. E.R. Dodds speculates that, as Proclus suggested, he might have put into verse some "revelations" of "some visionary or trance medium."[362]

Dodds also refers to the *Oracles* as "prescriptions for the magical evocation of gods" and notes that "later tradition represents the Juliani as potent magicians."[363] He does not offer any comments on what it is that would define the prescriptions as magical rather than religious or the Juliani as magicians rather than priests of some sort. He also refers to an interesting Christian legend that represented Julianus as competing with Apollonius of Tyana and Apuleius in a display of magical (religious?) powers. "Rome being stricken with a plague, each magician is assigned the medical superintendence of one sector of the city; Apuleius undertakes to stop the plague in fifteen days, Apollonius in ten, but Julianus stops it instantly by a mere word of command." It is again interesting to note that Dodds takes at face value that all three practitioners should be classified as magicians and their actions magical, however efficacious—and that Julianus is singled out as accomplishing the end of the plague through words that are commanding, not petitionary and are therefore apparently not to be confused with, say, prayer any more than his action should be confused

---

[359] See, for example, the *Epic of Gilgamesh*, in which the hero, (in tablet XI), seeking the Flower of Immortality, is able to journey to *dilmun*, where he encounters and receives guidance from the Mesopotamian version of Noah and his wife, living forever, like gods, in that realm. Note, too, that the word "paradise" in English (and its siblings in other European languages) derives from *paradisus*, a term contrived by St Jerome in his translation of the Bible into Latin—the so-called Vulgate—to refer to what in the Hebrew of Genesis is referred to as the Garden of Eden. Jerome created the word by merely Latinizing the Greek term, *paradeisos*, found in the Septuagint translation of the Bible. In turn, *paradeisos* was either a rendering of the Hebrew, *pardes*—or it came directly from the same Persian word, *paradeshu*, from which the Hebrew word derived. *Paradeshu* referred originally to the well-watered, beautifully cultivated park/garden found in the center of Persian cities, which was both separate from the otherwise dusty and unvegetal remainder of the city and also reserved for the exclusive use of the shah and his retinue.

[360] E.R. Dodds, *The Greeks and the Irrational*, (Berkeley and Los Angeles: University of California Press, 1951), Appendix II, 283-4, in which Dodds references Bidez as the source for this idea. "*Logos*" refers to a verbal account of some sort; by the time of New Testament Greek it most often means "word." Plato uses *logos* to mean a rational account (of indeterminate length), in contrast to *mythos*, but also to contrast with *ergon*, meaning "action"—which term shares a common root with the "*ourgos*" part of *theourgos*.

[361] *Theos*, of course, means god(s); *paradota* comes from *paradidomi*, which means to transmit/hand over. Thus *theoparadota* are "divinely transmitted things."

[362] Dodds, ibid, 284.

[363] Ibid, 285.

with miracles of the sort that Jesus or the apostles, or Moses and Aaron, were able to accomplish.

Others, interestingly, are also referred to by the term "theurgist," such as the third-century philosopher, Plotinus (204-70 CE), arguably the founder of Neoplatonism, and someone who on the contrary would have tried to draw a sharp line of distinction between philosophy and theurgy and the latter's *sacer*-focused ideology—and therefore Dodds vehemently disagrees with such an assessment.[364] The prevalence of syncretism among diverse systems of thought (as we have been seeing)—and in Plotinus' case, the idea that he was both born in Egypt and very knowledgeable with regard to Egyptian religion (and its supposed inherently "magical" elements) helps account for this potential definitional confusion.

Moreover, Plotinus' pupil, Porphyry, was certainly obsessed with oracles and their practitioners even as he was focused on Neoplatonic philosophy, and even though he is credited with directing challenging questions to theurgists, as we shall see (and of having unearthed and commented on the *Chaldaean Oracles*, as we have already noted)—and although he warned his readers that theurgy was a dangerous practice with potentially evil and not only good outcomes, and asserted that it could not, in fact, lead the soul back to its pure, divine source.

A better known commentary on the *Oracles* was penned later, by Porphyry's pupil, Iamblichus (ca 245-325 CE). It was apparently due to the latter's disagreement with Porphyry regarding the validity of the practice of theurgy that Iamblichus is said to have written the work that is best preserved among the many things ascribed to him, most of which have not survived. Thus his *De Mysteriis Aegyptorum* (*On the Egyptian Mysteries*) is in large part a response to Porphyry's criticism of theurgy.[365] Perhaps its most obvious doctrinal distinction from Porphyry's view is its assertion that salvation is achievable not through reason but through ritual.

The rituals that the embodied soul needs to perform in order to return to divinity— "doing/acting (*ourgos*, from *erga*) [the] divine (*theos*) [thing]"—were referred to by some students in late antiquity as *magia*, but Iamblichus seems pretty clearly to have considered the ceremonies to which he refers as sacramental religious rites. By contrast, Porphyry believed that salvation could only be achieved through mental contemplation; Porphyry's letter criticizing his student's ideas on theurgy led to the responsive publication of *De Mysteriis*.

In a nutshell, Iamblichus' view is that, since the transcendent realm—the ultimate spiritual, *sacer* reality—is supra-rational, then no amount of mental, rational engagement or contemplation can access and grasp it. The rituals of theurgy are intended to break through the barrier through which reason cannot penetrate, by retracing the divine "signatures" through the layers of being. Its symbolic language may be seen as offering a

---

[364] Pauly-Wissowa, the consummate encyclopedia of classical scholarship, (written in German), refers to Plotinus as a theurgist in its article, "Theurgie," for example.

[365] There are sufficient differences between this book and Iamblichus' other surviving works—in style and in some points of doctrine—to lead some scholars to question whether Iamblichus is the actual author. At the very least, the treatise originated from his school, and in its systematic attempt to give a speculative justification for the cult practices associated with that school, it marks an important point in understanding the shape of religious thought in the early fourth century.

kind of homeopathic approach to the trans-phenomenal world. Starting with correspondences of the divine in matter, the theurgist eventually reaches the level where the soul's inner divinity unites with God.

> Theurgic union is attained only by the efficacy of the unspeakable acts performed in the appropriate manner, acts which are beyond all comprehension, and by the potency of the ineffable symbols that are understood only by the gods… Without intellectual effort on our part the tokens by their own virtue accomplish their proper work (*de myst.* 96.13).

This proves significant because of how the world is spiritually evolving at this time. As Dodds points out, "[t]o the discouraged minds of fourth-century pagans such a message offered a seductive comfort. The 'theoretical philosophers' had now been arguing for some nine centuries, and what had come of it? Only a visibly declining culture, and the creeping growth of that Christian *atheotes* which was too plainly sucking the lifeblood of Hellenism. As vulgar magic is commonly the last resort of the personally desperate… so theurgy became the refuge of a despairing intelligentsia…"[366]

There is more. Similar to but not identical with the cosmology of Julian the Theurgist, Iamblichus posited a transcendental Monad, a "One" that is beyond normative contact, the first principle of which is *nous*. He suggested that there is a secondary "One"— also transcendent, called *psykhe* ("soul") that stands between the inaccessible "One" and "the many" produced by it. (This *psykhe* occupies a place and a role somewhat similar to that of Hekate in Julian's system.) *Nous* and *psykhe* together constitute the initial dyad. *Nous*, furthermore, is, albeit a monad, yet "divided" into two spheres, the intellective and the intelligible—the first of these the sphere of thought and the second the sphere of the objects of thought. Thus the primary dyad is also a triad (the divided *nous* plus the *psykhe*).

From the third part of this primary dyad/triad, creation proceeds: *psykhe* is the Demiurge—but this may also be understood as the *sixth* element, in that, as *nous* is both monad and dyad, and the dyad of *nous* and *psykhe* is both dyad and triad, we end up with a hexomad comprised of adding monad, dyad and triad together—and the Demiurge that produces our reality is actually the tail end of this progression.

There are three important issues that this brief discussion places before us. One is that the cosmological imagery is inherently paradoxic—various numbers co-exist with each other in the primary, transcendent *sacer* as they by definition cannot in the *profanus* world in which we dwell—and is therefore more familiar in the Jewish and Christian traditions in their mystical aspects rather than their mainstream aspects.[367] Second is that these as well as other numbers are handled with a strong emphasis on symbolic significance. We have noted and shall note further that numerology is part of the means by

---

[366] Dodds, Ibid, 288. *Atheotes* would mean "godlessness." As disbelievers in all of those diverse pagan divinities, the Christians seemed to be atheists to the pagan world—even more so, the Jews would seem so, whose sole god is entirely without physical form. By 325, the Christians would at least offer a fully human form for their singular god.

[367] For a brief discussion of mysticism in the Abrahamic traditions and how this issue of paradox applies, see Ori Z Soltes, *Mysticism in Judaism, Christianity and Islam: Searching for Oneness*, (Lanham, MD: Roman & Littlefield, 2008), chapters 2-4. Also, see below, 288-9, 373.

which the Jewish tradition, particularly in its mystical aspect, addresses and accesses the ineffable Name of the indescribable and **non-encapsulatable** God.[368]

Thirdly, this sort of numerological paradox is inherent in what eventually emerges, after the Council of Nicaea in 325, as standard, mainstream Christian doctrine: the triune God is both a monad and a triad, by definition. So not only is the relation16, ship between the thought of Iamblichus and that of Julian the Theurgist similar, but the thought of Iamblichus offers important similarities to aspects of Judaism and central Christian thought, which means that the world in which our discussion is ensconced is, again, far more complex than merely "Judaism vs Christianity vs Paganism" or "Judaeo-Christianty vs Paganism."

This brings us to two further points that are immediately relevant to our concerns. One is the sort of material, in somewhat more detail, that is offered in the so-called *Egyptian Mysteries*; the other is the matter of the influence of Iamblichus in the several generations after his death. The format of the work is as a series of 10 questions posed by Porphyry to the Prophet Anebo—the latter as if he were an Egyptian priest—with responses from Abammon the Teacher, (this would be Iamblichus), to whom Anebo has passed on the questions.[369] If it were to be proven that this work is definitely not authored by Iamblichus, it would still be important for our narrative, since the questions, beyond being arguably relevant to understanding Iamblichus are certainly relevant to our understanding of one among any number of *sacer*-focused perspectives within the Roman world of the early fourth century, when Christianity was on the verge of, or had recently become, legal and was poised to become hegemonic within a few generations.

"Porphyry"'s first question pertains to the gods: what are their particular attributes? And how are we to understand the hierarchy of divine beings: "are the *theoi* distinguished by [purely] aetherial bodies, the *daimones* by aerial bodies and *psychai* by bodies pertaining to earth?" He thus distinguishes Olympians from lesser divinites (think of Athena and Hermes versus Kirke or Kalypso in the context of the *Odyssey*, for instance) and both of these groups from the (presumably human) souls that are distinct from human bodies and connect us to the gods but at their most elevated are less than divine; he

---

[368] Regarding the Ineffable Name of God, see below, 285-6.

[369] The names themselves are interesting and perhaps of consequence. "Anebo," who is referred to as if he were an Egyptian priest, may well be the name Anabu or Anubis, the jackal-headed god who serves in classical Egyptian religion as a psychopomp—a guide for the soul across the boundary from the *profanus* of life to the *sacer* of death—and who is also a patron of sacred literature. He would therefore be an appropriate one to whom Porphyry would direct—or would be represented as directing—his questions regarding what are billed as Egyptian theosophic doctrines with regard to divinity and religious rites. Abammon strikes me—I am speculating—as a more interesting and complex instance of syncretism. I would propose that it is comprised of two elements, Av (Ab) and Hammon or Ammon. The first, a Semitic element, translates as "father." The second, if it is Hammon, is also Semitic and is part of the divine name, Ba'al Hammon, found from Canaan (Judaea/Palestina) to Mesopotamia. Ba'al Hammon—"lord of a multitude," his name also translated as "lord of the brazier (*hamman*)"—achieved particular success in Carthage, that North African offshoot of Tyrian/Phoenician culture against which Rome eventually fought three wars (the Punic Wars) for domination of the western Mediterranean region, in the third and second centuries BCE. If this second element is, rather, Ammon (aka Amun), then the name is not Semitic, but Egyptian, and refers to the "Hidden One", the consummate godhead and source beyond all other gods. Both Porphyry and Iamblichus were from the East: Syria, to be specific; and Porphyry was in fact from Tyre. Porphyry's own name was actually apparently *Molokh*—meaning "king" in Northwest Semitic—which was rendered by the Roman-era (third century CE) Greek writer, Cassios Longinos, (who may have been Porphyry's teacher), as *Porphorios*, a Greek rendering (rather than a precise translation) of Molokh, meaning "of [Royal] Purple").

distinguishes, further, among three of the elements that, since Empedocles and Aristotle, are understood by Greeks and Romans to comprise the universe. The most rarified is the *aither*—the blazing—the fiery element that we see when we look up into the distant heavens; the *aer*—the thicker substance through which we move, that extends from the earth and water up toward the *aither*; and of course, the heaviest, heavier even than water, earth.

How is it, he continues, that theurgic rites are directed toward them "as being of the Earth and Underworld? …How can the *theosophoi* [those with unique wisdom—*sophia*—regarding the gods] consider them as impressionable? …Why, then, are many things performed to them in the Sacred Rites as to impressionable beings? … it is implied that not only are the *daimones* impressioinable but so also are the *theoi*." Moreover, if "only the *theoi* are incorporeal, how shall the sun, the moon and the visible luminaries of the sky be accounted as gods? How is it that some of them are givers of good and others bring evil? … As the gods that are visible are included in the same category with the invisible, what distinguishes the *daimones* from the visible and likewise the invisible *theoi*?"

There are several issues being addressed then. The sacred theurgistic rites seem to treat both *theoi* and *daimones* as if their bodies are earth-bound—hence, "impressionable"—rather than aetherial or aerial. There is not only a question of how to understand the *theos/daimon* hierarchy, but where to place the most august of the *planetes* within the category of divinity: if *theoi* and *daimones* are generally invisible, then what about the sun, moon and other *planetes* that are visible?

In turn he asks (this is the beginning of the second query) how a *daimon* differs from a hero or demi-god or from a *psykhe*, and how does one know that a *theos*—or a divine messenger (*angelos*) or *daimon*, or *psykhe*—is actually present at a sacred ritual? Third: "what is it that takes place in divination?" For when we sleep and 8 we can be aware of things that are about to happen (because that condition connects us to the non-linear timelessness of the *sacer*). How is this different from the perception of the future that occurs during a condition of enthusiastic rapture? And what of other types of ecstasy—*ek-stasis* ("being outside one's ordinary sate of being")—such as that brought on by hearing

> cymbals, drums, or some choral chant; as for example, those who ae engaged in Korybantic Rites, those who are possessed at the Sabazian festivals, and those who are celebrating the Rites of the Divine Mother. Others, also, are inspired when drinking water, like the priest of the Klarian Apollo at Kolophon; others when sitting over cavities in the earth, like the women who deliver oracles at Delphi; others when affected by vapor from the water, like the prophetesses at Brankhidai; and others when standing in indented marks like those who have been filled from an imperceptible inflowing of the divine *pleroma* ["fullness"]… Some are affected by means of water, others by gazing on a wall, others by hypetheral air, and others by the sun or some other of

the heavenly luminaries. Some have likewise established the technique of searching the future by means of entrails, birds and stars.[370]

What we may recognize from this array of descriptions of modes of transgressing the *profanus-sacer* border is, yet again, some of the range and variety of classical and syncretistic religions that populate the Roman world in the era of Iamblichus, from Phrygia to Athens and from Apollo's sites to those of Dionysius, involving music and dance as well as noxious vapors.

Against this array, "Porphyry" asks what it is that makes divination distinct. "Diviners all say that they arrive at the foreknowledge of the future through *theoi* or *daimones*." But how is this so? For "I dispute," he asserts, "whether divine power is brought down to such subservience to human beings as, for instance, not to hold aloof from any who are diviners with barley-meal." This not only suggests compulsion rather than petition—which by at least one definition as we have encountered it, would classify divination as magic rather than religion—but it questions how it is that lesser beings (human) could possibly compel greater beings (gods), particularly with such an unimpressive substance as barley-meal serving as the means to compel.

"Porphyry" doubts the reality of *sacer* beings manifesting themselves in reality in response to efforts at divination, but that rather, the soul imagines these things—due to little sparks emanating from the soul, or "a certain mingled form of substance produced from our own soul and from the divine in breathing," or from strict imagination, or "that the emanations from the realm of matter bring *daimones* into existence through their inherent forces."

Again, in the fourth question, "Porphyry" expresses perplexity as to "how they who are invoked as superior beings are likewise commanded like inferiors." In his fifth question he doubts the utility of sacrifices: "The gods also require that the interpreters of the oracles observe strict abstinence from animal substances, so that they not be made impure by the fumes from these bodies, yet they themselves are [said to be] allured most of all by the fumes of the sacrifices of animals!"[371] Why and how would aetherial and aerial beings be drawn to anything having to do with such dross, earthbound material?

This earthbound/aetherial, impure/pure issue spills into the next question in which "Porphyry" notes that the seer—the one who has been initiated into a higher level of

---

[370] The Korybantes were the armed and crested dancers who worshipped the Phrygian (southwest Anatolian) version of the mother goddess, Kybele, with drumming and dancing. Sabazios was the nomadic horseman and sky-father-god of the Phrygians and also the Thracians. (To repeat: in Indo-European languages, such as Phrygian, the *-zios* element derives from **dyeus*, the common precursor of Latin *deus* and Greek "Zeus"). In any case, the Greeks eventually associated Phrygian Sabazios with both Zeus and Dionysios, as we have earlier noted. Mopsos, a son of Apollo, is said to have presided over a shrine in Kolophon, on the western coast of Anatolia, mentioned in the context of the return of the Akhaians from Troy; Delphi was of course Apollo's primary shrine, whose priestess stood over an opening in the earth's crust, breathing in vapors that induced semi-unintelligible rants; the second most famous shrine of Apollo was located at Didyma on the southwest coast of Anatolia, and was administered for many generations by the Brankhidai, a family said to have descended from a youthful beloved of Apollo, Brankhos.

[371] This fifth query is not found within the letter itself as we have it—the text goes directly from question four to question six—but from elsewhere in Iamblichus' writings; it is assumed by some contemporary editors to belong here, having been misplaced. The location issue is not essential one way or the other for our purposes, since it is the content, associated with Iamblichus or with his school, and at any rate with his era, which interests us.

understanding—must be pure from contact with anything dead, and "yet many of the rites used to bring the gods here are made effective through the use of dead animals," and he elaborates further on these last several issues. In the seventh question he asks what the prayers and *mythoi* mean: how does one distinguish symbolic from literal meanings? And why, "also, are terms preferred that are unintelligible, and of those that are unintelligible why are foreign ones preferred instead of those of our own language?... For the divinity that is invoked is possibly not Egyptian in race; and if he is Egyptian, he is far from making use of Egyptian speech, or indeed of any human language at all."

We recognize in this last question and its accompanying observation both what we have observed repeatedly where so-called magic is concerned—as discussed, for example, by Apuleius in his *Apologia*—that recitations that sound like gibberish are more likely to be thought efficacious, and that the Egyptians in particular, and therefore their language, are thought to have a strong connection to the *sacer*. But "Porphyry," like Apuleius, sees this perspective as absurd.

The place of Egyptian religion within the syncretism of the Roman period is particularly apparent in these middle questions—of a work that is, after all, entitled *On the Egyptian Mysteries*. In the further elaboration in question six of the absurdity of the notion that a human being, "inferior in dignity, should make use of threats...to the Sun-King himself, or to the moon or to some other of the divinities in the sky," reference is specifically made to the Arcana of Isis, the Egyptian goddess whose cult had become particularly popular by the Hellenistic period, and to "discourse among the Egyptians" in which last phrase "Egyptian" is a virtual synonym for "priest."[372]

So the reference to the preference for Egyptian as the language of invocation should not be a surprise. Nor the direction of the eighth question, which asks what the Egyptian Theosophers, specifically, believe the First Cause to be: *nous*, or something beyond *nous*, one or more than one, without physicality or embodied, whether the *Demiourgos* (creator of our universe) or something beyond the *Demiourgos*? What do they think constitutes Primal Matter—and was Primal Matter generated somehow or was it unoriginated and always extant? Within these interlocking queries the frame of reference encompasses what the Egyptians believe—and they are said to have associated the various gods with forces of nature: Osiris is said to be associated with the sun and Isis with the moon, for example.

The ninth question asks about *daimones* that serve as guardians, "how the Lord of the House assigns it. Interestingly, "Lord of the House," (in Greek: *oikoresmotys*) is a rendering of the Hebrew, *Ba'al Zebul*. If on the one hand we may recognize this as a discussion of astrological signs—thus there are twelve "houses" in the zodiacal subdivision of the heavens and the life of each of us is understood by astrology to be governed by the house associated with our birth date, and in the discussion here each house is served by a particular *daimon*—on the other hand the Hebrew phrase is one of the variant versions of the name Beelzebub. Given the evolution of that name toward an emphatically negative association in emerging Christian thought—with the forces of evil that oppose the

---

[372] We might note how the position of Egyptian *sacerdotes* is, in this context, 180 degrees removed from their position in the earlier Israelite context of Exodus 7 and 8 that we earlier encountered—and also from how the Persian magi are viewed.

goodness of the divine order—we are reminded of how all belief systems, including that associated with Iamblichus and his followers, can and will be associated by the Church with the negative engagement of the *sacer* and be delegitimized as magic or superstition or sorcery, rather than being considered religion.

"Porphyry" wants to understand whether within our souls there are subdivisions—one pertaining to health, one to figure, one to bodily habits; one to the body, one to the soul and one to the superior *nous*—governed by different *daimones*, and whether some of these *daimones* are good and others evil.[373] He asks, finally, in any case, whether there might be some other path to happiness besides the Sacred Rites. It is interesting that the Greek word for "happy", *eudaimon*, literally means "well-*daimon*ed." But perhaps *daimones* are not involved at all in human happiness and success, "Porphyry" will suggest at the end of this tenth question.

The response—presented as the *Reply by Abammon the Teacher to the Letter of Porphyry to Anebo*—is introduced with reference to the god Hermes, who is understood to be synonymous with the Egyptian god Thoth. As patron of learning and medicine, Thoth is credited with teaching humans how to invent hieroglyphic writing. His name is also rendered in Egyptian as *Tahuti*, meaning "thrice great," which in Greek became *Trismegistos*. Hermes Trismegistos was a particularly popular god by the Hellenistic and Roman periods and associated with esoteric wisdom. With this role in mind Iamblichus writes of the tendency to ascribe *all* esoteric works to him, and to label such works *Books of Hermes*—i.e., the so-called *hermetic* literature. It is as one who "*participates* in this god"—who is suffused with Hermes' wisdom-bearing essence—that "Abammon" responds to the questions sent to "Anebo, my pupil."[374]

Moreover, the syncretistic nature of the work to follow is made explicit, and its sources familiar ones:

> ...our answers are to be taken from many places and from different sources of knowledge. Some of these introduce fundamental principles from the traditions that the sages of the Chaldaeans delivered; others derive support from the doctrines that the prophets ["declarers (of the gods' will)"] of the Egyptian temples teach; and some of them follow closely the speculations of the philosophers [i.e., Pythagoras, Plato, Demokritos, Eudoxos and "many others of the Old Greeks"] and elicit the conclusions that belong to them.

He will, he informs "Porphyry," refer to different sources depending on the nature of the specific question to which he is responding.

He begins by asserting that there are two forms of knowing—and that the initial question posed to Anebo suggests the (wrong) assumption, that "the knowing of divine beings [is/can be] the same as the knowing of other matters... But there is no such similarity. For the perceiving of them is absolutely distinct from everything of antithetic

---

[373] The notion of body, soul and intellect may call to mind Paul's reference in his *First Epistle to the Thessalonians* V:23, to "spirit and soul and body."

[374] And see above, fn #370, regarding these two names.

character." We may recognize in this initial response the form that always can and most often is used by the believer in responding to critical questions from the non-believer: my belief system is inherently inaccessible to those who, not believing, do not and cannot understand—which is an inherently valid response, since by definition if one deals with the *sacer*, one is dealing with a realm that does not conform to the rational assumptions and convictions and the order of thought that shapes the *profanus* realm.

Iamblichus continues with respect to the attributes that distinguish different sorts of "superior beings," all of which "are to be considered as self-subsisting. The perfect ones take rank as *archon*s (heads/chiefs), and are separate by themselves, and neither have their substance from others or in others"—as opposed, that would be, to humans, all of whom derive their essence and their nature from sources outside themselves. Such beings are indeed organized according to the sort of hierarchy suggested by "Porphyry"'s initial question: *theoi, daimones* "and in like manner heroes (or demi-gods) and after the same course of things, of unbodied souls"—and moreover each of these four categories contains multiple sub-categories ("races").

Having established a workable direction for the inquiry, Iamblichus' Abammon proceeds to the questions by observing that the apex of the *sacer* hierarchy is "the Good: both that which is beyond essence and that which exists through essence. It is a special peculiarity of the gods, and is characteristic of all races that are included ith them; and hence, not being divided from this, but existing in a similar manner the same in all of them, it preserves their peculiar distribution and arrangement." We recognize a reflection of his Neoplatonic side and the sort of Absolute that Plato had referred to, among the Ideas/Forms that constitute his understanding of the eternal, immutable *sacer*.

But of course, the notion of a consummate, absolute entity at the apex of the *sacer* hierarchy, personified as a kind of individual variously engaged with the *profanus*— whereas the Good simply *is*, and is neither personified nor *engaged* with us—is found in any number of pre-Jewish/Christian/Muslim religions. Certainly Zurvan or Ahura Mazda fall into that category for Zoroastrianism; in the Indian religions of which Iamblichus seems to have had some awareness, Brahman constitutes that Essence, even if it comes to be variously understood as most consummately articulated as Brahma or Shiva or Vishnu or Krishna; and in Egypt, for the most part, Amun, in his capacity as the Hidden One plays that role—albeit at times identified with Ptah and sometimes articulated as Ra, and briefly, during the New Kingdom's 18th dynasty, under Akhenaten, replaced by Aten. The point is that we may see a synthesis of sources in this reference.

As for "souls that are ruling over bodies," they derive their goodness by means of "a certain participation in and habit of good." Between the inherently good gods and the souls are the *daimones* and demi-gods or heroes. The first of these "races... is closely allied to the gods (*theoi*), yet is in a certain sense inferior to them... accompanying in subservience to the good pleasure of the gods. This race causes the otherwise invisible goodness of the gods to become visible in operation." It is also the intermediate races that "complete the common bond of gods and souls and render the connection between them indissoluble..., bind[ing] these together in one continuous series, from those on high to the very last... [and] caus[ing] an outgoing influence to go forth equally from the superior to the inferior races and a reciprocal one from subordinate races to those ranking above them."

We can see how he is structuring his response to the question of how the inferior human species can be believed to have any influence on the superior, divine species: all the species ("races") are connected like links in the metaphysical chain and "influence" is like the flow of electricity that can both ascend and descend along the chain from one link to the next.

All beings, he further posits, are connected in that they share motion as part of their being—except the ultimate absolute, an unmoved mover (I am borrowing Aristotle's phrase; Iamblichus does not use it exactly) "that is firmly established in itself by unalterable law…that is immovable, and so is to be considered as the cause of all motion, that is superior to all things and has nothing whatever in common with them—are part of what might be called a continuous flow. And—obviously—the intermediate races of *daimones* and demi-gods/heroes are necessary for "the complete joining to gather into one of the first and last races (the *theoi* and *psykhai*)."

These highest and lowest races he examines in his next chapter. The gods are superior and perfect, souls are inferior and imperfect; the gods generate all things and are guardians of them, the souls are naturally disposed to yield, and so forth. "*Nous*, the leader and king of the things that actually are, the demiurgic art of the universe, is always present with the gods in the same manner, completely and abundantly, being established in itself unalloyed according to one sole energy. But the soul partakes of divisible and multiform *nous*, adapting itself to the supreme authority over all." The *daimones* and demi-gods fall between these extremes.

While articulating such a connected hierarchy in various terms, he rejects the distinction proposed by "Porphyry" that presents "the *theoi* being distinguished by aetherial bodies, the *daimones* by aerial bodies, and souls by bodies pertaining to the earth." He further suggests that "Porphyry"'s idea of the divine as transcendent –"that transcends all things [and] is itself transcended by the perfectness of the entire world"—suggests the banishing of "the presence of the superior races entirely from the earth, [which] is an abrogation of the Sacred Rites and theurgic communion of the gods with human beings. For it says nothing else than that the divine ones dwell apart from the earth, that they do not commingle with human beings, and that this region is deserted by them."

So, interestingly, Iamblichus seems to reject not only the notion of a hierarchy of purity that moves from the human soul to a point beyond the gods toward the Good but any inherent, *necessary* sense of a separation between the Good and humans. In other words, humans can achieve that height—and the theurgic *sacerdotes* are defined, in part, as humans who have accomplished that achievement, which is why the rites in which they engage are inherently legitimate. "For neither are the *theoi* limited to parts of the earth, nor are the inferior races about earth excluded from their presence." The Good is accessible because it is embedded within the *profanus*; it's merely a matter of understanding how to ferret it out of its hidden locales.

We may recognize here, as elsewhere in Iamblichus' arguments, a stepping off point endemic to every religion and belief system: that I believe because I believe. The stories narrated in the Hebrew Bible are believed by Jews and Christians to be incontrovertible because they believe that the text is inherently incontrovertible because it comes through the intervention of an interventionist God in human affairs. In the separation of the Israelite-Judaean tradition into Judaism and Christianity, those we term Jews believe that that specific kind of intervention ceased after the mid-fifth pre-Christian century, as we have seen; and conversely, those we term Christians not only believe that such intervention did not cease, but by the fourth century CE they believe that the consummate form of intervention by God was through assuming human form—mainly validated by the New Testament, which they believe but which Jews do not believe is a continuation and updating of the divinely articulated narrative of divine intervention in human affairs found in the Hebrew Bible aka Old Testament.

By the time God is universally understood by (non-heretical) Christians to have assumed human form as Jesus of Nazareth, God is also understood by both Jews and Christians to be all-powerful, all-knowing and all-good—a series of characteristics not so obvious and straightforwardly presented in the biblical text, as we have also seen. What is the basis for these differences in belief? Belief itself. I believe because I believe, because I was taught to so believe well before I reached an age when I might rationalize in this way or that. Iamblichus' argument makes perfect sense for those who believe as he does.

In the end, he will argue that the theurgic *sacerdotes* will be able to gain the assistance of the highest *theoi* against lesser *daimones* because we can achieve the Good as at least some of the latter cannot, and therefore we will be more attuned to the highest *sacer* powers that will, accordingly, support us even against other *sacer* beings—lesser *sacer* beings, *daimones*—that are less attuned to the *theoi* and the Good than we are. Such theurgic success may also recall—for it may be seen as parallel to—the sort of success we have seen Odysseus enjoy against Kirke through the intervention of the Olympians, Athena and Hermes—but that is not because of his moral superiority as a hero, but because Athena has a personal affection for him.[375]

Thus Iamblichus follows in the next chapter of his work with a discussion of rites, symbols and offerings, observing that the rites are both motivated by a *sense* of affiliation with superior beings and successful because they *are* in fact "affiliated by a kindred kinship relationship to the beings that are otherwise superior to us, and on this account the pure are attracted to the pure, and the impassive to the impassive"—which is not properly understood by the description of bloody animal sacrifices referred to in the "Letter to Anebo." And the imagery associated with them speaks in a symbolic, not literal language. Thus, for example, "we remark that the planting of 'phallic images' is a special representation of the procreative power by conventional symbols."[376]

---

[375] We have seen how Odysseus is assumed by the Homeric world to exhibit the "good" because the goddess loves and supports him—but that "the good" for that audience has no moral or ethical connotation; it is simply defined as connected to survival success, and it won't be until Sokrates steps onto the historical stage in the late fifth century BCE that "the Good" and its concomitants will begin to acquire moral and ethical connotations for the Greeks. We have also seen that it is difficult to determine whether that divine affection for Odysseus is a *result* of who he is and how he is successful or whether his essence and his success are *predicated* on divine support.

[376] This is also endemic to the history of art as it relates to the history of religion: we hope for survival through fertility—we cannot survive as a community or a species if we as well as our cattle and sheep and our fields are not fertile—but the concept "fertility" is abstract. So we concretize it by images that are incorporated into our religious rituals (e.g., phallic symbols, or small statues of females with enormous breasts, bellies and carefully delineated pubic areas) and help us express, explore and explain our need to ourselves and to the powers of the *sacer* upon whom we depend for success and survival. They serve as *symbola* (sing: *symbolon*)—stand-ins for the concepts that we cannot otherwise concretize. See Soltes, *Our Sacred Signs: How Jewish, Christian and Muslim Art Draw from the Same Source* (New York City: Westview Press, 2005), especially the introduction and chapter one.

So, too, the objection that "the invocations [to the *sacer*] are made to gods that are impressionable beings" expresses a misunderstanding. It is, rather, the case that, since "Divine Purpose" is, by definition, imbued with "Absolute Goodness," and that theurgic *sacerdotes* are ever in pursuit of "Absolute Goodness" that

> the gods being gracious and propitious, give forth light abundantly to the Theurgists, both calling their souls upward into themselves, providing them union to themselves in the Chorus, and accustoming them, while they are still in the body, to hold themselves aloof from corporeal things, and likewise to be led up to their own eternal and noetic First Cause.[377] From these Performances [of the Theurgic Rites] it is plain that what we are now discoursing about is the safe return of the soul [to the realm of the *sacer* whence it originally came prior to being embodied], for while contemplating the Blessed Spectacles [associated with the Theurgic Rites], the soul reciprocates another life, is linked with another energy, and rightly viewing the matter, it seems to be not even a human, for the most blessed energy of the gods.

Further, rites that are referred to in the "Letter" as intended as "propitiations of anger" need to be understood not to refer to the anger of the gods in the common parlance way in which we use the word "anger" in referring to ourselves, as exhibiting "an inveterate and persistent rage," but rather it refers to *our* "turning away from *their* beneficent guardianship... '[P]ropitiation' can turn us to the *participation in the superior nature* [emphasis added], lead us to the guardian fellowship of the gods, which *we* had cast from us, and bind to each other harmoniously both those participating and the essences participated... [B]ecause evil is present in the regions of the earth the 'expiatory sacrifices' act as a remedy and prepare us so that no change or passive condition may occur with reference to us." We recognize in this another standard reality of exploring and explaining the *sacer*: we can only do so by means of words that function as metaphors—if we speak of the Judaeo-Christian God as all-powerful and all-good, we can only understand these terms as far as we understand power and goodness from the *profanus* perspective of our own experience—and sometimes the metaphor falls very short. Similarly, there are times when the terms we use need to be adjusted away from their standard *profanus* meanings in order to apply them to the *sacer*.

The same is true with regard to the brief reference that follows to "what are called 'the necessities of gods.' The whole fact is this: The 'necessities' are the peculiarities of the gods, and exist as pertaining to gods, not indeed as from without, nor as from compulsion..."—so that, in other words, whatever might be construed as what the gods "need" must be understood as derived entirely from within them and their *sacer* realm, not in any way related to our sense of what "need" is, much less of the sort that could be

---

[377] His reference to a "Chorus" no doubt refers to what Plato, in his *Phaedros*, refers to when he offers the *mythos* describing how "divine beauty was splendid to the view when we, in company with Zeus, and others with other gods, beheld together with the Blessed Chorus, the divine Spectacle and were initiated into the perfective Rites, which are called most happy. Being ourselves entire and unaffected by the evils that await us in the days to come, being ourselves pure from earthly contamination..." (*Phaedros* 250B5ff).

satisfied by anything that we who stand (by definition) outside them, in the *profanus*, could offer. We cannot really even understand, therefore, what "need" means to the gods, much less presume to address or satisfy it. Even more absurd is the notion, therefore, that there is anything we can possibly do to compel the gods, as if, say, sacrifices might address and potentially satisfy some need or as if anything we might say or do could compel them, since that would require us to have the ability to give them something or to deny them something that they cannot otherwise get for themselves. If they accede to the Theurgist it is out of a sharing of love and of the Good.

So, too, the concept of "participating in the superior nature" referenced in the previous section of the discussion is not only not unique to Iamblichus' text within religious history, it is specifically found, for example, within the Christian text of the Second Epistle of Peter 1:3-4, where, in referring to Jesus' "divine power [that] has given to us all things that pertain to life and godliness, through the knowledge of Him...," Peter observes that through that knowledge—and it ought to be noted that "knowledge" here refers to the sort of knowledge conferred by faith, not the sort that is gained through rational analysis of, or in instruction in, the *profanus*—Jesus' adherents "have been given... exceedingly great and precious promises, that through these you might be participants/partakers/communicants of the divine nature." That sense of participation will in fact eventuate in Christianity as reinforced physically by the act of bread-and-wine communion—as we shall discuss further in chapter ten.

"Abammon" also addresses a question raised by "Porphyry" that would not have troubled the traditional Greek and Roman polytheists, but certainly will come to trouble Judaism and Christianity with their supposition of a singular all-good God: "How is it that some of these gods are givers of good and others bring evil?" The answer is simple: "they are all not only good, but... they are revolve [in their orbits] with reference simply to the One God, according to the beautiful and good alone."[378] That "One God" is, of course, the *Monad*, whose first principle is *Nous*, and not to be confused with the *personified* concept of the One God embraced in Judaism and Christianity, although the fact of its oneness reminds us that so-called Paganism in the Greco-Roman era—particularly as we follow it from the Hellenistic period forward—is not limited to the classical polytheism of the Homeric-Hesiodic world.

On the other hand, the notion of gods revolving around a central monad underscores the Iamblichean association between certain divinities—seven of them in particular—and the *planetes*. What this means, as we come to the end of this section, in which he concludes that "neither the gods [of the *planetes*] in the sky themselves, nor their gifts, bring evil," is that he seems to undercut the more popular association between astronomy and astrology: the *planetes*/gods are there, but do not rain blessings and curses upon humankind in accordance with their particular configurations at particular times. Gods respond in accordance with how successful we are—our Theurgists exemplifying those who are eminently successful—at addressing and importuning them.

---

[378] The phrase "beautiful and good"—*kalos k'agathos*—is taken directly from the Greek turn of phrase extending in use from Herodotos to Plato.

226

Fundamentally, as "Abammon" explains next, all of the so-called gods, however many of them may be perceived by us to exist, are aspects of a singularity—the Monad— for they all share the same essence, and that essence is Being itself. Thus "[i]nasmuch as the gods are all arranged as absolutely one, the primary [the *theoi*] and secondary [the *daimones*] races, even the many that are self-existent with them, preside together over the universe as one [i.e., the uncreated Monad], everything in them is one, and the first, the intermediate and lowest races coesixt as the One itself... for the self-same essence that is indeed in them is the one of their own substance."

This paradox, that the apparently many are ultimately one, may be recognized as a more extreme version of what will eventuate as Christianity, wherein the triune God is precisely that: simultaneously and paradoxically singular and triple. Moreover, the divine essence is ultimately "entirely non-corporeal [but is] united with the gods [in the sky; i.e., the visible *planetes*] that have bodies and are perceptible to the senses. For the gods that are visible are really outside of bodies, and therefore are in the world of *Nous*; and those of the world of *Nous*, through their unconditioned unity, encompass the visible divinities within their own substance..." Whatever their apparent physical forms, those forms are not what they truly are, but are only how they appear to us from our limited *profanus* perspective.

One could continue further through the extended discussion, but for our purposes we have followed far enough. The three most noteworthy lessons for us from a reading of Iamblichus are: one, that we recognize not only another term—theurgy—that must be juxtaposed with "religion" and "magic" and its various related terms in trying to understand what is what with regard to the engagement of the *sacer/profanus* relationship in the Greco-Roman world, even as the complicated delineation of that relationship extends several centuries into the so-called Christian era. Two, that those systems that are neither Jewish nor Christian in this period are both varied and that many of them share many features in common with each other and with both Judaism and Christianity—which is not surprising, since they all ultimately wrestle with the same problem: how to grasp or address the *sacer*. Three, that there are any number of elements within the Iamblichean system that bear a particular relationship and/or present a particular similarity or parallel to Christianity.

More fundamentally, as we shall subsequently see, the Iamblichean system is one among several that compete intensely with Christianity as it is moving from acceptability to hegemony in the course of the fourth century. After Constantine (d.337) every Emperor except one will at least nominally embrace Christianity—and by the time of Theodosius (r. 379-95), as we have briefly noted several times (and shall repeat again), Christianity will emerge as the only acceptable *religio* throughout the Empire. Along the way, the exception to the rule will be Emperor Julian (r. 361-3)—typically referred to by Western Christian historiography as Julian the Apostate. While the Porphyrean objections to Iamblichus' thought prevailed sufficiently so that the latter was not embraced within the Neoplatonic mainstream in the generation following Iamblichus' death in ca 325 CE—Eusebius of Myndus, a pupil of Iamblichus' own pupil, Aedesius, warns the future emperor Julian against "that stagy miracle-worker," the theurgist Maximus—Julian was nonetheless quite taken with Maximus and the teachings that Eusebius denigrated as "a perverted study of certain powers derived from matter." Julian asked his friend Priscus to get him a copy of

Iamblichus' commentary on his namesake, Julian the Theurgist, and when he became emperor, his patronage of theurgy made it quite popular.[379]

Indeed, Maximus became theurgic consultant to the imperial court—but in the post-Julian Christian response he was fined, tortured and ultimately executed in 371, on a charge of conspiracy against the Western and Eastern emperors. Theurgy remained rather quiet in the aftermath of that event, but the tradition did not die. It continued to be passed down in certain families and would be openly practiced again in the fifth century.[380] Most notably, Proclus, as we have previously noted, wrote a commentary on *The Chaldean Oracles* and other related works around mid-century.

Proclus would in fact refer to theurgy, (in his work, *Platonic Theology*, 63), as "a power higher than all human wisdom, embracing the blessings of divination, the purifying powers of initiation, and in a word all the operations of divine possession." Dodds, interestingly, comments that "it may be described more simply as magic applied to a religious purpose and resting on a supposed revelation of a religious character. Whereas vulgar magic used names and formulae of religious origin to profane ends, theurgy used the procedures of vulgar magic primarily to a religious end."[381] So on the one hand, he cannot and will not accept theurgy as the full equivalent of religion, reducing it to magic, even as, on the other, he distnguishes it from "vulgar magic" and recognizes that it has an ennobling ultimate *telos* (purpose) similar to the purposes of religion: "to lead one up toward the noetic fire" (quoting from *Mysteries*, 179.8). What lowers it from the level of religion for Dodds is his translation of the fact that much of Book III is devoted to techniques of divination and that Proclus claimed to have received revelations regarding the past and future from the *daimones* into a "this cannot be religion" conclusion.

We might ask how the teaching of divination techniques compares to the time spent in seminaries training priests in aspects of liturgical techniques, and culminating with the laying on of hands at ordination that accords them the presumed divinely ordained power to administer sacraments. We might also ask how prophecy in the biblical texts—and in particular apocalyptic works like Daniel and Revelation, or like the Enoch books that are canonical only in the Ethiopian church—is to be fundamentally distinguished from Proclean visions, beyond the obvious fact that the latter is not part of a canon embraced by either Jews or Christians, whereas Daniel is embraced by both groups, Revelation by one group, and Enoch by one subset of one group.

Dodds further observes that theurgic procedures are of two types, those that use symbols and tokens and those using an entranced "medium."[382] The first type works because every god has a "sympathetic" representative in the animal, vegetable and mineral world with a *symbolon* that connects to its divine cause. *Symbola* often take the form of statues that were expected to offer oracular comments based on their being in *sympatheia*—"feeling (*pathos*) with (*sym*)"—with the entity of which they are the symbolic representation. If on the one hand this suggests a very literal version of what we recall

---

[379] This is discussed in Dodds, Appendix II, 288.
[380] Ibid.
[381] Ibid, 291.
[382] Ibid, 291-2. Dodds places the quotation marks round "medium." We might more neutrally have used the term
sacerdos—but that is part of the point.

Frazer labeling sympathetic magic, on the other, as Dodds points out, "the art of fabricating oracular images passed from the dying pagan world into the repertoire of medieval magicians [in the Christian world]... Thus a bull of Pope John XXII, dated 1316 or 1317, denounces persons who by magic imprison demons in images or other objects, interrogate them, and obtain answers."[383] Thus a millennium after the legalization of Christianity, the head of the Western Church, although he denigrates what had been a theurgic activity as magic, certainly believes that the process works: it is by definition unacceptable as not part of the proper religious means of accessing the *sacer*, but it is real (and it is not necessarily nefarious in intention).

The importance of *sympatheia* is not limited to the *symbola* of statuary. Thus, for instance, the seven vowels of the Greek alphabet connect to the seven *planetes*—when properly pronounced or written down by a trained practitioner. The knowledge of how properly to either pronounce or write them so that they correspond properly was originally revealed by the gods themselves, and then transmitted from one theurgic *sacerdos* to the next, down through the generations.

The sense of the ubiquitous presence within the *profanus* of the elements of the *sacer*, discussed by Iamblichus, is not limited to his school of thought. Not only do other pagan belief systems express a consciousness of the ubiquity of *daimones* and other aspects of the *sacer* throughout the *profanus*, but there is a good deal within Jewish and Christian theology, particularly within their respective mystical traditions, which expresses the idea that the transcendent God is immanent throughout all of creation.[384] Moreover, the notion that esoteric wisdom can include the precise and proper articulation of letter-sounds—and in particular the idea that the very name of God is ineffable to everyday people and its proper articulation known only to the uniquely trained adept—is essential in particular to the Jewish mystical tradition as it begins to pick up pace during this era.[385]

While *symbola* had as a goal to induce and/or express the presence of the *sacer* within an inanimate receptacle, in order to offer oracles and/or to protect its user from the negative possibilities from the *sacer*—and on a small scale, such an image called a *telesma* (talisman), worn around the neck, was presumed to offer protection to its wearer—the other sort of theurgic procedure in effect temporarily incarnated the protective or informative divinity within a human being, entranced and in-spirited. In other words, the practitioner could make use of controlled possession—as opposed to the kind of uncontrolled possession that accounts for epileptic seizures and the like. Proclus writes of the ability of the properly trained soul to leave the body, commune with the *theoi* and return to its incarnate state.[386] The process of preparation for the experience involves purification with fire and water—which should recall to us Zoroastrianism and the Magi—and being specifically attired with garments decorated with the appropriate *symbola* as well as being

---

[383] Dodds, Ibid, 294.
[384] The notion of the One Creator present in all of creation is termed *panhenotheism*—not to be confused with *pantheism*. The latter sees individual divine bengs everywhere, personifying trees and rivers as *daimones*. The former recognizes the one (*heno*) God (*theos*) in everything (*pan*).
[385] See below, 285-6 and see Soltes, *Searching for Oneness*, chapter six.
[386] He talks of this in his commentary on Plato's *Republic*, II.123.8ff.

crowned with a garland made of plants known to help facilitate the process of crossing the *profanus/sacer* border.

Not everyone is equally suited to becoming a medium; not surprisingly, the most suitable types of individuals are "young and simple persons"[387]—in our terms, those who are not fully enfranchised members of the *profanus* and therefore by definition have an inherent place along the border between *profanus* and *sacer* and, as such, an inherently closer connection to the *sacer*.

In fact, non-expert—or more to the point, impure—practitioners can sometimes end up in contact with the wrong god, or what Iamblichus calls *antitheoi* ("antigods," that might be more functionally labelled in English as "evil spirits").[388] This is consistent with the principles of *profanus/sacer* relations that we have seen from the outset of our narrative: to invoke the *sacer* with an improper method will lead to its disastrous, rather than benign intrusion into the *profanus*. We have specifically seen this at a rather banal level in Apuleius' *Golden Ass*, where Lucius, failing to follow proper verbal procedure is transformed into a donkey instead of a bird—and can only eventually effect his restoration with what can be construed as a properly effected purification ritual. Later in our narrative we will encounter how a deliberate misapplication of the liturgy of the Catholic Mass will yield a Black Mass—black magic at its most fundamental—intended to connect its congregation to the Satan, whereas the religious Mass is intended to connect its congregation to God.

For the time being what we can recognize, to repeat, is the plethora of traditions and their texts that offer sometimes subtle parallels to and competition with the assertions not only of Judaeanism but, as time moves forward, of Christianity and Judaism as they are developing. And then there are texts that offer these features in a still more obvious and straightforward manner in being contrived of apparent combinations of diverse spiritual inputs. The Greco-Roman era is overrun with syncretistic texts the overlays in which are complex enough to leave virtually unanswerable the question as to whether or to what extent they are inherently Jewish or Christian or pagan, and with input from Paganism, Christianity or Judaism, as we shall begin to see in the following chapter.

---

[387] As Iamblichus asserts in *Mysteries* 157.14.
[388] *Mysteries* 177.7ff.

CHAPTER TEN

Christians, Jews, Judaeo-Christians and Pagans: Whose Charms, Amulets and Texts Are Whose?

In a thirteen-volume mega-work, *Jewish Symbols in the Greco-Roman Period*, written between 1953 and 1965, the scholar Erwin M. Goodenough (1893-1965) spends two extensive chapters (six and seven), in volume two, discussing charms and amulets. His work is particularly relevant to our own narrative because, in *that* double focus he begins by offering a double focus on the issue of magic versus religion and on the issue of Judaism, as a religion for which one might suppose that there should be no magic elements—but also, from our perspective, as a belief system to be distinguished both from Christianity or Paganism and from Judaeanism. He distinguishes the two modes of addressing the *sacer* (my term, not his) that form his subject by referring to "charms" "primarily [as] verbal incantations," whereas the term "amulets" refers to "objects to be worn on the person"— although he acknowledges that "the distinction often blurs, since capsules containing incantations were frequently worn as amulets, and talismanic figures were often drawn in the margins of incantations."[389]

To whatever extent this charm/amulet distinction will prove functionally effective (albeit not full-proof), it is the second definitional matrix that may prove more interesting to our inquiry. Goodenough notes that in the charms, Jewish names of God, of angels, and of Patriarchs are used with great freedom, often intermixed with pagan divine names, while on amulets Jewish names appear with figures of pagan divinities."[390] There are two issues that this observation will raise for us. One—and this is Goodenough's intention—is the question of how "Jewish" this "Jewish" material is, given the pagan elements within it. The second, which may impinge on the discussion of the first, is whether "Jewish" is in any case the correct term, or whether "Judaean" might not be more appropriate, given the time-period of much of the material under discussion. This second issue will also affect the analysis of the material with respect to whether there is any Christian substance within it, as we shall see, given that Judaeanism is ancestral to both Judaism and Christianity.

---

[389] E.R. Goodenough, *Jewish Symbols in the Greco-Roman World* (New York: Pantheon, 1953-65), volume two, 153.
[390] Ibid.

Goodenough poses the question, in fact, as to what the relationship between what he has just described and "Judaism" [his quotation marks] might be, and answers by suggesting that

> there was obviously some relation, or the Jewish names would not have been used; but ordinarily it has seemed enough to settle the problem with the phrase 'Jewish influence,' without trying to determine in what that influence consisted, or upon whom it operated. That is, the combination of Jewish and pagan elements has generally been taken to show that pagans borrowed the Jewish divine names to strengthen their pagan charms, while it has almost never been suggested that it may have been Jews who did the borrowing, or at least much of it. That pagans used Jewish names along with other 'barbarian words,' insisting that these lost their power when translated, is familiar. But the combinations seem to me often to go much farther in the direction of Judaism than merely introducing Hebrew words or names into a pagan context.

Goodenough's point is well taken. He notes further that others have suggested that the combinations on amulets may in fact be neither Jewish nor pagan but Gnostic—but he rejects that notion and concludes that, "once the Gnostics are removed as a possible *tertium quid* [third possibility], however, we are thrown back sharply upon the dilemma between Paganism and Judaism."[391] To this last sentence he adds a footnote, allowing that "a relatively small number of the amulets show Christian influence, but for our purpose these can be ignored"—but the question is: *can they*? It depends upon what he means by "Christian" influence versus "Jewish" influence—and the answer to that question may depend, in part, on where and whether one distinguishes these two categories not only from each other, but from "Judaeanism."

He speaks of the connection between the content and likely source of the amulets and the Greek Magical Papyri (some of which we shall subsequently examine) in which "Jewish and pagan names are used almost interchangeably, so that it is clear that pagans and Jews were profoundly influencing one another."[392] He also notes another group of charms from Coptic sources, and observes that "in many cases it is impossible to say whether a given charm was formulated by a Jew or a pagan, a Gnostic or a Christian," although he argues that he can establish criteria that "will distinguish a great number of them as primarily pagan or Jewish…"

So in this body of work we are confronted at the outset by the definitional issue as it pertains to the religious traditions in question. But we are also confronted by the definitional issue as it pertains to what constitutes religious tradition and what is magic. Goodenough, in considering most of his material as Jewish, inevitably asks next where it all fits into the Jewish tradition if most or even just some of it is deemed magical rather than religious in import. "True, such a distinction [between religion and magic] is no longer made by psychologists, and as regards anthropologists Ernst Cassirer could accurately say,

---

[391] Ibid, 154.
[392] Ibid, 154-5.

232

'It seems to be one of the postulates of modern anthropology that there is complete continuity between magic and religion'."[393] In other words, someone like Cassirer, writing toward the mid-twentieth century, has overcome the prejudices inherent in Frazer, Malinowski, Levi-strauss and others that cause them to relegate magic to a different category, inferior one way or another, from true religion.

Nonetheless, Goodenough continues in his next sentence, "historians of religion and, even more general historians still contrast magic or sorcery or the like with religion, on the ground that magic and its sisters use physical means [i.e., "fetishistic" objects or rituals or verbal charms] to effect spiritual or material ends [eg., curing or avoiding illness, escape from financial failure, success in love] while religion worships and prays in the spirit—or that in dealing with spiritual forces magic uses compulsion [i.e., conscripting gods or *daimones*], while religion uses petition." There are two issues here that are of particular interest to us. One is the question of what Goodenough himself thinks: in quoting the sort of definitional contrast that we have seen before, does he also embrace it, in spite of the likes of Cassirer? The second is, as he will himself point out: what did the *ancient* practitioners and purveyors of these materials themselves think of this sort of distinction? Will Goodenough impose his own sense of things on their sense as he analyzes their charms and amulets?

He exemplifies that tendency when he refers to the manner in which Kropp, in his *Zaubertexte* (*Magical Texts*), while admitting that the compulsion/petition distinction is not absolute, "since the imperative, even with 'quick, quick,' is often used in ecclesiastical liturgy. But he feels that ancients ought to have observed the distinction, and so he says that he translated a given Coptic imperative as *du sollst* ("you should") when its association seems to him magical, and as *moegest du* ("may you") when it seems to reflect ecclesiastical liturgy."[394] This is a perfect example of imposing one's modernist (or "pre-modernist modern") viewpoint on the material that you are presenting, and of how translation is always interpretation.

Goodenough wants to avoid Kropp's pitfall, and acknowledges that all three of these "magical" characteristics are often present in the "higher" religions. He quite properly points out that Campbell Bonner's comment regarding amulets, to wit that "'belief in the efficacy of amulets depends upon *certain primitive concepts of the mind* [emphasis added], namely, the notion that supernatural power may be inherent in some person, animal or material object, or that it may at least reside there temporarily,' ...puts him in a difficult position, for [this sort of belief] is linked with all ecclesiastical 'medals,' relics, crucifixes, and holy pictures and images—also with holy water, the materials used in the sacraments, the old Protestant's Bible, and the Torah scrolls of Judaism."[395]

Goodenough observes further that "[i]f we agree that use of such means is 'primitive,' we must admit that the 'primitive' survives to some extent in all of us, and

---

[393] Ibid, 155. Goodenough is quoting from Ernst Cassirer, *An Essay on Man* (New Haven: Yale University Press, 1944/5), 93.
[394] Ibid. Goodenough is quoting from A. M. Kropp, *Ausgewaehlte Koptische Zaubertexte*, (Brussels: Fondation Reine Elisabeth, 1930-31), Vol. III, 217f.
[395] Ibid, 156. He is quoting from Campbell Bonner's *Studies in Magical Amulets*, (Ann Arbor: University of Michigan Press, 1950), 45, a work that we shall shortly examine in some detail.

certainly in this sense persists in the highest religions.... Thus the contrast between religion and magic appears to be the reflection of a personal value judgment, not an objectively observable distinction."[396] He continues: "Material objectives, such as physical security, prosperity, and health, are the concern of people of every religious faith."[397] Indeed. This carries our own discussion back toward its beginnings in the comments by Frazer, et al.

Goodenough offers a most effective list of corroborating examples from Judaism and Christianity, from prayers for national peace to those on behalf of the sick or those journeying, from prayers on behalf of our armies to curses offered against our enemies and the Great Curse of the Church. "And we drop lighted candles as part of the cursing, that 'as these candles go from your sight, so may their souls go from the visage of God and their good fame from the world'," the expression of which sentiment certainly falls neatly into what Frazer would label homeopathhic magic.[398] And what of the Eucharist? Goodenough notes, in quoting from Charles Harris, how

> It is now widely taught and believed that the devout and well-prepared reception of the Holy Eucharist conduces to bodily as well as spiritual health. This belief... is psychologically sound, and in accord with the belief of the primitive Christians, who spoke of the Eucharist as 'pharmakon,' 'medicina,' 'sanitas,' in a combined spiritual and physical sense.[399]

Goodenough continues: "In the book from which I have just quoted it is said that magic is an 'action' which 'was believed to be the means of bringing about what was desired; it had a compelling power on the deity.' ...[I]t is hard to see how the healing power of the Eucharist, as defined in the statement above, lies outside the automatic power implied in the idea of compulsion. Every conception of a sacrament as an *opus operatum* seems to me logically to fall within the sphere of the 'magical' in this sense... Similarly, the consecrated oil is believed to heal the sick: it brings the power and blessing of God into direct action upon the sick body it anoints. In a word, it works"—and again, in Frazer's terms, it would be said to work through sympathetic magic; the individual who is ill comes into contact with a substance understood to have been in contact with God."[400]

The plot, as it were, thickens. For Goodenough asserts that "some advocates of ancient pagan magic come into what seems to me a full religious attitude when discussing it. I quote a paragraph from Iamblichus... 'The Theurgist commands mundane natures [which includes demons] through the power of the secret formula, and does so... as existing superior to these in the rank of the gods [and thus] he makes use of compulsions beyond those proper to his personal nature... a state into which knowledge of the secret symbols puts him.' I do not myself, of course, believe in all these powers allegedly operating the universe under the general tutelage of God or the gods, and I do not see how the theurgists

---

[396] Ibid.

[397] Ibid, 157.

[398] Ibid.

[399] Charles Harris, "Visitation of the Sick," and "Communion of the Sick," in W.K. Lowther Clarke and Charles Harris, *Liturgy and Worship*, (London: SPCK Publishing, 1940), 599.

[400] Goodenough, 158. He is quoting from the article by W. Oesterly in Clarke and Harris, 48.

had any such power... but I cannot see how one could deny that this is a paragraph written by a deeply devout man... of a rather fine religious point of view."[401] The point, from the perspective of our own narrative, is that referring to something as magical or religious which, from Goodenough's point of view, depends upon one's assessment—in this case, his open-minded assessment—of the intention and attitude and method of the practitioner, may also be seen to depend upon the attitude of the assessor. In other words, while he (Goodenough) recognizes what he commends as a religious sensibility on the part of Iamblichus, he still cannot bring himself to acknowledge that any of Iamblicus' claims could be true, because in the end Iamblichus is a theurgist and theurgists are classed with sorcerers and magicians and not with priests.

Thus he continues: "his [Iamblichus'] description of the power of the theurgist comes dangerously close to the orthodox description of the priestly power in all the Catholic Christian churches, though *there the priest has more than human power not through knowledge of formulae, but by virtue of a divine act of ordination...* [emphasis added]. Indeed, in baptism the water and the correct formula are sufficient in themselves, no matter who performs the rite."[402] Why indeed is this description *dangerously* close? Is it because it might assault our preconceptions regard *sacer/profanus* relations? And how is it that the Catholic priest performs his deeds legitimately through an act of ordination that Goodenough knows—because he believes?—is a divine act, whereas the acquisition of knowledge of the process of *sacer*-accession known by theurgists is assumed not to involve divine participation, because he does not believe in its legitimacy?

It might be noted—we shall discuss this in more detail later on—that the Albigensians in the twelfth through fourteenth centuries, self-proclaimed as Cathars ("Purists") emphatically denied the legitimacy of baptism. Their grounds were that, since baptism makes use of water, which, as a material substance, is by definition impure, it cannot possibly be efficacious for spiritually purifying those becoming Christians.[403]

Nonetheless, Goodenough, who in this last issue has stepped into the very Kropp-like trap that he hoped to avoid, emerges from it with the comment that "[m]agic seems to me then to be a term of judgment, not of classification. It is used subjectively, not objectively... The judgment is... one of personal taste and sympathy." This is precisely the point. But there is more, both for Goodenough and for our own discussion. For at this point he mentions mysticism, as offering the top "gradation" of every religion, at the bottommost level of which is demonism and magic—and he asserts that

> [w]hat holds such a religion together is the common use by "high" and
> "low" of the same symbolic objects or rituals. A person wearing the cross
> may be doing so from any one of a wide variety of motives. It may be to
> cultivate a constant mystic union with God—"the practice of the
> presence of God"—or just to ward off the evil eye... The practitioners
> of the "higher" approaches to religion have sometimes condemned as
> superstition the "lower" uses of the symbols of their own religion, and

---

[401] Ibid, 159.
[402] Ibid.
[403] For somewhat more detail, see below, chapter thirteen.

sometimes have condoned them... They have usually tended, however, to reserve such words as "magic" and "superstition" for the lower levels of *other* religions. Thus superstition has been defined as nothing but the faith of a conquered religion... [and] in our literature the words "superstition" and "magic," which describe... beliefs [in ghosts, demons, devils and the rest], or such practices of self-protection, are almost always words of condemnation, if not scorn, usually set off against "true religion," or "true" levels of our own religion.[404]

There are three comments that one might make on this—in examining Goodenough's words in reverse order, as it were. Thus his last sentence and a half could hardly be more to the point, given what we have read, beginning with Frazer: "what's mine is religion and what's yours is superstition and magic and myth"—terms intended to denigrate that which I don't acknowledge as legitimate and/or the elements of which I entirely dissociate from myself and my belief system. Second, the two and a half sentences preceding the last in fact describe the political reality of the Roman *imperium* for a long time, as we have earlier discussed it: *religio licita* refers to an accepted form of faith, and it was, for example, accorded to Judaeanism by Pompey the Great in 63 BCE. Later on, the competing views of Judaism and Christianity that each had evolved as the true continuation of the Israelite-Judaean spiritual tradition—*Verus Israel*—interwove the practical question, for the Roman authorities, as to which of the two would be accorded *religio licita* status.

With the exception of the late Hadrianic period, as we have seen, that status was accorded to Judaism. The alternative to *religio licita* status for a belief system was for it to be labeled a *superstitio*, but that term had less to do with wrong spirituality than with being—or at least being perceived as—politically subversive. If for the most part Christianity was either ignored or not recognized as a form of faith separate from Judaism for the first century or so of its existence, eventually it would be severely persecuted as a *superstitio*—most intensely under Diocletian—until Constantine eliminated the idea of political *superstitio* status altogether and with it, religious persecution, in 313, as we have also seen.

The third comment one might make, referring to Goodenough's first three sentences, pertains to what mysticism is—a term often used almost as loosely as is the term "magic". I would not call it necessarily the "highest" form of religion, but rather the most intensified form. The word itself comes from the Greek verb "*mystein*," meaning "to close," and by extension, "to hide." The mystic believes that there is a hidden, innermost recess within the *sacer* to which the ordinary practitioner does not accede. It is the mystic's goal to become one with that *mysterion* and as a consequence, help spiritually repair his/her community through the enlightenment that s/he has achieved through that intimate contact. But at various times in the history of the mystical traditions of Judaism and Christianity, among others, the mystic is perceived to have such an intimate relationship with the *mysterion* that s/he can accomplish extraordinary feats in the *profanus* that defy the norms of time, space and circumstance.

---

[404] Goodenough, op citum, 159-60.

Thus for instance in the Jewish mystical tradition, the great Rabbi Judah Loew of Prague (1525-1609), aside from engaging in the most esoteric processes of access to God's Ineffable Name, was believed in the late medieval tradition to have created a creature of river mud—the *Golem*—who did a range of everyday services for the rabbi and his community. The question is: where is the line to be drawn between mysticism and magic in this and other such traditions? The shaping and animation of such a creature—but is it truly be-*souled*; *anima*-ted?—for practical, everyday purposes is certainly not what is ordinarily associated with religion, much less its exalted, esoteric, mystical side, but with magic and sorcery. Yet the process of doing this is based on Rabbi Loew's profound knowledge of the *sacer* and its innermost hidden secrets, its *mysterion*. In later, hassidic Jewish mysticism, its founder, the *Ba'al Shem Tov* (ca 1700-1760) and his spiritual successors were associated with helping crops grow and curing illnesses through their intimate knowledge of God's ineffable Name—and so on.[405] Once again, then, conceptual lines typically drawn in everyday parlance and even by scholars prove to be blurrier than one might initially suppose.

In noting both actions and words set forth in the Gospels—which included passages in which Jesus is clearly depicted as believing in demons and demonic possession (and cures that include spitting in a blind man's eyes or touching with the fingers)—and the conclusion of various prayers with the formula "for Christ's sake" or "in His Name," or even "amen," Goodenough recognizes "magical" elements in the religion of Christianity. He asserts that there is a kind of evolution from the mind-set of the animal to that of "primitive man" to that of "civilized and intelligent" man—which means that, in the end, while there are "magical" elements in "religion" there is still a qualitative difference between the two, in hich the latter is superior to the former, even if the latter can never be fully free of the former.

While observing that "most religious symbols seem to have had at first such direct power as we now associate with the words "magic" and "superstition," and so long as they remain religious symbols, never entirely lose that direct operative power," he nonetheless comments in the following sentences that "when we deal with the so-called magical, then, we deal with the use of material means (words or objects or forms) to induce or compel divine forces to serve human ends," which religion does not do. So he seems to embrace that compulsion/petition dichotomy between magic and religion, although, as he prepares to move on to the discussion of "'magic,' 'charm,' and the like" he intends to do so "without prejudice or distaste."[406]

All of this brings him to the discussion of "Charms in Judaism." His starting point is to quote from Marcel Simon's important work 1948, *Verus Israel*, which focuses on the relations between early Judaism and Christianity during the period 135-425 (in other words

---

[405] The Ba'al Shem Tov's name/sobriquet, in fact means "Master of the Good Name." What does it mean to have *mastery* over that Name—certainly not to have *control* over it, for who would presume to *control* God's Name! It means to have intimate knowledge of that Name, through having an intimate relationship with God's hidden, innermost Being, (and vice versa: the knowledge of the Name yields intimacy with the Being of God, since a Name conveys its bearer's essence), and through that knowledge and that relationship, to be able to effect results in the *profanus* that one typically associates with God in God's occasional miraculous acts. For an explanation of "God's Ineffable Name," see below, 285-6.

[406] All quotes in this paragraph are from Ibid, 161.

the period beginning after the Bar Kokhba Revolt and continuing until the middle of the reign of Theodosius II). What is odd is that he takes at face value what Simon takes at face value: a characterization of "Jewish magic" based on his collection of "pagan and Christian references to the Jews as the leading exponents of magic." There are two issues here. One pertains to the obvious question of how objectively valid that view and therefore the characterization that flows from it can be expected to be in the intensely competitive spiritual atmosphere of that era that we have noted and about which we shall see further evidence shortly. More subtle might be the second issue: when are we dealing with Jews and when with Judaeans? Perhaps in this case, however, if we assume that the material pertains to the post-Bar Kokhba period, we can assume that it is indeed the Jews who are the focus, and that there is no Jewish/Judaean confusion.

So Simon observes that Jewish magic is characterized "by three features: first, a great respect for Hebrew phrases which were obviously not understood, but which seemed to the Jews to have magical power; secondly, a sense of the power of the name, an idea certainly not original with Judaism; thirdly, an overwhelming regard for angels and demons, which went over into a clear and elaborate angelolatry, so that to all appearances there was considerable justification for Aristides' statement that the religious activity of the Jews 'was directed to angels rather than to God,' as well as for the statement of the *Kerygma Petri* that Jewish cult practices were directed to 'angels and archangels, to the months and the moon'."[407]

What one might first question in this paragraph is the first feature: while it may certainly be true—would emphatically be true in the mystical tradition—that certain Hebrew phrases would command enormous respect, why would it necessarily be the case that these phrases were "obviously not understood" by the Jews who used and/or respected them? Christians and pagans would almost certainly not understand them, but every adult Jewish male would know at least enough Hebrew to offer prayers, and to hear the reading from the Torah three times weekly, so it is not clear why the phrases were *obviously* not understood by them. Interestingly, Goodenough comments in a footnote that "when Simon says [in *Verus Israel*, 407] that the barbaric distortions of Hebrew in the charms could not have been produced by Jews, but must be the work of pagan or Christian copyists, I cannot agree. The Jews of the diaspora in the third and fourth centuries seem to me to have been quite as far from any knowledge of Hebrew as the pagans and Christians."[408]

So one might say that there is an interpretive incline from Simon to Goodenough to Soltes, regarding this issue. It is not clear, meanwhile, as to what Goodenough's source is. While it is certainly true that, even in the Middle East and Eastern Mediterranean, the *lingua franca* for Jews was Aramaic, still, to repeat, every male at least would have had some Hebrew, and the rabbinic scholars would have had a good deal of knowledge— enough to comment on the Torah and on other biblical books and to further the amoraitic discussions of the *mishnah*.

The sense of the power of God's Name makes perfect sense, as we have previously discussed. The overwhelming regard for angels and demons does not inherently

---

[407] Ibid.
[408] Ibid, fn #27.

make sense. On the contrary, angels and archangels are named in the Intertestamental and New Testament literature that is rejected as non-canonical by Jews. It may well be that the Jewish angelology and demonology that shows up in medieval Judaism reflects Christian influence, rather than the other way around. One must keep in mind that, within the hierarchy of *profanus/sacer, sacer/profanus* border beings, Christianity develops the concept of saints—the very term is ultimately a French term derived directly from "*sacer*"—where Judaism does not.

This brings up the question of the reference to Aristides—a second-century saint in the Catholic and Orthodox churches, whose view of Jews as failing to effectively direct their religious activity to God can hardly be relied upon as objective or accurate, given the time period when he lived and the intense competition between Judaism and Christianity with regard to spiritual correctness.[409] Similarly, a quote from the fragmentary so-called "Preaching (*Kerygma*) of Peter"—a second-century combination of ideas found in a number of places in the New Testament (e.g., Acts 17, I Thess. 1:9f and Rom. 1:18ff) mixed with some elements that come from Jewish apologetic writings—hardly seems like a strong source for confirming the opinion of Aristides.[410]

The question that Goodenough is trying to get at is whether "magic" would have been part of mainstream Jewish thinking in the first few post-Christian centuries, and his conclusion is that it was. Again he turns to another source, Blau's *das Altjuedische Zauberwesen*—although he disagrees with Blau's formulation that the "characteristic feature of magic is thus any sort of act through which in a supernatural way a deed is accomplished."[411] Blau refers to "magic or superstition [as] a primitive and universal manifestation" that *precedes* religion in development. Blau calls religion "Faith" (*Glaube*, i.e., "belief") while he calls its predecessor *Aberglaube* ("superstition"). Goodenough, on the other hand, sees magic as still to varying degrees present in religion; he reminds us that Blau "asserts that religion… [is] something new which represses superstition…. Still, I feel that Blau is entirely correct in recognizing survivals of the primitive in all later religions, including Judaism."[412]

Having offered this extensive introduction to the material that he wishes to present, Goodenough turns to charms that he considers "unquestionably Jewish, based on Blau's assertion of the "widespread belief of Jews in a world of demons lying between man and God," to which demonic world "Jewish magic, like most magic, addressed itself primarily." One of the first things we recognize in this discussion, apart from the lack of clarity that we continue to encounter in the definitional distinction between religion and magic is the distinction between what a given religion—in this case, Judaism—teaches its believers and what those believers sometimes actually believe. Thus if it is obvious that for a faith that is emphatic regarding the singularity of the divine *sacer* as an all-powerful, all-knowing, all-good being, interested and involved in human affairs there can be no room

---

[409] The comment is made in Aristides' best-known work, his *Apology*, in which he asserts, in the second chapter, that there are four "races" in the world: barbarians, Greeks/Egyptians/Babylonians (Chaldaeans), Jews and Christians, whose respective attributes he describes in chapters 3-6; the Jews are described in chapter 5.

[410] The *Kerygma Petri* is in fact quoted here and there by Clement of Alexandria and Origen; no text *per se* exists.

[411] Lajos (Ludwig) Blau, *das Altjuedische Zauberwesen*, Budapest, 1898, 3. (One finds Blau referred to by both his Hungarian name and its German equivalent).

[412] Goodenough, op citum, 162.

for *daimones* of any sort, yet that has not prevented everyday Jews from believing, for whatever reason, be it influence from their non-Jewish neighbors or not, in such elements within the *sacer*. Goodenough points out that Blau demonstrates that even rabbinic leaders preaching and teaching against such beliefs themselves used charms against *daimones* in which they clearly believed.

"In Palestine, it is clear, verses from the Bible were used as magical charms, but rabbinic writings from Babylonia have preserved charms which appeal to demons and use barbaric language, although no names of pagan gods are included."[413] It would be interesting to know which "barbaric languages" were used, but the point would seem to be that, as always in the so-called magical process, the more unintelligible the words are, the better, and words in particular languages are assumed to have particularly strong efficacy, because they are associated with groups assumed to have particularly strong *sacer* connections. If Babylonians, Persians and Egyptians were assumed by Greek and Roman pagans to have those connections, and Jews might be assumed by Christians to have those connections, which pagan (barbarian) groups—Babylonians and Persians?—were assumed by Jews to have those connections?

Nonetheless, Goodenough asserts that written amulets or charms referenced by rabbinic sources "got their power chiefly from containing a divine name," which is what we might expect—but some of the rabbis found this a corrupt use of God's Name. Thus (as Goodenough quotes), "Benedictions and amulets, though they contain letters of the Name and many passages of the Torah, must not be rescued from a fire [on the Sabbath] but must be burnt where they li.e., they together with their Names"—whereas the work of rescuing a Torah scroll, per se, from a fire on the Sabbath (which would have meant performing "work" on, and thereby abrogating, the Sabbath) would not only be acceptable, but considered a *mitzvah* (a divinely commanded deed).[414]

Goodenough also quotes a formula from Talmudic tractate *Yoma*, 83b, in which protection is offered against the bite of a mad dog. The formula is doubly interesting. On the one hand it prescribes writing the formula on the skin of a male hyena. Is this homoiopathhic? Or is it putting into play the hierarchical notion (as in Hermes' power in protecting Odysseus from Kirke) that a wild hyena's body parts are more powerful than those of a mad dog)? On the other hand, the formula itself invokes "Kanti, kanti, kloros; Ya, Ya, *Yahweh*, *Sabaot*, Amen, Amen, Sela." The first three words are not Hebrew—and might be Latinized nonsense—where the next two are versions of the Hebrew-language Name of God followed by a corrupted version of the Hebrew "*Tz'vaot*," meaning "armies" (thus *Yahweh Tz'vaot* would mean "Lord of Armies"), and the last trio of words is a fairly common conclusion for mainstream Jewish (and Christian) prayers.[415]

---

[413] Ibid, 162-3. In the first several centuries after the destruction of the Second Temple in 70 CE, there were two major areas inhabited by Judaeans/Jews—Judaea/Palestina and "Babylon" (approximately today's Iraq). Each was led by its own group of rabbinic leaders. While they shared the same body of legalistic, mishnaic substratum, each rabbinic group developed its own series of commentaries—*gemara*—thus developing two basic Talmuds, the Palestinian and the Babylonian. The Babylonian community and its rabbinic leadership and Talmud were both larger than and continued to be prominent for a longer period of time than the Palestinian. When reference is made to "the Talmud," the usual intended source is to the Babylonian Talmud.

[414] The Talmudic passage comes from the tractate Shabbath 115b (in which, among other things, the issue of what may and what may not be done on the Sabbath is discussed). Quoted in Ibid, 163.

[415] More regarding "Sabaot" follows below, 245-6, 285.

He then takes an odd turn, apropos of Jews and Christians and the distinctions between them. He recalls, as Blau had, the story of Tobit, with its recognizable aspects of dealing with the *sacer*, from the killing of *seven* would-be husbands for Sarah by the demon, Ashmodeus, to the assistance accorded Tobias against Ashmodeus by the apparently more powerful archangel, Raphael (think once again of Odysseus, Hermes and Kirke)—which leads to Tobias' success at overpowering the demon "so that Raphael could catch and bind him." The apparent need that the archangel has for Tobias to follow the prescribed formula for conquering the demon, (as if somehow Raphael cannot do it himself) even as Tobias cannot accomplish this without the helpful intervention of the archangel, suggests a *quid pro quo* that follows the pattern of religious sacrifice summarized in the Latin phrase "*Do ut possis dare*": "I give that you may be able to give." At the same time, it recalls the questions to Iamblichus' Anebo posed by "Porphyry" regarding why it is and how it is that a more powerful god would or could be compelled by a theurgist to help out against a lesser *daimon*.

If the theurgy/magic/religion line is complicated by Goodenough's use of Tobit, so is the Judaean/Jewish/Christian line. For while he notes that this book was never canonized by the Jews, he refers to it as "part of the heritage of sacred books written in Greek which Christians took over from the Jews." He would seem to be somewhat off in this last statement. The book of Tobit, it is true, was never accepted into the Jewish canon— it would have emerged during the Judaean period, before either offspring of the Judaean tradition had fully coalesced—but is part of the intertestamental material in the Christian canon that was eventually rejected as non-biblical by Protestant denominations while continuing to be embraced by Catholic and Orthodox denominations. So it was "inherited" from the Judaean tradition, and whatever it offers as assumptions regarding religion and magic is part of that tradition, rather than being, per se, part of either the Jewish or the Christian traditions.

All of which brings us to Goodenough's discussion of Christian sources as sites preserving Jewish magical material. The double question will be—again—whether what Goodenough terms "Jewish" is Jewish or Judaean, and whether what he recognizes as Christian is Christian (and where Paganism fits into these evaluations), aside from the "magic versus religion" issue. Intertwined with this will be the question of how the information that he examines offers demonstrations of syncretism for these early centuries of Judaaism and Christianity.

To begin with, he offers a kind of hierarchy of definition: those that "are of course almost completely Christian… written by Christians *de novo*. [and] others [in which] the Christian elements are slight and quite easily recognizable intrusions in what appear to be very old Jewish forms."[416] He offers a Syriac charm that opens with an invocation to the Trinity (an unquestionable Christian element) and continues by quoting some lines from the Gospel According to John, but "then suddenly changes to what seems to me a purely Jewish invocation:

---

[416] Ibid, 164.

By the power of those ten holy words of the Lord God, by the Name, I am that I am, God Almighty, *Adonai*, Lord of Hosts, I bind, excommunicate, and destroy, I ward off, cause to vanish, all evil, accursed… adversaries, demons, rebellious devils… as are by night and by day; and Lilith, Malvita, and Zarduch, the dissembling (or "compelling") demon, and all pains… from off the body and soul, the house, the sons and daughters of him who beareth these writs, Amen! Amen!"[417]

So is this "purely Jewish"? Certainly the invocation of names for God, including the phrase "the Name" itself, and certainly "I am that I am" may be understood to be. Lilith—her name is derived from the root *l-y-l*, meaning "night"—is a night "demon" whose provenance could certainly be Jewish. She is referred to in early rabbinic literature as the winged first wife of Adam, who, refusing to be subservient to him was not only thrown out of Eden before Eve was created, but cursed by God so that a thousand of her babies per day would be destroyed.[418] As a consequence, she in turn, attacks human babies in their cribs, seduces adolescent males in their sleep and the like. But this is hardly certain with Malvita who, on the contrary, seems to be a Latin-based demonic name meaning "evil life," or the Syriac Zarduch—also known as Miduch, a female demon known as the Mother Who Strangles Children.

We might, then, accept this part of the charm as "partly Jewish," although it is written in Syriac, more often used by Christians—and in any case, the fact that it is prefaced by Christian invocations underscores its nature, more than anything else, as syncretistic. Why? Presumably because the lines are still not so precisely drawn between Christianity and Judaism at this point and those needful of such protective charms wish to cover all their sacerdotal bases, taking full advantage of the protective capabilities of the divine *sacer* as articulated from both sides of the fence.

The same may be said of the second Syriac charm referenced by Goodenough, "which opens with an invocation of Christ and closes with a call upon the Trinity," again, though, also invoking "'the glorious Godhead, and in the name of *ehyeh asher ehyeh* [I am/will be that I am/will be—spelled out in Hebrew in the midst of the Syriac], *El Shaddai, Adonai*, Lord *Sabaot*.'"[419] Distinct syncretism, made even more interesting and complicated, perhaps, by the last turn of phrase in the quoted "Jewish" part: as we have earlier noted, the proper words, from Isaiah 6:4, are *Adonai* [Lord] *Tzva'ot*. We have commented on the fact that, when in pagan texts that phrase has been altered as *Adonai Sabaot* it most likely represents a confusion between "*tzva'ot*" and *Shabbat*/Sabbath. So is this element Jewish—would a Jewish practitioner make that sort of error? Or is it, like the intitial invocation, derived from a Christian confusion regarding the Hebrew phrase—in effect, a continuation of that particular confusion from the pagan tradition?

---

[417] Ibid, 164. Goodenough's source is Hermann Gollancz, *The Book of Protection*, (Cambridge: Cambridge University Press, 1912) LXXIII f. This volume is a translation of and commentary on three manuscripts in Syriac of Eastern Christian charms and incantations—or at least all of which begin with an invocation to the Triune God.
[418] See below, fn #679.
[419] The source for Goodenough's quote is again Gollancz, XLIX, paragraph 40; L, paragraph 41 and LVI f, paragraph 53.

Goodenough next offers a Coptic charm, specifically a

Prayer of [for?] the Bread. The Lord God spoke to the Patriarch Abraham: "Arise, take thee bread, wine, water, and an iron vessel [perhaps "knife" would be a better rendering], go up to Mount Tabor and call three times, 'Man of God!' When Melkhitzedek comes out to thee, then cut off his hair, his nails, and the edges of his lips [his beard] and eat [these]... [And Abraham did these things] and [t]hen Melkhitzedek blessed Abraham by the inbreathing of his spirit.... So now, again, O Lord, be thou the one who blesses this bread, and give it to thy servant as [a token of] marriage.[420]

Goodenough comments: "No detail of this extraordinary prayer of consecration of bread suggest a Christian origin, though the ending shows clearly that the bread was to be eaten as a sacrament of mystic marriage of the devotee with God." I would propose quite the opposite: Melkhitzedek—with whom Abraham has a brief conversation in Gen 14, when he passes by the city of Shalem upon his return from his successful battle against the kings of the Cities of the Plain from whom he rescues his nephew, Lot, and others—has no particular significance in the Jewish tradition. At most he who is called "Priest of *El* Most High" may serve as a foil for Abraham, who serves "God Most High," and who, in their dialogue, makes it clear that the two God-concepts are not identical, even if the terminology of reference (*El Elyon*) is identical. For Abraham will not be keeping any part of the loot won in that battle for himself, in accordance with the oath sworn to his God.[421]

On the other hand, the early Church makes much of Melkhitzedek as a priest and as one of the important Hebrew Bible/Old Testament forerunners of the Apostles. There are, for instance, several sixth-century mosaics in Ravenna that depict important early priestly figures, and he is one of them.[422] Moreover, the idea of a mystical marriage—particularly one that is associated with bread—reflects a Christian sensibility rather than a Jewish one: a Eucharistic symbol that is broadly mystical in its implications for Christians has been synthesized to a concept that one may find present in St Augustine's writings—the symbolic marriage of the mystic's soul (for which the word in both Greek and Latin is grammatically feminine) with a God who assumes human form as a male. This idea will be developed more fully in the centuries to follow, and come to apply in particular to female saints and/or mystics in their relationship with God. But the idea finds little to no presence within the early Jewish tradition. So the question becomes: is there anything that is, per se, Jewish in this charm at all, in spite of Goodenough's inclusion of it among "Jewish charms" and assertion that here is nothing in it to suggest a Christian origin?

One of Goodenough's more interesting examples follows this last one. He suggests that it "seems to be an adaptation from Judaism made by the Sethian Gnostics"—

---

[420] Goodenough's source here is S. Gaselee, "de Abraha et Melchisedec," *Parerga Coptica*, (Cambridge, 1914), II, 6-8

[421] "*El*" is the name of the most powerful Canaanite god. While Abraham, in needing a name for the God with whom he has contact may be necessarily reduced to using that term because it is he most powerful god -name known to him, he may be understood to recognize that his God is very different from the Canaanite god.

[422] One site in particular stands out: the right tympanum of the Basilica of San Vitale, where Melkhitzedek is paired with Abel in offering sacrifices.

in other words, in one among many particularized versions of Gnosticism, associated with the son of Adam born after the death of Abel (and believed, by Eve, to have been provided by God as a "replacement" for Abel; Gen 4:25), that would be neither Jewish nor Christian but was among those forms of faith that competed with both, there are elements that are Jewish. But "no Christian intrusion appears in the text," he further asserts. Goodenough's finding of Jewish sources in the text is in part based on "the explicit stress… laid upon the value of the Hebrew language, 'the language of heaven'." Further, the charm "ends with the recitation of this 'Hebrew,' a series of degenerate magical syllables in which names end in –el."[423] He lists names for God that are identifiable in the charm—including *Sabaot* and including *Abraxas*, and admits that he sees "no way of distinguishing what Sethian Gnosticism may have added to the Jewish original"—an important point, since it underscores how the syncretism endemic to so much of this material is not always easily parsed.[424]

That it would not be Jewish, but gnostic, is evidently clear to Goodenough from the fact that the Hebrew is largely "Hebrew" and not truly *Hebrew*, reflecting the notion that Hebrew had become one of those "mysterious ancient" languages for non-Jews that would make it efficacious for invoking the powers of the *sacer*, analogous to how, in another context, say, Babylonian or Egyptian would be.

Conversely, he finds "no foreign element, however, in the Jewish charm which follows"—a lengthy text that, after a few lines that he refers to as magical syllables (presumably, again, nonsense syllables believed by the practitioner to possess power vis-à-vis the *sacer*) begins:

> Perform [it for me], Uriel,
> Perform [it for me], Michael,
> I adjure thee today, Holy Father,
> Thou who hast the breath of life on high…
>
> I adjure thee today, Davithea,
> Thou who liest there upon the bed of the Tree of Life….
>
> I adjure thee today, Davithea Eleleth,
> In the name of the seven holy archangels,
> Michael, Gabriel, Suriel, Raphael, Asuel, Saraphuel, Abael—
> That is those who stand at the right hand of the Father,…
> Come down upon this cup which stands before me,

---

[423] Ibid, 165.

[424] *"Abraxas"*—more commonly written as *"Abrasax"* (Greek writers typically spell it this way; the *PGM* and Latin writers tend to invert the last two consonants)—is the name of the Great Archon in the gnostic system associated with Basilides of Alexandria (see below, 259 and fn #441). He is the Emperor (*princeps*) of the 365 *ouranoi* (heavens; heavenly spheres) that govern the days of the year, because the numerical value of the letters in his name adds up to 365 (A=1, B=2, R=100, A=1, X =60, A = 1, S= 200)—as, indeed the seven letters of his name correspond to the seven *planetes*. More than half a dozen different theories obtain as to the etymology of the name—as coming from Egyptian, from Hebrew, from Greek or from a combination of Hebrew and Greek. My favorite is that of J.B. Passarius, who derives the name from Hebrew *ab*=father, Hebrew *bara'*=create, and Greek *a-* =un-/not—therefore "the uncreated Father"—since the meaning makes such perfect sense to me, although that derivation seems to offer one initial "a" too many and does not really explain the X/S…

Fill it with grace [*charis*] and a holy spirit [*pneuma*],
So that it will become for me a new plant within me...

Yes, come! I adjure thee
By the name of the seven letters [*stoikheia*]
Which are engraved upon the breast of the Father,
Which are *a e h i o u w*...

Iak, Mejak, Semjak,
The three decans [*dekanoi*], great in their strength,
Which stand upon the bed of the Tree of Life,
Give a sweetness to my throat!...

I have quoted a small part—about a third—of the overall charm as Goodenough gives it to us, to focus on the lines most relevant to our discussion. There are issues that stand out, it seems to me. One: there is the question that I have previously raised regarding whether one should properly view the articulation of specific archangelic names as Jewish or Christian, since we have them in the Book of Revelation but nowhere in the Hebrew Bible—which does not mean that they could not have evolved into use in both the post-biblical, early rabbinic Jewish tradition and the early Christian tradition.

Two: there is the issue of the name "Davithea"—a fairly clear combination of the Hebrew name "David" with the Greek word, "theos/thea," for "god/goddess." Aside from the question of why that second element, in being used as a suffix to the first element, is treated grammatically as a feminine (which does not in any case affect the point I am making), the larger matter is that the association of David with God is emphatically Christian—Christ is the descendant of David and is also God—rather than Jewish. Thus "no foreign element in this Jewish charm" strikes me as off the mark. Is it Jewish or Christian or a combination of these, regardless of whether "foreign" means Christian or Pagan (i.e., both of these would be non-Jewish) in Goodenough's terms.

Interestingly—this is perhaps a third point—Goodenough notes in his footnote, that Kropp (from whose volume II, 108 the charm is taken) "says that [Father, in line 3] refers to David, but I should guess it to mean God the Father, since David later seems an advocate with the Father.... Since complete identification of David with God the Father would go far beyond what we know of Jewish, Christian, or gnostic thought, it is safe to suppose that in this charm David is regarded as a mediator, a lesser figure than the Father."[425] The validity of this point, however, depends on how we view the name "David." If, as in my point in the previous paragraph, "Davithea" can be understood as an allusion to Christ, then he is—and thus, in a limited sense, Goodenough is correct—a mediator, but (and in this sense Goodenough is not correct) he is not a lesser figure than tha Father unless we presume that this text is much earlier than 325 CE and the Council of Nicaea. But there has been nothing to suggest this by Goodenough or by the material itself.

Four: the cup that is to be filled "with grace and a holy spirit, so that it will become for me a new plant within me," concerning which Goodenough states that "it would be

---

[425] Ibid, 166.

strange for this charm to be said over the cup of the Christian church, and nothing in its statements suggests Christianity," strikes me on the contrary as lending itself extremely well to a derivation from Christianity. What is the cup of the Eucharistic wine, if not a cup filled with grace and a holy spirit that, transformed within the body of the acolyte to the blood of Christ, becomes "a new plant"—rebirth, new life—within him/her? The plant, indeed, is an important verbal and visual symbol of rebirth and life in the Jewish, Christian and pagan traditions alike. Goodenough recognizes this last point, in fact—so why is he so certain that there is nothing in the imagery that could be considered Christian?

Five: In any case, there are other elements that can easily be seen as "foreign" rather than "Jewish," such as the reference to the seven Greek vowels. Aside from the universal idea of seven as important to the *profanus-sacer* relationship, which we have discussed and seen evidenced any number of times—derived from the idea of the seven planets—the specific use of *Greek* vowels as magically/religiously significant because there are seven of them and they are therefore construed in their number to afford a connection to the divine *sacer* (that, after all, as understood in the pagan Egyptian and Greek traditions, created writing and provided it to humans) reflects pagan, not Jewish usage.

Six: There is then, the question of the names of the "three decans," and the fact that there are *three* of them. There are all kinds of places within the Hebrew Bible and Jewish tradition where that number is important, but Christianity, in sharing that sensibility, connects it to the idea of the triune God, and the notion of the Trinity becomes central to Christian thought. Threeness is, in other words, more essential to Christianity than to Judaism—although not solidly until after 325.

The line that follows the reference to the three, with, for the second time in the charm, mention of lying on the bed of the Tree of Life, can, similarly, be construed as Jewish, since the Torah is spoken of, in Jewish metaphor, as "the Tree of Life." However, earlier and more emphatically within the Christian verbal and visual tradition, the Tree of Life is the Cross. *Lying* on the bed of the Tree of Life would seem to me a far more Christological than Jewish image. Christ dies as a human on the Cross; he lies (hangs, lies against, and lies in death) on the bed of the Cross—which (since he is not only human, but also divine) is the Tree of Eternal Life.

So at the very least there is a good deal of material in this charm that can be seen as "foreign"—i.e., not Jewish, even if we take it to be "Jewish" overall. Goodenough's sense that there is nothing foreign seems limited in vision, and the overall picture underscores the notion of syncretism as an important factor in this material. Interestingly, Goodenough goes on to point out that at the end of the text of this charm there is a drawing, "in which Davithea is himself presented, surrounded by, indeed covered with and holding, various forms of the solar cross." Such imagery can hardly help one to rule out a Christian, rather than a Jewish source—at the very least, in part.

Thus Goodenough's repeated assertion that he "can identify no Christian addition to the purely Jewish material" seems remarkably short-sighted. While the reference to David as a lyre player, playing in the tent of the Father may, as Goodenough points out, recall the imagery of a young David playing in the harp in the tent of King Saul, and his position as "the leader of the heavenly chorus who gathers all angels to hail the Father" may be construable as Jewish, it is also perfectly consistent with a more Christological view that associates David with Christ and Christ with a leadership position, (to say the least), in heaven.

The odd thing is that he notes that "David or Davithea appears also in more Christianized charms," such as a charm in which "the heavenly David is clearly a counterpart of David the Psalmist," which begins with the words "Hail David, Father of Christ, who in the Church sings psalms to those who are the first-born of heaven. Hail David, Father of God, with the lyre of joy...". In this charm that Goodenough describes as "shot through with Christian material" he asserts that there is nothing "Christianized about David except for the initial line." But not only would that be enough to underscore a Jewish-Christian syncretism, it also cannot help but raise the question in the first of these two "Davidic" (my turn of phrase) charms as to whether David as Davithea, who lies on the bed of the Tree of Life, might not also reflect a Christian sensibility, together with the other elements to which I have called attention.

We might, indeed, recall that David, as a young harpist, was brought to the court of King Saul when the Lord sent an evil spirit upon the king, and that David's music would drive the evil spirits out of Saul, who would be "refreshed and well, and the evil spirit would depart from him" (I Samuel 16:14-23). So David, filled with the spirit of the Lord (as he would assert to Goliath when the latter mocked him before David succeeded in killing him; I Samuel 17:45-7), could drive out evil spirits in a manner that Christians might view as anticipating the way in which Jesus would later drive out diverse kinds of evil spirits. There is, thus, much that can be seen as syncretistically Jewish and Christian in this charm.

Once more Goodenough examines a charm that, "except for the Christian introduction...looks to Iao *Sabaot*, though the magician calls upon various other spirits whose names, when they can be traced, seem to have Jewish roots." *Seem to have Jewish roots—why* do they seem to?—and then there is "*Sabaot*," again, and the question of whether that formulation is, rather than Jewish, a corruption and confusion of the Hebrew in other than Jewish hands. Further, the chief interest of *this* charm "lies again in the centering of the ritual in a cup." Given that it includes "the interchanging of water and wine" and that "there is reason to suppose that water and wine were often interchangeably used in the eucharistic cup of the early Church," and that he asks the rhetorical question, "[w]as the reference to the cup of the kiddush [the sanctification blessing over wine used in Jewish liturgy] if the charm was Jewish, to the cup of the Eucharist if the charm was Christian, or to the cup of the magician?"[426]—why, particularly given the importance of wine and water and the transformation of the latter into the former by Jesus, in the Christian tradition, does Goodenough suggest a lack even of the possibility of Christian influence in the earlier charm with its cup filled with Grace and the Holy Spirit?

One last instance from among the many that Goodenough offers, a Coptic charm that "has some definite Christian touches… [that present an intrusion] in a body of material basically Jewish." After instructions as to what one should do and what substances one should use, it presents the practitioner with the invocation that should be spoken:

---

[426] Ibid, 173.

> I summon thee today,
> Thou who ru[lest] from heaven to earth.
> From [earth] up to heaven,
> Thou great Unique One [*monogenes*],
> Hear me today, for I call upon thee,
> Father, Only One, Pantokrator,
> Though Mind [*nous*] concealed in the Father,
> First-born of all creatures and all aeons,
> > *Ablanathanaphla.*

The invocation continues for dozens of lines, and includes at one point the phrase "In the name of the Father and of the Son and of the Holy Ghost, Amen," as well as "Holy, holy, holy, Lord *Sabaot*, Heaven and earth are [fu]ll of thy glory." This last phrase is noted by Goodenough in his fn #83 as two lines "in Greek presumably from Christian liturgy, but...they may well have come from Jewish liturgy." Indeed they may have but, once again, if so, the Hebrew word *Tzva'ot* has been altered, as we have seen before in pagan and perhaps Christian contexts (the proper Hebrew phrase, from Isaiah 6:4 *is* part of the Jewish liturgy, of course, but the question is how to identify the phrase in its corrupt form). In any case, this last phrase follows the "In the name of..." recitation (the instruction is that this statement be repeated twelve times), which is an unequivocally Christian passage (which Goodenough identifies as such). What of the first nine lines that I have repeated? At first glance one might be inclined to insist that the use of the term "Unique One"—"single/only-born" is a more accurate translation of the Greek—is a Christian reference to Christ, which would certainly be appropriate, particularly juxtaposed with Pantokrator, ("All-powerful") a term used particularly in the Eastern Churches to refer to God/Christ. Goodenough notes, however, that the Greek word, *monogenes*, is used by Hesiod to refer to Hekate in *Theogony* 426, and therefore he sees "no reason to regard this line as a Christian intrusion."

Fair enough—but could one consider it Jewish? Highly unlikely, since at the very least God is never born but always existed, as far as Jewish thought it concerned. The point is that, to whatever extent this charm is "predominantly Jewish" it contains either a fair amount of Christian material and some pagan material, or more Christian material and less pagan material—and could in fact be viewed as primarily Christian with some pagan and Jewish intrusions (the use of the term, *Adonai*, is the only fairly obvious one) in it, rather than the reverse, which is how Goodenough reads it. One might take this spectrum of possibilities one step further, in noting the use of the phrase "all aeons." That last term, and the notion that the God worshipped by Jews and Christians is the chief among the aeons who rebelled against the true God, as we have earlier discussed, could suggest that this charm is—or is, in part; or is strongly influenced by—Gnostic thought. It is in any case exemplary of syncretism, regardless of which form of faith is understood to be its primary basis.

So we are left with a treble definitional question: is Goodenough correct in his distinctions between "Christian" and "Jewish" charms and is he correct, in any case, in calling "Jewish" what perhaps should be labeled "Judaean"? And is he wrongly ignoring pagan elements? We don't need to belabor this. What does makes clear sense is his reference to "such a Judaism of spirits and incantation [for which] the door must have been open to syncretism to an extent quite repellent to halachic Jews," except as Judaism was starting to shape itself, there may have been halakhic Jews who were not so uncomfortable with this syncretism, just as there were early Christians who were not.

What is most valuable in Goodenough is the large number of charms that he presents to the reader—I have only considered a handful of them—offering ample material with which to consider the question of Jewish/Christian/pagan interface during the first several centuries of the Common Era. In his discussion, he follows those that have been preserved in Christian sources with a group preserved in pagan—specifically, Greek—sources. He references two in particular: a spell upon a lead tablet from Hadrumetum, "where 'the demonic spirit who resides here,' that is, the local demon, whatever his name, is adjured 'in the name of Aoth, Abaoth, the God of Abraham; and Iao, God of Isaac; Iao, Aoth, Abaoth, God of Israma [Israel]' to bring Urbanus and Domitiana together in marriage. The god is described in terms of many Old Testament acts of his, especially in connection with creation." And the second is a "charm [in which] the Jewish God is adjured, with many references to Old Testament passages. But here, while the God of the Hebrew is elaborately specified, he is called Ammon, Joel, Ptah, Thoth, Ele, Elo, *Sabaot*, and a great number of other unrecognizable names. Indeed, one name given him is Jesus."[427]

Thus, as Goodenough notes, we are reading texts that reflect a very distinct syncretism. They are in Greek, not Hebrew (or even Aramaic) and Goodenough understands them to be essentially Jewish with pagan (and Christian?) infixes—although it is not entirely clear to me that one could not say the opposite: that they are essentially pagan, with very distinct Jewish (and possibly Christian) infixes. Goodenough suggests a means "for differentiating the pagan from the Jewish elements. That Ptah and Thoth, recognizable Egyptian gods, are named in the foregoing incantation did not keep us from feeling that it was basically a Jewish one, a feeling aroused by the fact that the charm as a whole is centered in the Jewish deity.... The Jewish elements are here central, not, like the pagan ones, tangential. 'Jesus,' as said, is a word so extraneous that it seems a late Christian addition in a charm essentially in its primitive Jewish form.[428]

I would add three observations to this. One, the idea that Goodenough's conviction that these charms are fundamentally Jewish is somewhat subjective is suggested by the fact that, as he points out, Bonner (about whom more in a moment) "says of this [second] spell that... it seems to him 'equally possible' that some pagan dragged in all the elaborate references to Jewish lore in order to enhance the power of his charm." So, objectively speaking, we may be back at a starting point of debate and confusion as to how to define the material we are looking at, with respect to its religious identity—which is apart from whether we label it and how we label it as religious or magical in the first place. Two, that the underlying point offered by the material we are perusing is the fact of syncretism, regardless of which identity we claim as primary and which as secondary or tertiary—which syncretism we might account for by suggesting that, in a world dominated by a strong consciousness of the ubiquitous presence and potential positive/negative power of the *sacer*, people are eager to cover all their *sacer*/sacerdotal bases in order to be maximally protected from the negative possibilities of the *sacer*.

This makes most sense for Paganism, with its multiplicity of gods, goddesses, and *daimones*. Syncretistic borrowing/inclusion from, say, Judaism, makes perfect sense in that

---

[427] Ibid, 190-91.
[428] Ibid, 191

sort of a pagan context. But it also makes sense for Christianity, which, while focusing on a single, all-good, all- powerful God, has embraced the notion of a Satan, an Adversary to that God, that is the embodiment of the dangerous, evil, negative side of the *sacer*. But this would even be true of Jews who, in theory, understand the *sacer* to be entirely under the governance of a single, all-good and all-powerful Being—who do not include the idea of the Satan and the notions of Original Sin and Eternal Damnation in Hell in their theology— but who, like their Israelite and Judaean ancestors, are wont to wander from a straight and narrow ideological path, a path that can be seen not only as intensely strict and demanding but as ignoring human nature and its foibles and worries.[429]

My third comment is that Goodenough leads us in two different definitional and textual directions with his last example. One is toward what are known as the Greek Magical Papyri—from which the last charm under discussion was extracted (from the so-called Great Paris Papyrus)—so that, in Goodenough's terms, we can continue to ask the question, in turning to that material, as to how to parse what would be called "mainly Jewish charms with some pagan material thrown in" as opposed to "mainly pagan with some Jewish stuff thrown in." So we need to examine some more of the Greek Magical Papyri. The second direction that he takes is that of defining charms versus amulets, and that will lead us to examine relevant material—amulets—collected and discussed both by Goodenough and by the aforementioned Campbell Bonner.

The so-called Greek Magical Papyri (*Papyri Graecae Magicae: PGM*)[430] once again carry us into the territory of a double definitional issue. They are primarily written, as the "name" indicates, in Greek and, both in terms of content and that particular language seem to reflect a largely pagan perspective. There are important elements, however, that reflect a Judaean or Jewish or Christian perspective, so the question arises as to how to explain these apparent spiritual cross-overs. Their content largely deals with instructions in how to invoke the powers of the *sacer* and spells that instruct the user in addressing those powers once they have been successfully invoked—material that might easily enough be termed magical. However, there is some material that is cosmological, asking questions regarding the universe and how it is shaped and how it operates—and these sorts of elements might just as easily be termed religious.

The so-called Paris *PGM* (*PGM* 1), concerning which Georg Luck asserts that it was written down as late as the fourth century CE (which does not necessarily mean that it did not have an prior oral history of some centuries in duration) includes a section that seems to address an all-encompassing figure in rather Christian-sounding terms: "... we have understood it, O womb fertile by the father's production; we have understood it, O everlasting presence of a fertile father. After having worshipped your infinite goodness, we can pray for only one thing: Preserve us in our knowledge of your existence, and help us never to go astray from this, our way of life (*PGM* 1:58). The "womb fertile by the father's

---

[429] In this regard, a comment by Goodenough is very relevant: "If we are not to proceed on the basis of a double standard, or of a presupposition that Jews could not have syncretized, we shall feel just as free to regard the charms at one end of the gamut as Jewish as we are to look upon those at the other end as pagan, and may suppose that those in between which are predominantly pagan were made by pagans, those predominantly Jewish by Jews" (Ibid, 206). The question that remains difficult to answer in an absolute sense is how one ought to draw lines among these three categories, (to repeat).

[430] The *PGM* came to light in the nineteenth century, when six such manuscripts were purchased in the Egyptian marketplace in 1827 by Giovanni/ Jean Anastasi (1765–1860) an Armenian from Damascus. The eventually much larger group was published a century later, in two volumes edited and translated (into German) by Karl Preisendanz, in 1928 and 1931. An updated second edition (also in German) was brought out by Albert Henrichs in 1974 and an English-language version was published in 1986, edited by H.D. Betz and others.

production" can certainly be read as a Marian womb, just as the "everlasting presence of a fertile father" can be read as Jesus. Luck suggests that "it is quite possible that its author was influenced by Christian theology, though not a Christian himself. The success of Christianity [particularly by the late fourth century] may have persuaded him that here was a powerful magic that might be used to good advantage, especially if the ancient magic did not work anymore."[431]

One might ask why he assumes that the ancient magic was no longer working. One might also ask whether the objects of the invocation could not be, say, Isis and Horus. Indeed, whereas Mary is no goddess, Isis is. So the apparent Christological influence may not be there at all—but the fact that Luck finds it there (and it is arguably there, if also arguably not there) is another reminder of the syncretistic possibilities offered by this literature. Earlier in the same long papyrus, a section offered a spell devoted to induce love. The spell is directed to the myrrh that is burning before the practitioner the entire time, concerning which he says "...Everyone calls you Zmyrna [myrrh], but I call you Easter and Burner of the Heart. I am, sending you to X, daughter of Y, to serve me against her and bring her to me."

As the practitioner expounds upon what he wants—"...[that] she may think only of me, Z, desire only me, love only me and fulfill my every wish"—and tells the smoking herb how to accomplish this, he evokes a handful of deities: "*Anocho, Abrasax,*[432] *Tro*, and ...those that are even more appropriate and more powerful—*Kormeiot, Iao, Sabaot, Adonai...*" We recognize names that we do not recognize, and those that we do—in particular the last three, from the group of four more powerful deities, which constitute two Hebrew God-names sandwiching between them a name that we have repeatedly seen as a confutation of two Hebrew terms. There is also the name, *Abraxas*... So might we say that this is a pagan text that exhibits a small but significant Jewish influence?

Later on in the same papyrus (*PGM* 1:83-87) there is another "love formula" that hardly sounds loving, that also references *Abraxas* and also *Adonai*. The instruction is to shape two figures in clay,

> ...one male and one female. Make the male look like Ares [the Greek god of war] in arms. He should hold a sword in his left hand and point it at her right collarbone. Her arms must be tied behind her back, and she must kneel. Attach the magic substance [the precise nature of which is unspecified]. On the head of the figure representing the woman whom you wish to attract, write: [gobbledy-gook *cum* magical words; there follows a list of other body parts upon which magical words are to be written]
>
> Take thirteen iron needles, stick one into her brain and say: "I prick your brain, X." [Other needles are pricked into other body parts, each time with the recitation: "I prick this part of the body of X, to make sure that she thinks of nobody but me."]
>
> Take a lead plate and write the same formula upon it and tie it to the figures in three hundred sixty-fve knots... and recite the "*Abrasax*, hold tight" formula that you know, and deposit this at sunset near the

[431] Georg Luck, *Arcana Mundi* (Baltimore: The Johns Hopkins University Press, 1985), 96.
[432] This name is a variant, by metathesis, of *Abraxas*. Or one might say, actually, that *Abraxas* is a variant, by metathesis, of the more common *Abrasax*.

tomb of someone who died before his time or died a violent death, with flowers of the season. The spell must be written and recited thus:

"I deposit this binding spell with you, gods of the underworld [gobbled-gook magical words] and Kore Persephone Ereschigal and Adonis, the [magical words] Hermes of the underworld, Touth [magical words] and powerful Anubis, who holds the keys of those in Hades, the gods and *daimones* of the underworld, those who died before their time... I conjure all the *daimones*... go to every street, into every house, and fetch and bind. Bring me X, the daughter of Y, whose magical substance you have, and make her love me, Z.... Let he not have intercourse... and let her not have pleasure with any other man except me, Z. Let her, X, not eat, not drink, not love, not be strong, not be healthy, not sleep, except with me, Z...

Yes, drag her by her hair, her entrails, her genitals, to me, Z, in every hour of time, day and night, until she comes to me...Do this, bind [her] during my whole life [to me] and force her, X, to be my slave...

For I am *Adonai* [magical words] who hides the stars, the brightly radiating ruler of the sky, the lord of the world...

Fetch her, tie her, make her love and desire me, Z... forever and ever."

Most of the ellipses in this formulation represent places where, for the sake of relative brevity, I have not quoted further details, but they would only reinforce the issues of interest to us. The goal of this charm is to make the woman love the practitioner, but his concept of love might be considered a bit odd—that she become enslaved to him. Perhaps a mere metaphor: she would become a slave to love—as presumably he already is? But that all her body parts (with an emphasis on the genitals) feel the effect of his needle, and that she be dragged to him, by her hair, entrails and genitals is hardly cuddly love.[433]

Indeed, the god of war is used as the primary instrument of compelling her love—or at least an image of that god—rather than, say, Aphrodite, but then the entire violent method would need to be replaced. The manner in which images are used as surrogates for the woman—and Ares for the practitioner/client—is consistent with the Frazerian idea of homeopathic magic that we have seen in use elsewhere. But the "God and *daimones*" issue offers interesting aspects in four directions. First, we are presented with a panoply of divine beings drawn from three pagan traditions (Ares, Kore Persephone, Adonis and Hermes are Greek, but Anubis and Touth are Egyptian and Ereschigal is Mesopotamian)—a by no means surprising synthesis, endemic to the Hellenistic-Roman period. But the figure commanding the others at the end, *Adonai*, is drawn from the Judaean-Jewish tradition, adding another layer of syncretism.

---

[433] The discussion of the relationship between love and strife in Greek and Roman (and other) literature and what that relationship reflects of the culture is a longer story for another time. See my forthcoming book *Eros and Eris: Love and Strife in Greek and Latin Literature and Their Offspring.*

The manner in which *Adonai* is presented is interesting, aside from the question of who he is understood to be (does the formulator of this text understand him as the all-powerful God worshipped by Judaeans/Jews?). Everything up to that point had been second person—you must do X and say Y—but the text suddenly becomes first person: *I am Adonai...* That would suggest, (this is the second interesting aspect), that not only do we have a blurry overlap between the practitioner and the client—the practitioner instructs the client but the client actually does and says all of these things—but an intended blur between the client and the *sacer* power(s) that he invokes: in performing all that he carefully performs, as he follows the *sacerdos'* instructions, he becomes a conduit through which the *sacer* power of *Adonai* speaks.

He speaks at that moment to the other *sacer* figures. Thus thirdly, where exactly are we with regard to the border between magic and religion and what distinguishes the one from the other? The necessary actions are to be undertaken at a precise border time (sunset) and in a border place (a tomb), involving particular kinds of dead people: those who have crossed the border from *profanus* to *sacer* precipitously—prematurely or violently. This is consistent with both magic and religion, is it not? Moreover, the element of precision encompasses the apparently necessary reiteration of the name of the woman and of the client/practitioner, lest the *sacer* powers make a mistake. Precision is certainly as endemic to religious as to magic ritual.

Moreover, *Adonai* is presented as if he (speaking through the conduit of the client) is more powerful than and can command all of the other gods and *daimones*. So if this is a pagan charm, does it nonetheless acknowledge the Judaean/Jewish God as the most powerful among the many? And is it "magical" because, in spite of invoking *Adonai* as most powerful—reminiscent, in a distinct way, of the story we have read in Exodus 7 of *Adonai*'s domination of the Egyptian gods through the domination of the Egyptian *sacerdotes* by Moses and Aaron—because it is essentially pagan? Or is it because of its personalized goal? Or is it because of its method?

That last-named issue leads us in the fourth interesting-aspect direction, and back both to Iamblichus and to a question that would have been asked by someone else, if not by him: is this method one of compulsion or petition? If the bevy of gods and *daimones* evoked is initially petitioned, when we get toward the end, the petitioner seems to use his position as conduit/persona of *Adonai* to *compel* them. How is it that powers of the *sacer* can be compelled, if they *are* being compelled? (And if they are compelled, does *that* cause us to call this magical and not religious?)

A range of complications attends these texts. Earlier on in the Great Paris Papyrus (*PGM* 1:76-79), the Egyptian pharaoh, Psammetichus—in spite of being perceived as immortal and therefore with an inherent connection to the divine *sacer*—receives instructions from Nephotes, the *sacerdos*, with regard to achieving contact with and thereby gaining information from the gods. He must "communicate with Helios (the sun) as follows (it can be at sunrise, provided the moon is in her third day). Climb up onto the roof of your dwelling... [I]n the presence of a mystagogue [a *sacerdos* who can guide one into the hidden depths of the divine *sacer*]... [w]hen the sun is in the middle of the sky, in the fifth hour, lie down naked on a linen sheet [with] your eyes veiled with a black strap. Have yourself wrapped as if you were a corpse."

So the pharaoh—at a precise, border time, in a precise manner—engages in acts that place him in a death-like condition, his eyes closed and unable to see, his body wrapped, presumably like a mummy. It is its own very particular homeopathic act vis-à-vis the *sacer* of death, in order to better facilitate contact with the divine aspect of the *sacer*—with which he already is and even more obviously will be associated when he dies. He is then told to utter a prayer—or is this an incantation?—to "[m]ighty Typhon, scepter-holder and ruler of the scepter-power above! God of gods! Lord! ABERAMEMTHOU. Shaker of darkness... IOERBET AU TAUI MENI. I am he who, along with you, searched the whole earth and found the great Osiris, whom I brought before you in chains. I am he who fought at your side against the gods...."

So the invocation is to the monster of monsters in the Greek tradition (who fought the gods and specifically, Zeus, but was defeated and buried under Mount Aetna, on Sicily). But the Greek-based idea is immediately wedded to an important story in the Egyptian tradition, in which Osiris is destroyed by his evil half-brother, Seth—with whom the later Greek historian, Herodotos (ca 484-25 BCE), in fact identified Typhon. The pharaoh who would be in communication with the gods and who will eventually dwell among them seeks assistance from one who is both one of them and inimical to them.

He continues, still addressing Typhon, as the most powerful of *sacer* beings: "AEMINAEBAROTHERRETHORABANIMEA. Give me strength, I beseech you, and grant me this favor that, whenever I order in my incantations one of the gods themselves to come, he will come and show himself to me." What follows is a long succession of nonsense words and syllables—NAINE BASANAPTATOU EAPTOU MENOPHAESME ... and so forth—among which three iterations of IAO are strewn. This is followed by Nephotes' description of how the pharaoh will know (after he has recited this last series of "words" three times) that communion has been achieved. "[Y]ou will [now] be in control of your godlike nature."

Nephotes further instructs Psammetichus regarding how to call Osiris or Serapis, a process that concludes with a lengthy invocation ending with a word 100 letters in length. Aside, then, from the issue of syncretism between different pagan traditions and the droplet of possible Judaean/Jewish influence suggested by the use of IAO, there is the different question of how this is to be construed as magical rather than religious, given the invocation of specific gods—but then perhaps, in spite of the reference to Egyptian gods, we should label this as magical because of its emphasis on compulsion, rather than petition. But again one wonders: how does one presume to compel gods?

Greek Magical Papyrus #2, found in Leiden and known as the "Sacred Book, Called the 'Monad,' or 'Eighth Book of Moses,' about the Holy Name" offers a fourth-century text many of the elements in which are, Luck suggests, two centuries older. This is less important for our purposes than other issues (although a text from the fourth century should underscore to us how the issues of Pagan-Jewish-Christian syncretism and religion-magic definition that we have been repeatedly noting extend into very late antiquity). For those issues, its salient parts (ls 98-102) include a ritual—that involves both an action and a recitation—for an exorcism. Thus: "if someone is possessed by a *daimon*, say the Name and hold sulfur and bitumen under his nose. He will speak at once and the *daimon* will go away."

We might note that bitumen came into the Roman world mainly from Judaea/Palestine (particularly around the Dead Sea; it was popularly called "Judaeans' pitch"—or later, if we make the distinction that I have been pressing all along: "Jews' pitch"). While this ancient form of pungent smelling salts was assumed, due to its objectionable odor, to drive *daimones* away, it is also noteworthy that the invocation of the Name—presumably the Name of (the Jewish) God—is expected to be stronger than any *daimon* and therefore have the power to help drive a *daimon* out.

To awaken a dead body, one is instructed to recite a formula culminating with the words that "it is I who perform this operation through the power of Thayth, the holy God" and then to "say the Name." So is the Name the Name of the Jewish (or Jewish/Christian) God? Or is it Thayth—presumably a corruption of the name, Thoth, the Egyptian god associated, among other things, with bringing writing into existence. Indeed, the next instruction, with respect to "how to unshackle fetters [involves saying] 'Hear me, Christ [but the proper reading could be 'helpful one'] in my torture...' [and then] for twelve days [to] whistle three times and say the whole name of Helios eight times, beginning with the Achebykro: 'Let every fetter be opened... let all irons break... and let nobody restrain me, because I am [say the Name]." So at the very least we seem to have a very syncretistic text—one component of which may be Christian and another possibly Jewish but most components certainly pagan.

Among the more interesting features of the *PGM* is the occasional recitation of the seven Greek vowels in a formulaic progression. Thus early in the so-called Great Paris Papyrus (ls 13-19) there are two columns in the first, left-hand side of which one sees a triangle configured of one *alpha*, two *epsilon*s, three *eta*s, four *iota*s, five *omicron*s, six *upsilon*s and seven *omega*s. To the right, the second triangle is upside down, going from seven *omega*s down to one *alpha*. Seven lines latter, the practitioner is instructed to "recite the following word:"—and what follows is a vowel progression from one *alpha* to seven *omega*s and then words of instruction or petition to a *daimon*. Sometimes the progression is of some extended word or phrase that is repeated multiple times but where in the second, the first and last letters are dropped, in the third line, the third and penultimate letters are dropped and so on, down to two or one letters. There seems to be no meaning even to the full word/phrase/line, so that the practitioner is reciting gobbledy-gook that serves as verbiage carrying beyond our *profanus* realm of verbiage and sense—rendered more incoherent by the reductive nature of the recitation.

Occasionally, imbedded within the Greek text there are entire passages—usually in Coptic, as in *PGM* IV, 120ff. Coptic is the last of the four Egyptian writing systems, of which hieroglyphs is the first (and hieratic the second and demotic the third). Its thirty-one-letter alphabet is comprised of forms of the 24 letters of the Greek alphabet and seven letters from Demotic. It continued in use until largely supplanted by Arabic writing in the seventh century, but remained and remains in use as a liturgical language by Coptic Christianity. So the intrusion might in some cases be construed as Christian, but in any case implies Egyptian (as opposed to Macedonian Greek) influence, and in fact, some of its words are recognizable as direct renderings of hieroglyphic passages.

The *PGM* also often include images, as well as words (as Goodenough noted in discussing one such text).[434] In *PGM* XXVI, 210, for example, there is a series of seven elements. Of particular interest to us is the first, a six-pointed cross, the sixth, a simple cross, and the fifth, a kind of square within which the word (in Greek letters, of course), IAO is inscribed. There is no inherent reason to associate the cross with Christianity—it will be some centuries before that association emerges—and even less so, the six-pointed cross/star with Judaism (it will be more than a millennium before that association emerges), but the casual viewer might mistakenly make those associations. In any case, the box with IAO within it may have the Judaean/Jewish or borrowed Judaean/Jewish significance that we have discussed before—and the seven symbols are, in fact preceded by the words "...bring me the favor/grace of all [of them], *Adonai*" (again, of course, in Greek letters, so we are in any case confronted with a certain syncretism.

More dramatically graphic are images such as that of an apparently mummy-wrapped anthropomorph around which a pair of serpents intertwine, their open mouth emitting forked tongues at what would be the ear level of the head. Directly above this image is one of a hybrid, its body more or less that of an upright anthropomorph and its head that of a horse seen in profile. It is marked by a kind of broken cross on its chest, wears a kind of fringed tunic from the left armpit to the knees, each of its feet is bifurcated, and it holds a circular entity in its outstretch left hand and a kind of rod in its outstretched right hand—and beneath that left arm is a progression of seven rows of Greek vowels, each letter repeated seven times. There are other figures on this papyrus fragment, together with

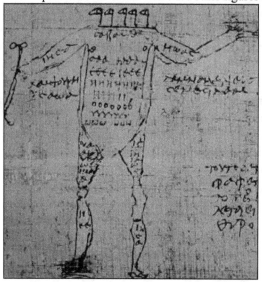

extensive lines of text. Yet another offers a figure without a head—in place of which is a series of five little pennants: they are eyes mounted, as it were, on sticks [FIG 3]. The body is filled in with the familiar handling of the heptapartite Greek vowel system in a progression down from seven *alpha*s to seven *omega*s, with *sabaot* written across the shoulders and inscriptions on the legs and upper arms, as well.

FIG 3: detail from *PGM* 2 ca 4th c ce

There is more, of course. But even from this small sampling, what we come away with is a sense of how blurry the lines can be among "pagan" and "Jewish" and "Christian" categories—and also, perhaps the line between religious and magical practice.[435]

[434] See above, xxx.
[435] We will have more to say about the *PGM* below, in Chapter Eleven, 292-300, and the consideration of John Gager's discussion of Moses.

We might note, however, that Goodenough, in his discussion, tends to use the term "magician" if he thinks that an element is neither Jewish nor Christian but is Pagan, which ought to remind us that he is thinking from a perspective that does not acknowledge how legitimate the diverse pagan forms of religion were to their adherents, and how, if the lines might have appeared clearer to contemporary practitioners than they do to us, on the other hand it would take some time until, mainly Christian and Jewish practitioners and writers would begin to look down consistently on pagans and their religious leaders as dealing falsely or weakly or nefariously with the *sacer*—and even longer for Christians and Jews to look at each other that way. We shall see that they eventually would, of course (although we will find more extensive evidence of this from the Christian than from the Jewish side).

The definitional issue of charms versus amulets offers an interesting sideline to the Jewish/Christian/pagan issue and an important addition to the religion/magic issue. Goodenough asserts in his first chapter on amulets that [a]ny line drawn between amulets and charms must be an arbitrary one."[436] He adds in the next few lines, however, that "[i]n the material we are discussing, we are for practical purposes distinguishing between charms as verbal and amulets as objects containing a graphic symbol: charms are ritualistic prescriptions, amulets are things with symbols on them which operate simply by being worn on the person, though objects which are amulets in themselves, the rabbits' foot as such, the opal or obsidian as such, liie outside our special interest. Even the distinction so made often breaks down, for many of the charms written on papyrus or parchments were worn on the person, or affixed to the house."[437]

So the line is blurry, since amulets can be verbal, like a charm, and don't necessarily need a graphic element—and we have already seen "Charms" that include graphic elements. Obviously a very long charm is far less likely to worn on one's person than a short one—which might then qualify as an amulet. One might also suppose that a charm is something used for a one-time purpose, where an amulet might be used or worn on a more ore less permanent basis to ward off evil. Goodenough himself mentions *t'fillin*, correctly recognizing them as Jewish amulets. These little boxes with their leather straps, containing small parchment scrolls with scriptural passages written upon them, would seem to have had that intention—at least partially. The Greek term for them, "phylacteries," emphasizes this, since *phylax* means "protector" in Greek. But the Aramaic term emphasizes their role as an adjunct to prayer (*t'filah*)—although of course by definition praying to God every morning and several times a day is part of the arsenal of maintaining a good relationship with God and therefore of being protected by God.

The question is therefore their use. If by the medieval period they were donned for morning prayers, in antiquity they were more frequently worn continuously; as Goodenough notes: "Rabbah bar bar Hana tells of Rabbi Johanan of the third century that he always had his *t'fillin* with him to protect him from the evil spirits," in the context of a discussion of whether one ought to take one's *t'fillin* with one into a privy or into bed with one's wife (thereby running the risk of soiling the sanctity of the protective amulet through

---

[436] Goodenough, 207.
[437] Ibid.

impure associations).[438] Similarly, when Jesus admonishes the Pharisees for wearing unusually wide phylacteries—presumably to (hypocritically) display their sanctity—in Matt. 13.5, as Goodenough points out, the Greek term is understood by modern scholars to refer to *t'fillin*, as subsequently it will certainly come to do.

One may also look, as Goodenough does, at the *mezuzah* as an amulet—not the doorpost, which is what the Hebrew term actually means, but the small container placed *on* the doorpost with a piece of parchment containing scriptural material written upon it. Placed by the opening into the house, it is clearly intended to protect it—particularly when the box is decorated with the Hebrew letter, *shin*, standing for *Shaddai*, God's power-protective Name. There are two issues of interest to us here. One is the broad one, which reminds us that the Jewish sense of the divine *sacer* as a singular all-powerful, all-good Being did not (and over the centuries continued not to) prevent Jews from protecting themselves from the potentially negative and dangerous aspects of the *sacer*, even if in theory they should not exist.

Second: the mode of protection, which we might expect to be that of singular, absolute reliance on God and God alone—the one, all-powerful, all-good (to repeat) God—turns out perhaps not to be limited to that form. Goodenough points to a study by Victor Aptowitzer, in which, from various testimonies it emerges that "not only were divine and angelic names written into the texts, but figures of angels were drawn on the scroll."[439] The implication is that multiple protective sources, albeit not pagan or Christian, per se, were being invoked. However, Aptowitzer's sources are medieval, and Goodenough himself references Maimonides (1135-204), so it is by no means clear that this was the case in antiquity. Goodenough continues by quoting a lengthy passage from the *Sepher Raziel* (*Book of Raziel* [the angel])—but this is a 13th-century text. The whole question of who first elaborated an angelology, the Jews or the Christians, is at play here. If, as I contend, it is Christianity, in the Book of Revelation, then arguably, over the centuries, Jews absorbed that influence and took it into their own sensibilities.

The classic modern compendium of amulets from Greco-Roman antiquity is that work by Campbell Bonner, organized in 1950 as *Studies in Magical Amulets*, and referenced several times, as we have seen, by Goodenough. In his introduction, in noting that the majority of amulets that he discusses are "Gnostic" amulets (his quotation marks), and observing that Gnosis refers to various "systems of religious philosophy... [that] manifested themselves as heresies in the Christian church of the second and third centuries," Bonner asserts that "amulets, though fundamentally magical, tend to take religion as an aid and ally, just as the converse is true... [furthermore] they are likely to invoke... the support of local divinities, and to absorb into themselves local religious ideas, or at least religious expressions and symbols."[440]

From these comments the most obvious question that one must raise—as we have felt obliged to do a number of times in the course our own narrative—is: what does Bonner understand to be "religion" and what is "magic"? He observes how "people regarded magic

---

[438] He is quoting from the Babylonian Talmud, tractate *Brakhot*, 23a, b.
[439] Goodenough cites, in fn 12 of his chapter on amulets, Avigdor (Victor) Aptowitzer's "Les noms de Dieu et des anges dans la mezouza," *REJ*, LX (1910), 39-52; LXV (1913), 54-60.
[440] Both quotes are from Bonner, *Studies in Magical Amulets*, 1.

that came from a distance as especially powerful"—a notion that we have already encountered. But what distinguishes religion from magic for them (Bonner does not say) or for Bonner (he also does not say this)? It would appear that the use of certain names, such as *Abrasax*, are regarded by him as magical because they are not divine names that he considers legitimately religious. He concedes that there is some overlap—that the two disciplines occasionally use each other as "an aid and ally"—but does not define the one and the other. If one invokes local divinities or local religious ideas, expressions and symbols, what is it with which one began that is presumably magical and not religious in the first place?

For that matter, he notes that the "writers [of many of these amulets] may or may not have belonged to a Gnostic sect; but the documents themselves... can seldom be regarded as monuments of Gnostic religion... [and] Gnosticism is merely one of several religious influences that have left their mark on these amulets."[441] So Gnosticism is a religion and its presence is felt, but not in strong enough terms to suggest that the amulets should be labeled as Gnostic, per se—and they are being called magical amulets, in any case, not religious amulets.

Of less concern for our purposes—except to remind us that the problem of definition extends in different directions where our subject is concerned—is Bonner's distinction between amulets and charms. The former he defines as "any object which by its contact or its close proximity to the person who owns it, or to any possession of his, exerts power for his good... [Further, t]he word 'talisman' is virtually a synonym of 'amulet'."

In then describing the amulets, he opines that these ingredients were magical."[442] He includes "charms and incantations papyrus [that have whereas other material person."

kind of material found in "the virtues ascribed to partly medical, partly as amuletic material written on small pieces of survived since antiquity, has not]...worn on the

FIG 4: Inscribed jasper snake-footed anthropomorph,

amulet with cock-headed, 1st-6th c CE; Bonner #172

So Bonner amulets as essentially point: that is, charms,

would see charms and interchangeable, up to a like incantations, are

words, but they can be used like non-verbal material as amulets, provided that the substance on which they are written can be folded up into a compact form and worn on the person

---

[441] Ibid. He takes issue, specifically, with scholars who classify amulets that mention *Abrasax* as Basilidian—which latter term refers to a Gnostic group founded in the second century by Basilides of Alexandria. The group flourished into the fourth century; its members practiced a five-year-long vow of silence and celebrated the baptismal day of Jesus as an annual festival spent partly in study.

[442] Both quotes are in close promximity in Ibid, 2. Bonner describes amuletic material found today (i.e., ca 1950) in bags around the necks of children in Egyptian hospitals and infers that the same material would doubtless have been used in antiquity, although none has survived the millennia.

like other substances are—stone, for instance, particularly those with presumed magical or medicinal qualities [FIG 4]. More significant is the question of what exactly distinguishes "magical" from "medical" for Bonner, since if the amulets he describes are half magical and half medical then we need to know which half is which—especially if "belief in the efficacy of amulets depends upon certain primitive concepts of the mind," and *we* don't wish to be perceived as primitive by confusing the medical with the magical. Alas, he has chosen not (or failed) to offer this definitional distinction. However, those "primitive concepts" are "notions that supernatural power may be inherent in some person, animal, or material object, or... may at least reside there temporarily,"[443] which presumably at least distinguishes them from more advanced, religious concepts, (such as our own would be).

"[C]ertain gem stones were believed to exert powers suggested by their color... [such as] amethyst, apparently because of its wine-like color, was believed to enable a man to drink heavily without becoming intoxicated." We recognize a form of what Frazer called homeopathic magic in this, although Bonner refers to it as the "idea of medicomagical power," again suggesting the unanswered question of what part constitutes the medical and what part the magical.[444] Bonner talks of the use of magic in antiquity—referencing the Kirke episode in *Odyssey* 10—and then observes how the Christian writer, Gregory of Nazianzos, in his sermon on Baptism, makes it clear that Christians among his community are using amulets, and that they should not do so, for "you have no need of amulets and incantations, *along with which the Evil One makes his way into the minds of simpler folk, stealing for himself the honor that belongs to God*" [italics added].[445] A later scholium discusses in some detail what constitute amulets (*periammata*) and what constitute incantations (*epasmata*), but main thing that we recognize is the use of amulets as a left-over from Paganism that Christian leaders like Gregory are trying to extract from the embedded religious arsenal of their flock. We also recognize that one of the dangers of customs and objects associated with Paganism is that they are coming to be associated with the Satan, whose role in Christian thought is becoming more substantial.

Bonner then offers a number of very interesting ancient Greek references to this sort of material—including a reference made by Theophrastos to an amulet (*periapton*) that no less a luminary than Perikles was wearing that the women of his household had hung around his neck when he was ill. With the use of "pendants and rings," he notes, "the contact with purely religious ideas is very close. Nowadays one type of Christian may wear the image of a saint in all reverence, gaining a certain comfort of mind from the constant reminder of a power beyond himself..."[446] For us this must again raise the question of what it is that makes the wearing of a saint's image around one's neck purely religious while wearing the image of Apollo or Aisklepios is magical, (albeit inflected with "purely religious ideas"), other than the fact that the writer is a Christian who, in the mid-twentieth century believes in the legitimacy of seeking assistance from the divine *sacer* through saints but views the hope for help from a pagan god as fundamentally false or at least flawed.

---

[443] Ibid.
[444] Both quotes are from ibid, 3.
[445] Bonner, 3, is quoting from Migne, PG 36, 381 A.
[446] Ibid, 6.

Bonner continues in this vein in observing that changes took place in the first century CE, for "we begin to find rings and pendants of semiprecious stones which show that *they are magical, either by designs of so peculiar a character as to admit of no other classification, or by the unmistakable evidence of inscriptions.* Brief petitions such as *diaphulasse,* "preserve," or *dos moi kharin,* "grant me favor," could be regarded merely as *a special development, in a religious direction...*" [italics added].[447] Why are these last statements inherently more religious than magical? Because they are petitions rather than commands? Or because (again) they are positive rather than negative in intention? The striking change to which Bonner refers is "a transition from an older national magic to a later international one," that combines Greek with "sometimes corruptions of Egyptian, Hebrew or Aramaic speech forms, sometimes unintelligible combinations of letters."[448] For our purposes, these changes are not what is important but rather the question of how one ought to—or Bonner does—distinguish the magical from the religious (or medical). And throughout his work we never find out with clarity what the distinction(s) is/are.

He concludes this part of his introductory discussion with a fuller exposition of the role of Egyptian, Palestinan and Babylonian influences on the amuletic material that he is studying. What he now terms Graeco-Egyptian magical amulets, he notes, have shapes that "differ little from those used for the later Greek and Hellenistic non-magical gems"[449]—meaning religious or meaning merely decorative? His physical descriptions are, of course, extremely interesting, but what we might find most significant is his comment that "such stones contradict Budge's view that 'the use of the amulet ... has never been, and can never be, connected with what is commonly called "Black Magic".' It is doubtless true that the magic of such amulets is usually 'white' rather than 'black,' yet there are Graeco-Egyptian amulets that express such wishes as might be scratched on a curse tablet (*katadesmos, defixionis tabella*). However, the true curse tablet, made for the sole purpose of destroying an enemy, is never worn by the person uttering the curse, but is hidden away or buried. When 'black-magical' words are inscribed on a gem stone it may mean that the stone was intended to be used in a ceremony (*praxis*) directed against an enemy, or that the inscription represents a desire so passionately felt that the person who expresses it wished to be constantly reminded of it."[450]

So we are seeing a distinction between two kinds of magic—which means that the positive/negative matrix cannot serve as a basis for a religion/magic definitional distinction. And there is nothing further to explain why, say, the image of a Christian saint around one's neck or of a *mezuzah* in which prescribed passages from the Torah are written on parchment differs from a "white-magical" pagan amulet—except that the latter is pagan—or, for that matter, why a "black-magical" inscription in that amulet, representing a "desire so passionately felt that the person who expresses it wishes to be constantly reminded of it" differs substantively (as opposed to subjectively) from the same level of

---

[447] Ibid, 6.
[448] Ibid, 7.
[449] Ibid, 9.
[450] Ibid, 10-11. His quote from the Egyptologist E.A. Wallace Budge comes from the latter's work, *Amulets and Talsimans,* Preface, XXIII.

passionate feeling leading to the saint medallion or *mezuzah*: to be ever reminded, in a concrete, tangible way, of (the Christian or Jewish) God's presence all around us.

And so on. He turns to the problem of diverse language-inputs into written material, including gibberish that seems altogether outside the ambit of known languages, and in summing up the tasks for the student of amulets notes that these are two-fold, one historical and the other descriptive. Thus in the first category is the question of what groups have contributed to what emerges as a given amulet: with diversely Egyptian, "Greek, Jewish, or Persian elements; and it goes without saying that in an age of syncretism two or more of these influences may often be detected in a single specimen. It is also necessary to inquire whether any of the prayers and invocations that are inscribed on some amulets express a genuine religious feeling, and if so, to determine its relation to known religious groups, such as the Jews, the Orthodox Christians, and the Gnostics...[or in some cases] where Greek mythology has suggested the design or the legend."[451]

Well and fine, but the issue of syncretism takes us back to the discussions of Goodenough that led us to Bonner, and the question of whether a given papyrus is, say, Jewish with some pagan influence or pagan with some Jewish influence. We might also note that, in using the term "Jewish" when perhaps the word "Judaean" would have been more historically accurate, he is inherently obscuring the distinction and overlap between Jewish and Christian material and between either of these categories and their Judaean predecessor. He has nowhere offered us the tools with which to determine what constitutes "genuine religious feeling"—as opposed to either magical or, since he brings up the phrase, Greek material that he refers to as mythological as opposed to religious.

The second issue, that of description, pertains, as Bonner explains, to the content: general prophylactics, or those "directed against the evil eye and other forms of enchantment... [or those] meant to prevent or cure various diseases... [and still others] grouped under the head of social (or antisocial) magic—love charms, charms meant to gain favor... charms to break up love affairs... charms to bring serious harm or death to an enemy."[452] It is interesting that he is astute enough to recognize the need to parse the amulets and charms into different goal-orientations, whereas so many other critical definitional issues remain invisible to him.

We might turn the screw of these two issues one further twist by a brief examination of a particular amuletic(?) kind of inscription that first appears on a wall in ancient Pompeii and offers offspring well into the medieval period: the so-called magic square. This phrase refers to a complex palindrome, made up of a certain number of words of a certain length that, when placed within a box-like format, offer multiple levels of palindromic contours. The most famous one, the so-called "*sator-rotas* magic square" consists of a succession of five five-lettered words, some or all of them presumably Latin. The earliest instance that we know of was carved as a graffito, in Pompeii—which means that the square had been developed before 79 CE (the year in which Pompell was buried by the explosion of Mount Vesuvius on August 24).

---

[451] Ibid, 21
[452] Ibid, 21.

Subsequent instances of the inscription have been found far afield. There is one at Dura Europos, Syria (a flourishing Roman border town that was overrun by the Sasanians in 254 CE and largely buried thereafter); and another in the excavations under the church of Santa Maria Maggiore—one of the four (later expanded to seven) major pilgrimage churches in Rome. An example has been found in the Luberon, in southern France and another at Corinium (modern Cirencester,) in England; and also one up in Gotland, Scandinavia—to name a few.

The five "words," in order, are: *sator arepo tenet opera rotas*. Organized in box-formation, they appear thusly:

S A T O R
A R E P O
T E N E T
O P E R A
R O T A S

Thus, they can be read horizontally, either right to left or left to right and also vertically, either top to bottom or bottom to top and in any of these directions the five words form a sentence of sorts. The grouping offers at least four questions of interest to us: what does the sequence mean? Is the language Latin, and if not, what language is it—or what language combined, perhaps, with Latin? Is it just a graffito, with nothing magical about it at all, or is it supposed to have some *sacer*-related significance? If the latter, with what tradition might it have been associated—pagan, Jewish or Christian—and is its intention, then, "magical" or "religious"? A fifth question which might impinge on our attempts to answer the others is: by what process was this particular combination arrived at?

The word *arepo* is attested nowhere else—it is a *hapax legomenon*, (a term that appears only once in the extant literature and therefore does not offer contexts through which to understand its meaning)—and most of those who have sought to analyze the meaning of the inscription have taken it to be a proper name. Thus, if we assume that the inscription is simply Latin, and if we take *sator* to derive from the verb *serere* ("to sow") and thus means "sower" or "plower" or "progenitor" the entirety would read: "the sower/farmer/ plougher Arepo holds (*tenet*) works (*opera*) wheels (*rotas*)." Less precisely, but less awkwardly: "the farmer Arepo uses wheels—i.e., a plough—for his work." But of what significance would this odd formula be?

What, too, about the name, Arepo? Various interpreters have seen it as derived from Celtic, (from a Gallic word for "plough;")[453]; or from Hebrew/Aramaic (a rendition, in turn, of Greek *alpha o*—*alpha-omega*—as that first-last Greek-letter combination is used in Revelation 1:8);[454] or from Egyptian *Hr-Hp* (meaning "the face of Apis," the bull-

---

[453] This view, perhaps not surprisingly, was proposed by the French archaeologist, Jerome Carcopino (1881-1970), after studying the example found in France.

[454] This view was expressed by David Daube (1909-99). A German-born Jew from a long rabbinic line, Daube managed to flee Germany for England at the beginning of the Nazi period. He was arguably the twentieth century's preeminent scholar of ancient legal thought, combining knowledge of Roman law and biblical law, with an expertise in Greek, Roman, Jewish, and Christian literature.

god);[455] or from a Latinized abbreviation of Harpokrates (god of the rising sun, sometimes referred to in the Hellenistic-period Greek of Egypt as *Georgos Arpon*, meaning "Earth-working Harpokrates").[456]

Henri Polge, in his 1969 article in the *Revue de l'histoire des religions*, argued that *arepo* was a made-up word or name used to facilitate the completion of the otherwise completed palindrome.[457] He suggested that the phrase, *sator tenet rotas*, once organized on five lines, then require a palindrome for the second and fourth lines, for which the vowels are already in place, which led to *opera* (a real word) and *Arepo* (a made-up word or more likely, name) but not to any significant meaning. Thus:

SATOR	SATOR	SATOR
	A E O	AREPO
TENET	TENET	TENET
	O E A	OPERA
ROTAS	ROTAS	ROTAS

Duncan Fishwick, in his 1964 article in Harvard Theological Review asserted that the sequence was an early Christian cryptogram; arguing that it must have begun with *Pater Noster*, from which the central element, *tenet*, was derived (i.e., the three main interior consonants—t-n-t—in that phrase and the twice-appearing "e").[458] If this word, as the intended center of a "magic square," is written in a cruciform, then each "t" on the ends must be flanked by vowels. A Latinization of the Greek, *alpha-omega*, (although Fishwick doesn't offer this as the reason) would easily enough yield A and O, after which, he claims, a "brief experiment" would yield *rotas/sator*, leaving P and R to fill in the remaining spaces and ending up with the finally square. Thus:

T	ATO	SATOR
E	A E O	AREPO
TENET	TENET	TENET
E	O E A	OPERA
T	OTA	ROTAS

There is a further variation on this last idea that deconstructs all of the letters of the square to yield a cruciform with *Pater Noster* extending vertically and horizontally from the central "n," and with the "a" and "o" offering a square in individual-letter counterpoint. The idea would be that the square was a secret symbol that Christians could and would mentally deconstruct, knowing what it was. The deconstructed form would be this:

---

[455] This is the view of J. Gwyn Griffiths, in his article, "'Arepo' in the Magic 'Sator' Square'," in *The Classical Review*, New Series, Vol. 21, No. 1, March 1971, 6–8.

[456] This is the view of Miroslav Marcovich in his "Sator arepo = ΓΕΩΡΓΟΣ ΆΡΠΟΝ(ΚΝΟΥΦΙ) ΑΡΠΩΣ, arpo(cra), harpo(crates)," found in the *Zeitschrift für Papyrologie und Epigraphik* Bd. 50 (1983), 155-171.

[457] Henri Polge, "La fausse enigme du carre magique," *Revue de l'histoire des religions*, 1969. Vol. 175, No 2, 155-63.

[458] Duncan Fishwick, "On the Origin of the Rotas-Sator Square." *Harvard Theological Review*, 1964. Vol 57, issue 01, 39-53.

```
            P
            A
            T
  A    E    O
            R
P A T E R N O S T E R
            O
  O    S    A
            T
            E
            R
```

There is a doubly interesting implication for this pair of closely related interpretations. If we assume that both *Pater Noster* ("Our Father") and the *alpha-omega* symbolism—of God's omnipresence; the beginning and the end of the Greek alphabet serving as a statement of divine time-space ubiquity—accurately depict the beginning points for this configuration, and if we associate both of these as we might, with Christianity, then this magic square could be seen as having served as a Christian symbol, although there is no evidence to date of a Christian community at Pompeii.

More problematically, the cross that would be the starting point in each variant would be serving as a Christian symbol several centuries before the cross is otherwise known to play that role. Moreover, early Judaeans for Jesus used Greek for their prayers (as opposed to the Hebrew used by early Judaeans not for Jesus—and as opposed to Latin). Furthermore, the use of the *alpha-omega* turn of phrase first appears in the Book of Revelation—that had not yet been written by the time Pompeii was buried in lava and ash. Yet another pair of suggested possibilities includes that is was a Mithraic formulation, although without an explanation of how it would have functioned as such; or that it was Jewish (i.e., "Judaean not for Jesus") in origin. We are aware of a small but substantial number of Jews—or at least Judaeans, pre-Jewish and pre-Christian—present in Pompeii by 62 BCE, following Pompey's eastern campaigns (which had brought him to Judaea and to Jerusalem, and which ultimately led to his declaring Judaeanism a *religio licita*, as we have noted earlier). Latin-speaking—as well as Greek-speaking and Aramaic- speaking—Judaeans and subsequently Jews were familiar, of course, with Hebrew, since it was their language of prayer and liturgy.

The Latin phrase, *Pater Noster*, could well have been a translation of the Hebrew, *Aveenu*, ("our father"), which is the centerpiece of a key part of the early Judaean/Jewish prayer cycle, the *Sh'moneh Esray* ("Eighteen [Benedictions]"). The *alpha-omega* configuration had an already-present Hebrew version—*aleph-tav*, first and last letters of the Hebrew alphabet, to suggest divine totality—in Isaiah 41:4 and 44:6. One might add that in palaeo-Hebrew writing, that flourished from the eighth century BCE until the second century CE, that last letter, *tav*, was shaped like an X—a diagonalized cross. But an X-shaped cruciform is not a T-shaped cruciform and one might ask whether Judaeans not for Jesus in Pompeii knew Latin well enough to translate *Aveenu* and to construct the complex magic square with all the necessary elements when the epigraphical evidence suggests that Pompeiian Judaeans/Jews wrote in fairly poor Latin. They still might have been able to make this translation, however.

We arrive at a further question and a comment. The question pertains to the use of the magic square—assuming that it was intended as anything more than a kind of mind game. One modernist source has observed that palindromes were presumed, in antiquity, to be effective instruments against negative *daimones*; they were immune to "tampering by *daimones*" since the latter would be confused by the repetition of letters. If so, then such a multi-leveled palindrome would be a powerful instrument indeed—but should it be called "magic" or "religious"? This last rhetorical question leads to the further comment, which is that different attempts to understand the so-called "*Sator/Rotas* Magic Square" lead in three directions, again, Christian and Jewish.

None of these is definitive, but the diverse possibilities remind us from this particular amuletic angle not only how blurred the line between magic and religion was, but of how intertwined these three types of religious tradition could be and often were in the Greco-Roman world.

The matter of distinguishing religious material from magical material but even more so, the matter of placing both kinds of material into a pagan vs Jewish vs Christian spiritual framework leads us chronologically back to a series of further texts, mainly in Hebrew, that present us with definitional issues analogous to those offered by the PGM— and forward again, to Origen, Hippolytus of Rome and ancient Christian writers for whom the categories of Judaism and Christianity, or Judaism and Paganism and Christian heresy, often have blurry boundaries.

CHAPTER ELEVEN

So: Ancient Jewish *Religion* or *Magic*?

This chapter continues to address the issue with which the previous chapter began, but from a different angle: texts that are written in Hebrew and therefore fairly reliably classifiable as Jewish (Jews and Christians and pagans alike might use Greek or Latin, but it would be rare for anyone other than a Jew to be using Hebrew extensively), but which offer abundant proof of the presence and influence of Paganism within them—and thus within the esoteric, presumably non-rabbinic mainstream Judaism that is taking shape in the second through fourth centuries. The texts upon which we focus attention are the so-called *Book of Secrets*—ascribed to Noah—and the so-called *Sword of Moses*, ascribed to the consummate Israelite prophet.[459] Both date from the second through fourth centuries—the early Jewish/Christian period—and both demand reflection regarding where the lines are drawn not only between magic and religion, within the early Jewish context, but between magic and mysticism and between mysticism and normative religion. Equally significant is the discussion with which this chapter closes—by way of a modern work (1972) by John Gager, *Moses in Graeco-Roman Paganism*—of how Moses was perceived in the pagan Greco-Roman world (particularly the Roman world) as the consummate magician (as opposed to as the consummate prophet). Where, yet again, is the line to be drawn between these two terms?

One might note that the tendency to ascribe to figures like Noah and Moses esoteric wisdom offers a parallel to what Iamblichus notes in the introduction to his "response" to the "questions of Porphyry": all books of esoteric wisdom are ascribed to Hermes. Hence they are called *Books of Hermes*. That is: where in the late Greco-Roman pagan tradition Hermes, both an aspect of the *sacer* (since he is an Olympian god), but also a *sacerdos* (since he is the consummate messenger of the gods to humans—as we have seen, for example, in *Odyssey* 10), and is thus viewed as the author of works offering knowledge beyond that used in everyday life or even everyday engagement of the divine *sacer*; so in the late Judaean-early Jewish tradition, great sacerdotal—prophetic—figures like Noah and Moses, to whom God spoke directly, as consummate *sacerdotes*, come to be seen as transmitters of knowledge even beyond what is conveyed in the Bible.

---

[459] The *Sepher HaRazim* such as we have it is a reconstruction by Mordecai Margolioth, based on no less than six separate manuscripts, each of them more recent than the presumed time of the original, with some of its parts missing. See Mordecai Margolioth, ed., *Sepher HaRazim, A Newly Recovered Book from the Talmudic Period.* (Jerusalem, 1966).

Noah has a special place among biblical sacerdotal figures: he is the only righteous man within his generation (Gen 6:4) and thus the only survivor, with his family and hand-picked animals, to survive the debacle that destroys all the rest of humankind. We are expected to understand that the work ascribed to him, *The Book of Secrets* (*Sepher HaRazim*),[460]is a revealed text; it recounts its own history in its opening pages, beginning with the assertion that the angel Razi-El (his name means "secret of the Lord") spoke it directly to Noah, who wrote it down with a sapphire stone—and that, just before Noah's death, he transmitted to his son Shem, who gave it to Abraham, and so it was passed down until it reached King Solomon, proverbial Wise Man, who as a consequence became expert in all the paths of understanding.

Noah learned from the book "to know the way of death and the way of life, to understand the evil and the good, to search the seasons and the moments... to interpret dreams and visions, to arbitrate combats and mediate wars, to rule over spirits and demons so as to drive them out so they will depart like slaves... to be wise to the peals of thunder, to elaborate the causes of lightning"[461]—among other things. As for the legend-bound King Solomon, "he ruled over all of his desires, over all the spirits and demons who wander in the world. From the wisdom of this book he imprisoned (them) and released (them), sent (them) out and brought (them) back, built and prospered."[462]From Solomon it continued its transmission down through the centuries, ultimately coming down to us (the "us" reading it in the late third century CE), "for many books were handed down by him, but this one was found dearer and more honorable, albeit more difficult than any of them."[463]

The text that follows this introductory material offers an interesting combination of what might be called cosmographical description—how the heavens are laid out and their components guarded by angelic beings—and recipes for accessing the power(s) within the heavens in order to accomplish very down-to-earth ends. In other words: on the one hand the notion of a singular Divine *Sacer* essential to mainstream, normative Judaism is potentially (but not necessarily) compromised by the multiplication of heavens and the *sacer*/sacerdotal beings who govern them. It is this sort of subdivisional thinking that is fundamental to early Jewish mysticism—merkavah mysticism, so-called because its primary inspiring text is the first chapter of the Book of Ezekiel, which contains the prophet's vision of a heavenly throne/chariot, referred to as the *merkavah*—in which the heavenly realm is divided into seven lower and three upper heavens. The successful mystic is not confused by this multiplicity, because he recognizes that there is no contradiction between God as one and the realm ruled and "dwelled in" by God as sevenfold or tenfold

---

[460] The opening lines of the work suggest that it was only one of several such works offering hidden, esoteric knowledge that had been vouchsafed Noah: "This is the book *from among the books of secrets* that was given to Noah... " [emphasis added].

[461] *Sepher HaRazim*, Opening, lines 11-15. Aside from direct or adapted quotes from the so-called Wisdom literature in the Bible, particularly Ecclesiastes and Job, it might be noted that "to know the good and the evil" (*lada'at et haTov vehaRa'*) is an idiom that means to have seen all sides of an issue and thus, by extension, to know everything. When Adam and Eve eat fruit from the "tree of good and evil," one of the rabbinic interpretations of the knowledge that they gain is knowledge of everything

[462] Ibid, lines 28-9. There are many legends regarding Solomon in the aggadic side of the rabbinic canon, including those that speak of his managing to put Asmodeus in his employ in the building of the Temple. This text evinces awareness of that tradition.

[463] Ibid.

or however-many-fold. The overall *sacer* can be multi-layered even as God, who "dwells" in the most distant of these subdivisions, is absolutely singular.[464]

So a mystical element—that offers an intense examination of the *sacer* in order to gain access to God, and that emphasizes God's awesome distance from us—may be seen here. More definitionally interesting for our purposes is the combination of "higher" issues that, according to one pattern of definition that we have encountered, are characteristic of religion, with "lower" issues that we have seen associated with magic. Moreover, there is a kind of hierarchy of nuance: the higher the practitioner gets into the heavens the more speculative the material (and briefer the text), so that one moves from simple charms with very straightforward *profanus* goals to the business of interrogating and potentially controlling spirits as well as seeing into the future and ultimately finding one's self standing before the heavenly throne.

One might say that the cosmographical material reflects a religious sensibility and the rituals offering outcomes in the here and now reflect a magical sensibility, if we accept that sort of religion/magic distinction; and, further, that the lower-heaven material pertains to magical concerns and the upper-heaven material to religious concerns. One would, however, need to acknowledge how blurry the line is between the two, and it might not be easy to determine exactly where that line is drawn. Each heaven is described in terms of its angelic overseers, whose functions are in turn described and thus the purposes that they can be induced to serve is articulated, together with the instructions for how to accomplish that service in terms of both physical procedures and verbal recitations.

Those recitations, while primarily in Hebrew, together with some Aramaic, also include a certain number of Greek words and phrases. This of course brings up the other definitional question that continues to preoccupy us: how do we draw the line between the presumably overall Jewishness (because of the language and also because of the overriding sense of the Divine *Sacer* as an all-encompassing singularity, rather than multiple gods and goddesses) of this text and possible embedded pagan components? Interestingly, in the introduction to his very fine translation of the *Sepher*, Michael Morgan asserts that it "seems likely that the magic rites have here been provided with a cosmological framework intended to make them seem legitimate Jewish practices... [in part because] all the Greek words and spells, as well as the few passages or words in Aramaic are all found within the spells and practices... It is the descriptions of the heavens which contain the Biblical quotations and the flowery descriptive literature."[465]

This suggestion in a sense begs the definitional question if the answer to that question is a clear delineation between Jewish and pagan sources. Rather, the question might be: who put this text together and where and when—and was that individual Jewish or pagan? It seems likely—and this may well be what Morgan means by his comment— that this material reflects the syncretism of the era in a specific manner echoing what we

---

[464] However, the potential danger to the average Jew seeking to understand this, who might be confused by the apparent paradox of singularity/multiplicity—and therefore drop dead, go crazy or apostasize—is what pushes the rabbis to try to pull their constituents away from just this sort of speculation.

[465] Morgan's translation of Margolioth's reconstruction of the text was part of his unpublished Master's Thesis, awarded by Columbia University in 1973. It later bècame the basis for his book, Sepher Ha-Razim: *The Book of Mysteries*.

have seen from the other direction in some of the PGM material: a Jewish author (or, if one prefers, transmitter of an original Noahide text!) has been heavily influenced by the predominantly pagan world around him/her, but has embedded the material that reflects that influence into a cosmological context with an identifiable and acceptable Jewish theology beneath it. This whole matter is further complicated by the fact that the myriad angelic names are drawn not only from Hebrew but from Greek—and even a few from Persian.

From a more detailed angle, after the introductory material with its genealogy of the text, the work is divided into seven parts, each one delineating one of the seven heavens through which the seeker must ascend, aiming toward the Divine Throne.[466] Sevenness, of course, has a long history of *sacer* association, as we have observed, ultimately derived from the fact that there are seven wanderers—*planetes*—that make their way across the heavens with a reliable periodicity against the backdrop of fixed stars. That concept of sevenness translates into the creation cycle in Genesis amd the concomitant commandment in Exodus 20 and Deuteronomy 5 to keep the seventh day sacred, which in turn leads to the shaping of a seven-branched menorah in the Temple in Jerusalem. Not insignificantly for our larger discussion, seven heavens are referenced in a range of both Jewish and Christian Apocalyptic literature—for example in the Testaments of the Twelve Patriarchs and in the Slavonic version of the Book of Enoch. Circling back to the pagan world, it also translates into the heptapartite concept of hell in the Babylonian tradition and of the soul in the Egyptian tradition—and so on.

In the *Sepher HaRazim* the sevenness of the heavens is complex. The first heaven is itself subdivided into seven encampments (*mahanot*), filled with wrath, each containing a throne and an overseer on it surrounded by bands of angels. The second heaven contains twelve levels (*ma'alot*; literally "ascents"), each governed by a certain number of angels. Within these two parts we find the lion's share of the *Sepher*'s text and most of the more practical types of magic. The third heaven is governed by three head angels, each surrounded by groups of ministering angels. The fourth heaven has two parts, the one embracing the angels who guide the sun by day, and the other containing those who guide it by night. The fifth heaven is an undifferentiated unit with twelve angels, one for each month of the year (and also corresponding both to the zodiac and to the twelve-tribe configuration of Israel). The sixth has an eastern and a western section, each governed by an angel and subdivided, with angels overseeing the sub-encampments. The seventh heaven stands apart from the others, for within it is the Heavenly Throne, described in detail, which description is followed by a doxology.

Within each section there is a description of the above-referenced particular magical actions of which angels in a given heaven are capable, offered in a rather Frazerian manner: the specifics of their essential natures correspond to the specifics of their capabilities in what might be termed a homeopathic manner. Thus an angel of silence may be invoked to silence one's accusers, an angel of healing may be invoked to heal an illness, and so on. The formula for gaining angelic acquiescence to accomplish one's desired ends

---

[466] There are alternative names for the book, including *Sepher Noah* (*The Book of Noah*) and *Sepher HaMa'alot* (*The Book of Ascents*).

is typically that, if you want X, first do Y, say the names of the angels A, B, C and then say certain prescribed words. There is a strong emphasis on ritual purity and whereas the cosmological descriptions show a relationship with apocryphal literature such that associated with Enoch as well as with early merkavah mystical material, the spells and vows and oaths as well as the emphasis on ritual purity resonate with passages in mainstream rabbinic legalistic literature.[467]

So: "The name of the first firmament is *shamayim*"—which is the garden-variety word for "heavens," used in Genesis I:1. "Seven thrones are prepared there and upon them are seated seven overseers... [and] these are the names of the seven overseers who sit upon the seven thrones: The name of the first is 'Orpani-El, the name of the second is Tigrah, the name of the third is Danah-El, the name of the fourth is Kalmiya', the name of the fifth is 'Asimor, the name of the sixth is Paskar, the name of the seventh is Bo'El. All of them were created from fire and their appearance is flaming... These are the names of the angels of the first encampment who minister to 'Orpani-El: Bomdi, Dimna', 'Anok, Qetibya', Patrop, Gamti', Pe'a'or, Nerantaq, Raqhati..."—and another sixty names follow these. Some of these names, like the first two and last of the overseer names, are formed in a recognizable Hebrew that is common in angelic names (eg, 'Avi-El—"The Lord is my Father"—or Netan-El: "The Lord is My Gift"), and others, like Bomdi, (and like the other overseer names), either draw from non-Hebrew languages or seem to be gibberish names. "These are the names of the angels of the second encampment who minister to Tigrah..."—and another long list is offered. And so on regarding each of the seven encampments that comprise the first firmament.

Each group is suited to its task, (to repeat): that of the first encampment must be sought out "if you desire to perform an act of healing," for which explicit instructions are given as to what to do and what to recite—and also the reminder to "purify yourself from all impurity and cleanse your flesh from all carnality and then you will succeed."[468] The second group can serve to destroy or harm one's adversaries—and the procedure is far more complicated than that to heal, involving seven days of preparation, a more complex ritual as well as specific recitations for different specific circumstances and/or outcomes.

The angels who minister in the fourth encampment to Kalmiya' include one whose name is Qristos, which raises an obvious question. This is the precise Greek version of the term that, in English, becomes "Christ," which could lead to the supposition that the syncretism of the *Sepher* includes very specific Christian elements. On the other hand, however, the Greek term, *khristos*, and its Hebrew equivalent, *mashiah* (from which the English word, "messiah," derives), simply mean "anointed." The earlier, Hebrew biblical context connected the Israelite kings Saul and David to that term and over the course of the centuries between the time of the Assyrian debacle of 722-21 BCE and the time of Jesus, it came to be used to refer to the hoped-for descendant of the House of David who would return Israel-Judah to the kind of glory that—particularly as time moved forward and that past became increasingly distant and increasingly romanticized—the nation remembered having experienced during the reigns of David and Solomon. So imputing the name

---

[467] One find oaths and vows of the sort found in *Sepher HaRazim* in *Brakhot* 2:I, 4b; *Pesahim* 6:I, 36a; *Ketubot* 9:5; *Baba Kama* 9:7; and in *Yoma* I:5; to name a few Talmudic sites.
[468] *Sepher HaRazim*, First Firmament, ls 28-34.

"Qristos" to one of the angels could simply be a function of the syncretistic use of Greek names together with Hebrew and other names with strongly positive (and often god-related) connotations.

The angels of the fifth encampment facilitate one's ability "to speak with the moon and the stars, to question a ghost, and to speak with the spirits." Skipping to the instructions for one who would wish to question a ghost, the instruction is to "stand facing a tomb and repeat the names of the angels of the fifth encampment [there are 62 of them]. Hold in your hand a new flask containing oil and honey mixed together and say this:

> *I adjure you spirit of Krephoryia, who dwells among the graves upon the bones of the dead, that you accept from my hand this offering and do my will and bring to me X son of Y who is dead. Raise him up so that he will speak with me without fear, he will tell me words of truth without concealing anything. Let me not be afraid of him and let him answer for me the question of which I need the answer from him.*

He [the ghost] should appear immediately, but if he does not, repeat it and say the adjuration up to three times. When the ghost comes forth, place the flask before him and then speak your words while holding a twig of myrtle in your hand. When you want to release him, hit him three times with the myrtle, pour out the oil and honey, break the cup, throw the myrtle from your hand and return home by a different route."[469]

There are, then, two obvious issues for us here. The first is that the evocation is not to *Adonai* or to *El Elohim* or some other version of the Name of God as it is used by Jews, but to an Aramaicized version of a Greek name, *Kriophoros*: Ram-bearer. This is a name for Hermes, the Greek god (his Roman equivalent is Mercury) who serves as a messenger as well, sometimes, as a psychopomp—the guide and in a sense protector of souls.[470] So this Jewish text makes explicit use of a pagan concept of the divine *sacer*. Is this because the all-powerful, all-encompassing Jewish God-concept would be too distant and disinterested in this sort of personal request?

But that leads to the second issue: the nature of the request. Is it a request or a command? Since it seems to be the latter, does that help identify this as a magical rather than religious procedure? That is, not only does it deal with a lower aspect of the *sacer*, but it does so by command, not petition. This in turn might raise the question raised in Iamblichus: how is it that one imagines it possible to command a god? Might that be the reason a lesser God than *Adonai* is invoked, since one would surely not presume to command *Adonai*? But how can a Jew for whom there is no God but *Adonai* believe in other gods who might then be invoked to be either petitioned or commanded? Clearly the creator and/or user of this text has much broader views of the Divine *Sacer* than "proper"

---

[469] *Op citum*, Fifth Firmament, ls 176-186.

[470] The origin of "ram-bearer" as a Hermes epithet is obscure, but may be due to what Pausanias asserts, which is that, in the Boeotian city of Tanagra the god was credited with saving the city in a time of plague, by carrying a ram on his shoulders as he circled the city's walls. (Pausanias, *Description of Greece* 4:33.4 and 9:22.1-2). Or perhaps it comes from that thread in the tapestry of the biography of Dionysios that presents Hermes, under orders from Zeus to protect his infant son from the wrath of Hera by carrying him off temporarily disguised as a ram. Hermes would be functioning both as a kind of messenger and, more importantly, as a protector.

mainstream Judaism supposedly permits—or was Judaism simply more belief-permissive eighteen centuries ago than we might suppose?

God is invoked, on the other hand, when Its power is felt to be useful to accomplish some end. Thus in the seventh encampment, where the angels in charge of the dream are located—"to make wise anyone who approaches them in purity"— the procedure of invoking them "by the sea shore or the edge of a stream in the third hour of the night... [is that, while] look[ing] toward the water and repeat[ing] three times the name of the overseer with the names of the angels of the encampment, when [one] see[s] a pillar of fire between heaven and earth, [one is to] say thus:

> *I adjure you by the One who has measured the waters in the*
> *palm of His hand, who has rebuked the waters so that they*
> *fled from Him..."*

Thus God is invoked as back-up for the invoker, quoting directly from Isaiah 40:12 (and other biblical passages, as the recitation continues), even as the recitation is directed toward a multiplicity of angels with diversely-sourced names who will assist the invoker in interpreting difficult dreams.

Let us fast-forward in the text to the seventh *firmament*, which brings us into the primary realm associated with God, and which "contains manifold light and its light illumines all the habitations; therein the Throne of Glory [is] planted upon the four Hayyot of glory"—virtually a direct reference to that part of the *merkavah* imagery in Ezekiel I. "And therein are the treasuries of life, the treasuries of souls and the perfection of the great light within is immeasurable; the entire earth is filled from the overflowing light"—an image that resonates from the first Divine creative act in Genesis ("let there be light! and there was light...") to the Jewish mystical tradition (albeit not explicitly until its kabbalistic phase, which arrives many centuries after the time of this text).

This—presumably allegorical?—description of God's greatness continues. Thus (for example), "His soldiers are standing before Him, but they do not see His appearance for He is hidden from every eye; there is none who can see Him and live!" We are reminded, first, of the words from the vision of Isaiah in the opening lines of chapter 6, of seraphim surrounding the Divine Throne and intoning "Holy, Holy, Holy, is the Lord of armies (*Kadosh, Kadosh, Kadosh, Adonai tz'va'ot*)." We are reminded, second, of the elaborate layout of the divine army of angels described in the Qumran "Battle Scroll," who will join with the forces assisting the Good Teacher to overcome the power of the Wicked Priest and his followers. We are reminded, third, that this is a Jewish text, for which a key aspect of its theology is that it ultimately looks to a God that is invisible, whose very Glory is a circumlocution the sight of which can reduce the viewer to ashes.

"He sits upon the throne of light and surrounding Him is the power of light. The *Hayyot* and *Ophanim* bear [the throne], and they are flying with their wings, each having six wings"—a conflation of Ezekiel's vision (of *hayyot* and *ophanim*) with that of Isaiah (in which all the seraphim possess six wings). The culmination of the work, after this description of God's awesome Being, is a long hymn of praise, in which the phrase "Blessed is His Name" repeats as the opening part of each verse, and the entirety ending with the words "Blessed is the Lord forever, Amen, Amen, Selah." So the text of the Seventh firmament has, so to speak, nothing magical about it, but draws from the sources and style that we might associate with Judaism as a religion.

In the end, we are confronted with material that offers what can be called religious—and also mystical—aspects, as well as what can be called magical aspects, (assuming lines between compulsion and petition, upper *sacer*-directed and lower *sacer*-directed), but still with some blurriness: is the need to heal someone or to be protected from one's enemies and the petition to a higher *sacer* source for assistance in either of these two enterprises limited to magic? How is the Jew who prays to God inside or outside the synagogue, alone or with the congregation, that his daughter be healed of her illness, different from the Jew who consults a "magician"—and where is the line drawn between the latter and the physician whom he might consult?

We are also, if dealing with a Jewish text and Jewish practitioners here, clearly dealing with a text and its users perfectly willing to do other than pray in a traditional Jewish manner for assistance in any of the matters addressed within the *Sepher*. The question one might ask is where such a text would have emerged. The answer might well be Greco-Roman Egypt with its large Judaean/Jewish population, so much of which was deeply embedded in the world around them that was both syncretistic as far as Greek, Egyptian and other elements were concerned and also, by virtue of being in Egypt, surrounded by the most recent version of religious traditions with several thousand years behind them in which, to the outsider, the religious and magical aspects seemed both consistently blurry and/or misconstruable along the lines of "what's mine is religion; what's yours is magic."

Noah, is, of course, not the only Hebrew biblical figure who is venerated as having a particularly strong relationship with the Divine *Sacer* and therefore possessed of esoteric knowledge within the Judaean-Jewish Greco-Roman world. On the contrary, he pales in comparison with the status achieved by Moses in that realm. Perhaps the most important work outside the Torah itself that is ascribed to Moses in late antiquity is the so-called *Sword of Moses*, an essentially three-part work in a mixture of Hebrew and Aramaic. The title presumably derives from Deut 33:29, where Moses, speaking just prior to his death, blesses the Children of Israel, offering specific words to each of the tribes and concluding with the rhetorical question and statement: "Who is like unto thee, a people saved by the Lord, the shield of thy help, and that [God; God's protection] is thy sword of excellence." Moses is, by definition, the consummate articulator and translator—wielder—of that sword, and in the context of this work, is understood to have grasped the very ineffable Name of God in his having come as face-to-face with a faceless God as one can come.

The first part of the *Sword*, which serves as a kind of introduction, including the presentation of the text's divine origin, is written predominantly in Hebrew, whereas the third part, primarily focused on prescription and formulae, is dominated by Aramaic. Sandwiched between these two parts is an elaborate presentation/discussion of the ineffable divine Name(s), contrived of often complex arithmetic combinations—this is indeed the sword which, wielded properly, can yield the results upon which the third part is focused— and, while the same writing system used by both Hebrew and Aramaic is used, the language of this second part is really a kind of gobbledy-gook that would not easily or straightforwardly be defined as either language.

The work begins by invoking "the Name of the mighty and holy God"—in Aramaic, and then by immediately asserting (in Hebrew) that

> Four angels are appointed to the "Sword" given by the Lord, the Master of secrets, and they are appointed to the Torah, and they see with penetration the secrets below and above;[471] and these are their names: SKD HUZI, MRGIOIAL, VHDRZIOLO, TOTRISI.[472] And over these there are five others, holy and mighty, who meditate on the mysteries of God in the world for seven hours every day.[473]
>
> And these are appointed to thousands of thousands, and to myriads of thousands of chariots, ready to do the will of their Creator, *Ahy Hay Hayah*, the Lord of Lords and the most-honored God (of Gods); and these are their names: MHYHOGTSAY PHDOTTGM 'SQRATHOO SHTAYNAYHOOM QTGNAYPRAY. And the [Master of] each chariot upon which they are appointed wonders and says: 'Is there any number of his armies?'[474] and the least of these chariots is lord and master over those four (above). And over these are three officers of the hosts of the Lord (*Ah Yavah Vav Vav*), who everyday make His eight halls tremble and shake, and they have the power over every creature.
>
> Under them stands a double number of chariots and the least of them is lord and master over all the above rulers; and these are their names: AS'HAHAY SHATRIS HAVAYAH SHTGY'YH. And the Name of the lord and King is PSKTYAH, who sits, and all the heavenly hosts kneel, and prostrate themselves before Him daily before leaving SHL'AH HO 'OHH, who is the Lord over all.
>
> And when you conjure him he will attach himself to you, and cause the other five officers and their chariots and the lords who stand under them to attach themselves to you just as they were ordered to attach themselves to Moses, son of Amram…[475]

---

[471] Moses Gaster uses the word "mysteries" to translate the Hebrew *razim*—the same word, however, used in the title of the *Book of Secrets* (*Sepher HaRazim*) that we have previously discussed; I'll stick with "secrets." He translates as "Lord" (as I have, for the sake of convenience) what is actually a series of disconnected syllable-ized renderings of Hebrew letters: *Ah Vah Yah Hah Hayah*—plays on the tetragrammaton, *YHVH*, out of order and with the Aleph that begins the Hebrew alphabet added at the beginning of the string (therefore five letters, not four). It was Gaster who discovered a 13th-14th-century copy of the *Sword of Moses* in the British Museum. He was able to publish it, with an introduction and translation, in 1896. The tetragrammaton (Greek for "four - lettered/consonantal [Name of God]") is the basic form of God's Ineffable Name. Referred to several times previously, this is explained below, 285-6.

[472] The Hebrew and Aramaic writing systems did not use vowels in antiquity; vowels emerge later on. So we can often not know for certain how these names, unrecognizable as known names in either language (or for that matter in Greek, Latin, Egyptian, et al), would have been vocalized. The entire text, in fact, is not only written without vowels but, like the Torah, it is also without punctuation.

[473] This time, instead of *razim*, *sitrim* is used, and "God" is actually *Ahiy Hay Yahay*—again using variations on syllabalizations of letters (consonants) from the tetragrammaton, which, incidentally, are derived from the root of the verb "to be," as we shall note below in the brief discussion of Exodus 3, (see below, 267-8).

[474] To repeat a point made earlier in reference to the Qumran "Battle Scroll": the word *tz'va'ot* is traditionally and typically rendered as "hosts" but it has a military implication—hence its use in modern Hebrew as "army"—and therefore I am rendering it as "armies."

[475] The original text is without the paragraph breaks that I have imposed for greater simplicity and clarity.

This first part of the text continues by repeating what the angels had communicated to Moses, to wit that

> if you wish to use this 'Sword' and to transmit it to the following generation, [then know] that the man who decides to use it must first free himself three days previously from accidental pollution from everything unclean, eat and drink once every evening, and must eat the bread from a pure man or wash his hands first in [salt?] and drink only water; and nobody is to know that he intends to use the 'Sword,' as therein are the mysteries of the universe, and they are practiced only in secret, and are communicated only to the chaste and pure. On the first day when you retire from [the world], bathe once and no more, and pray three times daily, and after each prayer recite the following blessing: 'Blessed are thou, QUSIM, O Lord our God, King of the universe, who opens the gates of the East and cleaves the windows of the firmament of the East, and gives light to the whole world and its inhabitants, with the multitude of His mercies, with His mysteries and secrets, who teaches Thy people Israel Thy secrets and mysteries, and have revealed unto them the 'Sword' used by the world... Unto Thee I call, *Ah Yavah Vav Vav*, Lord of the Universe, Thou are He who is called *Ah Yavah Vav Vav*, King of the Universe. Thou art called *Ah Yavah Vav Vav*, merciful King. Thou art called *Ah Yavah Vav Vav*, gracious King [nine more such formulaic descriptives follow, and then] Thou art called *Ah Yavah Vav Vav* and Thou hear my prayer, for Thou hearkenest unto prayer; and attach unto me Thy servants, the lords of the 'Sword'...

—after which introductory formulation the practitioner is to continue directly addressing the officers of the Lord's armies, beginning with the words: "I conjure you, Azliel called [gobbledy-gook], Ariel called [gobbledy-gook], Ta'aniel called [gobbledy-gook], Tafel called [gobbledy-gook], and the most glorious of these, Yofiel Mittron called [gobbledy-gook], the glory from above."[476] More of these beings with angelic names are conjured with the injunction that they all "attach yourselves to me and surrender the 'Sword' to me, so that I may use it according to my desire...; that you deliver unto me with this 'Sword' the secrets from above and below, the mysteries from above and below, and my wish be fulfilled and my words hearkened unto...Blessed are Thou, who understands the secrets and reveals the mysteries, and art King of the universe."

This lengthy prescribed invocation—it is implicitly delivered to the practitioner in the second person, but couched in the third person as describing what had been originally delivered to Moses as a prescribed invocation—is then followed by a further description of what Moses experienced, that Moses himself is depicted as recounting:

> A voice was heard in the heavens, the voice of the Lord of heavens, saying: "I want a light [swift] messenger [to go] to man and if he fulfills

---

[476] It is surely not accidental that the meaning of the last of these five figures is "Beauty (*yofi*) of the Lord (*El*)."

my message my sons will become proud of the 'Sword' that I hand over to them, which is the head of all the mysteries of which my seers have also spoken, that thus will my word be, as it is said: 'Is not my word like as fire?' saith the Lord" [Jer. 23:29] ...and the Lord over all commanded me: "Go and make this known to men who are pious and good and righteous and faithful..." I thus stood up...

This is the great and glorious Name that has been given as a tradition to Man—'HVH,[477] holy, glorious, glorious, selah. Recite after your prayers. And these are the names of the angels who minister to the son of man: MITTRUN, SGRDTSIH, MQTTRUN [and 25 other names]... and I adjure in His [God's] Name... His servants sanctify Him and praise Him with sweet melody, and say "Holy, holy, holy is the Lord of holy Name; the whole earth is full of His glory!" ...and I conjure you by this Ineffable Name, such as it was revealed to Moses by the mouth of the Lord over all, [gobbledy-gook], the Lord *Sabaot* is His Name.

This first part concludes with the instruction to

write with ink on leather and carry about with you during these three days of purification, and invoke before and after prayer the following Names communicated to Moses by MRGIIEL [and the other 12 officers listed at the outset, followed by a long string of gobbledy-gook names that were communicated to Moses]. For they have not hidden from him any of these sacred ineffable names of letters... these Names that constitute the mysteries of this 'Sword'; and they said to him: 'Command the generations that will come after you to say the following blessing prior to their prayer, lest they be swept away by the fire: "Blessed art thou, [gobbledy-gook], who was with Moses; be Thou also with me, Thou whose Name is 'HVH. Send me [gobbledy-gook], who is the cover of the Cherubim, to help me. Blessed art Thou, lord of the Sword."

Whoever is desirous of using this 'Sword' must recite his usual prayers, and at the passage "thou hearkenest to prayer," say: "I conjure you four princes..."

And he is not to touch this 'Sword' until he has done these things; afterwards he will be able to do whatever he likes, everything being written here following in its proper order.

After this lengthy and somewhat repetitive instruction regarding how to properly prepare one's self for the use of the 'Sword' in this first part, the second part offers the 'Sword'

---

[477] Since the tetragrammaton was and is typically vocalized as *Adonai*—although we cannot be certain exactly how early that circumlocutionary tradition began—then this may explain why the text offers AHVH instead of YHVH; that and, perhaps—*perhaps*—because this text is not a prayer offered in a standard religious service context and (again we cannot be certain when this tradition began) a traditional Jew only says "God," "Lord" (that is, their Hebrew equivalents, *Adonai* and *El/Elohim*), when reciting a standard religious prayer, precisely so as not even to utter those circumlocutions of the Ineffable Name in an insufficiently sacerdotal context). In any case, the full exfoliation of that Ineffable Name given in the *Sword* at this moment is something like IH BIH ATZ AH BAH HUI HU HU UH IA HU ZH UH UH AH IH IHU HH IHU IHU AQO HI HH HAH HH HAH HUAH HHUA HII HU HU HI—which intersperses the two root consonants of the Name—H H—individually and together, with all available vocalic combinations and permutations...

itself. The 'Sword' is a long series of largely unpronounceable or barely pronounceable (ineffable and certainly, as Gaster states, mysterious) Names of God and also of the various angelic officers, and the basic formula for using the Names and their power. Thus one recites: "With these your Names, and with the powers that you possess, like which there is nowhere anything, show me and search for me, and bring me So-and-So to do all my bidding in the name of X." Another list of names follows, from which to choose which one should be used in lieu of the "X" in a given situation. After the list of 134 such Names (the last seven are followed by HVYH—in other words, a jumbled form of the tetragrammaton), there is a concluding prayer/incantation to be recited:

> You sacred angels, princes of the armies of YHVH, who stand upon the thrones prepared for them before him to watch over and minister to the 'Sword'... you chiefs of all the angels in the world... I beseech you to do everything that I am asking of you, as you have the power to do everything in heaven and on earth in the name of YHVH, as it is written in the Torah: "I am the Lord, this is My Name!"

And so, onto part three, which articulates the actual instructions of what to do in the various particular instances where some outcome is desired. There are 136 of these and they range in ambition and thus specifics of whom to approach among the figures adumbrated in the previous two parts. They may have a singular goal or multiple goals. The first, for instance, informs the practitioner that "if at full moon, a man wishes to unite a woman with a man that they should be as one to one another, or to destroy winds [i.e., spirits], *daimones* and *satans* [literally: opposers], or to stop a ship, or to free a man from prison and for every other thing, then write on a red bowl from Tobar, and [address yourself to Tobat, and the others named in part two on the first list of Names, reciting the words indicated in part two (with these your Names, and with the powers that you possess... etc]."

On the other hand, the second prescription is for one desirous of "break[ing] mountains and hills, to pass dryshod through the water, to enter the fire, to appoint and to depose kings, to blind eyes, to stop the mouth, to speak to the dead, and to kill the living, to bring down and send up and to conjure angels to hearken unto [the practitioner], and to see all the mysteries in the world," who must write down the first two lists of Names from part two "upon the saucer of a cup and put in it the root of the juniper tree." Very different in ambition is Number 9, "for pains in the ear [against which one must] whisper in the painful ear" the Names from list number 9; so, too, Number 10 is (merely!) "for aches in the eye," for which one says those names in list number 10 "over water three days running in the morning and wash the eye with [that water]." Number 28 is "for a woman who has seen [menstrual] blood before the time, [for which you should] say [the Names in number 28] over an ostrich egg, then burn it, and she must be smoked with it." Number 42 is for a woman who has had a miscarriage: you recite the contents of Name-list 42 "over a cup of wine or strong drink, or water, and let her drink it for seven days; and even if she should see blood and she repeats it over a cup of wine, the child will live." Number 43 is for a man wishing to cure his baldness, but number 44 is to conjure a spirit, for which one should "write on a laurel-leaf: 'I conjure you, prince whose name is *Abraxas*, in the name of [the

Name-list 44] that you come to me and reveal to me all that I ask of you, and you shall not tarry.' And the one bound by you will come down and reveal himself to you."[478]

Number 46 offers a cure for leprosy, involving ablutions and a prayer/incantation—since it ends with the words "Amen, Amen, Selah" does that make it more of a prayer than an incantation? Number 55 is no surprise—sooner or later, love issues seem to be inevitably taken up with this sort of material: "If you want a woman to follow you, take your blood and write her name upon a newly-laid egg and say [the Names of list 55]." Conversely (number 68): "If you wish to kill a man, take mud from the two sides of the river and from it into the shape of a figure, and write upon it the name of the person, and take seven branches from seven strong palm-trees and make a bow from a reed(?) with the string of horse-sinew, and place the image in a hollow, and stretch the bow and shoot with it, and at each branch [i.e., shot arrow] say the words of [number 68, which is one of several composite names, together with the words] 'may So-and-So be destroyed." Number 77 prescribes that "if you wish to curse anyone, say in the 'Eighteen benedictions,' [the Names of list 77], in the name of So-and-So." "For a field that does not produce fruits [this is Number 102], take eight cups from eight houses and fill them with water from eight rivers, and put salt into them from eight houses and say over them [the Names from list 102] eight times, and pour two cups at each corner, and break them on eight paths." Number 125 pertains to one who wishes "to walk upon water without wetting the feet," for which one should "take a leaden plate and write upon it [the Names from list 125] and place it in one's girdle and then one can walk."

And so on. The end of part three offers the catch-all that "for every other thing that has not been mentioned, say [the Names in list 136, the last list] to the end of the 'Sword,' followed by the injunction that,

> upon every amulet that you write from the 'Sword' write first: 'In the name of the Lord of all the holy ones, may this 'Sword' be effective in accomplishing my services, and may the Lord of it approach to serve me, and may all these powers be delivered over to me so that I am able to use them, as they were delivered to Moses, the son of Amram, perfect from his God and no harm befalling him!'

This text provokes a number of observations and questions that are by now familiar to us. One can see, both by the range of its intended uses and by the nature of its invocations that can be distinguished from but incorporates elements from mainstream Judaism-as-a-religion within its bounds. Thus for instance the inclusion several times of the "Eighteen Benedictions"—we noted its usage for #77, but it appears elsewhere, as well—marks the inclusion of part of the most basic elements of the standard Jewish liturgy. Indeed, as we leaf through various among the 136 sets of instructions intended to serve their diverse purposes, we observe how the speaking of *words* certainly blurs the line, if there is one, between prayer and incantation (and thus between the categories religion and magic), and also between command and petition (and thus also, between the categories at

---

[478] Concerning *Abraxas/Abrasax*, see above, fnn #424, 432.

least of Jewish religion and magic)—whereas the accompanying *actions* all fall squarely outside standard Jewish religious practice (although occasional *aspects* of the actions, like purifying ablutions do not) and thus might be termed magical.

But as elsewhere, so here we might ask where the line is to be drawn between magic and medicine, since any number of the hoped-for outcomes pertain to curing maladies. And given the inherent size of the ambitions associated with actions like stopping a ship, or breaking mountains and hills, or walking dryshod through water, and accordingly, the scale and power of the Divine *Sacer* that one must invoke to accomplish such ends (the same could be argued, perhaps, with curing baldness, or causing a woman to fall in love with someone) raises the question of line-drawing with regard to higher versus lower aspects of the *sacer*. But then how *Jewish* is this invocation of such diverse powers within the *sacer* when the latter in its Divine aspect is understood to be singular in Judaism?

That part of the answer is relatively simple: if we may claim that mainstream rabbinic Judaism, theoretically, is insistently and rigorously focused on a single element within the Divine *Sacer*—thus distinguishing itself from the array of Paganisms among which it operates, and also, perhaps, from triune Christianity, which rabbinic Judaism might see as insufficiently rigorous in this matter—it nonetheless seems that Judaism more broadly and Jews more broadly were quite willing to turn away from that insistent rigor to accomplish certain ends. We *might* term that turn as a twisting away from Jewish religion proper and toward Jewish magic.

There would seem to be little doubt, in fact, that this text is Jewish, given its language—although there are the occasional turns of phrase or names that suggest at least some interest from other sources. Thus might the phrase "son of man" that appears in paragraph eight of the *Sword* reflect a Christian sensibility? Might the second part in the name Yofiel Mittrun referenced early in the second part be a name derived from Mithras? There are occasional, somewhat subtler suggestions of syncretistic thinking. Thus there is explicit reference to Jeremiah 22:29 in the second part shortly after the transition from a long invocation to a narrative ("A voice was heard in the heavens… 'Is not my world as fire?' saith the Lord"). Forty lines or so later, a quote from Isaiah 6:4, however, is approximate: Holy, holy, holy is the Lord of the Name"—rather than "Holy, holy, holy, the Lord of armies (hosts)." Moreover, the word for "armies/hosts"—*tz'va'ot*—is rendered a few lines later as *Sabaot*, which is the same sort of apparent conflation between "Sabbath" and "*tzva'ot*" that we have seen in use in pagan texts.

The issue of language as an identity-determining and definition-shaping factor is not just the issue of which language(s) is/are in use, but the fact that the entire text centers around the notion of God's Ineffable Name(s). There are two aspects of this that are relevant to our discussion. The first, as alluded to in fn #478, is that the very name of God is deemed both impossible to say—since there is no clarity, without vowels, as to how, exactly, to articulate it—and it would be sacrilegious to pronounce it if one could, since that knowledge and that right were limited to the High Priest in the Temple when the Temple still stood (and, to repeat, the Temple was destroyed in 70 CE). Exactly when this notion developed we cannot say for sure, nor can we say for certain when the cognate notion emerged that, with the advent of the messiah that knowledge and that right will re-emerge, out of the mouth of the messiah. Hence the various levels of circumlocution to which we have referred: not only is YHVH read and said as *Adonai*, but outside of prayer contexts *Adonai* is recast as *HaShem* (literally: "the Name") or takes some other form. Exactly when this custom began, to repeat, we also cannot know for sure.

Moreover—and this is the second aspect of ineffability—at some point (again, exactly how early we cannot know for certain) an extended exploration of the idea of the circumlocutionary divine Name begins. We do not see much of this in the garden-variety, everyday sort of mainstream Judaism and its texts, but it will become a mainstay of Jewish mysticism. This second aspect is connected to the fact that Hebrew is one of those languages (Greek, by the way, is another; the Latin alphabet, certainly as it used to write English, is not) in which each and every letter is also treated as a number, or rather, has a numerical value. Thus the first letter, *aleph* = 1, the second, *bet* = 2, the tenth, *yud* =10, the eleventh, *kaf* = 20, the twelfth, *lamed* = 30, and so on. The last five of the twenty-two letters of the Hebrew all-consonantal alphabet—*'ayin, quf, resh, shin, tav*—equal 90, 100, 200, 300 and 400 respectively. The outcome of this numerological handling of the alphabet is, among other things, that the combinations of letters that, say, make up God's Name can lead in different conceptual directions because the number-value summary of those letters coincides with certain important ideas.

Thus YHVH, for instance, "adds up" to 26. But those who focus on the numerological significance of God's Name readily recognized, further, that if one systematically reduced its basic consonantal elements—to YHV, YH and finally Y—then the outcome of 21, 15, and 10 added to the initial 26 would yield 72. That number becomes one of the most important numbers used to express the Ineffable Name of God by instead using a number, and because it is arrived at by a gradual and systematic exfoliation of the actual Name (Itself, I remind us, already ineffable in its basic tetragrammaton form), it is referred to as the *Shem* (Name) *HaM'forash* (expounded/expanded).

There is more to this of course. The number of 72 is arrived at, arithmetically, along any number of paths. One is 6 x 12—and six is the number of the days of creation and also the number of Hebrew words in the most basic credo in Judaism: "Hear O Israel the Lord Our God the Lord is One" (*Sh'ma Yisrael Adonai Eloheinu Adonai Ehad*); twelve is the number of Israelite tribes. Thus 72 symbolizes the relationship between Jews and God, in brief. Moreover, the very nature of God, particularly as a salvational figure—the consummate salvational figure—in Israelite-Judaean-Jewish history is conveyed by that number. Why? Because Exodus 14:19-21, in the context of the ultimate divine salvational act—the opening up of the Sea of Reeds for the Israelites and its closing over the pursuing Egyptians—offers three successive verses each of which possesses precisely 72 letters (consonants). And since all of the Torah is God's word and since no word of God can be accidental or incidental, this datum must have significance in assisting the Israelites and their spiritual descendants, the Jews, in engaging God with maximum effectiveness. "Seventy-twoness" must be a hidden, secret (mystical) expression of God in God's salvational aspect.

Other versions of the *Shem haM'forash* may also be found, ranging from other letter-combinations that add up to other numbers—42 is a particularly commonly used one, (discussed by the second-century rabbi, Rab, in the talmudic Tractate *kiddushin*, fol 71a)— to the notion that, if one were to recite the entire Torah from the first letter of Genesis to the last letter of Deuteronomy, in one breath, one would be pronouncing the Ineffable Name of God. This kind of thinking is important within Jewish mysticism, whereas everyday, garden-variety Jews would not be drawn to it. The mystic, however, is always looking for hidden—the Greek word *mysterion*, from which the word mysticism is derived, means "closedness" and by extension "hiddenness")—clues as to how to grasp God's essence, God's innermost hiddenmost essence, and thus to a more fully interpenetrating relationship with God.

Later on, as Jewish mysticism continues to evolve, there will develop other modes of articulating the *Shem haM'forash*, pertaining to systematic switches of Hebrew letters. Thus, for instance, *ATBa'SH* works by substituting the last letter (*Tav*) for the first (*Aleph*), the penultimate (*Shin*) for the second, (*Bet*), and so on. Variations on this kind of exchange (the process would be called *tzeruf* in medieval Kabbalah) were also practiced, such as substituting the twelfth letter (*lamed*) for the first, the thirteenth (*mem*) for the second, and so on—and one notes the significance of using the twelfth as a starting point; or a given letter for the one that immediately precedes it in the alphabetic order. A more complex variation on this idea is *AHaS BaTaN*, in which the eighth (*het*) *and* fifteenth (*sameh*) letters stand for the first, the ninth (*tet*) *and* sixteenth ('*ayin*) stand for the second, and the tenth (*yud*) *and* seventeenth (*pay*) stand for the third, and so on. Thus God's Ineffable Name could be written in many different ways while never actually being written, since other letters would be used to substitute and stand for *YHVH* (which is, I repeat yet again, in and of Itself, Ineffable)—and any of these variant substitute names would constitute a particular version of the *Shem haM'forash*.

The underlying idea that places particular emphasis on God's Name, while focusing on a range of words and phrases, is that the name of a being is understood to convey his/her essence. This is a widespread conviction, and not only in antiquity, although one finds the idea strongly expressed in the Greco-Roman era that is our focus. Thus, for example, when Odysseus returns home disguised by Athena as an old beggar, and his old nurse is told (in *Odyssey* 19) by his wife (unsuspecting, due to his disguise) to offer the old man hospitality, the nurse begins by rolling up his rags in order to wash his feet and legs. When she sees the scar above his knee she nearly collapses, because she realizes from that distinctive mark that the old beggar is in fact Odysseus. The narrative pauses to explain how he got the scar (as a child, hunting boar at his grandfather's farm, in which, being who he is, he outdistanced the grown-ups and got to and killed the boar—that simultaneously gored him in the leg, and the wound left a life-long scar), and thus offers an etymology of his name. It is said to derived from the Greek verb, *odyein*, meaning "to give or receive pain."

The text clarifies, then, that Odysseus' name and essence are the same: he is the long-suffering (one of his most frequently used epithets) hero who has spent ten years at war and another ten struggling against the god Poseidon himself to get home. And everyone who has had any contact with him—from his wife and son to his mother and father to Polyphemus to Kirke and Kalypso to the Trojans to his entire crew, (not a single one of whom survives the journey)—has been the emphatic recipient of pain at his hands. So his name conveys his essence, what he is most fundamentally about, and there is a sense in which, when I say "Odysseus" he (and all that he connotes) is in the room with me—and yet, it is not exactly the same as if he were to actually walk, physically, into the room.

But what of the substanceless, intangible, invisible God? We get the answer, as Moses does, in Exodus 3, when in response to the prophet's query as to the name of the Being that has communicated Itself to him, God responds: *Ehyey Asher Ehyeh*: I am/will be that am/will be. At first glance God might seem to be coy, responding to the question with a non-answer, but then one realizes that, on the contrary, God is being straightforward. It is as if God says to Moses: "you cannot box me in, define me, with a Name, the way humans are thusly defined and boxed in.[479] I am pure being—*isness itself*—without beginning and end [hence the imperfective form of the Hebrew verb, which I have translated as "am/will be"]; and indeed the very root of my Ineffable Name, YHVH, is 'to be'." So God has in fact answered Moses' question—"I and my Name are Isness itself," while explaining that it is impossible to truly know God's Name, as it is impossible to know fully God's essence or thus to know God Itself as it is impossible to really know pure "isness/being."

All of this leads us in several directions. One—the most obvious—is that the *Sword of Moses*" is centered on and obsessed with names and with the idea of God's Ineffable Name, which makes sense as a Jewish text that seeks to access a connection to God's power to accomplish its 136 potential ends. For there is a paradoxic sense in Jewish mysticism, that, to grasp the Name would be to have access to God's power, and the various circumlocutionary forms of the *Shem haM'forash*, as Gaster recognizes in his introduction, in spite of God's fundamental ungraspability, "took the place of the Ineffable mystical Name and were credited with the selfsame astounding powers.... The heavens were moreover peopled at a very early age with numberless angels arranged in a hierarchical order and each endowed with a special name, the knowledge of which was no less desirable for working miracles."[480]

To support this contention, Gaster references the Book of Enoch, ch 2—which he assumes is written in the last few Judaean centuries—with its long list of angelic names, and also the treatise associated with Dionysius the Areopagite that speaks of these angelic hosts in detail. If the Book of Enoch to which he refers (for we now know of three different versions, in three different languages and each dated differently from the other two) does indeed date from the second pre-Christian century—i.e., the Judaean period—it also incidentally raises the question of whether the idea of angelic hierarchies with a plethora of names associated with them moves from Judaeanism directly into Judaism or Christianity or both.

Thus a second direction in which we are led is to note that, as much as the *Sword* may be considered a Jewish text, it not only offers the occasional evidence of non-Jewish influence, through particular names or concepts that may come from the pagan or Christian worlds, as previously noted—and this could include the question of who influenced whom in the matter of hordes of specific angelic names—but the inclusion of an interest in

---

[479] We might keep in mind that the word "define" derives from the Latin root, *fin*-, meaning "boundary"—so to define something is to put a boundary around it, separating what is inside it from what is outside it; what pertains to it from that which does not pertain to it.

[480] Gaster, *Sword*, introduction, 8

numerology at least runs on a parallel track to that interest among those Greeks who follow a Pythagorean course of thinking. Pythagorean teaching placed considerable emphasis on numerology, and there may be many aspects of this that were picked up by the Judaeans and their Jewish descendants that mainly show up in the Jewish mystical tradition. We have also seen that numbers play an important role in the Qumran literature, especially in the so-called "Battle Scroll"—and in fact the *Sword*, among its eclectic possible sources of influence offers echoes of that text as well, since the *Sword* discusses various details regarding the armies/hosts of the Lord that will be used in the service of the Moses-emulating practitioner.

This brings up a third direction in which the *Sword* points us, that of a familiar definitional question: where are the lines drawn among Jewish, Christian and pagan labels for a text—in this case we can be pretty comfortable calling it Jewish, while recognizing other inputs and also recognizing how it broadens what may have been our prior view of what early Jews believed and what they practiced. At least some of them. But more to the point of definitional issues, the fourth direction is to ask not only where the line is drawn between mainstream, garden-variety religion and magic, but where it is drawn between mysticism and magic? Presumably whereas mysticism shares the same fundamental understanding of the Divine *Sacer* offered in mainstream religion, albeit presenting an intensified version of that understanding and an intensified sense of possibility and method for gaining access to the divine *sacer*—and to a hiddenness within it that the mystic believes remains inaccessible to garden-variety believers—magic offers different, presumably more selfish as well as more basic, everyday methods and different goals. Or at least that is a distinction that we have frequently encountered.

It is a truism of Jewish mysticism that the goal of the practitioner is both to become one with the *mysterion*, thereby gaining a transcendent esoteric *gnosis* that carries beyond ordinary knowledge, and to *return* from that experience and with that esoteric knowledge improve the community around him. Magic of whatever denominational sort has consistently presented itself—or been defined for us by various individuals, both ancient and modern—as seeking hidden knowledge that will yield more limited and down-to-earth results than those associated with *tikkun olam* (repairing the world). We have encountered the notion that magic deals with lesser, lower and religion with greater, higher aspects of the divine *sacer*; magic would be the opposite not only of religion but of mysticism as an intensified subset of religion.

The use on amulets of various forms of the *tzeruf* subset of articulating the *Shem ham'forash* reminds us that methods put into use by the mystic to seek a deep interface with the divine *mysterion* were put into use by practitioners seeking to offer down-to-earth protective services for their clients. Much later on, in fact—and we have briefly noted above and shall briefly reiterate—Jewish mysticism, as it evolved into the later phases of its kabbalistic period toward *hassidut*, would distinguish between "esoteric kabbalah" and "practical kabbalah" in which the latter is pre-occupied with the sort of ground-level miracle-making of the sort that peppers the *Sword* and other "magical" texts from the

Greco-Roman period.[481] So our definitional parameters, as we shall see, will not suddenly become clearer as we emerge from antiquity into subsequent eras.

As the *Sword of Moses*, then: there is certainly a good deal to associate it and its claims not only with magic in various broad senses, but specifically with what we have seen Frazer call homeopathic magic, both in the repeated correlations between "types" of *sacer* beings and their individual names and the outcome that the practitioner seeks, and in any number of processes, most obviously practices such as that exemplified in number 68, where one destroys one's enemy by shaping an effigy of him out of mud and destroying it according to a prescribed procedure. We have also earlier encountered the idea that magic claims to be able to compel *sacer* forces whereas religion is always and only about petitioning. Does the *Sword* claim that knowledge of its elements can yield to petition or to compulsion—or both? Given some of its curative intentions it also again raises the question of where to draw the line between magic and medicine. It offers a combination of words and actions—are those words prayers or incantations?

The first lines of Gaster's introduction to his 1896 translation present magic as either "part of the religion of the country, as was the case in ancient Egypt and Babylon and as it is now in some forms of Buddhism (Tibet), or lived an independent life side by side with the recognized religion... The belief in the witch and the wizard, and their powerful filters and charms, holds still stronger sway upon human imagination than appears at first sight."[482] We might note that he does not offer an account of magic's attributes that separate it from religion. What parts of Egyptian or Babylonian religion, exactly, are magical? And is the apparent distinction within them apparent to Egyptians and Babylonians, or only to outsiders—Christians and Jews, for instance—who see some of their practices as magical because of the nature of the gods that are addressed by them, which are not considered legitimate aspects of the divine *sacer* by Christians and Jews? If magic is *part* of religion, is it religion as opposed to magic that *contrasts* with religion?

Appositely, he speaks of the Egyptian exorciser as "pretend[ing] to constrain the god to obey his wishes and to give effect to his invocation if called by his true name; while in Chaldaea [Babylonia] the mysterious Name was considered a real and divine being, who had a personal existence, and therefore exclusive power over the gods of a less elevated rank, over nature, and the world of spirits." So his view is—for reasons that are not stated, but presumably derive from the same sort of pre-conceptions evinced by Malinowski, Levi-Strauss, et al, regarding traditions that are non-Abrahamic, or perhaps even not Judaeo-Christian—that the practitioner (like Quesalid and his colleagues in Levi-Strauss' narrative)[483] is only pretending to have contact with and/or control over aspects of the divine *sacer*. What is odd is that while he construes the Egyptian practitioner as pretending, he construes the Babylonians to really believe—in the power of certain divine names, in a manner analogous to that conviction in the Jewish tradition. This adds a new wrinkle to our definitional quilt: whether magical or religious, truly believing versus only pretending to believe.

---

[481] See above, 240, and below, 373.
[482] Gaster, *Sword*, Introduction, 3.
[483] See above, 23-25

In Egypt, in fact, Gaster adds, "even if the exorcisers did not understand the language from which the Name was borrowed, they considered it necessary to retain it in its primitive form, as another word would not have the same virtue... The use of such unintelligible words can be traced in Egypt to a very great antiquity."[484]The notion, however, that one must not alter a ritual, whether its physical or its verbal parts, without risking at least its failure to accomplish its purpose and at worst the production of a negative outcome, is a universal principle. Precision of time, place and circumstance, as we have noted at the outset of our own discussion, is essential to the success of *religio*, and given the inherent neutrality of the *sacer* toward the *profanus* and its potential to operate in either a positive or a negative manner—so it is odd or at least interesting that Gaster writes as if this care or its deeply ancient sources are something unique to the Egyptians.

The question of how to distinguish among magic, religion and mysticism (and medicine) remains unanswered as Gaster observes how in "the Middle Ages... magical art and practice were ruthlessly persecuted by the Church, and the [Church] Councils teem with denunciations against the work of the Evil One."[485] We can infer from this next comment that he associates magic, or understands the Church to associate it, with satanic opposition to proper, God-focused and good-centered religion—even if he had noted a few lines earlier that there are both "white or beneficial and black or evil magic" (which he refers to as a "peculiar subdivision") in various traditions. "Moreover, [magic] was connected to a certain degree with the teachings and practices of the various heretical sects, and the pursuit was anything but harmless."

So we may infer, although Gaster does not say this outright, that his understanding (or, again, at least his understanding of the Church's understanding) of magic is that it offers a negative engagement of the divine *sacer* as opposed to religion's positive engagement. We have already seen how that sort of dichotomy fails, not least of all because of so-called white magic as a category. We are at the edge of yet another definitional matter—heresy—for the significance for us of Gaster's offhand and unexplicated comment will in any case become apparent subsequently (in chapter twelve) when we consider Hippolytus of Rome and Origen, and when we also read Ramsay MacMullen and A.A. Barb and their discussions of heresy and also, incidentally, of Judaism vis-à-vis Christianity.

Gaster notes that the Gnostics offered a "spiritual interpretation with which they invested the forms and formulas of Magic... and especially those that lived in Egypt and Palestine adopted all the ideas that were floating about and transferred them into their system of superior Gnosis," so he associates Gnosticism both with syncretistic thinking and with presenting a kind of hybrid between magic and religion, although he does not offer details beyond noting that Gnostic teachings offered the means for the masses "to defend themselves against the attacks of unseen evil spirits, and to the more speculative minds it afforded a clue to the mystery of the universe."

He also notes how Gnosticism would provide a key antagonist to the early Church and would therefore be on the receiving end of both diatribes and (successful) efforts to

---

[484] *Sword*, Introduction, 6-7.
[485] Ibid, 4

destroy their (Gnostics') writings—a point that will also become significant for our own discussion when we arrive into chapter thirteen of this narrative, but it is the magic/religion category matrix that interests us for the moment, for Gaster goes on to reference magical papyri from Egypt concerning which he observes that "the very nature of a mystic formula prevents it from ever begin radically changed… [for] any change in *that* form would immediately destroy its efficacy [Gaster's italics]."[486] This is a point well taken, but his non-distinction between "magic" and "mystic" should reinforce for us the problem of definition as we have been encountering it all along.

Further, "…with the change of religion the charms also undergo changes, not in the form but in the name of the divinities invoked." This important point, which he illustrates with "a modern example"—a charm against the evil eye the form of which does not change but which invokes the name of Christ or of a saint in a Christian context, of Muhammad in a Muslim context, and of an angel or one of God's Names in a Jewish context—offers a distinction among religions but further muddies the religion/magic question since one might ask whether such charms are magical or religious in these three traditions that share in common the notion of the Divine *Sacer* as singular and all-powerful as well as all-good.

The manuscript that Gaster had at his disposal is dated, by his account, from the thirteenth or fourteenth century, albeit a copy from a much more ancient text—his manuscript (British Museum Cod. Heb., Gaster, 178) is filled with the copyist's errors and the evidence of his confusions—that he dates to the first four centuries CE. Its intended users were presumably Jews, as we have previously suggested, albeit Jews who were as comfortable with Paganisms as the creators and users of the so-called Greek Magical Papyri were with Jewishisms. What might most distinctly cause the *Sword* to stand out as Jewish rather than Christian *or* pagan, even before its contents are perused, would at first glance be the fact that it is ascribed to Moses, as his divinely-instructed sword; we might suppose that a Christian or a pagan would turn to a different figure for this kind of specialized esoteric instruction, for that would certainly be true in later centuries. But for this text in its time, our supposition would be wrong.

For what makes Moses interesting for our purposes is not merely the fact that such a work is ascribed to him or associated with his name, or that the text is syncretistic in a manner reminiscent of the *PGM*, among others and thus further symptomatic of a world in which the Divine *Sacer* was addressed from different sides of the sectarian fence not by remaining on a particular side of the fence but by reaching over and integrating elements from the other side onto one's own side, whether that side be Jewish, Christian or pagan. While all of this is significant, what makes Moses so particularly interesting is the manner in which he was viewed from the pagan side of the fence.

Moses' might as a transformer of natural elements by means of supernatural assistance—so mighty was he that he dwarfed the Egyptian masters at that exercise—that in the Greco-Roman pagan world of magical practice, as it moved through its emphatically syncretistic phases from the early Hellenistic period to the near-end of antiquity, he came

---

[486] Ibid, 5

287

to be regarded as just that: the consummate magician. This point was first made in a small but important book written by John Gager entitled *Moses in Greco-Roman Paganism*.[487]

Gager in fact points in particular to the *PGM* as a source for his assertion, and so, guided by him, we return briefly to that material, picking up from that specific discussion within the previous chapter. Gager points out places in the *PGM* where Moses figures prominently. He notes that, in *PGM* V, 108-18, Moses is himself the speaker, who addresses God and asserts: "I am Moses, your prophet, to whom you committed your mysteries that are celebrated by Israel... Listen to me! I am the messenger of Phapro Osoronnophris. This is your authentic name which was committed to the prophets of Israel [ellipsis added]."[488] For Gager, appropriately, the main issue is the prominent position of Moses in this erstwhile pagan text. For us it is both that issue and also the fact that the charm is dedicated to "Osiris the Headless," which means that it is essentially a pagan text—to which the fact that Moses refers to himself as the messenger of Phapro Osoronnophris lends further substance—but a text into which a distinctly Judaean/Jewish element has been embedded. The context also suggests that that element, Moses, is viewed as a most significant figure for divine/*sacer*-human/*profanus* intermediation.

This passage further helps to incidentally blur the line religion/magic line, since Moses is a key figure in the Judaean/Jewish (and Christian) religion(s), whereas here he is being utilized in what has been construed not only as pagan but as a magical text. Then again, of course, the construal is a modern one—by Preisendanz, Luck, Gager and everyone else who simply accepts all of the *PGM* texts as Greek *magical* papyri without considering the possibility that any of them might be considered *religious* texts (in this case, however, Egyptian and not Greek—albeit Greek and Egyptian are synthesized in the Hellenistic period, so in a sense, both) by their intended users. All of which brings the matter back to the religion/magic distinction along lines of method, purpose and mine-versus-yours.

As for the Judaean/Jewish/(Christian) versus Pagan nature of *PGM* V and/or its inherently syncretistic nature, Gager continues, by quoting the lines previous to those just quoted:

> I call you the headless one, who created earth and heaven, who created night and day, you who created light and darkness. You are Osoronnophris, whom no one has ever seen, you are Iabas, you are Iapos, you distinguished right from wrong, you made female and male, you pointed out seed and fruits, you made men to love and to hate one another (ls 98-108).

He notes in a footnote that Iabas and Iapos are "probably variants of Iao," which is reasonable but not necessarily the case. It seems to me that these names could just as easily—perhaps more phonemically easily—be variants of the Greek name, Iapetos.[489] The

---

[487] John Gager, *Moses in Greco-Roman Paganism*, Society of Biblical Literature Monograph Series, 1972. I am focusing for the purposes of this narrative exclusively on Chapter 4: "Moses and Magic."
[488] Quoted in Gager, 142-3.
[489] Iapetos—"the piercer"—was one of the pre-Olympian Titans, sons of Ouranos (Heaven) and Gaia (Earth). Led by Kronos, Iapetos and his brothers conspired against their father, ambushing Ouranos (the reasons are beyond our needs, but see Hesiod's *Theogony*, ls 170-82). Iapetos and three of his brother Titans were posted at the four

role of Iapetos in shaping the *profanus* is quite significant in early Greek thought.[490] For our purposes the "etymology" of these two names may not matter against the backdrop of the larger context of this discussion. However, if they derive from *Iao* and thus are, so to speak, more Jewish/Judaean than they would be if derived from Iapetos, the latter derivation would take a small percentage of the "embedded Judaean/Jewish component" away.

That still leaves the issue of Moses and his role in this text for its author/user, and the reference to the god being invoked as one "whom no one has ever seen." Moses is clearly enough the speaker given the lines that immediately follow, and the notion of the god's invisibility offers an obvious and interesting resonance to the Judaean/ Jewish God concept. It is also noteworthy, as Gager correctly points out, that nearly all of the verbiage of pairs (light/darkness, et al) are almost direct quotes from verses in the first chapter of Genesis. That would raise another question (not asked by Gager) regarding the putative pagan use of Moses as a figure in this text: was that pagan also not only apparently aware of Genesis, but of the Judaean/Jewish (and Christian) understanding of that text (and of the entirety of the Torah) as having been written down by Moses (taking dictation, as it were, from YHVH)? There is no way of knowing this, but the possibility introduces the notion that, at least at the sacerdotal, amulet-writing level, there was even more of an interwoven relationship between Pagans and Jews/Christians than we might otherwise have imagined.

Gager notes, by way of the quote from lines 108-118 of the phrase "your authentic name" that, specifically, the connection between Moses and knowledge of the Great Name—around which connection the *Sword* revolves, as we have seen—is also found elsewhere in the *PGM*. Thus in *PGM* II, 126-8, we read: "I am he who met you, and you gave me as a gift the knowledge of your greatest name," and in *PGM* III, 158, we read: "I am he whom you encountered and to whom you granted knowledge of your greatest name and of its sacred pronunciation," and in *PGM* XII, 92-4 : I am he whom you encountered under/at the foot of the sacred mountain, and you granted knowledge of your greatest name, which I will keep and transmit to nobody except to fellow initiates in your sacred mysteries."

While in none of these cases is Moses actually mentioned by name, Gager points out that scholars like Preisendanz have assumed that he is the intended speaker, and—particularly given the last quote, and the location in association with "the sacred mountain"—this certainly makes sense. One might further note the importance of the phrase "its sacred pronunciation," which would resonate from the issue of ineffability that we have discussed above (on pages 285-6) in the context of the *Sword* associated with Moses. Gager suggests that the similarity between these passages and the explicit Moses-Great Name connection previously pointed out in *PGM* V, 108-18 would militate in favor

---

corners of the world where they seized hold of Ouranos and held him fast, (this detail is part of a later, post-Hesiodic tradition; in Hesiod it's all Kronos) while Kronos, hidden in the center, castrated him with a sickle.
[490] Iapetos and his brothers represent the four cosmic pillars that, in earlier Near Eastern cosmogonies with which the Greeks were apparently familiar, hold heaven and earth apart. Iapetos himself was most likely the pillar of the west, a position which was later and more prominently held by his son Atlas. Iapetos may also have been regarded as the Titan of the mortal life-span. That he was understood to have a particular relationship with the *profanus* is signified by the fact that his sons Prometheus and Epimetheus were depicted as the creators of humankind and other mortal creatures.

of this interpretation. He then reminds his reader that the full title of *PGM* XIII is the *Eighth Book of Moses Concerning the Great Name*—and that there are other places where the association specifically between Moses and knowledge of "the Great Name" is found.

He brings in Josephus, which muddies the discussion, since Josephus is a Judaean Jew, not a pagan, so I am not sure how it validates the Moses-Great Name relationship found in the *PGM* except to reinforce the idea that that notion was out there. And if we are positing a strongly syncretistic relationship between pagan and Judaean/Jewish (and Christian) thinkers at around that time, then we can, I suppose, (albeit in a somewhat circular fashion), help validate the Moses-Great Name connection in the *PGM* by reference to the explicit articulation of that connection in the writings of a Judaean Jew who was well known for his close relationship with the Roman imperium.

The culmination of Gager's discussion of Moses within the *PGM* is his somewhat more detailed handling of *PGM* XIII (aka Leiden papyrus J395, also known, to repeat) as *The Eighth Book of Moses*)—to which he had a bit earlier referred, and which is dated to the late third or early fourth century CE. As he explains, the papyrus offers two recensions of the same essential text, to the first of which the "Moses" title applies, and in its entirety it consists of charms and an account of creation, with a kind of appendix to each of the two parts that are filled with magical names and charms.[491] The "title" actually appears five times in variant forms the reasons for which variations Gager discusses. For our purposes the details of that discussion are less important: what matters is the importance of Moses to the text, however we understand it, as a pagan work succumbing to syncretism or as an originally Jewish (or Judaean) text that has been appropriated by a pagan redactor.

Nonetheless, I find this last idea intriguing: that it originated as a Jewish (Judaean) text—based on the fact that already in the Hellenistic period, Judaeans (Gager uses the term, "Judaism") referred to the Torah as The Five Books of Moses, albeit as Gager notes (in his fn 42) there is no evidence for a sixth or seventh "Book of Moses." Three things occur to me on this front. One, of course, that two such books may have existed and have simply disappeared into the archaeological sands of antiquity like so many other ancient works. Two, along with this possibility, in the syncretistic world that we are investigating, one important group that we have not mentioned is the Samaritans—whose Bible consists of six books—Genesis through Deuteronomy and Joshua. So there is certainly an extant "*Sixth Book of Moses*," if not a seventh, even if the sixth was not acknowledged by Judaeans or their Jewish and Christian spiritual heirs.

Three, if Moses were understood by Judaeans/Jews like Philo Judaeus and Josephus (37-ca 100 CE) not merely to be the author (i.e., YHVH's "secretary") of the Torah but also of esoteric material (whether it is called magical or mystical)[492] then, again, this book could be a work that reflects that sensibility. And what, in the end is the *Sword*? Could it serve—be understood as—another such work? Might we call it the *Seventh (or Sixth) Book of Moses*? I am certainly speculating here, without presuming any sort of certainty, but either way, the *Eighth Book of Moses* speaks to the significance of Moses within the world beyond Judaism's borders in middle and late Greco-Roman antiquity.

---

[491] Gager, 146-8.
[492] See below, 296, 300, and 373.

So, too, yet another work, called the *Diadem of Moses*, is discussed by Gager.[493] The title appears in *PGM* VII, 620-8. At that point, amidst a scattered collection of magical charms, the text reads: "From the *Diadem of Moses*: 'Take a kynikephalidos plant, place it under your tongue when you lie down to sleep…" etc (its instructions continue, and include the recitation of "magical words," including *Iao*, *Sabaot* and *Adonai*); this, in order to gain the love of some woman. Gager notes that the origin of this charm is uncertain—and that there is no "strong evidence of immediate Jewish influence," since the only obvious Jewish elements are the mention of Moses as well as *Iao*, *Sabaot* and *Adonai*—but that it has been taken from somewhere else and embedded into *PGM* VII.

Gager had, just prior to the discussion of *PGM* XIII, gone on to point out other significant mentions of Moses in the so-called "Magical Papyrus of Leiden and London," (not to be confused with the Leiden Papyrus J395, which *is PGM* XIII), an Egyptian document written mostly in Demotic and Hieratic with frequent Coptic glosses, that is dated to the third century CE.[494] In this text "Moses appears twice as an ideal type of one who enjoys an intimate relationship with the gods. In the first passage, the speaker implores the god, 'reveal thyself to me here today in the fashion of thy revelation to Moses which thou didst make upon the mountain, before whom thou didst create darkness and light.' The second passage is part of a love charm in which the speaker requests the gods to awaken a longing between a man and a woman like the longing of God for Moses, 'the longing which the god, the son of Sopd(?), felt for Moses going to the hill of Ninaretos to offer water to his god, his lord, his Yaho, Sabaho, his Glemura-muse, Plerube… S Mi Abrasaz, Senklai…'."[495]

There is a good deal to dig into with these two passages, particularly the second one. In the first we again recognize familiarity with the idea that Moses communed with God on a mountaintop and perhaps the turn of phrase "before whom thou didst create darkness and light" in suggesting Genesis 1:2 in the second phrase implies that Moses was shown such an event so that he could write it down as we have that account in the Torah.

In the second passage, there is a series of unidentifiable names that Gager refers to as magical names and, as he points out, it is perhaps odd that the god longs for Moses and not the other way around. Gager also suggests that the hill is likely a reference to the mountain-meeting between God and Moses, although the name, Ninaretos, is unknown, and the water-offering is nowhere found in the biblical account. Furthermore, water was not used for rituals, he points out, before the exile (586-38 BCE)—in other words not until the Second Temple Period, but water libations were introduced during the Hellenistic

---

[493] Ibd, 151-2.

[494] Hieratic (Greek for "sacred") is a simplified and abbreviated form of the pictographic hieroglyphic ("sacred carving" in Greek) script, written almost exclusively from right to left, in which people, animals and objects depicted in hieroglyphs are too stylized to be easily recognizable. Developed as a shorthand for everyday purposes, it was in use until the 26th dynasty (664-525 BCE), when it came to be used mainly for religious texts. By then, Demotic—developed from a northern variant of the Hieratic script in around 660 BCE—became the preferred script at court. The Greek historian, Herodotos, named it "Demotic," but it was called "*sekh shat*" ("writing for documents") by the Egyptians themselves. During the third century BCE, after Alexander conquered Egypt, it was gradually replaced by Coptic writing, an alphabetic variant of Greek, to whose 24 letters seven letters from Demotic have been added to account for sounds not found in Greek. Its use became ubiquitous with the spread of Christianity. The term "Coptic" derives from the Greek word for Egypt, "*Aigyptos*" which was eventually Latinized to "*Copt.*"

[495] Gager, 145

period into the Feast of Tabernacles. "The rabbis justified this innovation by claiming that Moses had received it as part of his revelation on Mount Sinai."[496]

It is certainly true, as we have repeatedly seen, that gobbledy-gook names can be used in magical formulae—and it could well be the case that Yaho and Sabaho are confusions of the more standard Hellenistic-Roman Greek-language rendering of *YHVH* as Iao, as we have seen, and of *Tzva'ot* as *Sabaot*. The use of gobbledy-gook names is equally a feature, in a slightly different way, however, in Jewish mysticism, as we have also seen: any version of God's Name is in any case Ineffable.

Further, it becomes a central feature of Jewish mysticism—albeit, as far as we know, not until much later, in medieval Kabbalah, where God as loving rather than awesome is emphasized—to depict a reciprocal relationship between the mystic and God whereby each longs equally for the other and their successful merger—the mystic filled with the *mysterion*—is often likened to the coming together of lovers. So that sort of an idea may merely be earlier than is ordinarily supposed, and—yet again—the line between magic and mysticism as an intensified form of normative religion is blurred. Of course, the blur is even more complex when one keeps in mind that the passage in question comes from a document that is presumably pagan.

The question, then, of how much Judaean/Jewish (and given the time period of this document we can safely and comfortably say "Jewish") influence is present here, is also raised in Gager's raising the matter of the hill of Ninaretos, and that of the water-offering mentioned in the text. For it is also conceivable that the pagan author was, say, somewhat aware of the important biblical moment when Moses brought forth water from a rock for the Israelites, but misunderstood and/or misconstrued that moment as some sort of water offering—it would be the sort of misunderstanding/misconstrual that derives from an oral, rather than written awareness of the event: like a game of telephone, by the time the originally described act ends up in the Leiden and London papyrus, it has been significantly transformed. While I am of course merely speculating here, I also wonder from what source Gager derived his evidence for the introduction of water-libations in (and only in) the second part of the Second Temple Period—he offers no source—although the rabbinic discussion that justifies them through an association with Moses, (B. Suk. 34a) is clear.

Still earlier, before discussing the *PGM*, Gager had noted how certain important pagan writers, such as Pompeius Trogus, Celsus and Numenius mention Moses, but how "the bulk of the evidence is to be found among the documents of ancient magic and its half-sister, alchemy, where Moses was a stock figure."[497] As Gager points out and we have earlier seen, Pliny refers to Moses, together with several others, as leaders of a "magical sect" of Judaeans.[498] So, too, Apuleius, in *Apology* 90 not only refers to Moses, but—clearly alluding to his renown among his contemporaries—presents him in a manner distinct and different from the other "magicians" he lists (including Zoroaster):

---

[496] Ibid, 146.

[497] Ibid, 135

[498] Ibid, 137. Not surprisingly, he translates *Ioudaioi* and *Iudaei* as "Jews," thereby missing, as most of our contemporary sources do, the important conceptual and definitional distinction between Judaeans and Jews that this narrative has been at pains to point out. See above, fn 204.

"...Carmenides, Damigeron, *that Moses whom you know*, Johannes, Apollobex, Dardanus himself or any other magicians of note since the time of Zoroaster and Ostantes" [emphasis added].[499]

Gager adds to this the comment by Numenius (whom we have not discussed) in his work *On the Good*.[500] Numenius uses the name, Mousaios, which Gager supposes was intended to associate Moses with Musaeos, the teacher of Orpheus, which is a reasonable supposition (although I would suggest that it even more clearly connects Moses to the idea of the muses, who inspire poets and could be implicitly associated with the divine inspiration to which Moses was understood to have been subject—particularly given the fact that Numenius refers to Mousaios as "a man most powerful in prayer to God." Not only does Numenius apparently view Moses in a positive light, but the shape of that light—prayer, as opposed to, say, incantation or compulsion—sounds at least as much a part of the religious enterprise as of magic.

As a separate matter but equally interesting is that those who opposed Mousaios on behalf of the Egyptians are referred to by Numenius as "Jannes and Jambres, sacred scribes, men judged to be inferior to none in magic, when the *Ioudaioi* were expelled from Egypt... and of the disasters which Mousaios brought upon Egypt they appeared able to turn away even the most violent." So as much as the Egyptian *sacerdotes* are associated with *mageia*, they are called scribes—bookmen; learned men—with power equal to that of Mousaios. This is obviously a very differently-nuanced sort of depiction of the events that were depicted in Ex 7:11-13—and interestingly, does what many writers have done up to the present day: anachronistically refer to the Israelites as Judaeans or Jews.

Of further incidental interest for our purposes is the fact that the Egyptian *sacerdotes* are named—Jannes and Jambres—where they are not (important enough to be?) named in Exodus. As Gager points out, they are also named in one of the documents associated with the Qumran material, the so-called Damascus (aka Zadokite) Document (found, however, not at Qumran but in the Cairo synagogue *genizah*, by Solomon Schechter, and first published by him in 1910)—in other words, the late Judaean period, (which is contrary to how Gager frames this datum as Jewish), as well as in the New Testament (2 Tim. 3:8, which states that "Jannes and Jambres opposed Moses") and also the rabbinic tradition.

There is another apparent quote from Numenius that we might note, (not mentioned by Gager). According to several Christian sources, Numenius referred to Plato as the "atticizing [i.e., Greek] Moses."[501] If that were true, then it offers another instance not only of Numenius' awareness of Moses but it reflects his high regard for Moses, for we might have expected a reversed statement: that Moses was an Israelite or Judaean Plato. Perhaps he was just thinking in chronological terms (that Moses came first).

Perhaps the priority ordering has a different significance, for what makes this statement doubly noteworthy is that Numenius may not have made it.[502] The report of it

---

[499] See above, 182-88 (for Apuleius in more detail).

[500] Numenius of Apamea (in Syria) was a Neopythagorean philosopher who flourished sometime between ca 150 and 200.

[501] Clement of Alexandria, *Stromata*, i. 22; Eusebius, *Praep. Evang.*, xi. 10; Suda, *Numenius*.

[502] But see *On the Good*, First Book, Practical Questions 13, "Plato as a Greek Moses."

came from Church Fathers eager to connect Greek and biblical wisdom—who would be suggesting the supercessionist superiority (to be intentionally redundant) of Christianity—or, as we shall note below, in chapter thirteen, of Judaeo-Christianity[503]—over Greek thought by connecting Moses to Plato in a phrase that shows Moses to be prior to Plato and the standard against which Plato is being measured, rather than the other way around; and which phrase understands that Moses, the gold standard of wisdom, is the basis for Christianity (Judaeo-Christianity), not of Greek thought, and that therefore pagan Hellenic culture is inherently inferior to Christian (Judaeo-Christian) culture.

Toward the end of his "Moses and Magic" chapter, Gager turns from so-called magical texts where Moses is mentioned to what he calls alchemical writings attributed to him. This last part of his discussion raises several interesting issues. The first is his translation of *he theia kai hiera techne*—meaning "the divine and sacred art"—as "alchemy." Needless to say, the discussion of the past 250 pages should have made it clear that a term such as "alchemy" and its implications in the vocabulary of the last few centuries is very different in nuance from how the Greek phrase was used and understood by ancient practitioners of that *techne* (art).

So a *diplosis*—a recipe for producing gold from baser metals—is understood to derive from having a Divine *Sacer* connection, and Gager writes of an eleventh-century document in which the embedded *diplosis* is ascribed to Moses—the culmination of which instruction is "...and you will find, *with the help of God*, the whole to be gold [italics added]."[504] A second work, the *Maza of Moses*, is dated by Gager's account to the third century, and leads him to the conclusion that "no later than the third century, [there existed] at least one pseudonymous alchemical writing of Moses which was cited as an authority by [the third-century alchemist], Zosimus and later alchemists."[505] He also points out "the question of the possible Jewish origin of the [alchemical] writings in question. Some of the titles themselves... would seem to indicate that there existed a school of Jewish alchemy in the early centuries of the Christian era" (although he observes that, aside from these names and titles there is no evidence of Jewish alchemy at that time).[506]

"On the other hand," Gager continues, "as with the magical charms, the titles and the excerpts from the writings have been preserved in non-Jewish circles. Thus there is no way of determining with certainty whether the separate titles represent Jewish traditions or whether they were invented by non-Jews using the well-known name of Moses as a pseudonym. This much is certain: the two realms of magic and alchemy reflect in different ways the syncretistic environment of second, third and fourth-century Egypt, and in this world the name of Moses carried considerable authority."[507]

All of these issues underscore, albeit from different angles, not only the presence of Moses within pagan consciousness, mainly as a magician, but also the broader reality of Pagan-Judean-Jewish-Christian interface. Gager, in fact, when he discusses the title, *Key of Moses*, that appears four times in *PGM* XIII, does so in order to raise the comparison

---

[503] See 356.
[504] Gager, 153.
[505] Ibid, 155. "*Maza*" is a term referring to a lump of metal (such as, but not limited to, gold).
[506] Ibid, 155 and Gager's fn #66.
[507] Ibid.

with a renowned esoteric pagan work called the *Key of Hermes Trismegistus*, and with that comparison, the idea that this literature places Moses in a position of being a sacerdotal rival to Hermes. "Further evidence of the competition is line 14 of our papyrus [i.e., *PGM* XIII] where the writer charges that 'Hermes stole from this book when he named the seven sacrificial fumes in his holy book, the *Wing*.' On the Jewish side, the rivalry appears most sharply in the apologetic Moses romance of Artapanus where Moses performs the feats normally attributed to Hermes-Thoth and is dubbed Hermes by the grateful Egyptian priests."[508] So it is not only a matter of interface but—not surprisingly, given what is at stake with regard to effectively engaging the divine *sacer*—of competition, not only where Christianity vis-a-via Paganism is concerned, but with regard to Judaism vis-à-vis Paganism. And of course we shall see in the following chapter how that double-headed rivalry emphatically expands to transform Judaism and Christianity from allies vis-a-vis Paganism into forces engaged increasingly in inimical rivalry to each other.[509]

One further note before moving on to that discussion. Interestingly—and as in the Judaeans/Jews issue noted in fn #204, offering an important definitional and conceptual problem—is how Gager, in discussing the tetragrammaton, refers to it as "the starting point in Judaism of a widely held superstition concerning the power of the name."[510] He is blind both to the meaning of the term "superstition" as it is used in the period that he is discussing, and to the problematic of how and where to draw the line between *religion* and superstition, particularly given the importance of the Divine Name as we have discussed it above, in the context of the *Sword*, for Jewish mysticism and not only for Jewish "magic." That he is using it in the manner in which the term is used in common English-language parlance is not acceptable, it seems to me, in a book that is dealing with a key aspect of the issue of category definition with regard to this very sort of concept.

Similarly—perhaps more egregiously—is his reference to how Philo and Josephus both "knew Moses as a prophet and that both likened the Mosaic religion to *mysteria*." Aside from the question as to why he would invoke the names of two Judaean Jews in his discussion of Moses in Greco-Roman Paganism (although the chapter title is simple "Moses and Magic") is his quote from Philo, (in *On the Cherubim*, 49), "and I have been initiated into the greater mysteries of the god-beloved Moses." This quote shows that Philo regarded Moses as someone in possession of deeper, more esoteric, *mystical* knowledge of the Divine *Sacer* than he shared in the Torah with the everyday practitioner Israelites; it does not necessarily mean that the Mosaic teachings were, *per se*, *mysteria*. So the category distinctions among mainstream religion, mysticism and magic are untouched and unclear in Gager's otherwise interesting and important text.

Category distinctions between religion and magic—and superstition, theurgy, alchemy, medicine and even philosophy; and rivalries among Judaism, Christianity and various forms of Paganism—reach a particular sort of crescendo as we move into the later third and fourth centuries. This is the time period when Christianity shifts from enduring

---

[508] Ibid, 149.
[509] There are other apparent "Moses" works mentioned in *PGM* XIII briefly referenced by Gager: the so-called *Archangelical Book* and the *Secret Moon Book of Moses*—concerning both of which Gager raises the question as to whether there existed substantive works called by these titles beyond the brief mentions in *PGM* XIII.
[510] Gager, 142.

its most intense period of persecution at the hands of the Roman pagan authorities to acceptance and then to hegemony. It is through the lens of that process that we pursue the matter of definitions and conflicts into the following chapter.

CHAPTER TWELVE

The Competition for the Truth Regarding the Divine *Sacer*

We can recognize, through Pliny and Apuleius, that the terms *magia* and *magus*—which both writers recognize to be direct derivations from Persian terms referring to a legitimate sacerdotal class—have come, in common usage, to have a variously understood pejorative meaning by their respective eras. Moreover, we understand in particular from Pliny, that by his time the terms have become generalized, so that they don't even necessarily have a Persian-based connotation when he himself uses them: *magia* is associated by him with other "pre-Roman-and-uncivilized" Gallic Druids and even Italic pre-Roman tribes.

By Pliny's time, the Israelite-Judaean tradition is in the process of assuming an increasingly distinct bifurcation into what will become Judaism and Christianity. These two faiths will be engaged in a multiply-layered competition. They will exhibit a sibling rivalry that is both internally theological and informed by external political conditions that will effect the matter of which of them will inherit the *religio licita* status earned by Judaeanism back in 63 BCE, in the event that that status ends up not accorded to *both* of them. At the same time, they will be engaged in competition, on both theological and political grounds, with an array of pagan religions—some of which, like the old Olympian religion, are fairly distinct from Judaism and Christianity, and some of which offer many details that overlap details of Judaism or, even more so, of Christianity.

We may recall, in fact, that the shaping of Judaism and Christianity as two distinct faiths that we would recognize as fundamentally like they are (or appear to be) today is at the beginning of its process at precisely this time. It is not until the 120s or perhaps even the 130s that the pagan Roman authorities, specifically under Hadrian, can discern two distinct groups. It is not until around 140 that the canon of the Hebrew Bible has been solidified. It is not until 325 and the Council of Nicaea that a proper Christian understanding of Jesus as both fully human and fully divine has been defined—and there will continue to be Christians, followers of the perspective articulated at that Council by Bishop Arius, who deny divinity to Jesus, until the late sixth century in some parts of Christendom.[511] It is not until around 393-7, at the Council of Hippo, that the Christian biblical canon will be solidified.

---

[511] Thus Arianism co-existed with Trinitarianism in Ravenna, until 526, and prevailed in Visigothic Spain until 587. In fact, the complications attending the question of heresy are nicely encapsulated in the later, post-mortem biography of Arius himself. Where, as we have seen, the First Ecumenical Council of Nicaea deemed his views to be heretical, at the First Synod of Tyre (335) he was exonerated from the charge of heresy. After he died, he

Be these complications as they may, both Jews and Christians were ultimately wrestling with the same issue—how to understand God properly, given the fact that God created us and therefore was (is) assumed to have the capacity to destroy us: to help or harm, further or hinder, bless or curse us. Each side of the equation saw itself as the correct continuation of the Hebrew-Israelite-Judaean continuum that had forged a constantly evolving and ever-more-refined understanding of how to maintain a proper covenantal relationship with God. Each side saw the other as misguided, as having slipped off the correct path, although their respective senses of what sort of perdition that slippage offered is one of the key distinctions between the two emerging traditions. The Christian tradition the primary text of which culminates with the final battle and swallowing up of the enemies of God and followers of the Satan in a sea of fire would yield an increasingly complex and full-fledged concept of hell for all of those who fall off that path. Judaism's primary text ends with the narrative of the pre-return from Babylonian exile and, while offering the concept of the end of time and thus the end of the world as we know it, it contains nothing that corresponds to the Armageddon encompassed in Revelation 15:15ff or to the evolving Christian concept of Hell.

This distinction between the traditions grows out of their increasingly separate interpretive literatures. Jewish leadership continues along the path begun in strictly oral terms in the last few centuries of the Judaean period, eventually shaping an organized written literature of which there are two main types. The first, as noted in our Introduction, is called "*midrash.*" It offers a direct, often line-by-line (or word-by-word) elucidation of the Torah and other books within the Hebrew Bible, the point of which as often as not is to offer a moral lesson.[512] The second, called Talmud ("learning"), is formed over many centuries in two primary parts. The first part, *mishnah*, as we have also noted, is the original Judaean material that is organized and committed to a definitive form by the early third century. This process culminates with the formal written-down articulation by Judah the Prince of the rabbinic legalistic tradition in the organization of the *mishnah* into six orders and their sixty-three subset tractates, and in the centuries that follow, the layering over the *mishnah* of two bodies of further commentary, called *gemara*, over the next several centuries by further generations of rabbinical figures.[513]

Mishnah takes as its starting point some issue—rather than taking the text of the Torah as its starting point—from the question of the precise, proper time for morning prayers to the proper way to build a sukkah or proper sexual conduct between husband and wife. With the gradual dispersion of the Jewish community between the time of the destruction of the Second Temple in 70 CE and the aftermath of the Bar Kokhba Revolt after about 135 CE, there gradually emerged two primary Jewish communities, one in what was called Palestina after 135 and one in the by-then Parthian-governed Mesopotamian region, consistently referred to in Jewish tradition as Babylonia (today's Iraq). Each of these two communities produced its own rabbis and its own *gemara*, as a consequence of

---

was again anathemized and officially pronounced a heretic at the First Ecumenical Council of Consta ntinople, convened by Theodosius in 381.

[512] The word comes from the Hebrew root, *d-r-sh*, which means "to dig beneath the surface." *Midrash* seeks to dig out meanings from beneath the surface of the sacred text.

[513] As pointed out previously, the traditional date associated with Judah's organization of the *mishnah* is 212.

which there are in fact two Talmuds, a so-called Babylonian Talmud and a so-called Palestinian Talmud. The first is much more extensive than the second (for reasons beyond this discussion), but both direct themselves to articulating and accounting for the post-biblical foundations of a proper legalistic framework for Judaism—called *halakhah* ("the way to go").

Elements of *halakhah* may also be discerned in the *Midrash*, but its method tends to be more phantasmagorical, so it is regarded as offering the primary post-biblical foundations for *aggadah* (as noted earlier, literally: "telling," but with the connotation of "legend"). The Talmud offers some elements of *aggadah*, as well, although it is largely occupied with *halakhah*. Evolving as the street *lingua franca* of Judaeanism-Judaism is shifting from Hebrew to Aramaic, these texts are composed in varying degrees in both languages—typically, for example, the *mishnah* is mostly in Hebrew, whereas the *gemara* is mostly in Aramaic. Both talmudic and midrashic literature reflect the same methodology: discussion, whether between two or among four or five rabbinic figures—and the later figures, in continuing the discussion, do so as if the earlier figures are there in the room with them. There is therefore rarely a definitively correct, canonical interpretive conclusion, although most often one will be proposed as more effective than another. Both halakhic and aggadic types of discussion may be referred to as rabbinic literature.[514]

By contrast, what emerges as Christianity makes a deliberate choice to reject the rabbinic literature that had begun to be shaped during the late Judaean period. It develops its own literatures of interpretation, of which the first phase, carrying from the late second century until nearly the tenth century, in a manner analogous to the rabbinic traditions within Judaism, offers both exegesis of passages in the Hebrew Bible and New Testament and principles that become essential to the evolving faith. That literature is referred to as patristic.

One speaks in particular of four major figures in the West and four in the East as Church Fathers or Doctors of the Church.[515] Thus in the West—as decreed in 1298 by Pope Boniface VIII—Saints Ambrose (337/9-97), Jerome (347-420) and Augustine (454-530) together with Pope Gregory I (590-604, who is also regarded as a saint), comprise that four.[516] Jerome is best known for his translation of the Bible into what was the language of the people (*vulgus*), Latin. That translation, known as the Vulgate, reflects both his knowledge of Hebrew and Greek and his insightful recognition of how certain terms require unique renderings to effectively convey the uniqueness of their referents.[517]

---

[514] Strictly speaking, "rabbi" simply means "teacher," and was commonly used as a label of respect. Anyone regarded as knowledgeable in religious matters might be addressed as "rabbi." It is only in the past two centuries or so that the word has come to connote a formal title conferred on somebody through a prescribed course of study and a process of ordination.

[515] From Latin "docere," meaning "to teach" and referring to the particular significance of these individuals to the shaping of Church doctrines and principles.

[516] Beginning in 1568, under the papacy of Pius V, several dozen other figures (eventually including four women: Saints Catherine of Siena and Teresa of Avila in 1970, Saint Therese of Lisieux in 1977 and Saint Hildegard of Bingen in 2012) were elevated to the title of Doctor of the Church. The most recent was Saint Gregory of Narek, promoted to that title in 2015 by Pope Francis—but the original four are always treated as separate and, as it were, half a notch higher than other, subsequent honorees.

[517] Just two examples: the Hebrew phrase *gan eden* (Garden of Eden) referenced in the book of Genesis was rendered in the Greek Septuagint translation as *paradeisos*—a word derived from Persian, *para deshu*, that referred to the kind of exquisitely maintained garden/park, with trees, flowers, birds, flowing water fountains,

The final canonization of the Christian Bible at Hippo in 393-97 was in large part at the behest of Hippo's bishop, St Augustine. Augustine is renowned for offering a definitive articulation of critical doctrines that cement the foundations of Christian thought.[518] As such, he may be regarded as the most important of these early figures in the matter of shaping what was still evolving as Christianity. Interestingly enough, he spent perhaps the first thirty years of his life following in the pagan footsteps of his father, only after a revelatory experience choosing, rather, the path of his Christian mother, St. Monica and eventuating not only as a Bishop but as a theorist and writer of considerable power and originality.

Augustine's first important teacher was Ambrose, Bishop of Milan. Ambrose is famously understood not only to have prevented the spread of Arianism (still very much an issue at that time) to Milan but to have stood up to Emperor Valentinian himself in doing so—yet at the same time served successfully as the ambassador sent up into Gaul by the emperor to talk down Magnus Maximus as the latter had seized power in Gaul and was contemplating an invasion of northern Italy. At one point (in 390), he even excommunicated the Emperor Theodosius I (who had made Christianity the official religion of the empire) and received him back into the Church only after he performed the penance that Ambrose prescribed.

Particularly relevant to our narrative, Ambrose was also a strong opponent and even persecutor of Jews and pagans. When a synagogue in Mesopotamia was burned down by a Christian mob and Theodosius ordered that it be rebuilt at the expense of the local bishop, Ambrose convinced the Emperor to rescind that demand, writing, in part, in a letter that we still possess, that there is "no adequate cause for such a commotion, that the people should be so severely punished for the burning of a building, and much less since it is the burning of a synagogue, *a home of unbelief, a house of impiety, a receptacle of folly, which God Himself has condemned*"[519][italics added]. We can recognize in this both the ongoing development of interfaith hostility and its theological basis.[520]

---

reserved for the Shah and his entourage in the middle of an otherwise dry and tawny environment. Jerome, recognizing the specialness of the garden in Genesis, instead of translating it simply as *hortus*, the Latin term for garden, Latinized the Greek word, thus creating a unique term, *paradisus*—which has of course spilled into various European languages, as in English, for example: paradise.

    Similarly, the unique messenger between God and certain sacerdotal humans that in Hebrew is called a *mal'akh* and, in the Septuagint was simply called an *angelos*, which is a garden-variety Greek word for "messenger." (The garden-variety word in Hebrew is *shaliah*). Again Jerome chose not to use the garden-variety Latin word, *nuntius*, but created a unique word by Latinizing the Greek to *angelus*—and again, that word has made its way into European languages as "angel" and its equivalents.

[518] Augustine may be credited with offering the definitive discussions regarding the Trinity, the Virgin Birth and Original Sin that cement the foundations of Christian thought. It is perhaps symptomatic of the uneven parallels between the two Judaean offspring that Judaism arrives before Christianity at both the final decision regarding the biblical canon and the shaping of important theological discussions regarding doctrine—and also that both the talmudic and midrashic discussions are almost obsessively focused on how to live a covenantal life in the practical *profanus* sense whereas the patristic (and later, scholastic) discussions are more focused on faith and belief: how to understand the *sacer*.

[519] See Philip Schaff, editor, *Ambrose: Selected Works and Letters*, (Christian Classics Ethera Library) Letter XL.

[520] Ambrose is also traditionally credited but not actually known to have composed any of the repertory of antiphonal chanting, in which one side of the choir alternately responds to the other. However, it was called "Ambrosian chant" in his honor, due to his contributions to the music of the Church. He is credited with

Pope Gregory I "the Great" takes us, strictly speaking, just beyond our primary time frame focus, but must be mentioned because he is such a singular figure in the transition out of Roman antiquity into the medieval period. He is the first pope who really commands both a spiritual and, in the broadest sense, a political landscape.[521] Growing up in an aristocratic family, as Pope he gave away all of his wealth to feed and clothe the poor in a Rome that was a shrinking city, following the words of Jesus, "feed my flocks" literally. He negotiated with the Lombard barbarian chieftain, Agilulf, to prevent him from attacking and trashing the city—taking the initiative in negotiating with the Lombards that the imperial exarch at Ravenna (representing the Roman Emperor in Constantinople) had failed to take. He probably compiled the first biographies of the early, mostly martyred, Christian saints. And like Ambrose, he came to be associated with music: he is not likely to have composed any of the so-called Gregorian chants (these came later and probably in association with Gregory XIII), aka plain song or "Romish chants," but because of his multi-valent importance has been often mistakenly associated with them.

The eastern counterparts of these four figures were Athanasius of Alexandria, (c. 293/6–373), renowned for articulating the trinitarian argument against Arius at the council of Nicaea in 325; Basil the Great, a bishop and one of the so-called Cappadocian Fathers (c. 329–379); GregoryNazianzos, (329 – c. 390), who, together with Basil and the other Cappadocian Fathers, expended enormous intellectual energy both in bringing Arians into the Orthodox, trinitarian camp and in demonstrating the intellectual and rational legitimacy of Christianity relative to the Greek pagan thought of Plato and Aristotle; and John Chrysostom (347–407), archbishop of Constantinople and known in particular for his eloquence (hence the posthumous epithet, *chrysostomos*, meaning "golden-mouthed").[522] All eight of these "Fathers," in varying degrees and in diverse ways, would have wrestled with the theological relationship and in some cases political contention with various manifestations of Paganism, with the ongoing problem of heresy, and with Judaism.[523]

To repeat: Judaism was accepted as a *religio* by Roman authorities for several centuries into the Christian era, and during that time was actively proselytic among the pagans, but was never more than a spiritual minority, sometimes popular as a faddish oddity due to its significant differences from the pagan traditions: its invisible and

---

introducing hymnody from the Eastern Church into the West and was himself the composer of hymns, four of which have survived to our own time.

[521] Gregory is the turning point after which the Pope assumes a major political as well as spiritual position as a figure in the workings of expanding Christendom. However, Pope Leo I (400-61), was, like Gregory, an aristocrat and anticipated Gregory's bravery and clear-headedness vis-a-vis the "barbarians" when he came outside the walls of Rome to meet and negotiate with Attila the Hun in 452, persuading him to turn back from further incursion into Italy. Leo was the first pope to be referred to as "the Great" and was made a Doctor of the Church in 1568.

[522] Six of John Chrysostom's sermons, with their very strong anti-Jewish content, helped shape not only anti-Jewishness through the course of the medieval period, but were often quoted by the Nazis in t heir particular articulation of modern antisemitism.

[523] The Catholic Church refers to all eight of them as Doctors of the Church. This helps to separate them from a number of other individuals who were also called Church Fathers, but whose stature was somewhat less than these eight, although the later elevation of several dozen Fathers to the status of Doctor confuses the issue somewhat (see above, fn #517). To further complicate matters, only the last three of the Eastern hierarchs were and are typically treated as "Doctors" by the Eastern Church; it was really in the West that Saint Athanasius was included to offer a more complete four-for-four balance between East and West.

intangible God-concept, its prayers in a language decreasingly spoken on the street even by Judaeans and their Jewish descendants, its disturbing rite of circumcision, and its gastronomic prohibitions. Christianity, on the other hand, equally proselytic—even, it seems, when it was being viewed as a *superstitio*—when it finally rose above that status to become *religio*, in 313, was positioned to become hegemonic across the Empire by the end of the fourth century. One may recognize its astonishing growth as derived, in part, from its combination of Judaean roots and similarities to Judaism—a single, all-powerful and loving, engaged God-concept, a specific text that connects people to that God, one day a week of rest—and similarities to the pagan traditions, from the accessible human aspect of God to the *lack* of disturbing or difficult elements such as circumcision or gastronomic prohibitions.

This will be emphatically reinforced when, in the course of the fourth century, the position of Christianity within the empire shifts away from its *superstitio* status, as we have seen, by means of Constantine's edict of 313; and moves to a more important role within the Empire, as evidenced by Constantine's interest and important position in the Council of Nicaea in 325. Whether or not Constantine embraced Christianity before the Battle of Milvian Bridge, in 312, or the following year when he issued his edict, or on his deathbed in 337, or in between those dates—or not at all—he distinctly saw the faith as a glue that could help him hold the empire together and he favored it.[524] As a practical matter, moreover, every emperor after Constantine—with the possible exception of Julian, who is labeled by subsequent Christocentric historiography as Julian the Apostate—was Christian, so that Christianity grew not only from below, as a grass roots religious movement, but from above.[525] This, of course, culminated with Theodosius' decree around 381 reducing every form of non-Christian faith (including Judaism) to *superstitio* status.

Thus when one examines the religious developments of the second, third and particularly the fourth centuries in the Roman world from the perspective of our narrative, there is a logic to considering the situation particularly from a Christian, as opposed to a Jewish or Judaeo-Christian perspective, (albeit, as we shall subsequently see, the Jewish and particularly Judaeo-Christian perspectives will also have a role to play in our understanding of the era, overall). This becomes clear when one considers the forms of faith that were prominent and how they were likely to be competing more directly with Christianity on the rise than with Judaism the population of which was both dispersed and gradually leveling out.

As we have seen, there were many spiritual options—a smorgasbord of many available possibilities—for Romans across the Empire in the second, third and fourth centuries. The notion of other forms of faith (typically referred to in the literature as cults, but that, too, is intended to diminish their validity) is underscored by the Christian legend

---

[524] Our primary source for Constantine's Christian identity is his biographer, Eusebius (260/5-339-40) who, as a Christian polemicist certainly prefers to think of and to represent Constantine as having embraced the True Faith—earlier rather than later—and thus, in his *Life of Constantine*, written right after the Emperor's death in 337, that's how he tells it.

[525] However, we must keep in mind that some of those Christian Emperors were Arian or sympathetic to or at least tolerant of Arianism—notably, Constantius II (r. 337-361) and Valens (r. 364-78)—and since after Constantine the Empire was typically divided between Eastern and Western domains, one emperor might be Orthodox (triune) and the other Arian.

that reports on how the younger Julianus outdid Apuleius and Apollonius of Tyana in saving the city of Rome from a devastating plague: Whereas Apuleius could stay the plague in 15 days and Apollonius in 10, Julianus was able to stop it immediately by merely commanding it to do so. This not only extends beyond origins to capabilities as an issue, suggesting the greater power of theurgy than of other forms of engaging the *sacer*, but it further reminds us of how broad the range was of sacerdotal traditions with which early Christianity and Judaism were competing.[526] We can well understand how figures such as Apollonius would be presented in a manner intended to diminish them by the emerging literature associated with the Church Fathers.

Among the widest-spread forms of faith across the Empire, precisely during the period when Christianity was growing and Judaism was becoming more dispersed—and particularly popular with Roman soldiers, as we have noted—was Mithraism in its Romanized form. Since, as we have seen, there were some strong similarities between Mithraism and Christianity, we might ask how *much* competition there would have been for adherents. We might start by recalling some of the key similarities: the central ritual of a communal feast and the fact that the Mithraic New Year—the birthday of Mithras—was celebrated on December 25. But Manfred Clauss has asserted that "the Mithraic Mysteries had no public ceremonies of its own. The festival of *natalis Invicti* [Birth of the Unconquerable (Sun)], held on 25 December, was a general festival of the Sun, and by no means specific to the Mysteries of Mithras."[527]

David Ulansey comments, further, that, "[j]ust as Mithras is revealed as a being from beyond the universe capable of altering the cosmic spheres, so ... we find Jesus linked with a rupture of the heavens ... Perhaps, then, the figures of Jesus and Mithras, each regarded in his own tradition as ultimately coming from beyond our realm [from the *sacer* beyond the *profanus*, in our terms] are to some extent both manifestations of a single deep longing in the human spirit for a sense of contact with the ultimate mystery."

Where does this lead—or where did it lead—with regard to competition for adherents? Marvin Meyer has broadly observed that "early Christianity... resembles Mithraism in a number of respects—enough to make Christian apologists scramble to invent creative theological explanations to account for the similarities." Certainly early Christian apologists noted enough overlap between Mithraic and Christian rituals that they felt obliged to interpret the Mithraic rituals as negative—evil—reflections of Christian ones. Thus, for example, Tertullian wrote that as a prelude to the Mithraic initiation ceremony, the initiate was given a ritual bath and at the end of the ceremony, received a mark on the forehead.[528] He described these rites as a diabolical transformation and falsification of the baptism and Chrismation (the Orthodox and Eastern Catholic equivalent of Confirmation in the Roman Catholic Church). Justin Martyr (100-165 CE), an important Christian Apologist and the most outstanding interpreter of the idea of the Divine Word—

---

[526] See Dodds, *The Greeks and the Irrational*, 285, and his n #24 to Appendix II.

[527] Manfred Clauss, *The Roman Mithras*. (New York: Routledge, 2001), 70, fn #84. It was first published in German by C.H. Beck'sche Verlagsbuchhandlung in Munich, in 1990.

[528] Tertullian (ca 155 – ca 240 CE), from Carthage (modern Tunis) was the first Christian author to produce an extensive corpus of Latin Christian literature, including significant polemics against various heresies, among them Christian Gnosticism. He is perhaps best known for being the earliest extant Latin writer to use the term "*Trinity*" (Latin: *Trinitas*), that would later be adopted at the First Council of Nicaea in 325.

logos—of his era, contrasted Mithraic initiation communion (to its detriment) with the Eucharist.

The issue of Mithraism as a strong competitor of Christianity has been under discussion for the past 140 years. As antiquity came under more intense scrutiny in the 19th century, and in particular the study of the early Church began to make deeper inroads into the world of academic analysis, Ernst Renan, suggested (in 1882) that, under different circumstances, Mithraism might have risen to the prominence of modern-day Christianity. He wrote that "if the growth of Christianity had been arrested by some mortal malady, the world would have been Mithraic..."[529] On the other hand, Mary Boyce has argued that Mithraism was a potent enemy for Christianity in the West, but far less so in the East.[530] We have earlier noted how many more Mithraea have been found in the West than in the East, which would be part of the basis for her assertion. Others have denied the Renanian perspective as legitimate at all. Leonard Boyle wrote, in 1987, that "too much ... has been made of the 'threat' of Mithraism to Christianity," pointing out that there are only fifty known Mithraea in the entire city of Rome.[531] Appositely, J. A. Ezquerra holds that since the two religions did not share similar aims, there was never any real threat of Mithraism taking over the Roman world.[532]

Filippo Coarelli, however, in a 1979 study that we have earlier noted, tabulated forty actual or possible Mithraea by way of archaeological remains and estimated that Rome would have had "not less than 680–690" Mithraea.[533] Similarly, Lewis M. Hopfe states that more than 400 Mithraic sites have been found. These sites are spread all over the Roman empire from places as far as Dura Europos in the east (in current geo-political terms, in eastern Syria, not far from the Iraqi border), and England in the west. He too says that Mithraism may have been a rival of Christianity.[534] Certainly from a purely demographic point of view, if either of these two sets of numbers is even vaguely accurate, then Boyle's assertion is considerably weakened. Even while a scholar like David Ulansey

---

[529] Ernst Renan, *Marc-Aurele et la fin du monde antique*. Paris, 1882, 579: "On peut dire que, si le christianisme eût été arrêté dans sa croissance par quelque maladie mortelle, le monde eût été mithriaste." Also see Renan's 1880 *Hibbert Lectures: Lectures on the Influence of the Institutions, Thought and Culture of Rome on Christianity and the Development of the Catholic Church*, (Kessinger Publishing, 1898), 35f.

[530] Mary Boyce, *Zoroastrians: Their Religious Beliefs and Practice*. (Routledge. 1979), 99: "Mithraism proselytized energetically to the West, and for a time presented a formidable challenge to Christianity ; but it is not yet known how far, or how effectively, it penetrated eastward. A Mithraeum has been uncovered at the Parthian fortress-town of Dura-Europos on the Euphrates; but Zoroastrianism itself may well have been a barrier to its spread into Iran proper."

[531] Leonard Boyle, *A Short Guide to St. Clement's, Rome*. (Rome: Collegio San Clemente, 1987), 71.

[532] J.A. Ezquerra, (R. Gordon, transl.), *Romanising Oriental Gods: Myth, Salvation and Ethics in the Cults of Cybele, Isis and Mithras*. (Brill, 2008), 202–203: "Many people have erroneously supposed that all religions have a sort of universalist tendency or ambition. In the case of Mithraism, such an ambition has often been taken for granted and linked to a no less questionable assumption, that there was a rivalry between Mithras and Christ for imperial favour. ... If Christianity had failed, the Roman empire would never have become Mithraist."

[533] See Roger Beck and Wolfgang Haase, *Aufstieg und niedergang der roemischen welt [The Rise and Decline of the Roman World]*. (Walter de Gruyter, 1984). 2026f, who note that "a useful topographic survey, with map, by F. Coarelli (1979) lists 40 actual or possible Mithraea (the latter inferred from find-spots, with the sensible proviso that a Mithraeum will not necessarily correspond to every find). Principally from comparisons of size and population with Ostia, Coarelli calculates that there will have been in Rome 'not less than 680–690' Mithraea in all." Even if his estimation is off, let's say, by 300% there would still have been a large number of them.

[534] Lewis M. Hopfe, "Archaeological Indications on the Origins of Roman Mithraism," in Lewis M. Hopfe, ed., *Uncovering Ancient Stones: Essays in Memory of H. Neil Richardson*, (Eisenbrauns, 1994), 147–158; see especially 156.

refers to Renan's comment as "somewhat exaggerated," he nonetheless considers Mithraism to have been "one of Christianity's major competitors in the Roman Empire." Ulansey in any case understands that the study of Mithraism is important for understanding "the cultural matrix out of which the Christian religion came to birth."[535]

Nor, of course, was Mithraism the only competitor of Judaism and Christianity as time moved forward, nor was it the only form of faith possessed of certain features strikingly similar to those of Christianity. Thus in his *Seven Books against the Heathen* (3.33), the Christian writer Arnobius (284-305) observed that the Pagans "maintain that Bakkhos, Apollo, the Sun, are one deity" and that, to them "the sun is also Bakkhos and Apollo."[536] So the cult of Dionysios was recognized by at least one Christian writer to offer a broad, universal kind of place in pagan thought regarding the divine *sacer*. Moreover, precisely as in Christianity and its centering on Jesus, December 25th and January 6th are both traditional birth dates for the God-Man (to borrow St Anselm's later, eleventh-century term), these are also both traditional birth dates in the Dionysian *mythos*, reflecting a focus on the period of the winter solstice.[537] Indeed, according to the late Latin writer Macrobius (ca 400 CE), the date of the winter solstice associated by the Greeks both with the sun and with Dionysios was originally observed in early January but was eventually placed on December 25th. His point is that the winter sun god is born around this time, when the shortest day of the year begins to become longer—and for our purposes, there are obvious calendrical parallels to Christianity.

The situation may well have been more complicated than this. For one of the Church Fathers, Epiphanius (ca 350 CE) references the birth of the god Aion, son of the Greek goddess Persephone or *Kore* ("Maiden," who was carried off to the Underworld by Hades and thereafter became Queen of that realm and divided her time between residence within it and residence above, on earth, when she was in the company of her mother, Demeter—"Earth Mother"), at the time of the winter solstice.[538] The 20th century Christian theologian, Hugo Rahner, observes that "[w]e know that Aion was at this time beginning to be regarded as identical with Helios and Helios with Dionysios...because [according to Macrobius] Dionysios was the symbol of the sun... He is made to appear small at the time of the winter solstice, when upon a certain day the Egyptians take him out of the crypt, because on this the shortest day of the year it is as though he were a little child.... Macrobius transfers [this feast] to the day of the winter solstice, December 25."[539]

So: Dionysios is equivalent to Aion and was also said in some strands of the tradition to have been born of Persephone, the virgin maiden. Joseph Campbell also refers to this "celebration of the birth of the year-god, Aion, to the virgin Goddess, Kore."[540] He refers to Kore as "a Hellenized transformation of Isis," the Egyptian mother goddess who

[535] David Ulansey, *Origins of the Mithraic Mysteries*. (New York: Oxford University Press, 1991), 3-4.

[536] Alexander Roberts, et al, eds., *The Anti-Nicene Fathers*, (New York: Cosimo, 2007; reprint of 1886 edition), Vol VI, 472-3.

[537] The Western churches use the Gregorian calendar. Some Eastern churches use the Julian calendar; the Julian December 25 falls upon January 7 in the Gregorian calendar.

[538] The presumed logic is that ca nine months earlier, just prior to leaving the underworld, she conceived him and bore him just prior to, or just after, returning to the underworld, although the arithmetic does not really add up perfectly.

[539] Hugo Rahner, *Greek Myths and Christian Mystery*, (New York; Harper & Row, 1963), 139-40.

[540] See Joseph Campbell, *The Mythic Image*, (Princeton, NJ: Princeton University Press, 1974), 34.

was likewise called the "Great Virgin"—in inscriptions predating the Christian era by centuries.[541] (see below, 312, for more of a discussion of Isis, who was, after all, the wife of Osiris, who was killed by his evil half-brother, Seth. When she was able to restore him—there are different versions of both how he died and how he was revived—he was reborn as his son, Horus; so Isis is both the virgin mother of Horus and the spouse of Osiris. See also above, 139-40, and below, 308.)

We have earlier observed that, according to the farthest-flung tradition, Dionysios was the son of the god Zeus and the mortal woman Semele, but that in the Cretan version of the same story, which the (pagan) historian Diodorus Siculus follows, Dionysios was the son of Zeus and Persephone, who is commonly referred to as a "virgin goddess." In yet another version of the birth of Dionysios, Semele is mysteriously impregnated—miraculously—by one of Zeus's bolts of lightning. Thus she would obviously be viewed as a virgin mother.

Dionysios' oft-used epithet is "twice-born"—most commonly referring to his having been plucked, as a virtual fetus, from the ashes of Semele (who was incinerated by the glory of Zeus, when she asked to see that glory) and stored by Zeus in the god's own thigh until it was time for the baby to enter the realm of the living. A completely different source for the epithet, dealing with the "death" rather than the birth of Dionysios, and also common in antiquity at least by the second century, was the notion that he was resurrected after having been torn to pieces or otherwise killed. It was also said that Dionysios "slept three nights with Proserpine [Persephone]"—apparently referring to the god's journey into the underworld to visit his mother. As with Jesus, it is asserted of Dionysios—by the Church father, Justin Martyr (*First Apology*, 21)—that he "ascended to heaven".[542] Dionysios is depicted in this context as an *adult* (not a newborn baby), rising out of the underworld after death, with a horse-driven chariot like that of a sun god. Thus the repeatedly dying and resurrecting sun when it dies and is reborn enters into and exits from the cave (womb) of the world—an act of particular importance at the time of the winter solstice.

A different understanding of the etiology of the "twice-born" epithet comes from a less well-known third century Church father, Minucius Felix (writing in *Commodius*, XII) who, in addressing a pagan audience, observes that "[y]ou yourselves say that Father Liber (a name associated with Dionysios; see above, fn #222) was assuredly twice begotten. First of all, he was born in India of Proserpine [Persephone] and Jupiter [Zeus]... Again, restored from his death, in another womb Semele conceived him again of Jupiter...."[543] A different explanation from the same era asserts that Zeus gave Dionysios's torn-apart heart in a drink to Semele, who thereby became pregnant—offering another version of a miraculous virgin birth. Yet another variation on the virgin birth of Dionysios, son of *Zeus Pater* (God the Father) suggests that while the virgin Semele sat there, peacefully weaving a mantle on which there was to be a representation of the universe, her mother contrived that Zeus should learn of her presence; he approached her in the form of

---

[541] See also See D. M. Murdock, *Christ in Egypt: The Horus-Jesus Connection*, (New York: Stellar House Publishing, 2009), 120-197.

[542] Alexander Roberts, et al, eds., *op citum*. Vol I, 170.

[543] Ibid, Vol IV, 205.

an immense snake. And the virgin (Greek: *parthenos*) conceived the ever-dying, ever-living god of bread and wine, Dionysios, who was born and nurtured in a cave, torn to death as a babe and resurrected.[544]

This notion becomes reinforced and further complicated by the version of Dionysios' birth that makes his mother Persephone/Kore, a Virgin, (*parthenos*), according to Epiphanius, but also herself a symbol of death and resurrection, given the narrative of her being carried off into the underworld by Hades and of her annual return to the bosom of her mother, Demeter, with the advent of spring, as we have earlier noted.

There is more: Persephone's cycle of descent to and return from the underworld, we may also recall, is connected to the pomegranate: the number of pomegranate seeds that she consumed while resident/imprisoned in Hades' palace yields the decision by Zeus that she remain a corresponding number of months in the underworld each year. The pomegranate is a wide-spread symbol, throughout the Mediterranean and Middle Eastern worlds, of fertility, due in part to its many seeds, and perhaps to their reddish color, implying birth-blood.[545] But in referring to the Eleusinian Mysteries in his *Exhortation to the Greeks* 2:16, Clement of Alexandria asserts that the pomegranate tree was believed to have sprung from *the drops of blood of Dionysios* [italics added]. So the fruit from which Persephone ate, leading to her requirement to spend part of the year as a spouse married to Hades, (while spending the rest of the year as a maiden, in the company of her mother), who is otherwise understood to be the Virgin mother of Dionysios, is derived from that dying and resurrecting son.

The adult Dionysios, as the god of wine, is able to reproduce that liquid *ad infinitum*. At his annual festival in his temple of Elis he filled three empty kettles with wine (no water was needed—however he also enacted the miracle of changing water to wine, according to the account in Diodorus Siculus (*Library of History*, 3.66.3). And on the fifth of January, wine instead of water gushed from his temple at Andros. Surely we can recognize an echo of all this in the story of Jesus multiplying the jars of wine at the wedding feast of Cana (John 2:1-9). Most overt of parallels regarding wine and its transformation is the idea that the blood of Dionysios-Bakkhos-Zagreos (or, in still older, Sumero-Babylonian *mythoi*, Dumuzi-absu, Tammuz) is the wine drunk from a special, ceremonial chalice. Eventually the culminating moment in the Christian Mass will be the consumption of wine that is transubstantiated *by the words of consecration* into the blood of the Son of the Virgin.

Nor is "twice-born" the only epithet of Dionysios of significance with regard to parallels with Christ and likely competition with Christianity. Thus, in an Orphic hymn, Phanes-Dionysios is referred to by the Greek title *Protogonos* or "first-born" of Zeus—also translated at times as "only-begotten [son]," although the term *Monogenes* would be more appropriately rendered as the latter. He is also called "*Soter*" ("Savior") in various

---

[544] Joseph Campbell, *The Masks of God*, (New York, NY: Viking Penguin, 1976), Vol 4 (*Creative Mythology*), 27.
[545] It is arguable that the unspecified fruit that the Hebrew text of Genesis had in mind as shared by Adam and Eve—after which they became aware of their nakedness, were pushed out of the Garden of Eden, and had sexual relations for the first time, yielding Cain and Abel as their first babies—was a pomegranate. But that's another story for another day.

inscriptions, including on a bronze coin from the Thracian city of Maroneia dating to circa 400-350 BCE. Like Jesus in his aspect as the Father, Dionysios is called *Pater* ("father") in Greek. Typical, too, of the broad syncretism that defines the era, its texts and its terminology, the reference to Dionysios as "King of Kings" not only resonates to and from that phrase as it is used in late Judaean and early Jewish nomenclature, but echoes the phraseology used to refer to the Egyptian god Osiris in the late 18th and early 19th dynasties (c. 1300 BCE). His epithets include: "the king of eternity, the lord of everlastingness, who traverseth millions of years in the duration of his life, the firstborn son of the womb of Nut, begotten of Seb, the prince of gods and men, the god of gods, the king of kings, the lord of lords, the prince of princes, the governor of the world whose existence is for everlasting."

And of course, Osiris, too, by the Hellenistic period, has become popular not only as a god who presides over the dead but who arrived at the position by virtue of being a god who dies—destroyed, as we have noted above, (on 139, 254 and 306), by his evil half-brother, Seth—and is resurrected through the efforts of his wife/sister, Isis. In his reborn/resurrected form he is Horus, who is, in other words, simultaneously the son of the father, Osiris and Osiris the father himself; as he is both the son of Isis, born through parthenogenesis, and also her spouse (since he is also Osiris).

To summarize: Dionysios (and to a less detailed extent, Osiris/Horus) is yet another solar hero, like Mithras, who was depicted as having been born of a virgin on December 25th or the winter solstice, performing miracles and receiving divine epithets, being killed, giving his blood as a sacrifice, returning from the dead after three days in Hades, and ascending into heaven. All of these motifs also evolve as essential to the understanding of Jesus Christ as antiquity moves toward the medieval period; they thus underscore the fact that the emerging and evolving Church had more than just Judaism and one or two forms of Paganism with which to compete. One might argue that even details less essential than these in the narratives of Jesus and Dionysios offer parallels that would have challenged would-be adherents who were trying to choose between the two religions (aside from the many other choices). Thus for example, the episode picked up through its appearance in Euripides' play, *The Bacchae* (ca 415 BCE), in which Dionysios appears before King Pentheus on charges of claiming divinity *might* be said to be echoed in the passages in the Gospels where Jesus is interrogated by Pontius Pilate, although both the contexts and the contents of the two episodes are very different.

Nonetheless, the broad nature of the challenge of Dionysian/Bacchic faith to Christianity's gradual rise to hegemony in the course of the fourth century would have been further intensified if one accepts the proposal of E. Kessler that the Dionysian cult had developed into strict monotheism—for most of its Greco-Roman history, the cult of Dionysios placed him as one among many other gods, of course—by the 4th century CE; together with Mithraism and other sects, the cult formed one among several instances of "pagan monotheism" in direct competition with early Christianity (and Judaism) during late antiquity.[546] Even without this supposition the parallels and likely competition would have been considerable.

If the material in the previous several pages seems a bit overwhelming in its spiritual complexity and range of internal paradoxes, one can only imagine what the implications would have been for inhabitants of mid-to-late Roman antiquity, confronted with so many options, often with only subtle apparent distinctions among them—although for the most part, they would at least not have felt that they had to make a single definitive choice and leave it at that. Moreover, there is still more—an entirely other arena, so to speak—to be noted in that spiritually complicated world. For there were also hybrids between Judaism and Christianity on the edge of the Empire that have long been all but forgotten by everyday religious historiography. Thus for example the so-called Elkhasaites were a group that shared features in common with both Judaism and Christianity. The group enjoyed its greatest efflorescence in southern Mesopotamia during the Sassanian period (ca 251-643 CE).[547] Whatever might once have existed of their own literature has not survived, so that our understanding of their beliefs comes mainly from a trio of early Church Fathers, in their discussions of and commentaries on heretical movements, to whom we shall momentarily turn

There was more, however, with which to complicate the spiritual picture of the world of the third century. Yet another popular sect from this period, whose founder was raised by his parents in the Elkhasaite tradition, was that known as Manichaeism, founded by the Persian prophet, Mani (ca 216-74), who—according to the Cologne Mani-Codex—was born into an Elkhasaite family in what was then Arsacid (Parthian) Persia (250 BCE-224 CE)—he was born, specifically, in Mesopotamia—that became Sassanid Persia by 224.[548] The Manichaean tradition asserts that its prophet experienced his first revelations at the age of 12 and again when he was 24—and that during these years he gradually grew spiritually dissatisfied with the tenets of the Elkhasaite sect. The source for these revelations was what he referred to as his "Twin" (Aramaic *Ta'uma*; Greek *Syzygos*)—a kind of *doeppelgaenger/alter ego* that he also viewed as his Protective Angel or Divine Self.

This Divine Self brought him to full self-realization, transforming him into a *gnosticos* (someone who knows; who is possessed of divine knowledge—*gnosis*—and liberating insight), through teaching him the truths that he shaped into a religion. He thus claimed to be the Paraclete of truth—the embodiment of that helper referenced in the New Testament that is most typically identified with the Holy Spirit in Christian thought.

He may have been influenced by other contemporary Mesopotamian-based movements as well, such as Mandaeanism, and also by translations of Jewish apocalyptic writings similar to those found at Qumran, and by the Syriac dualist-gnostic

---

[546] Kessler offered this assertion in the symposium *Pagan Monotheism in the Roman Empire*, Exeter, 17–20 July 2006.

[547] They were presumably named for their founder, whose name is offered in slightly variant forms by our sources: *Elkhasi* (Ηλχασῖ, in Hippolytus), *Elksai* ('Ηλξαί, in Epiphanius), or *Elkesai* (Ελκεσαῖ, in Eusebius).

[548] The Sasanian (Sasanid) Empire was founded by Ardashir I, after the fall of the Parthian Empire and the defeat of the last Arsacid (Parthian) king, Artabanus V.

writer Bardaisan (who lived a generation before Mani).[549] He also seems to have been specifically influenced by the Enoch literature that had emerged during this period, vehemently rejected as apocryphal and pseudepigraphal by the Jewish and Christian mainstream leaders, but of strong interest to their mystical communities (particularly the early Jewish mystics).[550]

As far as is known, Mani composed seven written works, six of which were written in Syriac or Aramaic. The seventh, the *Shabuhragan*, was written in Middle Persian and presented by him to the most renowned Shah of Sassanian Persia, Shapur I. Although there is no proof that Shapur himself was a Manichaean, he clearly tolerated the spread of the new faith.[551] That changed with a change in the administration: the Sassanian Shah Bahram I (r. 271-4) apparently executed Mani—or Mani may have died in prison while awaiting execution—in 274.

Although most of Mani's original writings have been lost, a good number of translations and fragmentary texts have survived. From these we get a sense of a cosmological view that poses an ongoing struggle between a good, spiritual world of light, and an evil, material world of darkness. Through an ongoing process throughout human history, light is gradually removed from the world of matter and returned to the world of

---

[549] In recalling the earlier discussion of the putative influence of Zoroastrianism on the Qumran sect, particularly with regard to the dualistic emphasis of the "Battle Scroll," we might also recall the question as to whether and where the sect and its teachings survived after the destruction of Qumran during the time of the Judaean Revolt against the Romans (65-73 CE); and might add that, by the third through sixth centuries, the primary site of Jewish spiritual, intellectual and cultural activity was in Mesopotamia, and only secondarily in Judaea-Palestina.

Bardaisan (154-ca 225) was a Syrian or Parthian Christian gnostic who, *as* a Christian, sought to spread the teachings of the Church throughout the region, probably assisting the King of Edessa to shape the first Christian state in the early third century—but whose own teachings came to be viewed as heretical by the Church.

Mandaeanism is yet another gnostic-styled belief system (*manda* in Aramaic, like *gnosis* in Greek, means "knowledge") that emerged, perhaps by the second century CE, possibly originating in the Jordan River Valley but becoming established in Mesopotamia. Its essential principles include a view of the world in light/dark dualistic terms: all that is good, including the soul, derives from the World of Light and all that is evil—including the body and all of material reality—comes from the World of Darkness. The World of Light is governed by an entity—a Being too vast and unintelligible to be described in human words (i.e., ineffable) —variously referred to as "King of Light," "Lord of Greatness," "Great Mind," or "Life." An innumerable array of beings, emanating from the Light, surround and constantly praise It, although they inhabit a reality separate from that of this ultimate Being, and also separate from our own world. The Lord of Darkness, together with a female spouse, was formed from chaotic dark waters; the darkness that It governs is protected by a serpent/dragon-like being, called "Ur." These three entities created demonic progeny who govern the seven *planetes* and the twelve zodiacal districts of our heavens.

Our world is in fact a blending of light and dark shaped by the demiurge—named Ptahil—with the assistance of the dark powers. Adam was created by these dark beings, but his soul/mind was directly created by the Light, which is why humans can achieve salvation by means of our souls—albeit that "hidden Adam" component in us all requires an effort to be rescued from the dark, to ascend into the true heavenly realm of the Light. A key to redemption of the soul is baptism, which is performed not just once, but many times in the course of one's life. (John the Baptist is considered by the Mandaic tradition to have been a Mandaean, whose numerous baptisms helped push many humans toward salvation.)

[550] Enoch is found in the genealogy of the book of Genesis, chapter 5, which carries from Adam to Noah. Whereas concerning everyone else the standard litany is "X lived so many years, begat Y, lived so many years and died," where Enoch is concerned the end of that litany is "...lived so many years and walked with God, for the Lord took him." For early Jewish mystics obsessively focused on the text of the Torah as God's revealed word with nothing accidental, incidental or insignificant about its every syllable, this anomaly not only caught the eye but provoked an entire corpus of literature purporting to be Enoch's account of how he was taken up to heaven and entered the innermost hiddenness of God. See Soltes: *Searching for Oneness*, Chapter One.

[551] One might be reminded of Constantine, who tolerated—even actively supported the expansion of—Christianity, although it is not clear when or even whether he personally became a Christian.

light whence it originated. One can readily enough recognize the influence of Zoroastrianism, but with a more extreme emphasis on the dualism than had been articulated in the earlier faith as Ahura Mazda and Ahriman.

Further, Mani apparently travelled early on in his career to the Kushan Emipire that dominated much of the northwestern Indian subcontinent between the mid-first and mid-third centuries CE, which would account for what may also be the influence on his thinking of Buddhism. Most obviously, the idea of the transmigration of souls became a Manichaean belief, and the quadripartite structure of the Manichaean community, divided between male and female monks (the "elect") and lay followers (the "hearers") who supported them, may have been based on that of the Buddhist sangham.[552]

Of particular interest to our own narrative is the portrayal of him by Hegemonius as teaching that the God who created the world, the Israelite/Judaean/Jewish/Christian Jehovah (*YHVH*), was actually a satanic being.[553] Hegemonius reports Mani as saying, "It is the Prince of Darkness who spoke with Moses, the Jews [Israelites] and their priests.[554] Thus the Christians, the Jews, and the Pagans are involved in the same error when they worship this God. For he leads them astray in the lusts he taught them." Hegemonius continues: "Now, he who spoke with Moses, the Jews [Israelites], and the priests that he [Mani] says are the archons of Darkness, and the Christians, Jews, and Pagans are one and the same, as they revere the same god. For in his aspirations he seduces them, as he is not the God of Truth. And so therefore all those who put their hope in the god who spoke with Moses and the prophets have [this in store for themselves, namely] to be bound with him, because they did not put their hope in the God of Truth. For that one spoke with them (only) according to their own aspirations." Such teachings would suggest that Manichaeism shared fundamental views with Gnosticism—or might simply be called a version of Gnosticism.

There is still more to this with regard to emerging and evolving Judaism and Christianity in their conflicts with each other and with other forms of faith. For Mani is said to have had distinct views of Jesus as a being possessed of three qualities or identities: the Luminous, the Messianic, and the Suffering (*patibilis*). As Jesus the Luminous he was the ultimate revealer and guide—who awakened Adam from his long slumber and explained to him the divine origins of his soul, as well as the unhappy captivity of the soul

---

[552] Much of the pioneering research into Manicheaism that, among other things, has led to conclusions regarding this last issue, was done by Richard Foltz. See in particular his books, *Spirituality in the Land of the Noble: How Iran Shaped the World's Religions*. (Oxford: Oneworld Publications, 2004); and *Religions of the Silk Road*. (New York: Palgrave Macmillan, 2010).

[553] Hegemonius was a fourth-century Christian writer known only from his presumed authorship of the *Acta Archelai*, a work originally in Greek (a portion of which survives in the *Panarion*—a contemporary discussion of extant heresies by St. Epiphanius, Bishop of Salamis on Cyprus, venerated as a Church father in both the Orthodox and Catholic traditions) that survives in its totality in Latin translation. It is devoted to a discussion of Manichaeism. So there is something circular about this: we know about Mani from Hegemonius and we know about Hegemonius only that he presumably wrote about Mani. The significance of this last issue is enhanced in interest by the fact that the *Acta* is the oldest and most significant anti-Manichaean polemical text—so what it tells us about Mani is not objective. The *Acta* presents a fictional account of a debate between Mani and Archelaus, the Christian bishop of the city of Carchar in Roman-governed Mesopotamia, as well as a summary of Mani's teachings on cosmogony and also a version of Mani's biography. The work would continue to exert substantial influence on anti-Manichaean writings in Late Antiquity and into the Middle Ages.

[554] It is presumably Hegemonius, and not Mani who, for obvious reasons, errs in referring to the Israelites of Moses' era as Jews.

within the body through being mixed with physical matter. That analysis would, of course, apply to all of the offspring of Adam—in other words, to all of humanity—and truly recognizing this narrative would come through the acquisition of properly taught esoteric knowledge.

Jesus the Messiah is viewed by Mani as the historical figure who appeared as a prophet among the Judaeans and was his (Mani's) own forerunner. However, he was completely divine, never experiencing human conception and birth; the Manichean view of even the Virgin Birth is that it is obscene. Since the messianic Jesus is also the luminous Jesus, and thus Jesus was/is the Light of the World, where would that light have been while Jesus was in Mary's womb for nine months? His real birth came with his baptism, which was when the Father openly acknowledged his Sonship.

Similarly, the suffering, death and even resurrection of Jesus were illusory, since such acts have no salvational value except as an intensified model of the suffering and eventual deliverance of the human soul, and as a prefiguration of Mani's own martyred suffering and death. The pain endured by the Light Particles imprisoned throughout the visible universe, however, is real and part of the here and now. The wounds of Christ on the cross are a metaphor for the real wounds suffered by our souls. The Suffering Jesus, suspended on a mystical (i.e., hidden) Cross of Light, was/is the life and salvation of humankind; that Cross is ubiquitous throughout nature, in every tree, plant, fruit, vegetable, herb and even soil and stones. The entirety of the immanent world, in other words (or in our terms, the entire *profanus*) experiences and expresses the suffering of the soul imprisoned within that physicality.[555]

Thus Mani comes to see himself as an apostle and successor of Jesus. The tradition also claimed that he was the reincarnation of Krishna, Buddha, and Zoroaster. It would seem, in any case, that he believed that the teachings of these prior figures were incomplete and too limited in their focus, and that the revelations of which he had been the recipient and transmitter—the Religion of Light that he taught—were intended to be shared with the entire world more effectively than had been possible through these earlier figures. This may be understood as a classic supercessionist viewpoint, of the sort that is beginning to emerge for Christianity in the third century with respect to its relationship to Judaism, as we have seen implicitly articulated by Origen.

Manichaeism spread rather quickly in the mid-third century throughout the Aramaic- and Syriac-speaking parts of the Middle East and Eastern Mediterranean world, thriving until the mid-seventh century (when, like Zoroastrianism, it would largely be superseded by Islam). At the height of its demographic success, its texts and institutions could be found as far to the east as China and to the west across much of the Roman Empire. It reached Rome through the apostle Psattiq by about the year 280, and was apparently flourishing in the Fayum area of Egypt around 290. There were allegedly even Manichaean monasteries extant in Rome during the time of Pope Miltiades (ca 310-14). It was perhaps, even more substantively than Mithraism or Dionysianism, the main rival

---

[555] See the fuller discussion of this in Samuel N.C. Lieu's *Manichaeism in the Later Roman Empire and Medieval China*, (Tubingen: JCB Mohr, 1992).

to Christianity for a time—and arguably closer to mainstream Christianity than these other forms of faith, as classical Paganism was slowly being eclipsed.[556]

In terms of complexities and confusions for non-practitioners then or students today of the religious configuration of that era, one might note that among the angelic beings contained within the Manichaean worldview were two that were referred to by Persian-speaking Manichaeans as Mithra. Thus Mihrayazd (*Mithra-yazata*) was the name for the "living spirit" (*ruha hayya* in Aramaic), a kind of savior who rescued the "first man" (*adam kadmon* in the Hebrew of early Jewish mystical texts) from the Darkness into which he had plunged through his sinful nature. Mihr (*Mihr yazd*) is the "messenger" (in Aramaic, *izgadda*), who is also a savior, focused, however, on establishing principles that will liberate the Light that was lost when Adam was defeated (i.e., succumbed to sin) and thus plunged into the Darkness of sin by the Satan.[557]

In any case, the spread and success of Manichaeism were perceived as a threat to other religions, and it was widely persecuted in Christian, as well as Zoroastrian, Buddhist (and later, Muslim) cultures. Thus in 291, persecution arose in the Sassanian Empire with the murder of the apostle Sisin by Bahram II (r. 274-93), together with the slaughter of many of his fellow Manichaeans, a generation after the death of Mani himself at the hands of Bahram's predecessor. During the same approximate period, in 296, the Roman Emperor Diocletian, (who was in the midst of enacting the most serious persecution of Christianity in its history), issued a decree against the Manichaeans, declaring that "[w]e order that their organizers and leaders be subject to the final penalties and condemned to the fire with their abominable scriptures," resulting in many deaths in Egypt and North Africa. By the year 354, Hilary of Poitiers wrote that the Manichaean faith was a significant force in southern Gaul. In 381 Christian leaders requested that Theodosius I—who had assumed the Imperial purple less than two years earlier and was engaged, we recall, in the process of turning the Empire into a Christian state, in which any and all other forms of faith were coming to be considered *superstitiones*—to strip Manichaeans of their civil rights. He issued a decree of death for Manichaean monks the following year.

One of the more interesting aspects of all of this late fourth-century spiritual twisting and turning is that St Augustine himself had been a Manichaean in his younger years, formally converting to Christianity in 387, some five or six years after Theodosius' decree and shortly before the emperor made Christianity the only acceptable *religio* throughout the empire. In Book III of his *Confessions*, Augustine asserts that he joined the group as one of the "hearers," but by Book V he is beginning to question the idea that knowledge of any sort, however, esoteric, will lead to salvation.

Moreover, he rejects the notion that an inherently uncorrupted soul is corrupted by being mixed with the physical body: "I still thought that it is not we who sin but some other nature that sins within us. It flattered my pride to think that I incurred no guilt and, when I did wrong, not to confess it... I preferred to excuse myself and blame this unknown

---

[556] Manichaeism survived longer in the East than in the West, and it appears to have finally faded away only by the beginning of the fifteenth century in southern China.

[557] A yet further layer of this is that the essential terminology in play here would also find its way into (or found its way from) early Jewish mystical thought—in particular the idea of *adam kadmon* ("primordial man") and the *ruha hayya* ("the living spirit").

thing which was in me but was not part of me. The truth, of course, was that it was all my own self, and my own impiety had divided me against myself. My sin was all the more incurable because I did not think myself a sinner" (Bk V, Section 10). So rather than knowledge of a *pleroma*-like realm to which one can return one's soul, he embraces the notion that one's soul may be corrupted in and of itself and not because of a physical aspect to it, *per se*, and expressed the need to acknowledge one's sinfulness and to seek a way off the path of sin.

By Book IX, Augustine writes of his having determined that Manichaeism is insufficient and incapable of effecting change in one's life. He was baptized, subsequently becoming one of Manichaeism's most significant adversaries. This would be most distinctly evident in his writings against the Manichaean Bishop, Faustus of Mileve, Numidia (today's Algeria), whom Augustine queried at length regarding spirituality and salvation in 383. Soon after his conversion, having been impressed by Faustus' erudition but failing to find his spiritual questions answered, Augustine wrote a polemic, *Contra Faustum*.

Some modern students of St Augustine, however, have argued that he was influenced by Manichaeism in his exposition on good and evil (discussed in particular in his *Enchiridion*) and his view of hell, as well as with regard to his emergent hostility toward the physical body and in particular toward sexual relations. In any case, The Manichaeans preserved many Christian works that were left out of the final canon of the Bible and regarded as apocryphal, such as the *Acts of/Gospel According to Thomas*, which would very likely otherwise have been lost.

Certainly later heresies with which the Church struggled, most notably the Cathar or Albigensian heresy, at the very least echo aspects of the sort of thinking associated with Manichaeism, as well as Mandaism and other gnostic-like schools of thought that flourished alongside evolving mainstream Christianity, Judaism and slowly-fading classical Paganism in the second through fifth centuries. The Cathars (and other medieval heresies, like those of the Paulicians and the Bogomils, believed intensely in the sort of physical-dark/spiritual-light dualism endemic to these earlier forms of heretical (or quasi-Christian) thought. On the other hand, one obvious difference is that the Cathars were so profoundly hostile to anything physical/material that sacraments like baptism and rituals like communion were viewed by them as spiritually illegitimate—even associated with the Satan—since they involved material substances.[558]

Let us return, however, to the Elkhasaites, for a moment, and to the three Church Fathers who offer us source material on their beliefs. Hippolytus of Rome (ca 170-ca 236 CE) was one of the important third-century Christian theologians in Rome—certainly as a compiler and synthesizer if less so as an original thinker. He came into conflict with Pope Zephyrinus (199-217), whom he accused of being a modalist—one who believes that the entire Trinity dwells within Jesus, and that the names "Father" and Son" are only different designations for the same entity. Hippolytus was a champion of the *logos* doctrine: that

---

[558] The term "Cathar" is derived from Greek *katharos*, meaning "pure": they viewed themselves as spiritual purists, uncorrupted by anything material; they were called Albigensians because their largest and most central community was located in Albi, in the south of France. I will discuss this group a bit more in the following chapter.

God is simultaneously singular and indivisible and yet plural. Hippolytus may even have led a schismatic group, asserting himself as a rival Bishop of Rome—and thus he is referred to by many Church historians as the first antipope.

His disagreement apparently continued with Zephyirinus' successor to the papal throne, Calixtus I (217-22), and in turn with Urbanus I (222-30) and, finally, with Pope Pontianus (230-35). By the reign of Pontianus his primary disagreement apparently evolved toward the subject of what he saw as an overly indulgent attitude toward penances, a softness designed to encourage the influx of and to accommodate the presence of large numbers of pagans as new Christians. However, he is believed to have been reconciled with the mainstream Church shortly after having been exiled to Sardinia together with Pope Pontianus—and he died as a martyr, under the emperor Maximinus Thrax.

Hippolytus' most significant work is his *The Refutation of All Heresies*, written in Greek. From it one can gain a sense of the wide range of beliefs both rampant in the Roman world of the early to mid-third century and of how widely the term "heresy" was used to label systems that did not conform to the mainstream Christian understanding of the Divine *Sacer*. In Book IX we get the discussion of the Elkhasaites. Hippolytus asserts that a "Jewish-Christian" by the name of Alcibiades of Apamaea came to Rome during the papacy of Callixtus, and that he had with him a book that he claimed he had received from Parthia, and that the book had come to him from a just man named Elkhasai. According to Alcibiades the book had been revealed by an angel ninety-six miles high, sixteen miles broad and twenty-four across the shoulders, whose footprints were fourteen miles long and four miles wide by two miles deep. This giant figure, he further asserted, was the Son of God, who was accompanied by His Sister, the Holy Spirit, (who was of the same physical dimensions). Alcibiades announced that a new remission of sins had been proclaimed in the third year of the reign of the Emperor Trajan (which would be 100-101 CE), and he described a baptismal process that could bring about forgiveness even to the severest of sinners.

In the commentary that Hippolytus offers in Chapters 8 and 9, he writes that Alcibiades teaches the natural birth, preexistence and reincarnation of Christ but also that Alcibiades teaches circumcision and the Law of Moses—so his teachings emphatically synthesize elements from both Judaism and Christianity. Hippolytus then goes on, in chapter 10, to describe at length the group's teachings on baptism. For all sins of impurity, even against nature, a second baptism is enjoined "in the name of the great and most high God and in the name of His Son the great King," with an adjuration of the seven witnesses written in the book (sky, water, the holy spirits, the angels of prayer, oil, salt and earth). Baptism is offered also as a cure for certain maladies. Thus, for example, forty consecutive days of baptism in cold water is recommended for consumption and for the possessed. In Chapter 11 he discusses details that include Elkhasai's Sabbatarian teaching and also the astrological instruction not to baptize under certain constellations.

Later, Eusebius (ca 263-339 CE), in his *History* 6.38, summarizes a sermon on Psalm 82 delivered in Caesarea by Origen warning his audience against the doctrine of "the Elkhasaites." According to Eusebius, Origen—who would therefore be our second Church Father who is a source for this subject—regarded the heresy as recent, and asserted that the group denied the writings of Paul, claiming to have received a new book from heaven. "'I will show you,' Origen says, 'what evil things that opinion teaches, that you may not be carried away by it. It rejects certain parts of every scripture. Again it uses portions of the Old Testament and the Gospels, but rejects the apostle [Paul] altogether. It says that to deny Christ is an indifferent matter, and that he who understands will, under necessity, deny with his mouth, but not in his heart. They produce a certain book which they say fell from heaven. They hold that whoever hears and believes this shall receive remission of sins—another remission than that which Jesus Christ has given.' Such is the account of these persons."

Finally, a century and a half later, our third source, Epiphanius of Salamis (ca 310/20-402) claimed to have found this same book in use among the Sampsæans, descendants of the earlier Elkhasaites, and also among the Ossaens and various Ebionite communities. We learn further from Epiphanius that the book condemned virginity and continence, and made marriage obligatory—the opposite of what were evolving as mainstream Church teachings regarding ideal sexual (non-) relations. It permitted the worship of images if necessary in order to escape persecution, provided that the act was merely an external one, but was disavowed in the heart. Prayer was to be made not to the East, but always specifically toward Jerusalem from whatever direction. Not only was animal sacrifice condemned, but the book is said by Epiphanius to have denied that it had been offered by the patriarchs or under Mosaic Law. The Israelite prophets, he tells us, as well as the New Testament Apostles were rejected by the Elkhasaites, as was St. Paul together with all his writings.

This summary discussion of our threefold, rather varied, primary patristic source material regarding this group leads us to a further consideration of Hippolytus and Origen, since they are of broad interest to us with regard to the complicated range of faith options during the mid-third century. Within the sweep of Hippolytus' *Refutation of All Heresies*, the Elkhasaites are just a small part of his focus. Indeed, the *Philosophoumena*, as the first volume within his ten-book opus is typically called, and which is often regarded as the most important part of the larger work, offers us a distinct sense of how broadly that term is used.[559]

For it presents a comprehensive summary and discussion of the work of all of the Greek philosophers—hence its commonly-used title—from Thales and the Naturalists to the rest of the Presocratics to the thought of Sokrates, Plato and Aristotle to the ideas distinguishing the various Hellenistic schools. So his intention, it would seem, is not only to articulate what constitutes proper versus improper Christian belief, but to demonstrate that Christianity offers the most correct understanding of the Divine *Sacer* in comparison with *every* possible alternative belief system—and in directing himself toward these two goals he does not distinguish between misbelieving Christians and non-believers of whatever sort.

---

[559] Book I was in fact long mistaken for a work by Origen. Books II and III are lost and Books IV-X turned up, but without authorial attribution, among the many manuscripts in the Mount Athos monastery complex, in 1842. They, too, were attributed at that time to Origen when they were published by E. Miller, in 1852. That mis-attribution was subsequently rectified. I should add that some scholars use the title *Philosophoumena* to refer to the entire work.

In Hippolytus' Fourth Book, he mainly discusses astrology, its origins in Babylonia and its futility—he even refers to its absurdity (in chapter 7) with regard to engaging the Divine *Sacer* effectively. He considers astronomical calculations applied to heavenly objects—their sizes, distances, speeds, types of motion—and turns that discussion toward the art of identifying people's "type" based on their astrological birth-sign, on the one hand. On the other hand, in the midst of this he embeds a discussion (in chapter 28) of magicians, their incantations ("…uttering to [his assistant] several words partly in Greek and partly, as it were, in the Hebrew language [containing] the customary incantations employed by magicians") and rituals and, most of all, their tricks. We recognize the ever-present presumption regarding the efficacy of the Hebrew language for magical purposes and might wonder how Hippolytus views its use by ordinary Jews as a language of prayer. He does not make reference to this at all, although he does discuss the Jews, as we shall see.

He finally turns (in Book IV) to the Persian, Babylonian and Egyptian religions' intense emphasis on numerology—and how the study of any of this can lead to a heretical understanding of the *sacer-profanus* relationship. So there is a thin or perhaps just very blurry line between heresy itself and false belief systems that can *lead* one into heresy—or at least a lack of clarity as to what heresy is, which is an issue to which we shall shortly turn. Hippolytus' work in any case should reinforce for us the notion of how complicated the world of the third century was with regard (among other things) to knowing which form of which faith one ought to follow in order to be best off in this life—and possibly the next. Briefly summarized, in Book V he talks of the Nasseni—who ascribe their religious system to James, the brother of Jesus, and whose doctrine regarding the soul is found in the "Gospel According to Thomas"—as well as of the Peratae (whose spiritual system is largely astrological), the Sethians and the Justinians. In Book VI he begins with a brief reference to the Ophites, and then turns to a lengthy discussion of Simon Magus and the Pythagorean origins of his teachings, and also discusses Valentinus and his heretical teachings, as well as Marcus and *his* heretical teachings.

Book VII is largely preoccupied with the ideas of Basilides ("which are derived from Aristotle, not from Jesus Christ") as well as with Saturnilus, "who flourished about the same period with Basilides, but spent his time in Antioch, (a city) of Syria… He asserts that there is one Father, unknown to all: He who had made angels, archangels, principalities, [and] powers; and that by certain angels, seven [in number], the world was made, and all things that are in it. And [Saturnilus asserts] that man was a work of angels."[560] He discusses Marcion and his assertion that there are two different, contending sources that co-created the world—one that is good and one that is evil.

He also discusses the Ebionites, Theodotus, the Melkhisedecians, the Nicolaitans, Cerdon, and finally Apelles, who, influenced by Marcion, claims "that there is a certain good Deity, as also Marcion supposed, and that he who created all things is just, [and] was the Demiurge of generated entities. [But Apelles also maintains] that there is a *third [deity], the one who was in the habit of speaking to Moses, and that this [deity] was of a fiery nature, and that there was another fourth god, a cause of evils.* [italics added].

---

[560] Hippolytus of Rome, *The Refutation of All Heresies*, Bk VII, chapter 16, ls 1-3.

But these he denominates angels. He utters slanders, however, against the Law [i.e., the Torah] and against the prophets, by alleging that the things that have been written [in the Torah] are [contrived by] humans, and are false. Further, he selects from the Gospels or [from the writings of] the Apostle [Paul] whatever pleases himself, but he [mainly] devotes himself to the discourses of a certain Philumene as if these are the revelations of a prophetess. He affirms, however, that Christ descended from the power above; that is, from the good [Deity], and that he is the son of that good [Deity]—but not born of a virgin…"[561]

Book VIII focuses on the Docetae, on Hermogenes, on Monoimus, on the Quartodecimans, the Montanists and the Encratites, "who acknowledge some things concerning God and Christ in like manner with the Church. In respect, however, of their mode of life, they pass their days inflated with pride. They suppose, that by meats they magnify themselves, while abstaining from animal food, [and by] being water-drinkers, and forbidding to marry, and devoting themselves during the remainder of life to ascetic habits. But persons of this description are really Cynics rather than Christians."[562]

Book IX describes Noetus and Noetianism—and refers to Zephyrinus and "his assistant" Callixtus (i.e., two of the four Popes whom he opposed for their alleged heretical views) as followers of the doctrines of Noetus. It is in this book, to repeat, in chapters 8 through 22, that he offers most of his discussion of the Elkhasaites. He also turns in this book to a discussion of Jewish sects (chapter 13) and to an extended discussion of the Essenes (chapters 14-23), also briefly covering the Pharisees (Chapter 23), the Sadducees (chapter 24) and finally, as a kind of separate discussion and summary: of the Jewish religiion overall, in his last chapter (25).

In Book X, Hippolytus offers a brief, final summary of each of these heresies. There are three particularly obvious realizations to which we arrive in even merely perusing this last book. One: how extraordinarily broad the range of so-called heretical alternatives to mainstream Christianity was in the mid-third century across the Roman Empire— probably merely in Rome itself. Some of these—the Marcionites or the Montanists, for example—had substantial followings and a long enough historical shelf life to be familiar even today to those somewhat aware of the issue of heresy for the Church, and some of them were obscure enough that practically nobody today but a reader of Hippolytus would be aware of their existence at that time.

Two: in most cases, our knowledge of these various belief systems is derived from Christian writers *like* Hippolytus who are necessarily (and naturally) their detractors. Just as we are likely to raise our brows at the sort of accusations directed toward Christianity by its pagan opponents in the first several centuries after its birth—would we take seriously

---

[561] Ibid, chapter 26, ls 1-3. His discussion of the Melkhisedecians (in chapter 24) is particularly interesting, since they would appear to have taken the Priest, Melkhitzedek from the Abraham story in Gen 14, who is an important figure in Greek Orthodoxy (as evidenced, for instance, by the mosaics in Ravenna where he is depicted) and elevated him to a status even beyond Jesus—for this group "attempted to establish (the doctrine), that a certain Melkhisedec constitutes the greatest power, and that this one is greater than Christ. And they allege that Christ happens to be according to the likeness (of this Melkhisedec)." Or Hippolytus doesn't understand their ideology, given that he refers to "a certain" Melkhisedec (or I am wrong in my supposition regarding which Melkhisedec/Melkhitzedek is at issue here).

[562] Ibid, Bk VIII, chapter 13, ls 1-4.

the notion that Christianity is a form of political or spiritual *superstitio* or *magia*?—we must weigh very carefully what the Church's writers have left us with regard to the substance of any of these other belief systems before nodding our heads with a sense of absolute conviction that this is how and what they were.

Three: Hippolytus includes under the rubric "heresy" Judaism—including subset Judaean religio-political perspectives, like the Pharisees, Sadducees and Essenes—as well as all the schools of Greek philosophy. Under other, later circumstances, these would be considered varied forms of false belief, not heresy.[563] Significant for our purposes, Hippolytus concludes his discussion with a general exhortation to avoid heresy—significant because this is a problem that will still not be solved more than a thousand years later, as we shall summarily see in our last chapter, and the problem will have expanding implications not only for intra-Christian relations but for Christian-Jewish relations.

Hippolytus' slightly younger contemporary, Origen (184/5-253/4), was also an important Christian writer, whose work, *Contra Celsum*, also written in Greek, takes this issue of definitional lines in another direction: not between heresy and false belief as much as between Christianity and both Paganism and Judaism. One of Origen's key contributions to developing Christian theology was his articulation of the concept of the eternal generation of the Son by way of his formulation of the famous phrase, *Ouk en pote hote ouk en* ("There was never a when, when he was not") which would be repeated significantly in the discussions at the Council of Nicaea in 325 and its Arian-Athanasian controversy regarding the divinity of Jesus.

A substantial part of Origen's self-appointed task was to defend the developing Church from its primarily pagan assailants. This task really had two components to it. One was to assure the Roman government that Christianity was not a pernicious *superstitio*, contrary to what that government often seemed to believe during this period, as we have previously noted.[564] More specifically, during the reign of the Emperor Decius (249-51), two events combined to create the first really substantial persecution of Christians. The Emperor issued an edict at the beginning of 250 requiring that every adult across the empire offer a sacrifice to the gods. This was in part designed to restore a greater sense of piety to the Empire and in part to function as a signifier of loyalty for its inhabitants, since the sacrifices included a petition for the well-being of the Emperor as a central part of the ritual. Moreover, the sacrifices needed to be performed in the presence of a witnessing magistrate who was called upon to issue a signed certificate (a *libellus*) attesting to the carrying out of the act. (We possess actual examples of these *libelli*).

While there is no evidence that the decree was aimed, *per se*, at generating a persecution of Christians—there was nothing in the *libelli* demanding a renunciation of their faith, in contrast to what Pliny the Younger claims happened under Trajan, in 112 CE, when the Emperor allegedly require Christians to curse Christ—but it evolved that way. For as a practical matter Christians were forced to choose between death—which was the

---

[563] See the brief account of the difference among heresy, schism and infidelism above, fn 189.

[564] It might be recalled that Origen himself suffered torture as a martyr (he did not die, however) at the hands of the government under the Emperor Decius in or around 251—which prompted him to write his "Exhortation to Martyrdom." He was one of the first Christian writers to address the idea of martyrdom and its relationship to the mystic's goal of achieving oneness with God.

penalty for not obeying the edict—and their beliefs, for which sacrifices to pagan gods were by definition anathema. Around the same time there was the second outbreak of what was known as the Antonine Plague, which at its apogee between 251 and perhaps as late as 266, allegedly took the lives of 5,000 people daily in the city of Rome alone. Even allowing for considerable exaggeration, it was a fierce plague and the belief spread that it had been caused by magical activity that was associated with Christianity—already known, of course, as a *superstitio*. The need and search for scapegoats led logically enough to Christianity.

So the consequence of the confluence of these two events was that some Christians—it is not clear how many—were put to death for refusing to perform the sacrifices and others died due to the accusation of having fomented the plague through their subversive spirituality: acts of *magia* resulting from their adherence to a *superstitio*. Some went into hiding and others apostasized to save their lives. The outcome within the small but growing community was a good deal of hostility between survivors who had apostasized and those who had not—or claimed that they had not. On the other hand, the straightforwardly heroic handling of the affair by Christian leaders like St Cyprian, Bishop of Carthage, led to an influx of converts to the faith.

Given our overall subject, it is also interesting to note that the Jews were exempt from the decree. As we have seen, Julius Caesar, following Pompey's lead in granting *religio licita* status to the Judaeans, had formally articulated a policy that permitted them to follow their traditional practices without interference. That policy was continued by Augustus and subsequent Roman Emperors and eventually extended to Judaeans who eventuated as Jews—but not, as we have earlier discussed, to those who, after the Judaean schism led to a clear articulation of the two sibling forms of faith, to those who eventuated as Christians.

It was usually well understood by the pagan Roman authorities that the Jews would not and could not sacrifice to the Roman gods or burn incense before the image of the Emperor without contradicting their faith, but that they could be counted upon to be loyal to the state nonetheless, so they were typically exempted from the sort of edict such as the one Decius emitted.[565] Christianity, as a *superstitio*, was subject to hostility and fear and in the case of the Decian decree, persecution if they refused to sacrifice, and although the persecution died out by the time of the Emperor's death or even earlier, (and certainly well before the plague abated), the traumatic effect on the collective memory of the Church over the next few centuries was considerable. This brief time was retrospected as extended and horrific.

In any case, this was part of the context for Origen's activity during the middle of the third century. The other was that he sought to present Christianity to the educated classes as intellectually respectable and as having a venerable enough history to be of worth to them. (It must be remembered that the Church's starting point—from the Apostles

---

[565] The most notorious exception came during the last year or so of the reign of Caligula (37-41 CE), but his sudden insistence that the Judaeans place his image in their Temple to be adored along with the adoration of their God we may ascribe to the madness that seems to have overtaken the young Emperor—and it never evolved as the political problem that it might have become, since Caligula was soon thereafter assassinated by his own guards.

forward—was its appeal to the lower classes and the oppressed, in general, so Origen's redirection toward a more uppercrust audience represented a significant new development; not excluding the poor and the uneducated but broadening Christianity's appeal and its sense of inclusiveness).

Origen's treatise *Against Celsus* was probably written—originally in Greek, to repeat, not Latin, which suggests that Origen was himself part of the upper-class, well-educated intelligentsia that was a significant part of his intended audience—some time around 248,[566] during the very end of the reign of Phillip the Arab and before the Decian persecution began. Celsus was a pagan who apparently spoke and wrote vociferously against Christianity—he had referred to the Church as a secret (therefore seditious) society that was illegal (i.e., a *superstitio*) and should not, therefore exist. We may easily enough infer many of Celsus' specific remarks because Origen quotes them in order to respond carefully and fully to them. Thus (to choose a handful of examples) in the first part, section 3, where specific issues begin to be discussed, Origen writes:

> [Celsus] says that Christians perform their rites and teach their doctrines in secret, and they do this with good reason: to escape the death penalty that hangs over them. He compares the danger to the risks encountered for the sake of philosophy by Sokrates... I reply that in Sokrates' case the Athenians at once regretted what they had done, and cherished no grievance against him... But in the case of the Christians the Roman Senate, the contemporary emperors, the army, the people, and the relatives of believers fought against the gospel... [so that] it would have been defeated had it not risen above the opposition by divine power, so that it has conquered the whole world that is conspiring against it.

There are two particularly interesting issues here for us. The first is the accusation made by Celsus that Christians operate in secret, since we have seen numerous times, from Mauss to Apuleius, how that idea is used as a criterion for *magia* in its seditiousness. The second is that, in choosing to make a comparison with the persecution (or, rather, execution) of Sokrates, Origen's mode of distinguishing Christianity is to point out how far-flung and successful it already is and to suggest that, given the opposition to it, this proves that it operates with divine imprimatur—by implication, the imprimatur of the *true* divine *sacer*, as opposed to the misconception of what constitutes the divine *sacer* to which the pagans are subject. These two aspects of his argument are directed to his two audiences: the first to the Roman authorities and the second to those he would convert.

In section 6, we read that

> Celsus says: "Christians get the power which they seem to possess by pronouncing the names of certain *daimones* and incantations," hinting, I suppose, at those who subdue *daimones* by enchantments and drive them out." But...they do not "get the power which they seem to possess" by

---

[566] It may also have been written earlier, as early as the late 230s, but for our purposes the precise date is not important.

any incantations, but by the name of Jesus with the recital of the *historia* [apparently meaning: a phrase referring to his crucifixion] about him... In fact, the name of Jesus is so powerful against the *daimone*s that sometimes it is effective even when pronounced by bad men... [I]t is clear that Christians make no use of spells, but only of the name of Jesus with other words that are believed to be effective, taken from *divine scripture* [italics added].

So clearly Christianity is perceived by Celsus the pagan as a form of *magia*, on the one hand, and Origen wants to disprove that notion by distinguishing the invocation of lesser *sacer* beings (*daimone*s) from the invocation of the ultimate Divine *Sacer* being, and presumably the use of prayers from the use of incantations, (although he does not explicitly say this). We have seen the Apostles driving out *daimone*s, but through the power of Jesus—whose name is presented by Origen as having the kind of power that we have seen reflected so strongly in texts like the *Sword of Moses*. On the other hand, then, the Divine Name as a source of power is shared by Jews and Christians at this time, albeit for the Jews that Name is YHVH and its myriad *m'forash* sibling forms, whereas for Christians the Name is Jesus.

Of course the reference to "divine scripture" makes Origen's refutation argument circular: "believed" by whom?—by those (i.e., obviously, Christians) for whom the referenced texts are *believed* to constitute *divine* scripture and not, say, not-to-be-believed mythology. We must also keep in mind, however, that turns of phrase from the Gospels show up as spells, or parts of spells, in the *PGM*, reflecting at least a three-fold Jewish/Christian/pagan textual overlap and at most the embrace by at least some pagans of the at-least-potential-potency of those texts assumed by Christians (and/or Jews) to be divinely revealed.

In section 7, Origen continues: "[t]hen since he often calls our doctrine *secret*, in this point I must refute him. For almost the whole world has come to know the preaching of Christians better than the opinions of philosophers. Who has not heard of Jesus' birth from a virgin, and of his crucifixion, and of his resurrection... Moreover, the mystery of his resurrection, because it has not been understood, is a byword and a laughing-stock with the unbelievers." We might recognize an oblique echo of Apuleius' *Apology* here—moved from the personal to the communal: there is nothing that I (we) do that is done in secret, contrary to my (our) accuser's claims—and with that Apuleian echo we are reminded that *magia* was/is often defined as an action performed in secret rather than in public. Origen's angle of "performed in public" is not to refer to the *performance* (astutely, since Celsus' accusation is not specifically with regard to *performing actions* but to *holding doctrinal beliefs*) but to the fact that the far-flung renown of Christianity precludes assessing it as secret: it is well exposed in the public market of belief systems, in spite of its fragile position in the eyes of Roman law (to which Origen does not, however, call attention).

The notion of overlap takes a different, equally significant and, in a sense, more pronounced turn later on in his text. In section 19, Origen begins by asserting that "[a]fter this, secretly wishing to attack the Mosaic cosmogony which indicates that the world is not yet ten thousand years old..."—the significance of which, for our purposes, is that it underscored Origen's sense of a *Judaeo-Christian* perspective, as opposed to a *Christian versus Jewish pair* of perspectives, at least vis-à-vis the pagans. That sensibility is affirmed and expressed even more clearly shortly thereafter, in section 20, where he writes:

> If, to make their doctrine about animals [i.e., that wisdom exists in irrational animals] respectable, the Egyptians introduce theological interpretations, they are wise; but if a man who has accepted *the Jewish law and lawgiver* refers to the only God, the Creator of the universe, he is regarded by Celsus and people like him as inferior to one who brings God down to the level not only of rational and mortal beings but even to that of irrational animals... [italics added]. And if the Egyptians relate this mythology [of the transmigration of the soul, including into animals], they are believed to be concealing philosophy in obscurities and mysteries; but if Moses wrote for a whole nation and left them histories and laws, his words are considered to be "empty myths not even capable of being interpreted allegorically."

Not only is Moses "defended" as an important figure and explicitly (and positively) acknowledged as offering primary significance as a lawgiver for the Jews, but there is, of course, an incidental irony for us, who have just discussed how important Moses was—albeit as a magician, not as a lawgiver or prophet—to many pagans and pagan groups (above, 292-300). We are thus reminded yet again that, if Celsus is a denigrator of Moses, he represents a different pagan viewpoint from that studied by John Gager; and that there are diverse pagans, pagan groups and pagan viewpoints on various issues with which Christianity and Judaism are contending even as they contend with each other in the matter of correctly understanding and engaging the divine *sacer*.

This is still further amplified in the next section, 21 where Origen writes that Celsus says that "'Moses heard of this doctrine that was current among the wise nations and distinguished men, and acquired a name for divine power' [i.e., he did not originate the doctrines with which Jews and Christians credit him but picked them up from an earlier source]." To this Origen responds that, "supposing we grant to him [Celsus] that Moses heard an older doctrine and passed it on to the Hebrews, if he heard a doctrine that was untrue and neither wise nor holy, and if he accepted it and passed it on to the Hebrews, he is open to criticism. But if, as you say, *he accepted wise and true doctrines and educated his own people by them*, what did he do deserving of criticism? ...[T]he doctrine of the Jews and Christians which preserves the unchangeable and unalterable nature of God..." So in this last sentence he explicitly places the Jews and Christians in one group *contra* Celsus and his pagan perspective.

Astonishingly, even in discussing circumcision in section 22—a custom that emphatically separates Jews from Christians; and Origen points out that Jesus put a stop to circumcision for his followers, a custom that Celsus says came from the Egyptians—Origen may be seen to make common cause with the Jews by defending the non-Egyptian, biblical origins of the custom. He does this by reference to Abraham, whose name, he points out, is highly regarded even by pagans: for "many of those who chant incantations for *daimones* use among their formulas 'the God of Abraham'; they do this on account of the name and the familiarity between God and this righteous man…. They employ the expression 'the God of Abraham' although they do not know who Abraham is. The same may be said of Isaac and Jacob and Israel; although these names are generally known to be Hebrew they have been inserted within formulas in many places by the Egyptians who claim to produce some magical effect."[567]

The first half of this last sentence raises a small but interesting incidental question: how solid is Origen's knowledge of the Hebrew Bible, given that Jacob and Israel are one and the same—Jacob receives a new name, Israel, after his all-night wrestling match with God (Gen 32:25-30)—while his phraseology suggests that they are two separate characters? Keeping in mind that the New Testament will not achieve final canonization for another 150 years or so, but that texts like those of the Gospels and Acts have long been available, is it the case that, as a Christian, Origen primarily focusses on these books and only superficially on those of what, for Christianity, represents an Old Testament and an Old Covenant that has been largely superseded by the new?

It may have merely been a kind of stylistic choice of syntax, but it seems odd. That sort of attitude toward the Hebrew Bible would make his assumption of a common front for Judaism and Christianity even more compelling, to say nothing of subsequent history—that, as we shall shortly see, is not all that chronologically far away. In any case, he completes section 22 by noting that his reason for defending circumcision and its Hebrew antiquity is that "if he [Celsus] thinks that he will more easily prove Christianity to be untrue if he can show its falsehood by attacking its origin in Judaeanism," he is sorely mistaken![568]

Moses continues to be the key character in his discussion. So continuing into section 23,

> Celsus next says: "The goatherds and shepherds who followed Moses as their leader were deluded by clumsy deceits into thinking that there was only one God." Let him show how, since it was, as he thinks, without any rational cause that these goatherds and shepherds abandoned the worship of many gods, he is able to comment on the large number of gods among the Greeks or the other barbarian deities. Let him prove the existence and reality of Mnemosyne… or of Themis…or… the ever-naked Graces…. …Why are the Greek myths about the gods truer than, say, those of the Egyptians…? How much more certain and superior to all of these fantasies is it to be persuaded by the visible universe that the world is well ordered and to worship the one Maker of that which is itself one?

---

[567] What in part makes this even more interesting is the fact that the Egyptians are pretty well known, in any case, to have practiced circumcision in pagan antiquity. Sigmund Freud's *Moses and Monotheism*, published in 1938, takes a very Celsus-like general view of the Moses/Israelite story as beginning in Egypt—as opposed to beginning in Canaan, coming to Egypt and returning to Canaan—but that's another story for another day.

[568] Note that what I am rendering as "Judaeanism" would be rendered by most translators as "Judaism," but I am quite certain that Origen in his own time would have understood very well that conceptual distinction, although he would not, of course, have had the linguistic instrument with which to indicate the distinction, since he was writing in Greek.

It is interesting not only to note that he uses the word myth (i.e., the Greek word *mythos*) in a manner analogous to how we use it, to mean a fact-empty fantasy story—an evolution of its nuance 600 years old by his time from where it began with a "gods' truth account" nuance—but that he offers what is an inevitable perspective when the matter of the divine *sacer* comes up, whether in antiquity or, as we saw in our first chapter, in modernity: the perceived effectiveness of a given proof for a given viewpoint regarding divinity is dependent on the perspective brought by the viewer to his/her analysis of that proof and its viewpoint. Thus it is not only the case "that mine is religion and yours is superstition and/or mythology," but that "the world itself self-evidently *proves* my viewpoint—to *me*, at least."

In section 26, Origen focuses on how Celsus

> misrepresents the Jews when he says that "they worship angels and are addicted to the sorcery of which Moses was their teacher." As he professes to know the books of Christians and Jews let him declare where in Moses' writings he found the lawgiver enjoining them to worship angels. How also can there be sorcery among people who accepted the law of Moses if they have read the commandment: "Ye shall not cleave to enchanters or be polluted by them?" He next promises to teach us "how the Jews fell into error through ignorance and were deceived." If he had found ignorance about Jesus Christ among the Jews because they did not give heed to the prophecies about him, he really would have "taught how the Jews fell into error." But actually he had no desire to suggest this, and he suspects that the Jews are in error about things that are not errors at all.

This passage makes it clear that Origen maintains a strong conviction, as a Christian, that the Jews have erred in failing to recognize the Christhood of Jesus, but in this context his sense not merely of solidarity, but even of protectiveness toward Jewish thinking against the assault against it by a pagan thinker, trumps the competitive distinction between the sibling Abrahamic faiths. His text indeed underscores the legitimacy of this sort of metaphor: Judaism and Christianity are siblings and their sense of rivalry—be it for God's affection or for acceptance by the Roman authorities—can be intense, but if an outsider attacks one sibling, the other hurries to stand with him and defend him. That will, to repeat, gradually change over the next few generations.

There are other aspects of Origen's responsive attack upon Celsus, several of which are particularly interesting to our own narrative. Right before this just-discussed passage, in sections 24 and 25, he began by taking up Celsus' assertion that those "goatherds and shepherds [deceived by Moses] thought that there was one God called the Most High, or *Adonai*, or the Holy One, or *Sabaot*, or however they like to call this world…" which leads him to the subject of names, how they are conferred and whether there is an intrinsic relationship between them and the entities to which they are appended or whether names are arbitrarily attached to entities.[569] His reference in section 25 to

---

[569] Although Origen references Aristotle and Epikouros and the Stoics as the earlier discussants of this issue, it is actually Plato, in his *Cratylus*, who first takes up the subject in any sort of a systematic way. See Ori Z Soltes,

angelic names—and his link between that reference and the necessity of reciting a spell in its original language in order for it to succeed in its purpose—recalls texts like the *PGM* as well as the *Book of Secrets* and the *Sword of Moses* that we have previously discussed (above, 267, 274ff).

Jumping forward to section 60, we note his observation that "Magi are in communion with *daimones* and by their formulas invoke them for the ends which they desire; and they succeed in their practices as long as nothing more divine and potent than the *daimones* and the spells that invoke them appears or is pronounced. But if anything more divine were to appear, the powers of the *daimones* would be destroyed, since they would be unable to withstand the light of the divine power." So the term "*magus/magi*" continues to have the implication that it has had for several centuries: a sacerdotal practitioner engaging the lesser powers of the *sacer*, perhaps with nefarious intentions. The sort of *daimones* such as a *magus* might invoke lost their strength and became weak "at the birth of Jesus when, as Luke records *and I believe* [italics added], 'a multitude of the heavenly host praised God...' their sorcery was confuted and their power overthrown..." The truth of Luke's account is self-evident because Origen, as a Christian, believes that it is so.

The magi, however, are also already becoming what they become in the Christian tradition that treats them not necessarily as practitioners of lower *sacer*-engagement as much as exotic kings from beyond the world of Judaea. Thus (continuing at the end of section 60) "an angel rewarded the piety of the magi [expressed] in [their] worshipping [of] Jesus by warning them not to go to Herod but to return to their own country by another route."

Still further along, in section 68, he notes that

> Celsus pretends to grant that the scriptures may be true when they speak of "cures or resurrection to a few loaves feeding many people..." ...he puts them on a level with "the works of sorcerers who profess to do wonderful miracles, and the accomplishments of those who are taught by the Egyptians, who for a few obols make known their sacred lore in the middle of the marketplace and drive *daimones* out of men and blow away diseases and invoke the souls of heroes, displaying expensive banquets and dining-tables and cakes and dishes that are non-existent..." and he says "Since these men do these wonders, ought we to think them sons of God? Or ought we to say that these are the practices of wicked men possessed by an evil *daimon*?
>
> [Thus] he compares the stories of Jesus with tales of magic. They might have been comparable if Jesus had done his miracles, like magicians, merely to show his own powers. But in fact no sorcerer uses his tricks to call the spectators to moral reformation; nor does he educate by fear of God people who were astounded by what they saw... Sorcerers do none of these things, since they have neither the ability nor even the will to do so...

From Plato's Cratylus *to Levinas' "God and Philosophy": The Problem of Language for Philosophy.* (Lewiston, NY: Edwin Mellen Press, 2007).

Continuing at the outset of section 69 he asserts: "After this he muddles Christianity with the view of some sect as though Christians shared their opinions…"—and this sort of issue may be followed as the work moves forward, as in Part Two, section 51, for instance, where he accuses Celsus of "put[ting] together in one category things that really fall into two categories… what is accomplished by God's power is nothing like what is done by sorcery."

Origen has provided us here (and elsewhere; I have selected only a few passages that follow these sorts of lines of argumentation) with two large points relevant to our narrative. One point—and indeed we are reminded of passages in the Gospels and Acts that we have examined (see above, 190-5, 196)—is that extraordinary deeds of curing, or of providing bread for masses of people, or of transforming water into wine, viewed not from the inside by Christian believers, but from the outside by pagan non-believers, offer very little that objectively should cause them to be placed within the category of religion rather than magic.

To a pagan like Celsus, those acts are analogous to what he and others in the pagan world understood about Moses's miraculous acts; Jesus, like Moses, was an extraordinary magician. Given the negative view of magic by Celsus—consistent with popular opinion up to a point (as in Apuleius' need to defend himself against the accusation of being a practitioner), he has a negative view of Christianity. This is also consistent with the official Roman governmental view. What makes the issue further nuanced in terms of categories is that Celsus presumably also has a negative view of Judaism, but the Roman government does not. So the government places Paganism and Judaism on one side of the fence as *religiones licitae* and Christianity on the other as *superstitio* for legal purposes, whereas Celsus places pagan faiths on one side of the fence (presumably as *religiones*) and Judaism and Christianity on the other as *magia*—and Origen places Paganism on one side of the fence as *magia* and Judaism and Christianity on the other as *religiones*.

Origen's argument against the categorization of Christianity in particular as *magia* offers us a second large point: how—again—one distinguishes magic from religion and magical acts from religious acts. One could argue that this is evident in the New Testament texts in question: the matter of moral improvement. Magic and its practitioners are all about performing acts that contradict (or seem to) the ways of everyday *profanus* nature. Religion and its practitioners—in this case its star practitioner, Jesus—are all about moral guidance and education with regard to an ethically-based Divine *Sacer*, for which purpose acts that contradict everyday *profanus* nature are merely instrumental means to a greater end. So it turns out that there *is* an objective distinction between religion and magic that one may be able to read within these texts—but that distinction is not visible to Celsus. This of course is in part because he may not be reading those texts fully or carefully and it may be, more fundamentally, because he reads them with a gut-level prejudice that blinds him, and what's his is religion and what's Origen's is magic.

The Origenian distinction between the physical purposes of *magia* and the spiritual and moral purposes of Christian (and Jewish) *religio* is furthered in the last paragraph of section 51 when he refers to the "corollary from the existence of magic, [that it is] wrought by evil *daimones* who are enchanted by elaborate spells and obey men who are sorcerers" as opposed to someone (like Jesus or Moses) "who has been on pure and holy ground before God in his own soul and spirit, and performs wonders for the benefit of mankind and in order to exhort men to believe in the true God." Thus the distinction is not only between showing off performances and acting in order to push forward a moral agenda, but between acting with possibly nefarious intent and acting with pure and benevolent intent—and also, not incidentally, between having the capacity to *compel* these lesser, weaker daimonic elements within the *sacer* through "enchantments" and being assisted by the Divine *Sacer* to do extraordinary deeds in order to help people *recognize* the true Divine *Sacer*.

The topic of the company kept, as it were, by Moses, both backwards and forwards in time, provides the basis for Origen's refutation, in Part Four, section 33, of the attack by Celsus on "the first book of Moses entitled Genesis, saying that 'they [the Jews] shamelessly undertook to trace their genealogy back to the first offspring of sorcerers and deceivers…' It is clear that the Jews trace their genealogy back to the three fathers, Abraham, Isaac and Jacob. Their names are so powerful when linked with the name of God that the formula 'the God of Abraham, the God of Isaac, the God of Jacob' is used not only by members of the Jewish nation in their prayers to God and when they exorcise *daimones*, but also by almost all those who deal in magic and spells." Origen seems to make a clear distinction between Jews and Christians with regard to this genealogy, since Christians are not mentioned in it. In quoting the oft-used phrase naming the three patriarchs, from any number of places not only in the Torah but in the rabbinic literature, he views it as efficacious both for religious and for magical purposes—and usable not only by Jews, at that, but by anybody.

Indeed, his counter-challenge to Celsus is to explain how these biblical patriarchs cannot possess a divine character. Isn't it "shown by the fact that you [pagans] use the names of these three progenitors of a nation that, as experience shows, compel the performance of considerable miracles when their names are invoked? …How, then, was it shameful of the Jews to 'try to trace their genealogy back to the first offspring' of those whom Celsus supposes to have been 'sorcerers and deceivers,' and to trace themselves and their origin to those men whose names, being Hebrew, bear witness that the Hebrews, whose sacred books are written in the Hebrew language and alphabet, are a nation to them?" So both the historical role of the Jews (and again, the Christians are not explicitly included in this by Origen, who is also not always distinguishing in his choice of terminology among Hebrews, Israelites, and Judaeans or Jews) is defended as they are defended from the accusation of practicing *magia* and its concomitants, by way of reminding Celsus (and us) of the importance of Judaean/Jewish input into pagan *sacer*-engaging texts, such as we have seen evidenced in the *PGM*.

What makes this further interesting—and anticipates developments in the Christian-Jewish relationship that will soon bring problematic elements more emphatically into play—is that in the previous section (Part Four, section 31), Origen at first had refuted the Celsian assertion that the Jews "were runaway slaves who escaped from Egypt" by asserting that, on the contrary, "they were 'a chosen race and a royal priesthood,' [and] they withdrew themselves and avoided contact with the multitude lest their morals be corrupted." In the next breath, he notes that at times, when they sinned, God forsook them "sometimes for a short time, until under the Romans, because *they committed their greatest sin in killing Jesus, they were entirely abandoned* [italics added]."

So he both insists on the historical legitimacy of Judaism in its relationship to God and offers an emerging Christian perspective: that that relationship has dissipated due to Jewish reluctance to embrace Jesus as the *mashiah/khristos*. Indeed, this is one of the earliest instances of the Christian assertion that the Jews killed Jesus and that as a consequence God abandoned them, to which a supercessionist dogma will add a third corollary element, that God as a consequence turned primary divine favor instead toward the Christians, as *Verus Israel*: the True Israel.

Thus within the forest of defensive points on behalf of both Christianity and Judaism, treated largely as a common unit against the attacks by Celsus—in which, particularly in the later parts of his treatise, Origen separates his defense of the one from his defense of the other—he plants a seed that he obliquely nurtures here and there in subsequent passages, in returning to a singular adulation of Christianity alone. That seed will blossom in the generations that follow. It will become a tree of anti-Jewishness the roots of which are embedded in this threefold assertion, as we shall see. Moreover, we shall also see that in its first seasons of full efflorescence, that tree will barely distinguish Judaism from both Paganism and Christian heresy as closely allied fungi that need to be excised from a different tree—that of proper Christianity itself—lest *that* tree wither.

*　　*　　*　　*　　*

Let us conclude this chapter by considering two documents that further the discussion of the past several pages and its issues and also pushes forward into the century following Hippolytus and Origen: the chapter on "Magicians" in Ramsay MacMullen's *Enemies of the Roman Order*; and the article by A.A. Barb "The Survival of Magic Arts" in A. D. Momigliano's *The Conflict Between Paganism and Christianity in the Fourth Century*. Macmullen begins with an extensive discussion regarding Pythagoras, whom he refers to as a philosopher. He makes the point, however, that the stories about Pythagoras ascribe powers to him that suggest a magician but also a saint or other religious practitioner—he is presented as an incarnation of Apollo, among others, in Iamblichis (*Vita Pythagorae* 30), which would make him a Jesus-like figure. He is depicted as an object of awe among the Greeks, whom MacMullen quotes as saying that "the god revealed the way to the Egyptians and the Chaldaeans (for these are Assyrians) and the Lydians and the Hebrews."[570] So, embedded in the discussion of Pythagoras we find an understanding familiar to us, of the kinds of exotic other peoples that are believed to possess magical skills.

And at the same time, lack of clarity among terms reigns: MacMullen refers to the Roman Stoic *philosopher*, Seneca, who studied with a Pythagorean teacher and was subject to an emperor-demanded suicide under Nero—for this was an era in which "abstinence from certain foods was taken as proof of *superstition*."[571] A few pages later, in discussing a second-century Pythagorean, Peregrinus Proteus, who was influenced by the Brahmans

---

[570] Ramsay MacMullen, *Enemies of the Roman Order: Treason, Unrest and Alienation in the Empire*, (Cambridge, MA: Harvard University Press, 1966), 98. Routledge put out a new edition of the book in 1998.
[571] Ibid, 96.

of India—and also a "dabbler in a forbidden *religion*, Christianity"[572]—MacMullen observes that "later followers studied his *philosophy*, but turned more and more to that part of his heritage that could be called *religion* or even *magic* [italics added]." We are offered no explanation of how these various defining terms that I have italicized should be understood—but that will prove, in part to be his point, perhaps: that there was no clarity at that time. So, too, importantly for our narrative, MacMullen has offered us yet another group, (Pythagorean in general and in a specific iteration of/association with Peregrinus Proteus) that was competing with Christianity, Judaism and traditional pagan religions.

We come back, then, to philosophy and the blurry line between that discipline as a category and religion or magic, since "the last great pagan philosopher, Plotinus, joined the Roman invasion forces of 243-44 against Persia" in order to encounter the Brahmans of India, "while Christian contemporaries sent their saints, in imagination, to the same source, lest they should fall behind in reputation."[573] There will even develop a tradition (not mentioned by MacMullen) that Jesus journeyed to India during the long stretch of time between his Bar Mitzvah-age debate in the Temple with its learned leaders (*docti*: hence, misleadingly in English, "doctors") and the "journeys" throughout Judah, Samaria and Galilee that occupy his last three years of life on earth.

MacMullen's interestingly wandering essay notes how important the Temple to Isis in Rome had become by the second century—so that particular form of Hellenistic Egyptian *religio* had been emphatically translated to the Imperial capital—for "Egyptian worships had taken hold of the world, the ancient Egyptian primacy in the whole field of the occult was accepted with more absolute conviction."[574] Indeed, "Hadrian was the first to honor Serapis on imperial coinage, picturing himself in the Serapeum of Alexandria face to face with the god; and to his reign [r. 117-38] belongs that influential priest of Isis, Pachrates, who spent twenty-three tears in the crypt of the temple apparently learning everything the goddess could teach; for when he emerged, he had mastered the trick of riding on crocodiles and of transforming a door bolt into a robot helper... and he 'brought a man to the spot in a single hour, made him take to his bed in two hours, killed him in seven hours, and caused a dream to come to the emperor himself, demonstrating the entire truth of the magic through him'."[575] So Egyptian *religio*—or at least his version of it—is considered occult and called *magia*.

MacMullen, however, understands how thin (or blurry) the lines among categories can be: "...that, through the force of piety, like Plotinus', or of some unspecified virtuosity, like Pachrates', or of more vulgar tricks, like the market place Egyptians', one could wage war on weaker spirits. Within the second, third and fourth century world of mixed eastern magic or religion, and Neopythagoreanism, collision of fantastic powers could elevate or destroy a reputation."[576] The archaeological evidence offers a large number of curse tablets (*defixiones*), magical papyri, and amulets, which instruments (some of which we have studied, of course), dealt with the "dreads and desires of all social ranks, raking around

---

[572] Ibid, 99.
[573] Both quotes are from Ibid.
[574] Ibid, 101.
[575] Ibid, 101.
[576] Ibid, 102.

wildly in the rubble of eastern and classical superstition for any formula that would do the job. To the resulting muddle, the principal contributor was Egypt,"[577] as we have seen.

We have also seen the range of types of goals for such material that MacMullen summarizes:

> Aggressive magic was only one of many kinds, and by no means the most common. Among amulets, it was pain and sickness that were most often aimed at; among curse tablets, the wrong horse or chariot in the hippodrome... [but also] magical powers used for good purposes. Exorcism of unclean spirits occurs familiarly in the New Testament. [Such spirits] caused disease, especially madness, and experts could prescribe for their removal in various ways. More serious demonic forces cause plagues, earthquakes, floods, storms, or droughts. Occasion for such invasions might be offered by the presence of unholy people—Christians, said the pagans; Arians, said the Christians; or perhaps simply of "Jonahs."[578]

So not only are the lines between magic and religion thin or blurred, but those between magic and medicine—as well as those between proper *religiones licitae* (which are mine) and *superstitiones* (which are not mine, but yours), which lines are drawn according to the subjective criteria of who is in power. He is, thus, summarizing an era overrun with diverse modes and means of engaging the divine *sacer* and its cognate, the *sacer* of death (for a range of modes and means of "invocation raised the dead or deities to be questioned...").[579] Further, "the great object was to obtain *truth* guaranteed by its source [italics added]"—which turn of phrase suggests philosophy or religion and not magic or superstition as we have most often seen them distinguished.[580] Indeed, however, "[t]eachers for their part were obliged to present their philosophic or religious revelations wrapped up in the most absurd claims: an exclusive interview, *monos pros monon* ["one on one"], with Hermes, perhaps, or with Isis, or some other deity....the elder Julianus, known in Rome as a 'Chaldean philosopher' and author of a work on demons... 'demanded for [his son] an archangel's soul,' and 'conjoined him, when he was born [under Trajan], to all the gods and to the soul of Plato that abides with Apollo and Hermes.' The boy grew to a man, incredibly wise, and together with his father published the *Chaldean Oracles*... a whole philosophic system in which Platonism predominated. It purports to have been dictated by Apollo, Hecate, and others..."[581]

We have already encountered Julianus the elder and younger and are reminded by this passage in MacMullen that the lines separating philosopher, theurgist, and magician are neither completely clear nor certainly absolute. In the case of the two Juliani, this applies not only to them but to what they and their adherents apparently believe about Plato: that the supreme rationalist philosopher—but who again and again shows his

---

[577] Ibid, 103.
[578] Ibid, 103-4.
[579] Ibid, 105.
[580] Ibid, 106.
[581] Ibid, 106.

mystical side by turning from *logos* to *mythos* in his dialogues—is connected to the gods and seen as a source for theurgic invocation by the Juliani. In turn, as we have seen earlier, and as MacMullen points out, theurgy reaches the apogee of its popularity in the mid-fourth century under Iamblichus, when it attracts the attention of the Emperor Julian (r. 361-3), "abound[ing] in doctrines emanating from mysterious sources, promoted by mysterious beings half divine, as they claimed, able to work wonders, to warrant salvation, to reveal all truth"[582]—in short, making the sort of claims that, for instance, Christianity as a religion was making.

"Such revelations were in theory addressed only to initiates. Secrecy enhanced their attraction... [practitioners] promised [their adherents] elevation in knowledge far above the common herd."[583] That elevation in knowledge would be called *gnosis*, as we have seen, and if on the one hand we recall that that term is endemic to what the anti-Christian, so-called gnostic sects offered, we might also keep in mind the degree to which the idea of *mysteries* is endemic to Christianity itself, from the doctrine of the Virgin Birth and the Triune Godhead to the miracle of Eucharistic transubstantiation to the rituals performed in the Armenian Church behind a closed curtain, on behalf of the congregation but without it being permitted to witness or participate directly in them.

And the line between religion and philosophy (which is not the same line as that between religion and magic or magic and medicine) is, one might say, deliberately blurred by the "neoplatonists, [who] rather differed from the [Platonic] school they claimed to continue in making a religion out of philosophy. They hoped for salvation, not wisdom, for mystic union, not moral learning... Neither [Plotinus nor Iamblichus] believed it possible to establish philosophic truth by use of the mind unassisted. ...[T]he seat of power is the soul, not the mind. The mind, in fact, from the second century on, comes under increasingly open, angry and exasperated attack."[584]

It should not surprise us that, as MacMullen points out,

> [t]o cover the spectrum of men ranging from the semieducated charlatan to the most profound scholar in philosophy, including between ...various shades of philosopher, diviner, or magician, the words that should have indicated one type or another came to be used almost interchangeably. Some terms—*goes, agurtes, magicus, ariolus*—were always pejorative. They occur, however, joined casually with *philosophus, theurgus, mathematicus*, and *astrologus*, in the third and fourth centuries.[585]

We have seen how this conflation of terms was already afoot much earlier, as pointed out by Apuleius in his *Apology*, (and as MacMullen reminds us). The point is that the growing array of definitionally blurred terms—that expands the relatively simpler notion of religion-and-magic-as-a-pair-not-as-simply-distinguished-as-one-might-suppose — is reaching a peak precisely during the period in which Christianity is finally coming into its

---

[582] Ibid, 107.
[583] Ibid, 107.
[584] Ibid, 108-9.
[585] Ibid, 110.

political own, between the time of its legalization under Constantine and of its hegemony under Theodosius—and, as we shall see in the following chapter, this will have implications for the era that leads from this same period forward all the way into our own time.

There is more from MacMullen that is relevant to our narrative, as he reaches back into the first and second centuries before coming forward. He notes how

> people outside Greco-Roman Paganism reached in and filched "philosophy" as being properly descriptive of their own religion. We have seen this happening in 4 Maccabees and in Philo, too. To draw the comparison between *philosophia* and Judaism, the former term had to be applied to any life of piety, even gnosis or revelation. Christians of the second century followed suit, naming their religion a "philosophy" because it called for a way of life that led to God. Not that the old meaning disappeared among the church writers... [albeit not using the term] philosophy in the classical sense... their tendency was to apply the prestige of the word to all good believers... By Chrysostom's time "philosophy" had come to designate a life of Christian asceticism as well. Monks "philosophized"; so did martyrs, by their victory over the weakness of the flesh.[586]

He thus carries the issue as far back as the first and second centuries, since Philo wrote in the first half of the first century, 4 Maccabees is typically dated to ca 50-80 CE, and Justin Martyr (100-165 CE), the pagan philosopher turned Christian apologist (he went from Stoicism to Peripateticism to Pythagoreanism to Platonism before finding Christianity), whom he also references, was writing in the mid-second century—and forward again to the late fourth and early fifth centuries, since John Chrysostom lived between *347* and 407 CE.[587]

---

[586] Ibid 110-11. The Book, *4 Maccabees*, is a philosophical discourse written in Greek that praises the supremacy of pious reason over passion. It is considered apocryphal—in other words, not part of the Biblical canon—by Judaism and most Christian denominations, although it appears as part of the Georgian Orthodox Bible. It was also included in the 1688 Romanian Orthodox and the eighteenth-century Romanian Catholic Bibles, but is not included in Romanian Bibles today. The writer appears to be an Alexandrian Judaean/Jew, as Philo was, who, like Philo, used a philosophical (notably Platonic) angle to present his/her concept of piety. It is an important example of syncretism between Judaean/Jewish and Hellenistic thought. Interestingly, it was ascribed to Josephus both by the Christian exegete, polemicist and historiographer, Eusebius (263-339), and by St Jerome (347-420). This opinion was accepted for many centuries, leading to its inclusion in many editions of Josephus' works. Modern scholars, however, have recognized differences of language and style between Josephus and *4 Maccabees*. The book is nonetheless generally dated between the late first century BCE and the late first century CE; the latter dating makes more sense to me, for what it's worth.

[587] He was born in Flavia Neopolis (now Nablus), making him a pagan Judaean and thereby reminding us of the complication of both defining "Judaean" and distinguishing that term from "Jew/ish." Once Justin converted—perhaps at Ephesus—interestingly, he adopted the dress of a philosopher as he traveled about teaching. He arrived into Rome and started his own school during the last years of the reign of Antoninus Pius (r 138-61). During the reign of Marcus Aurelius (161-80), after a disputation with the cynic philosopher, Crescens, he was denounced by his opponent to the authorities, according to both Tatian (a student of Justin, who asserted this in his *Address to the Greeks* 19) and Eusebius (*Historia Ecclesiastica* IV 16.7-8). Justin was tried, together with six companions, by Junius Rusticus, who was urban prefect in 163-167, and was apparently beheaded. I am not sure that this is accurate, since the Roman mode of executing political subversives was still, at that time, typically crucifixion; this may be the later Christian retro-rendering of his martyrdom. Similarly, the account in the work known as *The*

Toward the end of his discussion, MacMullen offers a concise summary statement of the attitudes of the aristocracy in the first four centuries CE—we must keep in mind that part of Origen's goal was to *encourage* the aristocracy to recognize the validity and indeed significance of Christianity—to wit: "They were willing to grant the importance of portents in the first century, of oracles in the second, of apparitions in the third and later..."[588] Yet, he adds, after having referred to both Pliny and Apuleius, the latter in some detail, that "[t]here was no period in the history of the empire when the magician was not considered an enemy of society... How then to explain his open circulation in all social circles...? Set against the whole picture of magic in Roman society, the official attitude is a plain contradiction—resolved, however, by the very importance of magic. Not only could it not be eradicated from the common mind but the most enlightened people took it seriously..."[589]

The solution to this was to legislate not against "magic" *per se*, but against magic intended to harm people—so there "was black magic and white magic, there was the *goes* and the scholarly or benevolent practitioner... Like philosophy, magic thus presented two aspects, one accepted and even characteristic among good Romans, the other feared and unlawful. Initiates were found in the senate house or in the palace, and yet also in darkened crypts and temples, dragged forth to face arraignment before the civil authorities... Hence the ever-widening legislation to protect society from magic; [as] ...the decay of rationality among the best-educated men" increased.[590]

Barb's article further amplifies this discussion as it pertains in particular to the fourth century and the rise to hegemony of Christianity, as it re-angles our double helix of interest from the magic/religion issue to the Christianity/Judaism/Paganism issue. Indeed, Barb asserts at the outset that the "fundamental difference between magic and religion is still the same as it always was. On the one hand, we have the religious man, offering his adorations in humble submission to the Deity; always careful to add to any supplication the reservation 'if it be according to Thu will'. On the other hand, we have the magician, attempting to force the supernatural powers to accomplish what he desires and avert what he fears."[591] One must presume that "religion" as Barb understands it means the Abrahamic traditions, in which there is one God and the words "God" and "Deity" are habitually spelled with an initial majuscule letter, given that this is how he expresses it; his choice of term and punctuation does not give much hope that he regards religions with many gods, such as those of the Greeks and Romans, as *religions*.

Perhaps that's just a stylistic element offered without considering its consequences for this issue. He does acknowledge that there are "in ritual and liturgy

---

Martyrdom of Justin, may not be fully accurate. In it we read, in part: "The Prefect Rusticus says: 'Approach and sacrifice, all of you, to the gods.' Justin says: 'No one in his right mind gives up piety for impiety.' The Prefect Rusticus says: 'If you do not obey, you will be tortured without mercy.' Justin replies: 'That is our desire, to be tortured for Our Lord, Jesus Christ, and so to be saved, for that will give us salvation and firm confidence at the more terrible universal tribunal of Our Lord and Saviour.'" Would the anonymous author of *The Martyrdom of Justin* actually have been privy to this dialogue?

[588] Ibid, 120.
[589] Ibid, 125-6.
[590] Ibid, 126-7.
[591] A.A. Barb, "The Survival of Magic Arts," in A.D. Momigliano, ed., *The Conflict Between Paganism and Christianity in the Fourth Century*. (Oxford: Clarendon Press, 1963), 101.

elements which scarcely differ from magical acts and incantations," and clarifies: "Religion does not evolve from primitive magic; on the contrary magic derives from religion, which, as it becomes tainted by human frailty, deteriorates into so-called white magic (the Greeks called it *theurgia*—working things divine), gradually losing its whiteness and turning from more or less dirty grey into black magic, called in Greek *goeteia*, from the evil-sounding recitation of spells."[592] He thus reverses Malinowski's theory of the evolutionary relationship between religion and magic, but still maintains the methodological and, presumably, outcome distinction between the two disciplines. He also subsumes the positive/negative distinction into that evolution, rather than referring it to the fundamental distinction between them.

In this last regard, Barb goes on to observe how "[t]he task, which is not always easy, of drawing this line between fit and unfit supernatural fare, …has consistently been the concern of the lawful authorities"—or perhaps we might say, those in power, who assume lawful authority—"in Rome as elsewhere."[593] Appropriately enough, he observes the inherent ambiguity in a term like the Greek *pharmakon*, which we have observed in ambiguous action in *Odyssey* 10, in the story of Odysseus and Kirke; he follows that sort of ambiguity, by way of the Latin *venenum*, (the closest equivalent of *pharmakon*) through the evolution not only of the term's nuance but of the Roman legal relationship both to the term and to literature dealing with the *sacer*, in general.

At times, ambiguity of terminology and with it, the sense of distrust with certain books and certain objects reached a "point of absurdity, …[as when] the Emperor Caracalla [allegedly] condemned as criminals even those who wore magical amulets as a protection against malaria"—although he points out that it may have been the much later Emperor Constantius II who did this—but his point is that "we see this white magic treated on the same level as the blackest communication with the evil spirits of the dead."[594]

This is all, in a sense, preliminary to the direction that Barb takes and which is of primary significance for us. Given, however, his evolutionary viewpoint, it is not a surprise that he views certain developments in the fourth century as a function of the fact that

> the task of the Roman emperor as health officer in things supernatural became increasingly difficult when the syncretistic, rotting refuse-heap of the dead and dying religions of the ancient world grew to mountainous height… Perhaps it was never more difficult than in the fourth century. A thin but powerful layer of die-hard aristocrats and intellectuals tried stubbornly to preserve the religion by which their forefathers had built and cemented the Roman Empire. For them the new Christian belief must have appeared to be detestable oriental superstition, and where it

---

[592] Ibid, 101, for both quotes.

[593] Ibid, 102.

[594] Ibid, 102. Caracalla ruled 198-217. He reigned jointly with his father, Septimius Severus from 198 until Severus' death in 211. For a short time, he then ruled jointly with his younger brother Geta, until he had Geta murdered later in 211. Caracalla is remembered as one of the most notoriously unpleasant of emperors—according to the literate elite of his era—because of the massacres and persecutions he authorized and instigated throughout the Empire. If we accept that analysis of him, then the amulet proscription is certainly believable. Constantius II ruled 337-361, first (337-40) as co-ruler with his brothers Constantine II and Constans, then as co-ruler with his brother Constans alone (340-50) and finally, as sole ruler of the Empire(350-61).

was successful, it must have seemed even ore detestable magic, the more so, as for centuries persecutions had compelled Christianity to work of necessity in secrecy and darkness, those generally accepted characteristics of the magic arts.[595]

This makes sense, although I wonder if a pagan of that era would have described his or her religion as part of a "rotting refuse-heap of the dead and dying religions," or whether this is not—again—the perspective of triumphant Christianity looking back at the era in the aftermath of the long-fought battle and eventual victory of the True Faith within the complex morass that we have been encountering and describing.

Could not the negative view toward the Church simply be a generally competitive response to a form of faith that was most obviously different from the others (with the exception of Judaism) in rejecting any sort of multi-faith co-existence? If there is only one, all-everything God, then other faiths with other gods or other god-concepts are, by definition, false. Given a sufficiently strong position for the True Faith, the others would be (and were) reduced to being regarded as nefarious superstitions (to be intentionally redundant). "Die-hard aristocrats and intellectuals" is a phrase that certainly sounds less than objective in its nuance. "Die-hard" implies desperately hanging on to something that *is* dying and well past its time of efflorescence—but is it clear that this is the situation at that time for the faiths of these aristocrats and intellectuals as opposed to as it would seem from a later, Christian perspective?

Barb's last two clauses could not, conversely, be more on target: Christianity's position would have been circular up to 313: regarded as a *superstitio*, it had to function in secret; functioning in secret reinforced the view of it as a *superstitio*—regardless of whether or not its pagan competitors were rotting.

Be all these questions as they may, Barb's further elucidation of the century's *sacer-profanus* complications offers a straightforward and very informative picture. St. Peter, according to St Augustine, as Barb points out, was regarded as an arch-magician by certain pagans—a magician "who by his evil arts had brought it about that belief in Christ had survived for 365 years… [using] the number of days of the year which played a role in Gnostic systems [where that number refers to the number of heavenly spheres in the created universe] and is contained in the word *ABRAXAS* [who presides over those spheres]…".[596] And if "die-hard aristocrats and intellectuals" retained their stubborn Paganisms, on the other hand, Christianity, as it moved inevitably, (as Barb would seem to understand it, at least), toward a positon of power, coming into the open after 313, "and supported mainly by the less-educated masses, was tainted with all the superstitions of the man in the street." Thus their leaders were intensely obsessed with "the existence of evil demons (their legions swelled by all the pagan deities) and of powerful angels."[597]

Barb notes, accordingly, that the conditions "in many respects resemble[d] the worst witch-hunting centuries at the end of the Middle Ages," except that it was the temporal authorities, rather than the Church, that took the lead in fomenting and fostering

---

[595] Ibid, 104.
[596] Ibid. See above, fn #424 for the importance of *Abraxas* and how "365" is embedded in that name.
[597] Ibid for both quotes.

such conditions in the fourth century. The temporal leaders may have been influenced by Christian leaders, Barb admits. "[T]he emperors half-heartedly tolerated the old religious institutions which had been part and parcel of Roman public administration, but turned savagely against the prevalence of sorcery."[598] Our immediate questions, in reading this last sentence should be: how does Barb know that the toleration was half-hearted (and what about the Emperor Julian?)—but we'll let that one pass—and what did they regard as "sorcery" and why?

In anticipating this last question, Barb takes up the issue of the *haruspices*—those interpreters of animal intestines and celestial events whose office was extremely ancient— and suggests that they had decayed into "private dispensers of eagerly sought evil magic, apparently, according to Suetonius, already being limited to publicly witnessed consultations by Emperor Tiberius (14-37 CE). Under Constantine a *haruspex* was forbidden to enter a private house "not even that of his best personal friend, on penalty of being burned alive"—although citizens were still permitted to consult such sacerdotal sources in the open, "at one of the public shrines."[599] Does this mean, however, that a formerly religious institution of considerable import during the half-millennium of the Republic's history, (and perhaps still earlier), had already come to be looked down upon and/or feared by the early imperial period—in other words not, *per se*, during the fourth century when Paganism in general was becoming a "rotting refuse-heap" but as early as the time of the second emperor?

It would in that case also suggest both that the category of sacerdotal legitimacy/illegitimacy was in constant evolution or flux—and in this case, the defining attributes of the illegitimate category, whether one calls that category "magic" or "superstition" or "sorcery," were secrecy and nefariousness. The latest phase of flux and evolution coincides with the rise of Christianity, with certain consequences as to what is fresh-smelling and what is rotting, but the principle of flux, evolution and judging what is acceptable and what is not has neither changed nor evolved.

Barb notes that the Church Fathers do not distinguish *theurgia* from *goetia*—it's all bad stuff to them, for "[b]oth are founded on *idolatria*." The extremism with which they viewed such improper engagements of the *sacer* is reflected in St. John Chrysostom's praise for "the steadfast Christian mother who would rather see her sick child or her husband die than try on them one of those magic amulets which were generally used.... [They ought simply] to praise the will of God... [and] to make the sign of the cross." The first prescription is in lieu of an incantation and the second in lieu of a magical ritual. This makes sense, given the promises of the afterlife posed by the Church, but his discussion (and there are more details to it than I have repeated) also implies that there were still plenty of Christians turning to what Chrysostom considers illegitimate, idolatrous sacerdotal instruments as cures for the ill.

This last issue twists toward another ambiguous possibility: the development of what Barb refers to as "some kind of specifically Christian magic"—which turn of phrase sounds like a contradiction in terms—"[that] had in fact developed [as] is clear from rulings

---

[598] Ibid, 105 for both quotes.
[599] Ibid, 105-6. Barb's sources are Suetonius' "Life of Tiberius," lxiii; and the *Codex Theodiosianus* ix, xvi, 1-2.

of the Synod of Laodicea in the middle of the century when it was found necessary to forbid Christian clerics in major or minor orders to be magicians, charmers, soothsayers, or astrologers, or to fabricate amulets... [and also] to forbid the exaggerated cult of angels, which had apparently assumed the forms of magic..."[600] So it turns out that the border territory between Christian *religio licita* and various *superstitiones* is even broader and blurrier than we already have supposed.

Both the flux and the blurriness are implicitly acknowledged by Barb when he observes that "[i]t is one of the ironies of history that, while the fashionable pagan philosophers of the Neoplatonic school glorified 'white' magic as *theurgia*, the decrees of the Christian emperors of the same century were actually far more consistent with Plato's strict tenets of the criminal character of the magic arts, as he set them out in the *Nomoi* [*Laws*]," (as we have seen earlier).[601]

If, in fact, in response to these complications and potential confusions, the Church authorities could and did define an increasingly absolute dogma regarding legitimate versus illegitimate engagements of the *sacer*, the civil authorities of the fourth century, on the other hand, as Barb points out, were mired in a more nuanced wrestling match with *sacer* and sacerdotal categories. They "wavered between respect for the empty husk of Roman Paganism in which they no longer believed, and uncertain belief in a diluted Christianity, the full requirements of which they neither attempted to fulfill themselves nor dared to enforce on the state"[602]—where "they" refers to all the Emperors from Constantine to Theodosius. While it may be clear that they no longer believed in the old (and newer) Paganisms—although, again, Julian at the very least might seem to be an exception to this presumed truth—I am neither so sure that all that remained of those Paganisms was a series of husks nor am I clear on how Christianity was diluted at this point. On the contrary, it seems, from what Barb has just said prior to this comment, that Christianity was quite concentrated.

Certainly with regard to imperial ambiguity, however, Barb's account of Constantius II offers a case in point. When the oracle of Besa in Abydos, Egypt became popular, even consulted by the upper classes, and some of the petitions to the oracle were said to be subversive, the Emperor dispatched Paulus, his official witch-hunter, who established a court—and with it a reign of terror that extended from Alexandria to Antioch. Moreover, three imperial decrees, subsequently incorporated into the *Corpus iuris civilis* [the civil law code], demonstrate intense savagery against those using the "magical arts"— which group included spell-casters, *haruspices*, astrologers, Chaldaeans, soothsayers, interpreters of dreams and common sorcerers [*malefici*][603]—all of them subject to death, if found guilty of practicing their livelihoods. One notes both the inclusion of the once-venerable *haruspices* and also of Chaldaeans, so that this last term, in a pattern parallel to

---

[600] Ibid, 107.
[601] Ibid, 108. For the *Laws*, see above, 71-5.
[602] Ibid.
[603] Note that the etymology of the term *maleficus* is "evil-doer." "Sorcery" would be *maleficia*. One must also keep in mind that another term for this, *veneficia*, is more ambiguous in root-meaning and nuance, somewhat analogous in its ambiguity to that which might be used in sorcery but also in medicine, as we have seen (above, 58): a *pharmakon*.

that directed to the term *magus* itself generations earlier, has evolved from an ethnic designation to one that refers to one such nefarious livelihood.

But on the other hand, "we see that the intention of distinguishing magic from the old Roman religion was not abandoned. Like his predecessors and successors on the throne, including Valentinian I, Constantius retained among his titles that of *pontifex maximus* [High Priest]. When, for instance, during a threat of famine in Rome, the grain-ships were delayed by gales and the Prefect of Rome went to the temple of Castor and Pollux at Ostia to sacrifice to these patrons of sailors—with immediate success, as we read in Ammianus— there could be no question of his doing something prohibited."[604]

Again, then, both ambiguity of action on the part of the temporal leadership and ambiguity, or at least changes, in definitional categories, are manifest during this period. There is more, though, to the irregular shape of the century. Barb goes on to suggest that perhaps it was the harshness of the behavior of Constantius that "contributed to the momentum of the pagan reaction, which burst forth under Constantius' successor Julian the Apostate"—precisely when the "spell" of Peter the arch-magician was due to come to an end, according to the pagan sources referred to by St Augustine.[605] This is, indeed, the same Julian (r. 361-3) to whom I have twice alluded, who was a student of Maximus of Ephesus, (a pupil of Iamblichus), and who was apparently the last pagan emperor (which is why Christian historiography calls him "the Apostate"). He seems not to have been atypical of an upper-crust Roman pagan with regard to the syncretistic aspects of his thought that combined a traditional view of the gods with an almost monotheistic (Jewish/Christian-influenced?) sense of Zeus as the creator.

More to the point, as emperor, Julian began a religious reformation of the state that was intended to restore its "lost strength." He supported the restoration of polytheism as it had evolved in and since the Hellenistic period as the state religion. New laws tended to target wealthy and educated Christians; his aim was not to destroy Christianity as much as to drive the religion out of the governing classes of the empire. He restored pagan temples that had been confiscated since the time of Constantine (d. 337) and repealed stipends that Constantine had awarded to Christian bishops. He removed their other privileges, including the right to be consulted on appointments and to act as judges in private courts.

Most significantly, on February 4, 362, Julian promulgated an edict to guarantee freedom of religion. This edict proclaimed that all the religions were equal before the law, and that the Roman Empire must thus return to its original embrace of religious eclecticism,

---

[604] Ibid, 109-10. I assume that Barb mentions Valentinian (r. 364-75) in particular because he is typically referred to as the last "great" Western Emperor. Barb's references to Ammianus Marcellinus are to the *Res Gestae*. 19. 10. 4. Ammianus was born between 325 and 330 and died sometime between 392 and 400. He was a Roman soldier who served under both Emperor Constantius and Emperor Julian (whom he particularly admired), and he was a historian. He wrote the penultimate major history surviving from antiquity (the last was written by Procopius). Ammianus' work, written after he retired to Rome, perhaps in the early 370s, chronicled in Latin— although he was born in the Greek East, possibly in Antioch—the history of Rome from 96 to 378. Only the sections covering the period 353–378 have survived. From it we can deduce, by the way, that he was a pagan who was very tolerant of Christianity; when he criticizes a Christian it is not because of that individual's faith and conversely, he criticized his idol, Julian, for barring Christians from teaching in the newly reformed Roman education system.

[605] Ibid, 110. Barb is referring to his prior discussion (on 104) of Augustine's comment in *De civitate dei*, xviii. 53.

according to which the state did not impose any religion on its provinces. In practical terms, however, this had as its purpose the restoration of Paganism at the expense of Christianity. Indeed, Christians were barred from teaching posts in his education reforms.

Julian's preference for a non-Christian and non-philosophical view of Iamblichus' theurgy seems to have convinced him that it was right to outlaw the practice of the Christian view of theurgy and to demand the suppression of the Christian Mysteries. In one further twist to all of this, he made plans for the restoration of the Judaean Temple—by his time, of course, it would have been universally understood to have been the *Jewish* Temple—in Jerusalem. Ammianus Marcellinus writes that "Julian thought to rebuild at an extravagant expense the proud Temple once in Jerusalem, and committed this task to Alypius of Antioch. Alypius set vigorously to work, and was seconded by the governor of the province—when fearful balls of fire, breaking out near the foundations, continued their attacks, till the workmen, after repeated scorchings, could approach no more, and he gave up the attempt."[606]

Perhaps an earthquake—some sources claimed arson, presumably by Jews who did not embrace the idea that the Temple would be rebuilt by a Roman emperor and not through the advent of the messiah—destroyed the new foundations. This catastrophe coincided fairly closely with Julian's death in the indecisive Battle of Sammara against the Sassanids, in 363, so that both events were seen by subsequent Christian historiography, not surprisingly, as acts of God.[607]

In any case, the imperial pendulum would begin to swing back toward Christianity with Julian's successor, Valentinian I, who reiterated freedom of religion for Christians and pagans (and Jews) alike, as Julian had decreed it, in a manner recalling Constantine's Edict at Milan in 313, but with the beginning of a turn away from favoring the old Paganisms, and with an emphatic turn against *magia/superstitio*. The activities of *haruspices* were thus once again permissible, but woe unto those—capital punishment unto those—who were found to resort "at night to evil imprecations, magic rituals or necromantic [i.e., directed to the dead] sacrifices."[608]Indeed we receive quite a description by Ammianus of tortures and executions of those found guilty of this or that act of alleged

---

[606] Ammianus Marcellinus, *Res Gestae*, 23.1.2–3. The Emperor Hadrian, it may be recalled, had built a temple to Capitoline Jupiter around 135 CE, on that site some sixty-five years after the destruction of the Temple, at the same time that he renamed Jerusalem *Aelia Capitolina*.

[607] For what it is worth, Jerusalem is located close to a fault line between two tectonic plates in the earth's crust, thus making it somewhat more subject to earthquake activity than were its location otherwise. The Battle of Sammara took place during a retreat back to Roman territory after successes that included a victory before the gates of Ctesiphon, the Sassanian capital, but which failed to yield the conquest of the city. Apropos of the views and prejudices of different sources—specifically as that obtains with regard to Julian—in 364, Libanius claimed that the Emperor had been assassinated by a Christian who was one of his own soldiers, but this assertion is not corroborated by Ammianus (who was apparently a personal friend of the emperor) or by other contemporary historians. Fourteen years later, Libanius asserted that Julian had been killed by a Saracen—i.e., an Arab from the Lakhmid kingdom in what is now southern Iraq—an assertion perhaps derived from the story that Julian's doctor Oribasius, having examined the wound, said that it was from a spear used by a group of Lakhmid auxiliaries serving in the Sassanid army. Later, the Greek chronicler from Antioch, John Malalas (ca 491-578) claimed that Julian's death was an assassination commanded by St Basil of Caesarea. A much later variation on this last story was that St Basil, imprisoned by Julian at the outset of the Sassanid campaign, prayed to Saint Mercurius to help him and that Mercurius appeared in a vision to Basil claiming to have speared Julian.

[608] Ibid, 110.

superstitio under Valentinian (whom clearly Ammianus did not like). The most notorious is the trial in Antioch, in 371, in which

> hundreds of people of all classes were led to torture and execution, accused, justly or unjustly, of taking part in the attempts to replace the emperor Valens [Valentinian's brother and co-ruler at that time] by a brilliant young man of distinguished family and position, named Theodorus. ...[T]wo experts in divination, called Hilarius and Patricius [were employed], to discover by magical means the name of Valens' successor to the throne. ...[T]hey constructed from olive twigs—in imitation of the Delphic oracle of Apollo—a small three-legged table (which was actually produced in court), consecrating it with the usual secret incantations and lengthy ritual ceremonies. When this table had been placed in the middle of a house which had been purified thoroughly by incense, they laid on it an exactly circular dish made from an alloy of various metals. Round the rim of this dish, at carefully measured intervals, were engraved the twenty-four letters of the Greek alphabet. The celebrant—or should we say medium?—in ceremonial priestly attire, stood above the dish, holding a consecrated magic ring swinging from a thread. This ring jumped fitfully and finally halted above single letters which accumulated to form words, which in turn formed elegant Greek hexameters of the kind by which the famous oracles of old proclaimed their answers. When questioned about the name of the successor to the throne, the ring jumped to the letters *TH*, *E*, *O* and *D*..., at which moment one of those present cried out that inexorable fate had proclaimed the name of Theodorus—whereupon the session broke up, probably just as any spiritualistic meeting today would have to be discontinued after such an undisciplined incident.[609]

We might note before going further that the procedure involves, at least in part, imitation of the Delphic oracle—in other words, mainstream religion that was, or had been, central to Greek and Roman thought with regard to the *sacer* for centuries; and that the revelation was immediately subject to sacerdotal interpretation—but that the act of revelation itself, offered according to a prescribed procedure, was crucially interrupted, further opening the door to the possibility of mis-interpretation.

Indeed, interpretation assumes a still greater role as Ammianus' Barb-conveyed narrative continues forward. For the judges asked the accused "whether the magic oracle had not told them their own fate," to which they in part responded that the hexameters "foretold their own execution but also promised [that... t]he emperor, who was about to condemn them, was to die by 'evil fate while Ares rages on the plain of Mimas.'"[610] The two prisoners *were* duly tortured and executed, and the emperor, haunted by the prophecy, and thus studiously avoiding Asia Minor, where there was, he was told, a Mount Mimas,

---

[609] Ibid 111-12. Barb goes on to mention (112-13) the discovery of precisely this kind of stool/table and dish, with two magic rings, at an excavation at Pergamon, discussed in R. Wuensch's *Antikes Zaubergeraet aus Pergamon* (Berlin: Staatliche Museen zu Berlin, 1905)—so Ammianus' description of the equipment is right on.
[610] Ibid, 113.

did in fact die in battle—seven years later—at Adrianople, (*not* in Asia Minor). He was fighting the Goths, and died not far from the location of an old tomb the Greek inscription on which identified the deceased as a distinguished man named Mimas. And of course, Valens' successor—whose name had not been fully spelled out due to the interruption of the sacerdotal ritual—would be THEODosius.

We see in this account how even the "magic"-condemning Christian emperor sufficiently believes in the pagan magic that he condemns to be affected by it—sufficiently to help shape its message as a self-fulfilling prophecy. Or maybe there is a real reality to that pagan magic. Why, though is it condemned? Because it is *magic*? Or because it is *negative* magic? And is it negative magic because it is *pagan* and not *Christian*, or because the act of seeking to predict Valens' successor is taken to be a subversive act, as if the mere search could help to undermine the emperor's existence? Of course, Theodosius would finally do away with Greco-Roman Paganism altogether by declaring Christianity the only *religio licita*, the official *religio licita*, of the Empire (sometime between 381 and 395), as a consequence of which, all the still extant forms of Paganism, as well as Judaism, would be considered *superstitiones* thereafter.

As Barb points out in summary, "hand in glove with the Church, the emperors [following Theodosius] issued decree after decree against all the numerous heresies which had become rife on the fringes of Orthodox Christianity. These heresies, Jewish and Christian Gnosticism, Manicheaeism (the latter condemned as a kind of evil magic as early as the beginning of the century by Diocletian), NeoPaganism, and the rest were now thrown on the refuse-heap, a heavy bulk far more virulent and dangerous to spiritual health than the bones, by now rather dry, of the defunct religions in remote antiquity."[611]

Not only do we notice that the term heresy is a widely encompassing term— *everything* that is not considered proper Christianity, including Judaism—but the Paganisms with which most of these various heresies have been classed are already defunct or in the process of becoming defunct by the end of the century. This is obviously of consequence with regard to the side of our focus that is devoted to the beginnings of Judaism and Christianity, as we shall more fully discuss in the following chapter. On the other hand, Barb's further discussion of Ammianus Marcellinus in the last part of his article addresses the other side of our focus, on the relationship between religion and magic.

He asks rhetorically, "[w]hy, indeed, should Ammianus *not* have believed in magic?"—and continues, significantly: [e]verybody did so in antiquity except a few sceptics and agnostics—and they did not believe in religion either. If the more critical minds saw in much, or even most, of it a more or less fraudulent deception or superstition, that did not amount to dogmatic disbelief... All the Christian theologians believed in the existence of the magic arts; not to do so would mean disbelieving the stories of the Old and New Testament, from that of the Witch of Endor to that of Simon Magus. All of the fashionable pagan philosophers of the century, headed by the divine Iamblichus, believed in the magical arts of *theurgia* as part and parcel of their theosophic systems. The

---

[611] Ibid, 114. Barb's key source, as he indicates in his footnotes, is the *Codex Theodosianus* IX, 16 and 38.

Christians, however, anathemized the use of magic. The self-righteous pagan philosophers apparently did not do so. "[612]

We are, one might say, back where we began, then: magic is defined in terms of its alleged negative focus, but we are not provided with the specifics of what constitutes magical activity as opposed to religious activity. Where Christianity is concerned it is potentially anything non-Christian that purports to address, engage and make use of the *sacer*—a *sacer* that is conceived of as singular (albeit in a paradoxically triune manner). For Paganism, magic, again, must be more nuanced than simply to apply to anything that isn't "my" belief system, since it is a given almost always accepted by pagans who believe in many different gods and goddesses of different levels of power that there are many different religious directions and religious styles, methods and specific foci.

If "magic" is still being used to refer to a nefariously directed address, engagement, and attempted use of the *sacer*, the bottom line still seems to be—for pagan and Christian alike—that he who has the power to do so is the one who decides whether a practitioner is following a negative, magic-ridden sacerdotal path or a positive, religion-centered path. *Who* gets charged and *why* undergoes changes as we move from Constantine to Constantius II to Julian the so-called Apostate to Valentinian and Valens to Theodosius. Examples of this are multiplied by Barb by reference to the great orator, Libanius as well as to St John Chrysostom and to the anonymous author of *Lithica* (on the magical power of various stones).[613] He mentions how Ammianus reports that "after the sensational trial of 371 the judges ordered the wholesale public burning of vast quantities of codices and volumes containing in large part, as Ammianus insists, inoffensive scholarly literature," which act led book-owners to destroy their own libraries out of fear of fatal accusations of harboring nefarious magical texts within their collections. Ammianus' account reads like a passage from Ray Bradbury's *Fahrenheit 451*.[614]

"After all," Barb continues, "where was the unequivocal dividing line between Neoplatonic philosophy—say, like Iamblichus' *De mysteriis Aegyptorum* [*Concerning the Mysteries of Egypt*]—and Egyptian sorcery, between the criminal investigation into the future by the *mathematici*... and, say, the handbook of astrology written by Firmicus Maternus, the same uncompromising Christian who loyally addressed *De errore profanarum religionum* [*Concerning the Falseness of Profane (i.e., pagan) Religions*] to the emperors Constantius and Constans?"[615]

It is interesting that, in his discussion of *Lithica*, Barb suggests that most of these amuletic stones seem

> to have been fabricated in Egypt, that is in Alexandria, and it seems to
> me that Alexandrian Jews of rather dubious orthodoxy might have a good

---

[612] Ibid, 115.

[613] *lithos* means "stone" in Greek. The work addresses the magical benefits of minerals in combination with certain vegetable and animal substances and with the proper words of consecration as well as being engraved with certain images, names and formulae.

[614] Ibid, 116-17. Bradbury's novel is set in the future when the authorities improve their ability to control the minds of people by outlawing books; fahrenheit 451 is the fictional temperature level at which books burn; any books found by the authorities are burned, often together with their owners.

[615] Ibid, 117.

deal to do with their manufacture... Throughout this age the Jews share with Persians and Chaldaeans a reputation as expert sorcerers second only to the Egyptian past masters. The Alexandrian Jews, being, as one might say, naturalized Egyptians and having absorbed a considerable amount of the Persian and Babylonian heritage, could well have provided the outstanding specialists in the magic arts... The Fathers inherited the tradition of speculation on these jewels [the twelve gems on the breast-plate of the High Priest in the Jerusalem Temple] and christianized it... I am also inclined to see an Alexandrian Jew in Damigeron, who is named as author in a frequently copied lapidary...[616]

Again one might ask whether Barb is not assuming a prejudicial position based on centuries of medieval assumptions by Christians regarding Jews and imposing that view on both the anonymous author of *Lithica* and on Damigeron, whose Greek-language work was translated into Latin in the fifth century. I am not arguing that in both cases the individual in question could *not* be Jewish; I am merely offering a suspicion regarding the source of Barb's inclination, which would be a variation on the sort of inclinations that we have ascribed to Frazer, Mauss, Malinowski and Levi-Strauss in their approach to non-Western engagements of the *sacer*.

The fact that Jews shared a reputation with the Persians and Chaldaeans as expert sorcerers does not necessarily mean that they *were*, particularly when the "age" to which Barb is referring is one of intense *sacer*-engagement competition, as we have been seeing, and when by the fourth century, which is the time period he is discussing, most of our sources for that notion are Christian writers deeply embedded in that competition. We have seen, moreover, that the reputation, say, of the Persians, that leads to their term for priest, *maghos*, being treated as a term for "sorcerer"—and becomes the linguistic source for the term "magician" and its implications—is based on a misconstrual of what their priests are about, reflecting a mine-is-religion-and-yours-is-magic sensibility.

Indeed, Barb goes on to claim that his conjecture is "confirmed by the fact that a large number of the medieval magic lapidaries... introduce themselves as being written by 'one of the Children of Israel in the desert after their departure from Egypt'." Further, "... another jewel of Jewish magic, only superficially christianized, the *Testamentum Salomonis* [*The Testament of Solomon*, a work that is part of the medieval *Patrologia Graeca*, associated with the Greek Church Fathers]... is one of the many magical books... which that Jewish king and arch-magician was alleged to have written."[617]

We may recognize in this last pair of statements a reminder that in the medieval period Jews had acquired a firm reputation as wrongly-directed dealers with the *sacer* but that there also remained a willingness on the part of at least some Christians to follow in that wrong direction if it seemed necessary for survival, although they were not supposed to. Naturally any text pointing in that direction, however christianized, would be ascribed to a Jewish author. Whether or not the *Testamentum Salomonis* was a barely christianiized

---

[616] Ibid, 118.
[617] Ibid, 119.

Jewish text recalls that sort of question that we earlier raised with regard to the Jewishness/paganness/Christianness of the *PGM*.

The fact, moreover, that Barb refers to Solomon as a Jewish king and arch-magician presents two definitional problems that resonate with my proposal of his misdirected inclinations in refering to this material. One: as we have seen, Solomon was an Israelite king, the spiritual ancestor of both Judaism and Christianity, not a Jewish king, per se. The association of him with the Jews alone is both historically inaccurate and specifically issue-ridden in the period of the fourth and following centuries when both Jews and Christians claim to be the *Verus Israel* and when both lay claim to David as the consummate *mashiah/khristos*, who is, after all, Solomon's father.

Two: Solomon's position as an arch-magician is an amplification and transformation of the image of him as a wise king. The beginning point of that idea is arguably pagan (so, like Noah and especially Moses, he was thusly viewed by Paganism in late antiquity) and encompassed both Jewish and Christian interpretive literature. By the medieval period that encompassment is interwoven with the Christian view of Jews as magicians and thus to an association of them with Solomon as a magician. But Barb is retrofitting all of this onto an era in which these categories were still being shaped.

He notes that most of this stone-based material was used, in any case, for *white* magic, as opposed to the *defixiones*, sheets of lead (which sheets Barb calls *sinister*, as if the look of the material itself reflects its untoward uses) that pertained to *black* magic, reminding us yet again that the definitional borders are slippery: if mine is religion and yours is magic and superstition, then there is still the question of whether yours is nefarious—as a *superstitio* would be understood to be, by definition, and as whatever is construed as black magic would be—or whether it is innocent, as white magic would be. If, however, *any* sort of *magia* is illegal, then perhaps it does not matter what type you are practicing with regard to the punishment you may receive if found out.

Barb recognizes this, it would seem, when he concludes by noting that "magic is a rather more complicated business than it appears to be and contains a variety of ingredients. There is in it a large proportion of philosophy run wild—Neoplatonic philosophy, for instance; there is half-baked and misunderstood medicine stupidly popularized; there is the tendency to borrow clauses and stipulations from learned legal phraseology."[618] Indeed. Perhaps, though, the lines are not even that clearly blurred, (what is philosophy gone wild, for instance, and what exactly constitutes half-baked medicine?) and perhaps the placement of those lines is as dependent on who is drawing them, at least part of the time, as it is on inherent differences among these categories and between all of these categories and religion.

Where does this leave us and lead us with regard to the Greco-Roman world and how nascent Judaism and Christianity were faring within it? Barb has, in his very informative article, often slipped not only over the border into the fifth centiury but, in his last pages has jumped into the medieval period. This is where we need to follow, both to consider how that path leads back to Frazer and the others with whom we began our discussion, and beyond them toward our own era; and to sum up how the medieval and

---

[618] Ibid, 124.

post-medieval worlds need to be distinguished from the ancient world with regard to our double helix of religion/magic and Judaism/Christianity, while recognizing those ancient sensibilities that lay foundations upon which the sensibilities in the many centuries that follow from antiquity are built.

CHAPTER THIRTEEN

Religion, Superstition, Heresy and Definitional Confusion
into the Medieval Period

One might say that the topic that Peter Brown takes up in his "Sorcery, Demons, and the Rise of Christianity from Later Antiquity into the Middle Ages," picks up where Barb leaves off both conceptually and chronologically.[619] His thesis in the first part of his article "is that a precise malaise in the structure of the governing classes of the Roman Empire (especially in its eastern, Greek-speaking half) forced the ubiquitous sorcery beliefs of ancient man to a flash-point of accusations in the mid-fourth century."[620] Those accusations were being turned with greater frequency, he notes, toward the upper classes: "the senatorial aristocracy, for instance, and the professors of the great Mediterranean cities."[621] The context for this was the ever-widening circle of instability and insecurity, as "[p]ublic and continuous misfortune… was habitually explained, in this age of bitter confessional hatreds, by the anger of the gods or of God at the existence of dissenting religious groups—Christians, pagans or heretics."[622] So the concept of *superstitio* as political subversion has come more emphatically than ever to mean not only subversion against the state and its ruling administration but against the *polis* in the original sense of the Greek term: "community," and the range of potential objects of that accusation has broadened within the context of the increasing social upheavals of the late Empire. This, as opposed to a simple quantitative increase in the "fear of sorcery or in sorcery practices in the Late Roman Period," for it seems that there was not such an increase.[623]

And how was the period defined? By a tension between stability and change and by conflict between two kinds or systems of power: what Brown calls "*articulated* power, power defined and agreed upon by everyone (and especially by its holders): authority vested in precise persons; admiration and success gained by recognized channels. Running counter to this there may be other forms of influence less easy to pin down—*inarticulate* power: the disturbing intangibles of social life; the imponderable advantages of certain groups; personal skill that succeeds in a way that is unacceptable, or difficult to understand.

---

[619] Brown's article may be found in Mary Douglas, ed., *Witchcraft Confessions and Accusations*. (London and NY: Routledge. 1970), 17-45.
[620] Brown, 20.
[621] Ibid, 19.
[622] Ibid.
[623] Ibid, 20.

Wherever these two systems overlap, we may expect to find the sorcerer"[624]—or at least, I would add, the *accusation* of sorcery.

The accuser, as Brown multiplies his terminology, is typically "the man with the Single Images"—meaning that he understands only one, recognized and acceptable way of making one's way in the world, whereas the sorcerer (or the one accused of being a sorcerer, I would again add) is "the man invested with the Double Image... He has brought in the unseen to redress the balance of the seen... His achievements may [even] be admired, but they are, essentially, illegitimate."[625] So insecurity on the part of those with "fixed vested roles" leads to their feeling threatened by "holders of ambiguous positions of personal power" and to do what we have seen being done all the way back to the time of Apuleius—or, we might infer from the *Laws*, as far back as Plato's time (but most likely much further back than that)—they launch a *superstitio*-type accusation against those embodying that perceived threat.

And, in general, the more frequent the historiographic record of such accusations during this era, the more intense the condition of uncertainty, as we would not be surprised to hear. What is interesting—and hits its high-water mark of frequency during the reigns of Constantius II, Valentinian I and Valens—is the typical social configuration of this process. It usually involves the upper classes, but reflects new striations in those upper classes and a division between newly empowered and traditionally empowered members of those classes. More specifically, the use of the sorcery charge is "rarely made by the *parvenus* of the court among themselves; they are usually made by such groups against the holders of ill-defined, traditional status—to shake the pillars of the 'patrician class'."[626] Importantly, especially for our discussion, is the approximate correspondence between the latter and adherence to pagan beliefs and between the former and ascendant Christianity—for we can therefore see the sorcery-accusation process as a significant weapon in the war being waged by the Church against its spiritual competitors/enemies.

At the same time, as Brown notes, to reduce the accusations to nothing but that war may be overly simple. For he points out how Boethius and Mummolus, both eminent patricians who were destroyed in the sixth century, were brought down by charges that included the charge of sorcery. I would nonetheless argue that this may well be true by the sixth century, by which time Christianity has been the official *religio* of the empire and its post-Roman imperia for 150 years, but back in the fourth-century era of Constans, Valentinian and Valens that was hardly the case. And where Boethius, for instance, may have been accused of sorcery, this was not the main charge against him; treason against the Emperor Theodoric while serving in the senate was, leading to his execution in 524. So it seems to me reasonable to count the sorcery charges in the fourth century as having a decided Christian-versus-pagan aspect to them no longer paramount in the sixth century examples put forth by Brown.

It is, however, more complicated than that: the two fourth-century examples he offers are St Ambrose—not merely a bishop, but a Christian *saint*, after all—who was associated with no less than twelve deaths by sorcery; and Athanasius, Bishop of

---

[624] Ibid, 21-22.

[625] Ibid, 22.

[626] Ibid, 23-4. Brown is quoting Ammianus XXIX, ii, 9.

Alexandria (and essential to the conclusion of the Council of Nicaea of 325 in which Jesus was pronounced to be both fully human and fully divine), who also had a serious reputation for sorcery. Moreover, "[s]orcery was rife among the Syrian clergy of the fifth century. This is, of course, partly a tribute to their 'book learning' and thus to their reputations as guardians of the occult. But knowledge of sorcery was more precisely associated with a fluid group."[627]

Returning with Brown to that group that he originally mentioned along with patrician-types as being often on the receiving end of such accusations—"the professors of the great Mediterranean cities"—he notes that the supreme examples of men whose status was not fixed were "professors of rhetoric and philosophy, and poets (and, on a local level, in their own communities, the Jewish *rabbis*). They could become the *eminences grises* of the court... they were indispensable to the emperor as propagandists [toward their respective communities]... [T]he *rhetors*, at any period of Late Roman history... [offer us] situations of intense and insoluble rivalry... [Thus] the life of someone like Libanius was punctuated by accusations of sorcery: accusations by him and against him."[628]

We note in these last few paragraphs the significance of both the issue of ambiguity and the fact that Brown mentions rabbis as a subcategory of professorial recipients of the *maleficia* accusation. In looking back to our previous chapter and the writings of Origen and Hippolytus and also Barb's discussion we may recall the ambiguity among the categories of heretics, pagans and Jews; and in looking forward, we will see how as antiquity yields to the medieval period, this last-noted ambiguity will narrow in its focus to heretics and Jews and eventually and most often, to Jews.

There is at least one further issue that Brown raises that will offer significance in thinking back and in moving forward: the reminder of the role of St Augustine in introducing or firming up key tenets of Christianity—specifically, in this case, the concept of Original Sin. Brown points out how,

> [f]or pagan and Christian alike, misfortune was unambiguously the work of suprahuman agents, the *daemones*," and the late fourth and early fifth centuries offered an era particularly rife with misfortune, as we have seen otherwise noted, but the Christian Church offered an explanation of misfortune that both embraced all the phenomena previously ascribed to sorcery, and armed the individual with weapons of satisfying precision and efficacy against its suprahuman agents. ...[For w]hen we read the later works of Augustine... we realize that *his doctrine of the punishment of the human race for the sin of Adam has been widened so as to embrace all misfortune* [italics added]. ... Because of Adam's sin, God had permitted the demons to act as His 'public executioners'... The human race was the 'plaything of demons': damage to crops, disease, possession, incongruous behavior (such as the lapse of holy men), gratuitous accidents, and, as an insistent refrain, the untimely deaths of small children... *[God] has sent upon them the anger of His indignation,*

---

[627] Ibid, 26-7.
[628] Ibid, 24. See fn# 607 regarding the orator and historiographer, Libanius.

indignation and rage and tribulation, and possession by evil spirits
[italics added].[629]

A corollary of this, of course, is that individuals or groups who fail to recognize the Christhood of Jesus, who is the key to the door out of Adam-originated human misfortune—the solution to the otherwise insoluble problem of Original Sin—would be perceived as dangerous and threatening to the communities of which they remained part, so that they must be removed, by one means or another: think back to our initial discussion of the *lapis niger* and why the one who disturbs it must leave the community.[630]

Indeed, "[i]n the fourth and fifth centuries, therefore, the sense of a fixed identity in a stable and well-oriented world, that would encourage the blaming of sorcerers and would single out incongruities in public behavior as *the* misfortune *par excellence*, was being eroded in both the social milieu and the religious ideas associated with the leaders of Christian opinion. This situation changed as Late Roman society became more fixed. ... The idea of ill-defined guilt hardened into a sense of exposure to misfortune through the neglect of prescribed actions. At the end of the sixth century, it was plain to Gregory the Great that a ... nun who ate a lettuce without first making the sign of the cross on it would swallow a demon perched on its leaves."[631]

The implications of this for our discussion are treble: one, that besides the all-powerful, all-good God there are lesser, nefarious beings that are part of—occupying the lower part of—the *sacer*. Two: that to avoid the contradiction presented by this (for how can there be other *sacer* beings besides God, and nefarious, to boot, in an all-encompassing monotheistic reality?), they are, as we have seen Brown suggest, actually in the *service* of God to continuously punish humanity for Adam's Original Sin. Three: that an action such as making the sign of the cross can hardly be distinguished from actions that, in being non-Christian-specific, would be judged as magical, not religious—and almost certainly regarded as inherently nefarious. One might add a fourth implication, that the category "non-Christian" would, once Paganism has completely left the stage of history, be filled by heresy and Judaism, which might or might not be clearly distinguished from each other in the Christian mind.

The third of these points is acknowledged by Brown when he comments on how membership in the Church was deemed to protect one from those nefarious *daemones*: "the practicing Christian gained immunity from sorcery, [for o]nce inside the Christian Church, the Christian enjoyed, if in a form that was being constantly qualified, the millennial sensations of a modern African anti-sorcery cult."[632] Apart from the question of how this comment offers a contemporary Western perspective that necessarily delegitimizes such African cults, it is intended (obviously) to offer a delegitimization of at least part of the thinking that characterized Christians during the Late Roman era.

Of further relevance to our goal of understanding early Christianity and Judaism is Brown's observation that, in "the rise of Christianity in the third and fourth centuries...

---

[629] Ibid, 28-9.
[630] See above, 20.
[631] Ibid, 30-1.
[632] Ibid, 31.

we find ... a 'humanizing' of the suprahuman agent of evil."[633] Thus the problematic of multiple nefarious aspects of the *sacer* is gradually being "solved" by relegating that nefariousness to a more *profanus* sort of level. Thus the "Devil was the 'rival' of the saint: envy, hatred, and the deadly spleen of a defeated expert mark his reactions to the human race." Hardly the enormous supernatural being suggested by the Book of Revelation, whose only opposite in terms of power is God Itself (albeit he is ultimately, of course, no match for God, ending up consumed in a lake of fire), but barely more than a *profanus* being with a serious *sacer* aspect to him, as saints are.

"In the fourth and fifth centuries, ... the rise of Christianity should be seen as the rise of a new grouping of Roman society and as an attempt to suspend certain forms of human relations within the fold of the people of God. ... if there is misfortune, it is divorced from a human reference and the blame is pinned firmly on the 'spiritual powers of evil' [and] the new community... resolved its tensions by projecting [evil forces in the world] in the form of an even greater demonic menace from outside."[634] Brown either contradicts himself or, perhaps, intends to suggest that in the evolving competitive complications regarding the understanding of the *sacer* that carry us from the third and fourth to the fourth and fifth centuries, we move from that lowering of the status of the carriers of evil toward almost human level back toward their gradual re-elevation from the human plane that separates the sorcerer from the source of evil that he activates. One might suppose, however, that just that sort of separation would be very difficult for everyday Christians to recognize—and perhaps also difficult for many members of the clerical leaders of those everyday Christians, particularly if threats to their hegemony remained unresolved.

These complications would seem to be expressed, and perhaps, therefore, acknowledged by Brown in the brief concluding section of his article, which he begins by noting that the period 300-600 CE is "a recognizable whole," (rather than just a preliminary to the Middle Ages), but during which period, he asserts, a sorcerer was

> a man of undefinable *power*. In extreme cases, the ideal type produced by the traditional 'vested' culture would wear this ambivalent halo: the philosopher Apollonius of Tyana was widely known as a *magus*; many saints were spontaneously hailed as *magi*... Above all, the sorcerer is a man who enjoys power over demons, even over the gods. He can threaten the gods ... he *becomes* the god—'for Thu art I and I am Thou; whatever I say must come to pass.' In Christian sources, the demons act as servants of the sorcerer: he is the servant of the Devil only in a very generalized sense, for he is free to abandon him by destroying the books of his trade and by accepting Christian baptism.[635]

Presumably the sorcerer who has power over the gods and becomes a god through introjective identification is a pagan;[636] it seems somewhat odd that the Christian texts

---

[633] Ibid, 32, for both this and the following quote.

[634] Ibid, 33.

[635] Ibid, 34.

[636] Brown uses this phrase, in suggesting a formal similarity to the psychoanalytic process—which calls to mind the discussion of Quesalid in Levi-Strauss' narrative. (See above, 49-52).

would acknowledge any actual divine power in association with a sorcerer, in that case, since there can be no other gods, pagan or otherwise, aside from the real, Triune God, and obviously no human could compel or become that God—except Jesus, that is, who, by the mid-fourth century is understood by proper Christians to *be* God in human form (except, of course, by Arian heretics).

Where, again, does the saint fit into this? "[B]oth can command; but the saint has an effective 'vested' power, whereas the sorcerer works with a technique that is unreliable and, above all, cumbersome."[637] So we have come back to the underlying principle of Moses versus the Egyptian *sacerdotes*: their power is not non-existent and illusory; it is real but weaker than his because their gods are weaker than the God of Israel. So as Paganism is fading but still present in the fourth and fifth centuries, the increasingly powerful Church does not, by implication, deny the *existence* of pagan gods, it reduces them to a position that is both nefarious (of course) and weaker.

This notion, together with the idea of "'learned' sorcery," carries, Brown points out, into the medieval period, in which

> a man of occult learning could [still] placate, manipulate, even threaten suprahuman powers to his advantage... [This was particularly so] among societies that had remained in touch with their ancient roots—in Byzantium, Islam, and the Jewish communities. At the end of our period, however, it is joined by another theme. We meet the *witch* in the full sense, a person who either is born with or achieves an inherent character of evil... [T]he power is gained by a binding compact with the ultimate pole of evil—the Devil... The idea of the 'servant of Satan,' I would suggest, is a direct sequel of certain developments in Western and Byzantine society at the end of the sixth century.[638]

Brown adds the important note that the last notable cases of sorcery associated with worshipping pagan gods come in the 570s in the Eastern Empire, leaving "only one possible outsider in a Christian world—the Jew." Not by mere coincidence "the first widespread movements persecuting the Jewish communities of Africa, Byzantium, Visigothic Spain, and, sporadically, Gaul, with the choice of baptism or exile" date from this time period.[639] Even cases in which bishops are implicated, (of which there are several), the Jew plays a part, most particularly "because he always denied Christ—he was the 'apostate' par excellence."[640]

He notes that the Roman Imperial model has become solidified in two *sacer* directions by then: "Angels were the courtiers and bureaucrats of a remote Heavenly Emperor, and the saints, the *patroni*, the 'protectors,' whose efficacious interventions at court channeled the benefits of a just autocrat to individuals and localities," while at the other, negative end of the *sacer*, "the Devil also has grown in majesty: he, also, is a great

---

[637] Ibid, 34.
[638] Ibid, 34-5.
[639] Ibid, 35.
[640] Ibid, 36.

lord, a *patronus*; he also can welcome his servants." [641] If in theory, the most obvious candidates to be viewed as servants of the Devil are the Jews, then the question becomes: what, aside from the occasional accusation of sorcery, are the sort of accusations directed toward them and what actions might be taken against them besides expulsion and forced baptisms, if any? And while pagans are gone, what about heretics, and what might be done about them if they still persist—and are heretics and Jews clearly distinguished from each other by the Church and by everyday Christians?

*   *   *   *   *

The implications of the emerging and evolving complexities and complications that are discussed in the previous chapters attending the relationship between Judaism and Christianity in the early centuries of their side-by-side development continue to play out over the centuries that follow. As Christianity becomes hegemonic over a Roman Empire that, in the course of the fifth and following centuries is becoming medieval Europe, it continues to wrestle with challenges to its spiritual—and political—dominance. Among the traumas that would come with triumph, gradually, was the arrival on the scene of a further threat to both spiritual and political hegemony in the form of Islam, arriving by the early eighth century into Europe. Whereas monasticism had arrived into Europe by the sixth century, by the ninth and tenth centuries its ideals had been sufficiently compromised in certain quarters that a monastic reform movement was emerging—and by the twelfth century at least one monastic order, the Cluniac, was sufficiently large that its abbot was powerful enough to challenge the Pope on certain matters. The question of church and state—of the supremacy of the Pope as opposed to the Emperor—would be a frequent tug-of-war from the eighth through the eleventh centuries. A profound schism would eventually divide the Church in the mid-eleventh century (1054 CE) between the Catholic West and the Orthodox East.

Embedded within these complications were the two key issues that, for our narrative, most significantly reflect a continuation of problems developing in late Roman antiquity: that of heresy and that of Judaism—which latter really fit neither quite into the category of heresy nor quite into that of infidel belief (where Paganism and subsequently Islam would be placed) by the early medieval period. Eusebius, interestingly enough, refers to Judaism as a *superstitio* in his writings. For him that term seems still to have the meaning it had always had for the Roman authorities: a cult or belief system that is regarded as politically subversive and threatening either to the authorities or to the community or to both.

That Judaism was perceived to offer such a threat has an obvious logic to it, particularly when we take into consideration the thoughts expressed by Brown in the last

---

[641] Ibid. The *patronus-cliens* relationship was a staple of Roman society from the late republican period onward. A *patronus* offers protection to his *clientes*, who are expected to do favors that he might demand of them, such as voting as a block for a particular senatorial candidate, or even assembling to offer a show of force against an enemy of the *patronus*. This system would eventually evolve in a more layered complexity into the medieval feudal structure, in which a network of relationships of this sort would be governed by carefully defined hierarchies of loyalty. In more recent times, a somewhat simpler version can be seen in the structure of the *Casa Nostra*.

few paragraphs of his article, as discussed just above, centering on the Jewish denial of the Christhood of Jesus, and asserting both the ubiquity of negative *daemones* and the importance of Jesus for individual and communal survival from their would-be depredations.

FIG 5: Medieval English Caricature of Jews Attended by Devils, found on the *Rotulus Judaeorum*, 1233

In the black-and-white understanding of the *sacer*—which we have seen carrying from Zoroastrianism to Judaeanism, particularly in its Qumran outpost, and from there into Christianity as much as or more than into Judaism—if the Jews do not embrace the Christ, then there is only one alternative: they must embrace the anti-Christ. As the Christ is the Son of God by a Judaean virgin, the anti-Christ is the son of the Satan by a Judaean harlot. As by definition all Christians are working with those loyal to God to bring about the divine kingdom on earth, those who embrace the Satan and his son and, like them, are by definition disloyal to God, strive to undermine that effort. So, too, like the Satan and the anti-Christ, Jews came to be believed to have small horns on their heads—and sometimes even cloven hooves. Images, particularly in the Rhineland, depict Jews in concert with devils and demons, and/or horned or wearing horned hats —sometimes gathered around a great sow, particularly focused on its anal area [FIG 5].

There were various practical ways in which Christianity sought to solve its unrelenting Jewish problem as the centuries moved forward. One was a series of public debates regarding Jewish and Christian ideology, between various rabbis and bishops at various times and places. The outcome typically was that, if the rabbi was deemed to have been defeated, the Jewish community was expected to convert to Christianity. If the rabbi was deemed victorious, the anger against the Jewish community most often led to expulsion or some form of persecution.

A second means of dealing with the Jewish problem was the extensive legislation arrived at during the Fourth Lateran Council of 1215. Among the demands made of the Jewish community was that they wear a distinctive yellow badge on their outer garments so that they might be easily identified by their Christian neighbors who would not, therefore, get accidentally caught up in the nefarious practices of the Jews. More interestingly, in various parts of Europe it became a requirement that Jews wear a special hat—a horned hat, that would not only serve to identify them but reflect the fact and remind others of the fact that beneath the hat a pair of devilish horns was sprouting from the top of Jewish heads.[642]

More nefarious, and directly reflecting the sort of *religio/superstitio*, religion/magic sensibility that we have seen as endemic to the political and spiritual Greco-Roman world and the particular directions that sensibility had begun to take in the course of the second through fifth centuries, was the Blood Libel. One may see this idea—although we have no evidence of its appearance before the eleventh century, in the Slavic world of the Kievan Rus—as growing out of the New Testament, and in particular the Gospel According to John. That is, the notion that the "Jews" (fully conflated, by the medieval period, with the Judaeans) were responsible for the death of Jesus—which notion expands from the Synoptic Gospels to the Gospel of John to the Acts of the Apostles and various Epistles—lays direct conceptual groundwork for the blood libel, also referred to as the blood accusation.

There is a range of modes in which this notion manifests itself, but broadly stated, it offers two aspects. The first part (strictly speaking, the "blood libel") is that a Christian child is mock-crucified by Jews; the second part (the "ritual accusation") is that the Jews then use various internal body parts for this or that gastronomic purpose—the entrails, for example, for the *haroset* (sweet herbs) of the Passover meal—or to perform secret rituals. The classic accusation is that the blood is drained from the victim and then used as a key ingredient for *matzah*, the unleavened bread that is the consummate gastronomic aspect of and ultimate symbol within the Passover meal and within the entire Passover week. [643]

There is both a certain logic and an irony to this. The logic is that Passover occurs in close proximity to Easter, the time of year when the Passion of Christ is being most intensely reviewed in the Christian community, with Passion Plays filling out Passion Week, culminating with the Gospel stories that represent the Jews as responsible for Christ's death. And if they crucified him once, wouldn't it make a certain perverse sense, in the ongoing folk-level theological battle between the sibling faiths, that they would symbolically repeat that act year by year, particularly since mocking Jesus as the messiah would represent a reversal of the messianic hope so rampant for Christians (and, as we have noted, differently, for Jews) at Easter (and Passover) time? Wouldn't it make perverse

---

[642] In medieval Christian art, the color yellow developed an association with betrayal. Most obviously, Judas i s almost always depicted in yellow, and thus the color of choice for Jewish badges was yellow, thanks to the association between Jews and Judas through both the phonemic relationship between "Judaism" and "Judas," and the relationship between the by-definition-anti-Christ role of Judas in the Gospel narratives and the Jews' presumed anti-Christ relationship. It should be noted, by logical paradox, that Peter is also often depicted in yellow—albeit typically a more golden yellow than that of Judas—for although he was the Rock upon which Jesus would build the Church, he also denied his Master three times before dawn arrived on the night of Jesus' arrest.

[643] Connected to the notion of the Jews as in league with dark forces, and with the idea that, after all, black magic is tied to white religion—the most obvious linguistic reminder of this sensibility is the derivation of the magical phrase "hocus pocus" from the phrase that offers the culminating eucharistic moment in the mass: *hoc corpus est* ("this is the body [of Christ]")—there evolved a conviction that the Jews require Christian blood for their rituals and magical activities. Thus not only for preparing *matzah*, but in this place or that, for anointing rabbis, for circumcision, for curing eye ailments, preventing epileptic seizures, removing body odors, stopping menstrual bleeding, stopping bleeding from wounds, as well as to ward off the evil eye in general, and thus to fabricate amulets and love potions, as well as to anoint the bodies of the dead. See Willi-Erich Peukert, "*Ritualmord*," in the *Handwoerterbuch des Deutscher Aberglaubens*, Hans Baechthold-Staeubli and E. Hoffman-Krayer, eds., (Berlin, 1927-42) vol. 7, col. 734.

sense that the Jews in their nefarious, betraying ugliness, would instill within the flat bread that they eat at Passover the very element that emerges from the wine and flat bread of the Eucharist? And on the other hand, wouldn't it make sense that, since it is a universal truth that both magical and medicinal rituals require absolutely pure components to be effective, they would take pure body parts from pure little Christian children to accomplish their ends?

The irony is that the blood libel reverses the significance of the eucharistic ceremony within Christianity, in which the wafer and wine are transubstantiated into the body and blood of Christ, consumed by his followers so as to merge his being with theirs in a literal way: so the Jews are accused by medieval Christians of doing what they, the Christians, do, albeit in an indirect, symbolic and negatively nuanced way! They consume food infused with the blood of an innocent, crucified in mockery of the ultimate Innocent—the pure Lamb of God. The second irony is that blood is the most basic element that must emphatically be removed from food in order for Jews to consider it edible, i.e., kosher—acceptable in God's eyes for human consumption.[644] In the Jewish tradition, meat is typically drained and drained, pounded and cooked until it is well enough done so that not even the suggestion of blood that might be visually conveyed by the red juices of rarer meat will be in evidence when it appears on the plate. How likely is it that Jews, who so carefully avoid blood or anything resembling blood in their food, would incorporate it within *matzah*—plain, flat, unleavened bread into which not even yeast has been added?

Yet the canard of the Blood Accusation has a long history in Europe, beginning, to repeat, as early as the eleventh century in Russia.[645] The first *detailed* account of a blood libel, however was in Norwich, East Anglia—in what is today called England—in 1144. In that year a little boy named William disappeared into the surrounding heath woods on March 21, the Tuesday before both Passover and Easter. The court system in place at that time included local jurisdiction for secret cases of killing (i.e., murder, as opposed to open cases of homicide) and therefore it was the responsibility of the local authorities to deal with the body of a victim where it was found, even if, say, the body were identified as that of so-and-so who was known to have been living in a different district. One might further note that it was not until the 1180s that the idea of interrogating independent witnesses separately—found back in the deutero-canonical/apocryphal Book of Susannah and the Elders—was introduced under Henry II, and even then the system was only sporadically utilized.

As elsewhere in Europe, ground-level resentment toward the Jews derived probably not quite as much from religious sentiment as from the economic role they played. To be sure, that hostility was reinforced by the Church leadership, that—as a historical technicality, as it were—tended to emphasize the mocking-of-Christ's-passion-aspect of the blood libel canard, rather than the aspect that fantasized regarding the use to which the

---

[644]*Kashrut*, as it evolves, ranges with regard to the gastronomically impermissible from foods that are inherently off-limits, as stipulated in the Torah, such as pig meat or shellfish, or animals that don't have cloven hooves or chew their cud up and down instead of side to side; to animals that are not slaughtered according to a prescribed method; to meat that has not been prepared properly; to the mixing of certain foods, most notably milk and meat or even milk and meat products (no cheeseburgers!).

[645] In the context of the 1096 Polovtzian raid on Kiev, the monk Eustratus was said (in a later, thirteenth-century account) to have been sold to the Jews, who crucified him four years later in celebration of the Passover .

victim's blood or entrails might be put. So, too, the Crusades helped reinforce hostility to the Jews, as it also offered a means through which noblemen who had killed Jews in order to avoid paying debts could avoid having to offer justice for their actions, instead devoting themselves to God by going on a Crusade. The hostility toward Jews in England would culminate in the summary expulsion of them all in 1290.[646]

For expulsion was often the simplest way to deal with the Jewish problem, and was utilized any number of times in different parts of Europe down through the centuries. Arguably the most renowned expulsion of Jews was that from Spain, carried out in August, 1492, the point and purpose of which was to religiously "purify" the recently unified peninsula (the last Muslim kingdom in Iberia, that of the Nasrids, with its capital in Granada, had been defeated the previous January). But the expulsion was the culmination of a process, having nothing to do—at least theoretically—with the Jews, many generations earlier. That process has come to be known in English as the Inquisition. The original intention of the inquisitional process—that is, of *inquiring* into the proper/improper expression of faith of those made subject to inquiry—was to wrestle with the other long-term problem that had not been solved in the centuries since mid-Roman antiquity: heresy. Let us sum up the larger context of complications and issues attending the medieval Church, as we arrive into the twelfth and thirteenth centuries, in which the problem of heresy, like that of Judaism, was embedded. Thus beginning with the first Crusade declared by Pope Urban II in 1095, the stated goal of "carrying the Cross" was to deal with the infidel—and specifically, to reclaim control of the Holy Land from the Muslims. That First Crusade may be said to have achieved success. But the second (1147- 8), among whose most vocal supporters was St. Bernard of Clairvaux (the same who led a charge of heresy against Peter Abelard in 1141, in which Peter was protected by Peter the Venerable, the Abbot of Cluny), was not successful. Part of the reason may have been that the German crusaders expended so much of their energy—and St. Bernard was distraught about this—attacking, massacring and expelling Jewish communities in the Rhineland. Two years after Salah-ad-Din (known to Europeans as Saladin) retook Jerusalem for the Muslims in 1187, a third Crusade was declared (1189-92) that involved, among others, the English King Richard I (the Lion Heart). It included some victorious battles against the Muslims, but ultimately failed.

The Fourth Crusade culminated with the sacking of Constantinople in 1204, and the establishment of a "Latin" (theoretically loyal to Rome and its Catholic papacy) Imperium in Byzantium for a century (after which the Greeks, i.e., Orthodox, re-asserted themselves). In other words, the Crusaders decided that there was enough pillage to be accomplished in this heretical Orthodox Christian community; there was no need to continue on to the Holy Land to deal with the Muslim infidels. The line between heretics and infidels was considered far too blurry or thin for them to make the considerable added effort of moving on to Jerusalem and its environs.

This is the context in which Pope Innocent III (1198-1216) arrived into his papacy. In the very year when Constantinople was sacked and the Fourth Crusade came to

---

[646] For a fuller and more detailed discussion of both the case of William of Norwich and the Blood Libel in general, see Soltes: *Jews on Trial: Judges, Juries, Prosecutors and Defendants from the Era of Jesus to Our Own Time*, (Savage: Maryland: Bartleby Press, 2013), 76-101

an end, Innocent sent Diego de Acebes, Bishop of Osman, to preach in Southern France and Northern Spain, in the company of one Dominic of Caleruega. The focus of their preaching was the growing problem of heretical beliefs, of which the most disturbing, widespread and best-organized was that known as the Cathar or Albigensian heresy (see above, 238 and 318). On the one hand, what is often referred to as the Albigensian Crusade was declared in 1209. Its avowed purpose was to eliminate the Cathars who had spread through much of Occitania—what is now known as southern France. The bloody struggle lasted for decades, and was as much or more about the politics of northern France and its desire to incorporate the south into its domains as/than it was about spiritual concerns, but in the end both the heretics and the independence of the south were exterminated.

On the other hand, Diego and Dominic gradually gathered followers and so developed a mendicant order—a monastic order that moved, as preachers and beggars, from place to place, rather than establishing itself in a permanent monastic location, where it might become materially prosperous and, from the viewpoint of the Papacy, threatening—that was officially recognized by Innocent in 1215. This was the same year, as historical nicety would have it, when up in the England of King John, that monarch was being forced to agree to the terms of the *Magna Carta* drawn up by his rebellious knights at Runnymede.

So, too, in that year, at the Fourth Lateran Council, as previously noted, a call went out for the first time demanding of Jews that they wear distinctive badges, yellow and otherwise, on their clothing, or horned hats, so that their neighbors would be able to recognize these adversaries of the faith, in league with the horned anti-Christ and his father, the Satan. In our terms, the Jews, part of a *superstitio*, were understood to be associated with the negative, malignant side of the *sacer* and, to minimize the danger that they presented to the Christian *profanus*, needed to be marked in order to eliminate association with them as much as possible.

At the same Lateran council of 1215, polemics against Islam led Pope Innocent to call for a Fifth Crusade to the Holy Land—an effort that was ultimately engaged in the year following Innocent's death, lasting from 1217 to 1221 and, while achieving initial successes, it ended in the surrender of the Crusaders to Sultan al-Kamil, ruler of Egypt, and the agreement to an eight-year truce. Meanwhile, the mendicant order of which Dominic of Caleruega had quickly become the dominant leader continued to grow and spread until Dominic's death in 1221. At the same time, the mendicant order that had been established by St. Francis of Assisi in the early part of the century, that had begun seeking ordination from the Pope in 1209 and had achieved it *also* by 1215, became an elite clerical force within the Church by the time of St. Francis' death in 1226.

The following year, Pope Innocent III's successor, Honorius III, died and was succeeded as Pope by Gregory IX who at the outset of his own papacy pushed hard for a sixth Crusade—and excommunicated Emperor Frederick II for his failure to lead one in spite of the latter's many promises to do so[647]—at the same time that he began to augment the struggle against heresy. In that augmentation, the Pope initially called upon the

---

[647] Nonetheless, Frederick finally undertook the Sixth Crusade the following year (1228) and, ironically enough, managed through diplomacy rather than warfare to gain concessions from his Muslim counterpart who handed over Jerusalem, Bethlehem and Nazareth to Christian Crusader control for a ten-year period.

Dominicans to be his primary instrument, who were joined by the Franciscans by the mid-1230s. These were the two orders that, as mendicant orders and perhaps because of the psychological disposition of their respective founders and their followers, were most loyal to the curia.

Barb makes note of one of the more notorious directions an early version of this process took when he commented on the work of Paulus Tartareus—Paul "from Tartarus" (the deepest part of the Greco-Roman concept of Hades; "Paul of Hell" would not be a poor translation of his nick-name)—who in the mid-fourth century operated a reign of terror extending from Alexandria to Antioch on behalf of Emperor Constantius II.[648] Paulus was inquiring into accusations that professing Christians were consulting the oracles and priests of pagan gods.

Obviously, the issues with which the Inquisition dealt and the procedures that the Dominicans developed with which to deal with the issues had or should have had little or nothing to do with Jews and Judaism. Heretics, misbelievers from within the faith, are not infidels, unbelievers from without—but then the Jews, to repeat, fit awkwardly in both or neither of these categories. The most important Christian thinker of the thirteenth century—and arguably the most important Christian thinker of the entire medieval period—St. Thomas Aquinas (1225-74) argued strenuously against using force of any kind in trying to convince Jews of the wrong-headedness of their beliefs. "Belief is voluntary" he noted; to compel someone is to create a false believer. Only if Jews "hinder the faithful," must they be dealt with strongly.

So what, then, of Christians who, for one reason or another—perhaps as a consequence of this disputation or that—converted *to Judaism*? By 1267, Pope Clement IV enjoined the Dominican and Franciscan orders to direct their efforts toward prosecuting former Christians who had apostasized and become Jewish. They were to be regarded as heretics—on the grounds that, once baptized, an individual is considered a Christian, so for a former Christian to practice as a Jew constitutes mis-Christian practice, which is the *definition* of heresy. Moreover, Clement instructed his agents to punish any Jews believed to have *induced* such Christians into this form of heresy.

This redirection of the Inquisitional efforts of the two orders was repeated under the directing decrees of Popes Gregory X in 1274 and Nicholas IV in 1288 and again in 1290. We may recognize how all of these efforts—crusading against the Muslim infidel, inquiring into the faith of Christian heretics, and attacking Jewish thought through disputations as well as making special sartorial demands on Jews—were fundamentally linked. But beginning with Clement's decree of 1267 that linkage takes on a new, somewhat paradoxical twist: while the spiritual line between Christian and Jew is being drawn ever more emphatically (one cannot cross the line from the first to the second, *period*), the line of method regarding how to deal with heretics as opposed to with Jewish infidels is becoming more blurred—or rather, (hence the particular relevance to our

---

[648] Barb, op citum, 109. Barb translates his name as "Hell-fire Paul," which is not bad at all. He tells us, summarizing Ammianus (*Res Gestae* 19. XII.2ff), that Paul established a court in a secluded city of Palestine, halfway between Alexandria and Antioch, and developed a reign of terror. Even allowing, as Barb does, for the possibility that Ammianus exaggerates, it must not have been pretty, particularly given Paul's epithet.

discussion) *the blurriness of the third, fourth and fifth centuries is being restored*, as it were.

The institution of the Inquisition, led by the Dominican order, having continued its growth, came to encompass all the Jews in southern France by 1297—meaning that any of them could be subject to its attention based on the assumption that any of them could be involved in drawing good Christians into heresy: *the Judaizing heresy*, as it came to be known. With the same sort of concern in mind, the Christian authorities expelled all Jews from Apulia in southern Italy at around the same time.

Meanwhile, at just around the time when the great Muslim Umayyad Dynasty, with its capital in Cordova, was collapsing, (ca 1030), and with that collapse, the *reconquista* was beginning to succeed after 300 years of relative stasis, a socio-cultural silver age of the Jews in Spain was beginning to turn golden. That golden age began the gradual process of tarnishing in the middle of the thirteenth century, (following the Christian victory at the Battle of Las Navas de Tolosa in 1212), culminating by the end of the fourteenth. For in 1391, on Ash Wednesday, prompted by the torrid sermonizing of a preacher named Vincent Ferrer, the Christian community of Sevilla effected a serious violent attack on its Jewish community. The mood of virulent anti-Jewish sentiment spread quickly throughout Christian Spain.

The unrest continued virtually unabated for a generation, until 1415, the result of which is that perhaps a third of Spain's Jewry—some historiographers have asserted that there were nearly a million Jews among Spain's 9 million inhabitants by that time, making it by far both the most Jewishly populous country in the world and also the one with the highest *percentage* of Jewish inhabitants—left Spain; another third are said to have embraced Christianity under the stress of the oppressive conditions that emerged for the first time in nearly eight centuries. Jewish law is ambiguous regarding how to view conversion from Judaism—a real enough issue from the fifth century forward. In general, a distinction was made between a genuine conversion and one that was made under force and therefore might be viewed as fictitious rather than real. The very Hebrew word for "convert"—"*anoos*"—means "one who has been forced;" it is the same term used in contemporary Hebrew to refer to someone who has been raped.

This phenomenon had two aspects that defined it in Spain. One is that the fictional convert, while professing Christianity on the exterior—from having been baptized to going to church and celebrating Christian holidays—practiced Judaism on the interior: secretly praying on the Sabbath and on Jewish holidays, secretly baking and eating *matzah* during Passover and fasting during Yom Kippur. The second is that this complex double life might continue through several generations. The phenomenon was well enough known so that all *conversos*—all *Nuevos Christianos* (New Christians)—were at least theoretically suspected of being secret Jews: *crypto*-Jews. The frustration of "old Christian" neighbors who failed to reap the benefits they expected from the demise of their Jewish neighbors when that demise never set in, since those neighbors embraced Christianity, would have been exponentially greater if and when they suspected those neighbors of actually being crypto-Jews.[649]

Indeed, a specific term was directed toward *Nuevos Christianos*—or at least those suspected of being crypto-Jews: *marrano*. The word in the Castilian dialect of the time meant "swine," and it was applied both by Old Christians and also often by still-professing Jews whose non-converted status certainly doomed them to increasing poverty as the fifteenth century wore on. Of course, on the other hand, New Christians who were sincere in their profession of Christian faith—whether in the first generation or the second or third, as the strain of double-life marranism often led to gradual diminishment of or complete disconnection from spiritual or ritual connections to Judaism—might easily become more virulently anti-Jewish than their Old Christian neighbors, eager as they were to prove both to those neighbors and to themselves how fully Christian they truly were.[650]

If once baptized, one is unequivocally and irrevocably a Christian, then obviously a baptized Jew has now become a Christian and any Jewish religious behavior—despised, perhaps, but tolerated in an openly professing Jew—is by definition heretical. And in Christian Spain, from 1391 onward, the number of individuals committing, or suspected of committing such a heresy—the Judaizing heresy—would have expanded enormously. So the urge to put the Inquisitional process in motion in Christian Spain would have been—and obviously was—irresistible.

Consider the following handful of events reflecting the growing ugliness with regard to the condition of *Nuevos Christianos* in the second half of the fifteenth century: in 1468, Henry (the Impotent) of Toledo, whose confessor preached emphatically against the *Nuevos Christianos* decreed that no *converso* could any longer hold office within his domains. Five years later, in 1473, in Cordova, the self-styled "Christian Brotherhood" claimed that, during the procession of the image of the Holy Virgin, dirty water was tossed onto the image from the window of a young *conversa* and riots broke out that spread elsewhere in south central Spain—the most intense riots since 1391.

The following year, King Ferdinand of Aragon and Queen Isabel of Castile, ascended together to the throne of a unified Aragon and Castile. As these were the two largest Christian states within the peninsula that had been variously disunified since the Roman period, *Christian* Spain was virtually unified for the first time in the history of the

---

[649] What I mean by this statement of Christian expectation is that formerly Jewish *Nuevos Christianos* in the fifteenth century were disproportionately prominent in the law, as middle-level administrators of all sorts, in the army, the university structure, among the *literati*, even within the hierarchy of the Church. So many Old Christians could or would have been irritated by the fact that all of the positions that the former Jews (aka New Christians) held, but would have lost had they not converted, which positions would in that case have gone to Old Christians, did not go to them—especially if they suspected that some or all of their New Christian neighbors were falsely professing their Christianity.

[650] As a practical matter, it is difficult for the historian looking back at this period (1391-1492) to identify exactly who is who, religiously speaking, in Spain: Aside from Old Christians and Muslims (the latter still mostly inhabiting an independent state in Granada) there were three categories that cannot easily be distinguished from each other: New Christians who were genuinely Christian, New Christians who were actually crypto-Jews and may be referred to either as Christians or Jews depending on circumstances—thus, say, the Abravanel family, due to its importance in the court of King Fernando of Aragon, while nominally Christian, probably, was known by everyone including the king to actually be Jewish, and thus is typically referred to as Jewish—and openly professing Jews. See the concise discussion in Ori Z. Soltes, "Columbus, Catholics, Marranos and Jews: Who Was Who and What Was What?" in *Lexington Theological Quarterly*, Vol 28, No 3, Fall, 1993, 177-201.

reconquista. Within three more years—by 1477—the Christian Spanish civil war was functionally over and that unity was essentially complete. Within two years, the *reconquista* would resume, having as its goal to divest the Muslims of their control of Granada and thus to bring the *entire* peninsula under one administrative roof.

But sandwiched between the virtual end of the Christian civil war and the resumption of the effort at *reconquista*, in 1478 an accusation was lodged in Sevilla that, during the Passover Seder that coincided with Holy Week, some Jews had blasphemed the Christian Religion. Evidence (there is no record as to *what* evidence) was brought before the state court, the result of which was that the king sent an ambassador to Rome asking the Pope to emit a bull establishing the Inquisitional authority in Spain. This was odd, in a sense, since, to repeat, the Inquisition dealt not with Jews but with heretical Christians—unless we assume that the "Jews" accused of blaspheming Christianity were actually *Nuevos Christianos*, labeled as or misunderstood to have been Jews, by authorities then or since.[651] Pope Sixtus IV hesitated, out of concern that the Institution could well fall outside his control given the realities of distance and actual power, but finally complied, so that by the late fall, on November 1, the Spanish sovereigns were instructed by way of a papal bull to appoint three bishops over the age of 40 to assume jurisdiction over the shaping of an Inquisitional Board.

In 1480 the first activities of that authority began in Sevilla and in February, 1481 the first *auto-da-fe* ("literally, "act of faith," in Portuguese) was held: a public execution of unrepentant or confessed heretics who were burned at the stake (in order not to shed any blood, for the inquisitional policy called for death to be meted out "without effusion of blood"): six men and women were burned. All of them were *marranos*, accused of the heresy of Judaizing; the Inquisitional authority published a list of 37 signs by which such heresy might be recognized. The most obvious among these was evidence that an individual had celebrated the Jewish Sabbath by changing the bed sheets on Friday afternoon or not kindling a cooking fire on Saturday, or by reciting a Hebrew blessing over the wine or kindling candles on Friday evening and allowing them to burn out of their own accord; or by celebrating Passover by eating *matzah* or other foods associated with the Passover Seder; or by fasting and praying on the Day of Atonement.

By 1482, seven other Inquisitional centers had been established. The following year the entire system was unified under Tomas de Torquemada. Tomas was the personal confessor of Isabel—and had been since before she and Ferdinand were married. He was, moreover, the grandson of *conversos*, and therefore, perhaps, as fanatical an anti-*converso* individual as one could hope for. He now had the entire apparatus of the Inquisition in his hands with which to ferret out false *conversos*, the sort of crypto-Jewish *marranos* that gave his grand-parents and parents—and, should anyone know of his background, himself—a bad Christian name. His enthusiasm for his work naturally spread to the queen whom he confessed weekly. In turn that enthusiasm would have spread to the king, for two reasons. The first is that he, too, had *converso* blood flowing in his veins! His mother's mother was Paloma the Jewess, of Toledo (so that strictly speaking, he would be considered

---

[651] One might recognize a parallel between this "who is *actually* a *Jew*?" issue in fifteenth-century Spain and the "who is a *Yehoodi*?" issue discussed previously (above, 204), for ancient Rome.

a Jew by *halakhah*: Jewish law)[652] and more to the immediate point, he would have felt it of profound importance that he demonstrate to his wife and queen that his zeal to purify Christian Spain of heresy was as great as hers.

The second reason for Ferdinand's enthusiastic embrace of the Inquisition was one of the key features of its methodology. One accused of heresy and arrested by the inquisitional authorities was immediately deprived of his or her home and all of his or her belongings, the value of which was divided among three principals: the Church, the State and the accuser. If the fact that the accuser remained anonymous is added to this matrix, then we understand why such a method encouraged a reign of finger-pointing terror. But we also understand how, spiritual issues aside, both Church and State would have been eager to arrest more rather than fewer of the middle- to upper-management kind of individuals whose confiscated property would help fill their respective coffers—and Ferdinand's were remarkably empty.

For the purposes of our narrative, what is most important in all of this is that one might perhaps have expected that by the late fifteenth century the three "categories"—Christians, Christian heretics and Jews—would be fairly distinct from each other, contrary to what we have noted of the situation in the fourth and fifth centuries. That this was not the case, as we have seen, was in part a function of the unique issue of marranism, interwoven, perhaps, with the strong Iberian prejudice regarding the category of purity of blood (*limpieza de sangre*), which helped reinforce the distinction between "old" and "new" Christians. In the end, though, an institution that had been created to deal exclusively with Christian heretics evolved in Spain to directly effect practicing Jews and ultimately paved the way for their expulsion from the Iberian peninsula.

For—to sum up—by the late thirteenth century, the Inquisition's focus turned to former Christians who had become Jews. So how much more logical was it to turn, a century later, in Spain, to Jews who had become Christians—and from them to a focus on Jews who might be accused of encouraging backsliding into the Judaizing heresy among their former co-religionists? There was, too, a logic to expelling the Jews, lest in remaining in Iberia they continue to pose a threat to their former co-religionists of inducing them into backsliding toward the Judaizing heresy, and therefore present a threat to the Christian community overall in its ongoing battle with the forces of the Satan.

Interestingly enough, *conversos* were *forbidden* to emigrate. One might suppose that losing that population and the opportunities it offered for inquisitional confiscations of its material goods had something to do with that. For the Inquisition remained in place in Spain until the eighteenth century, and was carried over into Portugal and into the New World by the colonial administrations of both Spain and Portugal. There it lasted an equally long if not longer time. Interestingly, any number of its victims who had been genuinely faithful Christians abandoned that faith and reverted to Judaism as a consequence of its

---

[652] According to the Jewish legal understanding, an individual's Jewishness is carried through his mother. To the extent that this is understood in purely blood-line terms—in a literal sense, as the blood of the mother courses through the fetus and is carried by it out into the world beyond the womb—such an individual does not cease to be a Jew through the mere act of religious conversion. Given the notorious obsession with the idea of blood line—purity of blood (in Spanish: *limpieza de sangre*)—in Spanish culture, (as noted a few paragraphs below), Ferdinand's condition is fraught with irony (as is that of Tomas de Torquemada).

procedures. Both openly professing Jews by being forced and *conversos* by stealth managed to leave Spain in 1492 (and Portugal four years later) and in the years and decades to follow.

The consequences of the Inquisition and the Expulsion from Iberia for both Jews and Christians over the next five centuries is substantial—from the re-shaped lives of Jews from Spain and Portugal in Ottoman Turkey and the parts of Europe and the Middle East governed by the Ottomans, to the "excommunication" of the Dutch Jewish philosopher, Baruch (Benedict) Spinoza by the the rabbinical leaders of the Sephardic Jewish community of which he had been part, to both theoretical (blood-line concepts) and practical (torture) aspects of the Holocaust.

The point of this lengthy excursus on the development of the Inquisition in Spain, however, aside from where it points forward to our own era, is how its beginning point may be found in the late Greco-Roman world and three of its facets that we have observed. One is the fact that inquisition-style courts of inquiry were, as we have seen, already in place, at least occasionally, by the fourth century. Our poster-child for this is Paulus Tartareus and the court of inquiry he established on behalf of Emperor Constantius II in a Palestinian city sometime in the 340s, which created a reign of terror from Alexandria to Antioch, as reported by Ammianus Marcellinus and discussed by A.A. Barb.[653]

The second is the long-term ambiguity in what the Church perceived as threats to its spiritual and political hegemony. Thus what in late antiquity could often be a blurry line between heretics and Jews or heretics and Pagans emerges in fifteenth-century Spain as a blurry line between New Christians and Crypto-Jews or between Crypto-Jews and openly professing Jews, as far as the attacks on them by the partnership between the state and the Church in its inquisitional aspect were concerned. The third is the question of what, exactly, was deemed threatening to the state or to the Christian community: where is the line drawn between false religious beliefs and nefarious magical practices, between superstitions and *superstitiones*? And who is accused of what?

With this last question in mind, we might recall that amuletic kind of inscription that first appears on a wall in ancient Pompeii and offers offspring well into the medieval period: the magic square. I return to it because it appears, by the medieval period, to have acquired an association with Jewish magicians—specifically, we find an interesting text, *The Book of the Sacred Magic of Abramelin the Mage, as Delivered by Abraham the Jew unto his Son Lamech, A.D. 1458*, a book originally written in Hebrew, and then translated into French [FIG 6]. The French manuscript was found (among the then 8000 manuscripts and 700,000 printed books) in the French "Library of the Arsenal," by S.L. MacGregor Mathers, a noted Christian student of and writer on Kabbalah (medieval Jewish mysticism), at the end of the nineteenth century—in other words, we have come full chronological circle to the time period of Sir James Frazer—and translated by Mathers into English.

One might note the key phrase within the title. Referring to the contents as "sacred magic," seems to suggest that the contents deal with the "proper" *sacer* realm (the sacred), and yet not as religion would, but as magic would. This would seem either to mean that the intention is perfectly positive (since it is sacred) and/or that it deals with lower powers of

---

[653] See above, 363.

the *sacer*, (since it is magic). Either way the notion that there is more than one way or more than one level through which to deal with the divine *sacer* when it is in its entirety the realm of a singular, all-powerful, all-good God is a contradiction in terms for Judaism. This underscores for us the fact that, if theoretically there can be no magic, but only religion for Judaism, yet from antiquity through the late medieval period (and perhaps beyond toward the modern era) there were plenty of times and places across the dispersed Jewish world where one sees a belief in—and practitioners who reflected the belief in—magic.

FIG 6: Rembrandt: *A Scholar in His Study*.
Etching, 1650-54. The image has been taken by some to represent Faustus—or Abramelin the Mage

In his introduction, Mathers notes that the manuscript he found contained a note on the fly-leaf "in the handwriting of the eighteenth century" that includes the comment that "'Abraham and... Lamech, ...were Jews of the fifteenth century, and it is well known that the *Jews of that period possessing the Cabala of Solomon passed for being the best Sorcerers and Astrologers*' [italics added]."[654] I accentuate this last turn of phrase since—even, it would seem, in the late eighteenth century, the time of increasing "secular enlightenment"—Christians also believed in magic and, moreover, Jews were associated by their Christian neighbors pre-eminently with magic and the occult: the engagement of the (lower?) powers of the *sacer*, for both benign and malignant reasons. So, too, at least at that time, Kabbalah was associated with the legendary wise King Solomon, in a manner analogous to the associations between magic and Noah and Moses that we have noted for pagan, Christian and Jewish antiquity.

The work is divided into three parts and the first part is autobiographical—telling of Abraham's travels and of the "many marvelous works he had been able to accomplish by means of this system of Sacred Magic," as well as general advice concerning magic.[655] The actual "content" is contained within the second and third books, entrusted to Abraham the Jew (Abraham of Wuerzburg) by Abramelin, the Egyptian Mage. The style of these two books differs from that of the first in a number of ways, (the details of which carries

---

[654] S.L. Mac Gregor Mathers, *The Book of the Sacred Magic of Abramelin the Mage, as Delivered by Abraham the Jew unto His Son Lamech, A.D. 1458*. NYC: Dover Publications, 1975 (reprint of the 1900 edition published in London by John M. Wadkins), xvii.
[655] Ibid, xviii-xix.

beyond the needs of our discussion). The second book offers, in Mathers' introductory summary, a "general and complete description of the means of obtaining the Magical Powers desired, [while the t]hird book [presents t]he application of these Powers to produce an immense number of Magical results."[656]

Mathers further speculates as to the identity of Abraham the Jew, noting that he appears to have been born in 1362 and to have written the manuscript for his son, Lamech, in 1458, when he (Abraham) was 96 years old. This was a period, as Mathers understands it, "in which magic was almost universally believed in, and in which Professors were held in honour."[657] To become such a practitioner, it was expected that one would leave home and journey through much of one's life, seeking esoteric knowledge—undertaking a heroic spiritual/intellectual adventure. Abraham undertook such wanderings, which culminated with "his meeting Abramelin [whose name, Mathers notes, is spelled variously], the Egyptian Mage," from whom he received the instruction found in books two and three of this work.

"To the sincere and earnest student of Occultism this work cannot fail to be of value, whether as an encouragement to that most rare and necessary quality, unshaken faith; as an aid to *discrimination between true and false systems of Magic*; or as presenting an assemblage of directions for the production of Magical effects, which the author of the book affirms to have tried with success [italics added]."[658] So perhaps in this fifteenth century work, presented to the public at the end of the nineteenth century, in finding a distinction between true and false magical systems we may or may not be led to a clear distinction between magic and religion.

It is noteworthy that Abraham performed marvels for or against an extraordinary array of figures, including Emperor Sigismund of Germany, King Henry VI of England, and the rival popes Benedict XIII, John XXIII, Martin V, and Gregory XII—among other figures.[659] That datum underscores for us both the belief in alternative paths to engagement of the *sacer*—i.e., magical, as opposed to religious paths—and to the regard in which a Jewish practitioner might be held. This reflects two interwoven issues, ultimately: one, that the negative implications of the term *superstitio* and its conceptual cognate, *magia*, having evolved from the ancient pagan political context that we have, in part, explored, have also achieved a significant spiritual overlay—and thus, that Jews, like heretics, have arrived at a point of being regarded as political subversives (as Christians had once been considered by pagan Rome) because of their spiritual subversion and the danger that such subversion was perceived to pose to the Christian community at large.

Two, that the negative could also be treated as a positive, under the proper circumstances. Jews, inherently on the margins of the mainstream community, were almost

---

[656] Ibid, xix.

[657] Ibid, xx.

[658] Ibid, xxii.

[659] During the so-called Great Western Schism (1378-1417), in which there were popes in Rome and so-called anti-popes in Avignon (and sometimes also in Pisa), Benedict XIII was an anti-Pope presiding in Avignon (1394-1417/23), John XXIII was an anti-Pope presiding in Pisa (1410-15)—so that for five years they were rivals. Gregory XII and Martin V were rivals of both, serving as Popes in Rome during the same time period: Gregory served in 1406-15, (when he was forced to resign to end the Schism, as did John; Benedict refused to do so, was excommunicated, and fled to Aragon, the only state still recognizing him as Pope, where he died eight years later). Martin served in the reunified papal context (albeit theoretically also as a rival of Benedict) in 1417-31.

automatically *sacer*—if they are not part of the *profanus* they must be part of the *sacer*—and therefore, (particularly given the outsider quality of their liturgy, in Hebrew rather than, say, Latin or Greek or any of the evolving vernacular languages), could both be suspected of political and spiritual subversion and be sought out for their presumed abilities to access the *sacer* in other-than-ordinary ways. Even by Popes.

It is also noteworthy that, as Mathers, points out, Abraham "not only... insist[s] that this sacred system of Magic may be attained by any one, whether Jew, Christian, Mahometan, or Pagan, but he also continually warns Lamech agains the error of changing the religion in which one had been brought up."[660] The reason for the latter warning could not be more logical:

> Conversion to another religion invariably meant an absolute, solemn and thorough *renunciation and denial of any truth in the religion previously professed by the convert*. Herein would be the danger, because whatever the errors, corruption, or mistakes in any particular form of religion, all are based on and descended from the acknowledgment of Supreme Divine Powers. Therefore to deny any religion (instead of only abjuring the mistaken or erroneous parts thereof) would be the equivalent to denying *formally and ceremonially* the truths on which it was originally founded; so that whenever a person having once done this should begin to practice the Operations of the Sacred Magic, he would find himself compelled to affirm with his whole will-force those very formulas which he had at one time *magically and ceremonially* (though ignorantly) denied; and whenever he attempted to do this, the occult Law of Reaction would arise as a Ceremonial Obstacle against the effect which he should wish to produce, the memory of the Ceremonial Denial which his previous renunciation had firmly sealed in his atmosphere.... For of all hindrances to magical action, the very greatest and most fatal is unbelief, for it checks and stops the action of the Will.[661]

So, in a world in which fear of the other, as *sacer*, is interwoven with both fear of and hope from the larger, divine power of the *sacer*, Abraham exhibits an extraordinary perspective in regarding nobody as disadvantaged by way of his form of *religio* with regard to the ability to learn and practice the particular form of *magia* that he (Abraham) possesses.[662] More extraordinarily, he discourages the would-be practitioner from abandoning his birth-religion on the grounds that, since all forms of *religio* are ultimately directed to the same *sacer* realm—as is the *magia* that he or others with other systems might practice—then to deny *absolutely* any form of *religio* is to risk denying the power of the *sacer absolutely*.[663] Not to believe in the power of the *sacer* is inherently not to be able to access or engage it.

---

[660] Ibid, xxiii.

[661] Ibid, xxiii-xxiv.

[662] This lack of religious prejudice does not extend to gender: Abraham is very much a child of his era (and most eras) in denying to most women the *capacity* to practice his *magia*.

[663] To clarify: if as a Jew, let's say, I deny the validity of your Christianity, or as a Muslim I deny the validity of your Judaism, or as a Christian I deny the validity of your Islam, I am by no means necessarily denying your religion in its entirety—we disagree, let's say, on the divinity of Jesus, or on the prophethood of Muhammad or

Mathers goes on to define magic as "the Science [i.e., knowledge] of the Control of the Secret Forces of Nature"[664]—which raises for us the question of whether, as *part of nature*, albeit *hidden*, magic accesses and engages something different from that which religion engages (at least in Mathers' mind; certainly Abraham does not offer us such a definition, so we cannot gauge how he would view this distinction, although the content of the previous few paragraphs would suggest that he sees both disciplines, religion and magic, as pertaining to the same *sacer* realm, in which case he might object to Mathers' definition). He notes that white magic invokes angelic forces and that black magic invokes Evil Spirits (which would suggest the invocation of aspects of the *sacer*—unless we assume that for him, God is the *sacer* and everything else is *profanus*, but some of it revealed and some of it hidden).

He also explains that "all *ordinary material effects and phenomena* are produced by the labour of the Evil Spirits under the command usually of the Good."[665] If they are ordinary and material then they must be *profanus*—but these are the *phenomena*, not the power to *effect* phenomena. This would also explain—going all the way back to this question in Iamblichus (see above, 218ff)—why a magician, as a servant of the Good, can command Evil Spirits, but also why bad things happen in a world made by an all-powerful and all-good God: occasionally the evil spirits slip out from under the control of the Good, and they seek vengeance for their prior servitude!

Mathers adds, further, that the knowledge of the Higher and Good is necessary in order to control and obtain service from the Lower and Evil. He thus offers higher and lower as equivalent to better and worse—but both double categories are understood to be within the realm addressed by magic, as opposed to religion addressing the higher and better aspects of the *sacer* and magic the lower and worse. He also offers an apparent paradox: why would a magician inclined toward the Good *need or want* to command the Spirits of Evil—unless it were to keep them at bay, one might suppose.

Indeed, the religion/magic, positive/negative, upper/lower, greater/lesser matrix is interestingly reflected in its clarity/blurriness by Abramelin's/Abraham's exhortation in the first chapter of his Book Two, where he writes:

> I exhort you, ye who read, to have the Fear of God and to study Justice, because infallibly unto you shall be opened *the Gate of the True Wisdom which God gave unto Noah* and unto his descendants... this which I teach, is that same Wisdom and Magic, and which is in this same Book, and independent of any other Science [i.e., knowledge], or Wisdom, or Magic, soever [italics added]... [T]hese miraculous operations have much in common with the Qabalah... [in fact] from the Divine Mystery are derived these three kinds of Qabalah, viz.: the Mixed Qabalah, and the True Wisdom, and the (True) Magic.[666]

---

on what constitutes the ultimate revealed word of God. But Mathers understands Abraham to assert that if I convert, I am required to deny the validity, in an absolute sense and in its entirety, of the religion that I am leaving behind.

[664] Ibid, xxv.
[665] Ibid, xxvi.
[666] Ibid, 50-52.

So Abraham understands the content of this work to have a distinct association with God, and one that can only be efficacious if one's intentions are fully positive. At the same time, Abraham recognizes it as related to but separate from the mystical tradition (the secrets of which, as we know from the autobiographical parts of Book One, he passed on to his older son, leaving this work as compensation, to Lamech, his younger son), albeit related to it.

Mysticism, in brief, is an intensified subset of mainstream, normative religion. The mystic believes that there is a hiddenmost, innermost recess to God that everyday believers never access through their garden-variety prayers—but that the mystic can access. The goal of the Jewish, Christian or Muslim mystic is to gain that access—to be emptied of *self* and filled with *God*—and to return to the *profanus* from that state, positioned to better the community as a consequence of that experience. As Abraham recognizes, in the late kabbalistic phase of Jewish mysticism, there is a kind of bifurcation, between ever more esoteric formulae of access and accomplishing very down-to-earth goals through the capabilities that their use provides—so that the line between "practical Kabbalah" and magic could hardly be thinner or more blurred.[667]

This is the import of Abraham's last two comments. The significance of the first is to remind the user of his text that his (the user's) intentions must be good, or the system will either fail or worse, backfire. The potential to accomplish something, and the need to invoke the power of God Itself in order to do so, is clear from the "thorough list" to which Mathers had made reference in his introduction, found in chapter xix of Book Two. There the "four princes and superior spirits be: Lucifer, Leviatan, Satan, and Belial."[668] There are eight sub-princes and each of these has dozens of servient spirits answering to him.

Limiting ourselves to the "four princes" we recognize that three of the four have names used, by the medieval period, in mainstream Christianity and, to a lesser extent, Judaism, to refer to the major figure of opposition against God, whose place in the vocabulary of the *sacer* we have encountered in the first chapters of Job (the Satan), or in the Battle Scroll from Qumran (Belial), and translated in the Book of Revelation as the serpent in Genesis. "Leviatan" also appears in Job, where it is presented as a large and powerful reptile—perhaps a crocodile, but the later tradition easily enough connects that term, too, to the serpent in Genesis.

My point, then, is that the powers of *sacer* evil presented here are as extreme as possible, and thus a practitioner could only presume to be able to control these powers if God Itself were offering instruction and assistance—and that therefore this text, while referring to its content as "magic" draws from the consummate source of both Jewish and Christian *religion*, albeit from an angle very different from that used to invoke God in mainstream Christian or Jewish religion (and *that* is why it would be called *magical*).

This is all reinforced by Abraham's epilogic remarks regarding the symbols/figures that he shares in Book Three (to which we shall shortly turn), to wit: "there are many which one can employ of evil (purposes), … for often the secret judgments of God permit disgrace, hindrances, infirmities, and other vexing accidents to happen unto

---

[667] For more detail on mysticism in the Abrahamic traditions and specifically the question of its distinctness from magic, see Soltes, *Searching for Oneness*, introduction.
[668] Mathers, Ibid, 104.

Mortals, either to wake them from the lethargy wherein they be sunk so that they recognize not their Creator, or else to give them the opportunity by their afflictions of increasing their merit. And although God can in no way do evil, but always good, nevertheless… the Executioners and Executors of the Divine Justice be the Evil Spirits."[669]

He suggests taking counsel from one's Guardian Angel, a figure discussed in the denouement of Mathers' introduction. Mathers notes that if knowledge of the higher Good is the knowledge of the Higher Self, the point of Abraham's method is "by purity and self-denial to obtain knowledge of and conversation with one's Guardian Angel."[670] This being offers another variation on the multi-lateral theme of the *sacer* that we have been considering throughout this narrative. The notion of a particular positive aspect of the *sacer* that potentially connects to any practitioner runs parallel to the notion of individuals' patron saints. "[T]he thorough and complete classification of the negative Demons with their offices, and of the effects to be produced by their services," (as Mathers states it in summary form), also parallels both the proliferation of an array of saints and their domains of enterprise—and how these grow out of the range of earlier pagan gods and their domains—in filling out the *sacer-sacerdos-profanus* matrix.

That matrix also includes, less surprisingly—we may be reminded of Apuleius' *Apology* and his discussion of the accusation leveled toward him regarding his alleged use of a child in his "rituals"—"the employment of a Child as Clairvoyant in the invocation of the Guardian Angel."[671] From before Apuleius to after Abramelin and Abraham children have been understood to be inherently sacerdotal, since they are not yet full-fledged members of the adult *profanus*, but neither are they altogether outside the *profanus* of which their families are part—they are thus connected to the *sacer* but particularly useful because they are still part of the *profanus*.

All of this discussion leads us to the third book of Abramelin's sacred magic. The book is overrun with variants on the *Sator-Rotas* "Magic Square"—which is referred to as one of the Pentacles (referring, by way of the Greek root, "*pent-*", meaning "five", to its five-letter format) in the "Key of Solomon." We are reminded that the tradition of Solomon as not only preternaturally wise but as privy to esoteric divinely-received knowledge had grown by the medieval period so that, as a "source" he had joined or even overtaken Noah and Moses. We are also reminded that the Magic Square continued to be used and to be believed esoterically important for a millennium and a half beyond its first appearance on a wall in Pompeii. If its significance there remains debatable, it is clear that, by the time of its appearances here and there across the medieval period, it had achieved status as a key that can open doors into the *sacer* to access *sacer* power.

The exact nature of that *sacer* power brings us once again along the blurry border between religion and magic or superstition, and along that border we find fragments and variations on the original Pompeiian inscription. Thus, for example, an early Byzantine Bible offers the baptismal names of the Magi in the Christian Nativity story as Ator, Sator and Peratoras—all, it would seem, variants on *sator*, and there is a 10th-century reference in Byzantine Cappadocia to the Magi as Sator, Arepon and Teneton—obvious variants of

---

[669] Ibid, 248.
[670] Ibid.
[671] Ibid, xxvii.

the first three words of the "Magic Square."[672] In cases like these, the Square's terms are applied in what is obviously a *religious* context. On the other hand, the formulation offered in the Abramelin/Abraham text (the ninth figure in chapter XIX of his third book)—to be used for obtaining the love of a woman, and thus, we would say, in a magical context—is

```
S A L O M
A R E P O
L E M E L
O P E R A
M O L A S
```

Only the second and fourth lines correspond to the original Pompeiian square. The first word, *salom*, is a Latinized variant of Hebrew, *shalom*, meaning "peace." The third element, *lemel*, may derive from the Hebrew *le-* (meaning "to/for/unto") plus the Hebrew root, *m-l-'*—meaning "full," in which case we might translate it as "in/unto fullness." So the five-word phrase means something like "Peace *arepo* in fullness [His] works/creations *molas*." We are still left with uncertainty with regard to *arepo* (which is rendered by Mathers as "he distils"—which makes no sense in Hebrew or Latin (or Greek or Aramaic or Egyptian; he also translates *molas* as "in quick motion," which also makes no sense). Then again, perhaps it would not be a magic square if it easily made sense.

In any case, we might note three other features of the array of squares found in Book Three. One, that there are squares with as many as 12 letters per side (as in the last, seventh square in Chapter IX—the squares in the chapter focused on turning men into asses, deer, elephants, wild boars, dogs, wolves—and vice versa; the seventh square in this chapter is used specifically to turn animals into stones). Two, that many of the squares do not offer the double acrostic that the *Salom-Molas* and *Sotar-Rotas* squares offer; of those that do not, many are simply unfinished, so that they offer a single acrostic around the periphery, but nothing on the interior—for example, the first square in chapter VI—or only one term running along one vertical and one horizontal side, as for example, numbers 6 and 8 in chapter VI. (These three and the others in chapter VI are used to point out mines, to prevent them from falling in, to make them more workable, to separate gold from silver, and so forth). These particular three look like this; (the second and third would be called gnomons, rather than magic squares):

---

[672] The story of the Magi appears in only one of the four canonical Gospel narratives, in Matthew 2:1 -18, which in and of itself reminds us of how evolutionary even essential texts are in early developing Christianity and Judaism. We should also be reminded of the fact that the word "Magi" is the plural of the same Latin word, "magus," which is derived from Greek and in turn from Persian, and of the evolution of the understanding of the term not only from Persian to the Greeks and Romans, but from Roman pagan to European Christian thinking. In the latter tradition, the Magi have come to be thought of as astronomers/astrologers (since, as priests or magicians they would, among other things, be aware of and consult the heavens—and hence, they are guided by an unusual star to come to Bethlehem), and then, in subsequent variants, as kings or simply as wise men.

```
TELAAH          NAKAB           MARAK
E      A        A               A
L      A        K               R
A      L        A               A
A      E        B               K
HAALET
```

The third distinctive feature—not altogether surprising, given that the narrative was originally written in Hebrew, and given the importance of Hebrew, rather than Greek or Latin, as a liturgical language for Judaism—is that most of the *identifiable* words are recognizably Hebrew or derived from Hebrew, such as *macaneh* (chapter X, figure 5; from *makhaneh*), meaning "encampment" or, by extension, "fortification"; or *megilla* (chapter XII, figure 1; from *megillah*), meaning "scroll," but as a derivative of the verbal root, *m-g-l*, meaning "reveal"; or *basar* and *lechem* (chapter XV—which deals with compelling spirits to bring food and drink of whatever sort is desired—in figures 2 and 3), meaning "flesh" or "meat and "bread" respectively; or *tipharah* (chapter XVI, figure 1) meaning "glory" or "beauty." Chapter XIX, which deals with love and affection, includes terms like *dodim* (figure 1), meaning "lovers"; and *almanah* (figure 5), meaning "widow"; and *callah* (figure 6), meaning "bride." This is the chapter in which *arepo-opera* is found as part of the *salom-molas* magic square.

There are many other examples. So, too, there are other words that are identifiable as Hebrew *names*, such as *Ezechiel* (chapter XIII, figure 1), or *Iosua* (Joshua) (chapter XIII, figure 3); or *Belial* (chapter XVI, figure 9), referring to the greatest of Evil Spirits. Occasionally a non-Hebrew name *is* encountered. Thus, for instance, in chapter XVI, figure 10—a full magic square with five letters per line/side and doubly acrostic, horizontally and vertically—offers the name *Orion*, the famed hunter in Greek mythology who ended up as a clearly identifiable constellation in the heavens, which is overhead during the summer months in the northern hemisphere.

So the actuation of the magical capabilities laid out by this text is this array of magic square and gnomon figures (the text itself refers to them all as "symbols"). At the end of the book, its author returns to issues raised at the outset of Book Two. He informs his reader that he may share the Sacred Wisdom acquired through this work with a maximum of three trustworthy friends. He warns him that the "[t]he Evil Spirit is so subtle, so keen, so cunning… [that] the very first action to take especially with thy Familiar Spirits, should be to command them never to say anything unto thee of themselves."[673] He further accentuates "in any manner wherein thou canst aid and succor thy neighbor, [do so], and do not wait until he demandeth assistance from thee, but seek to know to the full his need even though it be concealed, and give him prompt aid. Also trouble not thyself as to whether he be Turk, Pagan, or Idolater, but do good unto all who believe in a God."[674]

This is clearly a work intended for good, and understood to offer a God-ordained means of improving the world—by paradox, through controlling the negative forces of the *sacer* that are commonly understood to oppose God, but which here are understood, when

---

[673] Ibid, 251-2.
[674] Ibid, 252.

properly accessed, to function as instruments for assisting God in the work of perfecting the world. Indeed, with regard to "the manner of treating and commanding the spirits, it is an easy thing unto whomsoever walketh by the proper paths"—in contrast to magical systems that are "imperfect, and their Authority proceedeth not from God by the intermediation of His Holy Angels, but proceedeth directly from express Pacts made with the Devil." Those, however, who attend with great care the instructions set forth by Abraham "will know that all thngs come unto us from God, and that it is He Who wisheth and commandeth that the Evil Spirits should be submitted unto us."[675]

If, as Abraham states emphatically, what motivates his system is Fear (or Awe) of God and a desire to fulfill His Commandments, and what underlies it is an incontrovertible faith in God, then—to repeat—this is mainstream religion, even as it is magic, due to its non-mainstream specifics. And even this is not fully the case, since "thou mayest make semblance of performing (thy cures) by prayers, or by ordinary remedies, or by (the recital of) some psalm, or by other like means."[676] So even the non-mainstream specifics can be interwoven with mainstream verbal sacerdotal norms to be effective. Indeed, the last words in the text are invocations of Divine Mercy, recognition of Divine Glory and prayers that the reader's final success be that which, at the end of his life, carries him to death "in His Holy Kingdom."

With the *Book of the Sacred Magic of Abramelin the Mage* we encounter the continuation and expansion of issues pertaining to the intention, method, content, and *sacer* level of religion versus magic—and the realization both that the latter term continues to evolve out of antiquity and that it is nearly impossible to assign a singular, distinct definition to it from the early biblical and Greco-Roman eras until nearly our own time. What most obviously identifies the text as "Jewish" is its author and the language in which it is primarily written—which distinguishes it from equivalent sorts of texts from antiquity that are somewhat similar. Both presumably at the time of its composition and even nearly 350 years later when being presented by Mathers the notion that such a text would have been written—particularly—by a Jew reflects a different angle of evolution regarding magic and superstition and the assumed potential role of Jews in those sibling disciplines: at once subversive and useful.

It is also noteworthy that Abraham the Jew presents a non-prejudicial view of non-Jews—be they Christian, Muslim, pagan, or idolaters (this last apparently a different category to him from "pagan")—that goes against the preponderant view that has extended from late antiquity through the era of the Crusades, as we have observed. This breadth of perspective is, however, occasionally reflected in the thinking of mystics like Ibn 'Arabi, Rumi, St Francis of Assisi and Abraham Abulafia in the twelfth and thirteenth centuries. It also emerges with some force in the Italian Renaissance, particularly in the thought of members of the Medici Academy in Florence such as Pico della Mirandola (1463-94—born a few years after Abraham's death). Such universalistic approaches to the Divine *Sacer* both will and won't carry forward into modernity and our own era.

---

[675] Ibid, 254-256, for all three quoted passages.
[676] Ibid, 258.

CHAPTER FOURTEEN

Conclusions: From the End of the Empire to the Modern World: Jews, Christians, Religion, Superstition and Magic

What is the difference between the various customs that Pliny discusses and the notion that emerges at some point in the medieval Jewish tradition that one should not initiate projects on Mondays? The latter is textual: rabbinic interpretation of the opening chapter of Genesis—God's word, and nothing in God's word can be accidental or incidental, if sometimes the message is admittedly difficult to dig out of the text—notes that, whereas, on most of the six days of Creation the last turn of phrase is that "…God saw that it was good," that phrase is missing from the concluding phraseology for day two (= Monday). By comparison, Pliny merely reports on customs without attempting to evaluate either their efficacy or their causes or analyzing their sources, textual or otherwise.

What the two communities share in common, however, most obviously, is, first, a consciousness of being surrounded at all times and everywhere by the *sacer*, so that one must always be cognizant of not offending it, even inadvertently—in the one case, because there are so many divinities, greater and lesser, all around; in the other because the One God is understood to be ubiquitous. More significant, in a sense, is the second feature shared by the two communities: a very blurred line between religion and magic, or between religion and superstition—or between what is "officially" part of the religion and what everyday practitioners actually believe. This makes perfect sense for Roman Paganism, given its omnivorous approach to the divine *sacer*. It is more theoretically disturbing for medieval Judaism, given its conviction that the all-encompassing God is all-good and all-merciful—and singular. On the other hand, it is *less* disturbing precisely because of the absolute and all-encompassing nature ascribed to God, and because, by definition, there are no other *sacer* powers to whom to turn if I am in danger of offending God, although if I am living a covenantal life, there ought to be no way that I could inadvertently offend God.

On the one hand, biblical texts like Jeremiah make it clear both that one can only offend God by failing to live up to the ethics of covenantal prescriptions—and one can be severely punished for having failed to do so, as the destruction of the First temple and the exile to Babylonia prove—and that, however severely one may offend God, if one turns back to God and the ethical divine prescriptions, God will turn back to you: it is never too late. On the other hand, a text like Job equally demonstrates that someone can suffer without having offended God—and without ever knowing why, even if, as in Job's case, the Lord responds to one's desperate query regarding one's suffering. So there is no definitive, absolute equation in any case between one's actions and the *sacer* reaction to them.

That the divine *sacer* can be offended and respond to that offense by harming the community that committed the offense is as old, textually speaking, as the *lapis niger*—although it is likely that such a truth has a much, much longer history than that. A corollary to this is the danger to the community should even one single individual from within it offend the divine *sacer*. This is true for the one who, theoretically, upsets the *lapis niger* even inadvertently, as it is true, literarily, for Oidipos of Thebes, even if his offenses—killing his own father and marrying, having sex with and producing four offspring by his own mother—were committed in ignorance of what he was doing to whom.

If *magia* or *superstitio* (or whatever term one might use) is antithetical to proper *religio*, then there is a logic to supposing that the practice of *magia* or *supersititio* might give offense to the divine *sacer* properly addressed by *religio*. Thus any practitioner of *sacer*-engaging processes that are not those of proper *religio* can represent a distinct danger to his or her community—and like Oidipos, must be removed from the community in order to protect it. While this is a truism within a polytheistic context in which the *sacer* is understood to have numerous aspects personified by numerous gods and goddesses, some more powerful than others—diverse *theoi* and *daimones*—it assumes a potentially even larger role on the stage of history when it encounters *religiones* with a conviction that the divine *sacer* is constituted by a single power.

Thus the notion of there being many different correct paths to engaging the divine *sacer* yields, over the last several centuries of the Greco-Roman period, to the conviction articulated by Jews and Christians that, not only is there only one, all-powerful, all-knowing as well as all-good divinity—one who is also interested in human affairs. But also, along the way, as we have seen, the lines separating proper from improper engagement of divinity begin to blur. The modes of potentially offending God and thereby endangering the community are perceived to be multiplying. Particularly as Christianity moves toward hegemony within the Roman Empire, practitioners of *magia* and *superstitio* come to be easily enough lumped together in the same pile with misbelievers—Pagans, of which there are so many variations—and with misbelievers *within* the proper faith: heretics; and with misbelievers who are not within the proper Christian faith but not as far outside as Pagans are: Jews.

Thus when the conviction that God can be offended—and that offense to God can endanger the community in which the offense was committed—is combined with the blurring of lines among the diverse modes in which the offense may be committed, the possibility that a given individual might find himself or herself accused of such an offense, and one way or the other be forced to leave the community (whether by exile or by death) expands exponentially.

We have seen how that would eventuate, only gradually, but relentlessly, in the perception of Jews and Judaism as dangerous by Christians and Christianity, as the last few centuries of the Roman era melted into the emerging and evolving Middle Ages. This perception also reflects a distinction between how Judaism and Christianity view *magia*. In considering Abraham of Wuerzburg's *Book of Sacred Magic of Abramelin the Mage* we saw clear evidence that, as Joshua Trachtenberg observes, "[t]he primary principle of medieval magic was an implicit reliance upon the Powers of Good, which was invoked by calling upon their names, the holy Names of God and His angels... It was the absence of the satanic element and the use of these names, that is, the employment of God's celestial servants, which stamped Jewish magic with a generally far from malevolent character."[677]

By contrast, as Christianity developed and, with it, the role of the Satan and his minions grew in perception, then *magia* as *superstitio* in the dangerous, malevolent, subversive sense, necessarily grew. And Jews perceived as practitioners would certainly be perceived as having at least the possibility, if not the certainty, of operating malignantly—particularly given that even everyday Jews could and frequently were suspected, as we have seen, of being in league with the Satan and his vicious offspring, the anti-Christ, with *increasing* frequency, as the centuries pushed forward.

There is a still further twist to this, for—as Trachtenberg himself observes—medieval Jews did in fact believe heartily enough in the same "middle world" as did their Christian neighbors: a realm "neither of the flesh nor altogether and exclusively of the spirit."[678] *Mal'akheem* (sing. = *mal'akh*) and *shedeem* (sing. = *shed*) formed part of an elaborate reality of what *our* terminology would label either lower *sacer* or upper sacerdotal, benevolent and malevolent beings: we would translate the first term as "angels" and the second as "demons"—perhaps. The angelic beings were deemed inherently more powerful than their demonic counterparts, however, so to be able to invoke the former was to provide effective protection against the latter, who were understood to possess a kind of implacable enmity toward humankind and toward the creation in general.

In fact, there is a more detailed vocabulary used to refer to these "middle world" beings. In addition to *mal'akh* (a biblical word that is used to refer to a messenger from God to humans) and *shed* (also found, but only in the plural, in the Bible), one encounters *mazzik*, meaning "one who damages, or destroys." So, too, the biblical word, *ruah* ("spirit" but also simply meaning "wind") acquires a partnering pair of adjectives: *tovah* ("good") or *ra'ah* ("evil"). These terms all tended to be used without distinction. One also find the phrase *mal'akhei habbalah* ("angels of destruction"), which proves how ambiguous even the term *mal'akh* can be, under certain circumstances. Yet another term, *lilit* ("night-demon"), acquired an entire tradition of its own.[679]

---

[677] Joshua Trachtenberg, *Jewish Magic and Superstition*, (New York: Behrman's Jewish Book house, 1939), 15-16.

[678] Ibid, 26—but see 26-43 for a fuller discussion of this topic.

[679] In brief: The word "*lilit*" is a *hapax legomenon* in the Hebrew Bible, appearing only once, in Isaiah 34:14, which makes its precise meaning less than obvious. It then appears several times in the Dead Sea Scrolls, and three times in the *Gemara* of the Babylonian Talmud—the third reference, (in *Sabbath* 1511b) offers R. Hanina noting that "...whoever sleeps alone in a house is seized by Lilith." It may be that, along the way, the term evolved through a confusion between the Hebrew word, *layil*, meaning "night" and the original figure of the Assyrian (Babylonian) *lilitu*, a winged wind-spirit with long and disheveled hair. In any case, it is the so-called *Alphabet of Ben Sira* (8th-10th c) that begins a serious elaboration of the figure of Lilith: as Adam's first wife, who unlike him, could fly. Ben Sira references her refusal—having been created, like him, from earth (and not, like Eve, later, from his rib)—to submit to him, and her exile and punishments: a thousand of her children are destroyed daily, which helps make her a creature who preys on unprotected human babies and pubescent boys. She also comes in for further discussion in the Kabbalah and later aggadic traditions. On might further note that the term is found in the plural (as *liliot*) early on but later exclusively in the singular, which underscores the idea that in the rabbinical tradition it evolved from a more general reference to night-demons to identifying one specific character.

We might note five things about all of this. One, that this full-fledged tradition was probably originally drawn from literary and oral sources found in Babylonia, Persia and Egypt—which we have seen to provide a good deal of the material for what ancient Pagans, Jews and Christians alike saw as the nefarious (or potentially nefarious) side of the *sacer*. Two, that tradition not only reached the folkloristic street-sensibilities of everyday Jews but is also attested in some of the rabbinic literature—so that "proper monotheistic Jewish religion," like its sibling, "proper monotheistic Christian religion," was much more fraught with beliefs that in theory should not be found within it, than one might suppose, certainly as we move from antiquity into and through the medieval period—although the non-rabbinic Karaites strongly opposed such beliefs, as did a number of key medieval Jewish thinkers, like Maimonides and Ibn Ezra.[680]

Three, that demonic forces are typically referred to as "spirits of uncleanness" and therefore associated with threats to both spiritual and physical well-being—they are obstructionists, rather than part of a team devoted to drawing humans away from moral goodness and to destroying the efforts to bring about the kingdom of God. If as a pious Jew I am supposed to wash my hands—and recite a blessing as I do so—before I eat, then the danger to me of such dirty demons would help remind me never to desist from this sacred obligation. On the one hand, the effective level of malignancy of demons is less than what we understand in Christian terms, and on the other, they are a species unto themselves, as opposed to a subset of fellow-humans who grow horns and possess other physical attributes that reflect their association with a creature like the anti-Christ. (This is a thin line, mind you, since there will be plenty of times and places in which Jews will be viewed by Christians as altogether a non-human species, rather than merely a dangerous subset of humans.)

Four, the tradition is much richer in the European Jewish world where the dispersed communities were surrounded by Christendom than among the Jewish communities of the Muslim world, from which we might infer that the firm belief in an elaborate world of demons (and angels) is in part influenced by Christian thinking, in which the idea of the Satan, the anti-Christ and their minions, and with this, the doctrine of hell as a realm in detailed opposition to heaven, is far more extensively worked out than it is in Islam. As Trachtenberg notes, Maimonides and Ibn Ezra were inhabitants of Muslim Spain, (Maimonides, after age 13, actually of Muslim North Africa), which may account for their opposition to the demonology with which the rabbinical communities of Christendom were so apparently comfortable.

In fact, demonology is far less well-developed than is angelology in the medieval Jewish world. And many of the names that emerge are direct and clear borrowings from their Christian neighbors—in Latin, French and German—by the thirteenth century (a century, we might recall, in which the issue of heresy and the desire to root it out was reaching a particular point of focus in Christendom). So whatever we might conclude of the underlying concepts, we can certainly assert that the terminology is borrowed into the Jewish tradition from that of Christendom.

---

[680] Ibid, 26. For a brief discussion of the Karaites, see above, 128-9.

Five: how could there *not* be some sense of the nefarious *sacer* for Jews, for the same basic reason that there is for Christians (and Muslims)? For how else does one begin to try to account for why bad things sometimes happen to good, apparently innocent people? Christianity, as we have noted, carries this issue so much farther—from the Satan and the anti-Christ and a final battle between these two and their followers against God, Christ and their followers; to increasingly detailed expositions, both visually and literarily, of hell—than does Judaism, which even lacks a proper term for "hell."[681] Yet, if the biblical Book of Job offers no clear explanation for why the innocent sometimes suffer, it also offers the beginning of an answer: that there is an Adversary, Questioner, Opposer—a *Satan*—who, while he is nothing compared to God in prominence, is yet accorded by God sufficient power to make negative things happen to humans for whatever reasons.

If Job's faith was being tested, perhaps ours is also, when we suffer without apparent reason—or maybe, like Job, we are simply not intended to understand why certain things happen when they happen. After all, the *sacer* is by definition beyond the understanding to which we of the *profanus* ordinarily have access. It is noteworthy that the Satan is not present at the end of the book, when Job is rewarded by God for his goodness and his faith. His role having been played, he does not even step back onto the stage for a bow, suggesting how insignificant he is compared to God—and even compared to a human like Job. So, too, as we have seen for Abraham and Abramelin, so, in general, where medieval Jewish engagement of demons is concerned, these beings "remain the creatures of God, subject to His will and respectful of His divinity, and actually subservient to the angels."[682]

We who dwell at a considerable distance from the beginnings of the spiritual and political competition between Judaism and Christianity, and the emergence and evolution of both, within themselves, in response to Paganism, and in competition with each other, are affected by the consequences that have carried through the long period intervening between that ancient time and our own era. We are wont not to remember, or never to have realized in the first place, that Christianity and Judaism took several centuries to develop, once they had effected a distinct split with each other and with each other's sense of how to build a proper edifice of faith on the Hebrew, Israelite and Judaean foundations that both religious traditions inherited.

In the transformation of the notion that "what is mine is religion and what is yours is magic or superstition" into the conviction that yours must be suppressed, expunged or even completely eliminated because otherwise the community of proper believers is in danger, as that translation and conviction has defined so much of the Christian-Jewish

---

[681] There are two words that end up being used in order to provide an equivalent for the Christian concept—albeit neither is ultimately any more its equivalent than Hanukkah is, as a Jewish holiday, a true equivalent of the Christian Christmas. *She'ol* is sometimes used, but it merely means "grave"—to tell someone to "go to *she'ol*" is really only telling him/her to "go to the grave"—and *gehenna* is a bastardization of the Hebrew phrase, *gei Ben-Hinnom*, "the valley of Hinnom," southwest of the old city of Jerusalem. This is the "valley of the shadow of death" through which, when I walk. "I fear no evil, for thou art with me," of Psalm 23:4. It seems to have been a kind of red-light district in antiquity—and apparently, before King David conquered the city and made it his capital, it was the site at which Canaanite/Jebusite babies were offered in sacrifice to the God, Moloch, by being burned. A scary place, in other words—but not the Satan-ruled hell depicted on so many church walls or described most definitively by Dante in his Inferno of ca 1310.

[682] Trachtenberg, op citum, 30.

relationship over the centuries, we find an increasing amnesia regarding how blurred the lines once were both between religion and magic—or superstition or myth, or even philosophy or medicine—and between Judaism and Christianity.

The implications of that amnesia have carried through the centuries from the end of the Roman period to our own time, encompassing public burnings and extermination camps from Sevilla to Auschwitz. Jews and Christians are still in the slow process of reconciliation based on a firmer idea both of their common roots and of their shared place within the larger arena of humanity. In understanding how complicated the beginnings of their turning away from each other were and how slow each was to become what we are typically taught in Sunday school they have always been, and in improving our memories with regard to those beginnings and that tardiness, we are in a better position to appreciate how and why we must turn back toward each other, however slow and complicated *that* process may be.

Brief Bibliography

Allegro, John, *The Dead Sea Scrolls: A Reappraisal*. Baltimore, MD: Penguin Books, 1965.

Ammianus Marcellinus, *Res Gestae (Later Roman History; 354-78 CE)*, Walter Hamilton, Transl. London: Penguin Classics, 1986.

Aptowitzer, Avigdor (Victor), "Les noms de Dieu et des anges dans la mezouza," *REJ*, LX (1910), 39-52 and LXV (1913), 54-60.

Barb, A.A., "The Survival of Magic Arts," in A.D. Momigliano, ed., *The Conflict between Paganism and Christianity in the Fourth Century*. Oxford: Clarendon Press, 1963.

Beck, Roger, *Beck on Mithraism: Collected Works with New Essays*. Aldershot, Hampshire: Ashgate Publishing LTD., 2004.

_____, "Merkelbach's Mithras," *Phoenix* 41.3, (1987).

_____, "Mithraism" in the *Encyclopedia Iranica*, 2002

_____, "On Becoming a Mithraist: New Evidence for the Propagation of the Mysteries," in Leif E. Vaage, et al, *Religious Rivalries in the Early Roman Empire and the Rise of Christianity*. Toronto: WLU Press, 2006

_____, "The Mysteries of Mithras: A New Account of their Genesis," in *Journal of Roman Studies*, 1998, 115-28

_____ and Wolfgang Haase, *Aufstieg und niedergang der roemischen welt [The Rise and Decline of the Roman World]*. Berlin: de Gruyter, 1984.

Berg, William, "Hecate: Greek or "Anatolian"?", *Numen* 21.2 (August 1974), 128-40

Betz, H. D. et al., eds., *The Greek Magical Papyri in Translation. Including the Demotic Texts*. Chicago: University of Chicago Press, 1986.

Bjornebye, Jonas, Hic Locus est Felix, Sanctus, Piusque Benignus: *The Cult of Mithras in Fourth-Century Rome*. (PhD Dissertation from University of Bergen, Norway, 2007)

Bonner, Campbell, *Studies in Magical Amulets*, Ann Arbor: University of Michigan Press, 1950.

Boyce, Mary, *Zoroastrians: Their Religious Beliefs and Practice*. NYC: Routledge, 1979.

_____, & Frantz Grenet, *Zoroastrianism under Macedonian and Roman Rule*, Part 1 (Leiden: E J Brill, 1975)

Brashear, William M., *A Mithraic Catechism from Egypt*. Vienna: Verlag Adolf Holzhausens, 1992.

Brown, Peter, "Sorcery, Demons, and the Rise of Christianity from Later Antiquity into the Middle Ages," in Mary Douglas, ed., *Witchcraft Confessions and Accusations*. London and NY: Routledge. 1970, 17-45.

Buber, Martin, *The Origin and Meaning of Hassidism*. New York: Harper & Row, Publishers, 1960.

Burkert, Walter, *Ancient Mystery Cults*. Cambridge: Harvard University Press, 1987.

Campbell, Joseph, *The Masks of God*. New York, NY: Viking Penguin, 1976, Vol 4 (Creative Mythology).

_____, *The Mythic Image*. Princeton, NJ: Princeton University Press, 1974.

Clauss, Manfred, *The Roman Cult of Mithras: The God and His Mysteries*. Richard Gordon, tr. (New York: Routledge, 2001).

Cumont, Franz, *Textes et monuments figures relatifs aux mysteres de Mithra*, in 1894-1900; (English-language reduction, *The Mysteries of Mithra*, was published in 1903 and re-issued by Dover, 1956).

Daniels, C.M., "The Roman Army and the Spread of Mithraism," in John R. Hinnells, *Mithraic Studies: Proceedings of the First International Congress of Mithraic Studies*, vol 2, 1975)

David, Jonathan, "The Exclusion of Women in the Mithraic Mysteries: Ancient or Modern?" *Numen* 47 (2): 121-41.

Dodds, E.R., *The Greeks and the Irrational*. Berkeley and Los Angeles: University of California Press, 1951.

Ezquerra, J.A., (R. Gordon, transl.), *Romanizing Oriental Gods: Myth, Salvation and Ethics in the Cult of Cybele, Isis and Mithras*. Leiden: EJ Brill, 2008.

Fishwick, Duncan, "On the Origin of the Rotas-Sator Square." *Harvard Theological Review*, 1964. Vol 57, issue 01, 39-53.

Foltz, Richard, *Religions of the Silk Road*. New York: Palgrave Macmillan, 2010.

_____, *Spirituality in the Land of the Noble: How Iran Shaped the World's Religions*. Oxford: Oneworld Publications, 2004.

Fox, Robin Lane, *Pagans and Christians*. New York: Harper&Row, 1988.

Francis, E.D., "Mithraic Graffiti from Dura Europos," in John R. Hinnells, ed., *Mithraic Studies*, vol 2, 424-445.

Frazer, Sir James, *The New Golden Bough (Abridged): Sir James Frazer's classic work on Ancient and Primitive Myth, Magic, Religion, Ritual, and Taboo. Revised and edited in the light of recent scholarship by Theodore H. Gaster*. New York: Criterion Books, Inc., 1959.

Gager, John, *Moses in Greco-Roman Paganism*, Society of Biblical Literature Monograph Series, 1972

Gaster, Moses, ed., *Sword of Moses*. London: British Library, formerly MS Gaster 78; now MS Or. 10678,

1896.

Gaster, Theodor H., *The Dead Sea Scriptures in English Translation*. Garden City, NY: Doubleday Anchor Books, 1957.

Geden, A.S. transl., *Selected Passages Illustrating Mithraism*. London: Society for Promoting Christian Knowledge, 1925.

Gollancz, Hermann, *The Book of Protection*. Cambridge: Cambridge University Press, 1912.

Goodenough, Erwin, R., *Jewish Symbols in the Greco-Roman World*. New York: Pantheon, 1953-65, vol. two.

Gordon, Richard L., "The Date and Significance of CIMRM 593 (British Museum, Townley Collection)," *Journal of Mithraic Studies* II, (1978), 148-74.

Graves, Robert, *The Greek Myths*, (Baltimore, MD: Penguin Books, 1955)

Griffith, A.B., "Mithraism in the Private and Public Lives of Fourth-Century Senators in Rome," in the *Electronic Journal of Mithraic Studies*.
http://www.uhu.es/ems/Papers/Volume1Papers/ABGMS.DOC

Guthrie, W.K.C., *A History of Greek Philosophy*. Cambridge: University of Cambridge Press, 1979.

Gwynn, David M., *Religious Diversity in Late Antiquity* Leiden: EJ Brill, 2010.

Harvey, Susan Ashbrook & David G. Hunter, eds., *The Oxford Handbook of Early Christian Studies*. New York: Oxford University Press, 2010.

Hesiod, *Theogony*, (Norman O. Brown, transl.). Indianopolis: The Bobs-Merrill Co., Inc., 1976

Hinnells, John R., "Reflections on the Bull-Slaying Scene," in *Mithraic Studies: Proceedings of the First International Conference on Mithraic Studies*. Manchester: Manchester University Press, vol 2, 290-312

Hippolytus of Rome, *The Refutation of All Heresies*, Orthodox Ebooks, 1984.

Homer, *The Odyssey*, (Richmond Lattimore, transl.). New York: Harper & Row, 1967.

Hopfe, Lewis M., "Archaeological Indications on the Origins of Roman Mithraism, in Lewis M. Hopfe, *Uncovering Ancient Stones: Essays in Memory of H. Neil Richardson*. Warsaw, IN: Eisenbrauns, 1994.

Josephus, *The Works of, Complete and Unabridged,* (William Whiston, transl.). Peabody: MA: Hendrickson Publishers, 1987.

Klauck, Hans-Josef, (Brian McNeil, transl.), *Magic and Paganism in Ancient Christianity*. Minneapolis: Fortress Press, 2003.

_____, *The Religious Context of Early Christianity: A Guide to Greco- Roman Religions*. Minneapolis: Fortress Press, 2003.

Jackson, Howard M., "The Meaning and Function of the Leoncephaline in Roman Mithraism," in *Numen*, Vol 32, Fasc 1 (July, 1985), 17-45.

Leon, Harry J., *The Jews of Ancient Rome*. Philadelphia: The Jewish Publication Society of America, 1960.

Levi-Strauss, Claude, *Structural Anthropology*. Garden City, NY: Doubleday Anchor Books, 1967.

Lieu, Samuel N.C., *Manichaeism in the Later Roman Empire and Medieval China*. Tubingen: JCB Mohr, 1992.

Lowther Clarke, W.K. and Charles Harris, *Liturgy and Worship*. London: Society for Promoting Christian Knowledge, 1940.

Luck Georg, *Arcana Mundi*. Baltimore: The Johns Hopkins University Press, 1985.

MacMullen, Ramsay, *Enemies of the Roman Order: Treason, Unrest and Alienation in the Empire*. Cambridge, MA: Harvard University Press, 1966.

Malinowski, Bronislaw, *Magic, Science and Religion and Other Essays*. Garden City, NY: Doubleday Anchor, 1945. (Reprint of the 1948 original edition by Free Press/Beacon Press, Boston, MA).

Marcovich, Miroslav, "Sator arepo = ΓΕΩΡΓΟΣ ΆΡΠΟΝ(ΚΝΟΥΦΙ) ΑΡΠΩΣ, arpo(cra), harpo(crates)," *Zeitschrift für Papyrologie und Epigraphik* Bd. 50 (1983), 155-71.

Margolioth, Mordecai, ed., Sepher HaRazim, *A Newly Recovered Book from the Talmudic Period*. Yediot Achronot: Jerusalem, 1966.

Mathers, S.L. MacGregor, *The Book of the Sacred Magic of Abramelin the Mage, as Delivered by Abraham the Jew unto His Son Lamech, A.D. 1458*. NYC: Dover Publications, 1975. (Reprint of the 1900 edition published in London by John M. Wadkins).

Mauss, Marcel, *A General Theory of Magic*. Robert Brain, Trans., New York: W.W. Norton & Co. 1975.

Merkelbach, Reinhold, *Mithras*. Berlin: A. Hain, 1984.

Meyer, Marvin W., "The Mithras Liturgy" in Amy Jill Levine, et al, eds., *The Historical Jesus in Context*. Princeton, NJ: Princeton University Press, 2006.

Morgan, Michael A., translation of *Sepher HaRazim*, Columbia University: unpublished MA Thesis, 1973.

_____, *Sepher Ha-Razim: The Book of Mysteries*. Chico, CA: Scholars Press, 1983

Murdock, D.M., *Christ in Egypt: The Horus-Jesus Connection*. New York: Stellar House Publishing, 2009.

Nock, Arthur Darby, "Paul and the Magus," in Frederick J. Foakes-Jackson and Kirsopp Lake, eds., *The Beginnings of Christianity*, London: Macmillan Press, 1920-33, vol 5.

Ogden, Daniel, *Magic, Witchcraft, and Ghosts in the Greek and Roman Worlds*. Oxford: Oxford University Press, 2009.

Olmstead, A.T., *History of the Persian Empire*. Chicago: The University of Chicago Press, 1959.

Pagels, Elaine, *The Gnostic Gospels*. New York: Random House, 1979.

_____, *The Origin of Satan*. New York: Random House, 1995.

Plato, *Collected Works*, Edith Hamilton & Huntington Cairns, eds., Princeton, NJ: Princeton University Press (Bolingen Series #71) especially *The Laws*.

Peukert, Willi-Erich, "*Ritualmord*," Hans Baechthold-Staeubli and E. Hoffman-Krayer, eds., *Handwoerterbuch des Deutscher Aberglaubens*. Berlin, de Gruyter, 1987-2001 (reprint of 1927-42 edition) vol. 7, col. 734.

Pliny the Elder, *Natural History*. (Harris Rackham, transl.). Cambridge, MA: Harvard University Press (Loeb Claisscal Library, Vol VIII of Pliny), 1958.

Polge, Henri, "La fausse enigme du carre magique," *Revue de l'histoire des religions*, 1969. Vol. 175, No 2, 155-63.

Preisendanz, Karl, et al, eds and trs., *Papyri Graecae Magicae. Die Griechischen Zauberpapyri*. Berlin: de Gruyter, 1928, 1931. (Second edition updated and edited by Albert Henrichs. Stuttgart: Teubner, 1974).

Rahner, Hugo, *Greek Myths and Christian Mystery*, New York; Harper & Row, 1963.

Renan, Ernst, *Marc-Aurele et la fin du monde antique*. Paris: LGF Livre de Poche, 1984 (reprint of original 1882 edition).

_____, *1880 Hibbert Lectures: Lectures on the Influence of the Institutions, Thought and Culture of Rome on Christianity and the Development of the Catholic Church*. Whitefish, MT: Kessinger Publishing, 1898.

Roll, Israel, "The Mysteries of Mithras in the Roman Orient: The Problem of Origin," *Journal of Mithras Studies*, Vol II, 1978.

Sandmel, Samuel, *Judaism and Christian Beginnings*. New York: Oxford University Press, 1978.

Sider, David, "Notes on Two Epigrams of Philodemus," in *The American Journal of Philology*, 103.2 (Summer, 1982:208-213).

Soltes, Ori Z., "Columbus, Catholics, Marranos and Jews: Who Was Who and What Was What?" *Lexington Theological Quarterly*, Vol 28, No 3, Fall, 1993, 177-201.

_____, *From Plato's* Cratylus *to Levinas' "God and Philosophy": The Problem of Language for Philosophy*. Buffalo, NY: Edwin Mellen Press, 2007.

_____, *Jews on Trial: Judges, Juries, Prosecutors and Defendants from the Era of Jesus to Our Own Time*. Savage: Maryland: Bartleby Press, 2013.

_____, *Mysticism in Judaism, Christianity and Islam: Searching for Oneness*. Lanham, MD: Roman & Littlefield, 2008.

_____, *Our Sacred Signs: How Jewish, Christian and Muslim Art Draw from the Same Source* (New York City: Westview, 2005

Speidel, Michael P., *Mithras-Orion: Greek Hero and Roman Army God*. Leiden: EJ Brill, 1980.

The Apocrypha. An American Translation by Edgar J. Goodspeed. New York: The Modern Library, 1959.

The Holy Scriptures, According to the Masoretic Text. Philadelphia: The Jewish Publication Society of America, 1966.

The New English Bible: New Testament. Oxford/Cambridge: Oxford & Cambridge University Press, 1968.

Theophrastus: "The Superstitious Man" from *Typoi (Characters)*, James Diggle, transl & comment., Cambridge: Cambridge University Press, 2004.

Thieme, Paul, "The Aryan Gods of the Mitanni Treaties," in the *Journal of the American Oriental Society*, 80.4 (1960), 301-17.

Thucydides, *The Peloponnesian Wars*. R.W. Livingstone, transl.). New York: Oxford University Press, 1960.

Trachtenberg, Joshua, *Jewish Magic and Superstition*. New York: Behrman's Jewish Book house, 1939.

Tripolitis, Antonia, *Religions of the Hellenistic-Roman Age*. Grand Rapids: Wm B. Eerdmans, 2002.

Turcan, Robert, *The Cults of the Roman Empire*. Oxford: Wiley-Blackwell, 1996.

_____, *Mithras Platonicus*. Leiden: EJ Brill, 1975.

David Ulansey, *Origins of the Mithraic Mysteries*. New York: Oxford University Press, 1991.

Vermaseren, Maarten J., *Corpus Inscriptionum et Monumentorum Religionis Mithriacae*. The Hague: Martin Nijhoff, 1956.

_____, "The Miraculous Birth of Mithras," *Mnemsyne* 4,1951, 285-301.

Von Gall, Hubertus, "The Lion-headed and the Human-headed God in the Mithraic Mysteries," in Jacques Duchesne-Guillemin, ed., *Etudes Mithriaques*. Bibliotheque Pahlavi, 1978.

Wilson, Edmund, *The Scrolls from the Dead Sea*. New York: Meridian Books, 1959.

Wuensch. R., *Antikes Zaubergeraet aus Pergamon*. Berlin: Staatliche Museen zu Berlin, 1905.

Yadin, Yigal, *Hazor: The Rediscovery of a Great Citadel of the Bible*. New York: Random House, 1975.

Zeitlin, Solomon, *The Rise and Fall of the Judaean State*. Three Volumes. Philadelphia: Jewish Publication Society, 1962, 1967, 1978.

INDEX

NB: footnote citations (fn) are according to the page on which they appear.

A

384

Christian, 11, 12, 20, 30, 31, 32, 41, 42, 45, 46, 98, 105, 115, 117, 118-121, 124, 126, 127, 130, 138, 146, 147, 149, 158, 161, 162, 163, 164, 191, 193, 195, 196, 197-8, 200, 204, 205, 206, 207-8, 214, 216, 217, 220, 224, 225, 226, 227-228, 229, 230, 231, 232, 235, 238-9, 241-249, 250-1, 254, 255, 257, 258, 260, 261-2, 264, 265, 266, 267, 270, 271, 280, 283, 284, 287, 290, 293, 294, 297, 298, 300, 301, 302-303, 305, 306, 307, 309, 310, 311, 313, 314, 315, 316, 318, 319, 320, 323, 326, 327, 329, 330, 333, 335, 336, 337-8, 339-40, 342, 343, 344, 345, 348, 349-51, 352, 354, 355-6, 357, 358, 359-363, 364-6, 369, 370, 376, 377, 378, fn 85, 87, 105, 117, 118, 121, 124, 132, 136, 140, 142, 143, 162, 224, 242, 263, 300, 302, 303, 305, 310, 311, 319, 333, 339, 340, 355, 358, 361, 367, 371, 379

Christian Brotherhood, 361

Christianity, 10, 13, 15, 16, 23, 24, 27, 37, 39, 40, 45, 52, 53, 60, 63, 67, 79, 88, 91, 94, 117, 118-121, 127, 129, 131-134, 135, 138-9, 144, 146, 147, 148, 151, 153, 159, 161-3, 164, 174, 189, 190, 195, 196, 199, 200, 203, 204, 205-206, 207, 208, 211, 217, 223, 226-7, 229, 230, 231, 234, 236, 237, 239, 241, 242, 246, 250, 251, 255, 256, 258, 265, 266, 280, 283, 286, 294-5, 297, 299, 300, 301-5, 307, 308-9, 311, 312-13, 314, 315, 316, 318-22, 323, 324, 325, 327, 329, 330, 332, 333, 334, 336, 337, 338, 339, 340, 342, 343, 345, 347, 348, 349, 350, 351, 353-4, 356, 360, 361, 362, 367, 369, 371, 376-7, 379-80, fn 64, 91, 113, 117, 119, 132, 133, 140, 151, 154, 158, 291, 300, 304, 310, 339, 361, 367, 371

Church Fathers, 294, 299, 303, 305, 309, 314, 337, 344, fn 301

Cicero, 14, 164

Circe, See Kirke

Circumcision, 97, 99, 119, 148, 302, 315, 323, 324, fn 324, 355

Clauss, Manfred, 161, 303, fn 151, 153, 157, 158, 159, 161, 162, 303

Clement of Alexandria, 147, fn 143, 147, 239, 293

Cleopatra, 96, 114, fn 96, 140

Cliens, fn 353

Cluny, 357

Coarelli, Filippo, 304, fn 153, 304

Codex Theodosianus, 342

Codrington, Robert Henry, fn 42

Communion, 11, 47, 143, 226, 254, 304, 314

Compulsion, 26, 33, 45, 219, 225, 233, 234, 237, 253, 254, 274, 285, 293

Contagion, Law of, 30, 32

Contagious Magic, 30-2, 167, 171, 172, 186, 197, 198, 210, fn 32

Contra Celsum, 319, fn 206

Conversion (religious), 99, 100, 101, 314, 360, 367, fn 101, 158, 363

Converso(s), 360-64

Coptic, 232, 233, 243, 247, 255, 291, fn 243, 291

Cordova, 360, 361

Cosmos. see Kosmos

Council of Hippo, 119, 297

Covenant 63, 85, 105, 106, 107, 116, 118, 119, 128, 149, 324, fn 114

Crete, 68

Croesus, 24

Crossroads, 75-8, 173, fn 213

Crusade(s), 357-8, 373, fn 358

Crypto-Jews, 360-61, 364, fn 361

Cumont, Franz, 150, 151, 155, 159, 160, 162, fn 150, 151, 159, 160

Curse Tablet, 261, 330, 331

Cybele, see Kybele

Cyrus (the Great), 24, 83, 149, fn 93

D

Daena, 92

Daimon(es), 15, 36, 75, 78, 188, 193, 194, 207, 208-10, 217-19, 220-24, 227, 228, 229, 233, 240, 241, 249, 252, 253, 254-5, 266, 278, 321-2, 323, 326, 327, 376, fn 170, 212

Damigeron, 293, 344

Daniels, C.M., fn 153

Dastur, fn 90

Davithea, 244-7

Day of Judgment, 116

De Antro Nympharum, 152-3, fn 152, 153, 161

Dead Sea (Scrolls), 88, 104, 114, 255, fn 107, 109, 112, 116, 377

Dead, the, 43, 59-60, 66-7, 77, 91, 93, 125, 126, 165, 170, 272, 278, 308, 331, 340, fn 90, 122, 142, 355

Defixionis/es, 261, 330, 345

Deisidaimon(ia), 75-8, 171, 189

Delphi, 17, 24, 39, 124, 142, 218, fn 124, 219

Demeter, 147, 305, 307

Demiourgos, 213, 220

Demiurge, 213, 216, 317, fn 156, 310

Deuterocanonical, 120, 121

Deuteronomy, 63, 270, 282, 290, fn 23

Devil, the, 40, 52, 126, 199, 351, 352-3, 373

Diadem of Moses, 291,

Diana, 20, 29, fn 77

Diego De Acebes, 358

Dilmun, 214, fn 214

Dio Cassius, 152

Diodorus Siculus, 193, 146, 306, 307

Dionysios, 41, 75-6, 139-46, 147, 148, 158, 162, 163, 180, 202, 209, 305-8, fn 76, 140, 142, 143, 144, 219, 272

Diplosis, 294

Divine Madness, 78

Do Ut Possis Dare, 27, 241

Dodds, E.R., 79, 214, 215, 216, 228-9, fn 79, 214, 216, 228, 229, 303

Dominic of Caleruega, 358

Dorpat, Russia, 32

Double Image, 348

Dragon, 124-6, fn 124, 310

E

F

388

Q

R

392

T

Printed in the USA
CPSIA information can be obtained
at www.ICGtesting.com
LVHW061200010823
754026LV00002B/74

9 780999 459492